The Great World War 1914-45

Volume 1

The Great World War 1914-45

Volume 1
Lightning strikes twice

Edited by
Dr Peter Liddle
Dr John Bourne
Dr Ian Whitehead

**To the generations who experienced
the lightning strikes
1914-1945**

HarperCollinsPublishers
77-85 Fulham Palace Road
Hammersmith
London W6 8JB

First published in Great Britain by HarperCollinsPublishers 2000

3 5 7 9 10 9 6 4 2

ISBN 0 00 472454 2

A CIP catalogue record for this book is available from the British Library.

Printed by Clays

Contents

Acknowledgements

A book of this nature has been, at every stage, a collective effort. The editors wish to thank all their colleagues for so generously devoting time and scholarship to the undertaking. The goodwill with which our colleagues and friends accepted a demanding intellectual challenge made the task of co-ordinating the result congenial, if no less daunting.

Many contributors assisted in bringing other historians to collaborate in the work. In particular, we should like to thank Imanuel Geiss and Werner Rahn from Germany, Dennis Showalter and Frank Vandiver from the United States, Bob Bushaway, Hugh Cecil, John Erickson and Gary Sheffield from the United Kingdom. A particular debt of thanks is owed to James Cooke for much valued assistance and support. We are also grateful to those authors who helped with the provision of illustrations, particularly Tony Lane and Jeff Tall. We should also like to thank Professor John Breuilly, Dr Robert Frost, Dr J.T. Lukowski, Dr E. Tinios and Dr S. Townshend for their helpful advice and recommendations.

The editors and contributors wish to express appreciation to the appropriate authorities for sanctioning the publication of quotations, photographs and facsimile illustrations and for all the help received from the custodians of material they consulted in their research. If there were to be any instance of omission of appropriate accreditation, the editors express in advance their regret and their readiness in a later edition to repair such omission. The editors thank the following institutions for permission to reproduce photographs and illustrative material: Liddle Collection, University of Leeds; Merrill's Marauders Organisation; Royal Navy Submarine Museum, Gosport; Second World War Experience Centre, Leeds; US Army Military History Institute. The reproduction of the final selection of photographs was undertaken by Media Studies: Photography in the University of Leeds, thanks to a link facilitated by Louise Liddle. We thank David Dixon, Colin Butterfield, David Bailey and counter staff for the quality of their service and the cordiality with which it was dispensed.

The editors warmly acknowledge the support of Claire Harder, at the Second World War Experience Centre in Leeds, experienced as she is in drawing together a book like this. They also wish to thank the Trustees of the Second World War Experience Centre who from the first recognised that the book would represent the distilled essence of the sort of material the Centre has been created to rescue. The sterling team of volunteers at the Centre has supported the book in a range of ways, especially in the work of Robert Carrington for the prisoners of war chapter and for the illustrations. In the case of transcriptions from tape-recorded evidence, the labours of Caroline Mumford have been invaluable. Tracy Craggs undertook the task of turning Peter Liddle's editorial notes into clear copy; her assistance was invaluable.

For all three editors this is the first time we have worked with HarperCollins. Our Commissioning Editor, Ian Drury, has been supportive and flexible. With good relations here and with our contributors, we have indeed been fortunate.

Finally, we ask our readers to note with sympathy that a factor in our morale has been the respective footballing fortunes of Port Vale, Sunderland and Manchester City. We hope that coping with euphoria and despair on a regular interchangeable basis has not resulted in any editorial sloppiness.

John Bourne
Peter Liddle
Ian Whitehead
May 2000

Editors' Introduction

Apart from debates about the international ramifications of the Treaty of Versailles, historians have tended to study the two world wars in isolation. This has been justified by the assumption that the two conflicts were qualitatively and quantitatively different. The First World War has more often than not been regarded as a 'bad' war resulting from failures in diplomacy, and a war characterised by the 'futile' sacrifices of trench warfare on the Western Front; standing in stark contrast to the justifiable and necessary struggle, between 1939 and 1945, against Nazi tyranny and aggressive Japanese militarism. In the First World War the civilian populations of the belligerent powers played an increasingly vital part in the war effort. But it is the Second World War, with its indiscriminate bombing of cities placing civilians in the front line, and technology taking man's destructive powers to new heights, that is more usually seen as the first truly 'total' war. To treat the wars separately in this fashion, however, is to ignore a significant historical reality – all those who were over forty years of age in 1940 would have had their adult lives in some sense defined by their participation, or non-participation, in these two global conflicts. It is this continuum of human experience that firmly unites the world wars, and which is the focus both of this book and its successor volume.

The aim throughout is to demonstrate the diversity of personal experience in the two world wars. This volume examines uniformed service and such aspects of civilian experience as occupation, displacement and genocide. It discusses the exercise of political and military leadership and details the difficulties of prosecuting coalition warfare. The later volume deals with the national experiences of both belligerent and neutral states and considers the role of civilians in war. There are also sections dealing with moral and cultural issues.

The comparative approach that underpins the book reveals striking parallels between the two global conflicts of the twentieth century. It is clear that in many respects lightning did indeed strike twice – when considering the development of modern warfare, its challenges and its impact, there is much that unites the two conflicts. Indeed, it is tempting to conclude that, in relation to human experience, there was nothing fundamentally new in the Second World War. There were, however, important differences, none more significant than the ideological basis of the struggle between Nazi Germany and her opponents. The First World War was, in part at least, the product of ancient Balkan savageries and the fate of the Armenians gave warning of the human capacity for organised atrocity on the scale of genocide, a word not yet then coined. But a new register is required to measure the consequences of ideological warfare in the Second World War. German and Japanese conduct of the Second World War was driven by racism and political dogma. This and the response it provoked from the Soviets on the Eastern Front, the Americans in the Pacific and the British and Americans in the skies above Germany and occupied Europe ensured that the Second World War extended the frontiers of human degradation and misery well beyond the boundaries 'achieved' in the earlier struggle.

PART I
THE FRONT LINE
EXPERIENCE

Chapter 1

A personal reflection on the two World Wars

J. M. Bourne

Dates resonate in history, and in life. Few dates in 20th-century history resonate more than '14-'18 and '39-'45. They are not only instantly evocative and significant in themselves, but they also give meaning to other dates.

'Would you mind telling me when you were born?' I asked an elderly Lancastrian while taking part in an oral history project 25 years ago.

'1903,' he replied. This was followed by an infinitesimal but palpable pause, a silence that has followed me down the years. 'A grand year, 1903,' he added.

'Why is that?' I enquired.

'Too young for the first war and too old for the second,' he explained with a chuckle.

I was born in 1949, too young for both wars; too young even for conscription. Old enough for the welfare state, antibiotics, mass working-class prosperity, the coming of television and the expansion of higher education. Like the vast majority of professional historians of my generation, my experience of war is entirely second-hand. It is, nevertheless, real.

No British child born in the immediate aftermath of the Second World War could possibly escape its influence. Samuel Hynes's felicitous description of the Second World War as 'Everybody's War' is certainly true in my experience.[1] Everybody appeared to have taken part in it. Not only fathers and uncles, but also mothers and aunts. I was taught by veterans of the war. My eccentric and charismatic English teacher, J. E. 'Boris' Simnett, landed in Normandy on D+3, carrying a wireless set that he promptly (and accidentally) broke, for which hamfistedness he was threatened with court-martial. My equally eccentric physics teacher, E. W. 'Daddy' Knight, enlivened lessons with tales of his time in bomb disposal.

As an undergraduate I sat at the feet of the Rev J. McManners, who fought in the Western Desert as adjutant of the 1st Battalion Royal Northumberland Fusiliers and later with the Greek resistance, and R. H. Evans, who spent much of the war with 7th Armoured Division and actually witnessed the German surrender to Field-Marshal Montgomery on Luneburg Heath. When I entered the world of work, as a civil servant, most of the middle managers were veterans. 'I slept next to my tank all the way from Normandy to the liberation of Belsen and never got a cold,' one wistfully recalled. 'Now if I go out without a hat, I risk pneumonia.'[2] The undoubted nostalgia that many seemed to feel for the war is apparent in the last remark. 'No one in this country comes alive until you mention the war,' observed a young American on his first visit to Britain in the early 1960s.[3]

Nostalgia was not confined to those who fought the war. Many in my generation grew up believing that they had missed something that was not only really important but also really exciting. This was due not only to the influence of adults but also to the new, powerful medium of television, especially perhaps to the long-running series *All Our Yesterdays*, which showed – almost nightly, it seemed – extracts from British newsreels from the same week 25 years earlier. In this way it was possible to live through the descent into war and the war years vicariously. And I did. Few major figures of the war adapted better to the new medium than Field-Marshal Montgomery. More even than Churchill, he was, for me, the great British hero of the Second World War. I cried the day he died. Churchill was a remote figure who appeared in newsreels and waved at the cameras from the steps of aircraft or the decks of Aristotle Onassis's yacht. Montgomery gave interviews. And what interviews. 'Now, I'll call you Cliff and you call me Monty,' he declared to the television journalist Cliff Michelmore, himself a veteran of the war. It was captivating stuff.

What television failed to achieve was completed by the cinema. War films were a staple of the British film industry throughout the 1950s and 1960s: *They Were Not Divided* (1950); *Albert RN* (1953); *The Cruel Sea* (1953); *The Colditz Story* (1954); *The Dam Busters* (1954); *Cockleshell Heroes* (1955); *Reach for the Sky* (1956); *Ill Met by Moonlight* (1956); *Battle of the River Plate* (1956); *The Bridge on the River Kwai* (1957); *Dunkirk* (1958); *Sink the Bismarck* (1960); *The Battle of Britain* (1969); and many more. Television repeated films made during the war itself: *The Foreman Went to France* (1941); *In Which We Serve* (1942); *Went the Day Well?* (1942); *The Bells Go Down* (1943); *San Demetrio London* (1943); *Desert Victory* (1943); *Western Approaches* (1944); and Olivier's *Henry V* (1944). Feature films tended to portray what were, to the British, key moments of the war. By the time I was ten I could recite the litany: the *Graf Spee*; Dunkirk; the Home Guard; 'the Few'; the Blitz; Coventry; the *Bismarck*; Tobruk; El Alamein; Singapore; the *Prince of Wales* and the *Repulse*; the death railway; Burma and the 'Forgotten Fourteenth'; Anzio; the Dambusters; D-Day; Arnhem; Doodlebugs and the V2; Belsen.

Samuel Hynes and Gary Sheffield have shown that young men who grew up in the 1930s and went to war in the 1940s did so with a war already in their heads.[4] That war was, of course, the First World War, or at least the First World War depicted in the 'anti-war' memoirs of a small number of middle-class veterans. By the time I reached my teens the war I had in my head was the Second World War. David Lodge's novel *Small World* has a hero who is writing a PhD thesis about the influence of T. S. Eliot on Shakespeare. There is an important sense in which it is possible to talk about the influence of the Second World War on the First. When, eventually, I came to read and think about the First World War, it was difficult to rid my mind of images of the Second. Doubtless, these distorted my view but they also illuminated it.

The Second World War in my head had several distinguishing features. First and foremost, it was clearly glorious. This is now a deeply unfashionable thing to say.

Many would regard the statement as wicked. It would be meaningless to my mother-in-law, a Pole, to whom the war brought nothing but suffering, loss and displacement. But most people in my childhood seemed to feel it. 'No English soldier who rode with the tanks into liberated Belgium or saw the German murder camps at Dachau or Buchenwald could doubt that the war had been a noble crusade,' wrote A. J. P. Taylor in the elegiac final paragraph of his volume in the Oxford History of England.[5]

Second, the noble crusade had been a quintessentially British victory. 'We' had won the war. This was the source of much national pride. Although the Second World War was a global conflict, fought by armies numbered in millions across four continents, the British always seemed to be at the heart of it and to be playing the key role. Persons who questioned this often got short shrift. The British were very proprietorial about their victory. During the 1960s an American television series about a US unit operating behind enemy lines in the Desert War had to be taken off by the BBC after a couple of episodes following howls of outrage from British Eighth Army veterans. Early attempts at revising the heroic 'myth' of 1940, by Len Deighton in *Fighter* (1977), also brought odium upon its author. Foreigners had only walk-on parts in this drama. Germans were efficient and brave in a bad cause. Italians were useless soldiers, worthy only of contempt. 'I've got no time for Italians,' one British veteran recalled. 'When we put them into the POW cages in Algeria they just sat around in their own shit. Not like Jerry.'[6] 'Japs' were cruel and unfathomable. One decent, humane, well-read, liberal-minded provincial Englishman recently observed to me that he still found it almost impossible to be civil to Japanese, whom he characterised as 'vicious little bastards'.[7]

Allies, except perhaps for the brave and exotic Poles, fared no better. The French (and the Belgians) had 'let us down'. The Yanks prevailed because they had lots of 'kit', not because they could fight. Eisenhower was no more than a glorified clerk, whose failure to submit to the military genius of Montgomery had handed half of Europe over to Communism; Patton was a madman who slapped shell-shocked soldiers. The war on the Eastern Front was vaguely recognised as bloody and important, but the war there had been won by a country that was now our mortal enemy, whose nuclear missiles were pointed at our shores. Wartime admiration for the achievements of the Red Army soon evaporated. Now, in middle age, I recoil with horror at the parochialism, narrow-mindedness and bigotry of these views, but they were commonplace in my childhood and many still share them.[8]

Third, the war was well-managed. After initial setbacks, mostly attributed to the malign influence of the 'Men of Munich', the British eventually got their act together. Churchill provided not only effective but also inspirational leadership at the political level. Montgomery and Slim emerged as 'great commanders', with an almost unbroken record of success. Both had learned from the mistakes of the First World War. They were prudent with men's lives. They left nothing to chance. They understood technology. They had the common touch. If, in Montgomery's case, it was that of a shameless vulgarian, no one seemed to care. But Slim was what would now be called 'cool'. He exemplified the ironic mode of late-20th Century heroism. Most of all, however, they had, in the words of Slim's own account, turned defeat into victory at a price that seemed worth the paying.[9] Casualties lie at the heart of British perceptions of the two World Wars. British casualties in the First World War were unprecedented in the national experience. British military casualties in the Second World War were hardly small (c305,000) but they were considerably less than half of those of the First. The superior nature of British military leadership and technology in the Second World War is still generally given credit for this by popular opinion.

Fourth, the Second World War was not only a war of national heroism but also a war of individual heroism. There was something almost bijou about Britain's war, a war of commando raids and operations behind enemy lines, small scale, human scale, dramatic, filmable and easy to follow. It was a war in which individuals and small groups seemed to make a difference: Douglas Bader; Guy Gibson; Orde Wingate; Vian of the *Cossack*[10]; 'Dickie' Mountbatten and the *Kelly*, the 'little ships' and their crews at Dunkirk; the Chindits; the Long Range Desert Group. When, in later years, I learned in the pages of Professor Fussell that the First World War had changed for ever the nature of heroism, it was the cause of some consternation.[11] The heroes of the Second World War seemed then, and seem now, to sit easily with those of the past: Grenville, Drake, Wolfe, Nelson.

Finally, the Second World War represented the triumph of brains. It was a war of the 'boffin' and the 'gadget'. Few books are better designed to lift the spirits of the Briton than R. V. Jones's *Most Secret War: British Scientific Intelligence 1939-1945*[12], in which a motley collection of mathematicians, linguists, classicists, engineers, chemists and physicists, even the odd historian, often eccentric and un-warlike individualists in horn-rimmed spectacles and decaying sports jackets, conspired to destroy the Nazi war machine. The centrepiece of this was, of course, the development of radar. Though the name of its originator, Robert Watson Watt, was well known, his personality was not. The iconic figure of the boffins' war became, instead, Dr Barnes Wallis, inventor of the 'bouncing bomb', a concept so bizarre that it must have been the work of a genius. Only later, however, did history offer up the pièce de resistance of the British war effort, Enigma. Revelations about the code-breakers' war at Bletchley Park, which appeared in the early 1970s[13], merely confirmed the importance of British brain power and discovered a new hero, the mathematician, cryptanalyst and computer pioneer, Alan Turing, who was not only a genius but also a tortured gay, very much a hero for the late 20th century.

During my childhood, the First World War struggled for visibility in the glare of attention paid to the Second. There was no one to reminisce with me about the Great War. Both my grandfathers died before I was born, one as the result of war service. My maternal grandmother died when I was three. My paternal grandmother was not a woman who invited questions. My first, dim, awareness of the First World War came through the powerful injunction never to wear a poppy. This stemmed from my maternal grandmother, Louisa Sheldon, a formidable personality who never forgave the war for killing her husband and leaving her in poverty to bring up a family of five, including four girls. She regarded poppies as a means of extorting money out of gullible people who could ill afford it for the enrichment of those who had done well out of the war.

Beyond the family, the First World War seemed to exist only as a guilty secret. My loud, childish enquiries about why some men had only one arm or one leg was met with a whispered, 'He lost it in the first war.' My native North Staffordshire was no stranger to respiratory disease: white lung for potters, black lung for colliers. During the early 1960s I began to notice coroners' reports in the *Staffordshire Evening Sentinel* in which the cause of death was given as 'pneumoconiosis, with gassing in the First World War as a contributory factor'. Gassing. The Second World War had gas masks, but no gas. The First World War evoked no nostalgia. Politicians did not summon the nation to show the 'spirit of the Somme' as they routinely did the 'spirit of Dunkirk' or the 'spirit of the Blitz'. It seemed to be a war of victims, not of heroes. It was, in short, a very different kind of war.

How different became apparent as soon as I began to read about it. My introduction was Alan Clark's *The Donkeys*[14]. It was not necessary to read far in this book to get the message. The caption of the first photograph, adjacent to the title page, read 'Donkey decorates lion'. Between pages 80 and 81 there were photographs of No-Man's Land showing 'human remains and detritus' and of an advanced dressing station (something that rarely seemed to adorn the pages of books on the Second World War) in a ruined farmhouse. These contrasted strikingly with the photograph of General Rawlinson, captioned 'Rawly', standing in the sun on the steps of a chateaux, immaculate in dazzling boots and leather gloves.[15]

When television finally turned its attention to the First World War, it did so with extraordinary effect. Tony Essex's epic documentary *The Great War* (1964) proved so compelling that it was repeated on BBC1 even before the 26 episodes had concluded on BBC2. Much of the modern British fascination with the First World War stems from the impact made by this series. The impact was not that intended by some of those who made the programme. The series's haunting, mournful music (written by Wilfred Josephs), its contemporary film (some of it now known to be fake) showing men 'going over the top' and dying 'on the old barbed wire', its still photographs of trenches deep in water and stretcher-bearers carrying wounded men through thigh-deep mud, its interviews with veterans, its extracts from contemporary memoirs, conspired to reinforce an image of the war that was completely at odds with the script of Correlli Barnett and John Terraine. The stage production of Joan Littlewood's *Oh! What a Lovely War* (1963) (followed by Richard Attenborough's film version in 1969), and A. J. P. Taylor's wonderfully readable, witty and damning *The First World War: An Illustrated History* (1963)[16] further discouraged the revisionist cause.

By the time I went to university, in 1967, there was a clear public consensus. The First World War was avoidable; the Second was not. The First World War was not really about anything, or not about anything important; the Second World War was about national survival at home and the defeat of a vile tyranny abroad. The First World War was hopelessly mismanaged by incompetent generals whose aristocratic, rural backgrounds ill fitted them to come to terms with industrialised war; the Second World War was well run by generals who understood technology, allowing them to fight a war of manoeuvre that avoided costly battles of attrition. The outcome of the First World War was futile, merely creating circumstances in which political extremism would fester, making another war inevitable; the outcome of the Second World War, sanctified by discovery of the Nazi death camps, was not only a military but also a moral triumph.

The differences embraced not only the origins, purposes, conduct and outcomes of the wars but also the ways in which they were experienced by ordinary soldiers. Trench warfare on the Western Front in the First World War has come to be regarded as the epitome of human suffering and degradation, a sort of hell on earth. Two of the books on the First World War recommended as further reading at the foot of this chapter contain the word 'hell' in their titles. This is rarely the case with books on the Second World War. The implication is that the business of soldiering in the Second World War was easier. Only after many conversations with veterans of both wars did I discover the extent to which they themselves often felt trapped by these stereotypes. People only wanted to learn from First World War veterans how 'terrible' it was, and from Second World War veterans how 'grand'.

How different was the experience of ordinary British soldiers at 'the sharp end' in the two World Wars? Some parameters need to be set. The First World War is unique in British history. It is the only war in which the British Army was engaged with the main forces of the main enemy virtually from the first day of the war until the last. The British Army mobilised on 5 August 1914. The first soldier to be killed, Private John Parr (4th Battalion Middlesex Regiment), died on 21 August. Two days later the British Expeditionary Force blundered into the German Army at the battle of Mons. The two armies remained in contact for the rest of the war. This is very different from the Second World War. Arguably, the British Army only faced the main forces of the main enemy once – and briefly – in 1940. British civilian casualties were higher than military ones until after the invasion of Europe on 6 June 1944. The campaigns fought by the British in Eritrea, in the Western Desert, in Crete, even – to some extent – in Italy, were what Gary Sheffield describes later in this book as 'big small wars'. From a German perspective, they were all essentially sideshows. The real big war was on the Eastern Front and, from 1944, in north-west Europe. The casualties on the Eastern Front, and the savagery of the fighting there, were far more severe than those of the Western Front in the First World War. British casualty rates in north-west Europe in 1944 and 1945 were comparable with those suffered in the infamous 'attrition' battles on the Somme and at Third Ypres that haunt the British national memory. They appear to have been even higher for officers.[17]

There is a persistent, and simplistic, popular view that trench warfare caused high casualties and that the absence of trench warfare in the Second World War, the result of superior technology, accounts for lower (British) casualties. This view needs to be 'unpacked'.

First, trench warfare developed in order to reduce casualties. The early battles of the First World War were closer to those of Napoleonic times than they were to the battles of 1916 onwards. Vast numbers of men, sometimes gaudily dressed (especially in the French Army), deployed into the open, rolling fields of northern France, where they met the withering fire of smokeless, breech-loading rifles, machine-guns and quick-firing rifled cannon (mostly firing shrapnel, deadly against troops in the open). Casualties were enormous. The decision to 'dig in', from which trench warfare evolved, was made through necessity by soldiers themselves. If they had not done this, it is difficult to see how the war could have been sustained for very long. The trench system, which began to be apparent from as early as September 1914, was routinised with remarkable speed. It was recognised that troops should spend only a limited amount of time there and that only a limited number should be located in the very front line. Regular systems of relief and rotation were organised, both into and out of and within the trench system. Although trench conditions were often extremely unpleasant, troops of all sides did not submit to them passively. They did their best to make themselves comfortable. Part of the experience of war, in both World Wars (perhaps in all wars), is learning how to achieve reasonable comfort in adversity. Official and semi-official campaigns were launched at home to provide 'comforts' for the troops. Vast masses of material were brought in to make the trenches more habitable. A single square mile of trenches contained 900 miles of barbed wire, 6 million sandbags, 1 million cubic feet of timber and 360,000 square feet of corrugated iron.[18] The logistical infrastructure to support this was huge and increasingly sophisticated.[19] Defending the trench system was never cheap. The experience of the 46th (North Midland) Division, the first Territorial division to be deployed to France (in March 1915), is instructive. 46th Division was involved in only three major attacks during the war, at the Hohenzollern Redoubt (13 October 1915), at Gommecourt (1 July 1916) and at Bellenglise (29 September 1918); 13 October 1915 was its worst day in the war. Casualties suffered on those three days account for a significant proportion of the unit total, but by far the majority of its casualties were incurred in the routine of trench-holding, from snipers, shelling, mortars and harassing machine-gun fire. The British Army during the Second World War was rarely subjected to this constant, expensive, piecemeal attrition.

Second, open, mobile or semi-mobile war is not less expensive than trench warfare. Fighting on the Eastern Front in the First World War was predominantly semi-mobile. The distances were greater than on the Western Front and the densities of men and equipment, especially artillery, were less. Casualties, however, were higher than on the Western Front. The British Expeditionary Force's worst calendar month for casualties during the Great War was, unsurprisingly, July 1916. The second worst was April 1917 (Arras). The third worst was October 1917. The fighting in all these months could be characterised as 'trench warfare'. But the fifth, sixth and seventh worst months were April, August and October 1918, all periods of semi-mobile war, the last two during a period when it is generally recognised that the BEF was well led, well resourced and operationally proficient. During the 'Advance to Victory' in the final hundred days of the war, from 8 August 1918, the British Tank Corps, the epitome of mobility and technology, lost a third of all its officers and men. Tanks crews were so vulnerable to disfiguring facial wounds, caused by 'metal splash', that they took to wearing chain-mail visors, reminiscent of medieval knights.

Nor is it true that the Second World War was won by 'manoeuvre' and the First by 'attrition'. The mobile war of the Blitzkrieg or the Western Desert or the break-out from Normandy was no more typical of the Second World War than slogging matches like Stalingrad, Cassino, Kohima and Imphal, Caen and the Falaise gap, or the Reichswald. The US Navy's freedom to 'hop' from island to island in the Pacific War was achieved only at the cost of epic attritional naval battles, such as Midway and the Coral Sea, fought principally by aircraft at long range. And once ground forces were landed, they faced an equally grim attritional struggle against ferocious resistance from Japanese soldiers, often dug into hillside bunkers and trenches, reminiscent (in a very different landscape) of the fighting at 'Passchendaele'. This process is usually known as 'winkling out', a typical cant phrase for what was a desperate business, contracted at close quarters, often with flame-throwers and grenades.

Third, trench warfare was not peculiar to the First World War. Trenches (saps) had always been part of siege warfare, the dominant mode of war for much of military history. They played a leading part in the final campaigns of the American Civil War in northern Virginia and in the Russo-Japanese war. They were also a constant feature of the Second World War, though they were generally less permanent and are, perhaps, better characterised by the American term 'foxhole', a rapidly dug slit trench for one or two men, exhausting to dig, often under enemy fire. Life in them, particularly for a prolonged period, was certainly worse than life in a First World War trench system. The key word here is 'system'. First World War trenches were organised places, with facilities – primitive maybe – but still real, and comradeship. (Rob Thompson has characterised the Western Front as 'trench city'.[20]) US troops in the Belgian Ardennes, in the harsh winter of 1944-45, found themselves occupying foxholes 4 or 5 feet deep, 2 or 3 feet wide and 6 feet long, for 10, 20, even 30 nights in succession. Trench foot, that spectre from the early days of trench warfare, made a reappearance, causing 45,000 men to be evacuated from the front line, more than were put out of action by the enemy.[21]

Fourth, technology does not save lives in war. The conceit that it does is often used to explain lower British casualties in the Second World War. It was repeated recently during the British television series *Great Military Blunders*[22]. The role of technology in war is to take lives, not to save them. First World War soldiers were killed by technology, high explosive, gas, aircraft, tanks, as were those in the Second. Many of the technologies used in the Second World War were deployed in the First. The 'all-arms, deep battle', utilising sophisticated artillery techniques, armour and ground attack aircraft, employed during the autumn of 1918 by Allied armies on the Western Front, was the true precursor of modern war. The contribution of 'boffins' was also apparent. The development of artillery in the British Army, on which its success in 1918 principally rested, owed much to the contribution of the scientist Lawrence Bragg, the engineer Harold Hemming, the cartographer Evan Jack and the brilliant meteorologist Ernest Gold. The Second World War had more sophisticated signals systems than the First (especially radar and the man-portable radio), its aircraft flew higher and faster and carried more ordnance, its tanks were better armoured, more potent and quicker, but there was comparatively little fundamental change in field artillery, small arms, mortars and grenades. A British soldier of the First World War would have felt quite at home with the Lee Enfield Rifle Mark IV, the Vickers machine-gun and the Mills No 36 grenade. The excellent Bren replaced the Lewis gun, but it would have held no mysteries for a First World War Lewis-gunner. Indeed, the generation of small arms used in the First World War survived in many armies until the 1960s.

Also, in both World Wars the reality of war at the sharp end was 'low tech'. First World War trench raiders favoured knives, knuckledusters and bludgeons. In the vicious, prolonged, hand-to-hand, street-to-street, building-to-building combat that characterised the battle for Stalingrad, one of the most prized possessions was a sharpened spade. Great claims are sometimes made for the 'war-winning weapon'. The tank has been portrayed in this way in the First World War; the Soviet T-34 tank and the P-51 Mustang (or its drop tanks) in the Second. There is no doubt that a technological lead, such as Fokker's development of the interrupter gear in 1915, allowing German aircraft to fire machine-guns through their propeller blades, gave them a decided (if temporary) operational advantage. But, in many cases, complaints about the enemy's superiority in technology merely disguise tactical inferiority. This was sometimes the case in the Desert War, where skilful German use of tanks in combination with the excellent 88mm field gun, rather then the inherent inferiority of British armour, was the decisive factor. The focus on quality disguises the importance of quantity. The T-34 was an excellent tank, but so was the German Tiger. The Soviets, however, produced far more T-34s than the Germans did Tigers, sufficient for the Red Army to survive a 75 per cent loss rate in armour.

This book is a study of comparative experience. What results it produces depends on what is compared. The true comparison is not between the experience of soldiers on the Western Front and in the Western Desert, but between soldiers at Verdun and Stalingrad, between the fighting of 1916-18 in France and Flanders and the fighting of 1944-45 in north-west Europe. Such comparisons show no dramatic lessening in the grim toll of casualties; indeed, quite the contrary. When like is compared with like, modern war is shown for the truly brutal and expensive business that it invariably is. Lower British casualties in the Second World War overall are explained not by better technology or by better generalship but by the smaller scale and lesser intensity of the ground fighting in which it was involved before D-Day. In the Royal Navy (and the merchant fleet), where seamen were involved from day one of the war with the main forces of the main enemy, casualties were higher than during the First World War.[23] High casualties were also central to the experience of Bomber Command, which spearheaded the British war effort against the main forces of the main enemy from 1942 onwards.

From these perspectives, the experience of the two World Wars seems much more similar than is often supposed, a view that is strengthened by consideration of some of the 'actualities of war'.

The first of these is 'the army'. The two World Wars were fought principally, though not exclusively, by organised military forces. The men (and women) who served in them, however, were not principally 'soldiers'. When war crept back on to British university syllabuses in the 1960s, it did so as a partner (a junior partner) in the relationship between war and society. War was considered worthy of academic consideration in proportion to the extent that it had social consequences. These were felt through the need of modern, 'total' war, in particular, to mobilise 'civilian' workers, including women, and the vulnerability of those civilians to enemy action through 'strategic bombing'. This ignores the fact that wars were fought, as well as supported on the home front, by civilians. The mass armies of the two World Wars are united by their essentially civilian natures. Sir William Orpen described the British soldier of the First World War as 'the British workman in disguise'[24]. Michel Corday depicted the French soldier, in similar terms, as 'merely a peasant in a steel helmet'[25]. The First World War had a higher proportion of volunteer soldiers than the Second did. The British Army was recruited wholly by voluntary means until the spring of 1916. The Australian Imperial Force was recruited by voluntary means throughout the war, as was the (British) Indian Army in both World Wars. But this was not the norm. Most soldiers, in most armies, in both World Wars, were conscripts, chosen because of their youth, their physical fitness and the degree to which their skills could be dispensed with by the war economy. In the British and American armies, with their traditional peacetime reliance on small, Regular forces, this meant that only a small number of wartime soldiers had any significant degree of peacetime training, something the conscript armies of Europe and Japan avoided. In both World Wars the British and American armies undoubtedly suffered from having to improvise large armies from small Regular cadres. This was, perhaps, particularly true of the British Army in the First World War, when it was allowed little 'preparation time' before being committed to combat. The civilian nature of armies also had consequences for their discipline and morale. In the German and Japanese armies potential problems were resolved by 'indoctrination' of an extreme kind.[26] 'Indoctrination' jars on Western liberal ears, but it produces formidable soldiers. It can also produce the most cruel and barbaric. On the whole, the British and American armies in the Second World War learned the lessons of the First. They recognised from early on that if the conscript soldiers of 'democracies' were to be asked to die, they had a right to understand the cause for which they were dying. Towards this end they mobilised an impressive array of talented writers, film-makers and artists. In the British case, Second World War practice built on that established towards the end of the First, and many exaggerated claims have been made for the political effects of the Second World War Army Bureau of Current Affairs.[27]

The process of converting civilians into soldiers and their 'blooding' has been a staple of feature films on both sides of the Atlantic. The dramatic effects achieved by following a group from civilian life through to combat, however, often required a stability of 'cast' that was often not achieved in real life. For many soldiers, as Sir John Baynes and Cliff Pettit point out later in this book[28], the reality was to be thrown into units, where they knew no one, after only the most exiguous training. War is a notoriously difficult thing to prepare anyone for. Far from coping with it as 'soldiers', many brought the resourcefulness, resilience and comradeship, rooted essentially in civilian values, to the business of mutual survival in extreme danger.[29] Although both World Wars were 'global', 'mass' affairs, at the sharp end they were fought by small groups, the infantry section, the machine-gun team, the tank crew. Combat effectiveness depended on the morale and cohesion of these groups. 'Comradeship' is a constant theme of wartime memoirs from both World Wars. It was undoubtedly a reality, deeply felt and never forgotten. But this somewhat cosy concept ought not to disguise the often brutal reality of military discipline, not least – perhaps – in the Italian army in the First World War and the Red Army in the Second. The Italian Army's attempts to bolster morale by a series of random executions would have done justice to a barbarian horde; the Soviet NKVD executed 15,000 Red Army deserters at Stalingrad alone.

The second 'actuality of war' that united soldiers of the two World Wars was the elements. The 'high tech' image of the Second World War, all speeding armour and diving aircraft, disguises the fact that war is a labour-intensive, physical, outdoor activity, which takes place at all hours and in all weathers. The front-line infantryman was a 'beast of burden'. Towards the end of the First World War, and during the Second, he may have obtained a lift into battle, but once he got there he had to carry everything he needed. Everything he needed seems to have weighed the same for centuries, certainly since Roman times, about 60lb. American slang for an infantryman, a 'grunt', is clearly well observed. In both World Wars, front-line infantrymen of all armies carried heavy burdens, worked long hours, and often got little sleep. They froze in the Iraqi desert at night during the First World War and on the Don steppe during the bitter winter of 1941-42 in the Second (the Wehrmacht boot, with its steel toecap and heels, might have been designed specially to induce frostbite). They were soaked to the skin in Flanders in the First World War and in Flanders in the Second World War. They burned under desert suns in the Sinai during the First World War and in Libya during the Second. They sweated through the African bush in the First World War and the jungles of Burma in the Second.

Both World Wars offered almost every kind of terrain. Some of it was familiar. Soldiers often commented in letters home on the similarity of the country through which they passed or on which they fought. But much was deeply foreign. German soldiers on the Russian steppe were sometimes demoralised by the infinite space and huge skies. This produced a desperate nostalgia (literally 'home-pain'), which, as James Cooke shows later in this book, often led to the idealisation of 'home'.[30] Wherever they went, on whatever terrain, soldiers would eventually make the acquaintance of mud. Mud is inseparable from war. British Army uniforms were dyed 'khaki', the Hindustani word for 'dust' (dried mud). American 'doughboys' acquired their name from the adobe dust of the Mexican border war of 1916-17 that covered their uniforms. German slang for an infantryman is *dreckfresser* ('mud-eater'). Learning to keep clean and to keep equipment on which your life might depend clean was part of the universal experience of soldiering in both World Wars. Few have better captured the image of soldiers adapting to these conditions than the painter Eric Kennington in *The Kensingtons at Laventie*, where functional efficiency has entirely replaced 'smartness' as a military virtue.[31] Apart from details of uniform and equipment, photographs of combat soldiers from the two World Wars are barely distinguishable. Dirty, unkempt, haggard, exhausted, prematurely aged, they look straight past us with the tell-tale 'thousand-yard stare' that transcends time and reveals a universal experience.

The final 'actuality of war' that bridged the experience of front-line soldiers in both World Wars to be considered here is 'artillery'. Both conflicts were wars of the 'guns'. Stalin called artillery the 'god of war', and in both World Wars, like the

Gods of Ancient Greece, it dealt out death with a chilling impartiality. Artillery was the major cause of death and wounds on the battlefield in both wars. It was also the major cause of psychiatric casualties. 'Shell shock' is often regarded as a phenomenon of the Great War.[32] I was never aware that it existed at all in the Second World War until I came across General Patton's famous assault on a 'shell-shocked' GI. The experience of being under prolonged artillery bombardment was among the most terrifying that anyone has invented. The German veteran of the Western Front, Ernst Jünger, likened it to having a giant continually aim blows at your head with a huge hammer and just missing. The chances of being killed by a high-explosive shell, fired from ten miles away, were far greater than being killed in single or small group combat, in which personal skill, training, equipment and determination might be a factor. This reality contributed to the fatalism of soldiers, remarked upon by many commentators. High explosive did not distinguish between the callow recruit and the old hand, between the brave man and the coward, between the willing soldier and the man who just wanted to go home. Knowing when to take cover, being able to see that tiny but significant fold in the ground that another might miss, helped to keep one man alive while another would perish. But, ultimately, it was a matter of luck (front-line soldiers on all sides in both World Wars were deeply superstitious). To be a front-line soldier in the two World Wars was eventually to recognise your mortality, that one day, not this day or even the next day, given long enough exposure to the 'God of war', he would deal death or wounds to you and that your fate was to 'lie on the litter or in the grave'.[33]

Notes on contributors

Dr J.M. Bourne, The University of Birmingham, UK
John Bourne has taught History at the University of Birmingham since 1979. He thought that the publication of Britain and the Great War (London: Edward Arnold, 1989, 1991) would be his first and last on that conflict, but he was mistaken. During the last ten years his work has become increasingly focused on the British Army during the First World War and he is currently completing a revisionist study of the British Western Front generals.

Recommended reading

Addison, Paul & Calder, Angus (eds) *Time to Kill: The Soldier's Experience of the War in the West 1939-1945* (London: Pimlico, 1997)

Donovan, Tom (comp), *The Hazy Red Hell: Fighting Experiences on the Western Front 1914-1918* (Staplehurst: Spellmount, 1999)

Ellis, John, *Eye-Deep in Hell: The Western Front 1914-18* (London: Croom Helm, 1976)
   The Sharp End of War: The Fighting Man in World War II (Newton Abbot: David & Charles, 1980)

Holmes, Richard, *Firing Line* (London: Jonathan Cape, 1985)

Hynes, Samuel, *The Soldiers' War: Bearing Witness to Modern War* (London: Pimlico, 1998)

Notes

[1] Samuel Hynes, *The Soldiers' Tale: Bearing Witness to Modern War* (London: Pimlico, 1998) Chap 4

[2] Sergeant Arthur Robinson, Royal Tank Regiment, to the author, 8 April 1971

[3] I owe this illustration to my colleague, Dr R. A. H. Robinson. The American was a former pen-friend of Dr Robinson.

[4] Samuel Hynes, op cit, Chap 2; G. D. Sheffield, 'The Shadow of the Somme: the Influence of the First World War on British Soldiers' Perceptions and Behaviour in the Second World War', in Paul Addison and Angus Calder (eds), *Time to Kill: The Soldier's Experience of War in the West, 1939-1945* (London: Pimlico, 1997) pp29-39

[5] A. J. P. Taylor, *England 1914-1945* (Harmondsworth: Pelican, 1970) p727

[6] Corporal R. Shirley MM, Grenadier Guards, to the author, 10 October 1986

[7] George Macdonald Fraser's unambiguous depiction of 'Jap' in his brilliant memoir of the Burma war, *Quartered Safe Out Here* (London: Harvill, 1993), led to accusations of 'racism' from some reviewers.

[8] At a research seminar at the University of Birmingham in the autumn of 1998, a decorated veteran of Bomber Command made remarks about the 'cowardice' of US aircrew so offensive that I was compelled to reprove him.

[9] Field-Marshal Viscount Slim, *Defeat into Victory* (London: Macmillan, 1986; originally published by Cassell, 1956)

[10] HMS *Cossack* was available as a plastic self-assembly kit, from Airfix, another potent medium through which the Second World War entered the heads of small boys in the 1960s.

[11] Paul Fussell, *The Great War and Modern Memory* (Oxford: Oxford University Press, 1975). I regret to say that I myself have repeated this conceit in print: see J. M. Bourne, *Britain and the Great War 1914-1918* (London: Edward Arnold, 1989) p235

[12] R. V. Jones, *British Scientific Intelligence 1939-1945* (London: Hamish Hamilton, 1978)

[13] F. W. Winterbotham, *The Ultra Secret* (London: Weidenfeld & Nicolson, 1974); see also Ronald Lewin, *Ultra Goes to War: The Secret Story* (London: Hutchinson, 1978)

[14] Alan Clark, *The Donkeys* (London: Hutchinson, 1961). The title of the book is taken from the supposed remark of the German staff officer, Max Hoffman, that the British soldiers were 'lions led by donkeys'.

[15] Ibid, between pp64-5. Another photograph, of senior French and British political and military leaders, between pp128-9, is captioned 'Polished boots'.

[16] A. J. P. Taylor, *The First World War: An Illustrated History* (London: George Rainbird, 1963). Taylor dedicated the book to Joan Littlewood.

[17] See John Ellis, *The Sharp End of War: The Fighting Man in World War II* (Newton Abbot: David & Charles, 1980) pp156-69, and Appendix, pp376-7, for the figures. Ellis's book captures better than any other the essential similarity of experience of front-line soldiers in the two World Wars.

[18] Denis Winter, *The First of the Few: Fighter Pilots of the First World War* (London: Allen Lane, 1982) p15

[19] For the British experience, see Ian Malcolm Brown, *British Logistics on the Western Front 1914-1919* (Westport, Ct, and London: Praeger, 1998)

[20] Rob Thompson, 'British Logistics on the Western Front, 1914-1918', paper presented to the War and Society Seminar, The University of Birmingham, 1 July 1999.

[21] Stephen E. Ambrose, *The Victors: Eisenhower and His Boys: The Men of World War II* (New York: Simon & Schuster, 1998) p301

[22] Shown on Channel 4 during February and March 2000.

[23] On British war memorials that record names from both World Wars, it is common for there to be three times as many names from the First World War than from the Second (Halesowen, in Worcestershire, is an excellent example). But war memorials in seafaring communities often have an equality of names from each war, or even more from the Second (Looe, in Cornwall, is a good example, as is the Royal Naval memorial in Plymouth).

[24] Sir W. Orpen, *The Outline of Art* (London: George Newnes, nd) p374. He was actually referring to the portrayal of British soldiers in the paintings of C. R. W. Nevinson.

[25] See Michel Corday, *The Paris Front: An Unpublished Diary 1914-1918* (London, 1933) pp154-5

[26] Every German soldier swore a personal oath of obedience to Adolf Hitler upon enlistment: 'I swear

by God this holy oath, that I will render unconditional obedience to the Führer of Germany and of her people, Adolf Hitler, the supreme commander of the armed forces, and as a brave soldier I will be prepared to lay down my life in pursuance of this oath at any time.'

[27] See S. P. Mackenzie, *Politics and Military Morale: Current Affairs and Citizenship Education in the British Army 1914-1950* (Oxford: Clarendon Press, 1992) for a measured analysis

[28] See below, Chap 2

[29] For an examination of this in the British First World War context, see J. M. Bourne, 'The British Working Man in Arms', in Hugh Cecil and Peter H. Liddle (eds), *Facing Armageddon: The First World War Experienced* (London: Pen & Sword, 1996) pp336-52

[30] See below, Chap 13

[31] Kennington painted the picture from experience and it contains identifiable soldiers of the 13th Battalion London Regiment (The Kensingtons), a Territorial unit. The painting is in the Imperial War Museum, London.

[32] A recent edition of the *Journal of Contemporary History*, 35 (1) (January 2000), devoted to 'Shell Shock', is almost entirely about the Great War. Psychiatric problems are, in fact, a constant feature of modern war; see Wendy Holden, *Shell Shock: The Psychological Impact of War* (London: Channel 4 Books, 1998). One of the Second World War's psychiatric victims was the real-life hero portrayed in the film *The Foreman Went to France*; see Holden, *Shell Shock*, p89.

[33] General Omar Bradley, quoted in Ellis, *The Sharp End of War*, p52

Chapter 2

Preparing for war: the experience of the Cameronians

John Baynes and Cliff Pettit

The aim in this chapter is to look sequentially at the experiences of men drawn into the preparations for war in 1914 and 1939, emphasising in the second half of the chapter the similarities and differences between these two threshholds to British active service soldiering in the two World Wars of the 20th century. The study is mainly based on the recollections of those who served in The Cameronians (Scottish Rifles), a regiment no longer shown in the Army List, but one of which both authors were proud to be members in their day.

1914-15

Although a few people in Britain foresaw the tragic consequences of the assassination of the Archduke Franz Ferdinand and his wife in Sarajevo on 28 June 1914, the speed of events that led to the outbreak of hostilities on Tuesday 4 August took most of the nation by surprise. Once the die was cast, however, virtually the entire population enthusiastically endorsed the decision to declare war against Germany. Mobilisation of the Regular Army, the Reserves and the Territorial Force was ordered on 5 August. Within days Lord Kitchener, the Secretary of State for War, also called for volunteers to join a new army, since he realised that troops would be required in far greater numbers than could be provided by existing organisations. By 25 August the first hundred thousand men, referred to as 'K1', had been enlisted, so he called for a further hundred thousand. Nearly double that number came forward.

To see how these events affected the various components of a particular regiment we shall look at the Cameronians (Scottish Rifles) at their home bases in Glasgow and the county of Lanarkshire, commencing with Captain R. M. S. Baynes, a Regular officer at that time at home on leave from a tour of colonial duty with the West African Frontier Force in Sierra Leone[1]:

'When war was declared I was at home in Kent and either that day or the day after I had a telegram telling me to rejoin the 1st Battalion at Maryhill

Barracks in Glasgow. When I got there I found intense activity: reservists coming in and all sorts of preparations being made. Also arriving were a lot of officers – veterans of the Boer War – many of whom had just dug out their uniforms, and looked as though they had just arrived from South Africa without having time to wash or change since arrival. I can't remember how long it was but it was two or three days after I got there, and we were really getting things going, when Kitchener made the announcement that he required a hundred thousand men, which were to be raised immediately. Robertson was commanding the battalion – always known as "Blobs" – and he sent for me and told me that he was very sorry, but as I'd been away from the battalion for some time, I must be one of the three officers who had to be sent off immediately to help with this business of raising a new army. It was a bitter disappointment, but there was nothing to be done about it. Off I went to the depot.

At the depot in Hamilton, instead of the intense activity of Maryhill we found utter confusion. Reservists had been coming in and were fitted out, and the staff were getting on with things fairly well, although the depot was extremely full. But immediately the announcement of the first hundred thousand was made, volunteers started pouring in: their tents were pitched in a sort of playing field in the middle of the barracks, and every available space was taken up by men sleeping. There was not enough preparation in the way of food and rations, and we had to send out into Hamilton and collect everything possible in the way of food. The first night things got so bad and the depot was so full that we had to close the gates and at intervals open them and then charge the people outside, thus keeping them from breaking in. All this first kind were a pretty rough lot, many of whom were unemployed, and they were only too anxious to join up and get some food and pay. After a few days I was sent off with a 2nd Lieutenant, 200 men and half a dozen or so NCOs from the depot. We were put on a train but we'd no idea where we were going.

We eventually found ourselves at Bordon in Hampshire. Nobody at Bordon knew anything about us either, but I met the garrison adjutant, whom I'd known before, and he told me that I'd better go and choose some barracks to live in. I chose Martinique barracks, which were nearest the station, and went in there with my 200 men.

Some days later another 200 men arrived and these were put into other barrack rooms, which we took over. Later came another 200, and then some officers of various sorts and kinds. I think the first officers were probably old volunteers dating back to the previous century. There were certainly two ancient majors, and then more odd people turned up. There were those who'd been on jobs in various strange places, odd Indian army people who'd been on leave, and so on. What was interesting was the sort of men who arrived with each party. The first lot that I had taken down were a pretty rough crowd who, as I said, had more or less broken into Hamilton and joined up for food and jobs. The next lot were rather better. They'd had jobs and had given them up and joined the army. Then later a superior class came down. These were all very well dressed, with a couple of them carrying suitcases, and later on came an even smarter variety. Also a lot of ex-NCOs who were most useful. One thing about it was that with all these men to select from there was no difficulty in finding somebody for any kind of job such as cooks, clerks and people who did all kind of mending such as bootmakers. I also found as mess president a man who was one of the directors of the Savoy Hotel in London.

To start with, as I said, we were more or less camping. We had absolutely nothing in the way of uniform or equipment or anything else. In spite of that we started marching quite soon, as one of the first things to do was to get the men as fit as possible. I think that broomsticks, instead of rifles, were the first equipment that we learned to drill with. Then a certain amount of uniform started to arrive. This was all old full dress uniform from every kind of unit, and you'd get a most extraordinary selection on parade. You'd see a man for instance in a rifle tunic and tartan trews, wearing a straw hat, next to somebody else in a red coat and some civilian trousers. At all events the men were clothed – in a way. The next stage was khaki, and everybody got fitted out not so very long after. There were no khaki overcoats available, and so a supply of civilian coats were sent down. This distribution was most amusing as in those days people wore very heavy overcoats, and senior NCOs, sergeant-majors and so on all took the large heavy double-breasted kind with belts. Other junior NCOs had double-breasted ones without belts, whilst the rank and file had to make do with the single-breasted ones which were not so handsome.

I can't remember how many hours training we put in per day, but the training syllabus came down from the War Office. We had to fit in so many hours on each subject for every company every week, and I had to make out a chart of the times and places of various kinds of training to ensure that we distributed it properly, as well as the training facilities such as ranges, assault courses, parade grounds and so on. These charts were always known by the company commanders as "my Chinese puzzles". The first great occasion was when we got a complete battalion on parade, though strangely dressed, and took them out for a route-march as a battalion. [After some confusion about its correct title the battalion was by now officially designated 9th Scottish Rifles.]

We then moved to Bramshott, and it was a very proud day when we got the whole battalion on parade, fully armed and with a certain amount of transport, and we were able to march out of the barracks at Bordon as a real unit, led by our pipers. I'd started getting pipers very early in the proceedings and one of the first was boy Gibson from Dunblane, who was 14 years old and afterwards became sergeant-major in the regiment. He was a tough lad who insisted on playing a full set of pipes, although I'd offered to buy him a smaller set, and went out on all marches. He never fell out, but very nearly burst from the amount of food and buns that were given to him at every halt by the local inhabitants. He was a most popular person and an enormous help to the battalion. I think eventually we had six pipers and they really were quite good.

It must have been either January or February 1915, certainly when there'd been a lot of snow, that the division was inspected by Kitchener. We were all drawn up along miles of road at Frensham Ponds on a bitterly cold day. Kitchener was late for some reason, so we were standing about in the snow for over an hour. A good many men were falling out or down.

All this time we were training pretty hard, and there was not much time for amusement, but we were now and again able to get up to London at weekends, where we had some very cheerful parties indeed. Of course we were all very keen to get to France. I shall never forget the shock we'd had earlier after the news of the Battle of the Marne, and then the advance from the Marne to the Aisne. We were all terrified the war would be over before we could get into it.'

Leaving the 9th, the regiment's first-formed K1 battalion, shortly before it crossed over to France, let us return to the first days of the war and look at one of the four Territorial battalions.

On 7 August there arrived at 261 West Princes Street, Glasgow, Headquarters of the 5th Scottish Rifles (created in 1908 out of the 1st Lanarkshire Rifle Volunteers), a very tall, rather irate subaltern who some years later was to become famous as the first Director-General of the BBC. Lieutenant J. C. Reith had been working for the firm of Pearson in London as an engineer on a big dock-building project, but there had been confusion over his mobilisation orders, which had been incorrectly telegraphed to him. The muddle was eventually sorted out, and he joined his company as described in his book *Wearing Spurs*[2] published in 1966, although he had actually written the account many years earlier:

'A Territorial battalion mobilised – On Active Service – a curious and interesting spectacle. We who had been amateurs had become professionals; what we had done in odd moments, voluntarily and in a sense unofficially, was now full-time, compulsory and very official. The authority of officer and NCO, in general the run of military law, had been observed almost on sufferance and on occasion; now they were mandatory and permanent. From being rather farcical, an officer's job had suddenly become very serious; the play-hour had merged into life itself and turned solemn reality – all rather bewildering. Camp each year was mobilisation of a sort, but the period was limited to a fortnight, and we were not On Active Service. It was these words which made the circumstances and conditions and atmosphere radically different. Trivial faults became crimes; minor crimes became major ones. Officers commanding companies were instructed to impress upon their men the awful import of the term; to warn them of the penalties of disobedience or neglect of duty. My OC company was thoroughly in form to do so. The death sentence was frequently to be found in the rubric. "And you're On Active Service now," he would with portentous solemnity interpolate, and glare along the ranks. We had no doubt about it.

We were shortly "to proceed to the war station" which sounded interesting; and we were given identity discs: "Lieut J. C. W. Reith Pres 5th SR". This, or rather what was implied, was something of a shock – the reference to one's religious persuasion in particular; so early and so far from actual warfare to be presented with the credentials for burial and record. Moreover, but quite incidentally, Territorials were available for home defence only, and no one had said anything about foreign service, though I for one had no doubt we would go abroad. The company OC told me to wear the identity disc day and night, but that struck me as being premature. As a matter of fact it was not worn until May 1915 – and then only par cause de pous.

Where was this war station and whither had two or three of the officers and about a hundred of the men disappeared? I sought enlightenment of my OC, thinking we might be going to some vulnerable spot on the east coast; Falkirk, he told me. "Falkirk – what on earth for?" As to the others, it was secret; but he had no doubt they were "in the trenches". I could not imagine what trenches there were in Scotland, nor why anyone should be living in them. His imagination was running away with him.

On Sunday morning, 9th, the Battalion paraded with its bands and marched down Great Western Road to church. It was an impressive performance. Every Friday night in pre-war drill seasons we had emerged from the seclusion of our training-ground and marched along the two miles of this spacious boulevard to a formal dismissal at Charing Cross. I never cared for this operation for, as senior subaltern of No 1, I had to walk beside the little company OC. The Territorials were always an object of amusement to a section of the community, and ribald youth along the route made the most of the sight of a very tall man in uniform marching by the side of a very little man. But it was different now. We had been playing at soldiers before; now we were soldiers. Status and potentialities recognised.'

Reith spent ten days at Falkirk before being detached with 60 men to guard two vulnerable points on the railway line south from Perth in the region of Larbert. For four happy weeks he ran his detachment in his own way with no interference from any senior officer. Then came the time to rejoin the battalion, when, soon after 20 September, the main body moved to Larbert as well:

'Next morning, with a heavy heart, I set out to attend an ordinary battalion parade which was to be followed by a route march. A route march! I was met by an orderly room messenger. He handed me a note from the Adjutant instructing me to take over command of Transport. Gosh, what a joy this was; the sun shone in an unclouded sky.

The Transport Officer was a somebody; an object of mystification, envy and even respect among his brother officers. He was not, as they, subject to parades and orderly duties. He was a power in the land; one with whom it was expedient to be on friendly terms; he could perform or withhold all sorts of services... Transport Officer. Magnificent – like the gold star.

The major issues of war are in the hands of God, politicians and the general staff. The regimental officer, realising his helplessness, is not greatly concerned about them. Apart from discharging to the best of his ability the particular little task allotted to him he is not exercised with schemes for the rout of the enemy. Beyond satisfying himself that there is an appropriate depth of sand or earth on his dugout roof, and choosing when available a cellar instead of an attic (or at any rate a room before reaching which a shell would have to pass through at least one other) the chances of his own survival and the general progress of the campaign do not figure much in his mind. He has too much else to do, and in the doing of them the Transport Officer is often of determining importance. A horse and cart at the right moment, or a few cubic feet of space in a cart, may make all the difference to his outlook on life. They may make war tolerable and perhaps, for the time being, enjoyable. A mighty and beneficent power to wield. Transport Officer 5th SR.'

For nearly all the men in the various units of the regiment, the first months of the war involved making many adjustments to military life. This applied to the Regular 1st Battalion, (always known as the Cameronians while the others were called the Scottish Rifles) because it was made up largely of reservists. With the 2nd being always kept up to strength at its overseas station in Malta, the 1st was usually short of men, especially during the summer trooping season when it sent out drafts of newly trained soldiers to its linked battalion. Thus in August 1914 it was ready to absorb all the reservists that came back to the colours, some of whom had been firmly settled in civilian life for many years. Although the men in the TF had a little military experience, their training, in Reith's words, had been 'done in odd moments and in a sense unofficially'. Naturally the New Army volunteers had the most adjusting to do, but the Regular reservists and TF men had their share of adapting, or readapting, themselves to military routine as well.

The problem of adjustment can be discussed under two general headings: physical demands and discipline. Under the first come general fitness, especially condition of feet; hygiene and medical matters; and food and drink. Under the second, obedience to orders and military law; the acceptance of a strict hierarchy of ranks; and loss of freedom.

Apart from the occasional long journey by train, and the rare trip in a bus or lorry, the infantryman of 1914 travelled everywhere on his feet, the condition of which was more than a matter of purely individual concern. During the retreat from Mons, which came so soon after the start of the war, the Regular reservists of the Cameronians and the other battalions of the British Expeditionary Force became fully aware of their boots not having been well worn in and their unhardened feet, as well as shoulders unused to carrying heavy packs and other accoutrements. However unpopular, long periods of foot drill, physical exercises and route marching were a major part of preparations for joining the army in France.

As described by R. M. S. Baynes, the volunteers who rushed to join the New Army were a cross-section of the population, ranging from well-educated potential officers to the unemployed only 'too anxious to join up and get some food and pay'. While members of the former group were normally healthy and kept themselves clean, many of the unfortunate ones at the other end of the scale were underdeveloped and had only rudimentary ideas about hygiene. Medical inspections, foot and skin inspections, inoculations, compulsory showers and other measures were applied to all, being resented by the various groups for different reasons, but accepted as an inevitable part of army life. As reaction to these basic health matters varied according to background, so did the views on army rations. Whether considered dull and inadequate by the better-off, or almost luxurious in comparison to the meagre diet of many of the poor, the basic ration scale was adequate to maintain stamina and fitness among men living unusually strenuous lives, and was more generous than most of the British population was used to.

Turning to the subject of military discipline, the first point to make is that it came as much less of a shock to most of the 1914 volunteers than it might to their few descendants in the Army almost 90 years later. Not only was British society more rigidly stratified than it is today, but at every level people holding any form of authority were expected to impose it on those below them with rigour, and in general were respected for doing so. It should be remembered that domestic servants, farm labourers and shop-workers constituted between them the major part of the working population of Britain; '...her farms employed more labourers than either business or her textile factories; and more men and women were engaged in paid domestic service than in all the metallurgical industries – from pin-making to ship-building – put together.'[3] In such employments hours were long and work hard, with graded levels from owner down to youngest farm-boy or kitchen-maid similar to the military hierarchy.

There were, however, places where hierarchy was not so readily understood. In those areas where the mines and heavy industry were the main employers, attitudes were different. In Glasgow and the surrounding smoke-grimed towns there were hard-faced mine and shipyard owners, with rough foremen to control the workforce, but their power was not so easily accepted. Scottish egalitarianism, supported by increasingly active trades unions, did not produce a type of man to take readily to being chased round a barrack-square. In *The First Hundred Thousand 'K1'*, a novel that was a best-seller in the war and long after, the author Ian Hay describes the reactions to military life of a Jock in the fictitious Bruce & Wallace Highlanders. Hay was in fact a captain in the Argyll & Sutherland Highlanders in 1914, commanding New Army men largely recruited from Glasgow and industrial Clydeside, and very similar to Scottish Riflemen.

'There are other rifts within the military lute. At home we are persons of some consequence, with very definite notions about the dignity of labour. We have employers who tremble at our frown; we have Trades Union officials who are at constant pains to impress upon us our own omnipotence in the industrial world in which we live. We have at our beck and call a Radical MP who, in return for our vote and suffrage, informs us that we are the backbone of the nation, and that we must on no account permit ourselves to be trampled upon by effete and tyrannical upper classes. Finally, we are Scotsmen, with all a Scotsman's curious reserve and contempt for social airs and graces.

But in the Army we appear to be nobody. We are expected to stand stiffly at attention when addressed by an officer; even to call him "sir" – an honour to which our previous employer has been a stranger. At home, if we happened to meet the head of the firm in the street, and none of our colleagues was looking, we touched a cap, furtively. Now, we have no option in the matter. We are expected to degrade ourselves by meaningless and humiliating gestures. The NCOs are almost as bad. If you answer a sergeant as you would a foreman, you are impertinent; if you argue with him, as all good Scotsmen must, you are insubordinate; if you endeavour to drive a collective bargain with him, you are mutinous; and you are reminded that upon active service mutiny is punishable by death. It is all very unusual and upsetting.

You may not spit; neither may you smoke a cigarette in the ranks, nor keep the residue thereof behind your ear. You may not take beer to bed with you. You may not postpone your shave till Saturday: you must shave every day. You must keep your buttons, accoutrements, and rifle speckless, and have your hair cut in a style which is not becoming to your particular type of beauty. Even your feet are not your own. Every Sunday morning a young officer, whose leave has been specially stopped for the purpose, comes round the barrack-rooms after church and inspects your extremities, revelling in blackened nails and gloating over hammer-toes. For all practical purposes, decides Private Mucklewame, "you might as well be in Siberia".[4]

1939-40

Any comparison of the respective attitudes of those joining the forces at the outbreak of the Second World War with the rush to enlist that occurred in 1914 must be considered in conjunction with the distinctive 1939 circumstance. Unlike 1914, where an isolated, unexpected event triggered the outbreak of hostilities, there had been an air of inevitability about war with the Axis powers. It profoundly influenced the population. For the many who could recall the grim reality of the earlier conflict, there could only be apprehension. This was confirmed by the introduction of conscription in May 1939 for what was intended to be six months' service of men aged 20, and the doubling in size of the Territorial Army. Thus when a declaration of war was made in September 1939, most felt that only force would defeat Hitler's tyranny and that this was essential for personal and national survival. There was no headlong dash to join up, although there were many volunteers. Recruiting was much more orderly than in 1914. This was only in relative terms, as the Depots struggled to cope with the recall of reservists, the conscripts already being trained, the established and newly formed Territorial units, in addition to the volunteers.

In many ways the recruit of the 1939-40 era faced less of a culture shock initiation into the disciplines of service life. Most who were conscripts, either of the May 1939 group or immediately after the outbreak of hostilities, had a much better preparation than their 1914 predecessors. Virtually all had parents or relatives who had served in that conflict. While many of this generation refused to recount tales of their time in the trenches – the memory often painful to recall – talk about service life in general was less difficult. The cinema, radio and improvement in literacy had given a much clearer picture of what to expect, as well as an indication of the true nature of Nazism and the consequences for those who failed to stand against it. Of his first impressions, an anonymous reservist wrote:

'On 13th July, 30 men aged 20 years and of various trades and creeds, were formed into the Ramillies Platoon of the Cameronians (Scottish Rifles). Most of these men had done very little physical training or swimming, and knew nothing of guns. Formerly they lived in quiet homes, each with a room to himself or shared with a brother. Now all this is altered. "The old order changeth yielding place to new." A fine spirit of camaraderie prevails, and we eat and sleep together, each man willing to help and share with his neighbour.

   In our physical training class and at the swimming bath our bodies are being developed. When we entered this life we were given a full kit, and some time was spent in cleaning our equipment, which was inspected on 29th July. If the cauldron of war should boil over, our country wants us to be able to protect ourselves against the atrocities of modern warfare, and so we have gas lectures in order to teach us to recognise the various gases, persistent and non-persistent, and how to treat our respirators properly. However, war may never come, and what then? Are the men of Ramillies Platoon just wasting six months of their lives? Certainly not, for habits of neatness and tidiness are being sown in the minds of these 30 men of this platoon, and what gives greater happiness than a disciplined life? So ends the first fortnight in the life of the first Militiamen of Ramillies Platoon.'

This quotation is part of an article that was printed in the Regimental Journal[5], and reasonably could be suspected of special pleading. However, it is unlikely that the writer would have sounded so euphoric, knowing the probability of his piece being read by his comrades, if it did not give a fair reflection of their general attitude. There were many similarities in the experiences of recruits joining the army at the beginning of both conflicts. The induction courses still operated along the same lines. Indeed, it is difficult to see where there could be much difference, as it is a basic necessity of any military arm to establish its own principles grounded on tradition, and the requirement of the acceptance and carrying out of orders.

   While the expansion of the armed forces was carried out in a much more structured manner – the chaos created by the too rapid formation of Kitchener's Army in 1914 being avoided – the absence of conscription until just before the outbreak of hostilities in 1939 resulted in a similar effect. Large groups of recruits had to be taught from scratch the rudiments of living collectively, on a long-term basis, and the peculiar disciplines of a military existence. It was acknowledged that this could not be accomplished overnight. Sensibly, it was achieved by the establishment of Infantry Training Units at Regimental Depots. These, in effect, were an extension of the Training Companies in being in 1919.

   This situation was endemic to all arms of the service. Frederick Hindmarsh[6], a civil servant and Royal Artillery trainee in 1940, said that his fellow recruits had a sober approach to the whole thing, although the lack of modern equipment produced an attitude of cynicism among his fellow conscripts. The standard of instruction was at times abysmal:

'Regular rankers were promoted and flung in at the deep end. Many had had no proper education. They knew nothing of teaching methods, and often couldn't understand the training manuals. So they learned everything by heart and repeated the words verbatim to the trainees – a question would throw them completely, and they simply repeated the last part of the lesson – relevant or not! Most conscripts were more intelligent than the instructors, and simply scoffed at the whole thing. I recall being given a talk on the Indian Mutiny in the wind and driving rain at the entrance to a shed which the noise of artificers at work made it almost impossible to hear, even if we had been interested. It was only two years into the war that things really began to improve.'

A comparison of the Infantry Training Manual issued on 10 August 1914 ('IT 1914') with that issued on 31 August 1937 shows some interesting variations that indicate that there was a clear acknowledgement of the need for a complete rewrite of IT 1914. The latter concluded its preface with a draconian warning on the authority of the War Office, that '…any enunciation by officers responsible for training of principles other than those contained in this manual, or any practice of methods not based on those principles is forbidden…'

By 1937 the approach had changed, with most rhetoric and exhortation removed. The preface to IT 1937 recognised that as a result of reorganisation, the manual reflected a period of transition:

'The new weapons and vehicles with which the infantry is to be armed and equipped, have either not yet been issued to the troops, or have been provided on a limited scale. There has therefore been little opportunity for studying the methods of training in peace, and leading in war, that may be necessitated by reorganisation, mechanisation and re-armament…'

The object of training is baldly stated:

'Above all he must be highly disciplined, for by discipline alone can morale be maintained; it is the bedrock of all training. It is the ingrained habit of cheerful and unquestioning obedience that controls and directs the fighting spirit and is the back-bone of a unit in a moment of crisis.'

IT 1914 provided for a course of 26 weeks, with about one-third devoted to squad and ceremonial drill, and the same for physical training. In IT 1937 there is a similar division in a more intense course of 18 weeks, about one-fifth of which, significantly, is to be devoted to educational training, a subject not part of IT 1914.

The state of training of the Territorials needed urgent attention. Charles Michie[7], a junior bank official, had joined the London Scottish, a Territorial unit, as a private soldier just after his 20th birthday in 1936:

'Training took place in the drill hall at Buckingham Gate, or at Easter and Whitsun Camps with a Highland battalion at Aldershot or at Dover Castle, or at annual camp. The weekend training taught me nothing except possibly to be a smarter soldier. Annual camp was better but our automatic weapons were mock-ups. In 1937 we did our annual march in Scotland: Tain, Dingwall, Inverness. This did help for later active service as we learned to march all day with sore feet! With the increase in size of the Territorials, I suddenly shot from private to Lance-Sergeant in a matter of months.'

At the antiquated Depot at Hamilton in Lanarkshire, it seemed that little had changed since 1914. While all entrants were kitted out with uniform and a rifle (the SMLE, but with no ammunition), there was a desperate shortage of equipment and accommodation. However, there were additional considerations to be taken into account. Bernard Kilpatrick[8], a railway clerk of Motherwell, was conscripted and joined the Regiment at Hamilton Barracks in March 1940:

'Strict blackout restrictions were in force. Once in the middle of the night there was an air-raid alarm. The drill was for us to parade on the nearby square. It was forbidden to turn on the room lights in case they shone out when we opened the door to double to the muster point. Once mustered, we then had to move, again at the double. To the racecourse, to stand about until the all-clear. The result was a mad scramble in the darkness of the hut for clothing as we dashed for the door. I remember one rather disorganised Jock ending up at muster point clad in nothing but his underpants.'

Kilpatrick is clear about the lack of any proper equipment other than the rifle for training purposes:

'A mortar platoon was formed, but there were no Universal Carriers, the prescribed basic transport for the men, weapons and ammunition. All that the platoon got to make it mobile was an issue of sit-up-and-beg bikes when the men paraded one morning. When the Platoon Sergeant gave the order "Prepare to mount", everyone had to put his left foot on the pedal. On the command "Mount", the Jocks did so. Some had forgotten to push their bikes forward at the same time, and promptly fell off the other side into the path of those who had. The result was a chaotic tangle of bodies and bikes all over the square. Our basic training, the NCOs and officers, I thought, were good. We all were keen enough to learn the principles of soldiering. After Dunkirk a "Duty Platoon" had to be available on constant standby in case of invasion. It had to remain fully dressed, with equipment to hand at all times. Having to sleep wearing our battledress and boots gave the feeling of being really involved in the great events taking place further south. We made route marches of up to ten miles, often being offered food by the locals – a great boost to making us feel that we were appreciated and serving a useful purpose.'

The pressure on accommodation in the barracks was such that every available space was utilised. Bob Baxter[9], a clerk, reported to Hamilton in January 1940 as a conscript, having had no previous experience of army life:

'We were billeted in the stables, and we all slept on the concrete floor on palliasses, hessian bags stuffed with straw. While the horses had been moved, the rats which often are their bedfellows remained. We had to accept at night they would crawl over our bedding, and sometimes over our faces. I had been an office clerk before call-up, and the primitive conditions were quite a shock for many of us whose life previously had been comparatively sheltered, even though we knew what to expect. We were taught the use of the Bren Gun on a wooden model. Being new to military life, we tended to accept everything we were told by the regulars as "gospel". It was only after a few weeks service that we began to realise that some of the very junior NCOs, old sweats who had received instant promotion after the rapid expansion of the forces, perhaps were not the ideal instructors. Even the over-officious Acting Unpaid Lance-Corporal was obeyed without question, as we soon learned that rank was all-important. I joined the Motor Transport Section. This consisted of a variety of military vehicles supplemented by an assortment of commandeered civilian cars, vans and lorries. Nevertheless, the usual moans of the private soldier apart, it was a sound introduction to military discipline and army life but nothing else.'

Rifleman W. W. Gallacher[10], a 1940 conscript, was astounded at the crudeness of some of the Regulars and reservists: '…they even used to spit in their tea to make sure no one would drink it while they queued for the next course, probably a legacy of service abroad in stations where water was in short supply.'

Thomas Laing[11] was a shop assistant in Edinburgh when conscripted in 1939. When asked on enlistment if he had any preference for a particular arm of the service, he explained that he was a musician and interested in organising entertainments. The response was immediate: '…it's the infantry for you!' He was posted to a training unit of the Cameronians in a hutted camp at East Kilbride, having had no previous military experience:

'We were all conscripts, and not allowed out of camp for the first three weeks, until we had acquired a semblance of soldierly appearance. Apart from the few malcontents which could be found in any branch of the forces, all of us realised we were there "for the duration", so there was nothing for it but to make the best of it. Having had to wait some time between enlistment and call-up gave us some time to prepare mentally for the abrupt change in our circumstances. I was able to escape the dreaded Church Parade by being detailed as an organist, and also to organise entertainments for the unit. I cannot recall that there were any complaints about the standard of catering, but some of our billets were pretty primitive to say the least, but we all mucked in and an excellent team spirit developed. While we were prepared to accept orders from our own officers, there was always objection taken to anyone not of our Regiment trying to tell us what to do. We had a strong sense of being part of the Scottish military tradition – I think even the Englishmen who joined us felt this, and adopted the same unwillingness to be messed about, especially by anyone we didn't respect.'

This was not always the case. The policy adopted in 1916 during the First World War of restricting the number of conscript postings to local regiments was continued – in order to avoid a particular area being severely affected in the event of that unit suffering heavy casualties. It was not a universal success. A Rifleman[12], who wishes to remain anonymous, joined at Hamilton in early 1940 to be squadded with several thoroughly disaffected East Londoners bemused by their alien surroundings, and intent only on returning to London and their former way of life in the criminal society of the city's East End:

'On our first leave, the Barracks shut down all training, and a special train was laid on to Glasgow to catch onward connections. The train had barely left the station when the Londoners changed into civilian clothes, threw their uniforms out of the window and produced false identification cards. I never saw them again...'

Unlike 1914 there was no immediate award of commissioned rank to men thought to be of the right social standing and background. Initially officers were selected mainly from the ranks of the existing Territorial battalions of the Army. However, in the Officer Cadet Training Corps a requirement of membership was the giving of an undertaking in the event of war to join HM Forces and go forward to commissioned rank. The potentiality of immediate commissioning occurred in September 1939 to David Liddell[13], a private in the only infantry battalion of The Honourable Artillery Company, a prestigious London Territorial regiment. He was a junior broker with Lloyd's, joining his battalion when it was mobilised. The HAC, in effect, was an Officer Cadet Unit, and membership then virtually guaranteed an offer of a commission after mobilisation, the timing of the offer being dependent on length of service as a Territorial.

'After a two-month crash course at Bulford in December 1939, I was awarded a commission. I was required to express a preference for a regimental posting. A friend of the family, Major Storey, MC, a Cameronian of many years standing whom I greatly respected, had urged me to apply to his regiment, and although I had no previous connection with it, I was delighted when accepted – so much so, that I was able to persuade three other friends, newly commissioned from HAC, to do so, and we all arrived at Hamilton Barracks at the turn of the year.'

The need to produce cadres of competent junior NCOs was quickly grasped.

'Training of new recruits was a priority. Soon after my arrival, still as a 2nd Lieutenant, I was given command of a platoon created to train potential

NCOs. At the conclusion of each course, my duty was to submit a report to Battalion HQ on the potential of each man. The quality of the Riflemen selected was uniformly high, and many of them joined the 12th Battalion, which was in the course of being made up to strength. I was privileged to be posted to that unit later in 1940, and was pleased to find that those men who had undergone this training were making their mark already as junior NCOs.'

Malcolm McNeil[14], formerly a member of Glasgow University OTC, who joined the Cameronians as a rifleman direct from taking a law degree, said of the four-month course that was to become the norm for Infantry OCTUs throughout the war:

'The standard of education set and the efficiency of instruction were pretty so-so. I don't think I learned anything more than I had done at OTC, but the difference was the 24-hour seven-day-a-week exercise and practice, and making soldiering a way of life... The proper training of the Home Forces only began seriously in 1942, when the influence of Alexander, Montgomery, and the GOC Home Forces began to apply to intelligent training – the setting up of Battle Schools, and the concentration on technical skills. Until then we were at sixes and sevens, and from what I saw of it, the 51st (Highland) Division was as poorly trained as we of the 52nd (Lowland) Division when they were sent out to Africa – where they had to learn pretty PDQ...'

Edward Scott[15], a Cheshire man with no Cameronian connections, had this to record:

'On the outbreak of war in September 1939 I volunteered for service in the army and was formally enlisted. I had undertaken to enlist as a member of the Officer Cadet Reserve, which I had joined on leaving the School OTC with Certificate "A". I was aware on enlistment that I would have to serve some six months in the ranks before being considered for a commission...'

While awaiting joining instructions he continued his legal studies. On the formation of the Local Defence Volunteers (afterwards the Home Guard) as a private, he joined the local unit. His opinion of its possible effectiveness, despite the undoubted enthusiasm of its members, most of whom were between 45 and 60 years or in reserved occupations, was somewhat circumspect:

'We were issued with a .303 rifle and ten rounds of ammunition with which to repel the German paratroops... Eventually to my surprise I received orders to report to the Infantry Training Centre of the Cameronians (Scottish Rifles) at Hamilton Barracks. I duly reported there on 14 November 1940, and found myself as a rifleman, in hutted accommodation in the company of some 30 young men from Lanarkshire and Glasgow, little of whose conversation I would at first understand. My comrades in arms were good-hearted and loyal to the group. They seemed to have readily, if resignedly, accepted the need to serve, accepted the firm but fair discipline, and showed keenness to learn. Regimental traditions and standards were soon imposed. The training, particularly in weapons, was of a high standard.

My Company Commander was Capt G. R. S. Drought. He was killed in action in Sicily in 1943. He had been an Army Boxing Champion, and it became clear to me that if I wanted a commission I had better enter the boxing ring. I did so one bitterly cold November night, suffering from a head cold and confronted by one Corporal Telfer, who seemed much bigger than me. He struck me on the nose in the first round, and I was covered in blood, but survived to be beaten on points over the three rounds…'

This exploit had evidently impressed the Company Commander, who put Scott forward for an interview with the Commanding Officer, as a result of which he was recommended for a commission. Scott attended 168 OCTU at Droitwich, then at Morecambe.

'At the conclusion of the four-months OCTU course, which did not impress me, cadets had the opportunity to choose three Regiments in order of preference. The time spent at Hamilton had been an excellent introduction to basic full-time soldiering, and I had no hesitation in selecting the Cameronians as my first choice, being thankful to gain acceptance.'

There was then no pre-OCTU course lasting six weeks, during which those unlikely to make the grade, for whatever reason, were weeded out. This did not become part of officer training until later in the war. Both in training and quality of instruction, in the early stages of OCTUs' existence it seems that they left a lot to be desired. Most who had been members of their university or school Officer Training Corps or Army Cadet Force felt that they had learned little new from the course. Standards did improve later as instructor cadres began to be filled with battle-experienced officers and NCOs.

Michie, by this time commissioned (in March 1940) and, like McNeil, a subaltern in the 6th Battalion The Cameronians, was very much of the same opinion:

'Early in 1940 I was sent on a short Junior Leader's Course at Esdaile, Kilgraston Road, Edinburgh, where an instructor read us a book called *Infantry Section Leading*. This excellent publication was issued to London Scottish NCOs in the summer of 1939, and I used to study it in the London Tube on my way to work – all the instructor did was to read from it… I could have taught him!'

Both Michie and McNeil served with the Battalion during its short stay in France in 1940. Of this period, Michie recalled:

'The platoon anti-tank weapon was the Boyes Anti-Tank Rifle, which could hardly open a tin of sardines. The rifleman in charge had more than likely come with me a week earlier as one of the 275 other ranks who joined the 6th.

He had to confess that he had never fired the weapon, and in fact didn't know how to handle it.'

MacNeil remembered:

'I'd had very good instruction on rifle, pistol, Bren Gun, 2-inch Mortar. Tommy Guns were issued in France in June 1940 – without even an instruction book. We relied on memories of US gangster films to get it working, per Edward G. Robinson.'

While the experience of recruits in 1939 was broadly similar to that of their predecessors in 1914, their instruction was different. They were more cynical about the nation's leaders, and less inspired by calls on their patriotism to rally them to the colours. The war was seen as a necessary evil to combat Nazi Germany's arrogance and drive for domination, but less of a crusade than it had appeared to many of those who rushed to enlist in 1914. Once part of an army unit, they settled down in much the same way as their fathers had 25 years earlier, accepting the trials and tribulations of wartime with as good a grace as possible.

Notes on contributors

Lieutenant-Colonel Sir John Baynes Bt., Independent Military Historian, Llanfyllin, UK.
Sir John Baynes served in the British Regular Army with the Cameronians (Scottish) Rifles and the Queen's Own Highlanders. He has written numerous military biographies and related books and is best known for his outstanding work, Morale: A Study of Men and Courage. The Second Scottish Rifles at the Battle of Neuve Chapelle (1967).

Cliff Pettit, Independent Historian and Author, Alnwick UK.
Cliff Pettit is a retired solicitor who served as an infantry platoon commander in North West Europe in the later stages of the Second World War. He has an extensive knowledge of the First and Second World War battlefields of Western Europe. He has presented, advised and assisted in television documentaries on Gallipoli, the Somme and Third Ypres.

Recommended reading

Milligan, Spike, *Hitler: My Part in His Downfall* (London: Michael Joseph Ltd, 1971). A humorous but
    nevertheless realistic account of barrack room life and the attitudes of conscript recruits.
Whiting, Charles, *Poor Bloody Infantry*, Chapters 1 and 2 (London: Guild Publishing, 1987)

Notes

[1] Dictated in old age, when he had become Lt Col Sir Rory Baynes, Bt, the memoirs of the then

Captain Baynes were published by The Pentland Press in 1990 under the title *A Tale of Two Captains* (Editors: John Baynes & Hugh Maclean).

2 John Reith (Lord Reith of Stonehaven),*Wearing Spurs* (Hutchinson, 1966) pp24-31
3 John Baynes, *Morale* (Avery Publishing, 1988) p168. Quoted from *Edwardian England 1901-1914* (OUP, 1964) p276
4 John Hay Beith, *The First Hundred Thousand 'K1'* (Blackwood, 1918) pp14-6
5 'The Covenanter', September 1939, The Regimental Journal of The Cameronians (Scottish Rifles). It is assumed that the writer was Rifleman W. Taylor. He and Rifleman J. M. Nichol were the first two militiamen to enter the Depot.
6 Later Major F. B. Hindmarsh, KOSB*
7 Later Colonel C. E. Michie OBE TD*
8 Later Sergeant B. Kilpatrick DCM*
9 Later Sergeant R. Baxter
10 A Rifleman throughout the war
11 Later Sergeant T. B. Laing MM
12 Later wounded in Normandy as a Rifleman Dispatch Rider
13 Later Major D. O. Liddell MC TD
14 Later Major M. D. McNeil TD
15 Later Colonel E. Scott TD

* The original accounts, obtained by or delivered to the authors, are deposited at the Archives of The Cameronians (Scottish Rifles), South Lanarkshire Council, Almada Street, Hamilton, Scotland ML3 0AA (Fax 0168 454728).

Notes on some military terms used in this chapter:

'Rifleman': in a Rifle Regiment this rank is the equivalent to 'Private Soldier' in other Regiments of the British Army.

'Universal Carrier': a tracked armoured open-topped vehicle, which had several versions (including the Bren Gun Carrier) used for the rapid movement of men and support weapons of an Infantry Battalion.

'Artificer': a Royal Artillery technician qualified to service and repair artillery pieces.

Chapter 3

Waging the undersea war: a British perspective

Jeff Tall

'It is essential to keep the standard high – nothing can be neglected – it is not a kindness to overlook slackness or mistakes, it is really great cruelty to do so – cruelty to wives and relatives of the man you let off and his shipmates and to yourself. There is no margin for mistakes in submarines; you are either alive or dead'[1] These words, spoken by Admiral Sir Max Horton when Flag Officer Submarines in 1941 to all submarine officers and men in Malta, carry a universal truth for all mariners, not just submariners. To cover the whole breadth of wartime maritime experience in the context of Horton's exhortation would fill several volumes; however, even the most gnarled sea-dog would probably concede that examination of the British submariner's story during the World Wars encapsulates his experience sufficiently well to justify this chapter's narrow focus on the craft and its inhabitants.

Of all the British fighting arms of the two World Wars, the greatest similarities are to be found in the Royal Navy Submarine Service. The platform itself had developed little in the inter-war years and, whatever improvements had been made, the tradition in the Royal Navy of putting the requirements for equipment above the comfort of the crew, prevailed. True, the submarine had become larger, which meant that it now had more torpedo tubes and greater reload capacity; the gun had a longer range and a bigger arsenal; its endurance had been enhanced through more powerful engines and higher fuel storage capacity; communications were now an integral part of submarine warfare; and a ranging form of ASDIC for mine detection had been added to its tactical capability. But all these enhancements called for a higher manning requirement, so there was no relief on the demands for internal space.

Thus, for the men, little had changed. Living conditions were cramped and sanitary arrangements were crude. Minor compensations were the fact that everyone smelled the same, and the daily tot of rum for the sailors (issued on surfacing) was served neat rather than watered down as 'grog'. Even though by the start of the Second World War the majority of submarines were fitted with Escape Towers and the Davis Submarine Escape Apparatus (DSEA), 'the war orders were that all escape and other hatches, except the conning-tower hatch, were not only to be clipped internally but also secured by a steel bar externally to prevent a hatch jumping its clips due to depth-charging.'[2] Thus the chances of escape once sunk were remote in the extreme.

The two areas of specialist operator growth witnessed between the two wars lay in communications and underwater listening. In the First World War, because of the lack of experience in Wireless Telegraphy (W/T) in the Submarine Service, it was necessary to call for volunteers from the ranks of Boy Telegraphists as they left training in HMS *Vernon*. There were 16 recruited throughout the war, the youngest of whom was 16½, and of these nine perished. There was a single Hydrophone Listener in the later submarines of the era. In the Second World War the W/T staff had grown to four in number, and the Higher Detection (HD) rating occasionally had an assistant, although a Radio Operator was often to be found on the ASDIC set.

In addition the submarines' modus operandi had changed little. Although they could travel further and stay on patrol longer, they were still weapons of position in that they relied on their targets to come to them, unless the playing field was levelled by mutual physical constraints of restricted waters; they were required in large numbers to be effective; they still relied on the cover of darkness to allow them to charge their batteries, the life blood of the submarine, and conduct their transits; the sextant and astro-navigation still told them where they were (some of the time); the torpedo was still essentially a straight-runner, whose reliability was sometimes in doubt; and the commanding officers still attacked by eye. In the First World War, in addition to being a torpedo boat, the submarine was used as a minelayer, anti-submarine patroller, shore bombardier and, on one famous occasion, a platform from which to launch a 'special forces' operation (HMS *E11* and a Turkish viaduct). In the Second World War they were used as gun-boats, minelayers, troop-carriers, store-carriers, tankers, navigation beacons to guide surface vessels, rescue stations to pick up downed pilots, reconnaissance units, survey ships, convoy escorts, anti-submarine vessels, power stations to supply electricity ashore, and for landing and taking off agents on enemy soil.

But above all else their primary role was to disrupt enemy supplies by sinking their shipping; they were weapons of attrition. However, unlike the Germans in the two World Wars and the Americans in the Second, who did most of their attacking on the surface at night in the open sea, preying on large convoys and relying upon their low profiles to avoid early detection, in both wars the British had to seek out their targets in heavily defended waters, much of it shallow and richly populated by mines. As a result they conducted most of their attacks submerged by day, or, if circumstances were favourable, by a brief visit to the surface to use the gun. It was constantly dangerous, and the virtually guaranteed outcome of an attack was a 'bollocking' either from escorting anti-submarine (A/S) vessels or aircraft. Commander Ben Bryant, who commanded HMS *Sealion* and *Safari* between 1939 and 1943, described the submarine as 'expendable'[3], and perhaps the final telling factor of similarity lies in comparison of loss rates for the World Wars. In human terms, the number of men lost was roughly equivalent to the number serving at the start of the conflict (First World War 1,200/1,418, Second World War 3,200/3,383), and in hull terms, losses were approximately 35 per cent of the total that saw active service (First 57, Second 74).

So lightning did indeed strike twice on a myriad of occasions in British submarines, but how and why, and what could possibly induce a young man to join a life redolent of sardines in a can and with a high chance of ending up just as dead?

Rudyard Kipling attempted to define the submariner in 1916 when he sought to find the origin of the sobriquet that had become attached to the service, still only in its 15th year of existence:

> 'No one knows how the title "The Trade" came to be applied to the Submarine Service. Some say the cruisers invented it because they pretend that submarine officers look like unwashed chauffeurs ... others think it sprang forth by itself, which means that it was coined by the lower deck, where they always have a proper name for things. Whatever the truth, the submarine service is now "the trade"; and if you ask them why, they will answer, "What else can you call it? The Trade's "the Trade" of course!"[4]

A very similar sentiment was expressed by another observer many years later. Following his analysis of the circumstance of every British submarine loss, A. S. Evans concluded that 'the small dank and foul-smelling interior [of a submarine] crammed with noisy and temperamental machinery, was no place for the faint-hearted; it took first-class men to withstand the unsavoury conditions and to perform skilled work with efficiency and with at least a modicum of cheerfulness.'[5] So, from the very beginning submariners had to be submarine 'types'.

In short, there was a submarine 'type' who wanted to belong to a 'trade', but this is still far too nebulous to lead to an understanding of why men sought to sign up. Perhaps a ready source of recruitment, consistent with the prevailing view that submariners were 'pirates', would have been the gaols, as suggested by Lieutenant Commander Williams-Freeman of HMS *H9* in 1915 when he wrote, 'I cannot conceive why they hang a man, when the foulest crime to be seen would be punished two-fold if they gave him life, and put him in submarines!'[6]

A better clue is provided by Captain W. R. Fell, a veteran of the Great War submarine operations and mentor of Charioteers (human torpedomen) and X-craft (miniature submarines) during the Second World War, when he stated:

> 'To serve in submarines is to become a member of the strongest, most loyal union of men that exists. During the First War and the 21 years of peace that followed, the Submarine Branch was an integral part of the Royal Navy, subject to its discipline and obeying its laws. But it was still a "private navy", inordinately proud of its tradition, jealous of its privileges, and, if slightly inclined to be piratical, the most enthusiastic, loyal and happy branch of the Service.
>
> Scores of people ask, "Why did men join submarines and how could they stick in them?" There are many answers to that question. For adventure and fun at the outset; then because of the intense interest, and because of the variety of tasks that must be at one's fingertips. The submariner must be a navigator, an electrician, a torpedoman, a gunnery type, and even a bit of a plumber. He must know men and get on with them, he must use initiative and

tact and learn to enjoy hard living. He must accept responsibility when young, and not misuse it. There is every reason why he should join and delight in joining submarines, but the greatest joy of all is the companionship, unity and feeling that he is one of a team.'[7]

It was not only the officers who felt the strength of the team. Telegraphist William Halter of HMS *D4* recounts his experience in 1914:

'It was an exclusive service because nobody but a submarine rating was allowed in a submarine. We got more pay and a very stiff medical examination. Your character had to be perfect to get in and we were regarded as something a bit special. We went to [HMS] Dolphin for training, messed in the hulk and slept in the Fort [Blockhouse]. Discipline was quite comfortable and after instruction you could lie in the sun on the ramparts; a very different navy altogether. When we got in the boats we were so near the officers ... every one was close to each other. No red tape, no falling in and out.'[8]

Certainly the experience of Lieutenant Leslie Ashmore bears out Fell's words concerning adventure. He relates: 'I had ambitions to get into some branch of the service that would give more scope to a junior officer. Watchkeeping and coaling were eating into my soul.' He found himself visiting the shipbuilding firm of Vickers Ltd in Barrow, Britain's principal builders of submarines and:

'...the sight of so many of these sleek little craft in various stages of construction seemed to suggest a solution to my yearnings. It was therefore not entirely by chance that I struck an acquaintance ashore with two officers, considerably my seniors, whom I knew from their conversation were submariners standing by HMS E18, which was nearing completion. The attraction of their mysterious trade for me must have been very obvious and I was soon being questioned by the senior of the two, Lieutenant Commander Halahan, captain designate of E18, as to what I was doing and whether I would like to transfer to submarines.

Evidently Halahan thought me likely material, for next time he visited the Admiralty, he pulled various strings with the result that I received orders to join the Submarine Depot ship HMS Bonaventure at Newcastle. In those days, entry into the submarine service was as simple as that. There were no organised training classes and the young enthusiast learnt the rudiments of his trade by going to sea as a "makee-learn" in an active service boat.'[9]

Although training became more formal as time progressed, nevertheless learning on one's feet continued as a basic principle. The 1940 experience of Lieutenant Phil Durham, though not typical, nevertheless underlines the principle. As a midshipman Durham had seen active service in a battleship, an anti-submarine trawler (of which he was second-in-command), a 'County' Class cruiser, a destroyer and a battlecruiser, and had earned a Mention in Dispatches, yet his goal remained service in submarines. While awaiting training class, he filled his time by joining the training submarine HMS *L26*, and spending a fortnight of 'daily seagoing, diving, gunnery and torpedo practice', after which he 'had made drawings of air and electrical systems and was able to trim and handle *L26* dived'. His enthusiasm made sense of the 'bewildering mass of pipes, gauges, dials, levers, switches, hand wheels, air bottles, electrical control boxes for rudder, fore and after planes, and centrally, the aluminium ladder leading to the conning tower and the outside world.' Like Ashmore his talent was also spotted by a senior officer, in this case the revered Commander Jackie Slaughter, who sent him off to join the recently captured German U570 (HMS *Graph*) with a warning to the Commanding Officer of Durham's lack of experience, but suggesting that since he had no knowledge of how a modern British submarine was handled, he had 'nothing to unlearn in finding out how a U-boat worked.'[10]

It was not until the trainee submariner got to sea that the real test of character began. Ashmore described conditions in the 'C' Class in 1915 as:

'…primitive in the extreme. There was one bunk for the Captain, but all the others had to sleep on the deck, there being no room to sling hammocks. When diving, the atmosphere quickly became foul, fumes from the petrol engine adding their quota to the normally fetid air… Sanitary arrangements consisted simply of a bucket passed up through the conning tower on surfacing. The periscope was raised and lowered by hand winch. By the time we had been dived for some 15 or 16 hours it was as much as one could do to operate it.'[11]

He also declared that 'during these early patrols I got to know the characters and temperaments of my fellow officers and of the ship's company in a way and a speed only possible in the cramped space, enforced intimacy, and shared responsibility of a submarine.'[12]

His sentiments concerning the atmosphere were echoed by 'Stoutfellow' in the ship's magazine of HMS *Oxley* of Second World War vintage:

'One soon gets used to the smell of feet
Of the bath drain blown on the bathroom wall
Of mildewed socks and of putrid meat
One gets to know and like them all

We get so we hardly notice
The smell of fuel and oil
And from ham and halitosis
No longer disgusted recoil

But there's just one smell like an angry skunk
That, wafted aft by the breeze
Keeps me tossing in my bunk
The smell of that blasted cheese!'[13]

Add to the smells the daily grind of watchkeeping and the hardships involved in conducting even the simplest functions, and one must begin to wonder if the enthusiasm of Ashmore and Durham (and thousands like them) was not totally misplaced. A letter home from Signalman Gus Britton of HMS *Uproar* in 1944 summed up the sailor's life and routine:

'We have lockers about the size of coffins ... and a small table in the fore-ends. Hanging from the ceiling there are about 15 hammocks, so if you want to move around you have to do so in a crouched position... Potatoes and cabbages are piled in one corner and, as it is as damp as Eastney beach, after six days there is the horrible smell of rotting vegetables, and refuse is only ditched at night; and on top of that there is the smell of unwashed bodies... At the moment we are doing about 18 hours dived every day so you can guess that it is pretty thick at night.

What a blessed relief when, at night, comes the order "diving stations" and about 10 minutes later "blow one and six". The boat shudders as the air goes into the ballast tanks and then up she goes! I am at the bottom of the ladder ... and then the captain opens the hatch and up rushes all the foul air just like a fog, and if I did not hang on I would go up with it as well. Beautiful, marvellous air ... we are provided with top-notch waterproof gear but the water always seems to find a weak spot to trickle into. Up on the swaying bridge, with a pair of binoculars which you try to keep dry to have a look around between deluges of water, soaked and frozen, you say to yourself, "Why the **** did I join?" Then when you are relieved, you clamber down the ladder, discard all the wet gear and go into the fore-ends, have a cup of cocoa, turn in and, as you fall asleep, you think, "Well it's not such a bad life after all."'[14]

Halfway through this catalogue of complaint Britton hastily points out to his parents (his father himself a submariner): 'Before I go any further don't think that I am complaining because I really love submarines and this sort of life, and I wouldn't swop it for anything.'

Not that surfacing at night, with the promise of the hot meal, a smoke, and the opportunity to 'ditch gash' was guaranteed utopia. It could be blowing a gale, and submarines, whatever the era, are wretchedly uncomfortable when on the surface in a storm. The misery was eloquently penned by Lieutenant Geoffrey Larkin RNVR, a human-torpedoman in 1942:

'I can feel, see and hear for a space
The blindness and the deafness both have gone.
Again I feel a love towards my race
Who recently I hated loud and long.
I feel an urge again to smell and eat
The faintest of a half felt urge to sing.
Strange, since my recent thoughts have been delete
And minus, strike out – leave not anything.

I know this saneness probably will last
And flourish just as long as we remain
At rest. Though still I hope this daily dying's past,
I feel tomorrow's dawn will see again
The same insensate blankness – nothingness.
A life of one dimension – of complete
And utter soul destroying hopelessness,
Longing for death and spared that final treat
Now for a while, tho' 'tis but short and sweet,
I smell and taste, and can appreciate
The beauties of this life, and can create.
When she begins to roll – I terminate.'[15]

Those who were sea-sick missed out on the delights of the submarine menu. During the First World War submarines did not carry trained cooks, and kitchen facilities were limited to one hot plate and a 'fanny' (water boiler). Submarine comforts (during both wars submariners got the best of provisions that were available) consisted mainly of tinned fare – soup, sausages, bacon, 'tickler' jam (even in the 1980s this was always plum-flavoured!), and bottled confections such as fruit. Ironically, fresh vegetables like onions and cabbage, sources of much-needed 'roughage', were invariably banned by Commanding Officers because of their residual smell! Bread and potatoes lasted only a few days, but by 1939 most submarines had trained cooks, and they would bake bread overnight for next morning's breakfast. The range of processed foods available to them had also improved. Tinned sponges – perennially referred to as 'Mrs B's' – became a firm favourite, and 'pot-mess', a conglomeration of left-overs, would make a regular appearance on the menu. As patrols became longer, food, like the receipt of mail, played a larger part in the 'morale factor' and chef's creations gave rise to many hours of debate.

Since the most basic of human needs is to relieve one's bowels, it is unsurprising that the 'heads' (or often the lack of them) are a common unifying bond for submariners of all generations. Constipation was a constant companion, but because of the limited diet, lack of exercise and, to begin with at least, sheer embarrassment at having to 'perform' in front of an audience, often only a 'pill' would sort out the problem. The most famous pills in RN submarine history were those taken onboard HMS *E9* in 1914.

Max Horton was engaged on a week's scouting duty in the Heligoland Bight early in the war, cruising with periscope awash by day and lying 'doggo' on the bottom at night.

'Five or six days of this cramped existence, living mainly on tinned foods, had affected very seriously the digestive apparatus of one of his officers. The latter, seriously perturbed, decided on drastic remedies, and before turning in one night demolished about 'half a guinea's worth' of a certain well-known brand of proprietary medicine. By the early hours of the morning the result of the experiment had passed his most sanguine hopes, but conditions in the confined and stagnant atmosphere lying on the ocean bed are not ideal ones for such shattering effect. That, at any rate, was the view taken by Horton and the rest of the crew. The latter sacrificed their morning beauty sleep without a murmur of protest when their commanding officer decided to rise to the surface an hour before the usual time. All on board were unanimous in expressing an earnest desire to fill the lungs with fresh morning air with as little delay as possible.

The boat rose slowly, Horton's eye to the periscope. The pleasing sight of the German cruiser Hela was reflected to his delighted gaze as she steamed slowly by, and within two minutes she was sinking, a torpedo in her vitals. It was that box of pills, undervalued at a guinea, that brought Horton to the surface at that propitious moment.'[16]

Horton, probably the greatest submariner in our history, strode the two World Wars like a colossus. His renowned attacking and leadership qualities during the First War carved out for him a glittering career and reputation, while his performance as Flag Officer Submarines in 1940-42, then as Commander in Chief Western Approaches 1942-45, earned him a place in the annals of outstanding national military leaders. He was also the first submariner to raise the Service's battle ensign – The Jolly Roger (JR). After his successful patrol he remembered Admiral Sir Arthur Wilson's words that 'all submariners captured in war should be hanged as pirates'[17], and raised the flag on entering harbour to denote his achievement. The practice of flying the JR on returning to home base, now adorned with symbols to depict a variety of activities, became standard practice during the Second World War.

However, back to basics; there are numerous stories from both World Wars about some submariners' total aversion to using the heads, but few took it to the extremes of Lieutenant Commander Robert Halahan, Commanding Officer of HMS *E18*. Leslie Ashmore tells the story:

'For Halahan I had great respect and affection. He inspired considerable devotion amongst his juniors and repaid it by resolute and fearless leadership. He had one idiosyncrasy, I remember, which used to cause us some anxiety. He could never bring himself to submit to the uncomfortable complications involved in the use of the submarine's rather intricate sanitary arrangements. He therefore insisted, no matter where we were, in taking the boat to the surface every morning so that he might exercise his natural functions in a simpler way over the side.'[18]

One day the inevitable happened and they were 'bounced' by a German airship. The Captain scrambled down the ladder 'pantalons en bas' and the boat escaped with a minor pounding.

However, the inability to handle 'intricate sanitary arrangements' that resulted in exploding heads discharge bottles did take their toll on the unsuspecting or the untrained, either at best by providing the operator 'with his own back', or, as on two sad occasions, death. This poem, from HMS *Torbay*'s 'Periscope Standard' in 1944, warns of the worst case:

'This is the tale of Joe McGee
Who couldn't work our WC.
He didn't realise when to vent
Nor did he know just what flush meant.
And so, with pressure ninety pounds
(Accompanied by explosive sounds)
He pushed on the lever "Hard a' blow"
With hull valve shut (cor stone a crow!)
A second later Joe was seen
Impaled upon the Fruit Machine
Where, there unto this day he sticks…
Grim warning to those men whose tricks
With submerged heads, with hands unskilled
Come close each day to being killed.
All because they do not know
When to flush and when to blow.'[19]

Living was hard enough, but to this must be added the strain of being under attack. Ben Bryant again:

'The swish, swish of the propellers of the hunter passing overhead, the waiting for the explosion of the charges as they sank slowly down. Had they been dropped at the right moment? Were they set to the right depth? The knowledge that there is no escape, that you must just wait for it. Then the shattering roar, the lights going out, the controls going slack as the power is cut, and the paint raining down. Then silence and the faint sounds of running water where a gland has started to trickle. It seems magnified one hundredfold – a serious leak is what you dread. For a few there is something to do, to make good the damage, provide alternative methods of control; others just have to wait for the next attack… For the CO being under attack was an absorbing business, you had far too much to think about to have time to be frightened. I always imagined it was very much worse for the crew, though most of them were kept pretty busy in controlling the boat as you twisted and turned, speeding up and slowing down. However, they never seemed to mind though critical interest was taken in the performance of the chaps up top – all of whom, judging by the remarks, had not only been born out of wedlock, but, blessed with amazing stamina, were credited with an almost continuous indulgence in the sexual act.'[20]

A typical attack of the Second War was survived by HMS *Sahib*, although dozens were not. By now A/S escorts of all nations were fitted with the sound-ranging device known as ASDIC, the pulses of which, according to Commander Edward Young, 'were as though someone was gently tapping on the outside of the pressure hull. I thought of Blind Pew's stick in *Treasure Island*.'[21] The Captain, Lieutenant John Bromage[22], starts the narrative after he had successfully attacked an escorted Italian convoy:

'Sahib was at 300 feet. The Climene took up position on the starboard quarter and maintained contact without difficulty in the perfect conditions … quite suddenly hydrophone effect [propeller cavitation], which was clearly audible to the naked ear in the control room, started up directly overhead. Very shortly afterwards the ASDIC office reported the unmistakable sound of depth-charges hitting the water.'

The helmsman, Leading Seaman Bobby Briard, takes up the story:

'As was usual in these circumstances, I just gripped the wheel a little tighter and stared unblinking at the lubbers line in the compass in front of me. The pattern of depth-charges was right on target and it felt as if some giant hand had taken hold of the submarine and was continually slamming it down. The shock waves inside the boat seemed to burst inside my head and dim my sight. The stunned silence that followed the attack was punctured by a sort of hissing roar coming from the engine room. "All compartments report damage to the Control Room." The Captain's voice contained a note of urgency. The gyro in front of me was spinning wildly. When I attempted to put correction on the helm, the wheel spun loosely in my hands, I listened to reports coming in.'

Bromage continues:

'I had ordered "full ahead group up" [high speed] when the very loud HE was directly overhead, and as a consequence by the time the depth-charges exploded the salvo must have been astern of the submarine. Nevertheless the result inside the boat was dramatic. A valve had been blown clean off the ship's side leaving a one and a half inch diameter hole through which water entered like a steel bar. No little Dutch boy could have put a stop to that! The pressure hull itself was leaking in the fore-ends, and under the after ends bilge.'

Briard concludes:

'The Captain's face was still expressionless but his words, when they came, seemed to hold infinite regret. "I'm sorry lads … stand by to abandon ship."[23]

Lieutenant Thomas Parkinson, First Lieutenant of HMS *J2*, in a report to Commodore (S), entitled ominously 'A submarine has no friends', provides a slightly different perspective:

'J2 was depth-charged on the first Monday in August 1917 at about 8am by British Light Forces returning home. The submarine was on the surface proceeding at 15 knots to the patrol area; the weather was perfect and the sea glassy calm. On sighting the ships the boat was dived; had an excellent trim and the Captain commenced an attack. Discovering the ships were British we went to the bottom, 125 feet on the gauge. Between 80 and 90 feet the steering gear jammed, and I was ordered to go aft to investigate. While examining the gear a depth-charge exploded quite near. The crew space filled with a white haze and the hands present, the tables and stools, were lifted clear of the deck. On arriving in the Control Room to make a report on the helm a second charge exploded shaking the boat from stem to stern; she was still sinking slowly. As she grounded a third and last explosion, this being nearer than the preceding two, and the lighting switches were thrown off the board. They were put to the on position… All valves were examined and tightened by wheel spanner. WC and [garbage] ejector locked, Sperry [compass] stopped and every necessary precaution taken against betraying our position. The boat was perfectly tight and nothing was broken. Books, magazines, papers etc were issued to the crew, and many of the older ratings turned in. Hydrophones were used and the listener ordered to make his reports in secret to the Captain so as not to disconcert the younger members of the crew though for a long time the ships could be heard quite plainly through the hull as they passed to and fro. How long they stayed I do not know as I turned in and slept until we went to the surface at 3.30pm. My reason for turning in was to try and convince the crew that all was well. We were up and proceeding to the patrol area at 4.00pm. I cannot praise too highly the conduct of the crew but am of the opinion it was due to the cool quiet manner of the old submarine ratings. The reaction was worse than the actual experience for whilst it was taking place the mind was fully occupied in carrying out the necessary duties knowing that a mistake might lead to destruction… To be depth-charged once is good experience; it adds to the keenness and efficiency of the boat's crew and shortens the time of a crash dive but it is something that no one could ever get used to. Familiarity would never breed contempt… I consider J2 was not lost for [one of] two reasons (a) The Light Forces were sure we were destroyed or (b) they lost our position.'[24]

To be sunk by the enemy is one thing, but to be sunk by one's own forces is the ultimate waste. But J2's 'blue on blue' experience was, regrettably, far from unique in the two World Wars, and such occurrences were generated by a variety of factors. In her case it was poor staff work by either the Light Forces Controllers/Submarine Controllers not operating the submarine in a 'weapons-tight haven', or one or other of the forces being out of position. Lack of knowledge of a friendly submarine's patrol area led to the loss of HMS H5 through ramming by the merchant vessel SS *Rutherglen* in the Irish Sea in 1918. Because the Admiralty was keen not to dissuade our merchant marine Masters from using one of the few counters to a U-boat attack available to them, the M/V was never informed of the mistaken identity, the usual bounty was paid, and the Master was awarded the DSO. A combination of one submarine being out of its patrol area (remember that accurate navigation was far from guaranteed) and failing to respond quickly enough to the daily recognition signal caused HMS *Triton* to sink HMS *Oxley* in 1939. Indeed, even firing the correct signal was no guarantee of immunity from attack, for in 1918 HMS D3's correct and speedily released recognition flare was taken as flak by a French airship, which responded to the 'attack' by sinking the submarine!

The 'fog of war' also left submarines particularly vulnerable to attack from friendly aircraft, and a combination of trigger-happiness by the pilot, poor navigation by the air-navigator and inadequate briefing before departure caused a number of incidents that often resulted in, at worst, the submarine's loss or, at best, its removal from the operational scene in order to conduct emergency repairs. Lieutenant Rufus Mackenzie, the Commanding Officer of HMS *Thrasher* in 1941, came under attack by a Royal Navy Swordfish aircraft as he left Alexandria Harbour. His boat suffered significant damage, including the loss of 90 per cent of his battery, and barely made it back to base. Rufus's punishment to the young airmen was simply to walk them through the submarine – they apparently refused the offer of a drink in the Wardroom after their tour![25]

Despite everything they had to suffer, the health of submariners during both wars was, to the onlooker, surprisingly good.[26] The present-day submariner would not be surprised, because it is now known that after 24 hours or so, individuals' germs become immune to each other! It is only on return to harbour and being exposed to others' 'foreign bodies' that submariners must rebuild their bacterial resistance with, in traditional fashion, alcohol proving a first-class catalyst. Indeed, letting off steam was a necessary relief to the pressures of patrol, and the role of the Depot Ship in this context was brought sharply into focus during the First War. The concept of the 'Mother' had been introduced from the earliest days of submarining (the first was HMS *Hazard* in 1902), but by tradition they tended to be hulks, with priority once again being given to workshop facilities rather than the comforts of attached crews. During the early conflict it was recognised that 'rest and relaxation', in as 'hassle-free' a scenario as possible, was the most beneficial recuperative tonic to get crews ready to go back to sea. It was concluded that a ten-day patrol needed four days rest to restore the balance (this compared with a ratio of 21:7 in the Second War in equivalent waters). Even those men who were showing the signs of neurasthenia were noted to recover rapidly after these few days in stress-free conditions.

In addition to comfortable bunks and good laundry facilities, there was a general call for the adjacency of a soccer pitch so that the crews could take exercise, although one cynical CO remarked that 'those that took exercise the most, missed it the most' and he was probably right. Four designated Depot Ships were built between the wars with, in addition to their routine comforts, rest-camps being established at every opportunity, although, hurriedly one should add, without the extremes of pleasure that were provided for German U-boat crews! These rest camps were much more appreciated than soccer pitches, and Leading Telegraphist Arthur Dickison of HMS *Safari* waxed lyrical about their recuperative qualities.[27]

Malta under siege and the base of the famous 'Fighting Tenth', however, offered few comforts, and in a renowned exchange between Captain Shrimp Simpson and Flag Officer Submarines (Horton), after the former had been taken to task for inviting HMS *Turbulent*, in the same signal that provided vital routing instructions, 'to bring plenty of booze', retorted to his senior:

'Sir, I would have you know that in all the time I have commanded the Tenth Submarine Flotilla, never have I known anything like the disastrous series of misses that have occurred during the last month. This has coincided with Lazaretto's supply of refreshment being completely exhausted. The two matters are not disconnected. I consider that anything to relieve the staleness of my overstrained COs is a matter of the most vital importance.'[28]

Ben Bryant commented: 'Malta at the end of the siege was dreary; men who are subjected to considerable strain do not readily relax and regain their resilience when all is dull and depressing; they go stale. A stale CO would be that second or two slower, the second or so that makes the difference between success and failure.'[29]

Bromage's action in *Sahib* in speeding up at the crucial moment was an example of the second between life and death. After one aircraft bomb (dropped on the area of torpedo discharge disturbance) and 56 depth-charges, *Sahib* managed to stagger to the surface, and the crew abandoned ship to be subsequently picked up and made prisoners of war by the Italians.

During each of the World Wars a number of British submariners became prisoners of war: 152 during the First, and 359 during the Second. To read the accounts of the manner in which they survived attack and remained alive to go into captivity is to appreciate the significance of the expression 'a hair's breadth' in war. To put this into context, every 2 feet of depth for a submarine equates to an extra pound per square inch of pressure on the hull, so at the 500-foot depth at which HMS *Splendid* (Lieutenant Ian McGeoch DSO DSC) began her recovery from a depth-charge attack by the German frigate *Hermes* that felt as 'if a gigantic sea-terrier had grabbed the submarine by the scruff of the neck with intent to kill'[30], she would have been subjected to 250lb per square inch. For her to reach the surface before flooding water under this tremendous pressure overcame the reserve of buoyancy required to maintain upward momentum, was a miracle, and testimony to McGeoch's speed of reaction. He and two-thirds of his crew became Italian POWs.

Others who survived from submarines attacked on the surface rather than dived were spared the gut-wrenching minutes of wondering whether the pressure hull would remain sufficiently intact to avoid its becoming their tomb, but their shortened experiences were nevertheless just as terrifying.

One of the unluckiest submarines to suffer such a fate was HMS *E20* in the Sea of Marmara in November 1915. She had been working with HMS *H1* as 'chummy boat'[31] and although they had both been surprised by the presence of FS *Turquoise*, they became a threesome. Part of the process of working together, in addition to conducting local water-space management and co-ordinating tasking, was to arrange a rendezvous to agree future tasking. HMS *E20* was waiting for *Turquoise* in the agreed position when, at about 5pm in glassy conditions with a slight haze, the party on the upper deck, enjoying a leisurely smoke, suddenly spotted a periscope soon followed by the wake of a torpedo. The subsequent explosion blew the British submarine in half. Lieutenant AN Tebbs RN, the First Lieutenant, describes how 'the wire for the heel of the foremast caught my foot and carried me down with the boat to a considerable depth. A rather curious fact was that the air which must have been forced out of the fore-hatch enabled me to take a breath before I actually got to the surface, and before I had got clear of the boat itself.' Eight other men survived and were picked up by their attacker, U-14, an Austrian-built boat manned mainly by Germans. 'We were treated with the utmost kindness and courtesy. Everything that could be done for our comfort was done.' Tebbs was to learn the circumstances of HMS *E20*'s loss from U-14's CO:

> '"You have the Frenchman to thank. We knew where you would be this evening from the Turquoise's chart." Some ten days previous to our being sunk we had arranged the rendezvous for the 4th/5th, and in the meantime, without informing us, she had attempted to go down the Straits once more, owing I believe, to lack of fuel. His periscope was shot away, and he surrendered his boat… On his chart was found, in writing, the time and place of the intended meeting with us.'[32]

Tebbs and his colleagues became Turkish POWs.

The experience of being well-treated once picked up was universal, but until that moment of recovery there was little respite from attack even though the submarine was evidently 'hors de combat'. McGeoch in *Splendid* lost 18 men out of his crew of 48 through the continued shelling of the *Hermes*, and Bromage in *Sahib* reported that although it was obvious that his submarine was being abandoned, she still came under heavy attack from two escorts and a Ju88 aircraft. After he had been rescued Bromage thanked the CO of *Climene* for not firing to hit his stricken submarine, but the latter said he had been! What this demonstrates, despite the gracious charm shown by his enemy when Bromage had been rescued, was the determination to sink the hated submarine without regard for the survival of the crew. A similar plight befell HMS *E13* when she ran aground in 1914 when attempting to enter the Baltic. Although in the neutral waters of Denmark she was repeatedly attacked by two German destroyers, and her crew fired upon by machine-gun when they attempted to swim to safety. It was only through the intervention of a Danish destroyer that the other half of the crew was not massacred.

In a similar vein, no comparison between the two wars would be complete without a brief mention of two actions that have been branded by some commentators as 'war crimes'. Each involves British submarine commanding officers. They were those of Herbert in *Baralong*[33] in 1915 and Miers in *Torbay*[34] in 1942. Both ordered the shooting of apparently unarmed survivors following attacks conducted by them (albeit Herbert was in command of a Q-ship). Their thought processes were very similar to those who pressed home attacks with men in the water – while they remained a perceived threat, and until their contribution could be guaranteed to be at an end, they were subject to the ultimate penalty simply by being in the wrong place at the wrong time. Ben Bryant reinforces this message: 'Submarining is often painted as a brutal game, but submariners are no more brutal than anyone else. Nobody should criticise the submariner unless he himself has been hunted, for it is when harassed that an animal becomes vicious.'[35] Both Herbert and Miers had been hunted, and were in the classic mould of submarine commanding officers.

In both wars there could have been few greater responsibilities given to a young man than to command a submarine. Onboard he was a 'Dictator' simply because it was his judgement and actions alone that could bring success, failure or death. As Captain Fell, a 'Captain Teacher' on two occasions, put it, 'He has no one to hold his hand, to advise or correct a fatal move. His eye alone can see, and his instinct sense, the correct and only tactic to pursue; on him rests all responsibility.'[36] Dictator, yes, full of determination, yes, but as Ben Bryant points out, 'no man relies more completely upon each and every member of his crew. A good submarine crew is far more than a team; they are as near as possible during attack, a single composite body using the CO as their eye and their director.'[37]

So perhaps there is after all an explanation of 'The Trade', but let a United States Air Force Officer have the last word on the subject. Colonel Bradley Gaylord was on board HMS *Seraph* for 'Operation Kingpin' in 1942 (the pick-up of General Giraud from Vichy France) when he noted in his diary:

'How could you have claustrophobia among these smiling boys whose easy informality was so apparently a thin cover for the rigid discipline on which every man knows his life depends upon the other fellow. It is so completely infectious. You suddenly realise that here is one of the essential points about war: there is no substitute for good company. The boys in the Submarine Service convey a spirit which quickly explains why they would sooner be in submarines than anywhere else.'[38]

Notes on contributors

Commander Jeff Tall OBE RN, Director of the Royal Navy Submarine Museum, Gosport, UK.
Commander Jeff Tall is the Director of the Royal Navy Submarine Museum in Gosport, a post he has held since August 1994 when he retired from the Royal Navy. A submariner for twenty eight years, he has served all over the world and commanded four submarines: HMS Olympus, HMS Finwhale, HMS Churchill and, finally, the nuclear powered Polaris Missile submarine, HMS Repulse. He served as Admiral Sandy Woodward's submarine staff officer during the Falklands Conflict in 1982. He was co-author, with the naval historian Paul Kemp, of HM Submarines in Camera, he wrote the historical element of the CD-Rom *The RN Submarine Service - Past Present and Future*, produced jointly with the Royal Naval School, which is available to the general public.

Recommended reading

Carr, William Guy, *By Guess and By God* (London: Hutchinson & Co, 1930)
Chapman, Paul, *Submarine Torbay* (London: Robert Hale, 1989)
Chatterton, E. Keble, *Amazing Adventure* (London: Hurst & Blackett Ltd, 1935)
Dickison, Arthur, *Crash Dive* (Stroud: Sutton Publishing, in association with The Royal Navy Submarine Museum, 1999)
Edwards, Kenneth, *We Dive at Dawn* (London: Rich & Cowan, 1939)
Mackenzie, Hugh, *Sword of Damocles* (Gosport: Royal Navy Submarine Museum, 1995)
McGeoch, Ian, *An affair of Chances* (London: Imperial War Museum, 1991)
Padfield, Peter, *War Beneath the Sea – Submarine Conflict 1939-1945* (London: John Murray, 1995)
Shankland, Peter and Hunter, Anthony, *Dardanelles Patrol* (London: Collins, 1964)

Wilson, Michael, *Baltic Assignment – British Submarines in Russia 1914-1919* (London: Leo Cooper)
Wingate, John, *The Fighting Tenth* (London: Leo Cooper, 1991)
Young, Edward, *One of our Submarines* (London: Wordsworth Editions, 1997)

Notes

1   Rear Admiral W. S. Chalmers CBE DSC, *Max Horton and the Western Approaches* (London: Hodder & Stoughton, 1954) p106
2   Rear Admiral G. W. G. Simpson CB CBE, *Periscope View* (London: Macmillan Ltd, 1972) p184
3   Rear Admiral Ben Bryant CB DSO** DSC, *One Man Band* (London: William Kimber, 1958) p49
4   Rudyard Kipling, *Sea Warfare* (London: Macmillan & Co Ltd, 19??) p97
5   A. S. Evans, *Beneath The Waves* (London: William Kimber, 1986) p16
6   RNSM File History of HMS *H9*
7   Captain W. R. Fell CMG OBE DSC RN, *The Sea our Shield* (London: Cassell & Co, 1966) p13
8   Captain John Wells RN, *The Royal Navy – An Illustrated Social History 1870-1982* (Stroud: Alan Sutton & Co, 1994) p73
9   RNSM Section Submarine Officers' Memoirs: 'Russian Scrap Book' by Vice-Admiral Leslie Ashmore CB DSO*, p6
10 Lieutenant Commander Phil Durham DSC RN, *The Fuhrer Led But We Overtook Him* (Bishop Auckland: The Portland Press Ltd, 1996) p90
11 'Russian Scrap Book', op cit, p81
12 Ibid, p7
13 RNSM File A1996/176, Bound Collection of Oxley Outlook
14 Commander Richard Compton-Hall MBE RN, *The Underwater War 1939-45* (Poole: The Blandford Press, 1982) p32
15 RNSM File A1984/117 Wartime Verses by Lieutenant G. J. W. Larkin RNVR
16 Commander C. L. Kerr RN, *All in the Day's Work* (London: Rich & Cowan Ltd, 1939)
17 Admiral Sir Reginald Bacon KCB KCVO DSO, *From 1900 Onwards* (London: Hutchinson & Co) p50
18 'Russian Scrap Book', op cit, p8
19 RNSM File 1980/090 HMS *Torbay* 'Periscope Standard'
20 Ben Bryant, op cit, p51
21 Commander Edward Young DSO DSC RNVR, *One of our Submarines* (London: Rupert Hart-Davies Ltd, 1952) p39
22 Later Commander J. Bromage DSO DSC* RN
23 A. S. Evans, p353-355
24 RNSM File History of HMS *J2*
25 Vice-Admiral Sir Hugh Mackenzie KCB DSO DSC, *The Sword of Damocles* (Gosport: Royal Navy Submarine Museum, 1995)
26 RNSM File Submarine COs and Medical Officer Post World War One Recommendations
27 Arthur P. Dickison, *Crash Dive* (Stroud: Sutton Publishing Ltd, 1999) p165
28 Ben Bryant, op cit, p194
29 Ibid
30 Vice-Admiral Sir Ian McGeoch KCB DSO DSC MPhil, *An Affair of Chances* (London: Imperial War Museum, 1991) p21
31 RNSM File A1918/20 War experiences of Petty Officer Moth
32 RNSM File A1997/077 Diary of Lieutenant A. N. Tebbs RN
33 E. Keble Chatterton, *Amazing Adventure* (London: Hurst & Blackett Ltd, 1935) pp134-45
34 Commander Paul Chapman DSO OBE DSC* RN, *Submarine Torbay* (London: Robert Hale, 1989) pp59-67, 164-6
35 Ben Bryant, op cit, p88
36 W. R. Fell, op cit, p18
37 Ben Bryant, op cit, p37
38 Terence Robinson, *The Ship With Two Captains* (London: Evans Brothers Ltd, 1957) p72

Chapter 4

The merchant seaman at war

Tony Lane

The development of submarine commerce warfare in the First World War and its extensive and systematic application in the Second World War ensured that in both wars merchant seamen were the only civilians to be killed in large numbers by military action: 14,679 in the First War, 28,000 in the Second. Where in each war the casualty rates suffered by merchant seamen were higher than those for Royal Navy seamen, in 1939-45 merchant seamen actually had a higher death rate than any of the armed forces. The wars produced a few epic encounters between lightly armed merchant ships and warships, and frequent examples of extraordinarily resourceful feats of survival in lifeboats and the nursing homeward of seriously damaged ships. Of the latter, there was the extraordinary case of the *San Demetrio*. Abandoned by her crew, then reboarded by those in a lifeboat unnoticed by a rescue ship, fires were extinguished and makeshift steering organised. With engines restarted, the *San Demetrio* limped home with her cargo of petrol – to be celebrated in a full-length feature film and a Government publication, *The Saga of San Demetrio*, by F. Tennyson Jesse (HMSO, 1942).

Seafarers could hardly have been unaware of their critical role in bringing in food and raw materials, or insensitive to the risks they ran; neither their exploits nor their crucial role in the supply chain seems in any way to have affected their everyday behaviour. They did not set aside their habitual independent-minded attitudes to shipboard discipline and become 'respectable' and orderly patriotic citizens. In both wars, merchant seamen unquestioningly adjusted to testing circumstances, but in their everyday actions they insisted on being themselves. They were intensely proud of their occupational culture, and at the heart of this fine mesh of norms and values was a profound belief in the legitimacy of resistance to breaches of customary rules of justice and fair play, and entitlement, when opportunity offered, to a 'good run ashore'. These beliefs were not set aside in the exceptional conditions of war, and merchant seafarers could therefore seem to be both heroic and a disorderly rabble. They were neither. They were themselves.

Ships, crews and war

Only 20 years separated the end of one war and the beginning of the next. It was therefore a relatively simple matter for those administering the direction and the organisation of shipping in the Second World War to draw upon the experience of the First. The Ministry of Shipping, which did not appear until 1916 in the Great

War, was operative in 1939 just six weeks after the outbreak of war, and had key senior officials who had held similar posts in 1918.[1] In 1939, as previously, this new ministry had overall control of the destinations and the cargoes carried, although day-to-day technical and personnel management of ships was left in the hands of the shipping companies. Military protection was of course the Admiralty's responsibility, and here, as in commercial operations, the Royal Navy was in 1939 much better prepared. Where in 1914 the Admiralty had been obliged to use the Lloyd's insurance market's global network of agents to advise shipmasters on avoidance of normal routes and on 'blackout' precautions, in 1939 the master needed only to open 'Envelope Z'. Previously lodged in his safe, it contained a single sheet giving the ship its secret call-sign and instructions on radio silence and blackout procedures. The Admiralty had also been providing training courses for merchant ships' deck officers since 1937 on the likely demands of war, and more than two-thirds of officers had attended them by September 1939. Gunnery training for officers began in the summer of 1938, and for ratings from early in 1939.

In the First War merchant ships only began to be equipped with defensive armament (stern-mounted 4-inch or 12-pounder guns) from 1916, and the typical gun crew was led by a recalled, retired naval gunner and assisted by volunteers from among the crew. In 1939 guns that were often relics from the Great War were quickly brought out of store and fitted between voyages when port-time and labour availability allowed. By 1943 every ship was armed with at least one large gun at the stern and lighter anti-aircraft weapons, and gadgets such as anti-aircraft kites. The deliveries in increasing numbers of American-built Liberty ships with purpose-built gun platforms and modern quick-firing guns from early 1943 finally provided the ultimate in armed merchant ships. By this time merchant ships were also being provided with professional gunners. Early in the Second World War gunners, as in the First, were either a mixture of recalled naval professionals and volunteers or wholly recruited from among trained crew members. By 1944 there were 24,000 naval gunners aboard merchant ships and a further 14,000 army gunners who were members of the specially formed Maritime Regiment of the Royal Artillery and universally known as DEMS gunners.

Britain's dependence on the ability freely to import great volumes of foodstuffs and raw materials was well enough known. And it was naturally better known in 1939 after the experience of 1914-18. Nevertheless, in 1939 the British merchant fleet's carrying capacity was 8 per cent smaller than in 1914, while both the British population and its per capita consumption of commodities had increased. For example, between 1914 and 1939 it was estimated that Britain's weekly consumption of sugar went up from 37,000 tons to 48,000 tons and grain from 27,000 tons to 38,000 tons, increases respectively of 22 and 29 per cent. The widened gap between the supply and demand for shipping services had been met by a growing dependence upon the shipping services of other nations, especially Norway, Denmark and the Netherlands. Ships of neutral nations had of course been important carriers of British imports in 1914-18. In the Second War the ships and crews of the neutral nations, which had escaped capture when their countries were occupied, made even more significant contributions; Norwegian tankers were especially valuable. Although the British economy had become increasingly oil-dependent in the inter-war years, it was Norwegian rather than British shipowners who had become tanker specialists.

The extent to which an adequate flow of supplies was maintained was necessarily a military matter, and the fundamental question was how best to protect merchant ships from submarines. After 12 months of the war at sea in 1914-18, 68 per cent of merchant ship losses were accounted for by submarines. The equivalent figure for 1939-45 was 44 per cent. The worst years for merchant seamen were 1917 and 1942, when respectively 94 and 77 per cent of sinkings were due to submarines.

In the First War it took the Admiralty a long time before it gave in to pressure, and finally, in April 1917, began to organise convoys. This was quite a policy turnaround considering that in January 1917 the Admiralty had issued a pamphlet that, in response to its critics, recorded that: '...the system of several ships sailing together in a convoy is not recommended in any area where submarine attack is a possibility.'[2] Convoying, however, quickly proved successful by demonstrating that unescorted ships were much more likely to be sunk than those sailing in company and with escorts. In 1939 there was still some residual Admiralty resistance to convoys, but the main problem – as indeed it had been in 1917 – was a lack of suitable ships and a general shortage of sufficient ships of any kinds.

The first homeward-bound convoy sailed from Gibraltar in mid-May 1917 escorted by two special service ships (small, armed merchant ships manned by the Navy) and three lightly armed steam yachts. Convoy escorts were not markedly superior in the earlier phases of the Second War. The SC7 convoy that sailed from Halifax, Nova Scotia, in October 1940 was escorted by a sloop and an armed steam yacht. After two days the yacht returned to port, leaving the sloop as the sole escort until joined after nine days by a corvette and another sloop. Of the 30 ships that began the crossing, 21 were sunk by submarines, 15 of them in one six-hour period. The war was almost two years old before North Atlantic convoys were escorted for the whole crossing. The most heavily protected convoys were those bound for Murmansk and Malta. Losses were especially heavy in the Malta convoys, which, although made up of the fastest and most modern ships in the British merchant fleet, came under heavy attack from aircraft and surface ships. Similar onslaughts were experienced in the Arctic convoys. These engagements were arguably the most significant military events in the war at sea in Europe during the Second World War.[3]

It may have taken the Admiralty a long time to develop effective tactics for the protection of merchant ships, but it was very quick to decide that it would like to impose military discipline on merchant seamen. In 1915 the two leading figures in the largest of the seamen's unions, Havelock Wilson and Edward Tupper of the National Association of Sailors and Firemen, were summoned to the Admiralty to be told by the Prime Minister of a proposal to conscript merchant seamen for national service. Apart from the fact that at this time conscription had not yet been introduced for the armed forces, the union leaders, who were well known as super-patriots, were outraged at the idea that, although still working for civilian employers, seafarers themselves would be subject to military law if conscripted.

The Prime Minister and his colleagues met with adamant refusal from the two union leaders and no more was heard of the scheme. However, the idea resurfaced in 1941 when Lord Marchwood, together with a group of retired admirals, some serving naval officers and members of the consular corps, were proposing that merchant seamen become an auxiliary service of the Royal Navy. This time the proposal lacked any superior backing and was quickly strangled by an ad hoc alliance of trade union leaders and shipowners.[4]

In both wars the Royal Navy took over large numbers of fast passenger liners for use as armed merchant cruisers, and many of their crews, including officers, volunteered to go with them and were duly entered into the Royal Navy. In the Second War, 50 of these ships were taken by the Navy and 15 were sunk, mostly by submarine, two of them, the *Jervis Bay* and the *Rawalpindi*, in hopelessly one-sided engagements with German battlecruisers. In the First World War 17 armed merchant cruisers were lost, also in the main to submarines. Other and similar merchant ships were taken up for Government service as hospital ships. Their crews stayed with them but retained their civilian status.

It was a matter for some understandable grievance that merchant seamen who stayed by ships transferred into the Royal Navy would be paid on service rates that were considerably lower than those paid to merchant seamen. In the Second World War the problem was pragmatically dealt with by paying these men a special rate. Generally, and as for other industrial workers, rates of pay for seafarers significantly increased in both wars. Able seamen who were earning £5 per month had doubled their wages by 1918. These gains did not survive the inter-war depression. In September 1939 the able seaman's wage, at £9 6s 0d, had only recently got close to the 1918 level. By 1945 wages had once again doubled, although seafarer's working hours were much longer than those in any other industry. In 1939 the basic working week before overtime was 64 hours, which was 20 hours longer than in the building industry and 17 hours longer than in engineering. Even when the basic week was reduced in 1943 to 56 hours, it was 10 hours longer than the all-industry average. The biggest wartime grievance, however, had little to do with either wage levels or working hours. What angered seamen was that their wages were stopped from the moment their ships were sunk. In the First War they had to wait until mid-1917, and until mid-1941 in the Second, before survivors were paid until their return to the UK.

In terms of more than just danger, the years 1917 and 1941 were significant ones for merchant seamen. For more than two decades before 1914 shipowners had fought a militant and highly organised campaign against the seafarer trade unions. By far the largest of the unions, the National Association of Sailors and Firemen, had a modest ambition – the creation of national collective bargaining machinery. In 1917, and at the height of the German submarine onslaught, the Government pressured the shipowners into creating the National Maritime Board, and also produced some significant symbolic gestures. A silver badge was struck for war-disabled seamen, a roll of honour to publicise brave deeds was to be issued regularly, and an Act of Parliament provided for the voluntary adoption of a standard uniform, identical in style to that of the Royal Navy and differing only in badge and insignia of rank. In 1941 the provisions of the Essential Work Order as applied to merchant seamen certainly tied them to their industry, but in return provided paid continuous employment, paid leave, paid study leave for approved courses, and proper compensation for lost effects in the event of shipwreck. In this war there was little additional need for symbolic gestures.

In 1928 the Prince of Wales had acquired the additional title of 'Master of the Merchant Navy and Fishing Fleets', and this then passed subsequently to the Monarch. Resentments in the First War at merchant seamen's ineligibility for medals and honours were laid to rest as the CBE, OBE, MBE, DSC, DSM, BEM and Mentioned in Dispatches all became available. In January 1940 Royal Assent was given to the production and distribution of a Merchant Navy buttonhole badge to be worn voluntarily. Merchant seamen, however, still commonly believed that they went unnoticed and unappreciated. Rarely practised but significantly often spoken of, the MN badge could be worn upside down as NW, to indicate 'Not Wanted'.

There were roughly a quarter of a million seafarers employed aboard British merchant ships in 1914 and almost 200,000 in 1939. In both years at least one-third of these were foreigners – mainly Europeans, but also Indian, Chinese, West African, West Indian, East African and Arab. Ships regularly employed in the trade to the Indian sub-continent were typically manned by British officers and Indian petty officers and ratings, and complements were high. In 1940 the *Clan Forbes*, for example, had a total crew of 108, of whom 87 were Indian. At the same time the *Biafra*, a ship trading to West Africa, had a total crew of 54, of whom 27 were from Nigeria and Sierra Leone. Manning levels per ship, whatever the nationality composition of the crew, changed little between the two wars, although average ship size increased considerably. The crews engaged in UK ports for coal-burning tramps averaged at about 42 men in both wars. Ships in the cargo liner trades, and with ratings recruited in India and China, rarely had crews of less than 80. Cargo liners with all-European crews comprised between 50 and 60. The fact of war made very little difference to crew size. In the First War the average foreign-going merchant ship doubled its complement of radio officers (from one to two) and in the Second three radio officers were carried but no other additional personnel were shipped, if members of the armed forces signed on as gunners are excluded.

Images and identities

In the Great War the mass media was in its infancy, unable to pick up and put into deep national circulation stories of the doings of merchant seamen. In the early decades of the 20th century far more people read local and regional newspapers than national ones, photo-journalism as a distinctive genre was under-developed, and the same went for cinema (even though the soundless newsreel could present actualité); books were relatively expensive and talking radio was still a few years in the future. In 1939 all these means of communication had reached high levels of technical development and, furthermore, were within the economic reach of the great mass of the population. But it was as much the politics of the Second War as the technical and economic development of the media that made merchant seafarers such an obvious and prominent focus for the attention of newspapers, radio and cinema. Where the First War was a patriotic war fought in defence of great power status, the Second was quickly announced as a 'people's war', to be fought in defence of democracy. The one war required examples of patriotic heroism and helpless victims of enemy brutality, the other needed patriotic heroic instances as before, but especially needed ordinary people being good citizens. Merchant seafarers were well cast for this role and no doubt for that reason received an enormous amount of publicity.

The weekly photo-news magazine, *Picture Post*, famous anyway for its celebration of the 'common people', regularly carried articles on merchant seamen. The following sequence appeared in 1940:

'ONE OF THE MEN HITLER CAN'T FRIGHTEN
Harry Townsend of the Dunbar Castle
Harry Townsend, 60 years old, is just one of over 150,000 men in the British mercantile marine. He had a berth as a cook in the Union Castle Line's Dunbar Castle. On a Tuesday, the Dunbar Castle strikes a mine off the south-east coast, and sinks in 10 minutes. With other survivors, Harry Townsend is picked up by a lifeboat. He reaches London wrapped in a blanket, a pipe stuck in his mouth. That was Tuesday. By Saturday, Harry Townsend has found another ship. He is at sea again.'[5]

'WHAT IT MEANS TODAY TO BE A MERCHANT SEAMAN
Lifeboats pull away from the sinking Clan Stuart
All day and all night ships are putting into the ports of Britain. They bring us food. They bring us metal. They bring us the needs of war and the comforts of life. They bring us them in spite of mines and submarines. They bring us them at the cost of heavy risk to our merchant seamen – the men of Cardiff, Glasgow, Tyneside, London; the men of Bombay, Singapore, and the little ports of the Near East.'[6]

'AND STILL THE CONVOYS COME…
The strain on merchant seamen's nerves is terrific, as the ships proceed at snail's pace over the ocean and nobody knows from minute to minute when disaster may come from under the sea, on the sea or in the air. The merchant seaman is given an inconspicuous little badge, about half the size of an air-raid warden's. He is paid (if he is an AB – a skilled man) £9 12s 6d a month, plus £3 danger money. For this he risks his life every minute of his day and night, awake and asleep … doing what is in the last analysis, the most important job of all – the job of keeping the nation fed, and its trade flowing.'[7]

Picture Post's only competitor, *Illustrated*, was no less concerned with celebrating the merchant seaman. A seven-page photo-article on the rescue of the crew of a sunken ship by a Royal Navy destroyer contained these captions:

'Rescued! The face of the Lascar survivor betrays his ordeal. His feet are frozen.'[8]

'James Fitzpatrick, junior wireless operator of the torpedoed freighter, is only nineteen years old. "I'm ready to sail again at any time," says James.' [9]

'Chief Steward Dumbill after being torpedoed four times, believes firmly in his lucky star. He was in his cabin rolling a cigarette when the torpedo struck the freighter. "I ran on deck to help with the boats then returned for my shipmates," says Dumbill, affectionately nursing his canaries.' [10]

The cinema and the popular daily press were no less attentive. There were seven documentaries, three full-length feature and at least 29 newsreel items. The *Daily Mirror* deliberately set out to champion the merchant seaman, as might be expected from the archetypal left-populist newspaper, but the patriotically populist *Daily Express* carried a similar number of stories. These two newspapers were certainly idiomatically different in their approach, but they were nevertheless staunch friends of the seaman. The same was true of the BBC, which broadcast at least 19 talks given by serving merchant seamen recounting experiences. The BBC also broadcast a number of charitable appeals on behalf of seafarers. Its greatest achievement was the programme *Shipmates Ashore*, which in its first six months went out as *The Blue Peter*. Devised as a light entertainment for merchant seamen of all ranks rather than about them, it had established a home audience of six million listeners by 1943. It went out at peak period on Saturdays, was one of the very few BBC programmes to be repeated on all its short-wave services, and was the only programme solely dedicated to an occupational group unless one were to include the musical offering of *Workers' Playtime*.

The press, film and radio output was supplemented by a number of novels and non-fiction books – at least 30 titles of each category. As we have seen, means of mass communication were of a different order in 1914-18, and there is therefore quite simply no comparison between the publicity attached to merchant seamen in the two wars. There were a number of 1914-18 wartime books that were wholly concerned with merchant seamen – but almost certainly less than ten titles. The idiom of the non-fictional books of this war, if just slightly more luxuriant than those of the Second War, was rhetorically interchangeable. The reader could have heard:

'Concerning the seafarer the slightest suspicion of degeneracy was never entertained. He toiled on in fair weather and foul, in every clime, in every season, all day and every day. He had neither the opportunity nor the desire to follow the path of the landlubber. Atlas-like, he supported Britain on his broad shoulders despite increasing hazards. The might of the navy is due to a very appreciable extent to the might of the Merchant Service, and it is the latter which is the real binding link of the Empire. Never before in our history have we so much appreciated the men who "go down to the sea in ships and occupy their business in great waters". The present conflict has accentuated our irredeemable debt of gratitude to them.' [11]

'Here then are the great arteries supplying Great Britain with survival power in the shape of food and raw materials; and over them every day and every night, in the piercing cold of winter and the blazing heat of summer, through fog and snow and ice and rain, with mortal danger hovering above and lurking below, go the brave obscure men of the Merchant Navy on whom now our hopes and our lives depend.'[12]

Just how far these images and implicit identities were heard, read and seen among seafarers themselves was finally what mattered. That the public at large and especially seafarers' families knew that seafarers were valued was of course important. But by being mostly absent for at least nine months in very twelve, it was unlikely that seafarers would themselves have had much opportunity to see themselves as others saw them. If, therefore, the imagery produced and distributed in the public domain was to percolate into the seafarer's own consciousness, it had to be passed on primarily by intermediaries who in most cases would have been family members.

In the First War at least, this two-step flow of communication was inevitably an imperfect process. The economic costs and the skills needed to consume the printed media must have meant that at best only a substantial minority of seafarers' families could have been aware of what was being said about their fathers, grandfathers, husbands, brothers or sons. And of those who did receive and pass on to their seafarer relatives the images in circulation, by far the great majority must have been officers' families. The two-thirds of crews of cargo-carrying ships who were ratings must surely only have seen themselves as they saw each other. Their image was their self-image. In the earlier war it is safe to say that most seafarers' experience of their conduct in war was little touched or influenced by the perceptions of the wider world.

The situation in 1939-45 was undoubtedly different. The economic costs of media consumption had fallen, the growth in scale and variety of the media had been enormous in order to feed the information demands of a developing democratic state and levels of literacy that were continually improving. On the other hand, the rhythms of the seafarers' life as dictated by the conditions of employment, passage times, trade routes and port stays changed very little in the inter-war years. In short, the pattern of sea life in 1939 was much the same as in 1918. This was an infinitely more closed occupational community than those of farmworkers, miners and quarrymen. Paid leave was still wholly unavailable to ratings and petty officers in 1939, and not much known among officers either. Being a seafarer meant being aboard ship for not less than 80 per cent of the year provided jobs were available, and that meant almost literally being out of touch with families and having only a sketchy awareness of world events. The enhanced pervasiveness of media messages in the Second World War, the introduction of paid leave and continuous employment, and the development of welfare services can only have brought seafarers 'closer to home' than was possible in the earlier war. But as we shall see, to be a seafarer was to live a life apart. All those carefully wrought images, as well as all the thoughtful and considerate good intentions, could not have weightily touched the Second World War seafarer. Although writing almost a century earlier, the Victorian poet Arthur Clough had found a universal measure:

'Where lies the land to which the ship would go!
Far, far ahead, is all her seamen know.
And where the land she travels from? Away,
Far, far behind, is all that they can say.'13

Custom, practice and intrusive war

David Divine, a well-known writer of middle-brow popular non-fiction in the 1930s, '40s and '50s, successfully caught the mundane social character of the crew of the *Heronspool* on her departure from Swansea in 1940:

'Except that she was painted in a dull unloveliness of greys and blacks there was nothing to mark this from a peace-time sailing ... perhaps the 4-inch gun mounted on the poop lent a point and purposefulness to the departure, but certainly there was nothing else. There was, for example, no grimness. It is one of the extraordinary characteristics of the seamen of the Merchant Navy that they do not go to sea grimly, even in time of war. They may go bad-temperedly, they often do, but a certain acerbity is the proper hall-mark of sailing day whether in peace or war. It is compounded partly of hangovers, and partly of regret for the absence of hangovers, and it has nothing to do with forebodings, or anticipatory hates.'14

Another prolific writer of popular non-fiction, Owen Rutter, also looked to realism for his characterisation of merchant seamen, and in doing so went very close to the seafarers' preferred version of themselves:

'They have been tough-livers, used to giving hard knocks and taking them, improvident and thriftless by standards ashore... They have always been, and still are, impatient of discipline, fiercely tenacious of their rights, and ready to combat any infringement of their independence... Among the industrial workers of Great Britain they are the supreme individualists ... [they] are nomadic in habit and temper, brooking no restraint...'15

There are two things to be said about this commentary. First, that it is a liberal political understanding of seafarers' attitudes and behaviour, and second, that the characterisation was only intended to describe ratings and petty officers. At no time in the modern period has it been possible to construct a social character for seafarers that was inclusive of all ranks. The simple popular stereotype of the seafarer as a roistering, insubordinate profligate can be made to work for able seamen and firemen, but not so easily for navigating and engineer officers. There is a great deal of reportage of the former and scarcely any of the latter.

In their own words and voice, the 'common people' are as absent in the case of merchant seafarers as they are everywhere else. They are there as objects of others' observations, commentaries and statistical aggregations, but rarely for themselves. What we have in evidence, when it comes to social behaviour, are descriptions of people acting that are written from within the perspective of people whom we might call the 'recording classes'. What we do not have are either the 'common people's' understandings of their own actions or descriptions of the social behaviour of the 'recording classes' as seen and understood by the 'common people'. This stricture can be relaxed somewhat when we get to the Second World War, where oral historians have tried to rescue the 'common people' for posterity. The rescues, however, have come at least several decades after the event and cannot therefore be used to equilibrate the recording classes' contemporary accounts. Oral history may be able to redress the imbalance when it comes to perspectives and interpretations, but not often reliably when it comes to the detail of patterns and sequences of events.

For the period immediately preceding the outbreak of war in 1914 there are substantial sources recording the character and behaviour of seafarers. The war years have mainly been recorded in published and unpublished memoirs, diaries, etc, of officers and in the surviving papers of Government records.

Writing in 1906 of his experience as a ship's engineer, William McFee commented:

> 'We were always losing men out of the fo'c'sle. At each port a small, ever-changing reservoir of convalescents, gaol-birds, wanderers and stowaways was drawn on for replacement. Our problem in Bremen was, we were going back to the States, winter North Atlantic, in ballast, the worst combination imaginable. British seamen could not be persuaded to sign on.'[16]

Captain John Carrington, highly regarded among his shipmaster peers, told a Board of Trade Committee of Inquiry in 1900:

> 'All those who have anything to do with shipping crews know that the majority of sailors are a very rough lot to deal with, and perhaps especially English sailors. The sailor is probably a man who has tried most things on shore, and gone to sea as a last resource, or he may have been a boy so thoroughly bad at home that his parents sent him to sea. That is the class of material we have to work with. Masters are put to a great deal of trouble to manage such crews.'[17]

As if writing in confirmation, F. T. Bullen observed at the turn of the century:

> 'Foreign seamen, especially Scandinavians, are not only biddable, they do not growl and curse at every order given, or seize the first opportunity to get drunk and neglect their work in harbour. Occasionally a truculent Norseman will be found who will develop all the worst characteristics of our own seamen, usually after a long service in British ships... But insubordination in the absence of any means of maintaining discipline is a peculiarly British failing.'[18]

Then, writing in his notebook during a voyage aboard a tramp in 1916-17, J. E. Patterson wrote:

> 'In the old days, when he was virile and wicked, [the seaman] got drunk and tried to paint the town red. But [he] paid for doing so... In these times of

degeneracy afloat, however, a man may be ashore, drinking instead of being at work; and if he is logged [punished] for doing so, especially in an American port, he just "jumps" the vessel... As for telling a man at sea that he is inefficient, or lazy, or is not sick when he lays up because he has stomach-ache or has tapped his finger with a hammer – well, the only result of such temerity and want of tact is to have the man say: "All rite, pay me off, then..."'[19]

While Patterson had an axe to grind and therefore places his descriptions within a coded political, explanatory framework – he complains of a loss of 'manhood' and attributes it to 'socialism [that] has made for the gutting of discipline [and] has put emasculated evils into the places of virile ones'[20] – there is no reason to question the actual behaviour. There may have been a war but there was no suspension of normal behaviour. Seafarers in the First War did desert, they did 'roister' and they were capable of voicing discontents.

Desertion was customary in the sense that it was long established and regarded by ratings and junior officers as a legitimate practice. In 1908 23,311 seafarers deserted abroad, roughly half in the USA and Canada and another 40 per cent in Australia and New Zealand, and there is no doubt whatever that desertions continued throughout the First War, though perhaps not on the same scale as in earlier years. The rate of desertion was especially high among sailing-ship crews. These were the ships where conditions were worst and therefore where desertion was customarily regarded almost as a means of redressing grievances. Towards the end of their epoch, and as they became more and more marginal economically, sailing-ships commonly depended on the labour of middle-class boys who were indentured as apprentices to learn the skills of a ship's officer. Apprentice deserters were common and it was not unusual for them to 'jump ship' in the company of able seamen. In 1915, when in New York, the *Naiad* lost four apprentices, one officer and three able seamen. All of them promptly engaged on the *Lusitania*, ten of whose crew had deserted. This was the voyage when the *Lusitania* was sunk by U-boat, and six of the ex-*Naiad* crew members were lost. The two apprentices who survived were brothers, and it was one of them who was on duty as a lookout when the liner was attacked. Leslie Morton, subsequently a key witness at the inquiry into the loss of the *Lusitania*, was awarded the Board of Trade's Silver Medal for Gallantry for his part in helping survivors to safety.[21]

Deserters rarely knew such prominence. Like the crew of the *Chepstow Castle*, almost all of whom deserted after port calls in Baltimore and New York in 1915, they typically melted away, in this case into the US seafarers' labour market where wages were almost double those paid on UK ships.[22] Desertion was almost certainly at a lower level in the Second War. The Ministry of War Transport recorded 1,850 cases in 1942 and 1,420 in 1943, and it is likely that perhaps as many as half of them were cases of crew members missing the ship's departure, but not deliberately. A detailed examination of desertions in US ports estimated that by the end of the second year of war some 3,402 Allied seamen had deserted, but that British seamen accounted for only 664, or 20 per cent of the total. The USA remained the most popular place to desert – 48 per cent of all deserters left in US ports and 32 per cent in Australasia. As in previous decades (and, indeed, centuries) most deserters found their way back on to ships – often British, but US, Norwegian and Panamanian ships were preferred, offering better wages and living conditions.

Shipboard discipline was almost entirely a problem for ships' senior officers in ports abroad. The following 'live' account from the personal log of an Elders & Fyffes master when his ship, the *Tortuguero*, was in port in Kingston, Jamaica, in 1940 could equally have been in 1914 – or at any other time, war or no war:

'August 12th 1940

The usual crew troubles in this port, with some of them getting ashore and getting insensibly drunk on the cheap rum. Firewater.

August 13th

Firemen break into chief steward's room and steal 6 bottles of whisky, one of rum, 40 tins of cigarettes and 1lb of tobacco. After a search some of the missing goods found in firemen's bunks.

Nine men logged… They are able to get very cheap rum from the bars and liquor stores adjacent to the dockgates, and in a very short time are drunk and incapable. Blotto, and can be seen stretched flat out on the pavement or the roadside in the blazing sun and police and people walk round these prostrate bodies with barely a glance, and they are left lying there…

August 15th

Greaser has deserted. This particular man is a hard worker and a good man at sea, but when he can get ashore at Kingston or anywhere abroad it is all over with him. This is the third ship this man has deserted from at Kingston.

Four men logged this morning were missing at sailing time and deliberately delayed the ship for one hour.

August 18th

At Santa Marta, Colombia. At 0800 hours two sailors came to see me and wanted passes to go ashore to church for confession. That's a good one, by Jove, I've heard some good excuses but that one is near the top of the list. I didn't let them go of course.

August 23rd

Now homeward bound at sea. The men who were logged are now working well and hard at their strenuous job.'[23]

Heavy drinking was not a problem confined to the non-officer ranks. In the First World War a young apprentice recorded two successive voyages with alcoholic chief officers. On the first occasion, during a ballast passage from St Nazaire to Barry, the chief officer had been locked in his room with his knife and razor confiscated. On the second occasion the replacement chief officer had taken to drinking bay rum and on passage from St Lucia in the West Indies to Cuba had been lashed into his hammock.[24] A comparable experience was recorded by a young engineer officer aboard the tanker *San Gregorio*. He noted that the chief engineer was perpetually drunk and so also was the master.[25] A similar story with different characters and 20 or so years later went into Leslie Harrison's diary in December 1939:

'December 5th

After a visit to a cinema and then a hotel in Port of Spain dropped in to ghastly Croydon Hotel for a few minutes to see sozzled Mate, 3/0, Sparks and Gunner in their element dancing in one of the lowest dives I've ever refused a drink in.

December 6th

3/0 in his usual alcoholic haze. Mate dozing on my settee as he sobered up.

December 7th

On passage from Port of Spain to Pte a Pierre ship runs aground. Mate and OM ['old man', the master] volubly convinced themselves that the buoy must have been out of position; but according to my (unannounced!) reckonings we'd made our course for Pte a Pierre jetty, and had been due to go aground ever since we started.'[26]

The official logs for both World Wars were commonly full of entries recording the misdeeds of, mainly, firemen, trimmers, able seamen and ordinary seamen. A sample of the logs of 85 ships for the whole period of the Second World War produced a total of slightly more than 2,000 disciplinary offences, of which 66 per cent were for absence without leave, disobedience in one form or another for 11 per cent, desertions formed 8 per cent, and drink offences 5 per cent. Engine-room ratings accounted for 42 per cent of offenders, catering ratings 30 per cent, deck ratings 23 per cent, petty officers 2 per cent and officers 1 per cent. Offences were predictably clustered where conditions were worst – aboard tramps the sample showed a ratio of eight offences for every ten non-officer crew members. Aboard tankers where conditions generally were much better, there was a ratio of two offences per ten crew members.[27]

Considering the level of reports of disciplinary offences in the secondary literature, it does seem likely that crew behaviour during port stays in 1914-18 was much the same as in 1939-45. There was, nevertheless, something of an official onslaught on seafarers in the later war and it is plausible to suppose that this was an attempt to prevent a recurrence of what had been seen as lamentable and reprehensible earlier. The Merchant Shipping Acts, which in their disciplinary provisions remained essentially unchanged between 1854 and 1968, provided shipmasters and shipowners with the power to levy fines, prosecute crew members in magistrates courts in the UK and colonies, and petition British consuls to set up special courts called Naval Courts in foreign ports. In a number of foreign countries – but not the USA – Treaty agreements even provided for the jailing of seafarers in those countries on Consular request.

Naval Courts were ordinarily little used – only three were convened between 1930 and 1939. But 505 were held between 1939 and 1944. Most cases – 415 of them – were held between May 1943 and June 1944 and were held in Mediterranean ports controlled by the Royal Navy: 90 per cent of all Naval Courts were held in Algiers, Bone, Oran, Alexandria, Port Said, Suez, Naples, Bari and Taranto. In these cases there seems little doubt that the Navy was attempting to impose on merchant seamen the disciplinary measures available for use on their own men under military law.[28] At home, in the UK, there was a comparable level of prosecutions through magistrates courts. From August 1942 the Ministry of Labour was responsible for these prosecutions after a filtering process by local tribunals whose members were employers and union officials sitting with an independent chairman. The range of prosecutable offences was also enlarged by a series of five Orders in Council under the Defence of the Realm Act.

The extent of the use of the legal system to prosecute civilians was both unprecedented and unparalleled in any other industry. It is certainly arguable that dockers and miners in the Second War presented the Government with far greater problems. That the state drew back from a legal attack on these occupational groups was almost certainly due to the kind of effective trade union organisation that was simply unavailable to seafarers.[29] There is no evidence to suggest that there was any comparable legal assault on merchant seafarers in the Great War – but enough evidence to suggest that crews were far from quiescent. During the Dardanelles campaign in 1915 a large part of the crew of the *Aragon* informed the master that they did not wish to work beyond the expiry of their agreement even though the ship was to remain at its anchorage. They were removed from the ship by a party of armed marines.[30] A similar event also took place aboard a White Star liner serving as a hospital ship in the Dardanelles. The master, Sir Arthur Rostron, subsequently wrote in his memoir:

'There was a day in Mudros when I had to go so far as to have a squad of soldiers lined up on deck because certain members of the crew had in fact refused duty – they were annoyed at being set some task when they had expected a spot of leave, but it was a job that had to be done – and I meant that it should be performed. When the soldiers were lined up with their rifles loaded with live cartridges I paraded the recalcitrant members of the crew with their backs to the bulkhead.'[31]

For ships' officers, particularly those of the cargo and passenger liner companies, the military style of discipline as represented by the Royal Navy was the model of practice to which they aspired.[32] But for ratings the point of reference was the shoreside workplace. For them the ship was just another example of an industrial working environment and one, therefore, in which refusal in various forms was believed to be legitimate. Here are two examples, both drawn from the Second War.

In 1943 a 20-year-old seaman was fined £2 by the Tynemouth magistrates for deserting his ship in a South Wales port. He told the court: 'I just left because the grub was not good. I was at sea before the war but that ship was the worst grubbed one I ever saw.' Asked by the magistrate why he had not complained to the master, he said, 'It's just one of those things. If you don't like a ship you don't sail in her.'[33]

The second example concerns a crew member of a ship in Port Said in 1944, where the master failed in an attempt to persuade the British Consul to convene a Naval Court. The story ran that the 4th Officer had told crew members to stop throwing bread to the labourers who were discharging cargo. The crew members were said to have crowded round the 4th Officer and abused him. The officer had then said to two men that he would have them logged, one of whom subsequently shook his fist in the officer's face and said:

"'Sh—" This was in reply to my repeated questioning as to what his name was, and then he said, "You are only a b—- Petty Officer, and that because you have a piece of braid on your shoulder you think that you can come along here shouting your —— mouth off; well, you can't. I have got a —— and two —— —— the same as you. I am just as good a man as you.'[34]

Here we have, so to speak, 'textbook' instances of seafarers' assertions of the legitimacy of customary behaviour in respect of their own actions, and outrage at officers overstepping customary boundaries.

Defence of customary practice and behaviour aimed at reasserting customary proprieties in the exercise of authority were, of course, only understood to be applicable in normal, routine daily practices where the technical and social division of shipboard labour was uncritically taken for granted. In extremity, pre-existing social arrangements were not necessarily turned upside down. But they might be. When sinking ships were abandoned and survivors subsequently – and literally – found themselves all in the same boat, the shipboard social organisation was never reproduced in its original form. Technical competence in boatwork was essential and it was not unknown for able seamen to be more competent than navigating officers. Furthermore, the limitations of space and provisions made privilege morally abhorrent, and anyway impossible to assert. Then there was the overpowering need for individuals skilful in morale maintenance. Where necessary skills for survival did not correspond with shipboard rank – prior rank became meaningless. However, this rarely meant that the world was turned upside down. Navigational skills were absolutely essential, and it was inevitable that wherever a navigating officer was present and not disabled, he would play a critical role, though he might not be the dominant person.

The evidence of the character of the social order of the lifeboat is ambiguous and is not equivalent for the two wars. In the First World War the submarine's operational range was limited and that meant that most ships were sunk relatively close to land and survivors were either picked up or made landfalls in boats within a matter of days. In August 1915, for example, none of the ships sunk was more than 100 miles from land. The situation changed somewhat in 1917 when submarine ranges had increased and convoying obliged submarines to hunt further afield. In April 1917 42 per cent of ships sunk were more than 100 miles from land. But in the Second World War, and certainly by the summer of 1940, ships' survivors were much more likely to be at some distance from either rescuers or land within a few days' sail. This was a far more testing time for merchant seaman survivors and produced far more cases of what can reasonably be called 'epic' voyages. There is extensive evidence of survival experience under such circumstances. A team of medical researchers was actively interviewing survivors, and so too were Admiralty intelligence officers. The former synthesised their data for statistical analysis and the original records have been lost.[35] The Admiralty records have survived – the ADM199 sequence in the Public Record Office, Kew – but the Navy's policy was to interview only the senior ranking survivor, and these persons were not necessarily those who had played key roles.

In August 1942 Captain George Robinson gave a BBC radio talk of his survival experience in the North Atlantic in December 1941. Although it is not mentioned in the broadcast, Robinson had had both of his frost-bitten feet amputated. There is no doubt that he had at least played a key role among the survivors of his ship, but it is equally plain that so also had one of the able seamen:

'That Christmas, dinner consisted of a mouthful of water and a ship's biscuit. One of the crew, a Scot named Patterson, used to sit reckoning up how much wages would be due when he got home. He even got to the stage of asking me how much overtime he was entitled to. This man was the toughest man I've ever had the pleasure to meet... He kept us all going and kept us all amused by reckoning up his pay in bottles of beer.

As we got weaker I noticed men reaching out for things that weren't there ... and I often wondered what it was they could see. Then, staring into the compass, I noticed a glass of beer go floating past and I realised I was seeing things too. I laid down in the bottom of the boat with a blanket around me and Patterson gave me a kick ... and yelled: "Hey, here's a ship coming!" After 18 days of sky and water one is inclined to think there are no ships left. After the rescue we were landed and hospitalised in Halifax but after a few days Patterson came up to say goodbye as he'd signed on a Dutch tanker that was sailing that night. He'd been ashore too long, he said.'[36]

One of the more celebrated boat voyages in this war was under the command of a 16-year-old ship's boy from the Hebrides. The survivor with six others of the *Arlington Court*, his background as the son of a fisherman equipped him with the skills needed to make a successful eight-day voyage.[37] There were many other cases where recognition was given to crew members whose boat skills had been critical. In what is now the standard text on survivors in the Second World War, the authors comment:

'It was fortunate for [fellow survivors] if pure chance placed them in a boat with someone like the Earleston's Newfoundland fisherman, the Peterton's chief engineer keen on yachting, the Aldington Court's Latvian bosun who was an expert boatman, the Ripley's West Indian able seaman who had spent most of his life in small boats, or the Larchbank's Bengali greaser who was familiar with river craft.'[38]

If there were some extraordinarily successful boat voyages[39], others were simply appalling disasters. In 1943 the Liverpool shipping daily published the first of these two reports from Port of Spain, Trinidad. The second was a survivor's report from the master of the tanker, *British Resource*:

'A delirious merchant seaman, who landed here two days ago, his life practically "baked out of him" after 76 days drifting in an open lifeboat ... was identified as William Colburn, aged 32, of Liverpool. Colburn, who survived 20 of his companions, could not give details of his ordeal, as he is still unable to talk... As days and weeks and finally months slipped by, the sun and lack of food and water took their toll, and one by one the other seamen died. Colburn did not have the strength left to throw the last five overboard, and when his tossing lifeboat was found he was huddled in the bottom surrounded by the bodies of his dead shipmates.'[40]

'After ordering the chief officer away in a boat with 30 men the vessel was torpedoed again ... throwing a high column of blazing benzine high into the air, setting the ship on fire from the foremast, right aft. The water on both sides was immediately covered with burning benzine. In spite of the port boat being 250 feet away from the ship it was filled with burning benzine and being a metal boat it soon melted. The occupants must have perished immediately... During three hours in the water before finding a raft I bumped into several of my men. I turned two of them over but they were beyond recognition, the flames had done their work only too well.'[41]

Both wars generated, among some of the more excitable jingoistic commentators, stories of brutal German warship crews. There were inevitably people who behaved cruelly, but the war at sea provided far more opportunities for acts of generosity and common humanity than were available to armies. When in the First World War the cruiser *Dresden* encountered the sailing ship *Penrhyn Castle*, the German captain allowed the ship to set a course for home unmolested on discovering that the sailing ship's captain had his wife and child aboard.[42] There were also numerous examples of submarine crews towing lifeboats to safety, providing first aid to wounded crew members, giving navigational advice, sending radio messages to neutral ships, supplying food, water and tobacco. In both wars some of these stories got into the press. The *Daily Mirror*, for example, reported in 1940 that an Italian submarine, after sinking the *British Fame*, towed the survivors in their boats to St Michaels in the Azores[43]. In 1941 an 18-year-old survivor recounted how, after survivors had got into rafts and a lifeboat, the submarine rose to the surface and the U-boat commander handed over a couple of bottles of rum and some tins of bully beef. He said goodbye and submerged.[44]

During the years of each conflict the war at sea killed thousands of seafarers. War is about damaging others defined as enemies, and this is well understood by the participants. But this engagement does not preclude the possibility of expressions of common humanity, whether it were between the formal enemies or among those on the 'same side', but commonly at odds with each other. Wars invariably demonstrate the absurdity of the condition itself. They also, and even more absurdly, offer some of the participants the opportunity of rediscovering the essential condition of life itself, that without solidarity there can be no life. Many survivors went to the edge and experienced that elementary lesson of interdependence – then forgot it again afterwards. It was bizarre and often remarked upon that survivors were quickly sorted out into officers and ratings. This was naturally regarded as essential because officers needed to be lodged in hotels of a certain class, and ratings in hotels of another class. Once back aboard ship – and it was the same in both World Wars – the rituals of encounters between persons of different classes carried on as usual.

In conclusion

The view of war as an imposition from a world of affairs that was 'nothing to do with us' was not unique to merchant seafarers, and was probably universal. In his novel *August, 1914*, Alexander Solzhenitsyn describes what he plainly takes to be the common response to the onset of war: 'People in the village did not discuss the war or even think about it as an event over which anyone had any control or which ought or ought not to be allowed to happen. They accepted the war … as the will of God, something like a blizzard or a dust-storm…'[45] Pre-revolution rural Russia, at least in terms of outlook on the world and thinking about the possibilities of human control over events, was perhaps not so far distant from Britain, which was in 1914 probably the most industrialised nation on the planet. Very little of the apparatus of the modern democratic state then existed in the UK. Property and residential requirements left roughly half the adult male population without the right to vote, and of course virtually all women were unenfranchised. A sequence of electoral reforms ensured that by 1939 almost all of the adult population had the vote, but the knowledge and experience of the democratic process beyond electoral politics was inevitably rudimentary. A young infantry lieutenant, Neil McCallum, noted in his diary during the Second World War that he found it ironic that if he and his comrades were fighting for democracy, why was it so 'hard to find an infantryman who could define democracy?'[46]

The merchant seafarer – or at least the ratings – came from the same stratum as McCallum's infantrymen and were no less hard-pressed to explain what the war was about.[47] Fifty years afterwards and thinking about how he and his shipmates had thought about the Second World War, Alan Peter, who had been a bosun, was surely right in his characterisation of attitudes:

> 'We had no control over the politics of war, had we? In the fo'c'sles of all the ships that I can remember or amongst the crew when we'd sit out on the poop at night chewing the fat just before the sun went down, there'd be fooling about among the younger ones wrestling or sparring up to each other, doing their hobbies or playing the mouth organ. That was the usual thing and occurred no less than in peacetime. There was no great discussion about the pros and cons of war.'[48]

It is impossible to escape the conclusion that most merchant seamen, despite feeling the full brunt of war, especially in the Second World War, felt that it had little to do with them. They kept it out of their lives even though it pervaded them.

Notes on contributors

Professor Tony Lane, Cardiff University, UK
Tony Lane is Director of the Seafarers International Research Centre at Cardiff University. He has written extensively on merchant seafarers in the nineteenth and twentieth centuries, including The Merchant Seaman's War (1990).

Recommended reading

Beckman, Morris, *Atlantic Roulette* (Brighton: Tom Donovan Publishing, 1996). Easily the best everyday account of a wartime voyage. Excellent.

Bennett, G. H. and R., *Survivors* (London: Hambledon Press, 1999). A very full account of Second World War merchant seafarer survivors.

Lane, Tony, *The Merchant Seaman's War* (Manchester: University Press, 1990, and Liverpool: The Bluecoat Press, 1993)

'The people's war at sea: work-discipline and merchant seamen, 1939-1945' in *Scottish Journal of Labour History*, 1995, pp61-86. Provides the only case study refutation of the 'people's war thesis'.

Thomas, R. Gabe, *Milag: Merchant Navy Prisoners of War* (Porthcawl: Milag Prisoner of War Association, 1995). A very detailed 'warts and all' account of the merchant seafarers POW camp, Milag Nord, in North Germany.

Woodman, Richard, *Arctic Convoys 1941-1945* (London: John Murray, 1994)

There have been no thorough studies of merchant seafarers in the First World War. Books published during the war or soon thereafter are neither in print nor readily available.

Notes

[1] Charlotte Behrens, *British Shipping and the Demands of War* (HMSO, 1955)
[2] Owen Rutter, *Red Ensign: A History of Convoy* (Robert Hale, 1943) p130
[3] See Georges Blond, *Ordeal Below Zero* (London. 1956), and P. Shankland and A. Hunter, *Malta Convoy* (London, 1961)
[4] See Edward Tupper, *Seamen's Torch* (Hutchinson, 1938) pp129-31, and Tony Lane, *The Merchant Seaman's War* (Manchester, 1990) p119
[5] *Picture Post*, 27 Jan 1940, p27
[6] *Picture Post*, 6 April 1940, p45
[7] *Picture Post*, 24 August 1940, pp18-9
[8] Ibid, p5
[9] Ibid, p8
[10] Ibid, p8
[11] Harold Wheeler, *Daring Deeds of Merchant Seamen in the Great War* (Harrap, 1918) p11
[12] Ivor Halstead's *Heroes of the Atlantic* (1941), p5
[13] C. Day-Lewis, *Palgrave's Golden Treasury* (Collins, 1968) p388
[14] David Divine, *The Merchant Navy Fights* (London: John Murray, 1940) p27
[15] Owen Rutter, op cit, p195
[16] William McFee, *The First Watch* (London: Faber) p34
[17] Report of a Committee Appointed by the Board of Trade on the Question of Continuous Discharge Certificates for Seamen (1900), Minutes of Evidence, Cmnd 136, Q1207, p41
[18] *The Men of the Merchant Service* (London: Smith, Elder, 1900) p140
[19] *A War-Time Voyage* (London: J. M. Dent, 1918) pp35-6
[20] Ibid, p36
[21] Leslie Morton, *The Long Wake* (London: Routledge & Kegan Paul, 1968)
[22] G. J. Whitfield, *Fifty Thrilling Years at Sea* (London: Hutchinson, nd – c1937) pp179-80
[23] Captain J. Bull, typescript memoir ms in possession of Professor P. N. Davies, University of Liverpool
[24] E. T. N. Lawrey, ms, Liddle Collection, University of Leeds
[25] R. D. F. Powell, ms, Liddle Collection, University of Leeds
[26] W. L. S. Harrison, ms diary, Imperial War Museum

27 Tony Lane, op cit, p112-6
28 PRO, MT9/51, 'Naval Courts'
29 Tony Lane, 'The people's war at sea: work-discipline and merchant seamen, 1939-1945', *Scottish Journal of Labour History*, 30, pp61-86
30 H. Atkinson, ms 249, Imperial War Museum
31 Sir Arthur Rostron, *Home From the Sea* (Cassell, 1933) p139
32 Tony Lane, 'Neither officers nor gentlemen', *History Workshop Journal*, 19 (Spring 1985), pp128-43
33 *Journal of Commerce*, 31 August 1943
34 PRO, FO 369/2987, 1944
35 R. A. McCance et al, *The Hazards to Men Lost in Ships at Sea, 1940-1944* (Medical Research Council, 1956)
36 Capt George Robinson, 'Adventure in a lifeboat adrift in the Atlantic', BBC Radio News Reel, 19 August 1942, BBC Sound Archive, No 4662
37 ADM199/2130, *Arlington Court*, report of Malcolm Morrison, deck boy
38 G. H. and R. Bennet, *Survivors* (London: Hambledon Press, 1999) p180
39 See F. West, *Lifeboat Number Seven* (London: William Kimber, 1960); S. W. Roskill, *A Merchant Fleet in War, 1939-1945* (London: Collins, 1962), which gives some detail of the excellent survival record of crews of the ships of Blue Funnel; Ralph Barker, *Goodnight, Sorry for Sinking You* (London: Collins, 1986); Stanley Simpson, 'Voyage to Tobago' in R. Hope ed, *The Seaman's World* (London: Harrap, 1982)
40 *Journal of Commerce*, 7 February 1943
41 ADM199/2140
42 J. Ifor Davies, *Growing Up Among Sailors* (Caernarvon: Gwynned Archive Services, 1983) pp84-5
43 *Daily Mirror*, 26 August 1940
44 *Journal of Commerce*, 9 September 1941
45 Alexander Solzhenitsyn, *August, 1914* (London: Book Club Associates, 1973) pp17-8
46 Neil McCallum, *Journey With a Pistol* (London: Gollancz, 1959) p142
47 Tony Lane, op cit, pp87-93
48 Quoted in Tony Lane, op cit, p9

Chapter 5

War in the air:
the fighter pilot

David Jordan

The first flight of an aircraft in 1903 created a new arena for warfare. In simple terms, the aircraft was another piece of machinery produced by advancing technology. Although from the perspective of the 21st century it is difficult to perceive the Wright Flyer or Blériot's monoplane as articles of cutting-edge technology, at the time of their construction they represented the height of innovation. They were also dangerous. Their newness made them unreliable, and herein lay the difficulties. If a piece of new technology failed to function on the ground, it did not usually lead to death or injury. The person operating the machine would simply note that it was not functioning and attempt to make it work. If he failed, he would send for technical assistance, either from the machine's inventor or the manufacturer. For a pilot this was not an option. If a piece of equipment failed, the aviator had no time for the luxury of sending out for help. Technological failure meant a rapid return to earth, with all the attendant risks. Although the knowledge existed to get a man into the air, the development of the parachute to get him down again was running some way behind. As a result, the public came to adore the 'magnificent men in their flying machines', ranking them as a special breed.

When the First World War broke out, their image was enhanced. The nature of warfare between 1914 and 1918 meant that the public at home could not easily find heroes from among the armies on the ground. The days of the knightly champion indulging in single combat were at an end. The great naval heroes of the 19th century were largely absent, thanks to the absence of great naval battles, leaving only the airmen. Initially, the acclaim they enjoyed related to the dangerous nature of flight rather than war, but within 12 months of the outbreak of conflict there was a new type of pilot to admire. The fighter pilot.

The need to prevent interference with operations by enemy aircraft led to the development of machines first equipped and then specifically designed for the task of fighting with other aircraft. The nature of this work provided heroes for the Home Front of every nation engaged in the conflict. Aerial combat seemed to possess the chivalry of old – man against man, machine against machine. Pilots, not just those in fighters, were eulogised as an elite band, engaged in combat that owed something to the age of chivalry. David Lloyd George informed the House of Commons:

'The heavens are their battlefield; they are the cavalry of the clouds. High above the squalor and the mud ... they fight out the eternal issues of right and wrong. Their daily, yea, their nightly struggles are like the Miltonic conflict between the winged hosts of light and darkness... They are the knighthood of this war, without fear and without reproach.'[1]

Lloyd George was not altogether accurate. In fact, fighter pilots knew fear, and they soon discovered that chivalric acts were just as likely to get them killed as to be to their benefit. Nonetheless, the image held. This leaves historians with a problem. The popular perception of fighter pilots of both World Wars is one dominated by the 'aces' – those pilots with five or more victories against the enemy. This neatly overlooks the fact that approximately 40 per cent of aerial victories have been achieved by around 5 per cent of all fighter pilots.[2] This means that to understand the fighter pilots' experience in two World Wars, we need to look beyond the aces; if we do not, we miss out of the equation large numbers of fighter pilots. They flew many hours on operations and scored only a few, if any, aerial victories. In fact, if the experience of fighter pilots, ace and non-ace, is considered, there is a remarkable seriality of experience. This applies to both conflicts and across national boundaries.

Although the popular perceptions of fighter pilots may be distorted, there are a number of truisms that can be drawn from the false imagery. Air combat is a difficult pursuit. Unlike other forms of warfare, it is fought in three dimensions, which adds to the challenge of being successful. The truly successful fighter pilot needs to possess great perception of what is happening around him; in the course of an air battle, this has proved to be extremely difficult. This 'situational awareness', or 'SA', is important to all fighter pilots. Those who possess the best SA have tended to be the high scorers. In the two World Wars pilots could not rely upon technology to guide weapons against enemy aircraft, and had to rely upon their shooting skills. For every crack shot, there were tens of others who were unable to bring a sufficient weight of fire to bear upon the enemy. This consideration applies across the board. It is notable that many aces have been described as only average pilots.

'Billy' Bishop was regarded as being a particularly ham-fisted pilot, but his shooting skills enabled him to become one of the leading aces. As will be discussed below, just how accurate was Bishop's total of claims is now open to serious doubt; nonetheless, there is enough evidence to state that he destroyed enough aircraft to be considered an 'ace' (although the Royal Flying Corps and its successor the Royal Air Force have never officially used the term), and his shooting skills were undoubtedly important. In comparison, the New Zealander Keith Caldwell, who ended the First World War commanding 74 Squadron RAF, was noted for his skilful flying and abysmal shooting. Mike Spick regularly makes the point that the adage 'good flying never killed anyone yet' holds a great deal of truth.[3] Spick also makes an important contribution by noting that the idea that the top-scorers were only average pilots is inherently subjective. As most, if not all, of the highest-claiming men possessed better situational awareness, they were able to use this superior judgement to avoid placing themselves in circumstances where superlative flying skill was required to save themselves.[4]

The debate over the importance of flying skill and shooting ability is not an easy one to resolve. The easiest way to score while avoiding trouble was to sneak up upon an opponent and press home an effective close-range attack before he knew what had occurred.[5] This apparently required only competent flying, but demanded good planning and accurate shooting. Although this type of attack fell outside the bounds of chivalric behaviour, this consideration did not worry fighter pilots. One of the leading British pilots of the Great War, Philip Fullard, firmly believed that his high score of victories owed more to his ability as a pilot rather than to superior shooting skills. Fullard was not shy in his self-analysis, calling himself a 'brilliant pilot'. He also remarked upon his penchant for getting so close to the enemy aircraft that he could see the bullets striking home.[6] Even if pilots were excellent shots, the need to get in close to the enemy was stressed time and time again. The second highest-scoring American pilot of the Second World War, Thomas B. McGuire, told new arrivals to his unit they should 'go in close, and then when you think you're too close, go in closer still.'[7]

With the arrival of batteries of wing-mounted guns in Second World War fighters, it is noticeable that the British aces all harmonised their guns to a set point, so that the rounds would converge. In the Battle of Britain a number of pilots had the harmonisation set at 50 yards.[8] This was in contrast to the initial alignment of the guns so that a 'shotgun pattern' was achieved. Although this was an admirable recognition of the lack of shooting ability of the vast majority of pilots, it did nothing to compensate, reducing the concentration of weight of fire. The same difficulty affected the Luftwaffe, where it was noted that the armament of the early versions of the Messerschmitt 109 created problems for the less experienced pilots. The Me109's armament of two rifle-calibre machine-guns over the engine and one cannon firing through the propeller hub demanded precise shooting for full effect.[9] The successful pilot invariably preferred to get in close. The leading 'ace' of the Second World War, Erich Hartmann (352 victories), remarked:

'You can have computer sights or anything you like, but I think you have to go to the enemy on the shortest distance and knock him down from point blank range. You'll get him from in close. At long distance it's questionable.'[10]

And:

'I liked the whole of my windscreen to be full of the enemy aircraft when I fired.'[11]

Getting in close reduced the need to possess deadly shooting skills; the major difficulty appears to have been that of judging distance. There are countless examples of pilots opening fire beyond the range of their guns, thus alerting the enemy and reducing their ammunition before closing to an effective distance. Hence, while the ability to shoot straight was important, the ability to judge range was equally imperative, especially when shooting with any degree of deflection.

Although the majority of pilots who followed the simple dictum of getting in close could score a few victories, the high-scorers were set apart by their ability to aim accurately while compensating for angles of deflection between them and their target. It will be realised that the majority of aerial combats did not involve straight and level flight. The twists and turns seen as aircraft manoeuvred for position meant that the ability to judge an aiming point became vital. It was therefore necessary for pilots to judge where their shells and the enemy aircraft would converge. This was true in both World Wars, but, coupled with the higher speeds of the Second, it made air combat a tricky business. More than anything else, this explains why shooting skills were arguably more important than flying ability.

In the First World War the French 'ace' René Fonck used to spend a great deal of time while on the ground practising his shooting. Although he used a shotgun or a rifle, the principles were the same. He ended the war with an official tally of 75 victories, a total that, in fact, may have been even higher. Fonck was also renowned for his ability to dispatch an enemy aircraft using remarkably few rounds of ammunition. In the Second World War the British 'aces' 'Johnnie' Johnson and Robert Stanford Tuck, both of whom went game shooting, were able to score highly (at least 38 and 29 victories respectively) as a result of their experience of judging both distance and movement so as to bring their guns to bear on a moving target. The closer the range, the less danger of miscalculation. Even with practice, be it gained from hunting birds or in the more official surroundings of a gunnery school, the shooting ability of the top-scorers relied heavily upon developed instinct. Gunther Rall, the third-highest scoring German pilot of the Second World War, with 275 victories, noted:

> 'I had no system of shooting as such. It is definitely more in the feeling side of things that these skills develop. I was at the front [for] five and a half years and you just get a feeling for the right amount of lead [ie angle of deflection].'[12]

A predecessor from the Great War, Captain Frederick Libby, was of the same opinion, claiming that, 'Aerial gunnery is ninety per cent instinct and ten per cent aim.'[13]

The truly successful fighter pilot therefore combined situational awareness with good judgement of distance and an ability to aim his guns to best effect. Possessing above average flying ability was helpful, but not essential. No matter how skilled a shot, fighter pilots nevertheless required more than all this. Their equipment, training and tactics also had a major role to play.

The development of air fighting in the Great War naturally demanded the consideration of both strategy and tactics. On the strategic level, the policies developed by the Allies, particularly the Royal Flying Corps, have received more attention than those of the German air service, while the tactical axioms developed by men such as Manfred Von Richthofen, Oswald Boelcke and Max Immelmann have been regarded more highly than those of the Allies. This is slightly misleading, as any study of what might be generically called 'pithy quotes by fighter pilots' from either World War demonstrates that there were master tacticians on both sides. The crucial point to be made is that the essential rules of air fighting remained very similar in both conflicts; furthermore, there were not a great many of them. Thus from the First World War we have Manfred Von Richthofen noting 'the aggressive spirit, the offensive, is the chief thing everywhere in war and the air is no exception'; while a whole conflict later, 'Johnnie' Johnson stressed that 'the only proper defence is offence.'[14] Although this gives the impression that the tactical development of the air forces progressed on similar lines, the RAF entered the Second World War at a tactical disadvantage.

The prescribed methods of flying and fighting laid down by Fighter Command manuals and routine orders predicated the use of either the three-aircraft section (or 'vic') and the line astern of four machines, with different types of attack profile being employed against fighters and bombers. The Luftwaffe, on the other hand, utilising its experience in the Spanish Civil War, adopted the more flexible 'schwarme' or 'finger four'. This formation, named in its English translation after the position of the fingers of a hand laid flat on a table to demonstrate the rough positioning of the aircraft within it, developed the notion of the 'wingman'. The aircraft in the four could, and did, divide into two sections, with each pilot certain that he was covered by his wingman. Although the pairs of aircraft usually had a designated (or de facto) lead and wing, if the wingman found himself engaged in a fight, he could usually rely upon his section lead to follow him, watching for any enemy aircraft that might try to engage. In spite of the fact that the 'finger four' was rapidly proven to be more effective than either the 'vic' or line astern, British pilots found that it was difficult to change a tactical system that had been carefully built up and protected by the entrenched bureaucracy of the inter-war years. This caused difficulties. The two wingmen in the 'vic' had to spend most of their time keeping formation, giving them little time to scan the sky for enemy aircraft, while the line astern simply enabled the enemy to work their way along the line.

Most RAF units circumvented the problem of tactical ossification in high command by ignoring the official way of doing things and using the best method, although this could lead to trouble from higher authority if discovered.[15] That the German method was far better is beyond doubt: the three-aircraft section left one of the aircraft without any cover for his rear quarter. When the problem of hidebound command was overcome – partly through the promotion of combat-experienced flyers to staff and command positions – the RAF was finally able to put the 'finger four' to good effect.

In a replication of the First World War, the Luftwaffe began to move towards defensive operations over occupied territory while the Allies took the war to them. This was, of course, first meant to be done through the use of bombers, but when it became apparent that the unescorted bomber was vulnerable, the emphasis of the offensive was transferred to the fighter arm. Thus, strategy laid down in 1916 re-emerged, putting the fighter pilot in the vanguard of aerial operations, even though pre-Second World War theory had given prominence to the bomber. The offensive use of fighters owes most to the thoughts of Marshal of the Royal Air Force Viscount Trenchard (in 1916, a Brigadier-General). Trenchard contended that:

'The moral effect produced by a hostile aeroplane is ... out of all proportion to the damage which it can inflict.

The mere presence of a hostile machine in the air inspires those on the ground with exaggerated forebodings with regard to what a machine is capable of doing.

The sound policy then which should guide all warfare in the air would seem to be this: to exploit this moral effect of the aeroplane, but not to let him exploit it on ourselves. Now this can only be done by attacking and continuing to attack.'[16]

Furthermore, Trenchard argued that:

'...An aeroplane is an offensive and not a defensive weapon. Owing to the unlimited space in the air ... it is impossible for aeroplanes to prevent hostile aircraft from crossing the line if they have the initiative and determination to do so.'[17]

For the remainder of the war, the British more than any other air service remained wedded to the doctrine of the offensive. The policy was designed to ensure that the RFC's army co-operation machines could operate without interference from the enemy; the safest means of doing this was to keep the enemy well behind the front lines. The disparity in losses between fighters and army co-operation machines suggests that the offensive policy worked, but it was extremely costly. Additionally, there were instances of patrols sent out over enemy lines and not meeting any opposition, but suffering losses as a result of mechanical failure or anti-aircraft fire.[18]

Arthur Gould Lee, an RFC veteran, felt that Trenchard viewed the offensive in terms of gaining territory:

'...for a British plane to be one mile across the trenches was offensive: for it to be ten miles across was more offensive... While we thus dissipated our strength, more often than not merely beating the empty air, the Germans ... concentrated forces superior in numbers or equipment and engaged our scattered line patrols in turn, and our Distant Offensive Patrols as and when it suited them. The result was that in 1917, British air losses were at times nearly four times as great as the German.'[19]

The Germans appeared to remain content to engage the RFC over their own lines, and never adopted offensive operations on the same scale. Of Manfred Von Richthofen's 80 credited victories, 62 were destroyed over German lines or No Man's Land. RFC 'aces' obtained most, if not all, of their 'kills' well over enemy territory.

The Great War first demonstrated a point that remained true in the Second World War, namely that the defensive fighter force had a number of advantages when compared to an air force pursuing an offensive. Pilots who were shot down on the defending side were able to crash land or (in the later conflict) parachute to safety on friendly territory, while the pilot from the attacking side who was forced down could look forward only to captivity or attempts to evade – which were rarely successful. In addition, the attacking force was compelled to consider its fuel state. In the case of the Battle of Britain, the Luftwaffe's efforts were greatly hampered by the fact that the Me109 was unable to remain over Britain for long because of lack of fuel reserves. British fighters, notably the Spitfire and the Hurricane, were similarly 'short-legged'. Nonetheless, this did not prevent the British from employing the fighter offensive after the threat of a German invasion of Britain had reduced. 'Johnnie' Johnson, as has been mentioned, was emphatic upon the value of offensive action, but he was talking about air combat. His views on the RAF's offensive against German-occupied territory in 1941 and 1942 were less than enthusiastic:

> 'We began to carry out low-level flights over France. These operations were known by the code name Rhubarb. The idea was to take full advantage of low cloud and poor visibility and slip sections of Spitfires across the coast and then let down below the cloud to search for opportunity targets, rolling stock, locomotives, aircraft on the ground, staff cars, enemy troops and the like…
>
> …I loathed these Rhubarbs with a dark hatred. Apart from the flak, the hazards of making a let-down over unknown territory and with no accurate knowledge of the cloud base seemed far too great a risk for the damage we inflicted.'[20]

It is hard to disagree with Johnson, since the effect of the operations was relatively small, and did nothing to compensate for the losses of experienced pilots. The famed Robert Stanford Tuck and Douglas Bader were both shot down and captured during the course of the offensive, while slightly less well-known 'aces' such as Howard Blatchford, John Gillan, Eric Lock and Paddy Finucane were all killed.[21] This is not to say that the use of fighters in an offensive role was without any value. Once the United States Army Air Force (USAAF) was equipped with long-range fighter aircraft, it was able to carry the war deep into Germany itself, escorting bombers and inflicting attrition upon the enemy fighter force. Among other things, this prevented the Luftwaffe from opposing the D-Day landings in great force, and began to remove experienced pilots from the fray. Indeed, Noble Frankland suggests that the use of long-range fighters over Germany was vital in winning the air war in Europe.[22]

Even though such strategic developments were of obvious importance, the tactical application of fighters in attempting to achieve these aims remained vital. Although the RAF had learned much about the use of the 'finger four' from encountering the Germans, this only applied to small groups of aircraft. Again, in a direct parallel with the First World War (although on a larger scale), pilots found that they were engaged in air battles involving increasing numbers of machines. The RAF had made attempts to use large formations during the Battle of Britain, most notably the famous 'Big Wing' led by Douglas Bader. This was a novelty for the RAF, for it had never previously attempted to use large formations of aircraft in a defensive situation. Although the German Spring Offensives of March-June 1918 had suffered greatly from air attack, actual air combat operations had been a secondary concern for the defenders. A further difference was the manner in which defensive air-to-air operations were conducted: in the Great War, the majority of combats were over enemy lines. During the Battle of Britain, then later the Battle for Malta, fighters worked almost exclusively over their own territory, without attempting to carry the war to the enemy.

While the gaining of air superiority was crucial, once won, the fighter force could have found itself with little to do. This was not the case, as fighter pilots found themselves engaged in ground-attack operations. The qualities of the fighter aircraft – speed, manoeuvrability and firepower – made it admirably suitable for the risky work of attacking ground forces. The RFC was arguably the first air service to make major use of its fighter aircraft for ground-attack, preferring them to developing machines specifically designed for such a role. Initially, pilots indulged in freelance operations as they were returning from patrols, but at the Battle of Arras in April 1917 the first co-ordinated operational orders for air support were issued. A combination of bad weather and inexperience meant that the missions did not achieve all that they might have done, but they showed great promise. At Third Ypres in July, the concept was proven to be effective, and came to the fore at the Battle of Cambrai at the end of the year. This had implications for a number of fighter pilots, who found themselves training for operations quite unlike any they had conducted before. Notable amongst them was Arthur Gould Lee of Number 46 Squadron. On 9 November, Gould Lee recorded his flying for that day:

'My other flying was a low cross-country and bomb-dropping practice. We were actually ordered to do the low-level flight, which normally is officially frowned on. Our machines have been fitted with racks under the fuselage to carry four 20lb bombs, and a target has been laid out… I wonder what's afoot?'[23]

This practice continued, until on 17 November he wrote home:

'Over the past four days we've been hard at it practising bomb-dropping… I found it surprisingly easy to get close results [with bombs], in fact mine were the best in the squadron… I hope this unexpected skill doesn't land me any awkward jobs!'

This cheerfulness masked his real concerns:

'Something unpleasant is certainly brewing. We all feel it. First 3 and 46 [Squadrons] both getting Camels in such a hurry. Then this intensive practice in low bombing and low … flying… Another squadron, 84, with SE 5a's under Major [Sholto] Douglas has arrived at the other end of the aerodrome… Every village in the forward zone is crowded with troops … obviously a big push is coming any time now.'[24]

The attack at Cambrai was launched on 20 November. Gould Lee was sent to attack enemy artillery batteries in Lateau Wood. His recollections of the incident were understandably vivid:

'The batteries below are firing producing more smoke ... there we are, the
three of us whirling blindly around at 50-100 feet, all but colliding, being shot
at from below and trying to place bombs accurately... In a sharp turn, I saw a
bunch of guns right in line for attack, so dived at 45 degrees and released all
four bombs... One fell between two guns, the rest a few yards away... I dive
at another group of guns, giving them 100 rounds. See a machine-gun blazing
at me, swing on to that, one short burst and he stops firing... A long column
of artillery limbers... I zoom [climb] then switchback along the column
spraying short bursts in each little dive.'

Gould Lee then became hopelessly lost, and landed alongside some men in a field,
hoping to discover his location. Unfortunately, the men were German. He took off
swiftly, and machine-gunned them:

'I swung over, dived and let them have it. Some horses and men tumbled, the
rest scarpered. I went down the sunken road they'd come from. It was full of
horsed traffic. I dived on them and let them have it too, and saw men falling
off stampeding horses. My dive carried me on to another road, with a column
of marching troops. As I fired, they bumped into one another, then broke into
the side fields.'[25]

Gould Lee recorded that the latter part of his attacks were easy, as there was no
ground fire. This was unusual, and was a significant difference from the
experiences of pilots in the Second World War, when there almost always seemed
to be some retaliation from the ground. Gould Lee in fact found returning to base
most difficult, as his compass failed and he could not navigate in the appalling
weather. As a result he had to forced-land. The strain of ground-attack began to
tell on his nerves. By 28 November his strain showed in his reference to the work
as a 'gardening spree'. His diary entry for the next day recorded:

'This trench-strafing is all becoming rather a strain. In air fighting, chance is
only one of the factors. But trench-strafing is all chance, no matter how
skilled you are. To make sure of your target you have to expose yourself to the
concentrated fire of dozens of machine-guns and hundreds of rifles... Of
course, strafing behind the lines is different, the odds against you aren't nearly
so great.'

Although trench-strafing of German troops may have enhanced the morale of
British infantry, it did nothing for the morale of the pilots. Attacks behind the
lines, on the other hand, were usually a complete success, causing panic and
confusion, even if they did not cause any injury to the enemy. The emphasis on
trench-strafing saw aircraft casualties at Cambrai average 30 per cent. This could
not be sustained, but did not dissuade the RFC from continuing such operations,
which, in fact, made a substantial contribution to halting the German Spring
Offensives of 1918, and in battles during the Hundred Days that brought the war
to an end. By this time, air superiority was largely in the hand of the Allies, with

the exception of a final German challenge in September. As a result, more ground attack work was carried out, and RAF fighter squadrons became highly proficient in the role. Number 73 Squadron, equipped with Sopwith Camels, specialised in attacking anti-tank guns, and did much to reduce the effectiveness of German field artillery pieces, which otherwise caused the advancing armour considerable difficulties.[26]

Having seen the effectiveness of ground-attack operations, the German armed services perfected air-ground co-operation after the Luftwaffe was formed, while the Royal Air Force forgot all the lessons learned. It was compelled to re-learn them in the Western Desert in 1941, again resorting to the use of fighter aircraft. The capability of virtually all fighters to carry bombs and later rocket projectiles was exploited to the full, and by 1945 the Spitfires of 2nd Tactical Air Force were being used as dive-bombers. The most famous ground-attack aircraft in British service at this time, the Hawker Typhoon, originated as a fighter, and was re-roled when it proved inadequate at higher altitudes. Its qualities of speed, firepower and toughness meant that it proved almost ideal for the job. The fame that the type won perhaps disguises the fact that, by 1945, the gaining of air superiority by the Allies meant that virtually all fighter types could be spared for ground-support operations and armed reconnaissance. Such work, however, was made extremely dangerous by the likelihood of liberal amounts of flak.

This is vividly recalled by many RAF fighter pilots, especially those who flew the Hawker Tempest. A development of the Typhoon, the little-known Tempest was one of the best fighter aircraft of the war at medium to low altitudes, and was a stable gun-platform. Although it did not normally carry bombs or rocket projectiles, it was still an ideal tool for ground-attack operations. This meant that the pilots regularly encountered heavy flak, as the former commanding officer of 486 Squadron, C. J. 'Jimmy' Sheddan, noted when recalling an incident early in 1945:

'Towards the end of the war trains often had flak carriages spaced throughout their entire length and it does nothing for your nerves when your aircraft seems surrounded by tracer and you know that for every one you can see there is at least four that are invisible. The Germans also used heavily armed trains as flak traps. One of my worst moments was when [Squadron Leader Warren] "Smokey" Schrader drew my attention to a train which I was trying hard not to see, as I knew in my heart that it was a plant – too much smoke, too little movement... I was between the devil and the deep blue sea. I had been at this game for longer than I cared to remember and knew that this was one train that I should keep away from, but with Smokey ... watching and waiting for my decision, I just had to take the risk and attack.

No sooner had I committed myself then all hell broke loose as the flak came showering up in waves. Crunch! About a foot of the end of my port wing folded over. Now I was in real trouble! Any sudden change of direction and that wing would stall, causing a spin. Down below was what looked like a train full of guns and all firing at a single aircraft... There was no way that my plane should have passed through the wall of lead without receiving further damage. However, I survived – just!'[27]

It was not only RAF pilots who suffered from this. One of the leading exponents of the P-47 Thunderbolt, Francis Gabreski (28 victories), was shot down when attacking ground targets, as were a number of other highly experienced men. Just as in the First World War, skill and experience could do little to save them from a well-aimed – or even a lucky – burst of flak. The random nature of ground-attack operations meant that they were often disliked intensely by fighter pilots. Pilots knew that, in aerial combat, skill, judgement and experience could greatly increase their chances of survival, whereas flak did not discriminate between good or bad flying. By 1945 all sides had the ability to make ground-attack a decidedly hazardous mission for participants. The most obvious example of this occurred on New Year's Day 1945 with 'Operation Bodenplatte', the Luftwaffe's attempt to cripple the Allied air forces on the ground. The operation saw the use of a large number of fighters, with somewhere between 700 and 800 aircraft being used. Although the mission saw the destruction of nearly 200 Allied aircraft, 'Bodenplatte' was a disaster for the Luftwaffe. Unbriefed German flak gunners shot down a number of their own aircraft as they headed to and from the lines, and the Allies were not caught totally by surprise, as some aircraft were already airborne. At the end of the operation, an estimated 300 German aircraft had been lost, along with over 230 of the pilots.[28]

This was perhaps the most extreme example of a fighter force suffering from its employment for ground-attack. The Luftwaffe especially was unable to sustain such losses since its fighter pilots were in almost constant action. Unlike the Allies, where pilots served an operational tour and were then sent to a second-line posting, German fighter pilots continued to fly until they were shot down and either killed or wounded badly enough to ground them. While this system meant that German pilots gained immense amounts of operational experience and scored enormous victory tallies, it also ensured that they became fatigued and less effective. Furthermore, they were generally unable to pass their experience on to new pilots at training schools. Although Allied pilots frequently felt that teaching new recruits how to fly and fight could hardly be described as a 'rest tour', they were at least able to pass on some of their experience (even if 'Johnnie' Johnson was moved to note that 'the right senior officer was not present' to explain how to win at air combat[29]). Thus the Germans were forced to throw inexperienced pilots into battle, where they proved to be hugely vulnerable to marauding American escort fighters. The pilots of the latter were becoming progressively more experienced, and as the quality of their opponents decreased, they were less likely to be shot down themselves. As Adolf Galland was moved to remark. 'A steadily increasing percentage of the young and inexperienced pilots were shot down before they reached their tenth operational flight.'[30]

This meant that the Luftwaffe was always struggling to keep up. As its pilots were outnumbered, even the huge experience levels of the *experten* were not enough to prevent them from being defeated. The lack of numbers became significant. In certain instances history had demonstrated that if an outnumbered air force possessed aircraft as good as or better than the enemy, it could at the very least cause serious problems for the enemy. By both 1918 and 1945 the Germans were in possession of splendid fighters, but the Allied aircraft were good enough to enable their pilots to defeat less-experienced opponents in a better machine. Von Richthofen rightly argued that the quality of the aircraft mattered less than the quality of the man who flew it, although if pilots of equal ability were in aircraft of differing quality, the one in the better machine was likely to win.

The Fokker D VII may have been the best aircraft of the Great War, but it was overcome by a combination of factors. The Allies had greater numbers of aircraft, and the fighters were of a nearly similar qualitative level. This was enough to minimise the effect of the Fokker. The same occurred in 1945. While the FW190D, Ta152 and Me262 could all claim to be superior in some way to their opponents, this was offset by the pilots of these types being outnumbered by aircraft that could at least match them if well flown. This applied even to the Me262, which although 100mph faster than any Allied fighter available, was shot down frequently by Mustang, Spitfire and Tempest pilots. This was in direct contrast to the experience of German and British pilots in 1941 and early 1942 when the first versions of the FW190 had been introduced. The Luftwaffe then possessed an aircraft that was superior to any in British service (until the Spitfire Mark IX arrived) and large numbers of experienced pilots. Although the RAF was able to give a good account of itself generally against the FW190, the problems it faced were serious. They were further intensified by the fact that the RAF was operating over enemy-held territory, thus ensuring that it was unlikely that pilots of shot-down aircraft would be able to return to battle.

The same could be said of the RFC's experience in early 1917, culminating in 'Bloody April'. Although the RFC possessed many highly proficient pilots, its equipment was simply not good enough to deal with the fighters in German service. This saw the loss of many experienced men, who had to be replaced by aircrew fresh out of training schools. This created a vicious cycle of losses, where newcomers to fighter squadrons were unable to remain alive for long enough to gain knowledge of how to fight, to be replaced by men who, as a result of the demand for them, had even less training, being even more vulnerable as a result. Once the Sopwith Camel, SE 5a and Bristol Fighter arrived in service by June 1917, the situation changed dramatically, and the Germans found it almost impossible to gain anything other than local air superiority for the remainder of the war.

This was not a phenomenon confined to the Western Front; the Soviet air force was virtually annihilated in the first weeks of the war by experienced pilots in better aircraft, and it took considerable time for the Russians to be able to make their numbers and manufacturing superiority show. In the Pacific the RAF was surprised to discover how proficient the Japanese were, with the result that the hopelessly outclassed Brewster Buffalo could do nothing to contain the Japanese advance. The Americans also found their aircraft were outclassed by the A6M Zero-sen, but found ways to overcome the difficulties. American fighters carried a far heavier armament than Japanese aircraft and were better armoured. This meant that if American pilots could at least get a shot in at the Japanese they stood a good chance of seriously damaging or destroying their opponent. As a result, the US air services sought to develop suitable tactics to force the Japanese to fight on terms that gave American pilots the opportunity to exploit these advantages in their equipment. This did much to rectify the problem initially, until new aircraft types entered service. Once the Vought F4U Corsair, Grumman F6F Hellcat and Lockheed P-38 Lightning arrived, the Japanese found that they were outnumbered and facing aircraft that were in many ways (if not absolutely) superior to theirs. Once again the Japanese began to haemorrhage experienced pilots as a result of this, creating what might be termed the qualitative-quantitative cycle of aerial attrition.

This applied in both World Wars. It was all very well having more experienced pilots, but if they were hopelessly outnumbered there was little they could do. If they flew machines that were clearly inferior to those of their enemies, the situation was the same. Alternatively, possessing an aircraft that was clearly superior to the opposing air force was of little use if the pilots were not experienced enough to exploit the advantages their machines possessed. However, where numerical and qualitative variables were more closely matched, the results of aerial combat (and the campaigns of which they were part) were less easy to predict. A smaller number of superior aircraft, coupled with well-trained pilots, could tilt the balance, even when numerical superiority lay in the hands of the enemy. A classic case in point may be said to have been the Battle of Britain. Although the RAF was outnumbered, it had two splendid fighter aircraft in the Spitfire and the Hurricane, which were able to deal with the German attacks. Had the RAF settled in the 1930s for vast numbers of the Gloster Gladiator, even if this type had outnumbered the Me109 and Me110, it is hard to perceive a positive outcome for the RAF in the summer of 1940. Although a slightly different case, the possession of large numbers of Fairey Battle bombers did little for the RAF's efforts in France in 1940 – a smaller number of Hurricanes equipped for the fighter-bomber role would perhaps have been better, though not sufficiently so to have changed the overall outcome of the German campaign against France and the Low Countries. As 'Johnnie' Johnson noted, 'Good aeroplanes are more important than superiority in numbers'.[31]

Air forces were of course not slow to recognise the importance of having machines that could match those in enemy service, and to have pilots capable of matching their opponents. Although the leading 'aces', as noted, possessed certain personal qualities that other pilots lacked, such as enhanced Situational Awareness, training organisations understood that fighter pilots tended to be slightly different. It was all very well possessing superior aircraft, but if their pilots were inferior they would lose. Von Richthofen argued that 'the quality of the box matters little. Success depends upon the man who sits in it'.[32] This was recognised by all air forces in both wars, although the losing side in each conflict suffered from an inability to obtain enough men with 'the right stuff'.

The term 'right stuff' has now entered the realms of cliché, but was applicable. In the case of the First World War, the pilots were regarded as 'intrepid aviators', who required great courage and fortitude to leave the safety of the ground in their potentially dangerous machines. This meant that many of the first men to enter into air combat were of a notably strong character, which in some cases manifested itself in eccentricity. Perhaps the most notable example here was the inimitable Louis Strange, who as well as being probably the first British pilot to conduct a ground-attack mission, survived falling out of his aircraft and hanging inverted on to the ammunition drum of his Lewis gun before managing to swing himself back into the cockpit. Strange ended the First World War commanding 80 Wing, RAF, flying Sopwith Camels, and then distinguished himself in the Second World War.

He managed to persuade the authorities that he was still capable of flying, and in June 1940 he found himself at Merville airfield commanding the efforts to transport men and equipment away from the advancing Germans. A number of serviceable Hawker Hurricanes were on the airfield, and Strange decided to fly one back to England. Although he had never flown a Hurricane before, he successfully took off, only to be 'bounced' by a flight of Me109s. Although the Hurricane was not carrying any ammunition, Strange simply outmanoeuvred the enemy fighters, including some hair-raising low-level flying. He returned safely to Britain, and was awarded a bar to the Distinguished Flying Cross, 20 years after he had first won that award.[33]

The RFC produced a number of pilots whose behaviour was extremely unusual during the Great War, but this was more by virtue of circumstances at the commencement of the conflict than by design. As the war went on, it was neither possible nor desirable to track down men who were noticeably unusual in their general behaviour in order to train them for air fighting. Instead, pilots were asked if they had experience of riding horses, or motor vehicles. The employment of the former question by recruiting officers has been ridiculed, but made perfect sense.[34] A man who could control a horse probably had the necessary reflexes and dexterity to control an aircraft. An interest in motor vehicles (which, by virtue of being considered more plebeian, does not receive the same level of amusement) was of use, and remained so. Robert Stanford Tuck, upon applying to join the RAF in 1935, was asked of his knowledge of 'ICE'. Tuck had no idea what his inquisitor was talking about, but managed to bluff an answer in general terms. Upon leaving the interview, he suddenly realised that 'ICE' stood for 'Internal Combustion Engines'.[35]

Technical aptitude was important, but was not the only factor. Even if fighter pilots did not need to be brilliantly adept at flying, they needed to be competent. The demands of air combat placed heavy psychological and physiological demands upon pilots. Not only did pilots have to cope with the violence, speed and ferocity of air fighting, they had to sustain heavy g-loadings, cold, and changes in air pressure, all of which had a cumulatively fatiguing effect. In the First World War pilots rarely had the benefits of oxygen supply, and the majority flew for their entire careers without it. At heights above 10,000 feet, the thinner air combined with the cold to make air fighting a difficult task. The effort required to change the ammunition drum on a machine-gun was substantial, as the thinner air made exertion more taxing. The lack of oxygen also had the effect of dulling mental agility, crucial to air fighting, which demanded swiftness of thought. The Second World War at least saw the use of oxygen, but sub-zero temperatures remained a challenge, even with the provision of heating systems in the enclosed cockpits. The physical stresses of flying in both wars meant that pilots became fatigued. This, coupled with psychological fatigue, created dangerous and often fatal circumstances.

The fighter pilot was invariably on his own in combat.[36] This required a certain type of person. Research conducted after the Second World War suggests that a combination of physical and psychological factors were important in selection of pilots. Good pilots were not anxious types and had good psychomotor adaptation and co-ordination. In addition, they tended towards introversion, but – crucially – had the ability to get on well with others when they wished.[37] The top-scoring 'ace' Erich Hartmann noted this, and contended, with the benefit of empirical observation rather than science, that fighter pilots tended towards individualism. This is supported by the historical examples of Billy Bishop, Georges Guynemer and Albert Ball from the First World War, and George 'Screwball' Beurling from the Second, all of whom preferred to operate alone.[38] This did not mean that they were anti-social on the ground, although Ball was famed for his solitary lifestyle, which included wandering outside his self-built cabin playing the violin.

In contrast to Ball and others, 'Mick' Mannock believed in teamwork, often 'setting up' kills for new pilots to give them confidence. Boelcke and Immelmann formulated their tactics together, and experience in the Second World War demonstrated the importance of fighting as a pair. The trust between pilots was important, since it was comforting to know that there was someone watching out for attack by the enemy. The nature of air combat demanded qualities that were apart from those required in other forms of fighting. Hugh Dundas noted this after his first combat in 1940:

> 'From the leading Messerschmitt came thin trails of grey smoke as the pilot fired his guns. The group faded into specks which, in an instant, disappeared beneath the thick black smoke cloud rising from Dunkirk…
>
> Perhaps this little cameo lasted before my eyes for about five seconds; it was a lightning personal introduction to the use of guns in earnest and to the terrifying quality of air fighting. But I did not at that time have so much as one second to reflect upon it, for I was suddenly aware that the formation in which I was flying … was breaking up in violent manoeuvre.'[39]

This marked the start of Dundas's first 'dog-fight'. He found it a terrifying and confusing affair:

> '…when, at last, I felt it safe to straighten out, I was amazed to find that the sky which only moments before had been full of whirling, firing fighters was now empty. It was my first experience of this curious phenomenon, which continually amazed all fighter pilots. At one moment it was all you could do to avoid collision … the next moment you were on your own.'[40]

The rapid nature of air combat – which could be made all the more sudden by a surprise attack from the enemy – was not the only confusing matter for pilots. In both World Wars, the fighter pilot could return from a particularly arduous mission feeling lucky to have survived, then find himself going out for a pleasant evening's relaxation before having to face the prospect of being heavily engaged the following morning. This imposed great levels of stress upon pilots, particularly for the Germans with their policy of not rotating men to training units. Unlike many other combatants, fighter pilots faced dramatic contrasts in their living conditions day after day. Coupled with the physical stresses of air fighting, this meant that even the most experienced pilots became heavily fatigued. Hugh Dundas, after scoring his first victory, noted a worrying 'inner voice' that urged him not to take risks. Although he heard this voice regularly, he was able to ignore it – to the extent of becoming a willing wingman to the aggressive Douglas Bader – until he approached the end of his tour. By mid-1941, he was in need of a rest, but:

> 'It did not occur to me to ask for a rest. Bader's influence had taught me that this was not an acceptable course. Indeed, I felt more strongly than ever that I must stick with the Squadron, continuing to fight … and helping to pass on to the new pilots the experience and knowledge I had gained…
>
> At the same time, I subconsciously shrank from battle. The instinct for survival, the inner urge to rest on my laurels, was very strong. I know there were a couple of occasions when I shirked from the clash of combat at the critical moment. Looking back on it later, I recognised that this was a time of extreme danger for me and also to some extent for the men I was leading. It was the stage of fatigue when many experienced fighter pilots have fallen as a result of misjudgement or a momentary holding back from combat.'[41]

Fatigue and misjudgement applied to all fighter pilots, and could not be avoided by the end of a tour of operations. For the Luftwaffe this meant either death or wounds that prevented flying, which was hardly the best fashion in which to husband experience. By the time of their deaths in action, both Albert Ball and Georges Guynemer were displaying signs of fatigue that may have contributed to their loss. Fatigue could affect pilots in other ways too – Philip Fullard fought with considerable aggression until November 1917, when he was injured in a football match at his aerodrome. Fullard informed Peter Liddle that he did not suffer from stress or nerves, but after his enforced removal from the front, his efforts to repress this caught up with him, and his nerves gave way, preventing him from returning to light duties until September 1918.[42]

It is clear that the personal qualities of fighter pilots were important. Although recruiting officers could never be sure, they attempted – usually successfully – to find men who could ignore or suppress their anxieties for considerable periods. The ability to be both introverted and personable suggests that perhaps the pilots were able to compartmentalise aspects of their lives, ensuring that they could cope with the stresses imposed upon them. Although individualism was important, it is worth noting that most memoirs by fighter pilots stress the importance to them of at least one other colleague, often their wingman. This was rarely so great as to cause breakdowns if that close friend was lost, and again suggests an ability to maintain professional detachment to a greater degree than others. This mix of individualism and teamwork was vitally important, along with the third major quality of aggression. In 1917, Trenchard noted:

> 'The battle in the air can only be won by taking the offensive and persevering in it … victory over [enemy] low-flying aircraft [will come] through offensive superiority [emphasis in original]… The aeroplane is a weapon that has no

exact counterpart ... but the principles which guide it in warfare, in order for it to be successful, are those which guide all other arms in all other elements of warfare, and the most important of these is the will and power to attack the enemy, to force him to fight, and to defeat him.'[43]

To do this an air force required pilots who were prepared to take risks and to operate in an offensive manner. The canard 'the best form of defence is attack' was expected to be an unconscious part of a fighter pilot's character. This applied across national boundaries in both World Wars; fighter pilots were required to be aggressive to be successful – and that success might be measured on occasion by whether they lived or died. Aggression could, and did, bring casualties when applied recklessly. Pilots also needed to judge when to be aggressive and when not to be. There was little room for men who were unable to think quickly and press home the advantage when they had it. This did not preclude some degree of fellow-feeling for enemy pilots. Most preferred it when the pilot of an aircraft they destroyed escaped alive. Arthur Rhys-Davids, the conqueror of Werner Voss, was heard to express his dismay that he was unable to have brought him down alive. Mannock, on the other hand, was a notable exception to the vague bonds of comradeship that fighter pilots had towards one another, and was not the only one. Pilots with these sentiments tended to be exceptions: even though the Vietnam war 'ace' Randall Cunningham argued that it was better to go into battle with some 'hate in your heart', this did not extend in either war to attacking a defeated opponent on the ground or in a parachute. Although this did happen, pilots from both sides on the Western front (in both wars) generally regarded such actions as unacceptable.

Whether an 'ace' or simply a regular squadron flyer, the fighter pilot has always been slightly apart from other warriors. Aggression, teamwork, popular recognition and adulation combined with danger, fear and the random nature of simple fate to make the fighter pilot's task demanding and different. Whether German, American or British, whether fighting in the First or Second World War, or whether flying a Fokker Triplane or Supermarine Spitfire, the fighter pilot's experience was remarkably similar. The nature of their task made it so.

Notes on contributors

Dr David Jordan, Joint Services Command and Staff College, Bracknell, UK
Dr Jordan is a Lecturer at King's College London, based at the Joint Services Command and Staff College. He was educated at St Edmund Hall, Oxford, and the University of Birmingham, where he took his doctorate. He specialises in air power and international relations and is currently writing a book on the development of tactical air power in the First World War.

Recommended reading

Gould Lee, Arthur, *No Parachute: A Fighter Pilot in World War I* (London: Jarrolds, 1969)

Lewis, Cecil, *Sagittarius Rising* (London: Greenhill Books, 1993 (1936))

Liddle, Peter H., *The Airman's War 1914-1918* (Poole: Blandford, 1987)

Richey, Paul, *Fighter Pilot: A personal record of the campaign in France, 1939-1940* (London: Leo Cooper, 1990)

Shaw, Robert L., *Fighter Combat: Tactics and Manoeuvring* (Annapolis: Naval Institute 1985, and Wellingborough: Patrick Stephens Limited, 1986)

Sims, Edward H., *Fighter Tactics and Strategy, 1914-1970* (London: Cassell, 1972)

Spick, Mike, *The Ace Factor: Air Combat and the Role of Situational Awareness* (Shrewsbury: Airlife, 1988)

Notes

[1] David Lloyd George, *War Memoirs*, Vol II (Odhams, 1936), p1115, and Parliamentary Debates (Hansard) Vol XCVIII, col 1247 (29 October 1917)

[2] Mike Spick, *The Ace Factor: Air Combat and the Role of Situational Awareness* (Airlife, 1988), pii

[3] Mike Spick, op cit, passim. The comment originates from Major Edward 'Mick' Mannock VC

[4] Ibid, piii

[5] This is the rationale behind the modern radar-guided missile, which engages 'beyond visual range' (BVR). It is less technically described as giving the ability to shoot an opponent in the face before he sees you.

[6] Peter Liddle, *The Airman's War 1914-1918* (Blandford Press, 1987) pp65-6

[7] Robert L. Shaw, *Fighter Combat: Tactics and Manoeuvring* (Annapolis: Naval Institute 1985, and Wellingborough: Patrick Stephens Limited, 1986) p17

[8] Douglas McRoberts, *Lions Rampant: The Story of 602 Spitfire Squadron* (London, 1985) p103

[9] The designation 'Me109' is used throughout this piece as a result of its common usage, both during the Second World War and afterwards. It is recognised that the designator of Bf109 is generally (but not universally) accepted as the correct one.

[10] Robert L. Shaw, op cit, p13

[11] Ibid, p21

[12] Ibid, p8

[13] Ibid, p16. Libby was an American who joined the RFC. He began his career as an observer, shooting down ten enemy aircraft, before becoming a pilot. He added another 14 victims to his tally by the end of the war.

[14] Robert L. Shaw, op cit, pp138, 221

[15] It seems that almost every memoir of distinguished fighter pilots from all sides gives an example of the protagonist incurring the wrath of higher command for innovation that went beyond the book. Examples of such 'rockets' from higher authority abound in pilots' memoirs and biographies. See, for instance, regular references in Roland Beamont, *My Part of the Sky: A Fighter Pilot's First-hand Experiences 1939-1949* (Wellingborough: Patrick Stephens Limited, 1989); J. E. 'Johnnie' Johnson, *Wing Leader* (1956; Goodall, 1995); Ralph Barker, *The Royal Flying Corps in France: From Mons to the Somme* (London: Constable, 1994); S. F. Vincent, *Flying Fever* (London: Jarrolds, 1972). On the other hand, Sir Hugh Trenchard positively encouraged innovation, so long as the idea was run past him first.

[16] RAF Museum, Hendon, Trenchard Papers, MFC 76/1/4

[17] Ibid

[18] H. A. Jones, *The War in the Air, Being the Story of the Part Played in the Great War by the Royal Air Force*, Vol III (Clarendon Press, 1931) p355

[19] Arthur Gould Lee, *No Parachute: A Fighter Pilot in World War I* (London: Jarrolds, 1969) pp217-8

[20] J. E. 'Johnnie' Johnson, *Wing Leader* (1956; Goodall, 1995), pp79-81. Johnson's reference to Spitfires refers to the type he flew. Hawker Hurricanes, Westland Whirlwinds and later the Hawker Typhoon and North American Mustang I were also among the types used for this type of operation.

[21] For details of these men, see Christopher Shore and Clive Williams, *Aces High: A tribute to the most notable fighter pilots of the British and Commonwealth forces in World War II* (London: Grub Street,

1994); Larry Forrester, *Fly For Your Life: The Story of R. R. Stanford Tuck* (London: Panther Books, 1959); and Paul Brickhill, *Reach for the Sky: The Story of Douglas Bader* (London: Collins, 1954)

[22] See C. F. Webster and N. Frankland, *The Strategic Air Offensive Against Germany* (HMSO, 1961, 4 volumes), especially Vol III, pp131-6; and Noble Frankland, *History At War* (de la Mare, 1998) pp70-4

[23] Arthur Gould Lee, op cit, p154

[24] Ibid, p158. Douglas had recovered from his equine-inflicted injuries and been given command of 84 Squadron on regaining fitness.

[25] Ibid, pp163-4

[26] See PRO War Office [WO] 95/94; AIR 1/725/97/10

[27] C. J. Sheddan (with Norman Franks), *Tempest Pilot* (London: Grub Street, 1997) pp132-3
[28] 'The March to the Rhine', *The Illustrated Encyclopaedia of Aircraft* (London: Orbis, 1984), p2543

[29] Robert L. Shaw, op cit, pix

[30] Ibid, p198

[31] Ibid, p291

[32] Ibid, p182

[33] See Peter Hearn, *Flying Rebel* (London: HMSO, 1994)

[34] It has been suggested that the question was designed to exclude members of the working and middle classes, who were far less likely to have ridden horses than their upper-class counterparts. Since the RFC recruited NCO pilots, this hardly bears scrutiny.

[35] Larry Forrester, *Fly For Your Life: The Story of R. R. Stanford Tuck* (London: Panther Books, 1959) pp32-3

[36] Exceptions were the pilots of aircraft such as the Mosquito, Beaufighter, Junkers 88 and Me110, for example.

[37] Peter Watson, *War on the Mind: The Military Uses and Abuses of Psychology* (London, 1978) p103

[38] It might be argued by cynics that Bishop preferred to fly alone so that no one could dispute his victory claims. Recent research suggests that Bishop's attack on an aerodrome that won him the Victoria Cross was a fabrication, and controversy rages over the veracity of his claims. I am grateful to Mr Miles Constable for providing me with this information.

[39] Hugh Dundas, *Flying Start* (London, 1990) pp1-2

[40] Ibid

[41] Ibid, p97

[42] Peter Liddle, op cit, p69

[43] RAF Museum, Trenchard Papers, MFC 76/1/4, 'A Review of Principles adopted by the RFC since the Battle of the Somme', 23 October 1917

Chapter 6

War in the air:
the bomber crew

Christina Goulter

'The principal operational elements in the strategic air offensive are: first, the calibre of the crews, which is a question of selection, training, experience, leadership and fighting spirit; secondly, the performance of the aircraft and of the equipment and bases upon which they depend; thirdly, the weather; fourthly, the tactical methods and, fifthly, the nature of the enemy opposition.'[1]

The authors of the British official history, *The Strategic Air Offensive Against Germany, 1939-1945*, which remains the best single work on the subject, acknowledged the importance of the human element in this campaign. This acknowledgement was overdue. The decades following the Second World War were dominated by interest in the technological and scientific contributions to Allied victory, and the development of nuclear weapons merely reinforced the idea that science had done away with the need for the clash of massed armies. The idea that all operational problems could be subjected to and solved by scientific principles and the application of technology was a particularly strong thread in US military thinking after 1945, and this has persisted, in spite of the Vietnam experience, which demonstrated that the hi-tech nation does not always win. In Britain such ideas were less strong, for reasons of economy and the fact that the nation was engaged in more counter-insurgency and brush-fire wars, but in both countries there was a tendency to de-emphasise the contribution of the individual and to emphasise the big picture, in which nuclear strategy in a bi-polar world was the prime concern.

Although Vietnam was not Britain's war, it had a profound effect on the way most of the world has thought about war, especially its human face. So, the ground was fertile for the proliferation of autobiographical and semi-autobiographical accounts of individual war experience, especially from the pens of the Second World War's aviators. What has been lacking, however, is the type of study that examines aircrew experience in the round: what motivated men, in general, to volunteer for aircrew service; whether their training equipped them adequately for the job they had to do; the contrast between expectation and combat reality; combat stress; and, finally, the re-adjustment to civilian life.

These are universal questions, which are valid for any combat flying under consideration, and, because we are dealing with the human element, there are striking similarities between apparently very different wars. Thus we are able to observe many parallels between the aircrew experiences of the First and Second World Wars, even though, some would say, the technological advances during the intervening time meant that the nature of the war differed substantially between the two conflicts.

Whether we are talking about historical examples or today, a prime motivation for joining the air force has undoubtedly been the glamour associated with aviation. This was certainly true of the First and Second World Wars, when aviation was a new and exciting science, and interest in the 'third dimension' pervaded society at large. For those who were coming from Allied countries, there was the added excitement of an overseas deployment. A New Zealand pilot reflected that he and his friends joining the Royal New Zealand Air Force in 1939 were 'moved more by the spirit of adventure' and a need to validate their manhood 'than by the burnings of patriotism', although, invariably, this developed and 'loyalty shone bright'.[2]

What is also almost universally true is that men volunteered for flying duties because they had their sights on becoming pilots, rather than other aircrew trades. To be a pilot was glamorous; to be an observer, navigator, wireless operator or gunner was not. So, almost without exception, those who joined to fly joined to be pilots, and, within the pilot hierarchy, to be a fighter pilot always held the greatest cachet. However, there were no guarantees in either the First or Second World War that those wishing to be pilots would necessarily end up as pilots. Depending on the aircrew selection process, or simple supply and demand, a pilot candidate could find himself channelled into other aircrew trades.

Those who volunteered to fly in one of the air services in the First World War had witnessed aviation's extraordinarily rapid development, from the Wright Brothers' 1903 flight of a few hundred yards to bombing aircraft capable of round journeys of hundreds of miles by the middle of the war. In Britain, Blériot's flight across the Channel in the summer of 1909 captivated the nation, and it was from this point, rather than later in the 1920s, that Britain became 'air minded'.[3] Few seemed to doubt that those nations possessing air power would fail to use it in the next war, and now that Britain was apparently within easy reach of potential aggressors, steps were taken by the Committee of Imperial Defence to establish a British air service. When the Royal Flying Corps was formed in April 1912 (originally with two branches, naval and military), there was no shortage of recruits.[4] Many would go on to fill senior positions in the RAF, most prominent among whom were Hugh Trenchard, Arthur Longmore, Sholto Douglas, and John Slessor. What these men, and other more junior flying personnel, had in common when they joined up was a driving ambition to fly. Their recollections record their fascination and wonderment as they commenced their initial training.[5]

Later generations have been drawn to aviation for the same reasons, but recruits of the late 1930s and early years of the Second World War also had a desire to avoid the horrors of trench warfare, which had consumed their fathers' generation. Although war experience after 1939 quickly demonstrated that service in the Air

Force was not necessarily a safer option than service with the Army or the Navy, the perception during the 1930s was that one's chances of surviving a war were far greater in the air, and that the quality of life, in the meantime, would be superior. A former Lieutenant in the Royal Flying Corps expressed it in this way:

> 'When we were flying at about 17,000 feet, it gave you a wonderful feeling of exhilaration. You were sort of, "I'm the King of the Castle". You were up there and you were right out of the war. I'd been in the infantry and we were always lousy, filthy dirty and often hungry, whereas in the Flying Corps it was a gentleman's life. You slept in a bed, put on pyjamas every night. You had a decent mess to come back to… So, altogether, it was much more pleasant.'[6]

Some aircrew candidates also believed that air power offered a more humane way to wage war, and this view was particularly prevalent among Americans in the 1930s. Not only did many Americans within the US Army Air Corps (and, later, the US Army Air Forces) genuinely believe that the US possessed the technological means to perform precision bombing, and would, therefore, be able to realise Billy Mitchell's vision of attacks on key nodes within an enemy industrial infrastructure, but there was also the view that precision instruments offered the means to avoid civilian casualties. According to one author, this satisfied the 'deep-seated American need for the moral high ground in war, while satisfying an American hunger for technological achievement'.[7]

Regardless of nationality, many aircrew candidates also seem to have believed that the air service offered the greatest possibility of a quick, decisive victory. Prior to the First World War, there were those who looked at the potential of aircraft in the military sphere and felt that aircraft represented a Revolution in Military Affairs (RMA), even if it was not expressed in this way. One such was a Major Herbert Musgrave, who transferred from the Royal Engineers to the Royal Flying Corps. He was closely involved with aeronautical research, and his work on wireless telegraphy and bomb aiming, in particular, laid the foundation for the long-range operations undertaken during the war. Musgrave felt that the impending war would be 'the hardest, fiercest, and bloodiest struggle' experienced to date, and that aviation would play a decisive role.[8] However, the idea that aircraft could deliver the 'knock-out blow' gained most currency during the inter-war period. Even though there was very little in the First World War experience to indicate that air power would be able to deliver the quick, decisive victory, strategic bombing theory dominated air power doctrine. In Britain, as a number of scholars have already demonstrated, the pressures of budgetary constraint and inter-service rivalry, which threatened the independent existence of the RAF, led to increasingly grandiose claims being made for air power. Chief of Air Staff Trenchard's debates with the Navy were publicised in the national press, and added to the 'air-mindedness' of the country. Air power's overwhelming success in Britain's empire policing role, followed by a series of bombing assaults on populated centres overseas by other air power nations (notably Japan against Shanghai in 1932 and combined Fascist forces against Guernica in 1937), merely reinforced the public's belief that the next war would be dominated by massed aerial attack. So, although most aircrew candidates in the late 1930s and early war years volunteered with the hope of becoming fighter pilots, it was widely accepted that the bomber would decide the outcome of the next war.[9]

Volunteers for flying duties in both the First and Second World Wars found that there was an expectation that aircrew candidates, especially pilots, would be 'gentlemen'. It was typical for recruiting offices to ask a candidate which sports he played, and 'rugger and cricket' were considered mandatory for pilot trainees. For First World War recruits, evidence of horsemanship was also demanded.[10] Equestrian sports were not only the preserve of gentlemen, but were also supposed to quicken reaction times and make men better judges of distances. Many who applied for aircrew training failed to meet the gentleman's criteria, and were either turned away or told to consider enlisting in a ground trade. One of those who found a 'class ceiling' was Leading Aircraftsman Harry Jones, son of a Birmingham brewery worker. When he visited the recruiting office in 1935, aged 18, he was told, 'You've got to be a gentleman to fly,' and he subsequently became a rigger attached to 37 Squadron, Bomber Command.[11] However, in both wars the demands for aircrew meant that the class criterion was relaxed, although even by the end of the Second World War it was still more common to find working-class men in non-pilot aircrew trades, especially as gunners.

As both wars wore on, educational criteria were also relaxed for aircrew. In the early part of the First World War it was considered desirable for aircrew candidates to have had a 'public school education, … good all round engineering training', as well as 'outdoor sporting tendencies'.[12] Initially, those recruited into the ground support trades were also expected to be highly skilled (as carpenters, mechanics, riggers, etc), and had to pass a trade test to get in.[13] By the mid-war point, possession of an aviator's certificate and medical fitness were generally considered sufficient criteria to join either the RFC or the RNAS.[14] Similarly, prior to the Second World War pilot and observer candidates were expected to have at least four years' secondary education, and ideally a University Entrance qualification. By 1942 'some secondary education' and a demonstrated 'aptitude for flying' were increasingly being seen as sufficient, as long as candidates could pass flying training examinations. Certainly by 1944 aircrew selection and classification had moved away from educational qualifications to measurements of natural aptitude, as it was felt that the RAF could no longer rely on a sufficient supply of privately educated candidates coming forward.[15] The relaxation of educational standards was ironic, as, in both wars, the development of aircraft and related technologies demanded greater knowledge and skills from aircrews.

During both wars, the respective training organisations had difficulty producing the quality of aircrew demanded by bombing operations. This was especially true of the first years of war, but also in both cases, as demands for aircrew increased and training courses were generally shortened, the quality of aircrew joining operational squadrons was often inferior. However, during the First World War there was a sharp contrast between the Royal Flying Corps and the Royal Naval Air Service product. The RNAS aircrew training was far more rigorous in comparison with that of the RFC, and this was in spite of the fact that the Flying Corps engaged in an increasing number of bombing operations as the war progressed. This difference in aircrew training standards was to have a major impact not only on operational efficiency during the First World War, but also in the first years of the next war. When the RFC and RNAS were amalgamated in April 1918 to form the RAF, the new service was closer in character and outlook to the RFC simply because it had provided the bulk of its personnel. Whereas the RNAS contributed 55,000 officers and men, the RFC's input was over 200,000. But, perhaps most seriously, the number of senior naval personnel being retained in the RAF was very small, and the Admiralty's long tradition of heavy investment in training (and research and development) was lost.[16]

In the RNAS, officer aircrew training required the entrant to undertake first a six-week course of theoretical training in navigation, engine construction, wireless telegraphy, theory of flight, and meteorology. After passing these subjects, a pilot trainee was then sent to one of five Preliminary Flying Schools, where he learned to fly two types of aircraft to 'a reasonable level of proficiency', completing at least 20 hours solo flying, some of which was cross-country. At this stage pupils were selected for specialised training in seaplanes, scouts or bombers, and after a number of weeks training on one of these types, additional instruction lasting one month was devoted to subjects such as signals, photography, and navigation. This advanced training lasted for three months. In 1917, when the RNAS's bombing and anti-submarine effort reached a peak, the length of navigation training for pilots was, in fact, increased, from two to three weeks. Meanwhile, observers, who fulfilled the role of navigator in two-seater aircraft, were given their own separate course lasting four months beyond their preliminary training. Most of these four months were devoted to instruction in navigation (including dead-reckoning and astro-navigation), but bomb-dropping and wireless telegraphy were also taught in detail. A pass mark of at least 85 per cent was required for a First Class Observer's Certificate, and at least 60 per cent had to be obtained to graduate. Then, in January 1918, the Admiralty inaugurated a combined course of navigation and bomb-aiming.[17]

Training in the RFC, meanwhile, was sketchy, even allowing for the fact that there was insufficient time to produce fully qualified aircrew because of the manpower demands of the Western Front. The trainee pilot undertook, on average, only six hours' preliminary flying before being sent to advanced training. During a month's advanced training, the emphasis was on artillery observation, photography, and air-to-air combat. Some instruction was given in bomb-dropping, but very little practical experience was obtained. A Pilot's Certificate was granted if the candidate could carry out a cross-country flight of 60 miles, but this was the extent of long-distance flying, and only if a pilot wished to graduate as a Flying Officer was navigational training undertaken. While the operations conducted by the RFC for most of the war (artillery spotting, reconnaissance and air-to-air combat) did not require pilots to be trained in long-range navigation, it had commenced long-range bombing operations in October 1917. The so-called 41 Wing was brought into existence when the War Cabinet called for a 'continuous offensive' against objectives inside Germany. From a base near Nancy, the Wing operated against industrial targets around Cologne, Frankfurt and Stuttgart, involving return flights of at least 280 miles. Even at the start of 1918, when the expansion of this role seemed likely, the RFC was still placing emphasis on artillery spotting and aerial combat in its aircrew training programme.[18]

The relative inexperience of RFC bombing crews manifested itself in a variety of ways, but the first most obvious manifestation was a high accident rate. Brooke-Popham, when an Air Commodore in 1919, reflected:

'During the last eighteen months of the war, the average wastage was 51 per cent per month, ie all the machines with squadrons in France had to be replaced once every two months or six times a year. In other words, each machine lasted an average of sixty days, which would mean a little over sixty hours' flying time per machine. As regards causes of wastage, that known to be due directly to enemy action never reached 25 per cent... Whenever we had heavy casualties in pilots it meant that a large batch of new pilots came out from England, who were unused to the country and lacking in experience; consequently, a heavy casualty list was generally followed by a large increase in the number of aeroplane casualties due to errors of pilots.'[19]

Operational performance was degraded by the lack, first, of navigational training among 41 Wing aircrews. For example, 55 Squadron had difficulty not only locating their German objectives during bombing operations in December 1917 as aircraft were compelled to navigate 'above the clouds', but the squadron's members were also recorded as having had difficulty finding their home base.[20] Crews complained that there were never enough maps to aid navigation, and *Bradshaw's Railway Guide* was used in order to navigate along railway lines. One of the best accounts of this practice comes from the memoirs of Air Commodore P. Huskinson, who held a post in the Directorate of Training in the late 1920s. Relating his experience of a cross-country flight in 1916, he wrote:

'I was solely dependent, as was the established practice, on the map contained in Bradshaw's Railway Guide. However, a close study of this, known throughout the Flying Corps as the Pilot's Friend, and by repeated low dives on stations along the line, I was able, in spite of the maddening fact that most of the stations appeared to bear no name but OXO, to grope my way home in reasonably good time.'[21]

Deficiencies in bombing training in the RFC had to be rectified by training on the squadron. Typically, one flight (six aircraft) on each squadron was set aside to carry out bombing training for new arrivals. However, as the RFC thought it unnecessary to offer written guidance in the matter, each squadron tended to develop bombing tactics through its own experimentation and experience.[22] After the war, Brooke-Popham made the comment that the RFC never achieved an extensive bombing capability in large part because there had been insufficient time to train pilots and observers in the art of bomb-dropping.[23] He also commented that there was a tendency among RFC bombing crews to select their own targets, rather than the objectives specified in their briefings, simply because targets of opportunity demanded less skill in navigation, and tended to present larger profiles.

In contrast, by the end of 1916 the naval aircrews were confident of their ability to find their targets and to bomb them successfully. Throughout the war, in addition to a superior training programme, the Admiralty had also devoted a great deal of time and thought to the design of instruments that would assist the pilot and observer in their work, and the area to receive the greatest attention was aids to navigation. By 1917 the RNAS had in its possession a number of valuable instruments, among them the Course and Distance Indicator, the Douglas Protractor, and the Drift Indicator. Such was the accuracy of these pieces of equipment that RNAS crews were able to fly confidently above the clouds over long distances, whereas the RFC crews had none of these supporting aids. By the beginning of 1917 navigation by Direction Finding wireless telegraphy had also been introduced to most naval squadrons. However, the War Office dismissed the system for navigational purposes, and, after the amalgamation of the RFC and the RNAS, no more work was done in the area of radio navigation until just prior to the Second World War.[24]

Also high on the list of the RNAS's technical problems to be solved was that of bomb-aiming. The difficulty was not so much in the design of a bombsight, but in the fitting of a sight to an aircraft. A number of RNAS personnel set about developing an effective sight, and the best product was known as a 'Course Setting Bombsight'. This allowed an aircraft to attack from any angle, irrespective of the direction of the wind, and it remained in use until the Second World War, little research and development having been undertaken in the interim.[25]

Evidence of the RNAS's efficacy is suggested by the fact that the Germans developed their air defences in those areas being targeted by the naval squadrons. When naval bombing operations began in earnest in October 1916, the Germans created an air defence command, and when a naval wing began operations from a base at Luxeuil, 80 miles south of Nancy, the Germans established what were described as 'very large aerial forces', and four new enemy aerodromes were constructed.[26] The official historian also records that extra barrage detachments were allocated to the Saar, Lorraine, and Rhineland industrial areas, and the morale effect of the naval bombing operations was said to be great, disproportionate to the number of raids and the material effects.[27]

With the amalgamation of the RFC and the RNAS in April, the naval bombing operations came to an end. The RAF continued bombing operations with its Independent Bombing Force (IBF), but reflecting the preponderance of RFC personnel in the new service, the targets tended to favour army bombing policy (enemy Lines of Communication and airfields), rather than the true strategic objectives targeted by the RNAS (ammunition factories and steel plants).[28] Former RFC pilots in the IBF soon found that their navigation skills were not sufficient for the job, as most operations were being conducted at night. It was recommended that aircraft be flown above white roads, or, if this was not possible, for distinctive landmarks to be noted and memorised before the flight. There was a heavy reliance upon old RNAS stocks of navigation literature or aids to navigation. For instance, just prior to the IBF's creation a Major wrote to RAF HQ requesting 12 RNAS Course and Distance Indicators and six copies of the RNAS book *Aerial Work*. These, it was said, would assist squadrons in cloud flying training and operations.[29] Similarly, virtually all the bombsights and bombing manuals were drawn from Admiralty sources.[30]

The legacy of the RFC's lack of interest and investment in research and development was apparent, not only in the last months of the First World War, but also during the inter-war years. During the 1920s budgetary constraint, and associated inter-service rivalry, compelled Trenchard, as Chief of Air Staff, to make increasingly grandiose claims for air power. By the end of that decade British strategic bombing doctrine claimed that not only would the bomber always get through, but that finding and destroying a target was a straightforward business. With this doctrine underpinning the inter-war RAF, there was little incentive to pursue research and development into aids to navigation and bomb-aiming, but nor was there a sufficiently strong research and development tradition remaining within the new service to act as any sort of counter-balance to the effects of air power dogma. As the 1930s unfolded, the race to achieve numerical parity with German air power meant that the focus was on expanding the RAF's aircraft establishment, rather than developing supporting technologies or increasing the number of personnel who would have to fly these aircraft.[31]

The RAF's expansion between 1934 and 1939 aimed at increasing the front-line aircraft establishment at home from 547 to at least 1,780.[32] Eight different expansion schemes were proposed during this time, each with slightly different emphases, but all with a main focus on bomber production. Far less attention was paid to the question of how to man this force. On the eve of expansion, in November 1933, the RAF employed just over 33,000 officers and men. It was not a size of force that would be able to service or operate the anticipated increase in aircraft numbers. Numerous measures were introduced to meet this challenge, but the development of the training organisation lagged far behind the material expansion of the RAF, and this was to have serious consequences in the first half of the war.

To begin with, recruits were attracted to the RAF by short service commissions, lasting four or five years on the active list, with renewable periods of service. These recruits were trained at civilian flying schools, which received a fee from the Air Ministry. Then, in 1936, a Royal Air Force Volunteer Reserve was formed with the object of providing ab initio training for pilots. Finally, University Air Squadrons were established, and these persuaded many undergraduates to take up flying and to acquire the technical knowledge that would be so much in demand once war started.[33]

These various measures succeeded in producing a seven-fold increase in the number of pilots trained each year. However, not until the late 1930s was it appreciated that other aircrew trades would also require expansion. As late as 1936 it was felt that one observers' school would be sufficient to train all the observers required by the new size of force, but, more seriously, it was also believed that other aircrew trades could be trained on the squadrons.[34] This was in spite of the fact that the expansion programme envisaged the introduction of aircraft capable of much longer ranges and of greater technical complexity, demanding much higher standards of piloting and navigation. Specialised navigation courses were not introduced until 1937, but even then civilian flying schools were to provide most of the navigational training. The product coming out of these civilian schools proved inferior to the service-trained individual, and the problem was exacerbated by the fact that the RAF engaged in no long-range navigation exercises before the war broke out.[35] Further, there was no separate navigator function until 1941, as it was considered sufficient to have two pilots in the longer-range aircraft.

Until 1938, almost all of the other aircrew trades (wireless operators, air gunners, etc) were on part-time flying duties only and were trained on a part-time basis. The system was economical during peacetime, but once war broke out the RAF found that it could not provide full crews. Direct entry into these trades was disappointing, as no one wanted to be anything other than a pilot. Again, specialised training was slow in inception. A Central Gunnery School was not created until October 1939, and not until 1942 were the gunnery and wireless operator functions separated out.[36]

One of the greatest obstacles to aircrew training during the late 1930s was a reluctance to divert not only qualified personnel into instructor roles but also potential front-line aircraft into training units. The emphasis on the RAF's quantitative strength in the front line meant that the it had little in the way of reserves, either to sustain losses during wartime or to provide a sufficient training foundation. So, for example, although the number of initial flying training schools had been increased from five to nine in 1936, these schools failed to meet their targeted output to the extent of 1,200 pilots by 1939, and this shortfall was not made up until the latter part of 1941.[37]

In the short term, the output from the various training schools was increased by the expedient of shortening course lengths, but it soon became apparent that aircrews were substantially below standard. Like the Royal Flying Corps, in particular, front-line squadrons during 1939-40 were having to bring new aircrew up to operational standard. The quantity and quality problem was not solved until the first products of the Empire Air Training Scheme arrived on operational squadrons in any numbers (towards the end of 1941). By the terms of the Ottawa Agreement, ratified in December 1939, Canada agreed to train Canadians, Australians and New Zealanders in 13 Elementary Flying Training Schools, 16 Advanced Flying Training Schools, 10 Air Observer Schools, 10 Bombing and Gunnery Schools and two Air Navigation Schools. In addition, Australia and New Zealand provided an additional 29 elementary flying schools.[38]

This was the depth of training organisation needed to support the RAF's operations in Europe, the Middle East and the Far East, but even when this was fully functional, deficiencies in the training of aircrew personnel were still apparent. One of the greatest problems was preparing bomber aircrews adequately for the type of missions they would face once they reached their operational squadrons. It was one thing for individual crew members to reach a standard of proficiency in a training type of aircraft; it was quite another to reach a point where an aircrew, as a unit, felt comfortable in the type of aircraft they would take into battle. So, the problem facing Bomber Command was twofold: first, 'converting' crews from their training aircraft to the types they would fly in combat, and, second, crew-building.[39]

Shortly after the war broke out, the AOC-in-C of Bomber Command, Air Chief

Marshal Sir Edgar Ludlow-Hewitt, took the bold step of rolling up 13 of the 33 operational bomber squadrons to form the basis of what would become known as Operational Training Units.[40] At these OTUs the products of the various training schools would come together, and the process of crew-building was described by one former bomb-aimer, Miles Tripp, in this way:

> 'On the first day, men were sent to a large hangar and told it was up to them to form crews among themselves; those who were too sensitive, diffident or withdrawn to respond to these conditions would eventually be crewed up with others of similar temperament. This arbitrary collision of strangers was basically a marriage market and yet the choice of a good flying partner was far more important than a good wife. You couldn't divorce your crew, and you could die if one of them wasn't up to his job at a critical moment.'[41]

Once crews had formed, the following weeks were spent on cross-country, night-flying and navigational exercises, and practice bombing, and it was hoped that any serious weaknesses among the new crew would manifest themselves at this point, rather than on operations. Miles Tripp found that his bomb-aiming skills were not up to standard when he reached his OTU, and he was held back for additional instruction.[42] But he also found out that the gunner in his crew had poor eyesight – only luck and bluff had secured his place at the OTU – and his navigator had failed on one of the cross-country exercises. These types of deficiency could be identified at this stage of final training, but there was always one variable that would not be known until the crews reached operational squadrons: how individual members would cope with combat stress.[43]

For the first two years of the war, crews could pass directly from this training to their operational squadrons, because the aircraft being used by the OTUs were generally of the same type as those on the front-line squadrons. However, with the introduction of the new generation of four-engined bombers, such as the Lancaster and Halifax, it was realised that new crews also required 'conversion' on to these more complex aircraft. So a Conversion Unit course lasting two weeks was added to the OTU programme. In sum, Operational Training gave crews a fighting chance of survival once they joined the front line, but the organisation was not without its flaws. It was acknowledged after a time that the most valuable instructors were those men who had seen recent operational flying, but such men were hard to obtain because of the pressures of maintaining the offensive against Germany. This was particularly the case at the start of the campaign in 1940-41. The problem was solved partially in 1941 by the Air Ministry's setting operational tours at 200 hours, after which an individual would have six months' rest, usually instructing at an OTU. Another difficulty arose when the new generation of bombers entered service, and there was great reluctance to withdraw these types from the front line. Many of those crews destined ultimately to serve in Lancaster squadrons found that most of their conversion training actually occurred on Halifaxes or Stirlings.[44]

Pressure on the training organisation was relieved to a certain extent in the early part of 1942 when the Air Ministry did away with the policy of having two pilots per bomber.[45] From this point, a heavy bomber would have just a single pilot. Pressure on the OTUs was also relieved somewhat by the establishment of Advanced Flying Training Schools and Personnel Reception Centres, which undertook refresher training for those aircrew trainees recently arrived from overseas Empire Air Training Schools.[46] It was often at this point that the extra training revealed weaknesses in aircrew skills, and it was common to see pilots being re-graded and sent off for navigation training. In fact, only 64 per cent of those who started flying training as pilots ended up as pilots.[47] At certain points in the war, there were also shortfalls in other aircrew trades, so that even those judged to be good pilots could sometimes find themselves retraining in another role. One such was Walter Thompson, who joined the Royal Canadian Air Force in 1941 and underwent pilot training. On arrival in Britain, he was asked what type of flying he preferred:

> 'They said that those who did best would have first choice. I chose night-fighters first, Coastal Command ship-fighters second and bombers third. I had worked diligently at flying and ground school, and graduated first in the class. On the 10th day of July 1942, my flying log book was endorsed… "proficiency as pilot on type – Above Average". What more could one ask? Then the world collapsed! I was told that I had received a high mark in Navigation and was, therefore, posted to commence a Navigation Instructor's course at the Central Navigation School at Cranage. As simple as that!'[48]

Even after the inception of Operational Training and these other measures, the relative inexperience of crews meant that large numbers of crews were lost in flying accidents, either at OTUs or shortly after arriving on operational squadrons. Lord Mackie, who joined the RAF shortly after the war broke out, recalled that three out of the six crews on his OTU course had been lost in accidents.[49] Throughout the war 8,117 men were lost in non-operational flying accidents, and 3,985 were seriously wounded. Compared with combat losses (49,585), this was a high percentage.[50] As Brooke-Popham found in the First World War, heavy combat losses were often followed by a high accident rate, as more inexperienced crews entered the front line.[51] Inexperienced aircrew were not popular additions to squadrons, especially if an established crew had to find a replacement for one of its members. One Sergeant Air Gunner recalled his posting to 10 Squadron at Leeming in September 1941.[52] His first operations were flown with a crew of sergeants who had already done several sorties. They did not speak to him all the way to the target and all the way back, and, on one occasion, he thought that they must have all baled out but he was too frightened to switch on his intercom and ask. This attitude towards new arrivals was endemic, as 'green' crew were inclined to make mistakes when subjected to the physical and psychological stress associated with the first few operations. A former Flight Sergeant in 75 (New Zealand) Squadron commented that one mission was a complete disaster for his aircraft because of a 'green' crew member, and how his aircraft was only just able to return to base.[53]

As good as the training organisation had become by the mid-war period, it could never fully prepare aircrew for operational reality. However, as in any war, the contrast between doctrinal expectation and wartime reality was greatest at the start of the war. As the official historians comment:

> '...when war came in 1939, Bomber Command was not trained or equipped either to penetrate into enemy territory by day or to find its target areas, let alone its targets, by night. There were, of course, some crews [who] had reached higher standards of navigation, bomb-aiming and gunnery. But the character of their aircraft and guns meant that it was impossible for them, however skilful and brave they might be, to face the enemy over his own territory in daytime.'[54]

The first two years of the war saw the skies being darkened by all the doctrinal chickens coming home to roost. The effects of dogma and budgetary constraint were most apparent in the quality of aircraft and supporting technologies.

The aircraft that would have to carry the offensive to Germany were either obsolescent or obsolete (Hampden, Wellington, Whitley). All these aircraft, but especially the Hampden, were notorious for their lack of crew comfort. Crews operating the Hampden were quick to christen it the 'Flying Coffin'. One member of 106 Squadron described the difficulties posed by the cramped conditions in the aircraft:

> '...if the pilot was hit or incapacitated, the second pilot – who also carried out the duties of bomb-aimer and navigator as well as being reserve pilot – had to drag him out from his seat by pulling him backwards out of his position, and then crawl into the pilot's position; a feat which ... called for a combination of strength, dexterity, and a blind faith that the aircraft would stay on an even plane during which time this hazardous operation was accomplished.'[55]

The Hampden also had a particularly draughty cockpit, and crews would return from operations numb with the cold. Frostbite was common among the crews of all these early bombers, which had rudimentary heating systems prone to failure. Having to operate at altitudes of between 15,000 and 20,000 feet, temperatures fell as low as -30 degrees C. Crews were compelled to wear bulky and restrictive clothing, and the extreme cold also affected the oxygen equipment, so that even the simplest tasks became almost impossible. A particularly graphic account exists of a Whitley crew engaged in leaflet-dropping over Frankfurt:

> 'Everyone was frozen, and had no means of alleviating their distress. The navigator and Commanding Officer were butting their heads on the floor and navigation table in an endeavour to experience some other form of pain as a relief from the awful feeling of frostbite and lack of oxygen.'[56]

In this respect, aircrew conditions had not improved markedly over the First World War flying in open cockpits.[57]

Nor had there been any advancement in aids to navigation or bomb-aiming. At the start of the war dead-reckoning and astro-navigation were the basis of long-range navigation. The early crews had none of the radar navigational aids that ultimately appeared in Bomber Command, such as 'Gee' and 'H2S'. The inter-war Air Staff had shown great indifference to, and ignorance of, long-range navigation problems, and this was highlighted by none other than Arthur Harris, when he was Deputy Director of the Plans Division in 1936:

'The trouble with service navigation in the past has been the lack of knowledge and of interest in the subject evinced by senior officers in the service ... pilotage and "Bradshawing" have quite wrongly been considered as adequate substitutes for real navigation.'[58]

There were many senior officers who shared the opinion of the Deputy Director of Staff Duties, Group Captain (later Air Vice-Marshal) F. H. Maynard, that navigation over long distances was a 'comparatively simple' exercise.[59] When changes to the navigational syllabus were proposed in 1938, this was at the behest of Coastal Command, but few of the revisions were in place by the time war broke out. As late as 1941, to provide bomber crews with an accurate target position before take-off was thought to be sufficient. But operations very quickly demonstrated that if training and equipment were lacking, such information was of little use.

The extent of navigational error during many of these early operations is illustrated by one account of 7-8 March 1940, when Whitleys of 77 Squadron were returning from a mission over Poland. A 77 Squadron aircraft flew for 11 hours using dead-reckoning navigation before making an emergency landing in an area calculated to be near its base at Villeneuve, some 30 miles south-east of Paris. The crew was astonished to find that the language spoken by a group of farmworkers gathering around the aircraft was German. It was only then that they realised the enormity of their navigational error, and only just succeeded in restarting the Whitley's engines as enemy troops arrived.[60] This is reminiscent of similar navigational problems faced by the RFC's bombing crews in the First World War. For example, in December 1917, 55 Squadron lost half of its formation during one bombing operation because the crews lost their way when they were forced to navigate above cloud. Only the flight commander was able to locate the home aerodrome and land safely.[61] As the official historians commented, 'What is surprising about the years before 1942 is not that so many crews failed to find their targets, but that more of them did not fail to find England on their return.'[62]

Even if aircrews succeeded in locating their targets, there was no guarantee that they would be able to hit them. The early aircrews of the Second World War were reliant upon bombsights developed by the previous generation. The most common was the Course Setting Bombsight, which dated from the closing stages of the First World War, and this was only partially automatic, so that the final settings had to be done manually by the bomb-aimer in the run-up to the target. The bombsight demanded that the aircraft be kept on a straight and level approach to the target, as the slightest deviations in the air resulted in large errors on the ground, so that crews were compelled to hold their nerve if they wanted to hit a target accurately. As a consequence, aircraft fell easy prey to enemy fighters and flak, as one 10 Squadron Whitley crew found during May 1940 when they attempted to hit an oil installation at Bremen. In order to have a steady run-up to the target, the pilot made six passes over the city at less than 1,000 feet, coming under heavy fire each time. When the aircraft returned to its Yorkshire base, 700 holes were found in the fuselage.[63]

The real impetus to improve navigational and bomb aiming standards came with the findings of an independent report into bombing accuracy instituted by Churchill's Scientific Adviser, Lord Cherwell. The so-called Butt report, issued in the autumn of 1941, concluded that of all the aircraft claiming to have attacked their targets, only one-third had arrived within 5 miles of them. Over the Ruhr, the proportion fell to one-tenth because of the heightened anti-aircraft defences and industrial haze obscuring targets.[64] In combination with developing Operational Research techniques, this study led to a more frank approach to operational problems experienced by aircrews. Not only was there subsequently far greater research and development into aids to navigation and bomb-aiming, which led to the introduction of radar equipment such as H2S, improved bombsights such as the Stabilised Vector Bombsight known as Mark XIV, and the specialist navigational group in Bomber Command known as the Pathfinders, but there was also a far greater understanding of the physical and psychological stresses placed on aircrew.[65]

Like so many other facets of the air war, the First World War experience cast its long shadow also in relation to attitudes towards combat stress. In the First War the prevailing view was that there was something cowardly about squadrons who lacked an offensive spirit or individuals who broke down under the strain of operations.[66] Trenchard, who was known for his advocacy of an offensive spirit, admonished one of his bombing squadrons in 1918 for having 'naval ideas', by which he meant the squadron was being overly cautious. The RNAS had developed a reputation for not flying if the weather conditions were considered marginal, quite sensibly, whereas the RFC, and then the RAF under Trenchard, had the 'habit of flying whenever possible, taking risks, expecting losses, and hoping for the best'.[67] The CO of the bombing squadron concerned (which had been in the RNAS) disagreed fundamentally with Trenchard: 'I think the question of morale in a squadron is very important and if a squadron does a great deal of work without losing any machines, it is doing as good work as a squadron which is doing slightly better work, but at a high cost of machines and personnel and consequently morale.'[68] As time went on, Trenchard's views prevailed, and what seems to have been the wise caution exhibited by the old naval squadrons evaporated.

After the First World War there was no attempt by the Air Ministry to examine the question of combat stress, as it was not considered an issue. Nor did the official historians of the air war devote any attention to the subject. The closest they came was a page and a half on 'the spirit of the pilot', in which Walter Raleigh spoke of Trenchard's belief that the morale of the air service depended on individual pilots being positive in everything they did: 'To think only of dangers and drawbacks, to make much of the points in which the Germans had attained a fleeting superiority, to lay stress on the imperfections of our own equipment – all this, [Trenchard] knew, was to invite defeat.'[69] There seems to have been little appreciation of the unnatural stresses placed on aircrews, or, indeed, the fighting man on the ground, during the First World War. But, for the airman, there was not even a term equating to 'shell shock'. Evidently it was felt that aircrew during the First World War did not suffer from combat stress, and this might have arisen because aviators were removed from the horrors of the land war. The fact that men volunteered for flying duties, which, in any case, were seen as glamorous, would not have helped.

Therefore, combat stress in the early part of the Second World War was little understood. Before May 1941 there was no conception of a limited tour of duty; aircrews continued to serve until they were killed, wounded or taken off flying operations for some specific reason. There was no organised investigation into flying stress among aircrews until the end of 1940, and the term 'flying stress' was not coined until the very end of that year. Flying stress was then used to describe a condition that might be observed in an aircrew member as a result of an abnormal strain being placed on an individual. Those who broke down as a result of this strain were categorised into three principal groups. The first comprised those men who were temperamentally unfit for flying duties. 'These men are brave, and prove it by determined and unavailing effort to make good. They are overcome by fear of their environment and not by fear of the enemy.'[70] Such men, it was thought, would break down in the space of five to ten missions, and their breakdown was believed to be permanent. The second type identified was the individual with less than average capacity for sustained effort. He was described as a 'good type' who undertook operational flying successfully, but who had less than average capacity for sustained effort on such duties. Being less able, he was more likely to be under strain. The third category covered the man with average or better than average capacity for sustained effort, but who collapsed suddenly, usually after a period of sustained fatigue.

In addition to these categories there were two others, which sought to explain the failings of men considered to be outside the three principal groupings. There was the 'constitutionally unsuitable for flying duty' type. 'These men are not brave, and they seek to evade the danger and discomfort of operational duty through any door of escape.'[71] Such men were thought to break down after one to five missions, and they were considered a 'serious danger to morale'. The other type was called the 'fair weather' individual, who used as a means of escaping from operational duties an alleged dislike of a particular aircraft or environment, which he attempted to use as a justification for asking to be transferred. He, too, was described as a serious threat to morale.

A good indication that the phenomenon of flying stress was not fully understood at this stage is suggested by the fact that most of the men listed as unfit for flying duties in the period 1 April to 31 December 1940 did not fall into the three categories of unfitness for flying caused by 'real' factors, but rather had their records endorsed 'LMF' (Lack of Moral Fibre), the term for cowardice.[72] Accusations of LMF were levelled on a regular basis during the first half of the war. Aircrews who returned early from operations, claiming mechanical failure or similar in their aircraft, were liable to be labelled LMF until their reports were corroborated by groundcrew inspection of the aircraft.[73] The accusation of cowardice was made usually within the confines of the squadron or the station, but it could come from higher levels. For instance, it was reported at the end of 1941 that a Squadron Leader from a Blenheim unit ordered a formation to return to base without dropping its bombs after they failed to find a target, mainly as a result of low cloud.[74] On return to base, he was asked why he had not dropped his bombs on Heligoland, to which he replied that at such a low altitude he did not think it advisable to do so owing to the wastage of aircraft likely to occur. The Air Marshal conducting the interview used the words, 'Yellow, were you?', and put an end to the questioning. Shortly after this incident, the Squadron Leader was ordered to send out his squadron to attack Heligoland, from which operation only two aircraft returned.[75] This particular incident was brought to the attention of the Chief of Air Staff Portal by the Minister of Aircraft Production, Moore-Brabazon, in December 1940. Unfortunately, no reply can be found, and it is not clear from what remains of Portal's private correspondence as to what his views were on the subject of LMF. What can be said is that there was no perceptible change in attitude towards the subject of cowardice until 1943, and this was due to the more rigorous investigation into the problem of flying stress, for which much of the credit must go to the Air Member for Personnel appointed in August 1942, Air Marshal Bertine Sutton, who stated that he deplored the term 'Lack of Morale Fibre'.[76]

A study of combat stress in the operational commands was begun in 1942, under Air Vice-Marshal Sir Charles Symonds, who was a consultant in neuro-psychiatry, and a Wing Commander Denis Williams. They submitted their first report in December of that year, and their main finding was that aircrew stress was caused by the combination of fear and fatigue.[77] Many causes of fatigue are fairly obvious: the length of sortie, the extremely low temperatures, having to concentrate throughout on instruments or the night sky, the effects of low oxygen, etc. However, there were the less tangible causes of aircrew fatigue, such as the strain caused by concern for wives or other relatives, and dependants, should they be killed or incapacitated.

Meanwhile, fear was seen to have many elements. The fear of death or injury manifested itself in numerous ways, depending on the individual, but there were common tell-tale signs.[78] Many former aircrew recounted the atmosphere in messes before operations, how many men were unable to eat and how vomiting became a daily occurrence. Many referred to the congestion in ablution blocks, as men visited the toilet for the umpteenth time before an operation. Many referred to the distinctive 'smell of fear' that pervaded dispersal areas and transports to the aircraft. Then there was the fear of letting down the other crew members, or letting down a commanding officer. Many, including Miles Tripp, feared being labelled LMF. After an attack of nerves during a mission over Cologne, he was anxious to go on another as soon as possible, reasoning that it was like falling off a horse or having a car accident, when one had to get back in the saddle or back into the driving seat as soon as possible.[79]

For some aircrew, fear and general stress were manageable until one particular event caused them to snap, if momentarily, like Miles Tripp. A number of former aircrew commented that they had coped with fear and stress over many months of operations, but how they were thrown off balance by the death of a friend in the squadron, the sight of an empty bunk bed next to them, or seeing mutilated bodies. One former navigator recalled having seen a bomber make an emergency landing at his base, and how groundcrews had to use high-pressure hoses to clean out the rear gun turret after the gunner was shot to pieces by an enemy fighter.[80]

Methods of coping with fear and general stress varied. Some men became superstitious and could be seen going through pre-flight rituals. Those of a religious persuasion carried rosaries or crosses. Heavy drinking and absorption in mess social life were also common, as was living for the day. Most aircrew abandoned long-term planning and concentrated on day-to-day existence.[81] But there were also mechanisms commanding officers could employ to boost morale and alleviate stress, and Symonds and Williams made a number of recommendations.[82] First, it was emphasised that it was very important for a commanding officer to explain the purpose of missions and where they fitted into the overall campaign, as far as OPSEC would allow. Second, it was vitally important for the results of missions to be articulated to the crews, especially the success stories, and recognition of hard-won success by a telegram from Command or Group HQ level was considered essential. However, it was felt that the most valuable praise was that from the immediate commanding officer at squadron or station level. The award of medals or other decorations was also seen as a significant factor in the maintenance of good morale.

Keeping the crews at the sharp end apprised of their contribution to the whole effort does appear to have been one of the keys to maintaining Bomber Command's morale as a whole at a reasonable level. Whatever criticisms we may level at Arthur Harris for his lack of strategic vision and dogmatism over the merits of area versus precision bombing, he was very popular with the aircrews because he believed in speaking frankly about Bomber Command's successes and failures, and his enthusiasm and determination filtered right down to grass-roots level. Even when Bomber Command was facing crippling losses during 1943 and 1944 during the Battles of Berlin and the Ruhr, when a heavy bomber crew faced less than a 44 per cent chance of surviving a first tour of operations, Harris remained a popular C-in-C. One former Flight Sergeant said of him: 'We had all the confidence in the world in his strategy. We felt that we and we alone in Bomber Command were winning the war.'[83] It required a unique type of leadership to convince aircrews to keep on putting themselves in harm's way, with little chance of survival. Harris had that ability, and his leadership style is worthy of a much larger study.[84] Harris, for his part, had tremendous admiration for the bomber crews under his command. He said:

'There are no words with which I can do justice to the aircrew who fought under my command. There is no parallel in warfare to such courage and determination in the face of danger over so prolonged a period, of danger which at times was so great that scarcely one man in three could expect to survive his tour of thirty operations... It was, moreover, a clear and highly conscious courage, by which the risk was taken with calm forethought, for their aircrew were all highly skilled men, much above the average in education, who had to understand every aspect and detail of their task. It was, furthermore, the courage of the small hours, of men virtually alone, for at his battle station the airman is virtually alone. It was the courage of men with long-drawn apprehensions of daily "going over the top".'[85]

It is interesting that Harris chose to use a First World War image, and it was entirely fitting, given the enormous casualty rate in Bomber Command (49,585 killed in combat, with another 8,117 lost in non-operational flying), which paralleled 1914-18's battlefield losses.[86] Bomber Command's own record demonstrated that to serve as aircrew was anything but a safe option. Further, it imposed unnatural strains on individuals, and demanded levels of technical proficiency largely unparalleled in the other services. As is often the case, many of the fundamental principles of strategic bombing were identified, at least by the RNAS, in the First World War, but were subsequently forgotten, so that a second generation of airmen had painfully to relearn the lessons. For this reason, and the fact that we are dealing with human endeavour, there were many parallels between the First and Second World War experiences.

Notes on contributors

Dr Christina J.M. Goulter,
Christina J.M. Goulter was educated at the University of Canterbury, New Zealand, and King's College, London, where she took her PhD in 1993. She worked for two years as a historian at the Ministry of Defence, London, and was later Associate Visiting Professor of Strategy at the United States Naval War College. She is the author of A Forgotten Offensive. Royal Air Force Coastal Command's Anti-Shipping Campaign, 1940-1945 (London: Frank Cass, 1995).

Recommended reading

Bartlett, C. P. O., *Bomber Pilot, 1916-1918* (London: Ian Allan, 1974)

Goulter, C. J. M., *A Forgotten Offensive: Royal Air Force Coastal Command's Anti-Shipping Campaign, 1940-1945* (London: Frank Cass, 1995)

Harris, A., *Bomber Offensive* (London: Greenhill Books, 1990)
    Despatch (reprinted by Frank Cass, London, 1995)

Hastings, M., *Bomber Command* (New York: Dial Press, 1979)

Messenger, C., *Bomber Harris and the Strategic Bombing Offensive, 1939-1945* (London: Arms & Armour Press, 1984)

Terraine, J., *The Right of the Line: The Royal Air Force in the European War, 1939-1945* (London: Hodder & Stoughton, 1985)

Webster, C. F. and Frankland, N., *The Strategic Air Offensive Against Germany, 1939-1945* (London: HMSO, 1961)

Wells, M., *Courage and Air Warfare* (London: Frank Cass, 1995)

Williams, G. K., *Biplanes and Bombsights: British Bombing in World War I* (Maxwell Air Force Base, Air University Press, 1999)

Wise, S. F., *Canadian Airmen in the First World War, Official History of the Royal Canadian Air Force*, Vol I (University of Toronto Press, 1980)

Raleigh, W. and Jones, H., *The War in the Air* (Oxford: Clarendon Press, 1922), Vols I-VI

Notes

[1] Webster, C. F. and Frankland, N., *The Strategic Air Offensive Against Germany, 1939-1945* (London: HMSO, 1961, 4 volumes) Vol I, p19

[2] Sanders, J., *Of Wind and Water* (Airlife, 1989) Prologue

[3] Raleigh, W. and Jones, H., *The War in the Air* (Oxford: Clarendon Press, 1922), Vol I, p231. See also Chap IV

[4] Ibid, p189

[5] See, for example, Longmore, A., *From Sea to Sky* (London: Geoffrey Bles, 1946) pp12-38; Probert, H., *High Commanders of the Royal Air Force* (London: HMSO, 1991) pp1-4, 31-5, 41-5; Bartlett, C. P. O., *Bomber Pilot, 1916-1918* (London: Ian Allan, 1974) p15

[6] Steel, N. and Hart, P., *Tumult in the Clouds: The British Experience of the War in the Air, 1914-1918* (Hodder & Stoughton, 1997) p286

[7] McFarland, S., *America's Pursuit of Precision Bombing* (Washington: Smithsonian Institution Press, 1995) pp5-6

[8] Raleigh, W. and Jones, H., op cit, Vol I, pp231-2. See also pp155, 175, 178-9

[9] Overy, R. *The Air War, 1939-1945* (London: Europa, 1980) Chap1; interviews by the author (1983, 1985, 1987, Christchurch, New Zealand) with Messrs L. Butler and Max Ruane, 75 (NZ) Squadron, and D. Tunnicliffe, M. Langley and R. Dunn, 489 (NZ) Squadron.

[10] Kingsford, A. R., *Night Raiders of the Air* (London: Greenhill Books, 1988) pp44-5; Norris, G., *The Royal Flying Corps: A History* (London: Frederick Muller, 1965) p44

[11] Hastings, M., *Bomber Command* (New York: Dial Press, 1979) p5

[12] Wise, S. F., *Canadian Airmen and the First World War, Official History of the Royal Canadian Air Force* (University of Toronto Press, 1980) Vol I, p30

[13] Steel and Hart, op cit, pp21-2

[14] S. F. Wise, op cit, p29

[15] Wells, M., *Courage and Air Warfare* (London: Frank Cass, 1995), pp12-3

[16] Goulter, C. J. M., *A Forgotten Offensive: Royal Air Force Coastal Command's Anti-Shipping Campaign, 1940-1945* (London: Frank Cass, 1995) p22

[17] AIR 1/663, 17/122/692 'RNAS Officers and Men, re method of training, Dec 1917'; AIR 1/664, 17/122/704 'Training of RNAS pilots in aerial navigation, 9 Nov 1916-15 February 1917'; AIR 1/678, 21/13/2082 'Summary of notes on training of RNAS personnel, 1914-1918', pp13-5. See also Goulter, C. J. M., op cit, pp22-3

[18] AIR 1/664, 17/122/696 'Training in the RFC', pp3-6; Letter to Lt Pulford RN from Captain [signature illegible] in RFC Staff Training Brigade, dd 2 Sept 1916 regarding training of RFC pilots. See also Goulter, C. J. M., op cit, p24

[19] Williams, G. K., *Biplanes and Bombsights: British Bombing in World War I* (Maxwell Air Force Base: Air University Press, 1999) pp90-1

[20] Ibid, p105

[21] Huskinson, P., *Vision Ahead* (London, 1949) pp15-6

[22] AIR 1/921, 204/5/889 HQ RFC memo: 'Bomb dropping attacks', dd 15 Feb 1915. See also Williams, G. K., op cit, p121; Jones, N., *The Origins of Strategic Bombing* (London: William Kimber, 1973) pp60-1

[23] G. K. Williams, op cit, p123

[24] C. J. M. Goulter, op cit, pp24-5

[25] Ibid, pp26-8. AIR 1/674, 21/6/77 'Short notes on the evolution and theory of bombsights', by Capt D. C. Murray, dd 8 Feb 1921; AIR 10/314, 2/3 'Instructions for use of RNAS Equal Distance Bombsight', 1916. See also notes 75 and 76

[26] N. Jones, op cit, pp117-8

[27] Jones, H., *War in the Air*, Vol VI, pp120-1

[28] Williams, G. K., op cit, pp133, 165

29 AIR 1/725, 97/5 'Notes on night reconnaissance and bombing', papers 22 Aug 1918; March 1919; Appendix II, p7; AIR 1/1084, 204/5/1710 'HQ RFC and RAF: Navigation Instruments, other than compasses, January 1918-10 February 1919'. See also Goulter, C. J. M., op cit, p25f

30 C. J. M. Goulter, op cit, p28

31 Ibid, Chaps 2-3

32 Webster, C. F. and Frankland, N., op cit, Vol IV, Annexes and Appendices: Appendix 7, 'Comparison of Expansion Schemes of Aircraft Strength, 1934-39'

33 C. J. M. Goulter, op cit, pp102-3

34 Air Historical Branch (AHB) (RAF) Narrative AHB II/116/9 'Aircrew Training, 1934-1942', pp29, 33, 34, 36, 37

35 C. J. M. Goulter, op cit, p86

36 AHB II/116/9, p38; Terraine, J., *The Right of the Line: The Royal Air Force in the European War, 1939-1945* (London: Hodder & Stoughton, 1985) p87

37 AHB II/116/9, p35; Terraine, J., op cit, p82

38 AHB II/116/9, p62; Goulter, C. J. M., op cit, p103. See also note 122.

39 AHB II/116/9, p34

40 Webster and Frankland, op cit, Vol IV, Appendix 38, Bomber Command ORBAT, 1939; Annex III, 'Operational Training Units in Bomber Command', pp25-30

41 Tripp, M., *The Eighth Passenger* (London: Heinemann, 1969) p9

42 Ibid, p16

43 See discussion below, pp26ff

44 Webster and Frankland, op cit, Vol IV, Annex III, pp25-30; Vol II, p111; AHB II/116/9, pp35-6; Tripp, M., op cit, p15; Messenger, C., *Bomber Harris and the Strategic Bombing Offensive, 1939-1945* (London: Arms & Armour Press, 1984) pp57-9

45 Harris, A., *Despatch* (London: reprinted by Frank Cass, 1995) Introduction, pxxxii

46 AHB II/116/9, p578

47 Ibid

48 Thompson, W., *Lancaster to Berlin* (London: Goodall Publications, 1985) p24

49 Lord Mackie, *Symposium on the Strategic Bomber Offensive, 1939-1945* (Bracknell: Royal Air Force Historical Society, Bracknell Paper No 4, 1993) p33

50 A. Harris, op cit, Table 15 'Personnel Casualties'

51 See page 9

52 Philpott, B., *RAF Bomber Units, September 1939 to June 1942* (London: Osprey, 1977) p38

53 Interview with Mr Max Ruane, 75 (New Zealand) Squadron, Christchurch, NZ, 1983

54 Webster, C. F. and Frankland, N., op cit, Vol I, p125

55 Bowyer, C., *Bomber Group at War* (London: Ian Allan, 1981) p29

56 Air Ministry, *Bomber Command* (London: HMSO, 1941) p33. See also pp31-2

57 See, eg, the published diary of C. P. O. Bartlett, *Bomber Pilot, 1916-1918* (London: Ian Allan, 1974), especially the entries for November 1916-January 1917. See also S. F. Wise, op cit, p269, and reports on RNAS crews suffering frostbite during operations in January 1917

58 AIR 2/2860 Minute to DSD, D of T, from Gp Capt A. T. Harris, dd 3 Nov 1936, p3. See also C. J. M. Goulter, op cit, p86f

59 AIR 2/2608 Minute to ACAS from DDSD, Gp Capt F. H. Maynard, dd 23 Oct 1939, p2

60 B. Philpott, op cit, p20

61 G. K. Williams, op cit, p105

62 Webster and Frankland, op cit, Vol IV, Annex I, p4

63 M. Hastings, op cit, p89

64 Webster and Frankland, op cit, p178

65 Ibid., Vol IV, Annexes I, IV

66 M. Wells, op cit, Foreword, ppxi-xii

67 G. K. Williams, op cit, p208

68 Ibid, p208

69 W. Raleigh, op cit, Vol I, p439

70 AIR 20/10727 'Report on Flying Fatigue and Stress observed in the RAF', nd (cOct 1940), p1; also p2

71 Ibid, p1

[72] Ibid, p2

[73] Interviews with the author, 489 (NZ) Sqn personnel: Air Commodore Peter Hughes, Messrs Jack Simpson, Reg Shand, J. Richardson, Ralph Dunn (April-May 1989); Messrs L. Butler, M. Ruane, 75 (NZ) Sqn (1983)

[74] Portal Papers, Christ Church, Oxford: Box C, File 4, Item 7, Letter to CAS Portal from Minister of Aircraft Production, Moore-Brabazon, 8 Dec 1941

[75] Although it is not clear from this letter which operation was involved, it is likely to have been one undertaken on 26 August 1941, when six Blenheims were despatched to attack shipping off Heligoland. Four of the six were subsequently reported as missing. AHB Air Staff Operational Summary, No 279, 27 August 1941, p1

[76] AIR 20/10727 Minute to DGPS from AMP, A/M Sutton, dd 18 Jan 1943. See also J. McCarthy, 'Aircrew and "Lack of Moral Fibre" in the Second World War', *War and Society*, Vol 2 (Sept 1984) pp87-101

[77] AIR 2/6252 'Investigation into Psychological Disorders in Flying Personnel', Section II. See also AHB Air Ministry Publication 3139 'Psychological Disorders in Flying Personnel of the Royal Air Force, Investigated During the War, 1939-1945' (HMSO, 1947), especially p74f

[78] Interviews with the author: Messrs Butler and Ruane, 75 (NZ) Sqn, 1983; R. Shand, H. Blampied, D. Tunnicliffe and A. Carr, 489 (NZ) Sqn, 1983, 1987

[79] M. Tripp, op cit, p39

[80] Interviews with the author, as above (note 78)

[81] Interviews with the author; M. Hastings, op cit, p96

[82] Air Ministry Publication 3139, 'Psychological Disorders', pp79-81

[83] C. Messenger, op cit, p205. See also AIR 8/739 'Table showing the theoretical proportion of crews completing one and two operational tours, based on SD 98 rates revised on operational experience', 4 Jan 1943; C. J. M. Goulter, op cit, p155

[84] One of the best remains Charles Messenger's book, *Bomber Harris*. See also Goulter, C. J. M., 'Sir Arthur Harris: Different Perspectives', *Challenges of High Command in the Twentieth Century*, Strategic and Combat Studies Institute, Occasional No 38, 1999, pp75-85

[85] Harris, A., *Bomber Offensive* (London: Greenhill Books, 1990) p267

[86] Refer to note 50

Chapter 7

The Desert War experience

Niall Barr

The numerous campaigns fought in the deserts of the Middle East during both World Wars form only one era in a long history of warfare in the region. The first recorded battle in history took place at Megiddo in Palestine between the Hittites and the Egyptians in 1468BC. During Allenby's 1917-18 campaign in Palestine, soldiers could not help but be aware that they were fighting in regions that had a long history of warfare. The British troops who marched across the Sinai desert in 1917 came upon dusty villages and towns whose names had been learned by heart at Sunday school and Bible class:

> 'And so we got to the end of the sand after a good many weeks and came to the first village in Palestine and that after seeing nothing but sand for weeks and possibly months it was – one saw this green and gold of – of what I suppose to the old Israelites was the promised land and one can well understand the aptness of the description.'[1]

The news that the British Army was fighting in Palestine, and that the news reports mentioned familiar, if exotic, names created a sensation in Britain. This gave the capture of Jerusalem in December 1917 a heightened significance, and some British troops even had the unusual distinction of fighting in the holy places. One British sapper was ordered:

> '…to make sure that in the Holy Sepulchre there was no Turks lying about. So, "Go in there with your platoon again, Mathews. And make sure there's nobody about. If there is boys, you know what to do." So Mathews went in with his platoon and we advanced. And there was nobody there. They'd all gone.'[2]

Clearly, for this toughened veteran, there was no real difference where he fought. While Allenby's men were familiar with many of the place names that they fought over, the commander of the British 60th Division was surprised to find himself connected to a previous English commander during the advance on Jerusalem. When his staff officers complained that they could not find any wells in the area around the town of Qaryet el 'Inab on the road from Jaffa to Jerusalem, General Sir John Shea went to the local monastery to see if the monks could help him. He related that the abbot:

'...looked at me, and then he half smiled, and said, "General, you are the second General who found he couldn't find any water when he came here." I looked at him rather in surprise, and said, "Oh sir, please forgive me for saying so, but you must be wrong because I know I am leading the army, there is nothing in front of me. The 60th is the leading division." And again he looked at me, and then he smiled and his whole body shook, and he said, "The General I was referring to was Richard Coeur de Lion."'[3]

The British troops of this century who served in the deserts of the Middle East shared their battlegrounds with many previous generations of soldiers. Richard the Lionheart's Third Crusade was far from Britain's only previous connection with the Middle East. Thousands of regular British troops had already marched and sweated their way across the Egyptian desert by the time the first soldiers of the Great War disembarked in Egypt for the Gallipoli campaign. Abercrombie's victory over Napoleon's army at Alexandria in 1801 had inaugurated Britain's modern involvement with the Middle East. The construction of the Suez Canal in 1869 meant that Egypt was of great strategic importance to Britain, and the Royal Navy's bombardment of Alexandria in 1881 and the invasion of Egypt that led to the battle of Tel el Kebir in 1882 began the British occupation and domination of Egypt, which lasted until 1952. The numerous campaigns fought subsequently, including the ill-fated attempt to rescue General Gordon at Khartoum in 1885 and the battle of Omdurman in 1898, were all part of Britain's experience of Empire.

Thus the troops who fought in the Middle East in 1914-18 and 1940-43 were following in the footsteps of previous generations of British soldiers, and in some respects the experience of soldiers this century was little different from their Victorian counterparts. The campaigns fought in the Middle East against the Turks during the First World War can be seen as an extension and continuation of Imperial interests, and even the desert campaigns fought in the Second World War can be seen as a form of traditional 'defence of Empire'. Yet in a very real sense, these campaigns represented a break from the past. They were not isolated actions fought against native opponents, but major struggles for dominance in the Middle East fought on an unprecedented scale. As an integral part of much wider World Wars, they brought far-reaching change to the region and sparked a new sense of Arab nationalism among the inhabitants.

The armies that Britain sent to the Middle East during the two World Wars were also very different from their forebears. Not only were the forces sent to the Middle East during the two conflicts far larger than any previous forces, but they were composed of volunteers and conscripts rather than the toughened regular soldiers of Victoria's army. They were also polyglot forces, which contained men and women drawn from across the British Empire. The 51st Highland Division noted proudly in its war diary on the eve of the Second Battle of Alamein that:

'It is interesting that in this, the biggest organised offensive yet put in by the British Army in this War, the Highland Division is the only Infantry Division representing Great Britain, alongside the Australians, New Zealanders, and the South Africans.'[4]

Even this list omitted the heavy contribution made by the Indian Army, not to mention the numerous armies in exile, such as the Free French, the Polish Carpathian Brigade and the Greek Brigade, which all served in the desert during the Second World War. Nonetheless, the Highlanders' pride in being the sole British representative among the Empire infantry was perhaps misplaced; there were many other British units serving alongside the more distinctive Dominion troops. This multi-national pattern was repeated in both wars, and lent a distinctive 'Imperial' character to the British armies serving in the desert.

Just as the armies sent by Britain to the Middle East were diverse and polyglot in character, so was there a bewildering variety in the campaigns in which they became involved. There were diverse campaigns fought against a range of enemies and conducted over a vast area of harsh terrain. One of the first took place in the North African desert along the Libyan/Egyptian border when the British suppressed a Senussi-led Arab uprising in 1915-16, while from 1917 onwards T. E. Lawrence, in the Hejaz, helped to support the Arab revolt against Turkish rule. Meanwhile, large-scale conventional campaigns were fought against the Turks in Sinai, Palestine and Mesopotamia. The Second World War saw an even greater variety of campaigns against a wide variety of opponents. There were short but sharp actions against the Vichy French in Syria, an Axis-sponsored revolt in Iraq, and a hard-fought campaign against the Italians in Ethiopia and Eritrea. However, the main campaign took place against the combined German and Italian forces in the Western Desert. This campaign certainly represented a break with the past, as, for the first time, the Western Desert became an enormous battleground for two major conventional opponents utilising high-intensity manoeuvre warfare.

Such a diverse mix of regions, opponents and fighting raises the difficult issue of whether it is possible to make valid comparisons between the experiences of British troops of both World Wars. While the conduct of the campaigns was often different, and the nature of the opponents and terrain often sharply in contrast, nonetheless the British soldiers of both wars who served in the Middle East were connected by their experiences of Egypt and the desert, of soldiering in a harsh environment, and through their experience of the British Army. British soldiers were aware, if only dimly, of the weight of history present in the region, and they were linked by tradition with the previous British soldiers who had served in the desert.

The desert campaigns fought in the First World War certainly influenced the soldiers of the Second World War. T. E. Lawrence, the British hero of the Arab revolt during Allenby's campaign in Palestine, influenced an entire generation with his book *The Seven Pillars of Wisdom*[5]. Many officers of the Eighth Army quite self-consciously modelled themselves on the independent spirit of Lawrence of Arabia. This was reflected in the rejection of army-issue clothing in favour of sheepskin coats, corduroy trousers and desert boots, or 'brothel creepers' as they were better known. The glamorous idea of the British officer as guerrilla leader also found its way into Eighth Army tactics. This was most noticeable in the formation of 'Jock columns', which were small independent forces of motorised infantry and artillery, designed for raiding and scouting rather than heavy fighting. Lawrence's influence also encouraged the growth of many raiding groups such as the Long Range Desert Group (LRDG), Special Air Service (SAS) and 'Popski's private army', which were used for deep raids and observation of the Axis positions.

All the British troops who served in the Middle East were linked by their experience of travel. While troops serving in Flanders or France travelled to a reasonably familiar corner of Europe, the men who served in the desert had to endure a long sea voyage to a very different part of the world. After the relative inactivity on board ship and the tedium of routine days, the first experience of the Middle East could come as a shock. One Second World War veteran, whose first landfall in the Middle East was on the barren, rocky shores of Aden, remembered that, 'I think one's first impressions when you go ashore at a place like Aden are so mixed, you're bewildered with the difference. It's all so utterly different from anything one's ever seen in one's life.'[6] This sense of entering a very different, alien world was common to all British soldiers who served in the Middle East.

Once the long journey was over, there was one experience that linked almost every British soldier sent to the Middle East. The sights and sounds of Cairo and Alexandria were familiar to thousands of British soldiers who first arrived in Egypt and who spent their precious hours of leave taking in the sights and indulging in the bazaars and fleshpots of these two cities. A visit to the surviving Ancient Wonder of the World was obligatory. E. A. Woolley, a First World War veteran, remembered that, 'I visited the Great Pyramids and went on top and also inside the Great Pyramid... I also went to the Sphinx ... seeing them as I did, one could not but be impressed by these fantastic constructions.'[7]

The pyramids remain a potent symbol of ancient Egypt, and thousands of British soldiers had their photographs taken next to these monuments as a reminder of their visit.[8] However, the soldiers' experience of Egypt went far beyond the ancient world. One veteran remembered being fascinated by:

'Cairo, the Nile, the souks [markets], the mingling of so many nationalities, the pleasant smells of spices and cooking borne on the warm evening air (but not the ghastly daytime smells of which there were plenty). I suppose it summed up for me what I'd always imagined the Orient should be like.'[9]

Many troops enjoyed the exotic and foreign experience that Egypt offered, while many others simply enjoyed Cairo's and Alexandria's bars and nightlife. These innocent pleasures were sometimes mixed with more base concerns, as a naval rating related:

'...three of us went ashore in Alex to the Fleet Club for a game of tombola and our ration of beer. We still had plenty of time, so we said to ourselves, "Let's go to Sister Street." We were young and curious to visit the most renowned of the Eastern Fleet brothels, and wondered what effect it might have on three randy young men.'[10]

Egypt's reputation as a part of the exotic Orient was certainly enhanced by encounters such as these, but these experiences, although welcome, tended to be short-lived and most soldiers found themselves serving far away from the Delta and its temptations.

It was the experience of the desert itself that united all the soldiers who fought there. The desert in popular imagination has long been a place of romance and mystery, but British soldiers soon found that the reality was very different. The intense heat, sand, dust and flies soon removed the mystery, and the most widely held belief among British soldiers in the Eighth Army was that, '"The blue" was ... a right bastard.'[11] Living in the desert brought a series of discomforts and irritants that were quite new to British soldiers more used to a green and temperate climate. The first unpleasant shock to be experienced by any soldier was the intense heat of the day and the chill that descended as soon as the sun went down. One veteran remembered that:

> 'In early July 1917 we found ourselves in the desert of Sinai about eleven miles south-east of Gaza, and there we found that the all-pervading heat ... almost struck us physically, so intense was it. There was no avoiding it [and] no shade whatever.'[12]

In the Eighth Army, during the Second World War, the mark of a desert veteran was to 'get your knees brown', which proved that you had been burned by the sun and served in the desert long enough to adapt to its conditions.

Another feature of the desert conditions was the sheer physical effort needed to march through sand. Marching through the night for the surprise attack on Beersheba on 29 October 1917, one soldier found it:

> '...particularly tiring to march through sand ... the desert may be romantic but we didn't see much romance about it that night. We marched and marched and marched through that desert the whole night long.
>
> The worst feature of all to me I think was the dust. There was choking dust flowing over us from the other columns on our sides. We were perspiring madly [and] the dust settles on your face. I remember seeing my own face next morning when I went to shave – it was nothing but rivulets of dirt or rather clean rivulets amongst the dirt on my face – I wouldn't have recognised myself.'[13]

The huge clouds of dust thrown up by the movement of thousands of soldiers were an unavoidable discomfort. Clouds of dust were ever-present, but they probably reached a peak at Alamein in October 1942, when the passage of thousands of tanks and vehicles along a set number of tracks ground the sand into a powdery dust:

> '...as much as two feet deep in places. Like fluffy snow upon the ground, it rises into the air and hangs like a thick fog in the darkness. Eyes, ears and noses are filled with it and it nearly chokes a man whenever he opens his mouth to speak.'[14]

These man-made dust clouds were uncomfortable, but could not be compared to the natural khamsin or sandstorm. A member of the first armoured car squadron in Egypt remembered his first sandstorm in 1915 vividly:

'I noticed what appeared to be a great bank of fog, moving towards us from the southward. The Egyptian interpreter who rode in my car cried out that it was a sandstorm, and we ran the cars quickly to the lee side of the fort, while a violent wind arose and swept the swirling sand about us, until nothing could be seen at the distance of a yard. Breathing was almost impossible, and the darkness was eerie, while the grains of sand which were continually whipped against our hands and faces by the hot wind stung like the points of needles.'[15]

Sandstorms could sometimes last for days, making life in the desert a real misery. This unwelcome natural phenomenon reinforced the soldiers' perceptions of the desert as a harsh, sterile and alien environment.

However, the main reason for this perception lay in the nature of the desert terrain itself. The character of the desert could change dramatically from soft sand to a rocky limestone bed within a few miles, and each desert, from the Western Desert of Egypt to the Sinai or Sudan, was very different. One veteran of the Western Desert and Eritrean campaigns in the Second World War noted that, 'The Western Desert was sandy, scrubby and from time to time stony, but there was very little vegetation of any sort … [while] the Nubian desert is just an endless plain of golden sand.' Even though desert veterans soon learned to recognise the differences between areas of desert, the main impression was still one of a barren landscape filled with sand. One Eighth Army veteran noted his first sight of the desert with disgust:

'By late afternoon we've reached our destination, Jerawla, a few miles short of Mersa Matruh. Why anyone troubled to confer a name on the place or what anyone could have found to stick a label on, heaven alone knows – there's just miles of blank sand in every direction.'[16]

Soldiers found that places marked on the map were often just that – names on a map. The featureless nature of the terrain meant that good navigation was essential; as one staff officer commented, 'You can't wander around the desert, it's a dangerous thing to do.'[17] One veteran remembered that his training in Egypt during 1915 placed a premium on navigation, and that the troops:

'…had to learn to cross the desert from one place to another without any maps – there were no maps of the district, the only maps I ever saw out there were signed H. H. Kitchener Lieutenant, presumably made in the 1880s. There were no roads, no charts, no signposts.'[18]

Navigation in the desert with outdated maps, even if they had been produced by the famous Kitchener, was no easy matter. However, one solution adopted in 1917 was the use of wire-mesh 'roads', which assisted in both navigation and marching. One veteran remembered that the Battle of Gaza in 1917 was:

'…to me the climax of a walk of about 130 miles across the Sinai Desert – we left the Suez Canal knowing that eventually we were going to meet our friend

the Turk again after the Romani scrap – but we didn't know where it was to
be and that crossing was … made possible only because somebody had the
simple and brilliant idea of laying wire netting across the loose sand and that
helped us considerably.'[19]

While such methods could be useful on an approach march, they were of no help
in the Western Desert, where the majority of Middle Eastern battles were fought
during the Second World War. By 1940 soldiers did have access to good-quality
maps and the sun compass[20], which made the task of navigation much easier, but
one feature of all the desert fighting was the frequent confusion caused by map
errors and the inability to pinpoint a position in the middle of the desert.

Another reality of desert life was the scarcity of water and the discipline that had
to be enforced to cope with a meagre water ration. Ensuring that there was
sufficient water for the troops was a major task in both wars. One quartermaster
sergeant remembered the effort required to sustain Allenby's advance through the
Sinai in 1917:

'…now there were troops moving for that advance from all directions and
they all had to be watered. There were twenty miles of waterless desert to cross
and that water was carried by camels. On that particular occasion there were
over 20,000 camels carrying water alone.'[21]

Even with the best efforts of the engineers and the Army Service Corps to bring up
water and store it for use, water remained a constant preoccupation for most
soldiers. One Australian Light Horse trooper remembered that, 'Hunger never
worried us at any stage of the game but water did.'[22] Yet most soldiers found that,
with practice, they could survive on very little water. One veteran of Allenby's
campaigns related that:

'Then too there was the question of water and thirst. We had to discipline
ourselves to use only two pints of water a day … the troops had to learn to do
without it and they did. They can do it and they did do it.'[23]

Water supply for the Eighth Army was not based on camels but on trucks, which
eased the problem considerably. Nonetheless, the transport of water up to the front
remained a major task and water was still the most precious commodity consumed
by the army. Soldiers in the LRDG and SAS patrols who served in the deep desert
received the same ration as soldiers in the First World War – just 2 pints of water a
day. Ironically, the situation in Tobruk during its famous six-month siege in 1941
was slightly better, but still meagre:

'In Tobruk water was a scarce commodity at half a gallon per man per day, and
that was for drinking straight, as tea, for all ablutions and for washing clothes,
etc. One got used to it, but when someone came up from Alexandria with a
bottle of real water and a bottle of whisky the recipients drank the water neat
and left the whisky!'[24]

This Second World War anecdote was an echo of a truth discovered by a First World War veteran, who wrote that, 'Water is the staff of life in the desert, and its quality varies so much that half a pint of good water there is a gift of more value than a half dozen quarts of the best champagne in Europe.'[25]

Of course, these harsh climatic conditions had been present for centuries and the Bedouin tribespeople who inhabited the desert were inured to these difficulties. British troops also managed to adapt to the conditions. In fact, most soldiers adapted well to the desert conditions so that they could stand the heat of the day and the chill of the night, navigate themselves through the featureless terrain and cope with the strict rationing of water.

However, there were still some discomforts that most soldiers never really learned to live with effectively. The armies fighting in the desert found that no matter how carefully they disposed of the rubbish, detritus and waste that they inevitably produced, their rubbish dumps and latrines formed perfect breeding grounds for hordes of flies that followed the army wherever it went. This meant that the men could never be free from the attentions of these persistent insects. A First World War veteran explained that:

'...there were millions of flies, literally millions. They were in everything and on everything. They were in our food, they were in our clothing, they were in our ears, wherever we turned there were millions of flies. If you put a piece of paper down it would be black with flies in a few moments. We were living in bivouacs at the time and I had a little pet chameleon who seemed to appreciate the unlimited rations, but he made no difference whatsoever to the population of flies. They were simply intolerable.'[26]

Soldiers in the Second World War also kept chameleons as pets, but also realised the futility of trying to kill the flies:

'We did everything we could to reduce their population by trying to swat them, which was ridiculous, because it was hopeless. One thing we used to do was to burn up the guy ropes of the tents. They would congregate there after sundown and you could literally burn them, but it wouldn't make the slightest difference to the irritation of them next day. For every one you killed there seemed to be ten to take its place.'[27]

Flies, then, were a constant, ever-present and maddening discomfort. One common desert complaint that was exacerbated by the flies was the 'desert sore', which could develop from even a small scratch. The wound would not heal and could spread across the skin:

'Some people just developed these wretched sores and in the heat of the day they would be little rings of flies feeding, it was perfectly revolting, if you continually have to brush them away from the sore because it was difficult to cover, difficult to cover the sore itself.'[28]

While desert sores were an unpleasant, if relatively minor, complaint, one constant problem was dysentery, which could decimate an army faster than enemy action. The flies, feeding on refuse and the latrines, carried disease and dysentery to the men. One man remembered that, 'The heat, coupled with the flies, coupled with the effect of the flies on the health and the problems of dysentery and general sort of stomach upsets ... they pole-axed you, there was nothing you could do about it.'[29] Life in the desert, let alone combat, brought its own series of hazards.

Just as the terrain and climate conditions exerted their grip on the conduct of all of the campaigns, so did the iron laws of logistics. The desert could supply nothing of value to support an army, which meant that all of the armies sent to the Middle East experienced great difficulties in bringing up sufficient quantities of supplies for their needs. Ammunition came second only to the need for water, and this meant that the soldiers' rations took a fairly poor third. In the First World War fresh food was virtually unobtainable and soldiers had to subsist on biscuit and bully beef for days on end:

'At times we frequently had to go without decent food at all, the only thing we relied on were biscuits, and occasionally bully beef. We ate bully beef cold, we ate it stewed. The army biscuits were almost like chewing dog biscuits. After some weeks we heard that bread was coming up the line ... when the bread came up it looked just like gorgonzola cheese. To me it was uneatable.'[30]

Soldiers in the Second World War fared much better due to the motorisation of the logistic chain, although bully beef and biscuit still formed the bulk of their diet. Some troops even found themselves linked physically with the previous conflict – soldiers eating bully beef in 1942 found the date 1918 stamped on the tins! Soldiers still suffered from the unremitting diet, but their German opponents, subsisting on black bread and Italian tinned meat, known as 'Alter Man', fared worse. Even Rommel suffered badly from jaundice caused by the poor diet.[31]

While the relative scarcity of petrol – or any other flammable substance – meant that tea-drinking before or after action was rare during Allenby's campaign, the troops in the Second World War had the relative luxury of the regular desert 'brew-up'. A crew or section could boil water for tea with the aid of half a petrol tin filled with sand and petrol, and this became one of the rituals of the Eighth Army in the desert.

Another experience integral to soldiering in the desert was the sense of the unending monotony of life. An Australian Light Horseman who served in Sinai and Palestine remembered that, 'Life on the desert consisted of riding maybe on a patrol; you'd go out all day [and] come back at night to camp.' This same routine day after day led to monotony: 'It wasn't the fighting in the desert that worried the soldier, it was the monotony.'[32] Given this endless routine it was easy to lose track of time in the desert. One soldier recalled that:

'It was not until one of our platoon asked what day it was, that we realised no mention, record or check of days or dates had been kept by any ORs [Other Ranks]. It was yesterday, today and tomorrow, and that was sufficient when in uninhabited regions.'[33]

Losing track of the passage of time, and the seemingly unending time spent in the desert, could lead to psychological disorders, quite separate from reactions to battle. One man felt that:

'There's a sort of psychological complaint some chaps get after long exposure on the Blue called "desert weariness" ... for months now we've been cut off from nearly every aspect of civilised life, and every day has been cast in the same monotonous mould. The desert, omnipresent, so saturates consciousness that it makes the mind as sterile as itself... For weeks more, probably months, we shall have to go on bearing an unbroken succession of empty, ugly, insipid days.'[34]

The psychological roots of 'desert weariness' were not unique to the desert. Doctors had first diagnosed soldiers with the complaint of 'nostalgia' in 1678[35], as a reaction to the boredom of garrison duty and separation from home. This separation anxiety could affect men in every theatre of war, but soldiers do seem to have been more prone to the condition in the desert due to the barren and bleak nature of the terrain, and the complete isolation from civilisation.[36]

Yet soldiers this century could occasionally feel that they were in touch with home in a way impossible for soldiers in previous centuries. One signaller serving in Palestine in 1917 remembered that, by squeezing the best performance out of his wireless set:

'It was possible to get news even from England. One of the reasons why we were so welcome to the other personnel, particularly in the artillery, was that we could pick up news even from our station at Poldue in Cornwall and that was something that was appreciated very much by all those who were able to know how things were going at home and in other war areas.'[37]

While such broadcasts were informal and occasional in the First World War, by the Second World War there were radio stations in Cairo broadcasting to the troops in the desert, which helped to alleviate this sense of isolation. These radio stations also helped to develop a distinctive culture in the Eighth Army. The most famous song of the Desert War was 'Lili Marlene', a German song, which was picked up and enjoyed by the Eighth Army as well. 'Lili Marlene' was unique in that it was the theme song of both the German and British armies in the desert.

Desert warfare has always been very different from the nature of combat in Europe, and the campaigns fought in both World Wars were no exception. While desert terrain poses enormous problems in terms of distance, climate, water, supplies and navigation, it also provides opportunities in terms of space and freedom of mobility. The close, attritional nature of the struggle in Gallipoli, Salonika and on the Western Front during the Great War was not replicated in the Sinai or Palestine. Instead, the fighting was much more open and mobile and generally against lighter opposition. General Sir John Shea pointed out that:

'...there was a tremendous difference between fighting in France, and the fighting in Palestine. Because in France it was purely trench warfare. Hard work and frustration. You really could not see what you were doing. Whereas the great part of it was that you were in open warfare. It was a war of movement. You were keeping going. You could see what your troops were doing and you could use your reserves as you wished, when it was necessary. It was entirely different and it was a great happiness to fight there compared to the frustration of trench warfare in France.' [38]

Units that had become accustomed to the open, mobile fighting in Palestine found the Western Front an unpleasant change of environment. The 74th Yeomanry Division was transferred to France during the crisis of April-June 1918 and found its first taste of combat in France on 2 September 1918 altogether different from the conditions in Palestine.[39]

British troops in the Second World War also experienced the tactical opportunities offered by the wide open space of the desert:

'…the thing about desert warfare is the mobility, the fact that you could just go anywhere within your limits. You couldn't go too far south or you'd set off into the soft sands and you couldn't do that. You'd come to a dead halt. I suppose the mobility is the thing, the capacity to be able to continually outflank each other.'[40]

However, there was an important distinction in the nature of mobility between the First and Second World Wars. While tanks were used during the Battle of Gaza in 1917, and the Duke of Westminster's armoured car squadron was the first experiment with motorised warfare in the Western Desert, most soldiers in the First World War were restricted to the mobility offered by horses and their own legs. The Australian Light Horse gained fame for their ability to ride around the Turks – quite literally – but one British infantryman remembered that all his travels in the desert had been, 'All on foot. Never had a ride on a horse or anything… But I think I walked every inch of the way from the Suez Canal, Kantara, right up to Jerusalem. Every inch was covered on foot. Not in one day – not in two days either!'[41]

While the soldiers of the First World War were restricted to age-old forms of transport, the British Army that fought in the desert in the Second World War was almost wholly motorised. The mechanisation of the Army, and the opportunity for mobility that this conferred in an area devoid of natural barriers, meant that the fighting in the Western Desert in the Second World War was more fluid, chaotic and confusing than any before. During the 'Crusader' battle in November 1941, one soldier's battalion met with German tanks:

'The tanks fire a few shots after, but we're soon out of range, and keep moving at fair speed for ten miles, with hundreds of other vehicles streaming in concourse. It looks like a stampede, but everything's under control. Apparently these "scarpers" are accepted desert technique; when there's no cover at all and no particular bit of ground is tactically worth much sacrifice, getting thrown up against heavily superior enemy forces leaves no option but to clear out, the quicker the better – discretion proving the better part of valour every time.'[42]

This unparalleled mobility also had some unforeseen effects. With few features or places worth fighting for (with the exception of Tobruk), the armies could seize and relinquish vast areas of ground in a matter of days. As each army advanced, its supply lines became stretched, and its spearheads consequently weaker, while the enemy, retreating on to his supply lines became correspondingly stronger. This see-saw effect led to the famous 'Benghazi stakes' in which the armies found themselves advancing and retreating over the same desert five times in the space of two years.

The mechanisation of the armies in the Second World War was only one area of contrast. During the Palestine campaign of 1917-18, the Australian Light Horse had thought nothing of mounted charges against Turkish trenches, as one veteran related:

'The Turks, on the whole, right through the whole campaign, didn't seem to like the steel – you were safer with them at 100 yards than you were at 600 yards. At 600 yards they were wonderfully good shots and they'd shoot you right up to the trenches, but the minute you got amongst them with the steel it was always a surrender.'[43]

While the Australian Light Horse gained a fine reputation for the speed and daring of its mounted actions in Palestine, such exploits were a thing of the past by the Second World War. An episode during the Eritrean campaign demonstrated just how much had changed after the 20-year interval. During the advance to Keren, the headquarters of Gazelle Force, a reconnaissance unit commanded by Colonel Messervy, was charged from the rear by a squadron of Eritrean cavalry:

'Out of the scrub they burst, galloping furiously and throwing those little Italian hand grenades at anyone they could get. The guns were rapidly turned round and opened fire at point blank range. Gazelle headquarters dived into their slit trenches and started to fire with everything available. But the charge was stopped less than thirty yards from the guns and the few surviving cavalrymen fled, pursued by an armoured car. Out of the sixty men who made the charge, twenty-five dead and sixteen wounded were left on the ground. It was a most gallant affair. It demonstrated beyond all doubt that this obsolete arm could not be used to attack troops armed with modern weapons.'[44]

Horsed cavalry had had its day by 1939, but a mounted Yeomanry cavalry brigade was sent to Palestine in 1939. However, by the time these troops saw action at Alamein, their horses had been replaced by armoured steeds.[45]

While Allenby's men were familiar with the names of the settlements they fought over in Palestine, the featureless nature of the Western Desert meant that the few landmarks and towns in the area took on heightened significance during the campaign fought in the Second World War. Benghazi, Tobruk and Mersa Matruh became household names in Britain, but there was little to remind soldiers of past military history. Bir Hacheim, identified only by two hummocks in the middle of the desert, had been the site of the rescue of the prisoners from HMS *Tara* in 1915 during the Senussi campaign, but gained greater fame during the Battle of Gazala in May 1942 for the tenacious defence of the French Foreign Legion.[46] Just as their forebears had named trenches on the Western Front after familiar domestic landmarks, so soldiers in the desert identified positions with familiar names to bring some element of home to the barren landscape. The Guards defensive position or 'box' during the Battle of Gazala, known as 'Knightsbridge', is one of the most famous. But although one of the fiercest tank battles of the Desert War raged there, there was nothing to distinguish this piece of desert from another apart from the name.

One unique feature of the Desert War in the Second World War was the development of the 'Krieg ohne Hass' (War without Hate). With the battle areas largely devoid of population (with the exception of the townspeople of Benghazi, Bardia and Tobruk), the armies could concentrate simply on fighting one another. Although the fighting was certainly intense and bloody, a mutual respect developed between the armies to the extent that Rommel became an almost mythical figure amongst the British troops. This spirit also manifested itself in the generally correct and proper treatment given to prisoners and wounded. While this was obviously a clearer distinction for the Germans, who enacted such brutality on the Eastern Front, it also provided a contrast with the desert campaigns of the First World War. British soldiers respected the fighting qualities of the Turkish soldier in much the same way that they admired the skill of the German soldiers 20 years later. General Sir John Shea emphasised that he 'respected the Turk as a soldier, and was always careful to make my plans as best I could … I thought he was a good stout-hearted soldier, and he fought well.'[47] While there was a mutual respect between foes in the First World War, there was no development of a similar spirit of a 'War without Hate'. Turkish treatment of British prisoners could be appalling and this seems to have been reflected in the harsher style of war between the two armies. One British soldier tasked with the capture of some Turkish machine-guns led by German officers related that:

> 'When I gave the word, we all dashed forward… There wasn't one left alive after we'd finished with them. We captured the guns and finished them off. And the German officers, they had the first packet, believe me.'[48]

Although such an attitude to fighting was also common on the Western Front in the First World War, this kind of incident does not accord with the idea of a spirit of 'chivalry' engendered by desert fighting.

Yet even though there are numerous contrasts between the two wars in the desert, the similarities remain more important. Both armies experienced the hardships of the desert and the sense of isolation, intensified by distance and enhanced by the harsh climate. Both developed a distinctive identity as desert warriors, quite separate from the wider identities found on the Western Front in the First World War, or of Slim's Fourteenth Army in Burma in the Second World War. Both armies shared the experience of defeat and eventual victory, and this veteran's account of taking Turkish prisoners in Palestine in 1918 could easily have been an Eighth Army veteran speaking of O'Connor's offensive of 1940-41 or the final pursuit in 1942:

> 'And the troops went forward then and of course captured prisoners on the way, just like that. Thousands and thousands of them being captured. They were all fed up with the war and everything else. We were just enjoying ourselves then. They were on the run.'[49]

Perhaps the final experience of victory after hardship was the most important common bond running through the two wars in the desert. Yet some men could feel bitter about their personal experience in the Desert War. Peter Bates stated that, 'My own involvement was a 12-hour engagement with the enemy that ended in capture, and like many who served at Alamein, for all I accomplished I might as well have stayed at home.'[50] Perhaps the words of a veteran of the Eritrean campaign, written in 1941, sum up the experience of many in the numerous campaigns of the Desert War:

> 'I have seen the most ghastly sights and heard noises which I shall remember to the end of my days. I've seen unparalleled bravery and self-sacrifice and have seen all the horrors of modern warfare magnified a hundredfold by the intense heat, flies and filth. There's nothing glorious about it at all, only stark reality.'[51]

Notes on contributors

Dr Niall J.A. Barr, Joint Services Command and Staff College, UK.
Dr Barr is a Lecturer at King's College London, based at the Joint Services Command and Staff College. He is an authority on the history of the British veterans' movement and has a deep interest in the history of both world wars. Having recently worked with J.P. Harris on a collaborative study, Amiens to the Armistice: The B.E.F. in the Hundred Days Campaign 8 August-11 November 1918, he is currently researching the Alamein campaign of 1942.

Recommended reading

Black, Donald, *Red Dust: An Australian Trooper in Palestine* (London: Jonathan Cape, 1931)

Caccia-Dominioni, Paulo, *Alamein 1933-1962: An Italian Story* (London: George Allen & Unwin, 1966)

Crimp, R. L., *The Diary of a Desert Rat* (London: Leo Cooper, 1971)

Crisp, Robert, *Brazen Chariots: An Account of Tank Warfare in the Western Desert November-December*

1941 (London: Frederick Muller, 1959)

Dinning, Hector and McBey, James, *Nile to Aleppo: With the Light Horse in the Middle East* (London: Allen & Unwin, 1920)

Gilbert, Adrian (ed), *The Imperial War Museum Book of the Desert War 1940-1942* (London: Sidgwick & Jackson, 1992)

Gilbert, Vivian, *The Romance of the Last Crusade* (London: D. Appleton-Century, 1935)

Graham, Domick, *Against Odds: Reflections on the Experiences of the British Army, 1914-45* (Basingstoke: Macmillan, 1999)

Hughes, C. E., *Above and Beyond Palestine* (London: Ernest Benn Ltd, 1930)

Warner, Philip, *Alamein* (London: William Kimber, 1979)

Notes

1   Carless, 4052/B/B, Sound Archive, Imperial War Museum (SA, IWM), London
2   Leslie Joseph Mathews, 8232/08, SA, IWM
3   General Sir John Shea, 328/1, 4227/C/B, SA, IWM
4   51st Highland Division War Diary, 23 October 1942, WO169/4164, Public Record Office, Kew
5   T. E. Lawrence, *The Seven Pillars of Wisdom: A Triumph* (London: Jonathan Cape, 1935)
6   Major D. A. Blake, 7392/11, SA, IWM
7   E. A. Woolley, 316/08, SA, IWM
8   On 'Brightstar 99', the joint United States-Egyptian exercise held in Egypt, it was ordered that all US personnel had to be given the opportunity of visiting the Pyramids.
9   Ben Coutts, *A Scotsman's War* (Edinburgh: The Mercat Press, 1995) p41
10 Frank Dey, *Swinging the Lamp: Recollections of the Fleet Air Arm 1939-1945* (Edinburgh: Frankin Press, 1993) pp41-2
11 James Lucas, *War in the Desert: The Eighth Army at El Alamein* (London: Arms & Armour, 1982) p49
12 John Bolton, 4029/B/B, SA, IWM
13 Ibid
14 P. W. Pitt, *Royal Wilts: The History of the Royal Wiltshire Yeomanry, 1920-1945* (London: Burrup, Mathieson & Company, 1946) p149
15 S. C. Rolls, *Steel Chariots in the Desert* (London: Jonathan Cape, 1937) p32
16 R. L. Crimp, *The Diary of a Desert Rat* (London: Leo Cooper, 1971) p18
17 Brigadier R. B. Scott DSO, 008235/05, SA, IWM
18 John Bolton, 4029/B/B, SA, IWM
19 Carless, 4052/B/B, SA., IWM
20 Invented by Major Ralph Bagnold, creator of the LRDG during his explorations of the Western Desert in the 1930s
21 John Bolton, 4029/B/B, SA, IWM
22 Pollock, 4200, SA, IWM
23 John Bolton, 4029/B/B, SA, IWM
24 Ben Coutts, op cit, p45
25 S. C. Rolls, op cit, p99
26 John Bolton, 4029/B/B, SA, IWM
27 Major D. A. Blake, 7392/11, SA, IWM
28 Ibid
29 Ibid
30 E. A. Woolley, 316/08, SA, IWM
31 F. W. Von Mellenthin, *Panzer Battles: A Study of the Employment of Armour in the Second World War* (London: Cassell & Co, 1955) pp146-7
32 Pollock, 4200, SA, IWM
33 Maurice Merritt, *Eighth Army Driver* (Tunbridge Wells: Midas Books, 1981) p49
34 R. L. Crimp, op cit, p29
35 Richard Gabriel, *The Painful Field: The Psychiatric Dimension of Modern War* (Westport, Ct:

Greenwood Press, 1988) p15
36 Robert H. Ahrenfeldt, *Psychiatry in the British Army in the Second World War* (London: Routledge & Kegan Paul, 1958) p180
37 E. A. Woolley, 316/08, SA, IWM
38 General Sir John Shea, 328/1, 4227/C/B, SA, IWM
39 C. H. Dudley Ward, *The 74th Yeomanry Division in Syria and France* (London: John Murray, 1922) pp208-18
40 Major D. A. Blake, 7392/11, SA, IWM
41 Leslie Joseph Mathews, 8232/08, SA, IWM
42 R. L. Crimp, op cit, p52
43 Pollock, 4200, SA, IWM
44 Brigadier R. B. Scott DSO, 008235/05, SA, IWM
45 P. W. Pitt, op cit, pp119-20
46 S. C. Rolls, op cit, p54
47 General Sir John Shea, 328/1, 4227/C/B, SA, IWM
48 Leslie Joseph Mathews, 8232/08, SA, IWM
49 Ibid
50 Peter Bates, *Dance of War: The Story of the Battle of Egypt* (London: Leo Cooper, 1992) p3
51 Major D. A. Blake, 7392/11, SA, IWM

Chapter 8

War in the Pacific

Eric Bergerud

Between December 1941 and August 1945 the United States and its allies fought an unrelenting war against the Japanese Empire. Although only one portion of what Japanese leaders called the Greater East Asian War, Pacific operations were certainly the most decisive in the military sphere. Even though more people died in China and South East Asia than in the Pacific, it was Allied victory in the Pacific that determined the nature and duration of the overall conflict.

Although East Asia had been racked by tumult for decades before 1914, it was spared the military ferocity of the First World War. Tsing Tao in 1914, still less Rabaul in the same year, simply do not register on any scale of comparison with the warfare experienced in the Pacific a generation and a half later. Nevertheless, the Great War did much to shape the military geography of the Second World War. Japan seized German possessions in China and the Central Pacific. Many of these islands became battlefields when the US drove into the Central Pacific in late 1943. While Japan was picking German plums, Australia was also active, taking north-west New Guinea and the nearby Bismarck Archipelago, which included the islands of New Ireland, New Britain and Bougainville. Much of this area early in the Second World War fell to Japan. Centred at their great bastion at Rabaul on New Britain, the Japanese developed a base system in the Bismarcks that served as a major bulwark of their maritime defence line protecting the precious resources in the East Indies. Efforts to take or neutralise Rabaul drove on the campaigns in both New Guinea and the Solomon Islands and constituted the major Allied effort in the Pacific for a year and a half.

Inter-war events in Europe also had a crucial bearing on the road to war in the Pacific. Japan's aggression in Manchuria and later against China would have been unthinkable without the paralysis caused in the Western world by the Depression and later the looming war clouds in Europe. Hitler's early triumphs accelerated events tremendously. The Japanese Government, controlled by the military and supported by militant expansionists, saw the defeat of France and Britain's apparent doom as a priceless opportunity to move in and occupy mineral-rich South East Asia, then controlled by the European empires. Because of antagonism over China and the strategic position of the American-controlled Philippine Islands, a move into South East Asia would also almost certainly mean war with the United States. When Hitler struck Russia, again there was delight in Japan.

However, the Japanese Army insisted that it keep its core on the Manchurian border to take advantage of a Soviet collapse. This meant that the Imperial Headquarters would part with only 11 divisions for 'southern operations', which the army considered the responsibility of the Japanese Navy.

It is important to understand the relationship between the war in Europe and the Pacific War. On the one hand the wars were essentially separate conflicts. Although allies on paper, Germany and Japan never co-ordinated action in a meaningful way. On the other hand, Japan was absolutely dependent upon a German victory. If Hitler went down to defeat, Japan would face a massive array of enemies alone. Indeed, given a German defeat, it is best to view the course of the Pacific War in terms of nature and duration, not outcome. For Japan there was cruel irony in that two days after Japanese carrier aircraft attacked Pearl Harbor, the Red Army launched its devastating counter-attack outside Moscow.

Japanese juggernaut

In the short term Tokyo experienced victory beyond expectation. Japan's strike against Pearl Harbor was a spectacular success in the tactical realm. By May 1942 imperial forces had seized American bases on their perimeter, crushed the British in Malaya, moved into Burma, pushed into the South Pacific and finally captured the Philippines. Most importantly, the resource-rich islands of the Dutch East Indies were in Japan's hands. Looking at the map, it had conducted a spectacularly successful military campaign. This cavalcade of victories came quickly and intoxicated Japan. If these gains could be maintained through an eventual peace agreement, a Japanese empire would have come into existence via the semi-divine imperial sword.

Assessing these early Japanese victories is important in judging Japan's overall war effort. Closely defined, the Japanese armed forces displayed every major military virtue in the grim craft of war. Like Hitler in Europe, the Japanese could not have picked a better time to begin their war. The hard-pressed British were crippled by strategic muddle over the defence of Singapore. Similar muddle existed in Washington concerning the Philippines. With the Pacific Fleet and Britain's naval task force destroyed in the first days of war, Allied naval forces were pitifully small when compared to their Japanese opponents and were easily overwhelmed. On land the bulk of Allied forces consisted of ill-trained colonial levies. With a few notable exceptions these units were unable to face the Japanese in serious combat. The Japanese Army's major opposition came from a very small number of Regular Allied ground units. British and Australian units in Malaya were incompetently deployed, vulnerable to infiltration and were seriously deficient in air power.

Although obscured by the euphoria of victory, Japanese commanders might have looked at land operations against the Americans with concern. American ground forces on the Philippines conducted a skilled retreat to the Bataan Peninsula. Supported by artillery and a few tanks, these forces mauled the first force of Japanese invaders. Although Japanese victory was inevitable, it took heavy reinforcements to accomplish it. American capitulation in May was due more to a collapse in logistics than military defeat.

Some sober Japanese officers like Admiral Isoroku Yamamoto, Chief of the Imperial Combined Fleet (the Navy's core of operational warships), realised that the Japanese victory was far from complete and that Tokyo's easy victories were not likely to be repeated. Disappointingly, neither Washington nor London showed any signs whatsoever of defeatism. What Tokyo's pessimists partially sensed was that local Allied weaknesses had allowed a string of Japanese victories that were so easy that they masked serious deficiencies in all of the Japanese armed forces. Within a year, all of these weaknesses would be evident to both sides.

Nevertheless, their lightning victories gave the Japanese an aura of invincibility for a brief moment. At the front, Allied morale was shaken. Indeed, it is difficult to overrate the shock effect when explaining early Japanese victories. Jim Morehead, soon one of the first American fighter 'aces', was one of a small number of American fighter pilots sent to aid the Dutch against the Japanese onslaught upon Java. Later Morehead described the odd chemistry at work in a unit that concludes it is beaten:

'Whereas youth is normally optimistic about fate, forever feeling that if bad things happen, they will never happen to me, now there was a reversal. Unlike any combat circumstance I was ever exposed to, it switched. The attitude changed to, "I am a goner, the next one lost will be me, I know it will be me." How many times I heard, "We're just flying tow targets. We are all on suicide missions!" Such conclusions were only logical. Anyone's arithmetic can figure out how many missions you are likely to last if ten go out and only five come back. While an alert shack is normally boisterous with laughter and wisecracks, silent anxiety was the mood in those days.'[1]

In the rush of events the Japanese made a tremendous blunder. Tokyo could never decide how to deal with Australia. However, the splendid harbour at Rabaul in the Bismarcks was an obvious target and was seized, along with some nearby points in New Guinea in January 1942. However, the Imperial Army's parsimony with ground troops came into play. In January the remaining Australian bases on New Guinea were almost undefended and could have been seized with a few imperial battalions. Had Tokyo done this all of New Guinea would have been in Japanese hands. It is very doubtful that, given their limited naval resources, the Allies would have attempted an amphibious attack from northern Australia against southern New Guinea. With foresight, Tokyo could have shut down the New Guinea front before it started. As it happened, the Australians reinforced Port Moresby in south-eastern New Guinea and the Americans launched a carrier raid in the area.

This potential weakness was very important. Japan had made brilliant plans on starting the war but had no clear road toward ending it. As an attack against the United States mainland was out of the question, Tokyo planned to establish a maritime perimeter of air bases, which, supported by Combined Fleet, the fighting core of the Japanese Navy, could guard their new empire. Any major break in this chain, however, left vulnerable either the oil and minerals required for industry or the Japanese home islands themselves.

Finally realising the potential danger from Moresby, the Imperial Navy formed a powerful force to attack these targets. By this time the United States was firmly committed to defending Australia. In May 1942 the Japanese carriers protecting the invasion fleet met their American counterparts in the Coral Sea. Tactical laurels went to Japan, but imperial forces suffered serious losses and the all-important invasion of Moresby was postponed. In the meantime two crack Japanese fleet carriers were out of action for Yamamoto's grand plan for the Central Pacific, which began three weeks later.

In keeping with the central tenet of Japanese fleet operations, Yamamoto was eager to entice the remainder of the American Pacific Fleet, particularly its aircraft carriers, into a battle of annihilation. In late May, Combined Fleet threw everything it had into a complex and powerful drive toward the north-central Pacific designed to force a battle. In early June, Combined Fleet's carrier force was mauled at Midway.

Trench warfare in the South Pacific

In most accounts of the Pacific War the Battle of Midway is considered the 'turning point'. This is true only to a very limited extent. Had Yamamoto been successful in destroying the American fleet, Washington would have had trouble. However, the nature of naval battle in the Pacific had been badly obscured by Pearl Harbor and the destruction of Task Force Z off Singapore. The engagement in the Coral Sea proved a much more reliable indicator of results. If enough ships were at sea and enough aircraft in the air, both sides were going to suffer losses. Luck showed a tendency to even itself out. (The 4-1 carrier loss suffered by Japan at Midway was largely reversed a few months later when Japanese submarines sank one US fleet carrier, and damaged a second carrier and a precious fast battleship.) Taken together, the two carrier battles in the fall of 1942 (Eastern Solomons and Santa Cruz) were a draw. Carriers played an important role in important moments during the early battles for the South Pacific, but in essence they had soon committed an unintentional suicide pact. Between October 1942 (the Battle of Santa Cruz) and June 1944 (the Battle of the Philippine Sea) there were no major carrier actions.

For well over a year the Pacific War revolved around land bases. Implicit in this geometry was an unprecedented number of engagements between surface ships. Somewhere between the firepower of warships and aircraft were thousands of infantry facing a fearsome enemy and an inhuman environment.

The South Pacific was the most unlikely battlefield of the Second World War. (I define the 'South Pacific' as did the natives: a vast area including New Guinea, the Bismarcks, the Solomons, and New Hebrides Islands.) There was nothing in the entire area, New Guinea included, that had intrinsic value except, of course, Australia. The issue was forced in the first months of the war, with Japan victorious everywhere, when Franklin Roosevelt decided to reinforce Australia, even at the expense of 'Europe First'. Australia received precious US infantry, US air units and logistic support for an airbase network to support New Guinea. Roosevelt ordered General Douglas MacArthur to take command of forces in the theatre. On its part, Canberra withdrew home two veteran divisions from the Middle East immediately, and a third on the way. In addition, Australian territorial divisions began receiving very serious training. Canberra naturally concentrated its forces where Australians lived – the south-eastern quadrant of the country. In fact, the Australian Government had no idea what Japan might do. Neither had the Japanese.

MacArthur, given the precious toe-hold taken by the enemy at Port Moresby, was convinced that the war should be brought north. In this he was supported by the Australian Government. When the two precious veteran Australian divisions finished reforming in Queensland, both were sent to New Guinea to face Japan's last ferocious assault. They were joined by an American division and a growing Allied air force. The United States and Australia had, in fact, reacted to the Japanese threat with startling speed and keen purpose. Japan's military honeymoon proved very short.

By summer 1942 the Japanese Army, in contrast to its stance six months before, believed that New Guinea must be secured. In early summer an elite Japanese regiment, usually called South Seas Detachment, began an overland assault from Buna on the north coast of New Guinea toward Port Moresby on the south. Between the attackers and their target lay the Owen Stanley Mountains. After some bad moments the Australian defence stiffened. By September the Japanese force was facing malnutrition. A Japanese amphibious attack at nearby Milne Bay in late August failed badly and constituted Japan's first major land defeat of the war. In September Tokyo decided that South Seas Detachment must retreat to the north coast. In hot pursuit, the Australians mauled the Japanese in November. The retreat, however, led the armies to one of the worst battlefields on earth at and near Buna.

Before South Seas Detachment headed over the Owen Stanley Mountains, the US Navy decided to take advantage of the Midway victory and ordered one of the most audacious and successful amphibious campaigns in history – the invasion of Guadalcanal. Prior to its launch, the Navy's newly made construction branch, the 'Seabees', created vital bases in the New Hebrides Islands. Soon American intelligence learned that Japan was building an airfield on Guadalcanal and a frantic pace overtook preparations. On 7 August 1942 an Allied task force, including three aircraft carriers, escorted 12,000 men ashore on Guadalcanal and the small island of Tulagi. Marines pushed away some Japanese-led construction workers on Guadalcanal and occupied the nearly completed airfield. The small Japanese garrison at Tulagi, foreshadowing the extraordinary brutality that characterised the Pacific War, fought to the last man.

As it slowly became clear that the American force represented a major operation and not a raid, Yamamoto and others surveyed their situation with growing concern. The Australians and Americans were building up in New Guinea and northern Australia. With the Marines in the Solomon Islands, a two-pronged thrust was aimed at Rabaul. If the Allies could get by Rabaul, there was nothing to stop a thrust into the Indies. What appeared to outsiders as two separate campaigns – New Guinea and the Solomons – was seen as a single blow by Japan that threatened to unhinge its entire position. The threat was clear, but the response was slow and unco-ordinated.

The soldiers and airmen who entered the South Pacific encountered some of the world's most malignant terrain. There were no roads, no real towns, no sanitary facilities, no electricity, no supply of fresh food and no European women. The indigenous population served both sides as porters, and some assisted the famous Australian coast watchers. For the most part, however, the civilians were bewildered onlookers to events they did not understand and in which they had no obvious stake.

What did exist was a miserably hot and humid climate that generated a medical nightmare for interlopers. Malaria was rampant and caused more casualties than battle. Tropical diseases of all types posed baffling problems. Dysentery was a constant danger because of poor sanitation. 'Rot', a tropical relative to the Great War's 'trench foot', threatened to turn the smallest cut into a serious infection. Combat units did a good job maintaining morale under these daunting conditions, but stress was undeniable. (The rate of psychological breakdown among US forces was much worse in the South Pacific than any other theatre in the Second World War.)

Situated directly on the equator, the South Pacific was above all home of what an earlier generation called 'the jungle'. American soldier Robert Kennington described it:

'Jungle was really rough. We were hit by the heat, mosquitos, leeches and a little bit of everything else. Guadalcanal was about 96 miles long by 35 miles wide. Except along the beach and the top of the ridges there was nothing but jungle. The jungle had big trees that grew about 100 feet high. Vines grew out of them and dropped to the ground. Some vines grew as wide as your leg. We called them "Wait A Minute Vines". They had big hooks on them like a rooster spur. When you tried to get through on patrol and ran into one of those vines you either stopped or you were cut up. When tangled you backed out. You learned not to try to bull through them because those hooks were like a razor. I still have scars from them. In the afternoon you'd really notice a kind of dead smell. Probably from all the decaying matter. Mosquitos were so thick you could wipe them off your arm in handfuls. You wade through the rivers and you'd come out with leeches you didn't even know were there until you felt a sting. You'd look down and there was this creature on your leg full of blood.'[2]

If anything, New Guinea was more daunting than the Solomons. The Australian and Japanese soldiers that crossed the Kokoda Trail traversed an area with trees so tall that the sky was dim at noon. On the coast, combat soldiers confronted the horrid New Guinea mangrove swamp. In 1942 an Australian coast watcher forwarded a description of where the Mambare River reaches the sea. This point was a few miles north of the miserable battlefield near the pitiful settlement of Buna:

'The Mambare debouches into the sea between low, muddy banks along which nipa palms stand crowded knee-deep in the water. Behind the nipa palms, mangroves grow, their foliage a darker green dado above the nipa fronds. Here and there a creek mouth shows, the creek a tunnel in the mangroves with dark tree trunks for sides, supported on a maze of gnarled, twisted, obscene roots standing in the oozy mud. Branches and leaves are overhead, through which the sun never penetrates to the black water, the haunt of coldly evil crocodiles.'[3]

Mobility through the jungle was severely limited. Most movement took place along paths made by native peoples or animals. As the Japanese found out to their grief, moving through the jungle itself made co-ordinated operations almost impossible and utterly exhausted troops prior to battle. Consequently, 'control' was a very abstract term in the South Pacific. One side or the other would seek to control strategic points – almost always airfields. The bulk of the terrain, however, was unoccupied. In this bleak environment, if an objective could be isolated through gaining air dominance and thus control of the sea lanes, it would be put under siege. If besieged, the defenders became immediately a wasting asset. If the attackers wanted the position occupied, starvation of the defending garrison soon became one of their most potent weapons. The Allies soon learned that it was better to bypass the defenders, rendering them irrelevant as military forces.

Although the campaign lasted nearly two years, the Japanese lost the war in the South Pacific in the first six months. I have already noted the imperial retreat up the Kokoda Trail. This was followed by a miserable siege of some 8,000 Japanese soldiers, sailors and engineers near the village of Buna. An American division involved was effectively finished as a fighting force by January 1943 when the Japanese garrison finally perished. Even experienced Australian troops found the area a nightmare and suffered more casualties in that zone than anywhere else in the Pacific.

Guadalcanal was an equal disaster for Tokyo; there (and at Buna) the Japanese command structure showed serious defects. The US Navy had gained rough equality in terms of strength in carriers, but remained inferior in all other warship types. If they stretched their range, Zeros could escort bombers from Rabaul to Guadalcanal. Had Tokyo ordered Yamamoto to hit Guadalcanal with everything available, including major ground reinforcements, it is very possible that Japan could have isolated the Marine garrison and destroyed it. Such a move would have been risky with the American carriers still about, but an American defeat might well have caused Pentagon believers in 'Europe First' to shut down offensive operations in the Pacific for an extended period – exactly what Tokyo needed. Conversely, Japan could have accepted the loss of Guadalcanal and chosen a more favourable battlefield closer to Rabaul. In practice it fell between two stools. Japan was determined to recapture Guadalcanal, but tried to do it with minimum forces when an all-out effort was required.

Yamamoto ordered major naval reinforcements and slowly landed a sizeable force of infantry. However, the Americans, holding the only air base on Guadalcanal, could help to protect their own supply convoys and make extremely risky the embarkation of Japanese men and supplies from proper troop transports. Thus, although the Japanese landed a large number of men from small ships and barges, they were always desperately short of artillery, ammunition, medicine and food. Trying to compensate for superior US firepower with spirit and guile, the

Japanese launched a number of night ground assaults on the Marine perimeter. All were crushed by American firepower and courage.

While the ground and air struggle at Guadalcanal was taking place, both sides established the pace of naval operations that existed with some variation throughout the Pacific War. The great fleet engagement that mesmerised a generation on both sides of the Pacific would not take place. Instead, aircraft proved mortal enemies to the most powerful warships during the day, making airbases the most important places in the Pacific. At night, if the fleets were close enough, warships could engage in violent and helter-skelter night surface actions.

Also, the many battles that took place, including all of the carrier engagements of the Pacific War, dealt with the attack or protection of an invasion fleet. This did not fit with pre-war doctrine, particularly in Japan. In 'classic' actions like Tsushima or Jutland, fleet fought fleet unencumbered with troop convoys. During the Pacific War there was not even a small Jutland. In each clash, one side was trying to bring in troop ships and the other side was trying to keep them out. Even Midway, despite Yamamoto's intentions, fits this description.

The two carrier battles of the South Pacific and all of the night surface actions of 1942 were directly connected with troop reinforcement to Guadalcanal. These were deadly affairs. The US Navy lost nearly 5,000 men killed off Guadalcanal, several times the number of infantry deaths due to action. Japanese manpower and tonnage losses were worse. The major work off the well-named 'Iron Bottom Sound' off Guadalcanal, the graveyard for nearly 50 warships from both sides, was done by the cruisers and destroyers of the US and imperial fleets in night battles. The Japanese proved for a time to be better at night combat. Superior Japanese training proved more valuable than early American radar, and US destroyers, submarines and aircraft were crippled by miserable torpedoes until late 1943.

Ted Blahnik was a crewman on the American cruiser *Helena* and participated in one of the largest naval battles off Guadalcanal in November 1942. A three-day affair, the Imperial Navy deployed a large force, including two battleships, intended to bombard into oblivion American air units at Guadalcanal. With their small window of superiority, Tokyo planned to land two more divisions with large troop transports and destroy the Marines. It was a plan by the Japanese that should have been tried two months earlier, but it resulted in a naval bloodbath, as recalled by Blahnik:

'My battle station was on a 20mm anti-aircraft mount. Like most ships then, Helena had seen its share of air attacks. When planes struck, I cannot remember fear. Everyone was so busy there was hardly time to think, although you got a little shaky after the action was over. It was very different when Helena went in on the night of Friday the 13th, 1942. I was still at my 20mm, but we all knew that anti-aircraft weapons would play no part of the battle. Instead we were passive observers. Because we weren't doing anything, all of us were scared as hell – inactivity does that. The battle was extraordinary. At night the main armaments firing like crazy and emitting huge sheets of flame from every gun. The noise was deafening. When a large shell leaves a gun at night, the heat of the barrel gives it a glow that you can see as it flies off. In the

distance you could see other ships firing and searchlights scanning for the
enemy. Everyone fired at everyone and we later found out that some of our
ships had been firing at friendly vessels. Ships blew up or caught fire. All of
this took place in a relatively short period of time and men who watched
things but didn't shoot were caught between a deep fear and tremendous awe.
We lost two admirals and several ships. What was left of our task force headed
for home in the early morning. We had, however, left one sinking Japanese
battleship and other victims.'[4]

Blahnik's description was accurate. Two nights later the fleets came together again
and the Japanese had the indignity of losing a second battleship. Imperial
destroyers wrought terrible havoc, and not for the last time. Nevertheless, the
Japanese troop convoy heading to Guadalcanal was obliterated by American
airmen. Accepting the obvious, Japan ordered an evacuation of Guadalcanal in
late January 1943 at the same time that Buna was in its death agony. (Ominously,
so was the German force at Stalingrad.) East and West, the Empire had been
defeated and would never again make another major offensive move.

By the time Guadalcanal and Buna were finally cleared, the terrible dynamic of
ground combat in the Pacific War was all too obvious. Since the war, scholars have
often attempted to ascribe the extraordinary ferocity of combat in the Pacific to
racism on both sides. No doubt an abstract racism added fuel to the fire and
contributed greatly to the American and Canadian Governments' shameful
decision forcibly to relocate citizens and residents of Japanese descent living on
the West Coast to camps inland. However, at the point of fire, grim lessons learned
on the battlefield, many sadly true, were far more important than pre-war racial
antagonism in turning the conflict between the United States and Japan into
something resembling a war of annihilation.

At the root of the terrible dynamic of savagery in the Pacific War was the unique
and tragic military ethos propagated by the Japanese Government and military in
the generations before Pearl Harbor. By 1941 Japan was the most intensely
militarised nation in the world. Military service or training was a part of life from
cradle to grave. The time spent in these programmes in any given year was often
not great. Yet indoctrination and discipline were stressed, as were the twin notions
of self-sacrifice for the nation and obedience to the Emperor.

In the famous Imperial Rescript to Soldiers and Sailors promulgated by the
Emperor Meiji in 1882 (and carried by every Japanese fighting man in the Second
World War) a set of virtues similar to the traditional samurai code of bushido was
enumerated to serve as a guide for the Japanese soldier. The paramount duty was
loyalty, even at the cost of one's life: 'Duty is weightier than a mountain, while
death is lighter than a feather.' In the same period the Emperor dedicated the
Yasukuni shrine in Tokyo, a place where the Meiji and his successors came to pray
for the spirits of those who died in the service of the Emperor. Thus, a connection
was made between the military, the people and the Emperor. Over the years, this
connection took on an increasingly mystical quality, initially generated by pride,
eventually by desperation.

These conditions had important military ramifications. Many Japanese officers realised that their army could not hope to match the firepower of a Western army. The Japanese therefore were forced to make the best of a bad situation. They did so by trying to develop advanced infantry tactics, and by increasing indoctrination through personal example and spiritual training.

It is essential to understand the Japanese concept of 'spirit'; it did much to shape the nature of battle in the Pacific. Educators, following government guidance, taught Japanese youth that they belonged to a special race that was culturally and morally superior to the decadent and materialistic West. Officers and nationalist educators passed on to recruits their contempt for American and European soldiers. (The Japanese defeats suffered in 1939 against the Red Army were a closely kept secret.) The spectacular victories at the start of the war seemed to confirm the lessons learned in school and training camp.

But the notion of 'spirit' had a deeper connotation. It included the belief that the human will could surmount physical circumstance. Japanese officers taught their men, and most themselves believed, that they could do things no other army could simply because Japanese troops would not be denied. All Japanese recruits knew of great acts of heroism in both the distant and recent past of Japanese history. Most icons had one thing in common: they and their followers died in battle. Death in battle was portrayed as an honour to the family and a transcendental act on the part of the individual. Surrender was a disgrace to the soldier, and a disgrace to the family. No doubt some soldiers believed government propaganda that the enemy would butcher them if they were captured. However, for the most part, there can be no doubt that the astounding physical courage shown by Japanese soldiers came from spiritual indoctrination.

The most remarkable behaviour shown by Japanese soldiers was their willingness to accept orders that meant certain death and their refusal to surrender. The death of the young is one face of war. All societies know this. Unfortunately for all concerned, the Japanese extreme veneration of death was unique and came dangerously close to becoming a cult of oblivion.

Japanese views also struck at the very nature of the warrior code as understood in the West. In the West, death in war had value only if it had purpose. Soldiers were asked to risk their lives in battle, not commit suicide. An officer intentionally putting his men in a position where they had no reasonable chance of survival would in all likelihood not be obeyed in a Western army. (Every Western army had its equivalent of the Alamo, but these were very much the exception.) If conditions showed that further resistance was futile, surrender was honourable. The Japanese took this attitude as a sign of weakness. Although the Japanese did not understand it, surrender in a Western army was viewed very differently. Honourable surrender in the Western tradition prevented the needless squandering of one's own men. It also prevented the needless squandering of the enemy's life. It was a mutual agreement, manifested over centuries of history, that served as a brake on the worst excesses of war in Europe and in many other parts of the world. If Japanese officers did not hallow the lives of their own soldiers, they were likewise showing a contempt for the lives of the foe.

The cult of death, which ultimately became the heart of Japan's combat ethos and shaped the battlefield tactics employed, was obvious very early in the war. The early American soldiers going to New Guinea and Guadalcanal were miserably trained in military basics and there was no time for organised political indoctrination. (Pearl Harbor, naturally, was the ultimate proof that the Japanese were warlike, cruel and, most importantly, devious.) However, in all the South Pacific battles, examples abounded of the refusal of Japanese troops to surrender, regardless of circumstance. Stories multiplied on Guadalcanal and New Guinea of Japanese soldiers pretending to surrender only to fire upon their potential captors at the last moment. Soon most Allied infantry believed it was dangerous to try to take prisoners. Naturally the 'rumour mill' inherent in war made the perception even more vivid. Yet the image was valid enough.

Stanley Larsen, at the start of an extremely distinguished military career, was a young US Army battalion commander attacking one of the last Japanese strongpoints on the almost impenetrable jungle ridges on Guadalcanal in January 1943. Japanese resistance was hopeless and the garrison of about 200 near starvation. Larsen got a tank up the ridge in the morning and crushed what was left of the Japanese line. At a time when there was no hope, what was left of the Japanese garrison attacked at night. It was a good example of the famous 'banzai charge'. Larsen described what took place:

'We gave them a chance to surrender but they wouldn't. That night after the tank attack, the enemy made a banzai attack against a company which was overlooking their water hole. It was a steep slope. I've only been in two banzai charges, and they are terrifying. In this one 85 Japanese were killed. Twenty-one were officers and the rest enlisted. F company did not lose a single man. We had a bulldozer up there and we bulldozed a mass grave and all were buried there. That was the end of the Japanese strongpoint.'[5]

What should be noted in Larsen's narrative is the high number of officers and the lack of American casualties. The attack described was a method of suicide. Larsen's story is only one of many from Guadalcanal and gives credibility to the even more miserable accounts of the end at Buna.

In the last days of the Buna campaign, the newly arrived US 41st Division helped liquidate the Japanese garrison in January 1943. Sergeant Joe Murphy later recounted to the 41st Division's historian a horrible battle at a Japanese field hospital:

'Company G opened up on the shacks with all possible firepower. A hut collapsed under a stream of bullets. We flanked the shacks and picked off riflemen. From the nearby cemetery the Japanese light mortar fired only three or four times before we killed it. Meanwhile, grenades began exploding among the huts as able-bodied defenders and hospital invalids blew themselves up – or tried to blow up G Company. Some Japs fought in the open, some fought from foxholes and trunks of large trees. Others ran and were cut down. And in the huts our tense riflemen found live Japs under blankets and dead Japs under blankets. And G Company had no chance to check each corpse with a stethoscope – not when a pale hand might reach out to blast a grenade in your face. So G fired first and pulled blankets off corpses later. Some Nips were dead or dying of wounds, malaria, dysentery and blackwater fever. Some patients held live grenades under blankets and tried to blast us or blow themselves up. I saw one Nip rifleman with an amputated leg – prone and firing from the floor of a hut. We found newly dead grenadiers hiding under blankets beside skeletons.'[6]

The murderous result of this dynamic can easily be imagined. Allied soldiers did take prisoners throughout the war when conditions were right. (In action, a high percentage of prisoners early in the war was of imperial soldiers found unconscious.) However, Allied soldiers believed that an apparent surrender might be a trick. They also believed, with reason, that the Japanese took no prisoners on an active battlefield. The obvious effect was that Allied soldiers became less likely to attempt to take prisoners. Sadly, until the end, the Japanese ethos rejected surrender. It is also undoubtedly true that, as the war progressed and the Allies engaged more common Japanese infantry units, Japanese troops attempting surrender were shot out of hand. This in turn reinforced Japanese propaganda that the Allies would murder any Japanese in their clutches (including civilians). The Second World War's most tragic self-fulfilling prophecy was well in action early in the Pacific War.

The tide began to turn at Buna and Guadalcanal, but the South Pacific remained a fierce struggle throughout 1943. A slow advance up the Solomons and the coast of New Guinea finally allowed the Allies to bypass Rabaul in early 1944. They were, however, still far from Japan. Many American soldiers sardonically quipped 'Golden Gate in 48' or 'Join Mac and never come back'. In reality the long fight in the jungle proved well worth the cost.

Drive to Tokyo

Although not obvious in early 1944 Japan had suffered its Stalingrad in the South Pacific. Losses in aircraft, pilots, warships and seamen had been crippling and put serious strain on Japan's limited production capability to replace these losses. The qualitative edge in both air and sea operations had shifted to the United States. Although large numbers of Japanese aircraft rose to contest the skies in 1944-45, Japan's best pilots had perished in the South Pacific and the Allies were now beginning to pile up a colossal 'kill ratio' in their favour. Obviously, better US planes and pilots were also accompanied by a quantitative edge growing rapidly after mid-1943.

The change in tempo of operations after Allied victory in the South Pacific was striking. Early in the war imperial forces had the edge. The long struggle in New Guinea and the Solomons was hard fought. However, once Rabaul was bypassed and the Allies moved into the open waters of the Pacific, every major engagement between fleets and air units was a crushing and decisive US victory. In June 1944, when the Americans attacked the Marianas Islands, knowing the island of Saipan was within range of Japan for the secret B-29 'Super-fortress' bomber, the Imperial Navy sortied the core of the fleet in search of the 'decisive battle'. Despite decent odds for Japan on paper, American fliers and submarine crewmen humiliated the once proud Imperial Combined Fleet.

In October 1944 the Imperial Navy threw the dice for the last time. Attacking a massive American armada invading the island of Leyte in the Philippines, Combined Fleet made another futile attempt to defeat a major American invasion and thus gain some kind of leverage for an optimistically anticipated compromise peace. Despite some American errors, the resulting Battle of Leyte Gulf was an air and sea calamity for Japan. In the ensuing battle for the Philippines the Japanese Army Air Force was also shot to ribbons. Japan's plight became so desperate that, for the first time in modern history, suicide became an integral part of a nation's military apparatus when kamikaze air attacks were first employed over the Philippines.

Also the line moved much more quickly after the Allied neutralisation of Rabaul. The front in the South Pacific moved relatively little in nearly two years. Within a year of victory in the South Pacific, an American invasion fleet, in early April 1945, was heading for Okinawa on the doorstep of the Japanese home islands. By the time the fleet set sail, American submarine blockade and intensive air attack on cities had brought Japanese industry to a state of near paralysis.

Another major reason for the impressive quickening of operations lay in the South Pacific debacle. The Japanese Army was shaken by the prospect that the Allies would crack the Rabaul position and move into South East Asia and recapture Japan's irreplaceable sources of raw materials. Consequently, generals stripped the army's reserves from Japan itself and Manchuria and moved them into the South Pacific or Indies. By late 1943 there were 40,000 troops on Bougainville, 100,000 on Rabaul, 250,000 on New Guinea, 125,000 on the Malay Barrier. The garrison in the Philippines was also increased, ultimately reaching 450,000 men.

This was a miserable distribution of manpower. As Rabaul was coming under pressure, the United States was making ready an additional advance into the Central Pacific. Saipan was one of its first targets. MacArthur's advance did indeed threaten South East Asia, but the US Navy's drive through the centre was aimed at Japan itself. Nevertheless, because so many men were allocated to defend South East Asia, there were few remaining to ward off a blow in the centre. To give an idea of the depth of the calamity, there were more Japanese infantry defending Bougainville than on Saipan or Iwo Jima. There were more imperial troops on Rabaul than on Okinawa.

Once the Americans bypassed Rabaul there was nothing to prevent them from crushing by siege the huge Japanese garrisons sent south. Indeed, the bulk of the Imperial Army sent to the South Pacific and South East Asia was simply bypassed with very little loss to Allied forces. Japanese troops on New Guinea, so desperately needed elsewhere, sat on the coast of the primitive island, serving no military purpose and trying to ward off starvation. When the American Army deployed its vastly superior firepower and mobility on the relatively open spaces of the major Philippine Islands they crushed the Japanese opposition and forced them to retreat into the Philippine hills and mountains where they also became not a foe but an annoyance.

The Philippine campaign did include one of the most violent and senseless engagements of the Pacific War. When MacArthur's troops invaded the main Philippine island of Luzon in January 1945, his Japanese counterpart, General

Tomouyki Yamashita, believed that the city of Manila was of no strategic worth and ordered it abandoned. (Ironically, MacArthur himself had declared Manila an 'open city' in 1941, also realising that it was impossible and pointless to defend.) Incredibly, the imperial naval and army troops defending Manila refused to obey their commander and deployed in long-prepared defences inside and outside the city. The murderous chemistry inside Manila was as bad as that of Saipan or Okinawa, but very different. The Filipino people had been the most difficult for the Empire to subdue. Guerrilla warfare had begun in 1942 and only increased in intensity.

The 15,000 Japanese soldiers and sailors ordered to defend Manila were hated by the population and the emotion was returned in full measure. When the siege of Manila began (most of the fighting was in the southern part of the city) the city's population, expecting rapid American victory, was in place and the Japanese garrison in a state of suicidal fury. The result was that the long-suffering civilians of the Philippines were caught in nightmare pincers. Japanese troops, often within eyesight of American artillery observers, raped and murdered thousands of civilians. Artillery, mortar and small arms crossfire coming from both sides probably killed more. American tanker Tom Howard was in the middle of the siege for the southern portion of Manila:

'The state of siege had settled down into a condition where bodies of civilians and Japanese were still strewn over the streets, in gutters, on lawns and in the middle of the pavement. Attempts to remove them were met with sniper fire, so instead of removal, when dusk came, the bodies were covered with quick-lime to hasten their deterioration and to stifle the smell.'[7]

Despite the insubordination of Japanese leaders defending Manila, a decision which may have cost 100,000 civilian lives lost, the Japanese were blown out of their positions by American tanks and artillery by early March 1945. Some 12,000 Japanese died in Manila and the remainder fled to the hills to face starvation. Isolated, the huge Japanese garrisons in the Philippines joined their neighbours in the theatre as useless military units. Indeed, the South Pacific and much of the Indies became, in effect, history's biggest POW camp.

Unfortunately for the United States, the Central Pacific advance proved a far more bloody affair. The American nemesis, met before on a smaller scale at Buna and Guadalcanal, was the battle ethos of the Japanese infantry. The islands and atolls of the Central Pacific were small and the medium-sized garrisons found on them had enough time to build elaborate systems of caves, tunnels, beach obstacles and minefields. Most of these positions were difficult or impossible to spot from the air. Nor was it simple to bypass Japanese garrisons in the Central Pacific. The Americans believed that the road to Tokyo could only be travelled under the cover of land-based airpower. Unfortunately, the number of islands in the Central Pacific was much smaller than in South East Asia. If the Americans wished to employ land-based airpower there was often no alternative to direct assault on these Japanese positions. When Combined Fleet was crushed off Saipan, the Army realised that victory in a given battle was almost out of the question. With

Combined Fleet almost helpless, all of these garrisons would be cut off hopelessly as soon as an American invasion fleet arrived. The strategic goal on the Pacific islands was no longer victory but simple attrition. Japanese generals told their soldiers to 'withstand assault by a million men for a hundred years.'[8] Tokyo hoped that if the Japanese infantry could hold every position until the bitter end they might inflict enough casualties on the Americans to force Washington to accept a compromise peace. In fact, Tokyo badly underestimated American will. Yet what ensued was a bloody and brutal struggle that was interspersed by some of the largest-scale instances of politically inspired mass suicide in world history.

The fierce Central Pacific advance began in November 1943 when an American Marine Division invaded the atoll of Tarawa in the Gilbert Islands. Badly outnumbered, the 5,000-man imperial garrison put up a furious resistance for 72 hours on its small rock. The Japanese commander cabled 'May Japan last for 10,000 years!' Altogether 17 wounded Japanese survived and were made prisoners. However, the Marines had lost nearly 1,000 men killed in three days – more than they had lost in battle during the entire Guadalcanal campaign.

Worse came on Saipan in June 1944. As noted previously, the Saipan invasion precipitated the crushing American naval victory during the Battle of the Philippine Sea. Although isolated after the US Navy's smashing victory, the Japanese garrison of 30,000 men fought with desperate tenacity. A night attack early in the battle very nearly broke the American line. Yet once on shore, the Marines and soldiers employed the techniques used to defeat the fanatic defenders on all of the Pacific isles.

American troops on Saipan, as on later islands, had the support of naval gunfire and aircraft throughout the campaign. Strike forces attacked beaches in armed amphibious assault craft. They also had large shallow-draft landing-craft that could deploy tanks as soon as a solid beachhead was secured. Once the tanks and land artillery were on shore, a type of military mathematical equation took over. If the Japanese were conservative (almost always bad news for American invaders) they would wait until US infantry closed and open fire with mortars and machine-guns from one of the hundreds of prepared positions. Inevitably Americans died, but the position was eventually seen and the advantage switched. American tanks proved a very difficult problem for the Japanese. Japan had only a handful of tanks deployed in the Pacific, and American armour found it simple to obliterate those found in the open. Japanese anti-tank guns were in short supply and too small in calibre. Thus, imperial infantry had to put down a withering small arms and mortar fire against an American tank-infantry team, hoping to drive off US troops and attack tanks with hand satchels of explosive. In the right circumstance, this technique led to the death of many American tanks and soldiers. It was, however, obviously a desperate tactic. Usually those with the satchel charges died under the American support fire.

Once identified, a Japanese strongpoint was dead. A machine-gun emplacement, if spotted by a tank, was usually destroyed by the tank at point-blank range, with the tank driving over the remnant to ensure destruction. If a strongpoint was more heavily held, tanks, machine-guns and artillery would keep up a covering fire while American soldiers climbed on top of the cave entrance, hurled grenades inside and prevented escape unless the cave had another opening. If possible, combat engineers got into place with their flame-throwers. If flame-throwers could operate, the defenders would either die immediately or retreat if possible. Americans were always on the look-out for a prepared cave that would have some kind of ventilation. Once found, US infantry employed incendiary devices of all kinds. If trapped, imperial soldiers either burned to death or were buried alive. (The Japanese called the American tactics of sealing and destroying caves 'the horse-mounting technique' and feared it greatly.) Japanese would retreat if necessary and if possible. However, ultimately the defenders ran out of space and supplies. The obvious solution in such circumstances was surrender. In practice, for Japanese forces, the response was suicide.

After two weeks of vicious fighting the Japanese position cracked on Saipan. The 'end game' disintegrated into barbarism remarkable even for the Pacific War. The Japanese commanders committed suicide. Previously they had ordered a pointless banzai assault against US infantry that cost the lives of 2,000 Japanese troops. After this grim prelude insanity gripped the island. Saipan had been Japanese territory since the First World War. Consequently it possessed a civilian population of approximately 25,000. Terrified by bogus propaganda that US forces would rape and murder them, thousands of women and children committed suicide, many within view of shocked American Marines. According to American testimony and interrogation of survivors, many civilians were forced to die by enraged and often drunken Japanese soldiers as an adjunct to their own suicide. Americans estimated that two-thirds of Saipan's civilian population perished. Only a handful of prisoners came from the dead garrison. The Japanese inflicted 14,000 casualties on US forces, the worst so far of the Pacific War. It should be emphasised, however, that US losses were very slight during the blood-crazed last days. Saipan, and many battles that followed, duplicated on a large scale the pattern first seen at Buna: initial fierce Japanese resistance, slow American dominance due to superior firepower and Japanese isolation, and a final act of pointless Japanese suicidal violence.

Events followed this grisly pattern every step on the way to Tokyo. Marine Eugene Sledge, a veteran of the terrible struggles at Peleliu in 1944 and Okinawa in 1945, later tried to express the almost unimaginable stress put on the combat infantry:

'The struggle for survival went on day after weary day, night after terrifying night. One remembers vividly the landings and the beachheads and the details of the first two or three days and nights of a campaign; after that, time lost all meaning. A lull of hours or days seemed but a fleeting instant of heaven-sent tranquillity. Lying in a foxhole sweating out an enemy artillery or mortar barrage or waiting to dash across open ground under machine-gun or artillery fire defied any concept of time.

To the non-combatants and those on the periphery of action, the war meant only boredom or occasional excitement; but to those who entered the meat grinder itself, the war was a nether world of horror from which escape seemed less and less likely as casualties mounted and the fighting dragged on and on. Time had no meaning; life had no meaning. The fierce struggle for survival in the abyss of Peleliu eroded the veneer of civilisation and made savages of us all. We existed in an environment totally incomprehensible to men behind the lines – service troops and civilians.'[9]

All the small islands such as Biak, Kwajalein, Eniwetok, Peleliu and Iwo Jima assaulted in the 18 months of war were ruthless 'slugfests' with relative violence controlled only by the size of the forces involved. It was both logical and fitting that Okinawa, the last battle of the Pacific War, was the most violent single encounter of the war and the one in which the Japanese leadership incorporated suicide most deeply into the essential fabric of imperial warmaking.

Because it was south of the home islands and relatively close, both sides knew that, if in American hands, Allied land-based aircraft of all types could wreak havoc across Japan and cover the already planned assault on Kyushu. After witnessing the enormous size of the American fleet that had assaulted the Philippines, Tokyo knew that when the Americans inevitably hit Okinawa, they would do so in great force. In a very real sense, Okinawa was a suicide mission in every respect. The Imperial Army hoped that a huge 'butcher bill' delivered to Washington might convince a hopefully war-weary America to consider the cost of attacking the Japanese homeland prohibitive and thus make the Americans willing to agree to some kind of compromise peace. No one in Tokyo expected the 100,000-man Japanese garrison on Okinawa to survive.

On 1 April 1945 the Allies (a large British task force participated in naval support) attacked Okinawa. Although initially unopposed, Marines and soldiers soon found themselves in an all too familiar fight against an entrenched and fanatical enemy. As before, the invaders had copious support from carrier-based aircraft and heavy naval gunfire. Convinced that their pilots no longer had the skill to contest Allied airmen, the Japanese sent some 2,400 kamikaze aircraft against Allied ships. Nearly 5,000 Allied sailors died in these attacks, a total slightly larger than the carnage in the Solomons 2½ years before. Allied sailors viewed their enemy with bewilderment, later expressing attitudes ranging from profound respect for Japanese courage to the view that they were fighting men who were pathologically insane. One witness, Vice Admiral C. R. Brown, later expressed the ethical confusion wrought by the kamikaze attacks:

'Among us who were there, in the Philippines and at Okinawa, I doubt if there is anyone who can depict with complete clarity our mixed emotions as we watched a man about to die in order that he might destroy us in the process. There was a hypnotic fascination to a sight so alien to our Western philosophy.'[10]

Against the advice of many combat officers, Tokyo decided to expend what remained of the Imperial Navy on a suicide mission. The Navy ordered a task force based on the super-heavy battleship *Yamato* and eight smaller warships to sortie to Okinawa. Shadowed from the outset, the small force received its first American air attack barely 100 miles south of Kyushu.

Ensign Mitsusu Yoshida's battle station was to serve as liaison between the bridge of the *Yamato* and its air-search radar, giving him a unique vantage point for the tragedy to follow. Early in the battle an American bomb scored a direct hit on the heavily armoured radar room. Yoshida rushed to the scene where many close friends and comrades served. He described the psychological hammer-blow of war at its worst:

'It is as if someone had taken an axe and split a bamboo tube. The bomb, a direct hit, must have sliced way in at an angle and then exploded.

Tuned and retuned in preparation for today's decisive battle, the instruments have been scattered in all directions. I don't recognise the debris. Not even any pieces left.

Just as I begin to think that everything must have been blown away, I notice a chunk of flesh smashed on to a panel of the broken bulkhead, a red barrel of flesh about as big around as two arms can reach. It must be a torso from which all extremities – arms, legs, head – have been ripped off.

Noticing four hunks scattered nearby, I pick them up and set them in front of me. To the charred flesh are stuck here and there pieces of khaki-coloured material, apparently scraps of military uniform. The smell of fat is heavy in the air. It goes without saying that I cannot tell where head and arms and legs might have been attached...

What emptiness! How did they die, those beings who only a moment ago were so real? I cannot stop doubting, stop marvelling.

It is not grief and resentment. It is not fear. It is total disbelief. As I touch these hunks of flesh, for a moment I am completely lost in thought.'[11]

Three hours after the first bomb fell, five imperial ships, *Yamato* among them, were on the bottom, and four surviving destroyers were heading back to Japan as fast as possible. In one afternoon the Imperial Navy lost 3,500 men, almost as many sailors as the Allies lost to aerial kamikazes throughout the entire Okinawa campaign. In return, Japan gained nothing.

The garrison at Okinawa, because it was close to Japan, received an unusual number of artillery pieces of medium field level (105mm) and above. American infantry had a multitude of standard land artillery and was, despite kamikaze attack, continually supported by powerful naval gunfire. Artillery is the great killer of the modern battlefield. When added to the fierce effectiveness of machine-guns, grenades and rifles held by fanatical Japanese troops in hundreds of hidden strongpoints, Okinawa became a blood-soaked siege lasting ten weeks.

Marine Eugene Sledge had the unfortunate fate of going from the fierce battle at Peleliu to Okinawa. His unit entered the fray in early May just prior to an ill-advised Japanese counter-attack on entrenched American positions. The description of battle would have been familiar to someone at the Somme in 1916:

'There was the brassy, metallic twang of the small 50mm knee mortar shells as little buffs of dirty smoke appeared thickly around us. The 81mm and 90mm mortar shells crashed and banged all along the ridge. The whizzbang of the high-velocity 47mm gun's shells, which was on us with its explosion almost as soon as we heard it whizz into the area, gave me the feeling the Japanese were firing them at us like rifles. The slower screaming, whining sound of the 75mm artillery shells seemed the most abundant. Then there was the roar and rumble of the huge enemy 150mm howitzer shell, and the kaboom of its explosion. It was what the men called the big stuff. I didn't recall having recognised any of it in my confusion and fear at Peleliu. The bursting radius of these big shells was of awesome proportions. Added to all of this noise was the swishing and fluttering overhead of our own supporting artillery fire. Our shells could be heard bursting out across the ridge over enemy positions. The noise of small-arms fire from both sides resulted in a chaotic bedlam of racket and confusion.'[12]

Despite furious Japanese resistance, American numbers, firepower and skill left the issue in no doubt. By June the Japanese were driven to the southern portion of the island. In his memoir, Colonel Hiromichi Yahara, the highest-ranked Japanese survivor of Okinawa, gave a vivid description of the ruin of a once beautiful portion of Okinawa toward the end of the campaign:

'Two weeks of battle changed the scenery completely. Hills were flattened and reshaped by tanks and bombardments. It was now a wasteland, the darkened terrain exposing a gateway to hell. Early one morning I left the cave and saw dark clouds rolling turbulently across the sky with gun smoke creeping across the land. For a moment the roar of the guns ceased. I was overwhelmed by the ghostly sight of the battlefield that had sucked the blood from thousands of soldiers. As a wise old man once said, "Even the demons of the world would mourn at this sight." The hilltop was covered with corpses.'[13]

With the outcome of battle decided, a final bloodbath ensued. Thousands of Okinawan civilians had been killed in military operations throughout the battle. As the end neared, hundreds more emulated the innocents on Saipan with useless suicide. Japanese soldiers had preceded them. As the Americans pushed back imperial forces, the Japanese faced the problem of evacuating the seriously wounded under relentless fire. In practice it was impossible and the result can be imagined. Colonel Yahara explained the situation:

'The army should, of course, make every effort to carry the wounded to safe areas and prevent their capture by the enemy. The fact was, however, that we were unable to care for such large numbers. How to handle this situation? …The army directive on this matter stated: "In facing an emergency every Japanese soldier should act proudly." In fact, many wounded soldiers shouted "Long live the Emperor!" as they took their lives with hand grenades, satchel charges or cyanide. In other cases, doctors injected patients with cyanide.'[14]

As the end loomed, thousands of imperial soldiers joined their wounded comrades. Young intelligence officer Frank Gibney was led to the headquarters cave of the

Japanese 24th Division and observed one of the largest of the 'suicide caves' on Okinawa. The dreadful event had taken place about a week before Gibney discovered the carnage:

'With 7th Division intelligence officers, I went down to one of the cave entrances and crawled in. After a walk through a long tunnel we came on a huge underground cavern and one of the ghastliest sights I ever saw. Here lay General Amamiya [24th Division commander], surrounded by his staff and some two hundred officers and men. They had all killed themselves, most with grenades, although Amamiya had thoughtfully given himself a lethal injection to avoid the rigors of ritual suicide. The cave floor was literally carpeted with corpses.'[15]

Resistance began to collapse on 20 June 1945. The last act was the ritual suicide of Okinawa's commander, Lieutenant-General Mitsuru Ushijima, and his chief of staff, Major-General Isamu Cho, at dawn on 23 June. Although already ordered to make his way somehow to Tokyo and report on the battle, Yahara was drawn to witness the final scene:

'General Ushijima quietly stood up. General Cho removed his field uniform and followed with Paymaster Sato. Led by candlelight the solemn procession headed for the exit, with heavy hearts and limbs.

When they approached the cave opening, the moon shone on the South Seas. Clouds moved swiftly. The skies were quiet. The morning mist crept slowly up the deep valley. It was as if everything on earth trembled, waiting with deep emotion.

General Ushijima sat silently in the death seat, ten paces from the cave exit, facing the sea wall. General Cho and Sato sat beside him. The hara-kiri assistant, Captain Sakaguchi, stood behind them. I was a few steps away. Soldiers stood at the exit, awaiting the moment.

On the back of General Cho's white shirt, in immaculate brush strokes, was the poem:

With bravery I served my nation
With loyalty I dedicate my life.

The master swordsman, Sakaguchi, grasped his great sword with both hands, raised it high above the general's head, then held back in his downward swing, and said, "It's too dark to see your neck. Please wait a few moments."

People were still nudging me toward the cave exit when a startling shot rang out. I thought for a moment it was the start of naval gun-firing, but instead it was Sato committing suicide outside the cave. When that excitement subsided, the generals were ready. Each in turn thrust a traditional hara-kiri dagger into his bared abdomen. As they did so, Sakaguchi skilfully and swiftly swung his razor-edged sword and beheaded them. Ushijima first, then Cho.'[16]

In a narrow sense, the Japanese garrison on Okinawa had succeeded admirably. Although losing some 100,000 men to the inferno, they had inflicted the unprecedented total of 12,500 killed and 36,000 wounded on Allied forces of all types.

Such losses caused tremors in Washington but in no way halted the build-up for an invasion of Kyushu scheduled for 1 November 1945. Indeed, the tempo of the offensive increased. In July the Australians took the oilfields on Borneo. The British were planning an amphibious strike deep into South East Asia. The USSR, as Japanese intelligence knew well, was building up forces in Manchuria.

The powerful and growing 'peace faction' inside the Japanese Government realised that Okinawa was another great defeat. A large and well-entrenched Japanese garrison was crushed by an American army only half again larger than the defence force. Okinawa had cast great doubts on the Imperial Army's claim that a 'decisive battle' on Kyushu could be anything else than a hopeless struggle leading to the destruction of much of the Japanese nation.

Undoubtedly some of the Japanese garrison were thinking along these lines also. In the weeks after the battle the Americans were astounded to find that nearly 7,000 Japanese soldiers crawled from unseen caves and surrendered, a total without precedent until that time. Japan was beginning to crack.

Japan itself possessed an undernourished population, its industry was crippled and its urban centres in ruins. The strategic bombing campaign directed against Japanese cities by American B-29s was savage but effective. Learning that Japanese industry, like that found in German cities, was not concentrated, the Americans abandoned their 'pin-point bombing' tactics employed in Germany in favour of area attacks against Japan's densely populated urban areas. Knowing Japanese cities were made of wood and would burn furiously, the B-29s launched low-level night attacks, dropping thousands of small incendiary bombs. The result was a nightmare that overwhelmed Japanese attempts to protect its populace from immolation or asphyxiation in the inevitable firestorm. On 10 March 1945 journalist Masuo Kato witnessed one of the first and largest incendiary raids launched against Tokyo. On that occasion fortune conspired against the citizens of Tokyo as a fierce wind was blowing before the bombs dropped, which, as Kato recalled:

> '...whipped hundreds of small fires into great walls of flame, which began leaping streets, firebreaks and canals at dazzling speed. The flames roared on, gulping great drafts of oxygen, and thousands of human beings died in shelters, in the streets, in the canals and even in large open areas, like so many fish left gasping on the bottom of a lake that has been drained... On some broad streets, as far as one could see, there were rows of bodies where men, women and children had tried to escape the flames by lying down in the centre of the pavement. There were heaps of bodies in schoolyards, in parks, in vacant lots and huddled under railway viaducts.'[17]

We shall never know if further violence was required to goad the Emperor into forcing his military to cease the conflict. In the event, the atomic bombs dropped on Japan in early August provided a justification for capitulation, a justification used by Hirohito. Although the military chiefs pleaded for a last battle, even after the atomic bombs, the Emperor demanded an end to hostilities. After a brief flurry of diplomacy, Japan surrendered on 15 August 1945.

When the Emperor addressed the Japanese people to announce surrender he urged them to 'endure the unendurable and bear the unbearable'. The exhausted population was glad to comply. Apprehensive American troops began almost immediately to occupy key points in Japan. To their delight and amazement they encountered almost no violence and met with almost universal co-operation. For their part the Japanese civilian population soon recognised that the American occupation would be benign and temporary. It is such an irony that the Japanese and Americans, implacable foes during one of the most terrible wars of modern times, soon developed mutual respect and political friendship that has endured to this day.

Notes on contributors

Dr Eric M. Bergerud, Lincoln University, San Francisco, USA
Eric Bergerud received a PhD at the University of California, Berkeley in 1981. He is now Professor of History at Lincoln University, California. His works include Dynamics of Defeat: The Vietnam War in Hau Nghia Province (Boulder, CO. and Oxford: Westview Press, 1991); Red Thunder, Tropic Lightning: The World of a Combat Division in Vietnam (Boulder, CO. and Oxford: Westview Press, 1993); and, most recently, Fire in the Sky: The Air War in the South Pacific (Boulder, CO. and Oxford: Westview Press, 2000).

Recommended reading

Bergerud, Eric, *Fire in the Sky: Air War in the South Pacific* (Boulder, Colorado: Westview Press, 2000)
   Touched with Fire: The Land War in the South Pacific (New York: Viking Press, 1996)
Dower, John W., *War without Mercy: Race and Power in the Pacific War* (New York: Pantheon Books, 1986)
Dull, Paul S., *A Battle History of the Imperial Japanese Navy (1941-1945)* (Annapolis: Naval Institute Press, 1978)
Gailey, Harry, *The War in the Pacific: From Pearl Harbor to Tokyo Bay* (Novato, California: Presidio Press, 1995)
Goldstein, Donald and Dillon, Katherine V. (eds), *Fading Victory: The Diary of Admiral Matome Ugaki, 1941-1945* (Pittsburgh: University of Pittsburgh Press, 1991)
Harries, Meririon and Susie, *Soldiers of the Sun: The Rise and Fall of the Imperial Japanese Army* (New York: Random House, 1991)
Sledge, Eugene B., *With the Old Breed: At Peleliu and Okinawa* (New York: Oxford University Press, 1990)
Spector, Ronald H., *The Eagle Against the Sun: The American War with Japan* (New York: Vintage Books, 1985)

Notes

[1] James Morehead, *In My Sights: The Memoir of a P-40 Ace* (Navato, California, 1999) pp65-6

[2] Eric Bergerud, *Touched with Fire: The Land War in the South Pacific* (New York, 1996) p70

[3] Ibid, p73

[4] Interview with the author, June 1998

[5] Eric Bergerud, op cit, pp197-9

[6] Ibid, pp420-1

[7] Gerald Astor, *Crisis in the Pacific: The Battles for the Philippine Islands by the Men Who Fought Them – An Oral History* (New York, 1996) p399

[8] Meriron and Susie Harries, *Soldiers of the Sun: The Rise and Fall of the Imperial Japanese Army* (New York, 1991) p429

[9] E. B. Sledge, *With the Old Breed: At Peleliu and Okinawa* (New York, 1990) pp120-1

[10] Hiromichi Yahara, *The Battle for Okinawa* (New York, 1995) pxix

[11] Yoshida, Mitsuru, *Requiem for Battleship Yamoto* (London: University of Washington Press, 1986) p70-1

[12] E. B. Sledge, op cit, pp206-7

[13] Hiromichi Yahara, op cit, p135

[14] Ibid, p109

[15] Ibid, p201

[16] Ibid, p155-6

[17] Editors of Time-Life Books, *Japan at War* (Chicago, 1980) pp172, 179

Chapter 9

War in the Tropics:
East Africa and Burma

Phillip Parotti

I f war is complicated, war conducted in the tropics seems doubly so; this is a fact to which even cursory studies of the First World War in East Africa and the Second World War in Burma abundantly attest. Physically distant from the main venues in which the ultimate defeats of Germany in the First World War and Japan in the Second were being decided, East Africa and Burma seemed to lodge in contemporary Western consciousness as military backwaters, so much so that combatants in those out-of-the-way theatres of war often came to think ironically of themselves as fighting on or as having fought on 'secret'[1] or 'forgotten'[2] fronts. Invalided home after two years of combat in the East African bush, W. E. Wynn recalls this incident:

> 'The majority of people in England knew nothing about the war in East Africa, and even if they did have a vague idea that something might have been happening down there, they were not in the least interested. There was plenty to think about nearer home. Of course, the average man, or woman, in the street had never even heard of East Africa.
>
> A very stern and leathery faced female once stopped and seized me by the arm. With an accusing ring in her harsh voice she began to ask me searching questions. First, she demanded to know why I was loafing about England, instead of fighting for my country.
>
> I feebly remarked I had just come home from East Africa.
>
> "Young man," she angrily declared, "you've no right to be here. You should be at the front."'[3]

To the men fighting in these distant geographical regions, their fronts, of course, were really neither secret nor forgotten. Rather, they were vicious fields where life was played out against death in never-ending battles with an elusive and implacable enemy. To make matters worse, nearly every element of climate, geography, health, diet, logistics, and the unexpected, seemed to conspire in multiplying the degree of difficulty with which tropical campaigns were conducted while compounding the stress and intensity with which they were fought. If war is trial, war in the tropics has proved twice so.

Given the particular nastiness of bush and jungle warfare, one might well ask why men would ever fight in such environments. Obviously, men fight where wars find them or send them, and not on the fields that they might choose. More to the point – and this was as true of Burma as it was of East Africa – motives of duty, honour, country, and comradeship defined the dominant considerations in each man's commitment right down to moments of final sacrifice. Placing these important issues aside, one notices at once an outlook, an illusion, held by men going to war in East Africa that was greatly toned down or utterly missing among the men who fought in Burma. Recalling his departure for East Africa in February 1916, Deneys Reitz says:

> 'Before Smith-Dorrien could take over he fell ill, whereupon General Smuts assumed command of the campaign, and he left South Africa in December 1915. I decided to go too. I had no animus against the German people, but I thought then, as I think now, that a victorious Germany would have been a disaster to human liberty. Also, my chief was going and, further, I could not hang back while so many of my countrymen were moving forward to an adventure in the wilds of Africa.'[4]

Reitz's sense of duty and his loyalty to Smuts are indeed the primary motives here, but the romantic drive to adventure that Reitz expresses appears again and again in the recorded memoirs of veterans from the East African campaign. W. T. Shorthose, writing in *Sport & Adventure in Africa*, recalls, 'Needless to state, we were all agog with excitement… The common opinion was that the war would end very soon, and our only anxiety was lest we should miss a chance to fight!'[5] Christopher J. Thornhill, who was 18 when the war began, remembered, 'I felt I could hardly breathe until I joined something,'[6] so at the first opportunity he joined the 'Rag-time'[7] soldiers of the East African Mounted Rifles, who, without any training whatsoever, had joined the war straight off their farms. Although he was in northern Canada near the Arctic Circle when the war commenced, Angus Buchanan hastened to return to England, where he joined the 25th Royal Fusiliers. As his unit began its voyage from Plymouth to East Africa, Buchanan speculated, 'Were they not, after all, starting out on the greatest adventure of all – the stern pursuit of a perilous quest?'[8] One does well to remember that the men writing these memoirs are, like Conrad's Marlow, older men reviewing their lost illusions. Nevertheless, early in the war the illusion existed that the war in East Africa would prove to be soon ended and relatively easy, something of a boy's lark, and a romantic adventure not unlike a chivalric quest.

For a period of time, the chivalric, romantic delusion persisted. W. E. Wynn provides a telling incident when he recalls the pre-sailing conference held before Force B embarked for the ill-fated 1914 invasion of Tanga:

> 'The General [Aitken] apologised for our being associated with such a simple affair as the taking of German East Africa. After that had been accomplished he promised he would do his best to have us all sent to France; all who had, in the meantime, been well behaved.

"There is one thing, gentlemen, about which I feel very strongly," he said, as a finale to the meeting, "that is the subject of dress. I wish officers and men to be always well turned out." He looked sternly down the table. "I will not tolerate the appalling sloppiness allowed during the Boer War."[9]

In the beginning, matters of character, demonstrated through smartness and keen romantic élan, were going to be accorded precedence over professionalism. Following the disastrous battle but prior to the British withdrawal, Richard Meinertzhagen, then an intelligence officer with Force B, negotiated with the Germans to assist British wounded with medical stores; in his 5 November 1914 diary entry, he says:

'My letter to the German commander was sent through to him and I was conducted to the hospital with my medical stores... The Germans were meanwhile kindness itself and gave me a most excellent breakfast which I sorely needed. Several German officers who were present at breakfast expressed their admiration at the behaviour of the North Lancs, and we discussed the fight freely as though it had been a football match. It seemed so odd that I should be having a meal today with people whom I was trying to kill yesterday. It seemed so wrong and made me wonder whether this really was war or whether we had all made a ghastly mistake. The German officers whom I met today were all hard looking, keen and fit and clearly knew their job and realised its seriousness. They treated this war as some new form of sport.'[10]

Later, in the event that one or the other might be taken prisoner, Meinertzhagen and German Captain Hammerstein exchanged names, addresses and pledges of assistance.[11] And still later, on 19 January 1915, W. E. Wynn was a member of the attacking force sent to relieve Jassin, and he reports yet another chivalric moment:

'A little after the following day's dawn, with troops ready for attack, two figures were seen through the morning haze. They were the two British officers who had been at Jassin post. With ammunition gone they had been forced to surrender.
    Colonel von Lettow had offered them parole in tribute to their gallant defence. As a further compliment the German commander drew up the German troops in ceremonial order. The troops presented arms and the two British officers were courteously conducted down their ranks, privileged to inspect the men they had been fighting.'[12]

Thus we see the war's chivalric beginnings, but eventually disease, continual hardship and the indiscriminate death derived from technological advances like the modern machine-gun would reveal the war's hard edge. In response, chivalry would evolve into professional respect for a hard-fighting opponent, and romanticism would be cut to shreds by the killing power of modern weaponry loosed upon the unsuspecting amidst the worst of tropical environments.
    Speaking about the men who fought in Burma, one can say with relative

certainty that when they went to war they knew more about it than had their First World War counterparts. This is not to suggest that they were more experienced, better trained, better motivated, or more logistically prepared than the soldiers of the Great War; rather, that they had a knowledge that their First World War counterparts could not have had: they had a knowledge of the First World War. Psychologically, writers like Graves, Owen, Sassoon, Hemingway and Remarque, a variety of realistic war films and the talk of veterans had better prepared them for the horrors of 20th-century war. Gone was the assumption that war would offer a romantic adventure; rather than setting out on a quest, the men who fought in Burma knew that before they could return home in order to recover mundane normalcy they had to do an extremely difficult and dangerous job, and about that work there was little that one could call romantic. This is not to say, however, that they were free from illusions of their own.

At the outset, the men fighting in Burma suffered from two equally debilitating delusions. In his well-written memoir, *Defeat into Victory*, Field-Marshal Viscount Slim offered this personal observation:

> 'To our men, British or Indian, the jungle was a strange, fearsome place; moving and fighting in it was a nightmare. We were too ready to classify jungle as "impenetrable", as indeed it was to us with our motor transport, bulky supplies, and inexperience. To us it appeared only as an obstacle to movement and to vision; to the Japanese it was a welcome means of concealed manoeuvre and surprise.'[13]

In order to win in Burma, fighting men had first to dispense with their belief that the jungle was impenetrable, then they had to disabuse themselves of the idea that the Japanese were invincible. Experience, observation and direct contact with the enemy were the keys to exploding these myths, and as a result of his first forays behind the Japanese lines in Malaya, F. Spencer Chapman concluded, 'The Japanese troops I have seen are good second-class material, well trained but poorly equipped. Their lines of communication should prove singularly vulnerable to attack by trained guerillas.'[14] Later in the war, Orde Wingate's Chindits, the OSS, and a host of irregulars drawn from the native tribes were among the first to defy and dispel the assumptions about Japanese invincibility, and their contributions to overturning the accepted wisdom of the time proved invaluable in changing the thinking behind the entire Allied effort in Burma.

One final illusion, widely subscribed to during the First World War in East Africa, was greatly toned down if not altogether absent during the Second World War in Burma. This delusion – no doubt derived from a colonial habit of mind, from an imperial outlook and attitude – had to do with what might be interpreted as false assumptions about racial inferiority and the potential fighting quality of native troops. Having watched a native stretcher-bearer nurse a fire in the dry centre of a mealie cobb, Francis Brett Young speculated:

> 'With this slow-burning tinder he had nursed a smouldering fire all night, and the sight of him brought swiftly to my mind the Promethean legend and the

Titan's hollow stick of fennel, so that in this chill dawn I seemed again to be riding in the dawn of the world: and indeed this land was as unvexed by man as any Thracian wild and the people as simple as those to whom the son of Zeus brought fire.'[15]

If this recalls a Victorian/Edwardian concept of the civilised West high-mindedly carrying 'the white man's burden', one must also recognise the downside. Meinertzhagen, who invariably favoured expansion of the native King's African Rifles, reported this exchange with General Aitken who commanded Force B at Tanga in 1914:

'When I was in East Africa in 1906 I visited the German military station at Moshi and was shown everything by some friendly German officers. I formed a high opinion of their efficiency and reported them as better trained, disciplined and led than our own King's African Rifles. I told this to Aitken, who said with some heat: "The Indian Army will make short work of a lot of niggers."'[16]

As history has shown, General Aitken, soundly defeated, would have cause to reconsider his judgement. Arnold Wienholt, another British officer serving with the Intelligence Corps, seems to express the general attitude when he calls the natives 'big children'[17], but at the same time – and this eventually became the general view – he speaks for the mature army when he concludes that, 'The German East campaign proved, at any rate, that, with training and discipline, the negro can become a first-rate soldier.'[18] Although slow to change, attitudes nevertheless changed, and among the men who fought in East Africa, former prejudices were humbled.

In Burma during the Second World War racial attitudes were much changed. General Stilwell, for example, said, 'If I can prove the Chinese soldier as good as any Allied soldier, I'll die happy.'[19] This is not to say that Stilwell was without prejudice – his ludicrous references to the English as 'limeys' were legion – but such nonsense was always professionally and politically competitive.[20] British and Americans who served with the Karens and Kachins invariably spoke highly of them. Brigadier Bernard Fergusson has paid continual tribute to the Karen scouts of the Burma Rifles who were assigned to serve under his command[21], and about the Kachins, OSS man Neil H. Barrett said this: 'Any time a movement was started to fight the Japs the Kachins were the first to respond and, I might add, they were fearless, ruthless fighters, and the Japs feared them.'[22] Vague notions that Wingate harboured a prejudice against the Indian Army were put to rest by Brigadier Michael Calvert who described the multi-ethnic character of the Special Force in these words:

'In all there were seventeen British battalions, five Gurkha battalions and three West African battalions in the Special Force. No Indian battalions were used, owing to the difficulty, at that time, of special feeding, cooking, camp followers, etc, insisted upon by the Indian army, whereas all the battalions in Special Force could, and did, eat any type of food, although certain special provisions were sometimes made for the Gurkhas.'[23]

With admiration, Calvert later wrote, 'At one time my brigade major, Francis Stewart, had to compete with seven different races in Brigade HQ, comprising British, Indian, Burmese, Karens, Chinese, West African, and Gurkhas.'[24] Finally, on the basis of his personal experience, Slim offers this appreciation, an appreciation that puts some of the racial delusions entertained early in the East African campaign fully and finally to rest:

> 'In Burma we not only fought against an Asian enemy, but we fought him with an army that was mainly Asian. In both respects not a few of us with little experience of Asians had to re-adjust many ideas, among them that of the inherent superiority of the white man as a soldier. The Asian fighting man is at least equally brave, usually more careless of death, less encumbered by mental doubts, little troubled by humanitarian sentiment, and not so moved by slaughter and mutilation about him. He is, by background and living standards, better fitted to endure hardship uncomplainingly, to demand less in the way of subsistence or comfort, and to look after himself when thrown on his own resources.'[25]

One subject about which no man fighting for any side, either in East Africa or Burma, harboured a single delusion was the difficulty to be faced in contending with raw nature. And raw nature in the tropics was a matter far divorced from raw nature as it was experienced in Europe. With the vagaries of weather everyone had to contend, but there all similarities between the fronts ended. To the lasting misfortune of the men who fought in the tropics, the threats and dangers imposed by nature arrived in a multiplicity of forms.

Occasionally, one supposes, soldiers fighting in Europe were bitten by dogs, scratched by cats, or bedevilled by lice and insects; if so, their problems with the animal kingdom were minuscule when compared with those of the tropical fighting man. Writing about East Africa, Christopher J. Thornhill recalled:

> 'Charging rhino were to be a feature of this campaign – we had to get used to them and more or less dodge their cyclonic onslaught; for nothing but death will stop a rhino once he takes it into his head to charge, and it is not always prudent to let off firearms when enemy patrols are about. That day I counted no less than eight full-grown rhino disturbed by our advance, three of which charged, two of them being shot.'[26]

At Maktan on 3 September 1915, Angus Buchanan recorded this diary entry:

> 'Out on reconnaissance, to position enemy holding about eight miles west of our camp. Moving quietly through bush – our party two whites and two porters. On outward journey ran across a rhinoceros, who charged on hearing stick break underfoot; but he stopped about ten yards short, when he then got

our wind, and cleared off rapidly with a quick turn and snort, apparently afraid of us. Self and companions, at the sound of the rushing crash of the charge, had backed behind stoutish trees, with rifles ready, but the natives, in an incredibly short moment, had squirmed frantically into the bushes overhead.'[27]

As W. E. Wynn wrote, 'In peace we laughed at the rhino, behind his back... In war the rhino was no longer funny. He was a nuisance. To my own knowledge eight men were killed by charging rhinos.'[28] W. T. Shorthose, after reporting a number of men killed or wounded by buffaloes, went on to state: 'Not only from German rifles did our men suffer in the East African campaign. I am correct in stating that numbers of carriers were taken by lions, also sentries, others crushed to death by elephants or tossed by buffaloes and rhinos, and many poisoned by the bite of snakes.'[29] Given the incredible abundance of East African wildlife and the utterly uncertain nature of its reactions to man, the threat it posed was ever-present. Francis Brett Young describes a fine bull oryx several times charging his column before a thin line of machine-gun porters finally parted from before its straight horns, which allowed the cornered beast to escape into the bush.[30] The aggressive African honey bee – today called 'the killer bee' in the United States – several times disrupted entire military columns on the march.[31] And at least once, at Tanga, the viciousness of the bees played a significant role in a British defeat:

'As a matter of fact, wild bees worried the Lancs a good deal. It sounds ridiculous, but I saw it myself. Apparently wild bees were in abundance in some of the palms, and bullets happened to break up their nests. They all came out angry and stung anything in their way. I myself got stung twice by angry bees, and some of the Lancs were stung all over by hosts of these little pests. Of course, they said the Germans had let bees lose on them, but this must be nonsense.'[32]

When a predator was involved, a sudden attack could be far more threatening:

'The enemy soon got to hear that we were in their neighborhood, especially as we were getting in the Government tax food from the various villages, to prevent it falling into the enemy's hands. However, we had our own troubles close at hand, for a few days after making our temporary camp and erecting shelters, a leopard, coming into the camp at night (we had, of course, no fires), seized and terribly mauled my white companion. The horrible beast, sneaking in, had seized his victim by the head, and, dragging him off his stretcher, had actually taken him away some fifteen yards before we were able to help him. Being asleep at the time, I was rather muddled for a few seconds when his shrieks started, and I fear was all too slow in coming to his assistance. It was not till he had cried out "chui" (leopard) that the situation was made plain to me, and meanwhile the man-eater was worrying him.'[33]

Minutes later, at the opposite end of the camp, the same leopard attacked and attempted to drag away an askari. Throughout the East African campaign, raw nature could be as dangerous as the enemy.

In Burma, the threat – if slightly different – proved no less ubiquitous and appeared again in a variety of forms. When the 7th Armoured Brigade arrived in Burma straight from combat in the North African desert, Rangoon was already under attack and in a state of chaos. Captain the Rev N. S. Metcalfe, Chaplain to the 7th Hussars, went with the transport officer to the zoo in order to recover some RAF vehicles thought to have been abandoned there: 'Fortified by the report that all the animals of a dangerous nature had been destroyed, we made our entry only to discover that some were very much alive, and outside their cages! There was a tense moment when it was discovered that a "tree trunk" was really a crocodile, and a "rope" … a full-size boa constrictor!'[34]

Training in eastern India before Wingate's 1943 penetration into Burma, David Halley relates a narrow escape:

'One dark and starless night, a Gurkha sentry was standing to his post, alert and keen as Gurkhas always are. The jungle here seemed to us thick enough by day, as the visibility was never more than about fifteen feet, but at night it was impenetrable. The Gurkha strained his eyes this way and that. It was coming near the hour of dawn, when the enemy is most likely to make his attack. The slightest unnatural movement would herald his arrival. At last came the sound for which he had been tensely listening, a stealthy crackle in the undergrowth… He crouched, ready to spring. A slinking shape materialised, blacker against the surrounding blackness. The Gurkha leaped and clutched, then, with a startled cry, let go his hold and departed at speed into the night.

It was a tiger he had grabbed. And the tiger, equally startled, lost no time in departing at an equally high rate of speed.'[35]

After waking up one morning to find that a few of his 'friends' had put a baby tiger into his bed, Neil H. Barrett goes on to report a far less innocuous event:

'Three men from the quartermaster outfit driving along the Burma Road in a jeep saw a tiger jump from the brush on the side of the road and lope slowly towards the opposite side. At this point, one of them did a very foolish thing. He fired at the tiger with a .30-calibre carbine, hitting him just hard enough to wound him. It takes a much heavier weapon than this to kill a tiger. The tiger turned in a blind rage and attacked the jeep. Of the three occupants, only one lived to reach the hospital. The jeep was a complete wreck – the hood, radiator, and windshield were completely torn off by the terrific power of the tiger's paws.'[36]

If tigers were the most powerful animals that men had to contend with during the Burma campaign, snakes were, perhaps, the most unnerving. In Back to Mandalay, Lowell Thomas records a story told to him by Dick Boebel, one of Col Phil Cochran's Air Commandos, whose glider broke loose and crash-landed beyond the Chindwin but before reaching the 'Broadway' jump zone where it was supposed to have landed. In his party were four Americans, five Burmese, and eight 'Britishers', and after they had escaped from the crash site, they stopped to rest:

'When we thought we were safe from Jap pursuit we crouched in a thicket to rest. We were worn out. I was lying exhausted when in the darkness a noise started crackling. I saw the shadow of a snake coming down the side of the gully to my right. There was enough light to see that the thing was about five inches in diameter, a huge python... Luckily, I remained still. He came down. It all took about ten seconds. It seemed eternity. The python crossed over my right foot, straight across my left, and up the other side of the gully. He never hesitated a second, never slowed down. He must have been twelve feet long.'[37]

On 8 February 1945 Slim moved his Tactical Headquarters to Monywa:

'The Japanese had left behind a number of booby traps which were disconcerting, but my chief frights came from snakes which abounded in the piles of rubble. They seemed specially partial to the vicinity of my War Room which lacked a roof but had a good concrete floor. It was my practice to visit the War Room every night before going to bed, to see the latest situation map. I had once when doing so nearly trodden on a krait, the most deadly of all small snakes. Thereafter I moved with great circumspection, using my electric torch, I am afraid, more freely than my security officers would have approved. It seemed to me that the risk of snake bite was more imminent than that of a Japanese bomb.'[38]

Having set up a target range upon which to teach Shan tribesmen marksmanship, OSS man Neil Barrett found his first training exercise suddenly and swiftly broken up by the appearance of a king cobra not more than 20 feet behind him. 'His head was puffed out at the sides as it is when he is attacking. I was running in a zigzag fashion, because this is supposed to be the only way to keep one of them from running you down. They practically have to stop to turn.'[39] Eventually the snake gave up the chase, but the curious Barrett turned and followed from a distance, attempting to shoot the cobra with his .45-calibre pistol. When the snake turned on him a second time, Barrett gave up both his interest in the cobra and his target range.

Setting aside the threats of immediate death posed by tigers and snakes, the armies fighting in Burma had daily to deal with a wide variety of other annoying creatures. Duncan Guthrie, dropped into the Karen Hills in order to raise native levies, reported waking one morning to find his clothes, rucksack, and all of its organic contents eaten by big brown and white ants.[40] David Halley wrote of clouds of disease-bearing flies gathering around wounds and the difficulty of sleeping in the bush when covered by thousands of ants.[41] Leeches were among the worst of these annoyances, and throughout Burma, they were ubiquitous. Brigadier John Masters has written:

'Our short puttees, tied tightly round the join of boot and trouser, kept out most of the leeches, but a halt seldom passed without an oozing of blood through the boot eyelets telling us that some particularly determined beast had found its way in. Hair-fine when they passed through the eyelet holes, they fed on our blood, and when we had taken off puttee, boot, and sock it was a bloated, squashy, red monster the size of our little finger to which we applied the end of a lighted cigarette.'[42]

Fred O. Lyons, one of Merrill's Marauders, even reported leeches crawling into men's ears and noses, 'so the medics would hold a cupful of water under the leech-sufferer's nose or ear. As the leech reached down, the medic would tie a loop of string to the tail and pull tight.'[43] A lighted cigarette would then be applied and the leech removed so that the head would not break off beneath the skin and start an infection. 'All of us were more or less bloody all the time,'[44] Charlton Ogburn Jr judged. But still, nature had not finished with the tropical combatant.

In both East Africa and Burma, flies, mosquitos, airborne and waterborne micro-organisms, and general fighting conditions visited so many and such debilitating diseases on the troops that it is difficult to keep track of them. Slim, writing about 26 days of combat during the 1944 monsoon, reported that 9 Brigade 'had only 9 killed and 85 wounded, but lost 507 from sickness.'[45]

In East Africa, the profile was much the same: 'By 1916 the ratio of non-battle casualties to battle casualties was 31.4 to 1.'[46] Malaria, typhus, jaundice, blackwater fever, dengue fever, spotted fever, dysentery … the list was endless, and sooner or later almost every man who fought in a tropical theatre of war was struck down by something. Indeed, many British officers who later wrote compelling personal accounts of the war in East Africa –Meinertzhagen, Wynn, Young, Buchanan, Thornhill, and others – were eventually knocked straight out of the theatre, not by the enemy but by fever and ill health. Returning to Burma, on 25 May 1944, Col Charles Newton Hunter reported that before Myitkyina where the American Galahad Force was fighting, 'Almost every member of the unit was suffering from either malaria, dysentery, diarrhoea, exhaustion, or fever.'[47] Weeks later, conditions were worse: 'The rains continued to fall heavily as the June days dragged inexorably on. Three or four days of steady rain would be followed by a day or two of searing humid heat. Men sitting endlessly in wet foxholes began to develop trench foot. Malaria, fungus, and fever were afflictions common to most everyone.'[48] Writing of approximately the same time, Mike Calvert reported the same problem in 77 Brigade: 'We fought and lived most of the time in mud and water and everything and everywhere was at best damp and at worst soaking.'[49]

Alongside the men, animals and, consequently, transport were powerfully afflicted. Throughout East Africa men and animals continually passed through belts of tsetse fly; as a rule the men managed to avoid infection with sleeping sickness, but mules and horses did not, and they died by the thousands, delaying transport and clogging the roads with their rotting bodies.[50] Eventually, animal sickness became so widespread and so problematic that it seriously disrupted supply, particularly the supply of food and medicine, and this in turn caused the general health of the army to deteriorate further. By war's end, animals were being replaced by porters, and there was fairly general agreement that trying to use beasts for tropical transport had been a mistake.[51] In Burma both Wingate and Merrill placed heavy emphasis on animal transport, and while the animals were prized and even loved, the rigours of the tropical climate exacted a staggering toll. Injury, the enemy, and finally disease felled the mules right and left. Charles Ogburn Jr, for example, recalled that leeches plagued Galahad's mules more consistently than Galahad's men: 'Their fetlocks were generally red and slimy with blood. In addition, eggs deposited in their lesions by a kind of fly hatched out into screw worms.'[52] As Wingate and Merrill's campaigns wore on, more and more animals went down, and with each animal's death the fighting efficiency of its parent unit was reduced.

Too frequently, the impact of raw nature manifesting itself through disease was brought on by, or compounded through, serious problems with the food supply. And even when sickness was not an immediate result, obtaining food adequate to keep up one's strength remained a consistent difficulty through both campaigns. Owing to breakdowns and slowdowns in motor and animal transport, Francis Brett Young's narrative of the march down the Pangani is the record of a march made continually on half rations.[53] Frank J. Magee RNVR, helping in 1915 to drag the gunboats *Mimi* and *Tou-Tou* north from South Africa so as to sweep the Germans from Lake Tanganyika, reports having to hunt frequently in order to keep up the meat supply and having to shoot crocodiles in order to provide food for the expedition's porters.[54] Captain Shorthose often had to live off the country, and some of the most difficult fighting that he saw came in 1917 when he was hard pressed for food and fighting the Germans for the possession of native grain fields.[55] In 1916 Deneys Reitz reports several times being hungry: 'Meanwhile we were living under famine conditions. There was little or no game in the forest, nor any cattle in this tsetse-haunted region [near Kissaki], and the millet fields lay mostly reaped ... and for the next few weeks we lived on very spare diet.'[56] Buchanan, who fought against food shortages daily, eventually purchased a hen so as to guarantee himself a steady supply of eggs; the system worked well for several months until the hen 'was stolen by someone whose hunger overcame his scruples'.[57] Arnold Weinholt recalled some of his porters going so far as to eat some 'awful-looking red and yellow toadstools' to satisfy their hunger; the result was not fatal, but it came close.[58]

For the Germans in East Africa, conditions were not much better, but resourceful improvisation often came to their aid. Of necessity, General von Lettow-Vorbeck had to rely on carriers for his transport, so in most cases this kept his food supplies abreast of his army. Invariably, von Lettow reports that he foraged, the supreme guerrilla tactician living off the land. Mtama, a kind of millet, was pounded into a native flour, which, when mixed with stocks of European flour, made excellent bread, the staple of the askari's diet.[59] Watching flocks of birds gave von Lettow the idea that maize crops could be harvested and used before they were ripe, experiment soon showing him that the grain could be artificially dried before being made into very good meal.[60] Fruits were collected by primitive gathering techniques in the bush, water was often collected from inside coconuts and bamboo, and meat was derived from both hunting and native herds. Finally, hippos were used as a source of fat: 'The quantity varies: a well-fed beast provides two bucketfuls,'[61] providing that an expert was present who knew where to find it. These measures notwithstanding, food remained a persistent problem for the Germans, and on 27 November 1917, while Smuts's famous scout, Major P. J.

Pretorius, watched from the top of a gorge, Captain Tafel marched to within one mile of von Lettow's approaching column before turning away and altogether missing their intended rendezvous. On the following day, ignorant of the fact that he had come so close, near starvation but unable to replenish his stocks of food, Tafel surrendered '3,400 askaris, nineteen officers, a hundred Europeans, and a thousand porters.'[62]

In Burma, for the men engaged, food often proved as much of a problem as it had been in East Africa, and the lack of it proved equally debilitating. During Wingate's first raid, David Halley recalled how the Burma Riflemen of his intelligence section helped the regulars to supplement their diet by catching small sprat-like fish with their mosquito nets: 'Then they impaled five or six of them on a bamboo splinter, stuck their splinters into the ground beside a fire, turned it round once or twice, and they were ready for eating,' bones and all.[63] Later, during the walkout, when his own party faced starvation, Halley attempted to quell his hunger by swallowing a small piece of soap, while, 'Our two Burmese plucked little bamboo shoots and the tenderest and greenest pieces of grass they could find and made themselves a sort of stew.'[64] In a Burmese jungle village, Neil Barrett faced the possibility of having to dine with the local headman upon white worms drawn from beneath a manure pile and stewed, the whole mess being served with an accompanying dish of roasted wasp. Diplomatically, Barrett and his companion 'insisted that we didn't want to eat up his food, which was very hard to obtain'.[65] During the move forward to begin the second Chindit operation, Richard Rhodes James, John Masters's signals officer, made this observation: 'The rations themselves were a throwback to the bad old days – bully, biscuits and a few dried apricots. We were expecting something rather good on this trip, but the supply services ... fell down badly.'[66] Later, throughout the rigours of the second Chindit penetration, stretching three days rations to cover a five-day period became the standard procedure.[67] Given the particular strain of the Chindit operation, malnutrition contributed significantly to the near collapse of the units involved:

> 'Beginning about June 1 1944, a man with a cut finger would probably show anaemia; then the cut would go bad; then his whole body would droop, and in a day or two, he would die. Men died from a cold, from a chill, from the exertion of a patrol to the nearest village four miles away. Mild malaria cases became helpless, men with jungle sores or dysentery collapsed... Desmond Whyte was a fighting doctor and, when I called all the medicos together for a conference, he and the others assured me that a high proportion of the British troops, officers and men, were in fact on the threshold of death from exhaustion, undernourishment, exposure, and strain. It needed only a small push to send such men over.'[68]

With the Marauders of the Galahad Force, the food situation proved tragically similar: surviving on C, D and K rations – none of which provided enough nourishment to sustain operations for long periods – the men first became obsessed with food and then, gradually, went into a physical decline that brought the whole unit near to collapse. Charles Ogburn Jr described the intermediate stage:

'Supper – Preparations same as breakfast with exception chocolate bar and bouillon instead of fruit bar and coffee and too often with corned pork loaf – vile concoction with a perfume flavor from apple flakes... Some made cocoa from D-Bar. For a while Sam's trick of shutting eyes and chewing together with soft biscuit gave illusions of eating a chocolate cake.

After an hour's interval we again hungry. Followed a period of old-maid's gossip of our eating habits at home: the best meals we'd ever had, ideal menu for first repast on getting out, etc. Voluptuous lingering over details like Latins discussing mistresses... At last sleep, but after midnight constant waking up to gnawing in belly.'[69]

Even in the face of such misery, after the fact, men tended to treat it humorously in order to shield loved ones from the deprivation they had suffered. In 1944, following his combat experience in the Arakan, Lt Cedric Carryer of 44 Royal Marine Commando sent his mother this recipe:

'Take one pint of water; if it is black, don't worry because it will be blacker still in a little while. Take three monsoon beetles and ground them up finely. Add some flies legs (these flies must be fully fledged and mature). Mix up with the hearts of a Preying Mantis, and the head of a tarantula. Now add corn beef indefinitely, and heat rapidly, and leave it to get cold by mistake. This dish will be found to be most delicious, if you close your eyes, hold your nose and think about "Christmas".'[70]

In both East Africa and Burma – after contending with climate, the savagery of nature, the onslaught of disease, and logistical nightmares – the men engaged in tropical warfare still had to confront the enemy, and when they did, the range of individual experience seems to have run a gamut from the absurd to the deadly. In both theatres of war the initial problem often involved nothing more complicated than finding and recognising the enemy. Von Lettow-Vorbeck, in a reflection that could serve to describe either war, begins with a specific miscalculation:

'After midnight, that is, quite early on the 22nd March [1916], I arrived at Kissangire Station, and discovered to my very great astonishment that all the reports about strong hostile forces moving on that place were erroneous, and that our withdrawal had therefore been unnecessary. This incident afforded me the remarkably striking proof of the extraordinary difficulty of observing the movements of troops in thick bush, and of the great care every commander must exercise in estimating the value of such reports.'[71]

Christopher Thornhill stated quite bluntly that, 'The greatest secret in this type of bush warfare is to see your enemy first.'[72] Thus, the men walking point for a column or a formation were almost always in the most responsible and the most dangerous position with regard to the enemy. Brett Young defined the problem more precisely: 'When our forces stumbled on a prepared position in the bush – and indeed the first evidence of its existence was generally a burst of maxim fire – they lost heavily in the first minute. There was no way out of it; these were losses which were inherent in the type of warfare and not to be avoided by any refinements of caution.'[73]

Throughout the Second World War, initial contact proved as difficult and nerve-racking in Burma as it had been in East Africa. At least twice in March 1945, Duncan Guthrie slept peacefully through the night, hidden by jungle foliage, only to wake in the morning to discover that Japanese patrols had passed within 15 feet of where he was sleeping.[74] To capitalise on the terrain, both sides made a virtue of concealment, and where Angus Buchanan had worn moccasins on night patrols in East Africa so as to avoid alerting the enemy to his whereabouts[75], David Halley resorted to simple fire discipline in order not to disclose his presence.[76] The Japanese, masters of camouflage, took nature a step farther in their attempts to avoid air attack; according to Neil Barrett's experience, 'The Japs used caged monkeys for air-raid warnings because monkeys are deathly afraid of aircraft. They would screech minutes before a plane would arrive. This would give the Japs sufficient time to find cover.'[77]

One might assume that making contact in the bush or the jungle at least resolved the problem of locating the enemy, but in practice the issue seldom proved so simple. In a remark that could, again, be applied to both battle zones, W. T. Shorthose declared that, 'It is extremely difficult in the African bush to distinguish friend from foe.'[78] Recalling a reconnaissance he conducted in 1917, P. J. Pretorius underscored the problem:

'During this period I had to move rapidly within a week from one camp to another, in much the same manner as a bird hops from one tree to the next, for the Germans sent out party after party to capture or kill me. On one occasion two companies converged on my camp, but – thanks to information brought to me by my native spies – I wasn't there! Instead, I was squatted on a neighbouring height watching a sharp engagement lasting an hour between the two companies of Germans, who each thought the other was my party.'[79]

To show that this particular kind of error knew no nationality, one has only to review von Lettow-Vorbeck's recollection of an incident that took place in 1918:

'I now followed slowly with the main body. Our rearguard, under Captain Koehl, had quite a series of little collisions, which in bulk caused the enemy not inconsiderable losses. One of our Askari patrols had been surprised and captured by a stronger enemy patrol when engaged in foraging for food. These Askari subsequently looked on while this English patrol fought quite a bloody action with another English detachment in the thick bush and the occurrence gave them their opportunity of escaping.'[80]

In what became one of the more celebrated incidents to occur during the 1916 advance toward the German's Central Railway, Arnold Weinholt, Christopher Thornhill and some others who were engaged in a long-range reconnaissance carried out an exploit that depended entirely for success on the difficulty in differentiating friend from foe, and on Weinholt's ability to speak German. As Thornhill recalled:

> 'Just then through the scattered trees and long grass we saw a small convoy of pack donkeys, in charge of a Greek or two, followed by hundreds of natives carrying loads on their heads. As we watched there seemed no end to the long line, which appeared to stretch out for miles. We let the first lot of askaris and pack donkeys go past and when they were out of sight we cut in upon the road, finding only one remaining askari in charge. He must have thought we were Germans for as we came up he stood and waited, making no attempt to flee or defend himself, so we walked right up to him, and Weinholt relieved him of his rifle, which he handed over quite willingly. By this time there was quite a little knot of carriers standing before us.'[81]

While Thornhill directed the German carriers to throw down their loads and start a high fire, Weinholt bolted up the trail after the extended line of porters. 'Shouting and cursing at them in German, I got these puzzled fellows to turn back with their loads.'[82] Half starved and gorging themselves on German sausage, Thornhill and Weinholt nevertheless supervised the destruction by fire of nearly 200 loads before making their rapid retreat at the head of a few captured prisoners whom they had loaded down with German provisions.

In Burma, the inability to distinguish friend from foe quickly produced some equally tense moments. During the walkout from the first Chindit expedition, near Hintha, Brigadier Fergusson had this narrow escape:

> 'As usual when using tracks, I was leading the Column, and I halted it as a precaution while I went on with a Burma Rifles sergeant, as interpreter if I needed one, to check that the village was clear. As a further precaution I had a grenade in my hand with the pin out.
>
> We reached the crossroads without incident, and from there I saw a fire on the track thirty yards to my left, with four men sitting around it. Still without misgiving, I approached them and asked a question in Burmese. They looked round startled, and the Karen sergeant said "They're Japs!" at the same moment as I realised it myself. I dropped the grenade – indeed, I was so close that I almost placed it – on the fire between them, and ran. They were so surprised that they made no move. It was a four-second grenade, and when it went off I looked round. All four men had fallen outwards from the fire, and only one showed any sign of life.'[83]

On 18 June 1944, during the advance on Mogaung, the Lancashire Fusiliers and the King's put in a particularly difficult day cleaning more than 100 of the enemy from some rice paddies into which they had driven them. Brigadier Calvert, who commanded the brigade's operation, reported what happened next:

> 'At twilight that day as the Fusiliers were finishing cooking their evening meal in their newly won positions, a patrol of seven men came in, heaved a

sigh, lay down their rifles, and took off their equipment. It was only then that one of the Fusiliers saw that they were Japanese. A rush for weapons ensued, and the Japs were soon all overpowered and killed. They were a patrol who had been away for twenty-four hours and did not know that their position had been captured.'[84]

If tropical warfare compounded the difficulty of telling friend from foe, all sides – in order to gain the advantage over their enemies – engaged in deadly and sometimes elaborate deceptions. In 1915, in order to stop an educated Arab at Mwanza who had been capturing British intelligence agents, Richard Meinertzhagen employed the stratagem of sending the man a letter of thanks along with 1500 rupees in German currency as a supposed reward for his services. Intercepting the letter and believing that Meinertzhagen had succeeded in turning one of their most effective spies, the Germans reacted as Meinertzhagen had hoped that they might: they arrested the Arab and shot him for treason.[85] During their 1916 retreat, one of von Lettow-Vorbeck's Schutztruppen laid an ingenious minefield on a mountain road using 4-inch shells recovered from the SMS *Königsberg*, the German cruiser that had been sunk the year before in the Rufiji delta.[86] Having been stopped by the mines, which had proved particularly deadly, Thornhill eventually cleared the road by bringing up a herd of oxen and driving the sacrificial beasts through the minefield.[87]

In Burma, where the Japanese were notorious for setting booby-traps, one trap in kind proved especially insidious. During the first Chindit expedition, David Halley reported his unit, exhausted and half-starved, entering a deserted native village to find a succulent ham hanging from the doorpost of a native basha; the first two men to approach the ham were instantly killed by the Japanese who had sighted a machine-gun on the morsel.[88] Neil Barrett reported a similar instance later in the war near Loi-Lem. This time the Japanese used the body of an American officer as bait, but, sensing a trap, Barrett's men were not drawn; instead, they waited: 'The second evening two Japs started out of some nearby brush toward the body, but that was as far as they got.'[89] In fighting south of Tamu on 20 March 1944, British Major Perrett, leading his Lee tanks to the rescue of a force of infantry that had got pinned down, advanced into an attempted Japanese deception that he modestly called 'most confusing and rather dangerous.'[90] The Japanese, after having given considerable thought to the technical aspects of their ambush, had positioned their infantry on one side of a narrow jungle road and six well-camouflaged Type 95 tanks on the other side of the road. Their apparent intention in so arranging themselves was to tempt the Lees into confines where the British tanks would not be able to bring their guns to bear. Perrett solved the problem by bolting straight through the ambush into the clearing beyond:

'The position of the combatants was now exactly reversed – the Japanese were themselves sandwiched between infantry on one side and tanks on the other.

Suddenly, the enemy infantry began to melt away into the jungle, and the Japanese tank crews panicked. Instead of reversing into deeper cover, which

would have put the British tanks' bigger guns at a disadvantage had they tried
to follow, they broke out of their ambush position and tried to drive past the
Carabiniers.'[91]

This disastrous move resulted in the destruction of five Japanese tanks and the
capture of a sixth.

Finally, across the course of both tropical wars and with some qualification for
their enemy's perceived weaknesses, men on all sides developed a blunt admiration
for their opponents' bravery and devotion to a cause. On 25 March 1916, near the
Himo River, Meinertzhagen made this entry in his diary:

> 'We all under-estimated the fighting qualities of the German native troops.
> They have proved themselves quite first-class, stubborn fighters and cheerful
> in adversity. It speaks highly of German training and discipline… The
> Germans have every reason to be proud of their men and von Lettow has
> every cause for congratulation on his leadership under harder conditions
> than we have experienced.'[92]

Indeed, Meinertzhagen's personal appreciation of both von Lettow-Vorbeck and
the army he led in East Africa became and has remained the accepted fact. Looking
at the issue from the opposite side, von Lettow-Vorbeck, although sometimes
critical of his opponents' tactics, nevertheless admired the British for their bravery
and their drive.[93] About his Portuguese opponents in Portuguese East Africa, von
Lettow seemed to have decidedly less respect.[94] In Burma, where the Japanese had
initiated the fighting by showing perfect contempt for their Western opponents,
their attitude was slow to change, but change it did. Shown the Allied
determination at Kohima, Imphal and Myitkyina, the Japanese became more wary
of offering battle. In the vicinity of Myitkyina, as the battle entered its last stages,
Bert Butler, a British officer attached to Kachin HQ, saw a large body of Japanese
troops making their way through the jungle a few yards from the radio shack.
'Japanese morale had gone. A hundred of them crept solemnly past the little HQ,
making no attempt to attack it.'[95] Such stories crop up constantly in reading about
the Japanese retreat from Burma; clearly, one can deduce, the Japanese had been
forced to develop a new respect for the American, British and Chinese armies
ranged against them. About the Japanese themselves, the Allies never had the
slightest doubt. Slim thought them 'ruthless and bold as ants while their designs
went well'[96], but found their inflexibility to be their undoing. Indeed, from the
beginning, Slim knew how to defeat them, having learned the secret from a
Chinese general:

> 'His experience was that the Japanese, confident in their own prowess,
> frequently attacked on a very small administrative margin of safety. He
> estimated that a Japanese force would usually not have more than nine days'
> supplies available. If you could hold the Japanese for that time, prevent them
> from capturing your supplies, and then counter-attack, you could destroy
> them.'[97]

About the hardihood of the Japanese army, the individual bravery and tenacity of its soldiers, Slim said that he knew of no army that could have equalled them.[98] Major Peter Gadsdon, who earned the Military Cross for the action he describes at Letse, makes the point more explicitly:

'We then worked through the village ahead killing about ten. They just fight to the last – typical example of one wounded – my chaps put a round over his head and shout "hands up!" He puts his hands up. We start to close in on him. He goes for a grenade – we all dash for cover! Then we start again, until he throws the grenade whereupon my chaps fill him up with lead… We only got the officer because he was past reaching for a grenade.'[99]

If the Japanese soldier's refusal to surrender in the face of certain death was not always understood by the British and Americans who contended with him, the bravery with which he fought was well recognised and admired.

War, any war, is never what men expect it to be. Instead, as philosopher J. Glenn Gray has noticed, 'War compresses the greatest opposites into the smallest space in the shortest time.'[100] In the process, as civilised, well-developed environments are stripped away, men are reduced to their essence, and upon this, for long periods, they are forced to rely. This, more than anything else, typified war in the tropics as made manifest in East Africa and Burma. It was at once what made both conflicts so utterly simple and so absolutely complex. Fighting to a final decision through jungle, bush, and thorn, men were forced to move forward stripped of everything but themselves.

Notes on contributors

Professor Phillip Parotti, Sam Houston State University, Huntsville, Texas, USA.

Professor Parotti graduated from the United States Naval Academy in 1963, served four years at sea, and enrolled at the University of New Mexico to pursue graduate studies, receiving his PhD in 1972. In addition to having published essays, professional articles, poetry and short fiction, he is the author of The Greek Generals Talk: Memoirs of the Trojan War (1986), The Trojan Generals Talk: Memoirs of the Greek War (1988), and a novel, Fires in the Sky (1990).

Recommended reading

Calvert, Michael, *Fighting Mad: One Man's Guerrilla War* (London: Leo Cooper, 1996)
  Prisoners of Hope (London: Leo Cooper, 1996)
Farwell, Byron, *The Great War in Africa: 1914-1918* (New York: W. W. Norton, 1986)
Fraser, George MacDonald, *Quartered Safe Out Here* (London: HarperCollins, 1993)
Gardner, Brian, *On to Kilimanjaro* (Philadelphia: Macrae Smith Co, 1963)

Masters, John, *The Road to Mandalay* (London: Corgi, 1973)

Miller, Charles, *Battle for the Bundu: The First World War in East Africa* (New York: Macmillan, 1974)

Nunneley, John, *Tales from the King's African Rifles* (Petersham: Askari Books, 1998)

Page, Malcolm, *KAR: A History of the King's African Rifles* (London: Leo Cooper, 1998)

Slim, Field-Marshal Viscount, *Defeat into Victory* (London: Papermac, 1988, originally published by Cassell, 1956)

Tuchman, Barbara W., *Stilwell and the American Experience in China, 1911-1945* (New York: Macmillan, 1971)

Notes

[1] Wynn E, Wynn, *Ambush* (London: Hutchinson, 1937) p5

[2] C. Inman Leonard, 'Letters Home: A P-47 Thunderbolt Pilot Reports to the Home Front from the CBI Theatre', 9 April 1945, online posting, http://www.cbiinfo.com/letters_home.htm.

[3] Wynn E. Wynn, op cit, pp250-251

[4] Deneys Reitz, *Trekking On* (1933; London: Faber & Faber, 1947) p78

[5] Captain W. T. Shorthose, *Sport & Adventure in Africa: A Record of Twelve Years of Big Game Hunting, Campaigning & Travel in the Wilds of Tropical Africa* (London: Seely, Service & Co, 1923) p88

[6] Christopher J. Thornhill, *Taking Tanganyika: Experiences of an Intelligence Officer, 1914-1918* (London: Stanley Paul & Co, 1937) p16

[7] Christopher J. Thornhill, op cit, p9

[8] Capt Angus Buchanan, *Three Years of War in East Africa* (1919; New York: Negro Universities Press, 1969) p6

[9] Wynn E. Wynn, op cit, pp26-7

[10] Colonel R. Meinertzhagen, *Army Diary, 1899-1926* (Edinburgh: Oliver & Boyd) pp97-8

[11] Ibid, p101

[12] Wynn E. Wynn, op cit, pp118-9

[13] Field-Marshal Viscount Slim, *Defeat into Victory* (1956; London: Papermac, 1988) pp117-8

[14] F. Spencer Chapman, *The Jungle is Neutral* (London: Chatto & Windus, 1949) p37

[15] Francis Brett Young, *Marching on Tanga* (1917; New York: E. P. Dutton & Co, 1927) p44

[16] R. Meinertzhagen, op cit, p105

[17] Arnold Weinholt, *The Story of a Lion Hunt: With Some of the Hunter's Military Adventures During the War* (London: Andrew Melrose, 1922) p197

[18] Ibid, p197

[19] Darrell Berrigan, 'Uncle Joe Pays Off', *Saturday Evening Post*, 17 June 1944, p20

[20] Frank Dorn, *Walkout: With Stilwell in Burma* (New York: Thomas Y. Crowell Company, 1971) p28

[21] Bernard Fergusson, *The Trumpet in the Hall: 1930-1958* (London: Collins, 1970) p143

[22] Neil H. Barrett, *Chinghpaw* (New York: Vantage Press, 1962) p39

[23] Michael Calvert, *Prisoners of Hope* (1952; London: Leo Cooper, 1996) p40

[24] Ibid, p41

[25] Slim, op cit, p538

[26] Christopher J. Thornhill, op cit, p28

[27] Angus Buchanan, op cit, pp27-8

[28] Wynn E. Wynn, op cit, p139

[29] W. T. Shorthose, op cit, p100

[30] Francis Brett Young, op cit, p50

[31] Arnold Weinholt, op cit, p146

[32] R. Meinertzhagen, op cit, p94

[33] Arnold Weinholt, op cit, p208

[34] Bryan Perrett, *Tank Tracks to Rangoon: The Story of British Armour in Burma* (London: Robert Hale, 1978) p30

[35] David Halley, *With Wingate in Burma* (London: William Hodge & Co, 1946) pp33-4

[36] Neil H. Barrett, op cit, p18

[37] Lowell Thomas, *Back to Mandalay* (New York: The Greystone Press, 1951) p236

[38] Slim, op cit, p417

[39] Neil H. Barrett, op cit, p128

[40] Duncan Guthrie, *Jungle Diary* (London: Macmillan & Co, 1946) p17

[41] David Halley, op cit, pp93-4

[42] John Masters, *The Road Past Mandalay* (1961; London: Corgi Books, 1973) p256

[43] Capt Fred O. Lyons (as told to Paul Wilder in 1945), 'Merrill's Marauders in Burma', on-line posting, http://www.cbiinfo.com/merrilsm.htm.

[44] Charlton Ogburn Jr, *The Marauders* (New York: Harper & Brothers, 1959) p143

[45] Slim, op cit, p358

[46] Byron Farwell, *The Great War in Africa: 1914-1918* (New York: W. W. Norton, 1986) p293

[47] Colonel Charles N. Hunter, *Galahad* (San Antonio: The Naylor Company, 1963) p131

[48] Ibid, p160

[49] Michael Calvert, *Fighting Mad* (London: Airlife, 1996) p177

[50] Lieutenant-Colonel Charles Horden, *Military Operations in East Africa*, Vol I (Nashville: The Battery Press, 1941) p394. See also Farwell, op cit, p306

[51] See Christopher J. Thornhill, op cit, p73; Arnold Weinholt, op cit, p251; and Francis Brett Young, op cit, p53

[52] Charlton Ogburn, op cit, pp143-4

[53] Francis Brett Young, op cit, pp68, 103-4

[54] Frank J. Magee RNVR, 'Transporting A Navy Through The Jungles of Africa in War Time', *The National Geographic Magazine* 42 (1922), pp335-6, 347

[55] W. T. Shorthose, op cit, pp135-40

[56] Deneys Reitz, op cit, p104

[57] Angus Buchanan, op cit, p112

[58] Arnold Weinholt, op cit, p194

[59] General Paul von Lettow-Vorbeck, *East African Campaigns* (New York: Robert Spiller & Sons, 1957) p124

[60] Ibid, p162

[61] Ibid, pp146, 219

[62] Major P. J. Pretorius, *Jungle Man* (New York: E. P. Dutton & Co, 1948) p205. See Charles Miller, *Battle for the Bundu: The First World War in East Africa* (New York: Macmillan, 1974) p297, for conflicting figures

[63] David Halley, op cit, pp67-8

[64] Ibid, p165

[65] Neil H. Barrett, op cit, p26

[66] Richard Rhodes James, *Chindit* (London: John Murray, 1980) p38

[67] Ibid, pp76, 98, 148

[68] John Masters, op cit, pp255-6

[69] Charlton Ogburn, op cit, p155

[70] Cedric Carryer, 'To My Darling Mummie', 29 June 1944; *Despatches from the Heart: An Anthology of Letters from the Front during the First and Second Word [sic] Wars*, ed Annette Tapert (London: Hamish Hamilton, 1984) pp106-7

[71] Paul von Lettow-Vorbeck, op cit, p110

[72] Christopher J. Thornhill, op cit, p68

[73] Francis Brett Young, op cit, p136

[74] Duncan Guthrie, op cit, p53

[75] Angus Buchanan, op cit, p30

[76] David Halley, op cit, p74

[77] Neil H. Barrett, op cit, p72

[78] W. T. Shorthose, op cit, p151

[79] P. J. Pretorius, op cit, p200

[80] Paul von Lettow-Vorbeck, op cit, p241. See p240 for an incident in which the English mistake the Germans for their friends

[81] Christopher J. Thornhill, op cit, pp162-3

82 Arnold Weinholt, op cit, p162
83 Bernard Fergusson, op cit, p155
84 Michael Calvert, *Prisoners of Hope*, p218
85 R. Meinertzhagen, op cit, p128
86 Jim Burbeck, 'The Last Voyage of the SMS *Königsberg*', 10 May 1999, on-line posting, http://www.wtj.com/artdocs/konig.htm.
87 Christopher J. Thornhill, op cit, pp188-9
88 David Halley, op cit, p96
89 Neil H. Barrett, op cit, p153
90 Bryan Perrett, op cit, p101
91 Ibid, p101
92 R. Meinertzhagen, op cit, p178
93 Paul von Lettow-Vorbeck, op cit, pp134, 153, 195
94 Ibid, pp208-77
95 Ian Fellows-Gordon, *The Magic War: The Battle for North Burma* (New York: Charles Scribner's Sons, 1971) p143
96 Slim, op cit, p537
97 Ibid, p18
98 Ibid, p337
99 Major Peter Gadsdon, 'To Mum and Dad', 21 March 1945; *Despatches From the Heart: An Anthology of Letters from the Front during the First and Second Word [sic] Wars*, ed Annette Tapert (London: Hamish Hamilton, 1984) p122
100 Glenn Gray, *The Warriors: Reflections on Men in Battle* (1959; Lincoln: University of Nebraska Press, 1970) p12

Chapter 10

Hitting the beach: the amphibious experience

Geoffrey Till

'**E** ach one of us had our own little battlefield. It was maybe forty-fifty yards wide. You might talk to a guy who pulled up right beside of me, within fifty feet of me, and he got an entirely different picture of D-Day.'1

Introduction

The first thing that needs to be said is that there was no 'amphibious experience' of either war. Experience is both an input and an output. People have immediate experiences of personal events, but in slower time they can process them into accumulated knowledge of previous related events to be used to guide them in the next. Moreover, personal experiences covered a range that was determined by which operation they were involved in, and what their role was in it. But as one participant noted, even when these two variables were the same, it was extremely difficult to generalise:

'And yet the great story of the Royal Marines [in the Normandy landings] can never be told as a single adventure: there were so many different craft, different jobs, different experiences in the same job.'2

Because the conduct of amphibious operations is an activity of infinite variety, so also are the experiences they generate. One of the major determinants in shaping this experience was the strategic circumstances of the country. In Britain there was a widespread view that though amphibious operations were difficult, they remained feasible; however, unless there were a major collapse in the Maginot line there was unlikely to be an early requirement for amphibious operations in Europe; in the Far East they could only be waged against Japan once sea and air command had been assured, and this too would take precedence. For all these reasons, there were more important things to be done in the meantime. While the development of Britain's capacity for amphibious operations was not neglected to the extent often claimed, it was certainly far from being its top priority. British amphibious experience in Norway and French West Africa unsurprisingly reflected that fact.3

It was different for the Americans, whose strategic circumstances appeared so much simpler and whose vision of the future was therefore much clearer. The

Japanese would attack first, seize the Philippines and other islands, forcing the Americans to fight their way back across the Western Pacific. Assaulting a whole series of island bases through carrier airpower and amphibious operations of the most rigorous kind was therefore central to the American view of their strategic future in a way that simply was not true for the British. In due course, American experience would reflect that fact.

But, more immediately, the Americans had no such experience, other than a few largely uncontested 'administrative' landings in Nicaragua, Mexico and Haiti during the inter-war period. This was important because the experience of one campaign could, and frequently did, act as the basis for a universal desire that things should be different the second time around. Those involved in the planning and execution of the Normandy landings, for example, were grimly determined that it would be as different as they could make it from Dieppe, or still more from Gallipoli.

In the inter-war period the United States Marine Corps was well aware of its problem in this regard. At Quantico, its officers decided to make the fullest use of British experience at Gallipoli:

'In the [Gallipoli] campaign, we have at our disposal the results of actual experience in the planning and conduct of overseas operations; experience that can become our own through the medium of study ... it is the only combined or amphibious operation of that war which corresponds in any degree to the conduct of an overseas campaign which our own country might some day be obliged to conduct against a distant enemy.'[4]

As a result, the 1932-3 course engaged in a major exercise in reverse engineering, taking apart every aspect of the British conduct of the Gallipoli campaign, with a view to identifying what would need to be done differently for the Americans to be successful in a large amphibious operation like this.

Six committees were set up to investigate Naval Activities, Landings, Signal Communications, Naval Gun Fire, Intelligence, and Services and Supply. Their conclusions were eminently sensible and contributed to the appearance of the Tentative Manual For Landing Operations in 1934. In some respects, however, the Americans struck out in new directions, particularly in the development of what became known as 'Storm Landings', where the Japanese were dug in, could not be avoided and had to be overwhelmed by frontal assault.[5] This too had a profound effect on the American experience of amphibious warfare in the Second World War. However, as a comparison of the fundamentally divergent methods employed by the Marines in the Central Pacific and MacArthur in the South so clearly shows, there were basic differences even in the Pacific theatre.[6]

Against this background, it should be possible to deconstruct the two archetypal amphibious operations of the First and Second World Wars, Gallipoli and the Normandy landings, to identify their common stages and to compare and contrast the experience of both.

Planning the campaign

Planning a large-scale amphibious operation was and remains one of the most complex undertakings confronting the military planner because it involves operations at the interface of the sea, land and air dimensions of war, and because it seems to require activities that put the attacker into a situation of severe risk, especially at the early stage of the operation. During the first four months of 1915 Britain's planners were perfectly well aware of this and of their dearth of experience of anything but unopposed or administrative landings in modern military conditions. As General Charles Callwell observed:

> 'There was no precedent to point to and no example to quote. The subject had been studied tentatively and as a matter of theory, and certain conclusions may have been arrived at, but few works treating of the art of war concerned themselves with the matter at all, and the problem involved had hardly received the consideration to which it was entitled either from the point of view of the attacking or the defending side. Still, all soldiers who had devoted attention to the subject were in agreement on one point. They realised that an opposed landing represented one of the most hazardous and most difficult enterprises that a military force could be called upon to undertake...'[7]

The Gallipoli planners' ability to cope with all these notoriously difficult problems was limited by two key factors. First, as a considerable literature shows, there was gross indecision as to the purpose and nature of the whole operation. Was this to be a naval operation, or one with substantial Army support so that the Royal Navy could pass through the Narrows and threaten to bombard Constantinople? How much Army support was envisaged? Who was to have priority? Was this, instead, to be a Combined Operation? None of these things was clear; worse still, the strategic ideas seeping down from London were frequently ambiguous and seemed often to change.[8] This lack of clear direction from on high meant that theatre commanders at the operational level were in a continual state of uncertainty, and this in turn cascaded on downwards to the unfortunates who had to try to put the policies into effect at the tactical level, and whose experience of war was determined by it.

The second factor was the very short notice under which the Gallipoli planners were forced to operate. The decision to launch the landings on 25 April was made at a conference on *Queen Elizabeth* shortly after the failure of the Navy's attempt to force the Straits on 18 March. In short, the planners had just over a month to prepare for what was the recognised to be 'one of the most hazardous and most difficult enterprises that a military force could be called upon to undertake'. Worse still, the whole planning, and indeed the whole command system itself, was thrown together at the last minute, to the despair of many of those involved in it.[9] It is therefore hardly surprising that journalists at the time, the Quantico committees, and historians ever since, have been able to find major errors in almost every aspect of the campaign plan. What is perhaps more surprising is that in the circumstances, the planners did not do so much worse.

This is all in strong contrast to the deliberate and considered pace of the Normandy landings. This operation benefited first of all from the fact that it was not the first in the war. All previous experience, and particularly perhaps that of failures like Dakar, Norway and Dieppe, contributed hugely to the planners' understanding of the problems that confronted them. Dieppe, for example, pointed to the dangers of assaulting a defended port, and determined the whole shape of the Normandy battle. The inadequacy of naval gunfire and air support and the failure of the tanks at Dieppe all provided lessons that the planners were able to take to heart.

Moreover, the planners had time to absorb the lessons, reflect on them and take the appropriate remedial action in a process that went on recognisably for the better part of a year. Admiral Ramsay was designated Allied Commander, Naval Expeditionary Force, on 23 April 1942, and specifically appointed to command 'Operation Neptune' in July 1943. Of course conceptions changed as events unfolded, and there were disputes and arguments all the way through, but crucially there was time for this military dialectic to work. After the landings Ramsay wrote, '...because it all went so smoothly it may seem to some people that it was all easy and plain sailing. Nothing could be more wrong. It was excellent planning and execution.'[10]

It was all helped by the fact that despite the turf battles and the inevitable personality clashes, the command system worked well – in strong contrast to the gross inefficiency of the German military command system that was effectively wrecked by the Fuhrerprinzip.[11]

The planners were helped also by the fact that by 1944, no one on the Allied side was in any doubt either about the fact that this was to be the major strategic operation of the war, or about what its basic purpose was. It was top priority and generally commanded the resources it needed, if they existed.

The result was 'the most thoroughly planned amphibious operation in history.'[12] The outline plan was ready by late March and the ideas it contained were successively and practically put into effect in the weeks following. Finally, a full-scale simulation was conducted at St Paul's School in London on 15 May. Voluminous operational orders were issued in April, several inches thick. Many Americans were appalled at the level of detail. As the Commander of the Western Task Force, Rear Admiral Alan G. Kirk, US Navy, ruefully reported:

'The planning done by the ANCXF was of a very high order, but at the same time this operation illustrated once more the great difference in planning methods and concepts of command between the Royal Navy and the US Navy. British plans are issued in great detail from higher to lower echelons. American naval tradition tends to leave details of execution and planning to the officers who are actually charged with doing the job.'[13]

But whether the Americans liked it or not, great detail was what they got from Admiral Ramsay, a leader noted for his precision and enormous attention to detail.

The result of so much deep planning was in huge contrast to earlier experience at Gallipoli, where key issues over the conduct of the naval bombardment, for example, were left unresolved and where, in the awestruck words of the Official History, the '...naval orders [for the Anzac landings] with their various tables and appendices, amounted to no less than twenty-seven typed pages of foolscap.'[14] Planning at Gallipoli was as thorough as it could be, but not as it needed to be.

For all the planners, though, the activity was frantic and sustained. The Admirals, Generals and their staffs worked unstintingly:

'The generals set a pace that left other men in their early fifties panting and exhausted. They were typically on the road by 6.00am each day, inspecting, driving, training, preparing their men. They ate on the run, field rations or a sandwich and a cup of coffee. They did not return to their quarters until well after dark. Eisenhower averaged four hours sleep per night, Rommel hardly more.'[15]

Ramsay did better, managing golf on Sundays and some dinner parties in London, but for all of them the real contrast was between the preparation and the execution phases. Once Eisenhower's much-described order to go was given, all the generals became irrelevant for a while. Eisenhower gave no orders on D-Day. Bradley, head of the US First Army on USS *Augusta* off Easy Red section, Omaha Beach, was desperate for information, little more than a helpless observer of the awful events ashore.[16] At Gallipoli, Hamilton felt the same.

The result of all this processing of past campaigns and planning for the next, was a great sense that the problem of amphibious operations was now solved. What had to be done was known. In Admiral Kirk's words:

'It is my opinion that there has now been developed a technique of amphibious assault, which, when properly implemented can be counted upon to ensure a successful landing. Experience of joint British-American forces in the Mediterranean and in this theater, coupled to those acquired in the Pacific and Southwest Pacific theatres, prove by their unbroken series of successes that our system is correct.'[17]

Training for the campaign

To effect such a landing under the sea and shore conditions obtaining and in the face of enemy resistance requires careful preparation and training.[18]

As with planning, the desperate haste of the Gallipoli operation and the lack of advanced warning about its real amphibious nature left little time for specific training for the tasks ahead. Worse still, many of the main units, the 29th Division, the Naval Division, the Australians and New Zealanders, were not well schooled in the basics of the military art anyway. The 29th, for example, had never exercised at the Brigade or Divisional level. The Naval Division arrived without artillery or transport.

The month before the landings gave some opportunity for the rehearsal of small boat work off Mudros. For the sailors this involved practising the lowering and towing of cutters, picket boats and steam pinnaces. For the soldiers it was a question of learning how to clamber in and out of small boats when heavily laden. It was all very necessary, and good fun no doubt, but hardly sufficient. There was little training for the key tasks of subduing Turkish defences or for getting off the beach.

There was far more opportunity for extensive and thoroughly professional training for 'Overlord', many months for most troops, several years for the Canadians and Americans who arrived in Britain during the early part of 1942. In camps and bases scattered throughout the country, but mainly clustered in Southern England, the sailors, airmen and troops honed their basic general military skills and practised for their particular part in the invasion to come. For the Royal Marines, who manned two-thirds of the small craft used in the landings, it was a question of learning for months on end how to operate LCAs, LCMs or LCVPs in places like Dartmouth, Hove and Hayling Island. For the soldiers it could be any of a dozen specific skills, such as how two men should deal with pill-boxes.

If two men were attacking a pill-box, one would put continuous fire on the embrasure while the other crept up on it from the other side. When the advancing man drew fire, he went to ground and began firing back while his partner crept closer to the objective. Eventually one crept close enough to toss a grenade into the pill-box. 'We enacted this scenario countless hundreds of times from 1941 though 1943, often with live ammunition.'[19]

For the combat engineers and demolition experts it was how to deal with the countless underwater obstacles with which the Germans had bestrewn the invasion beaches.

And then as the day approached, it was a question of full-scale dress rehearsals through April and May 1944, usually with live ammunition and a reluctant expectation of casualties. The beaches of Southern Devon were thought appropriate places for the Americans to train their men in landing techniques. A little to the east, Major Howard of D Company, the Ox and Bucks, rehearsed his men for the assault on Pegasus bridge at a place near Exeter where a river and a canal ran close by one another.[20] And finally, on the eve of the invasion itself, unit commanders clustered round sand tables or scale models showing their particular objectives, when all was finally revealed, often even the names, so at last they knew where they were going.

Thorough though it was, training for Normandy was criticised for two things. First, as things turned out the training was too light in some areas. In a general way there was probably too much focus on hitting the beach and too little on the techniques needed to get off it and to develop the bridgehead. It seems that the biggest single omission was the failure to anticipate the difficulties of coping with the Normandy bocage, such a feature of the hinterland behind the American beaches. In a dry, post-action report, Lt-Col P. H. Bethune outlined the problem for Americans who at home had no experience of such things:

'A hedgerow is usually an earthen wall four or five feet tall and varying from four to six feet thick at the base. Usually trees and other shrubs grow in them. Almost every field seen in the combat zone in Normandy was surrounded by hedgerows. The Germans, when they have time to dig in, organise their defenses along hedgerows. The fields in front of the position are covered with inter-locking fires from automatic weapons.'[21]

How it was that this intelligence failure occurred, especially when the area where so many Americans were stationed in Devon was filled with just such hedgerows, is one of the great mysteries of the Normandy campaign. There were other failures in technique, too, most obviously perhaps the provision of close air support for troops in combat – techniques that had to be learned on the job.

But perhaps they were too well prepared, for the second criticism is that there was too much training and schooling for specific activities, and that the whole fragile structure would come tumbling down if the unexpected happened – as it did on Omaha. The Americans and Canadians who first arrived in Britain in 1942 had a second, closely related complaint. There was just too much wearisome, repetitive training. Men got bored with it, sometimes demoralised, sometimes restless, looking for fights in garrison towns and local pubs. The British, too, practised so much that people got 'browned off', especially towards the end when they were sealed into their concentration areas. But when all was revealed, the prolonged effort and the frustrating restrictions seemed justified:

> 'They sealed the Camp, no one in, no one out. We started the briefing sessions and the area of the intended landing and our job, oh boy! A table with a scale model of the Area and the objective, maps to scale with bogus names for the actual places. We were treated like fighting cocks, and the meals were the choice of American rations.'[22]

But in the end, despite its deficiencies, the training clearly worked and the men were well-prepared for the tasks ahead. On Gold Beach, according to one well-schooled British Marine:

> 'One wasn't conscious of being in the middle of a hurly-burly. Everything was very well ordered. Things were arriving, being unloaded… It was absolutely like clockwork. We knew it would be. We had every confidence. We had rehearsed it so often, we knew our equipment, we knew it worked, we knew given reasonable conditions we would get off the craft…'[23]

Of course, no plan survives first contact with the enemy, at least not in its entirety, and things did go wrong, when troops were landed in the wrong place, or obstacles proved more difficult to deal with than expected. Sometimes things were harder than had been thought, sometimes easier, but generally the Allied soldiers on the ground had been trained enough to cope. It was otherwise with the German defenders, whose capacity to cope with the unexpected revealed the disadvantages of Rommel's emphasis on the construction of defences at the expense of training.[24]

Shaping the battlefield

In amphibious operations, 'hitting the beach', while it is often the most intense and deadly phase of the campaign, is but one of them. It is preceded, and followed, by many others that can also do much to determine the final outcome. But, since getting ashore was recognised as a deeply hazardous activity, the function of navies and air forces was to do as much as possible to shape the battlefield so as to make the prospective operation as easy as it could be.

Indeed, at Gallipoli the initial idea was that a naval operation forcing its way through the Straits would make a large-scale contested operation unnecessary. But in the end it was found impossible for the Navy both to deal with the guns ashore by direct fire, and to get through the Straits themselves because of the Turkish mines, howitzers and mobile artillery. So, after all, a large-scale amphibious operation proved at the last moment to be necessary. The battlefield seemed to have shaped the naval action rather than the other way around.

Worse still, the whole effort devoted to a Navy-only, or Navy-mainly, operation gave ample warning and preparation time to the Germans and the Turks awaiting attack. It was, as so many people realised even at the time, a lost opportunity of major proportions. Had an amphibious operation been planned at the outset, things may have been very different. Even the young Lt G. C. C. Crookshank on the battleship HMS *Agamemnon* could see that this was clearly the case. After weeks of largely futile operations against the Turkish shore and three days before the actual landings, Crookshank confided in his diary:

> '…the southern end of the peninsula is altered altogether, the last month or so, and is now a mass of trenches and entanglements… If our troops had been ready in Feb[ruar]y after the destruction of the entrance forts, they could have strolled ashore smoking – now thousands of lives will be lost in landing.'[25]

But, of course, in the last month before the landing the Navy and the planners did what they could to facilitate it by feinting operations to north and south. The largely unprepared Naval Division hovered about at sea in a menacing fashion (or, in modern parlance, 'poised') off the Bulair lines to the north. The young Lt-Cmdr Freyberg volunteered to swim ashore and cause as much chaos and confusion as he could. Naked, painted black and greased against the cold (for there was a touch of frost in the air), he swam ashore for 2 miles carrying a revolver and a knife and towing a small canvas raft for flares. This took 2 hours. Once ashore, his teeth chattering with cold, he lit flares, investigated the Turkish trenches and sparked off a fire fight that drew in the gunfire of the fleet. He was eventually rescued and awarded a VC for his efforts.[26] Away to the south, the French staged a temporary landing on the Asiatic shore of the Straits.

The aim of both operations was to fix the Turkish Divisions in the area and to provide as much opportunity for the landed troops at Anzac and Helles to get ashore and break out of their bridgehead. The much-noted concentration of naval gunfire support at either end of the Allied assault on the peninsula was likewise designed to limit the Turks' capacity to reinforce the beaches' immediate defenders, and so, more distantly, were the operations of Allied submarines through the Straits themselves.

In the Normandy campaign, both sides devoted considerable attention to the requirement to shape the forthcoming battle in as helpful a way as they could. The Germans constructed a complex beach system (to which the commonly used phrase 'Atlantic Wall' does much less than justice) of interlocking .75 and .88

guns, heavy machine-guns, minefields and obstacles of every kind focused on the tactical need to force the invaders into pre-set killing zones. Heavy guns further back, plus extensive minefields at sea, were designed to impose attrition on the way in. Subsequent air and naval attack and the movement into the battle area of forces kept back from the beaches in reserve were the only active part of this defence system. The Germans' problem was that so much of their defensive system was static and was therefore vulnerable to plotting and subsequent evasion.

The Allied method of shaping the battle was much more ambitious than this. It incorporated an extensive deception plan intended to convince the Germans that the invasion would take place anywhere but Normandy. It involved thousands of people erecting dummy tanks in Scotland, flying aircraft in streams towards the Pas de Calais, poring over intelligence intercepts and photographs to see whether their secret had been guessed, liaising with the French underground, guarding against loose talk in the concentration areas, and so on and so forth. Their experience of 'Overlord' was enormously varied by their task but played a huge part in determining the outcome of the campaign.

Nearer the time, those remarkable people the COPP (Combined Operations Pilotage Parties) provided swimmers whose task was to investigate the topographical features of the beaches. One pair went ashore on New Year's Eve in 1943, as the sea was getting up:

'Eventually we got a signal from the beach to pick them up. By this time the surf was quite something. So these poor devils, weighed down by augers and soil samples [carried in 12 10-inch tubes worn on a bandolier] and measuring chains, had to swim out to us through this very heavy surf. We couldn't get any closer or we'd have overturned. Two very strong young men, but they came up absolutely exhausted. We hauled them back on board. "Happy New Year," they said.'[27]

Other COPP activities involved the use of midget submarines taking photographs of the beaches from wave level to help increase landing accuracy. But it was all carefully controlled so that untoward accident would not give the game away. To this end, beaches in the Pas de Calais were surveyed as well.

On the eve of the actual invasion an extensive bombing campaign was combined with French Resistance attacks to interfere with the free movement of German reserve forces behind the assault area by disrupting rail and road communications. But once again it was important to avoid giving the game away, so for every bomb dropped behind the Normandy area, two were dropped elsewhere. The US and British air forces also sought to soften up the German defences in a campaign that slowly mounted in intensity as D-Day approached.

In the hours before the main assault, parachutists were landed on both of the main flanks, partly to seize key points essential to the movement into the area of the Germans' immediate reserves, partly to facilitate a breakout from the bridgehead area, and partly to spread as much confusion as possible about the Allies' real intentions. It is hard to be sure about how effective all this was, but at the strategic level the Germans remained unsure that the Normandy landings were the main attack for several weeks afterwards, and so did not move forces into the area as speedily as they might have done. In due course they did find it difficult to move their strategic reserves as fast as the situation warranted. Operationally and tactically, and even in the immediate area behind, say, Utah and Omaha beaches, the arrival of crucial reinforcements was fatally delayed, partly because of the deficiencies of their command system, but partly because they had been so thoroughly confused by the Allies.

Much was expected of this aerial assault, not least by the troops themselves. On the way over, one RM officer on a LCVP of a more than usual poetic bent wrote:

'The sun climbed in a sky of windy blue, and soon we saw the whole arch of the heavens stippled with silver specks: masses of planes, coming and going, as thick as starlings, and all ours.'[28]

With so many resources devoted to the task and with such careful attention to ensuring that the conditions were as favourable as possible, what, the optimists wondered, could go wrong?

Approaching the beach

Because the amphibious operation against Gallipoli was mounted at such short notice, there was little chance for the attacking forces to develop much anticipation for the specific undertaking that lay before them. But they did realise that they were going gallantly to war in a beautiful and fabled spot, with the fate of empires resting on their efforts:

It must not be imagined that the situation seemed to those on the spot anything but reasonably promising at this time. It is indeed poignant to recall the high hopes with which the Naval Division had started out to the scene of war. Rupert Brooke has left on record his own peculiar enthusiasm: 'I had not imagined,' he wrote, 'that fate could be so benign… I am filled with confident and glorious hopes.' He was not alone in his excitement. The Englishman's protective irony could not indeed be expected to survive the splendour of that voyage through the Mediterranean, when the first breath of spring was in the air, the sea was brilliant like a jewel and 'sunset and dawn divine blazes of colour.' [29]

The contrast between the beauty of the scene and what was actually happening became greater the closer they approached the action. The Official History, when describing the approach to the second battle of Krithia, captures the extent of this contrast in a long and vivid passage that deserves inclusion not just for its own sake, but because it captures a point made less elegantly in so many recollection accounts:

'The scene that unfolded itself from the forward slopes of Hill 114 still lives in many memories. The grassy slopes that crown the hills are carpeted with flowers. The azure sky is cloudless; the air is fragrant with the scent of wild thyme. In front, beyond a smiling valley studded with cypress and olive and patches of young corn, the ground rises gently to the village of Krithia, standing amidst clumps of mulberry and oak; and thence more steeply to a frowning ridge beyond, its highest point like the hump of a camel's back. Away to the right, edged with a ribbon of silvery sand, lie the sapphire arc of Morto Bay, the glistening Dardanelles, and the golden fields of Troy. On the left, a mile out in the Aegean, a few warships lie motionless, like giants asleep, their gaunt outlines mirrored in a satin sea; while behind them, in the tender haze of the horizon, is the delicately pencilled outline of snow-capped Samothrace. As far as the eye can reach there is no sign of movement; the world seems bathed in sleep. Only high on the shoulder of Achi Baba – the goal of the British troops – a field of scarlet poppies intrudes a restless note. Yet in half an hour that peaceful landscape will again be overrun by waves of flashing bayonets; and these are the last moments of hundreds of precious lives.'[30]

But for the troops approaching this golden shore, their concerns were more immediate and much more practical. For the most part they were cramped together in small warships, and were already exhausted after hours of standing or perching in tiny spaces. Some of them were debilitated by inoculations or the effects of stomach upsets. Some of them inevitably were sick, even in that calm sea.

For the August landing at Suvla, the men of the 11th Division in SS *Partridge* had been on their feet for 17 hours:

'One by one we began to nod and doze, like old tired carthorses standing asleep in their stalls. And one by one we began to lean heavily against each other, to lurch and sag and give at the knees, until at last we sank slowly down into a sprawling overlapping heap. We had been on our feet since dawn. Most of us had "gyppy tummy" and many were suffering from sand-fly fever, a mild form of dysentery.'[31]

Many of them were also suffering the effect of recent cholera inoculations on top of all this. The troops' slow start, and their desperate desire for water when they reached Suvla, could perhaps only be expected.

The adrenaline began to pump around them as they scrambled into the small boats that were to take them to the beaches, and, as the naval gunfire support began apparently to devastate the shore-line, revived them.

'The soldiers in my boat were simply enthralled with the sight of the cliff's face being literally blown away by the ship's guns and the spectacle of the ship steaming in firing was magnificent... The change in their attitude towards what lay ahead during that short run in alongside the ship was quite phenomenal.'[32]

And when the Turks began to open fire with their machine-guns on the crowded helpless cutters and picket boats coming ashore, it needed to be, for desperate, unimaginable courage was called for.

Looking back on some of the catastrophes of the April landings, it was the sheer courage of all those involved that most impressed Lt Bampton of HMS *Prince of Wales*:

'General impressions after Dardanelles: The extraordinary coolness under fire of our boat Midshipmen who after all are only boys. Their trips to the beach several times daily through a zone of shrapnel fire was taken quietly as a matter of course. The coolness of everyone during the first landing in the dark which was a creepy business, and the irremovable courage of the men crowded in the boats under heavy rifle and shrapnel fire and the extraordinary determination and spirit in the Australians' first charge for the hill considering that they'd been in crowded boats shivering with cold for so long and had been under fire while quite helpless in the boats and that a large proportion of them were facing the music for the first time.'[33]

Lt R. W. Wilkinson of HMS *Ribble* approached Anzac Cove in bright moonlight:

'…and they opened fire on us from the cliffs at a range of about 300 yards. I was towing six boats alongside and before we could get them away I had 2 killed and 15 wounded on my decks… I had a bullet through my sleeve… The ship's side was ringing from the bullets … the Australians were fine. I felt proud that I was a Briton. They pulled in singing a song "Australia will be there". A good many lost their rifles in their eagerness to jump out of the boats, and I could see them scaling the cliffs, waving their sword bayonets, and heard them "cooing" like mad… In some of the boats everyone was either killed or wounded, and two boats drifted ashore where it was not possible to get at them, and the poor wounded must have died lingering deaths. The midshipmen in the boats were grand. They were mostly boys of 15 or 16 straight from Dartmouth. We felt very proud of them and it was wonderful and marvellous to see the way they took charge of and handled the big Australians.'[34]

But of course the experience of the approach varied from beach to beach, from time to time, from boat to boat. The first wave nearly always suffered much more than reinforcement forces coming in later in the day. The forces approaching stealthily in the darkness had tiredness to contend with and the tension of anticipating the first shots from the shore.[35] But the men coming ashore at V or W beach were plunged into instant and terrifying horror in awful scenes that defy description, but which can be inferred from the cold statistics of loss. For those coming ashore at Y beach, or S Beach and Suvla in August, on the other hand, it was almost an anti-climax.

The Captain of HMS *Pincher* saw both worst and the best of it. On 25 April he was a horrified observer of '…the poor wretches from *River Clyde* falling off the gangways like ripe plums to the water, it was awful to see…' But on 6 August he led the forces approaching Nibrunesi Point just south of Suvla Bay, tense lest he either point up the landing place incorrectly or by some incautious move spark the Turks on the assumed strongpoint on Lala Baba into action:

'…we eased down the anchor and I eventually found out we were only 2 degrees out in our proper bearing and almost 100 yds too far out, so I was rather pleased and not a sound ashore except a dog barking some way inland. So far so good!! We showed our light towards Kephalo and screened it well and it must have been a success as not a shot was fired at us so we evidently weren't seen. It was a fine sight to see the 7 destroyers slowly emerge from the pitch darkness, stop abreast of me, slip their motor lighters and in less than five minutes ... 3,500 were ashore and still not a sound.'[36]

Later that day there was some resistance, but the new armoured landing craft, the Beetles, proved their worth. Months later still, the acquired skill and specialised equipment of amphibious operations were demonstrated in the complex business of evacuating the force from under the unsuspecting noses of the Turks, without significant loss. It showed how much the British had learned of the business of conveying an assault force on to a hostile shore during the Gallipoli campaign.

Getting the troops to the beach was a much more complex affair at Normandy. The troops and their equipment were loaded into many different and specialist types of landing craft at scores of large and tiny ports of embarkation all along the southern coast of England. There were large assembly areas for the shipping around the Isle of Wight, and even the sight of this vast maritime concourse filled many of the troops with confidence.

Ahead of them, air and sea control had been assured and an extensive operation of clearing and marking a way through the German minefields had been laboriously completed. Picket ships and submarines were deployed to mark the way.

As they slowly approached the Normandy coastline, the distant sounds of battle began to make themselves felt:

'By this time, the whole horizon was twinkling, and the thunder of the guns became louder and more insistent – it was like an Autumn electric storm, with thunder and lightning rumbling in the distance. Just as we were debating whether the dark smudge on the horizon was the French coast, we were ordered below.'[37]

Closer in, the noise became deafening as air attack and naval gunnery seemed to be devastating the German defences:

'I went up on the bridge at 6.30am and from there I had my first view of the beaches. And what a view!! Just at that moment the RAF started their concentrated bombing – four times they flew up and down the beaches, and what had been all quiet a second before became a raging inferno. I saw the ground just rise in a sheet of flame and the noise was terrific. Even the ship shuddered violently and to me it seemed impossible that any human being could remain alive in the beach areas.'[38]

But, in fact, it was the same story at Normandy as it had been at Gallipoli. Naval gunfire support and, in the latter case, bombing proved less effective than it looked in the initial assault, and indeed for some time after the invaders had struggled

The First World War: British soldiers of the 8th Battalion Leicester Regiment move up into flooded trenches in France in the winter of 1915; a painting by soldier-artist 'Dick' Read. *I. L. 'Dick' Read, Liddle Collection, University of Leeds*

Above A generation later: the Second World War. *US official photograph, Second World War Experience Centre [SWWEC], Leeds*

Below British Eighth Army infantrymen move warily past a weapons carrier abandoned in Aquino, Italy, on 27 May 1944. They are searching for snipers among the ruins. *US official photograph, SWWEC, Leeds*

Above Pitching in the Bay of Biscay, 17-26 December 1943. 'Convoy scattered, structural damage to carrier HMS *Fencer* [shown here], multiple aircraft crashes and "right offs".' B. *Vibert, SWWEC, Leeds*

Below Resuming course after the storm: 'at 22 degrees, half our biggest roll'. B. *Vibert, SWWEC, Leeds*

Above 'The real Dad's Army': a British Home Guard unit under inspection. *E. C. Eshborn, SWWEC, Leeds*

Below Scuttling of the *Graf Spee*, 17 December 1939. *A. Bennison, SWWEC, Leeds*

Above A concert in the hangar of HMS *Furious* by the Soviet Northern Fleet. *B. Vibert, SWWEC, Leeds*

Below Submariners from HMS *D2* pose for a photograph immediately on return from patrol. This submarine was lost with all 26 hands on 25 November 1914 during her eighth patrol after an interaction with a German TB off Western Ems. During the war the D Class carried an additional officer for navigation duties. In *D2*'s case this was Lieutenant F. E. Oakley, an England Rugby International. *Royal Navy Submarine Museum, Gosport*

Above One of the legacies of Admiral Sir Max Horton to the Royal Naval Submarine Service was its battle ensign – the 'Jolly Roger'. Pictured here are members of the crew of HMS *Turbulent* commanded throughout her short but dazzling career by Commander 'Tubby' Linton VC DSO DSC. The 'Jolly Roger' was the symbol of shared danger and achievement of all on board, and was shown off with great pride. The bars represented ships sunk by torpedo, the stars ships sunk by gunfire, the daggers represented covert operations, and the 'U' was a U-boat sunk. Two 'oddball' symbols appear on the bottom left of the flag – the train was blown up by gunfire in St Ambroglio station, near Cefalu, and the lorry symbolised an attack against a car park in Sirte. HMS *Turbulent* was lost with all hands to a mine off Madellana during March 1943. *Royal Navy Submarine Museum, Gosport*

Below The Mercantile Marine: New Year's Eve, 1942, in a convoy, a 'Sam boat', that is a Liberty ship, British-designed, American-built, in bad weather off Cape Hatteras, viewed from SS *Atlantian*. *W. E. Williams, per Tony Lane*

Above German nightfighter pilots being reviewed by Reichsmarschall Goering. *H. A. W. Thomas, SWWEC, Leeds*

Below German paratroopers at a Luftwaffe base in Germany, Christmas 1942. Robert Frettlohr, nursing a broken arm, is in the centre, with his pipe and dagger. *Robert Frettlohr, SWWEC, Leeds*

Above Somewhere in Italy, 25 May 1944: Italian crew members reload the guns of a Macchi fighter plane after it has completed a mission over Yugoslavia, harassing the German withdrawal. *US official photograph, SWWEC, Leeds*

Below Flying Officer Harry Elderfield and crew being debriefed after a raid on Stuttgart on the night of 14/15 April 1943. Two nights later the crew ditched 6 miles off the French coast after a raid on Pilsen; the Second Pilot and the Bomb Aimer were drowned. Elderfield, on the right, tried to swim to the French coast to get help, as the dinghy was holed: drowned aged 28, no known grave. *Mrs Rhoda Elderfield*

ashore. 'The results,' concludes Stephen Ambrose, 'for the most part, were terribly disappointing.'[39] The German defences proved extremely resilient and were hard to spot; and in many cases the Germans were able to recover sufficiently quickly to open fire on the invaders when the Allied bombardment lifted. Many of the air attacks, moreover, were rather too far inland.

But while the bombing and the gunfire support were rarely as decisive as had been hoped for, the morale effect on the troops landing on the beaches was encouraging. And they certainly needed it, since for them the voyage over had been otherwise quite miserable.

The landing craft, varied as they were, big and small, all shared one characteristic – their flat bottoms meant they were not good sea boats. Nearly everyone was sick, many desperately so. 'Most of the crew was sick,' wrote one unfortunate. 'I actually took to sitting on a bucket and wondered how I could use it at that end and be sick at the same time.'[40]

Sometimes vomit even clogged the bilge pumps, making the landing craft still less seaworthy. Although this kind of reaction was so common as to be almost universal, it is difficult to generalise about the soldiers' feelings at this time. All were cold and tired, particularly the men en route to Utah, since many of them had spent much of the previous day at sea before the first attempt was called off in bad weather. But whatever their objective, the men were cramped, uncomfortable, often wet, some simply terrified, others wildly excited; but most were desperately anxious to get off their boats. As one Commando explained:

'The reason we stormed Normandy like we did was because the soldiers would rather have fought the whole German Army than go back on the ships and be as seasick as they were going over. My God! Those soldiers couldn't wait to get on dry land. Nothing would have got in their way... They would have torn tanks to pieces with their bare hands.'[41]

Hitting the beach

But for many of them, hitting the beach added to their problems rather than reducing them. In quite a few cases, as at Gallipoli, they found that they were being landed on the wrong beach, or on the right beach but in the wrong order. Experience at Anzac and Suvla seemed to show that accurate night landings were particularly difficult. In the Normandy campaign, the Utah landings were on the wrong part of the beach; the US Rangers heading for the strong-point at Pointe du Hoc were taken to the wrong headland and had to steam slowly down the coastline being heavily fired on by the Germans on the cliffs above them. The landings on Omaha were chaotic with the elements from the two Divisions (the 1st and 29th) jumbled up in a way that made a coherent attack very difficult.

For the Australians and New Zealanders at Anzac, landing a mile and a half from their intended beach had its compensations even if it did so confuse their order that coherent exploitation of their landing success proved impossible. The Turkish defences at their intended landing sight were much stronger and the attackers' initial losses would certainly have been greater. As it was, by the end of the day they had suffered some 2,000 casualties for 15,000 troops landed.

Away to the south, the 29th Division faced a different but equally difficult situation at Helles. Here the Navy had insisted upon a daylight landing because of the currents and navigational hazards inevitable with the tip of a peninsula. There were five beaches to be dealt with, two in the centre (V and W) and three flanking beaches (X, Y and S). The 86th Brigade was to form the bulk of the initial assault (or Covering force) for all five beaches, with the 87th and 88th Brigades as the main body reinforcing later in the morning. Anticipating action against V and W, the Turks had concentrated their defences there; the other three beaches were but lightly defended.

The experience awaiting the invaders depended clearly on which beaches they faced, and on whether they were in the initial assault or the follow-on landings. All three of the flanking beaches were taken with relatively few casualties, if any. The landings of the follow-on forces here could even seem quite civilised. Thus for Major Cuthbert Lucas of the 1st Border Regiment, landing at X, it was:

> '…a bright sunny morning, dead calm sea, not a shot fired. I had a bag in one hand, a coat over my arm, and was assisted down a plank from the boat by an obliging sailor, so that I should not wet my boots. The only thing missing was the hotel.'[42]

Inevitably, as more Turks arrived during the course of the day the situation became less civilised, especially at Y where, by the end of the day, of the 2,000 or so who had landed, 700 were casualties. Here it proved impossible for the attackers to consolidate their position and the men more or less evacuated themselves.

It was realised that the Lancashire Fusiliers at W faced a very difficult task, and a massed, rather than a sequential, assault was decided on. The troops were debarked from HMS *Euryalus* in a single sweep of eight tows, each comprising a steam picket boat pulling four cutters. The problem was that the picket boats drew 5 feet, so would have to cast off the cutters some 50 yards from the shore, from where the sailors would row the soldiers ashore. Facing them, after the initial naval bombardment, were perhaps 100 Turks with several heavy machine-guns and a good deal of barbed wire. But a straight numerical comparison between attacker and defender is meaningless, for as the Official History points out, 'while the defenceless troops scramble out of their boats, and struggle waist-deep in water, they can be shot down as easily, and almost as safely, as bottles at a fair.'[43]

This is indeed what happened. As Lt Clayton of the Lancashire Fusiliers reported:

> 'We thought nothing could survive the ship's guns, but they bombarded too far inland and the trenches overlooking the landing beaches were not touched, so the rifle and machine-gun fire poured into us as we got out of the boats and made for the sandy shore. There was tremendously strong wire where my boat landed. I got my wire cutter out but could not make the slightest impression. The front of the wire was now a thick mess of men, the majority of whom never moved again. The noise was ghastly and the sights horrible.'[44]

Worse still, the soldiers, encumbered with about 88lb of equipment, either left it behind in the boats or dropped their rifles in the water. Desperately they tried to clean the rifles with oil and brushes while under fire. The fact that eventually the Lancashire Fusiliers got though the wire and up the cliffs against such odds was nothing short of a miracle. But of the 950 men who disembarked from HMS *Euryalus* 530 were dead or wounded.

The outcome was similar at V beach, where a landing force of 2,800, mainly from the Royal Dublin Fusiliers, the Royal Munster Fusiliers and the 2nd Hampshires, came ashore in six tows on the left and the SS *River Clyde* (a collier imaginatively converted to disembark troops on to pontoons to the shore from holes cut in the sides) on the right. The 600 or so Dubliners in the tows suffered in much the same way as did the Lancashire Fusiliers, losing well over half their number in the process. Some of the boats drifted off with everyone dead; many Dublins were killed as they waded ashore, and many who were wounded, drowned.

Attempting to put men ashore from the SS *River Clyde* directly under the unsuppressed fire of machine-guns in the fort Sedd-el-Bahr was a serious mistake. The casualty rate amongst the first 1,000 men who sought to get out was terrible, perhaps one man in six reaching the shore. The last 1,000 came out under cover of darkness, or even on the following day. Second Lieutenant R. B. Gillett, leading his platoon out of the ship, was horrified by what he saw:

> 'The sight that met our eyes was indescribable. The barges now linked together and more or less reaching the shore were piled high with mutilated bodies – and between the last barge and the shore was a pier formed by piles of dead men. It was impossible to reach the shore without treading on the dead, and the sea around the cove was red with blood.'[45]

But in contrast to events at Y, where a good situation deteriorated, the situation at V and W slowly improved, and by the end of the day the British had 12.5 battalions ashore at Helles on a disappointingly narrow and vulnerable beachhead, at a cost of some 3,000 casualties.

The explanations for the high casualty rate and the 29th Division's failure to reach its objectives are many and various, ranging from failures in command, through insufficient resources and inadequate logistical and medical organisation. But what stands out, especially at V and W, was the failure of the close naval gunfire support so essential to contested amphibious operations in daylight. The contrast between the excellent performance of HMS *Albion* at V beach on 26 April, when the ship came in close, and its toothless performance on the crucial day before when it stood off as apparently directed, suggests that there was nothing inevitable about this failure.

It was a curiously similar story at Normandy. Here the need for heavy preliminary and close-in support from naval gunfire and aircraft, to compensate for conducting the landings in daylight, was fully realised, but here too its effects were disappointing. Again personal experiences depended on which beach and in which phase of the operation soldiers found themselves. Overall the Normandy casualty rate was about 4,900 from about 175,000 men landed by the close of D-Day. The luckiest, despite what they probably felt on their long (and repeated) voyage, were the men going ashore at Utah, who suffered some 200 casualties for the 23,250 landed. Worst were the Canadians at Juno, with losses of 1,250 casualties for 25,000 landed, and the Americans at Omaha, with 2,200 casualties for 35,000 landed. The American overall loss rate in one day was therefore about 6.5 per cent. Awful though that was, it is dwarfed by the 13 per cent rate of the Anzacs and the 20 per cent rate of the 29th Division at Gallipoli. In all cases, however, casualties were particularly heavy among the first wave, especially at Omaha, where losses approached the rate of the covering force at V or W beaches.

The German defences at Normandy were relatively much stronger, with a complex system of interlocking fires aimed principally down the beaches, rather than out to sea. Just as at Gallipoli, the troops were initially quite relieved at their apparent invulnerability on the run-in. Thus Corporal Andrews of 47 (RM) Commando approaching Gold :

> 'Started the run in, which was uneventful until a few hundred yards off-shore, then it was clear they did not want us to land, and the shells started to come down with great accuracy, many hitting the water [with] instant explosions. Capt O'Hare was in the front of the craft by the ramp, and kept saying, "Piece of cake. Piece of cake." We bumped, then the ramp went down, we all got ashore without getting our feet wet really, due to the consideration of the Coxswain.'[46]

However, many craft were hit on the way in, especially at Omaha, and heavy machine-gun fire often opened up on the hapless Americans just as the ramps of the landing craft were lowered. The sea state caused tremendous problems too, making it difficult for the men to scramble into the landing craft and unexpectedly keeping some of the obstacles covered. Fully laden landing craft and amphibious tanks often proved barely seaworthy, especially in deep water. Even finding a spot clear of debris and wrecks in which to get ashore frequently proved a problem. Some craft got stuck on sand-bars too far out, while others were almost wrecked on landing. As he approached Juno, Major Flunder, 48 (RM) Commando, observed all the chaos ashore:

> 'The shore line was under bombardment, there were sinking craft ... and ... it didn't look as if the Canadians who had landed just before us had actually secured the beach. Things didn't look particularly good, but I certainly didn't realise we were under direct small arms fire until I saw two men collapse and fall overboard from the craft on our starboard side. [We] ...grounded on an obstacle... [lowered the ramp] ...and off I went. I wasn't half-way down before a big wave carried the boat off the obstacle ... and somersaulted the ramp and me into the sea. I saw the great bows coming over me and the next thing I remember is finding myself walking up the beach, wet through of course, and with some of my equipment torn off, including my pistol, but still clutching my stout ash walking stick.'[47]

Ashore the noise was deafening, and at Omaha and parts of Juno everything seemed chaotic. The sights were often horrible, and many survivors took away with them awful memories of the carnage around them; a friend casually killed at one's side, unseeing tanks driving over their own wounded infantry, or the sight of mutilated corpses:

> 'There was body rolling with the waves. And his leg was holding on by a chunk of meat about the size of your wrist. The body would roll, then the leg would roll. Then the leg would roll back and then the body would roll back.'[48]

American survivors of the assault wave, shocked by their experience and deprived of leadership by the loss of so many officers, huddled for shelter and comfort, like the Lancashire Fusiliers before them, under a sand and shingle bank, until other officers, or NCOs or brave individuals, took them in charge and led them through the defences where their chances of survival and of success were so much higher. It was a classic case of small unit initiative led by people like Brigadier Cota at Vierville and Lt Spaulding at Colleville.[49]

The tanks that got ashore in fighting condition (all too few at Omaha since the amphibious variety were unloaded too far out), were invaluable, taking strong-points under direct fire and providing aiming points of reference for the warships, which were close in, anxious to help but often unsighted.

Captain de Loraine Scott recalls:

> 'Now the infantry came pouring ashore and our job was to fire over their heads and deal with any strong points which caused them trouble. Tank commanders had orders to have a go at these on their own initiative. Just in front of me was a large pill-box and we were pumping shells into this as hard as we could go. Over on my left I saw my Troop Lieutenant and another of my Troop tanks giving all they'd got to a large house almost surrounded by trees and from which machine-gunners were making things uncomfortable for the leading infantry. I saw them get several direct hits on the building and they blew most of the top floors to pieces.'[50]

By such a variety of means did the invaders of Normandy get and stay ashore. Only for a brief while at Omaha was there serious doubt that the Allies would prevail. Interestingly, the German defenders at Omaha, the 352nd Division, lost about 1,200 killed, wounded or missing, about 20 per cent of their fighting strength. The balance of advantage between amphibious attacker and land defender had plainly shifted since Gallipoli.

Back-up and break-out

'…you had to get off that beach. Get off the beach. Never mind anything else, get off the beach. That'd been drummed into us. They wanted to get this beachhead formed. That was the only thing that mattered. Get us off the beach so they could bring in more behind us. This time they were going to pile

the stuff in. Mulberry Harbour. Pile the stuff in. That's why it [Normandy]
succeeded.'[51]

And this is also why Gallipoli failed. At Anzac, V and W beaches, the key beaches
for reinforcement, the heroic survivors had struggled ashore, survived, held on; but
they ran out of steam. The main body arriving later had first to consolidate the
landing before pushing on. On that fatal delay more Turks had arrived and the
attacker/defender balance had shifted. In the extremely difficult country above
the beaches, military operations took the form that was normal for other
battlefields of that war. Krithia II and III were like other deadly encounters of the
time, except for the flies, the broiling heat and the narrowness of the gap between
the front line and the so-called rest areas. Accordingly it proved impossible to
expand the bridgehead, as the planners had wanted.

The result of all this was a very narrow area that did not allow for sufficient
storage for spares, on-shore medical facilities, landed artillery and for the assembly
of sufficient reserves. The Royal Navy was therefore doomed to provide close
support to the forces ashore, in very hazardous and unfamiliar circumstances, for
months on end. The absence of sufficient reserves, the relative undermanning of
so many of the units engaged, acute shortages in artillery, shells, even grenades, all
made it impossible to recover the momentum so fatally lost on the day of the
landings. The wonder is that the Allies managed doggedly to hang on at Gallipoli
and, even more, to evacuate so successfully when the time came.

The planners of Normandy were determined that none of this should happen
again. The plan was to have 11 Divisions ashore by D-Day, 13 by D+1, 17 by D+4.
Stores of every sort would flood in. Huge resources were to be committed to the
campaign. In the expectation of high casualties, many units were over-manned.
Moreover, in the critical initial period few German reinforcements, even those
theoretically in close support, arrived in time. But despite all this, the break-out
was still difficult.

Soldiers who had struggled through the experience of the landing felt
overwhelming relief and euphoria at having survived and having succeeded.
Above the Easy Red section at Omaha, Sgt John Ellery of the 1st Division recalled:

'The first night in France I spent in a ditch beside a hedgerow wrapped in a
damp shelter-half and thoroughly exhausted. But I felt elated. It had been the
greatest experience of my life. I was ten feet tall. No matter what happened, I
had made it off the beach and reached the high ground. I was king of the hill
at least in my own mind, for a moment.'[52]

Not surprisingly there was something of a very natural human tendency to rest on
one's laurels and to leave the exploitation to someone else. In Normandy on 7 June
1944, as on the Gallipoli Peninsula on 26 April and 8 August 1915, a new range of
experiences lay ahead.

Notes on contributors

Professor Geoffrey Till, Joint Services Command and Staff College, Bracknell, UK
Professor Till is Dean of Academic Studies at the Joint Services Command and Staff, College, Bracknell, and Head of the Defence Studies Department. He is also Visiting Professor in Maritime Studies in the Department of War Studies, King's College, London. In addition to many articles and chapters on various aspects of defence, he is the author of a number of books. His work has been translated into eight languages and he regularly lectures at defence and academic establishments around the world.

Recommended reading

Gallipoli
Aspinall-Oglander, Brigadier-General C. F., *Military Operations: Gallipoli* (London: William Heinemann, 1929) Vol 1
Callwell, Major-General Sir Charles, *The Dardanelles* (London: Constable, 1919)
Gillon, Captain Stair, *The Story of the 29th Division: A Record of Gallant Deeds* (London: Thomas Nelson, 1925)
Hargreave, J., *The Suvla Bay Landing* (London: Macdonald, 1964)
Liddle, Peter, *Men of Gallipoli* (London: Allen Lane, 1976)
Steel, Nigel and Hart, Peter, *Defeat at Gallipoli* (London: Macmillan, 1994)

Normandy
Ambrose, Stephen, *D-Day 6 June 1944: The Climactic Battle of World War II* (New York: Simon & Schuster, 1994)
Bruce, Colin John, *Invaders: British and American Experience of Seaborne Landings, 1939-1945* (London: Chatham Publishing, 1999)
Hastings, Max, *Overlord: D-Day and the Battle for Normandy 1944* (London: Bookclub, 1984)
Love, Robert W. (ed), *The Year of D-Day: The 1944 Diary of Admiral Sir Bertram Ramsay* (Hull: University of Hull Press, 1994)
Miller, Russell, *Nothing Less Than Victory: The Oral History of D-Day* (London: Michael Joseph, 1993)
Ryan, Cornelius, *The Longest Day* (New York: Popular Library, 1959)

Notes

[1] Stephen Ambrose, *D-Day June 6 1944: The Climactic Battle of World War II* (New York: Simon & Schuster, 1994) p420
[2] Anon, *The Men of the Little Ships* (Eastney, Portsmouth: Royal Marines Museum, afterwards RM Museum) Arch 7/19/5
[3] See David Massam, 'British Maritime Strategy and the Development of Amphibious Warfare 1900-1940', DPhil thesis, Oxford, 1995
[4] Cdr L. W. Townsend, US Navy, 'The Dardanelles Campaign', lecture delivered at Marine Corps Schools, 1922. USMC Archive, USMC University, Quantico, Va (afterwards USMC)
[5] Joseph H. Alexander, *Storm Landings: Epic Amphibious Battles in the Central Pacific* (Annapolis: Naval Institute Press, 1997) pp4-5
[6] Ibid, p88
[7] Major-General Sir Charles Callwell, *The Dardanelles* (London: Constable, 1919) p105
[8] For this, see my 'Brothers in Arms: The British Army and Navy at the Dardanelles' in Hugh Cecil and Peter H. Liddle (eds), *Facing Armageddon: The First World War Experienced* (London: Leo Cooper, 1996)
[9] Discussed in my 'The Gallipoli Campaign: Command Performances' in Gary Sheffield and Geoffrey

Till, 'Challenges of High Command in the Twentieth Century' (Camberley: SCSI Occasional No 38, 1999)

[10] Robert W. Love (ed), *The Year of D-Day: The 1944 Diary of Admiral Sir Bertram Ramsay* (Hull: University of Hull Press, 1994) pxxxvii

[11] Stephen Ambrose, op cit, p68

[12] Ibid, p107

[13] United States Fleet, Task Force One Two Two, Report, 25 July 1944, 'Amphibious Operations: Invasion of Northern France', p6, USMC. Hereafter cited as Kirk

[14] Brigadier-General C. F. Aspinall-Oglander, *Military Operations: Gallipoli* (London: William Heinemann, 1929) Vol I, p172

[15] Stephen Ambrose, op cit, p68

[16] Ibid, p435

[17] Kirk, op cit

[18] Joseph H. Alexander, op cit, p9

[19] Stephen Ambrose, op cit, p131

[20] Ibid, pp141-2

[21] 'Report on Observations on Normandy Operation Headquarters Army Ground Forces, 7 Sept 1944', Box 124, USMC

[22] Ted Ford, *The Nearly Man* (Wolverhampton: privately published, 1997; RM Museum)

[23] Stephen Ambrose, op cit, p521

[24] Ibid, pp115-6

[25] Diary entry, 22 April 1915, The Papers of Captain G. C. C. Crookshank, Imperial War Museum (IWM)

[26] Douglas Jerrold, *The Royal Naval Division* (London: Hutchinson, 1923) p80

[27] Colin John Bruce, *Invaders: British and American Experience of Seaborne Landings, 1939-1945* (London: Chatham Publishing, 1999) p176

[28] *Men of the Little Ships*, op cit

[29] Douglas Jerrold, op cit, p67

[30] C. F. Aspinall-Oglander, op cit, p343

[31] J. Hargreave, *The Suvla Bay Landing* (London: Macdonald, 1964) p78

[32] Letters from the then Midshipman Stanley Norfolk to Captain Hughes Lockyer, RN, 2 Sept 1936, cited in Nigel Steel and Peter Hart, *Defeat at Gallipoli* (London: Macmillan, 1994) p84

[33] Undated reminiscence, Papers of Captain J. Bampton (IWM)

[34] Letter of 1 May 1915, Papers of Captain R. W. Wilkinson (IWM)

[35] C. F. Aspinall-Oglander, op cit, p173

[36] Diary entry for 25 April and 6 Aug 1915, Papers of Captain H. W. Wyld (IWM)

[37] Undated memo, Papers of J. K. Emerson, Arch 7/19/5 (RM Museum)

[38] Memo of 8 August 1944, Papers of Captain John de Loraine Scott, RM, Armoured Support Group, Arch 7/19/5 (RM Museum)

[39] Stephen Ambrose, op cit, pp269-70

[40] Ted Ford, op cit, p50

[41] Stephen Ambrose, op cit, p521

[42] Quoted in Captain Stair Gillon, *The Story of the 29th Division: A Record of Gallant Deeds* (London: Thomas Nelson, 1925) p21, and cited in Steel and Hart, op cit, p97

[43] C. F. Aspinall-Oglander, op cit, p222

[44] Cited in Field Marshal Sir Nigel Bagnall, 'The Human Story', Gallipoli Memorial Lecture Series, 1992, p4

[45] 2nd Lieutenant R. B. Gilbert, Sound Recording (IWM) cited in Steel and Hart, op cit, p106

[46] Papers of Sgt W. A. Andrews of 47 (RM) Cdo, Arch 7/19/5 (RM Museum)

[47] Papers of Major D. Flunder, 48 (RM) Cdo, Arch 7/19/5 (RM Museum)

[48] Stephen Ambrose, op cit, p353

[49] Ibid, pp339-40 passim and 349-52

[50] de Loraine Scott papers, op cit

[51] Cited in Bruce, op cit, p140

[52] Stephen Ambrose, op cit, p382

Chapter 11

British Special Forces operations behind enemy lines

Julian Thompson

'They [special forces] contributed nothing to Allied victory. All they did was to offer a too-easy, because romanticised, form of gallantry to a few anti-social irresponsible individualists, who sought a more personal satisfaction from the war than of standing their chance, like proper soldiers of being bayoneted in a slit trench or being burnt alive in a tank.'[1]

This remark is attributed to a choleric General officer in a work of fiction by John Verney, who served in Lord Jellicoe's Special Boat Squadron – thinly disguised as 'Bomfrey's Boys' – in the Mediterranean in the Second World War. This war has been called the golden age of British special forces, and certainly neither before nor since have so many private armies flourished and behind-the-lines operations been mounted; albeit with varying success. Certain sections of British special forces also received much adulation in the press, both during and after the war, and patronage from the highest political and military figures. Despite this publicity and support, or perhaps because of it, special forces were not universally admired, especially by their fellows, and by some senior commanders, as the above quotation demonstrates. Although the remark may be apocryphal, it was not untypical. Field Marshal Slim condemned 'private armies' as 'expensive, wasteful and unnecessary', saying that they could 'only be employed for restricted periods', while conceding that 'there is, however, one kind of special unit which should be retained – that designed to be employed in small parties, usually behind the enemy, on tasks beyond the normal scope of warfare in the field.'[2] The Field-Marshal was persuaded to insert the exception above by his son, then Major John Slim, serving in the Special Air Service (SAS) in Malaya in the 1950s.[3]

Behind-the-lines operations in the Second World War were the province of what were loosely called Special Forces; at least as far as the British were concerned. For the purposes of this chapter, my definition of a special forces soldier is one who operated in the enemy's rear areas, but usually fought in uniform expecting to be treated by the enemy in accordance with the laws and usages of war (in the event an expectation that was not always met). This excludes most Special Operations Executive (SOE) operations. This chapter is confined to describing the activities of units that operated behind enemy lines for protracted periods, and omits some of the units that in the Second World War were often loosely grouped under the heading 'special forces', although passing mention of some of them will be made. Some, as we shall see, were neither 'special', in the sense that they had undergone rigorous selection, nor consisted of men of an especially high calibre. There were far too many 'private armies' to include even passing mention of all of them in a single chapter. Instead, following a brief overview, it is intended to outline Special Forces operations within the framework of some of the activities of the Long Range Desert Group (LRDG), the Special Air Service (SAS), and the Chindits, while mentioning some others.

The First World War saw no 'private armies', as defined above, in the British order of battle. The fronts were usually static for long periods, and especially on the key Western Front there were no flanks. The means of strategic and tactical mobility were limited and constrained by the nature of the war and the available military technology. No attempts were made to raise forces even just for reconnaissance when special circumstances arose – amphibious operations, for example. General Sir Ian Hamilton, when planning the Gallipoli landings, could not call upon such expertise. Had appropriate teams been available, the troops at Anzac might have landed in the correct place thanks to proper terminal guidance; the beach and underwater obstacles at Helles should have been accurately plotted together with enemy strengths and dispositions there; while weak or undefended spots on the peninsula might have been identified as the best places at which to direct the main point of effort – to name but three areas in which, for lack of proper reconnaissance, the Gallipoli operation was seriously flawed. Even in the desert – the exception, in that flanks and opportunities to exploit mobility existed – T. E. Lawrence and the small band of officers and men engaged in the Arab Revolt were rather like United States advisers in Vietnam in the 1950s and 1960s, or seconded personnel, and were not a special force in their own right.

The proliferation of 'private armies' a mere two decades later owes much to the nature of the Second World War and the advance of military technology. By 1942 the war was being fought over a vast geographic area, and in many theatres. However, with regard to continental Europe, the fall of Denmark, Holland, Belgium, Luxembourg and France had excluded Britain from North Western Europe, then, after German victories in Greece and Crete, Balkan campaigning was precluded too. Special Forces offered a way of getting at the enemy that did not incur the risks or require the resources for an invasion, impossible as this was without the support of the United States. The sheer size of enemy-occupied territory presented the opportunity of open flanks, and long lines of communication vulnerable to attack, and often many choices of approach by sea, land and air. The scope of activity in the Second World War, and especially the great Allied amphibious and airborne operations, demanded that they be preceded by covert parties, mainly for reconnaissance, but also for deception and destruction. The Combined Operations Pilotage Parties (COPPs), responsible for beach reconnaissance before amphibious landings, are one example of such parties. The SAS teams inserted on the flanks of the intended Allied beachhead early on the night of 5/6 June 1944 to spread alarm and draw enemy forces away from the main landing areas are another.

In the 22 years since the end of the First World War, aircraft had been produced that were capable of flying long ranges carrying quite heavy loads. Troops could be launched into battle, and be supplied, by parachute. Heavier equipment, including guns, light tanks, engineer plant and large numbers of troops, could be brought in by gliders towed by powered aircraft, and landing strips could be constructed for follow-up waves flown in by transport aircraft. The military radios of the early 1940s, although nothing like as small, light and versatile as today's equivalent, were sufficiently powerful and portable to enable the passage of information from operations deep behind enemy lines, and allow command and control of these activities over long distances. Wheeled vehicles capable of operating over rough terrain were available in quantity, thus extending the 'reach' of behind-the-lines operations. A soldier in the Second World War could usually call upon a weight of firepower and array of support undreamed of by his forebears two decades before, including small, light, hard-hitting weapons such as the Vickers K-gun, the shoulder-fired PIAT anti-tank projector, 2-inch and 3-inch mortars, and the .5-inch Browning heavy machine-gun. An individual could control fighter-bombers to strike targets far behind enemy lines. Transport aircraft could keep him supplied, reinforce him and evacuate him if he were wounded. He might even have a vehicle flown in for his use.

Special forces in the Second World War had, and still have today, three functions: offensive action, the gathering of intelligence, and operating with indigenous resistance groups, which sometimes included transporting and escorting agents. Of course these functions often overlapped, and it would be incorrect to assume that the first two were always conducted independently of resistance groups. For example, the escape of the partisan leader Tito, when his headquarters at Dvrar was attacked by the Germans in May 1944, was greatly assisted, at his request, by British special force operations in Dalmatia both in concert with partisans and independently.[4 & 5]

The dilemma facing special forces supporting partisans, Maquis, call them what you will, was that to be effective the guerrilla force must be active. As Brigadier Michael Calvert, the outstanding Chindit leader and SAS brigade commander, once remarked:

'As a guerrilla you don't achieve anything by just being present. No regular force of any nation in the world is really frightened of guerrillas unless they can see the result in blown bridges, their friends being killed, or trucks being ambushed. There were cases in Burma and elsewhere, for example in Europe, where missions just existed, were supplied by the RAF at great risk, and did nothing.'[6]

Yet activity against a ruthless enemy often brought down retribution on the heads not only of the partisans, but also on the local population. An Australian officer trained by Calvert, after blowing a railway bridge in China, learned that the Japanese had hanged a hundred villagers from the telegraph posts along the line. A repeat effort by the officer concerned resulted in the Japanese hanging a thousand villagers, men, women and children.[7] Thereafter fear of Japanese reprisals effectively closed down guerrilla activity by British officers in China.

One answer to this dilemma lay in engaging in 'stand-alone' operations, that is having little or no contact with the local population, and certainly not relying on them for support. This was only possible when the terrain and circumstances, such as a very low population density, allowed. The British operated behind the lines in a variety of terrains, but perhaps the two that offered the best conditions for protracted stand-alone operations, were the North African desert and Burma. But terrain is not necessarily the overriding factor in determining whether an operation can be 'stand-alone'. T. E. Lawrence could not have operated in the desert without support from Arab tribesmen. His operations were the opposite of 'stand-alone', which is not to say that they were ineffective, but they illustrate the difference between the methods he was forced to adopt and those used in another desert in the Second World War. It was the advance of military and other technology, discussed earlier, that allowed the LRDG and SAS to operate 'stand-alone'. Although the Light Car Patrols (LCP) in the First World War had patrolled the Egyptian frontier with Cyrenaica in Ford cars over some of the ground covered by the LRDG in the Second, they did not penetrate behind enemy lines, so their ability to operate 'stand-alone' was not tested.

June 1940 saw the first British special forces raised in the Second World War – the commandos in Britain and the LRDG in Egypt – each with a different purpose in mind. On 22 June France concluded an armistice with Germany, but before this, on the 6th, Winston Churchill minuted General Ismay, his Chief Staff Officer and personal representative on the Chiefs of Staff Committee, on the subject of striking back at the enemy-held coastline[8]; immediately the call went out for volunteers for what became known as the commandos.

The first two commando raids in 1940 were not successful, two others the following year moderately so. Eventually more raids were conducted, perhaps the most notable being the Dieppe operation and the raid on St Nazaire, in both of which the commandos distinguished themselves. But although conceived as a raiding force, most commando operations in the Second World War were not conducted behind enemy lines, nor were those by parachute battalions. Of the 38 battle honours on the Commando Association Flag in St George's Chapel, Westminster, three are raids, the remainder commemorate activities in support of main force operations, such as North Africa, Sicily, Normandy and so forth. However, the early days of commandos are interesting because some of the characters who joined them were to emerge later in other special units, and the manner of their raising was to be mirrored in later 'private armies'. To begin with, much of the recruiting was by word of mouth – who you knew and whether your face fitted counted for much. Selection, where it existed, was mostly by your peers. For example, Number 8 Commando was formed from troops in London District by Lieutenant Colonel Laycock of the Blues, and mainly consisted of officers and men from the socially smart Guards and the 60th (King's Royal Rifle Corps). 'It was White's Club in the Army,' commented Lieutenant the Lord Jellicoe of the Coldstream Guards.[9] Jellicoe was later to serve in the SAS in the Desert under Stirling (Scots Guards), another Number 8 Commando member. Later still, Jellicoe raised and commanded the Special Boat Squadron (SBS), an offshoot of the SAS. The founder of the Special Boat Section (also called the SBS – whether this served to confuse the enemy is difficult to establish, although it confuses many people to this day) was another founder member of Number 8 Commando, Lieutenant Roger Courtney, KRRC. He eventually broke away from the commandos, and the SBS became an entirely independent organisation. This separation of new 'private armies' from existing 'private armies', rather like amoebae, was another feature of British special forces in the Second World War, and led to the proliferation of such forces as alluded to earlier.

In the same month that commandos were being formed in the United Kingdom, Italy declared war on Britain and France, and British garrisons in the Middle East were threatened by substantial Italian forces in North and East Africa. The most immediate menace was the large Italian Army in Cyrenaica, which greatly outnumbered the British force in Egypt. The LRDG was the brainchild of Major Bagnold, who had spent his leaves in the inter-war years exploring the Western Desert in Model-T Ford trucks.[10] He persuaded the Commander-in-Chief (C-in-C) Middle East, General Sir Archibald Wavell, that a mobile force would be invaluable to watch the Italians and report on their activities, and, if they proved to be supine, which in the event they did, he would mount offensive operations. Within six weeks the LRDG was born and carried out its first patrol.[11]

In the North African desert during the Second World War, the supreme exponents of behind-the-lines warfare were the LRDG, followed later by the SAS. The LRDG's navigational and driving skills were such that if they said they would arrived at a certain point a thousand miles from base on a certain day, on most occasions they did. One of the early patrols, led by Captain Crichton-Stuart, raided Murzuk, in Libyan Fezzan, covering 4,300 miles between 7 December 1940 and 9 February 1941, in the process crossing the Egyptian Sand Sea:

> '...about the size of Ireland, from Siwa Oasis in the North, almost down to the Sudan, along the Libyan frontier. The parallel lines of dunes run almost north and south, rising to some 500 feet above the desert floor in the centre of the Sand Sea. Here and there the great, smooth, "whale back" dunes break into sharp, twisting crests and ridges, falling almost sheer on one side, utterly impassable except with the greatest labour on foot. Packed and shaped by the prevailing wind over thousands of years, this Sand Sea compares in shape and form with a great Atlantic swell.'[12]

The Italians, thinking the Sand Sea impenetrable, felt safe behind this barrier, but the LRDG had already found a way across, and lost no opportunity to prove them misguided.

The LRDG's radio operating expertise also ensured that messages usually got through. It is perhaps not coincidental that Bagnold was in the Royal Signals. Their high standards of driving and maintenance under the most testing circumstances were never surpassed and seldom equalled by their imitators.[13] They were self-supporting for fuel, water and rations. Most of their information was self-acquired, although they did sometimes rely for information on Senussi tribesmen in Cyrenaica through agents, for whom they themselves often laid on a 'taxi service'.[14] In general, however, the LRDG, and later the SAS, neither expected nor wished the tribesmen to involve themselves in operations, nor provide material support of any kind. One of the most successful agents with the Senussi was Vladimir Peniakoff ('Popski'), a Belgian émigré of Russian extraction.[15] His biographer, who knew him well, judged him to be 'a little cavalier with the facts, and it is not always easy to disentangle the truth.'[16] As an aside, Peniakoff provides a good example of self-invention, or the 'amoeba' tactic, by abandoning his original special forces function and creating another. After operating with the LRDG, he raised his own jeep-born force, which became known as 'Popski's Private Army' (PPA).[17] Although he did some good work in a conventional reconnaissance role in northern Italy in the closing months of the war, the public image of the PPA as a behind-the-lines unit, assiduously cultivated by 'Popski', is a sham; throughout the Second World War it spent a total of seven weeks behind the lines.[18]

The LRDG engaged in the two classic special force activities: information gathering and direct action. Of the former, the most effective, and highly valued by GHQ in Cairo and the 8th Army, was road-watch.[19] One of the principal lines of communication for the German and Italian forces in Libya and Egypt, and indeed for the British, was the only tarmac road from Tripoli to Alexandria. The battles of the North African campaign were fought along the shores of the Mediterranean; large forces could not penetrate far inland because their supplies were brought to them on the coastal roads and railways, and by sea. Few, if any, roads existed more than about a hundred miles inland. On the critical tarmac road, road-watch patrols counted the numbers and types of enemy vehicles heading in either direction, and reported their findings to Cairo by radio, usually via LRDG headquarters at Siwa Oasis. If the enemy was building up for an offensive, the intensity of the traffic and types of vehicles would be an indication. A patrol might be on watch for two weeks or longer, and the operation maintained for months. For example, the LRDG road-watch 35 miles west of Agheila was in place from early March to 21 July 1942.[20]

The road-watch patrol set up a base usually in a wadi in which the vehicles could be camouflaged. The principal danger was from enemy aircraft. The observation post (OP) by the road would normally be occupied by two men for 24 hours. They would keep about 300 yards from the road by day, and approach to about 20-30 yards by night. Change-over was usually between midnight and dawn. Sometimes the terrain demanded that the vehicles were hidden several miles from the road, and the LRDG thought nothing of walking a dozen miles at the beginning and end of each 24-hour watch, laden with personal weapon, ammunition, water and, in the winter, a greatcoat. Sometimes the scrub was sparse, and, except in a sandstorm, the watchers had to remain motionless throughout the day. The hazards varied from Arabs with goats and camels, road repair gangs, or enemy convoys pulling off the road to cook, answer the call of nature, or camp for the night. The soldiers back in the patrol base could not walk around for fear of leaving tracks, but lay under the camouflage nets; sweating in the summer and shivering in the winter.[21]

Apart from a few ineffective commando raids, for the first year of the campaign the LRDG was the sole British special force operating in the Western Desert. As well as deep reconnaissance, they also mounted direct action operations against targets such as airfields and other military installations. With the arrival of the SAS on the scene there was an attempt to 'rationalise' the roles of the two organisations. The LRDG would continue with long-range reconnaissance, and the SAS would do 'beat-up' operations, in the slang of the time. In fact, the LRDG continued with 'beat up', sometimes on a large scale, both in company with the SAS and others and on their own. One of the most daring of the LRDG-only affairs was the raid on Barce airfield in mid-September 1942.[22] Two patrols, totalling around 30 men, in 12 trucks (Chevrolet or Ford 30cwt) and five jeeps, drove 1,155 miles from Kufra to Barce. Here, in darkness, one patrol attacked the airfield, and the other 'beat up' the barracks in town as a distraction. After destroying 35 aircraft and engaging with Italian light tanks in town, the two patrols withdrew. They succeeded in fighting their way out of an ambush by about 150 Tripolitanian troops, although not without loss of some vehicles. Enemy aircraft, which almost invariably posed the greatest threat to LRDG and SAS patrols, found them at daybreak, and from about midday until nightfall set about them as they twisted and turned in the open scrub. By last light only one truck and two jeeps remained working. The medical officer took a jeep and a truck with six wounded men and eventually reached a rendezvous (RV), where a patrol had been sent to meet them. Eleven members of the party walked to another RV on foot, but one of them had a wounded leg that was turning gangrenous. That did not prevent him and one companion from covering some 150 miles, mostly by night, navigating by the stars, before being betrayed by Arabs. Others with the remaining jeep loaded with water and rations made the RV. Total casualties to the LRDG were eight taken prisoner after fighting in the town, and six wounded.[23] & [24] These long walks were by no means the only example of endurance by members of the LRDG, usually after their vehicles had been destroyed or damaged by aircraft.[25]

The SAS did not have an auspicious beginning. The unit had originally been formed by Lieutenant Stirling in mid-1941 to raid airfields after insertion by parachute. On their first raid in mid-November 1941, all the aircraft missed the Dropping Zone (DZ). High winds blew the soldiers miles out into the desert, and only 22 men, including Stirling, out of the 60 who had been dropped turned up at the RV, manned by an LRDG patrol. The patrol commander suggested to Stirling that they abandon parachuting, and be carried to the target by the LRDG.[26] Stirling eventually agreed, and for several months, until the SAS got its own transport, the two organisations worked closely together, and continued to do so on occasions thereafter.[27] The SAS was eventually equipped solely with jeeps, which were fitted with four Vickers K guns, taken from obsolete biplanes. These had a very high rate of fire, 1,200 rounds per minute each. In a typical raid such as that on Sidi Haneish, Stirling took 17 jeeps, which drove round the airfield firing their Vickers K guns, destroying some 35 aircraft, for the loss of one man.[28] In one minute the 68 jeep-mounted Vickers K guns could unleash over 80,000 rounds.

At the end of the desert campaign, the SAS went on to operate in Italy and France, usually in support of partisans, with mixed success.[29] There were a number of reasons for this, mainly the uneven quality of the partisans with whom they had to work and rely for information and support, the unsuitability of some of the terrain for jeep-borne operations, and, in a few cases, hubris and lack of professionalism on the part of the SAS.[30] 'Operation Bulbasket' near Poitiers provides an example of these failings. To begin with all went well with the SAS task of disrupting the rail network that German formations based in southern France would have to use to move to the Normandy battlefront. Eleven trains of fuel wagons were destroyed by fighter bombers called in by the SAS working with the Resistance, and the railway was cut in 12 places. After three weeks the SAS base was attacked by the Germans, and only eight SAS men escaped; 31, including four wounded, were taken prisoner. One of the wounded was tied to a tree and beaten to death by the Germans with their rifle butts; all the others were shot. This treatment was meted out to most SAS captured in France, despite operating in uniform. Of the hundred or so recorded cases of SAS being taken prisoner, only six survived. Officially 'Bulbasket' was betrayed by collaborators, but it is likely that carelessness, including the fundamental error of staying in one place too long, was the main cause of the SAS's downfall.[31]

There were, however, many very successful SAS behind-the-lines operations. In 'Operation Houndsworth', near Dijon, a force consisting of 144 SAS officers and men spent three months behind enemy lines, disrupting the rail network. They demolished the lines 22 times, and reported targets for air strike on 30 occasions. About 200 enemy were killed, and 132 taken prisoner for the loss of 18 casualties: 14 of these were killed in one aircraft that apparently hit a hill in low cloud. The SAS party was supplied by air drop with 1,129 containers, 73 panniers, nine jeeps, and two 6-pounder anti-tank guns.[32] In 'Operation Gain', 58 officers and men of 1st SAS Regiment attacked the railway communications in the Rambouillet-Provins-Gien-Orléans-Chartres bottleneck between 14 June and 19 August 1944. For the loss of ten killed, including the squadron leader, they inflicted much damage, covering some 1,500 miles in their jeeps, and, as a variation to demolishing the line, attacked German troop trains by machine-gun fire from stationary jeeps.[33] The twin Vickers K gun could cut a truck in half at a range of 50 yards. SAS jeeps by now could be fitted with extra fuel tanks, giving them a range of 6-700 miles. Some were armour-plated and mounted up to five Vickers K guns, or Brens and bazookas, and carried 3-inch mortars (these last had to be dismounted before firing).

Perhaps the most successful SAS jeep operation behind enemy lines was 'Operation Wallace' led by Major Roy Farran. On 19 August 1944 the party set off in their jeeps from Rennes, by then occupied by American forces, driving some 380 miles to their operating area, 200 miles behind enemy lines. In one operation they killed over 100 Germans, wounded many more, and destroyed 12 enemy vehicles. Operating over a wide area, they eventually inflicted over 500 casualties on the enemy, destroyed 65 vehicles, a complete goods train, and 100,000 gallons of petrol.[34]

Farran later operated in Italy alongside partisans on 'Operation Tombola'. When he first encountered the local resistance division, of about 1,200 men, he found all but about 200 of them useless. Farran described his first encounter with them:

'I was very shaken by the raw material. It looked like a tableau of Wat Tyler's rebellion. The men were all young, but nearly all of them had some physical defect... They were the worst partisans in the valley and had only arrived recently from the plains to avoid conscription for labour by the Todt organisation [German 'slave' labour system].'[35]

The partisan leaders were worried by '...a suspicion that they were to be a shock force to carry out actual operations, instead of sitting in military splendour in the mountains like the majority of partisans.'[36]

From this organisation he formed a small battalion stiffened with 42 all ranks of his own SAS Squadron. Farran narrowly avoided court martial on two occasions. On the first, when specifically ordered not to take part in 'Operation Tombola' himself, he 'accidentally fell' out of the aircraft; having first briefed the dispatcher. Until he sent his first radio message Army Headquarters believed him to be dead. On the second occasion, having been forbidden by 15 Army Group to attack German 51 Corps Headquarters, he nevertheless went ahead and did so.[37] His final operations involved harassing the German withdrawal routes with considerable success.[38]

The LRDG still retained its title after leaving the desert, and after a thorough re-organisation into smaller, mainly foot-borne patrols trained for parachute and sea-borne insertion, experienced an unhappy period in the unsatisfactory Dodecanese campaign, where they were mis-employed on a number of occasions. They subsequently found their niche in the Adriatic, mainly in Yugoslavia and Albania.[39] As well as 'beat up' operations, they put their communications and observation skills to fruitful use on ship-watch operations along the Dalmatian coast and islands, and the Istrian Peninsula. Through radio links to Italy, they were able to wreak havoc on the German coastal traffic by calling down and directing air strikes even when the vessels were hiding under camouflage nets in secluded bays and inlets. On occasions the pilots of attacking aircraft could not distinguish the target from its surroundings, and only when the post-strike report was received from the LRDG, giving the score in damaged and sunk ships, would they know what they had achieved. Information was also passed to the Navy in order to allow it to intercept and sink enemy ships transiting the mine-free areas. The enemy was well aware that patrols were operating in this manner, but thanks to good fieldcraft the LRDG were never located.[40] The LRDG was the first true special force raised by the British in the Second World War, and during the five years of its existence carried out more than 200 operations behind enemy lines, and throughout those five years there were only two periods of five months when no patrols were operating behind enemy lines.

The largest force of British soldiers to operate behind enemy lines in the Second World War was the Chindits in Burma, 20,000 in all. The force was under the command of Major General Orde Wingate. Chindit is a corruption of 'Chinthe', the mythical beast that guards temples and monasteries in Burma, which Wingate chose as his brigade formation sign. He was given command of the 77th Indian Infantry Brigade to put into effect his ideas on long-range penetration (LRP), which he had sold to the C-in-C India, Field-Marshal Sir Archibald Wavell (who had authorised the raising of the LRDG when C-in-C Middle East). Wingate believed that a brigade operating behind Japanese lines in jungle terrain could cause damage to the enemy out of all proportion to the brigade's numerical strength. The brigade could be supplied by air and dispense with a long and vulnerable line of communication. Japanese communications would be ideal targets for an LRP force. Wingate was given two low-quality battalions, one of average British soldiers, and one of under-age Gurkhas, and an experienced battalion of Burma Rifles.[41] The only volunteers for LRP were in the Commando Company, consisting mainly of demolition teams.[42]

Wingate organised his brigade into seven 'columns', each consisting of about 400 men. The nucleus was an infantry company, and to this was added a small headquarters, a reconnaissance platoon of Burma Rifles, two 3-inch mortars, two Vickers machine-guns[43], a mule transport platoon, an RAF officer and radio operators to communicate with the air base whence resupply would come, a radio detachment to communicate with other columns and brigade headquarters, a sabotage squad, and a doctor and two orderlies. The column's supplies and heavier weapons were carried on mules. Wingate's tactical concept was that the columns should march independently, be self-supporting for a week, and be supplied by air. He hoped thereby to achieve mobility and security. By not having wheeled transport and being tied to a land line of communication, he could, in theory, go where he wished. His security was based on the assumption that the enemy would have difficulty finding mobile columns in the jungles and teak forests of northern Burma; if located and outnumbered, the columns could still disperse, evade, and subsequently rendezvous to carry on with their task.

We need not concern ourselves with following the fortunes of the 77th Indian Infantry Brigade.[44] The results were mixed, and no great damage was inflicted on the Japanese lines of communication, other than putting the railway from Mandalay to Myitkyina out of action for four weeks. About six to eight Japanese battalions were drawn off to hunt down Wingate's columns. However, as the Japanese were not under pressure anywhere in Burma at the time, neither interruption was significant. One of the reasons for the Japanese not being heavily engaged was their perception that the country astride the Chindwin was so inhospitable that it could not be crossed by large bodies of troops, hence their reluctance to invade Assam and India. They contented themselves with remaining on the defensive in this sector, and indeed in all of Burma.[45] Now, having seen Wingate's force cross this terrain, the enemy made plans to make the same journey in reverse, thus setting the scene for the Japanese Army's first major defeat in the Burma theatre, in Assam the following year, and subsequently, after a year of hard fighting, its eventual destruction. Perversely, perhaps, this was the most important outcome of Wingate's first expedition. His brigade suffered some 1,000 missing, of whom 450 were battle casualties. Apart from some Kachins and Shans who remained in their homes with Wingate's permission, all the missing were dead or prisoners of war. The majority of those who returned to India were unfit for further service through malnutrition, malaria, and other diseases. Despite this, Wingate, on his return to India, found himself a hero, lauded in the press and summoned to attend the Quebec conference with Winston Churchill.

Before Wingate crossed into Burma, Wavell had already given orders to convert the 111th Indian Infantry Brigade into another Chindit formation; this and the

77th Brigade would carry out LRP turn and turn about. Despite a warning being sounded by General Auchinleck, who had taken over from Wavell when the latter became Viceroy of India, that the LRP force should not grow too large, Wingate returned to India to command not only the original two LRP brigades, but in addition the first-class, well-trained and battle-experienced 70th Infantry Division, turned into what became known as 'Special Force'.[46] Later the 3rd West African Brigade was added, and Wingate eventually had six infantry brigades at his disposal. His Special Force, although containing few specially selected volunteers, was in a different league from the two very low-grade infantry battalions in his first expedition. The majority of the infantry was Regular or Territorial Army. Again the battalions were broken down into columns.

This time Wingate had secured the services of the so-called Number 1 Air Commando USAAF, consisting of 100 WACO gliders, 100 short take-off and landing (STOL) L-5s and L-1s, 30 P-51A Mustang fighter-bombers, 20 B-25 Mitchell medium bombers, 20 C-47 (DC-3) Dakotas, 12 UC-64 transport aircraft, and six Sikorsky helicopters (the first ever to take part in operations). The Air Commando was Wingate's for 90 days only, and needed the assistance of the RAF when towing large numbers of gliders. The support provided by the light aircraft in particular meant that wounded now had a chance of being flown out rather than at best being left with Burmese villagers, who usually turned them over to the Japanese, and at worst being left to die.

Wingate's tactical concept this time involved setting up brigade strength strongholds, sitting on or near the Japanese line of communication, which the Japanese would be forced to attack. To this end he planned to fly in all his brigades by glider and Dakota, except one, which would walk. In particular Wingate hoped to seize an airfield at Indaw, into which a conventional division would be flown. This was part of Wingate's private aim of reconquering Burma, and holding it north of a line corresponding with the 24-degree parallel. He had been told by the Commander of the Fourteenth Army, Lieutenant-General Slim, that no division was available for such a task. To no avail Wingate badgered Admiral Lord Louis Mountbatten, the C-in-C South East Asia Command (SEAC), to overturn this decision, in the process going over the head of Slim (the Army Commander) and the Army Group Commander.[47]

Ultimately, one block, nicknamed 'White City', dominating the main north-south railway line, and commanded by the redoubtable Calvert, succeeded in its aim, until the block was lifted. Wingate's aim of capturing Indaw was never realised, not least because his plan for doing so was flawed. Eventually, after Wingate's death in an air crash, the whole Chindit force, less one brigade, was ordered north to assist the US Lieutenant-General Stilwell's Chinese/American advance from north Burma. Here there is no doubt that efforts by the Chindits, by now fighting as conventional troops but lacking the fighting power of a standard division, were of assistance to Stilwell in realising his aim of pushing forward the road connecting India with China. This was the route by which the Americans planned to supply Chiang Kai-shek for his offensive against the Japanese – an offensive never came about because he husbanded his resources for the forthcoming struggle with the Communists. Chindit operations against the enemy line of communication with the Assam front were only partially successful. The lack of supplies reaching the Japanese in that area, once they started their offensive aimed at the Imphal Plain, owed more to their own incompetence and their wildly optimistic logistic plan based on living off captured supplies, than Chindit action.

Overall, the large numbers of casualties suffered by the Chindits were not justified by their achievements, especially bearing in mind the manpower, which arguably would have been better employed in a conventional division, and the huge investment in air resources to insert it and maintain it. Over 900 were killed or died of wounds, over 2,400 were wounded, and 450 were missing. But greater numbers were sick – those admitted to hospital represent a figure of over 100 per cent of the original force, whereas battle casualties represent just over 24 per cent. In one brigade the ratio of sick to battle casualties was 7.8:1; in contrast, in Calvert's brigade it was 1.2:1, a measure of the high standard of morale and leadership in his brigade, which did more fighting than any other.[48] The strain on men, even in a well-led formation, shows in a letter from an officer describing the period just before Calvert's Brigade captured Mogaung, their final operation:

'By now everyone was very tired and jumpy. I know I never felt more depressed and exhausted during the whole show. In my early days in White City, my sergeant and I would often sit out in the open and finish boiling water for our tea, although the evening shelling was landing all around us.'[49]

Later, describing the march out at the height of the monsoon:

'It took us a fortnight of marching through mud and water, of crossing deep and fast-flowing rivers and of miserably damp nights; for the last two days of it I was sick with jaundice and had a temperature of 102. The leeches by now were really thick on the ground, and at the end of every halt, after sitting down, there were always half a dozen of them to be burnt off [with a cigarette]. Most days it was too wet to light fires, so that hot drinks or food were rare.'[50]

Slim wrote to one of his corps commanders, referring to Wingate's operations: 'Compared with those of a normal corps they were painfully slight.'[51] This should not be taken to be any criticism of the Chindit soldiers, who on the whole did all that was asked of them, and more; marching, suffering and dying. In effect Wingate was trying to fight an air-mobile war, but without the means of mobility, which did not exist at the time, not least in the form of medium and heavy-lift helicopters vital to success in this type of operation. Once his troops had been delivered by glider or aircraft, they had the mobility of the boot. Wingate's successor, Major General Lentaigne wrote:

'A column has NOT [sic] got superior mobility to the enemy in the jungle [one of the main pillars in Wingate's argument for LRP]. The rations and supplies carried by the man are heavier than carried by the enemy, whilst the heavier weapons and W/T [radios] which make the column self-supporting entail a mule train, which inevitably slows it down and also makes it very vulnerable when attacked on the march.'[52]

So, finally, what about the charge by the General quoted at the opening of the chapter? In reality the majority of those volunteering for special forces joined for action, not to dodge it. One of the problems that beset commanders of special units was the restlessness of their soldiers if they were left unemployed for protracted periods and saw their parent units engaging the enemy. An officer in an airborne unit, not strictly special forces, but whose soldiers were all volunteers and of exactly the same persuasion as those in the SAS, LRDG and others, wrote of the tedium and frustration of training and waiting for operations:

'For years now we had sat on our arses, living in what passed for comfort in wartime, while the infantry were slaughtered in Burma, Africa, Italy and France. How ironic it was! Most of us had left one of those infantry battalions to try to find a quicker way to the fighting, only to be trapped in a never-ending round of training exercises.'[53]

Their wish was about to be granted. About ten days later, the writer of that passage was one of the only three officers and 43 soldiers of his battalion to get back across the Rhine after the Arnhem operation.

The largest special force of all, the Chindits, contained few volunteers. In the first expedition particularly, the majority would not be regarded as special in any way; and the men were only remarkable for either being too old, or too young, and poorly trained. The Chindits, of all British special forces operating behind the lines in the Second World War, constantly found themselves fighting in exactly the conditions endured by conventional infantrymen, but without some of the benefits. John Masters, who had commanded a Chindit brigade when his commander took over the Chindits on Wingate's death, describes the soldiers of the 19th Indian Infantry Division the day he joined it as the GSO I: 'It [the division] was on a regular supply line and the men looked fit and full of fire, very different from the gallant, ragged, deadbeat scarecrows my Chindits had become when I left Burma.'[54]

The contribution of special forces is hard to measure, because it cannot be calculated solely in terms of enemy equipment destroyed. Other gains have to be considered, such as the effect on morale, both enemy and Allied, the enemy reaction in terms of movement of troops to counter the threat, and in the bolstering of an ally, as in Yugoslavia, but subjective evidence to support this is often difficult to establish. Even in the realms of intelligence it can be difficult to say that a particular piece of information, gained by a spectacular coup, was the sole key to a success. The gathering of intelligence is usually more mundane; often many pieces of information, laboriously garnered, go to complete the puzzle.

In the end the judgement must be in favour of the special force that produces results out of all proportion to the resources invested in it. The supreme example in the British order of battle in the Second World War was the LRDG, not only in the desert but later in the Aegean, Adriatic, Yugoslavia, Albania, Greece and Italy over a period of five years from June 1940 to May 1945. At the other end of the scale were the Chindits. In between there were other units by no means all mentioned here, their experience of action and effectiveness in action as wide-ranging as the two special forces upon which this chapter has focused.

Notes on contributors

Major-General Julian Thompson, King's College, University of London, UK. Major-General Thompson served in the Royal Marines for thirty-four years in many places round the globe. His commands included a Royal Marines Command, the Commando Brigade in the Falklands War of 1982 and Royal Marines Special Forces. He has been visiting professor at the Department of War Studies, King's College, London. He has published seven books on military history subjects, and contributed to four others.

Recommended reading

Bagnold, R. A., *Libyan Sands: Travel in a Dead World* (Hodder & Stoughton, 1935)
Bidwell, Shelford, *The Chindit War: The Campaign in Burma, 1944* (Hodder & Stoughton, 1979)
Calvert, Michael, *Chindits: Long Range Penetration* (Ballantine, 1973)
Courteney, G. B., *SBS in World War Two* (Hale, 1983)
Farran, Roy, *Winged Dagger: Adventures on Special Service* (Fontana, 1956)
Fergusson, Bernard, *The Trumpet in the Hall* (Collins, 1970)
Lloyd Owen, David, *The Desert My Dwelling Place* (Cassell, 1957)
Masters, John, *The Road Past Mandalay* (Four Square, 1967)
Slim, Field-Marshal Viscount, *Defeat into Victory* (Cassell, 1956)
Strawson, J. A., *History of the Special Air Service Regiment* (Secker & Warburg, 1984)
Warner, Philip, *The Special Boat Squadron* (Sphere Books, 1983)

Notes

[1] John, Verney, *Going To The Wars* (Collins, 1955) p147
[2] Field-Marshal Viscount, Slim, *Defeat into Victory* (Corgi, 1971) pp463-5
[3] Conversation with the author
[4] Fitzroy, Maclean, *Eastern Approaches* (Reprint Society, 1951) pp349-52
[5] Michael, McConville, 'Knight's Move in Bosnia and the British Rescue of Tito: 1944', in *Journal of the Royal United Services Institute*, December 1997, pp61-9
[6] Calvert interview, 9942/21, Sound Archive, Imperial War Museum (SA, IWM)
[7] Ibid
[8] Winston S. Churchill, *The Second World War*, Vol II, *Their Finest Hour* (Cassell & Co Ltd, 1949) p217
[9] Jellicoe interview, 13039/5, SA, IWM
[10] 'Early Days of the Long Range Desert Group', transcript of lecture by Brigadier Bagnold to Royal Geographical Society, 15 January 1945, p32
[11] Ibid, p33
[12] Report by Captain M. D. D. Crichton-Stuart, Scots Guards, 'Patrol by G Patrol LRDG', in Lloyd

Owen papers, P 219-225, Department of Documents, IWM

13 See 'LRDG Training Notes', ibid

14 'LRDG's Part in 8th Army Operations, April 19th-May 26th [1942]', sheet 7, Lloyd Owen papers, op cit: 'Of recent weeks, LRDG has found itself more and more in the position of "universal aunts" to anyone who has business in the desert behind enemy lines. An increasing stream of commandos (European and Arab), L Detachment (SAS), bogus Germans, lost travellers, escape scheme promoters, stranded aviators, etc, has continued to arrive at Siwa needing petrol, rations, maintenance, information, training, accommodation, and supplies of all kinds.'

15 See Military Cross citation for War Service, Captain, Temporary Major, Vladimir Peniakoff, of Libyan Arab Police Force, dated 1 October 1942, in Lloyd Owen papers, op cit

16 John, Willett, *Popski: A Life of Vladimir Peniakoff, Commander of Popski's Private Army* (Macgibbon & Kee, 1954) p30

17 See General Sir John Hackett, 12022/4, SA, IWM, for an account of the raising of this force

18 John Willett, op cit, p120

19 For examples of the high regard in which the LRDG was held by GHQ and the 8th Army, see letter GHQ to HQ LRDG, 7 April 1942 and 2 May 1942; signal 8th Army to LRDG, 12 April 42, and letter, 12 April 42; and Montgomery letter to Prendergast, 2 April 43, in Lloyd Owen papers, op cit

20 Kay, R. L., 'Long Range Desert Group in the Mediterranean' (Wellington, New Zealand: War History Branch, Department of Internal Affairs,1950) p5, Lloyd Owen papers, op cit

21 For example, see 'LRDG's Part in 8th Army Operations, Feb 6-Apr 18 1942', sheet 2, Lloyd Owen papers, op cit

22 'LRDG Operations, September 11th-October 23rd, 1942', p2, Lloyd Owen papers, op cit

23 See citations for Distinguished Service Order for Major Easonsmith and Captain Wilder, and for Military Medal for Trooper Dobson, dated 1 October 1942, Lloyd Owen papers, op cit

24 R. L.,Kay, op cit, pp7-10

25 For example, see reports by Troopers Martin, Ramsay and Brown, Gunners Stuttard and Walsh, and Signalman Fair, dated 3 December 1941, Lloyd Owen papers, op cit

26 Interview with author

27 'LRDG's Part in 8th Army's Offensive, 25 December-5 February 1942', Lloyd Owen papers, op cit

28 Jellicoe interview, 13039/5, SA, IWM

29 In France alone from June to October 1944, the SAS carried out 43 operations. Otway, Lieutenant Colonel T. B. H., 'Airborne Forces', in the series 'The Second World War 1939-1945' (Army, War Office, December 1951, reprinted by Department of Printed Books, IWM, 1990) p239

30 For examples of the quality of Italian partisans, see reports by Captain Greenwood, Appendix C to 'LRDG Op Report No 120', dated 27 June 1944, and Lieutenant Bramley, attached to 'LRDG Op Report No 123', dated 1 July 1944, Lloyd Owen papers, op cit

31 For an assessment of the state of training of the SAS and lack of professionalism during 'Operation Bulbasket', see Hastings, Max, *Das Reich: Resistance and the March of the 22nd SS Panzer Division Through France, June 1944* (Michael Joseph, 1981) p207

32 T. B. H. Otway, op cit, p240. Containers dropped by parachute varied in size from cylinders 6 feet long and 15 inches in diameter to the biggest version, 11 feet long by 1ft 6in square, designed to fit in the 2,000lb bomb cell in Halifax, Stirling and Lancaster aircraft. Panniers were packing-case-sized boxes made of basketwork in which stores such as ammunition, rations and other unbreakable items could be dropped by parachute. Jeeps were dropped under a cluster of three 32-foot canopies. The jeep was fitted with a frame, and a 'crash pan' underneath to take the shock of landing.

33 Ibid, p241

34 Ibid, p249

35 Roy, Farran, *Winged Dagger* (Fontana, 1956) pp284-5

36 Ibid, p285

37 Ibid, pp269, 293

38 T. B. H. Otway, op cit, pp252-3

39 See 'Summary of Operations' in memo from LRDG to Land Forces Adriatic, dated 7 May 1945, Lloyd Owen papers, op cit

40 'Land Forces Adriatic to LRDG', 8 July 1944, Lloyd Owen papers, op cit. See also the 'Official History' in the Lloyd Owen collection, prepared by the Southern Rhodesian official observer in

Italy and the Adriatic, which gives examples of these operations, mainly by the Rhodesian Squadron of the LRDG, including Appendices giving examples of strike success, and messages of congratulation from senior Allied commanders.

[41] Mainly consisting of Karens, Kachins and Chins; the Burmese were either pro-Japanese or anti-British, or both, having deluded themselves that if the Japanese won the war it would grant independence to Burma

[42] For the state of training of the battalions in the 77th Indian Infantry Brigade, see Wingate papers, 97/20/6-12, 'Report on LRP' by Major Bromhead, Brigade Major, p2, Department of Documents, IWM

[43] The tripod-mounted First World War-vintage Vickers medium machine-gun, not the Vickers K

[44] For account by Wingate, see 'Report on the Operations of 77th Indian Infantry Brigade in Burma, February to June 1943', by Brigadier O. C. Wingate, Wingate papers, op cit

[45] Kirby S.,Woodburn, *The War Against Japan*, Vol III (HMSO, 1961) pp1-2

[46] Auchinleck's views are contained in a note signed and dated by him on 18 August 1943, appended to Wingate's 'Report on the Operations of the 77th Indian Infantry Brigade', Wingate papers, op cit

[47] For example, see Slim's signal to 11 Army Group, 21 January 1944; Wingate to Mountbatten, 20, 26 and 27 January 1944, and 10 February 1944; and Mountbatten to Wingate, 9 February 44, Wingate papers, op cit

[48] For a full analysis see F. A. O.,Crew, *Medical History of the Second World War: Army Medical Service, Campaigns*, Vol V (HMSO, 1966) Appendix B

[49] Papers of Captain N. Durant, 80/49/1, Department of Documents, IWM

[50] Ibid

[51] Papers of General Sir Geoffrey Scoones, 96/43/1, Department of Documents, IWM, letter from Field Marshal the Viscount Slim dated 20 May 1956

[52] 'Note on Special Force', by Major General W. D. A. Lentaigne, Wingate papers, op cit

[53] Tom, Angus, *Men at Arnhem* (Leo Cooper, 1976) p14

[54] John, Masters, *The Road Past Mandalay* (Four Square, 1967) p281

Chapter 12

Partisans and guerrillas

Malcolm Mackintosh

Any attempt to analyse the role and character of partisans and guerrillas and their type of warfare in the First and Second World Wars must surely begin with a definition of terms. Guerrilla warfare, whose title in modern times originated in the struggle of the Spanish and Portuguese peoples against a French army of occupation in the Iberian peninsula in the Napoleonic invasion of 1808-1814, has been described as 'warfare carried out by irregular forces employing unorthodox military tactics to fight small-scale, limited actions against orthodox civil and military forces'.[1] Traditionally, guerrilla warfare has been carried out against a foreign invader, but it has also been used to oppose a domestic government in power, including its method of rule or its political ideology. The underlying principles of guerrilla warfare include the harassment of the enemy until sufficient military strength is built up to defeat him in battle or until enough political or military pressure is applied to force him to seek peace. A further aspect of successful guerrilla warfare is the importance of terrain. If a guerrilla force is to survive, let alone prosper, it must control safe areas from which operations can be mounted and extended to attack towns and enemy lines of communications, and to which it can retire in periods of setbacks for recuperation and repair of arms, clothing and equipment, and where recruits can be mustered, trained and, perhaps, indoctrinated. In both cases mobility and familiarity with the terrain are vitally important. In many European instances of guerrilla warfare such areas are located in remote, rugged terrain such as forests, woods and mountains, as we shall see when we discuss guerrilla and partisan conflicts in the Balkans during the Second World War, when the principles outlined above were particularly applicable.

When examining guerrilla and partisan operations in the Second World War an important distinction must be made, because of the nature of the subject and the demands of space, between partisans or guerrillas fighting on a battlefield and other kinds of political and military resistance to enemy forces occupying the national territory. The latter includes the nationwide resistance to the Germans and to the Vichy regime in France, including fighting in specific areas and sabotage, which cannot be covered in one brief chapter. Similarly, resistance in Belgium, Holland, Norway and Denmark was carried out with great courage outside the kind of partisan operations with which this chapter deals. Nor can the chapter include risings by trained and disciplined troops directed from Allied capitals, such as the

Warsaw rising in Poland in 1944 or the Slovak rising in Czechoslovakia in the same year. The guerrilla and partisan activity in this chapter refers exclusively in the First World War to the role of guerrillas in the Arab Middle East in 1916-18, and in the Russian Civil War in 1918-22. In the Second World War the chapter concentrates on national and ideological insurgency in the Balkan countries, Yugoslavia, Albania and Greece, the Soviet-German war of 1941-45, with a look at the brief partisan operations in northern Italy at the end of the war.

The First World War

When the Ottoman Empire entered the First World War on Germany's side in 1914, the British attempted to launch three strategic offensives against the Turks: the first in Gallipoli in 1915, with the Australians and New Zealanders, the second in Mesopotamia (now Iraq), and the third from Egypt, where Britain maintained a peacetime garrison. The fate of the unsuccessful Gallipoli and Mesopotamian expeditions is well known, but the advance led by General Sir Edmund Allenby in late 1917 and 1918 led to the defeat of the Turks in Palestine, Jordan and Syria in the final phase of the war. A significant factor in the British success was the Arab Revolt and the guerrilla campaign in support of Allenby led by Colonel T. E. Lawrence, an Oxford University Arabic scholar then serving in military intelligence in Cairo. It must be noted that Lawrence was not the only British officer involved, but 'history', with a helping hand from Lawrence, has left him wearing the laurel wreaths of victory.

Lawrence persuaded his military and political masters to allów him to make contact with the most influential Arab tribal chiefs in what is now Jordan and Saudi Arabia. From his base in Jeddah, Lawrence gained the confidence of the Amir Faisal and his family, partly through promises of British support for Faisal's political aims involving dynastic control over that part of the Arab world, which were not to be realised after the war. In 1917, however, Lawrence helped the Amir to turn his tribal mobile forces into a disciplined army – in Arab not Western style – and personally led them in raids against Turkish garrisons and railway communications including vital bridges. In all his operations he collaborated with, and greatly assisted, the regular advance of General Allenby northwards towards Damascus, a city that Lawrence's guerrilla army entered in October 1918 just ahead of British forces. At the end of the war Lawrence's guerrilla campaign had trapped 600,000 Turks, killed or wounded 35,000 of them, and suffered few losses itself. Lawrence was scarcely an objective critic when he wrote, 'Guerrilla warfare is more scientific than a bayonet charge.'[2]

In the wider scale of the war, and despite paying tribute to Lawrence and to the Arab irregulars with their 'unrivalled endurance and mobility as guerrillas', C. R. M. F. Crutwell did not consider the military importance of their joint exploits to have been 'great', but General Sir Edmund Allenby acknowledged in his report that the Arab army had 'rendered valuable assistance, in cutting the enemy's communications before and during the operations.'[3] Cyril Falls, who described Lawrence as a 'partisan', stresses too that the Arab strength compensated significantly for the loss of some of the best British troops returned to France in the 1918 crisis there.[4]

The point might well be made that as with irregulars in the Second World War the Arabs had their own rivalries and their own agenda, an agenda that had of course a relationship to, but was not circumscribed by, their paymaster's overriding priority, defeat in the field of the forces of the main enemy.

The other main appearance of guerrilla warfare in the period of the First World War – though not an integral part of it – came during and after the Russian Civil War. In that conflict the Russian Imperial Army had disintegrated after three years of campaigning on its Western front; the Communist (Bolshevik) Party had seized power in St Petersburg in October 1917, and, with a German-Austrian-Hungarian Army in occupation of Ukraine and Belorussia, White Russian officers and men established anti-Bolshevik armies on the periphery of the State. Lenin and his colleagues faced the task of raising a battle-worthy 'Red Army' to crush this resistance, and small groups of dedicated supporters of the revolutionary regime known as 'Red Guards' assembled to form such an Army, but they proved inadequate when facing professionally experienced officers of the 'White Guards'. Lenin and Trotsky decided to re-mobilise the population into a regular 'Red Army' assisted by former officers entitled 'military specialists'. Nevertheless, revolutionary advocates of a 'guerrilla' war continued to exert influence, and many of the battles against the Whites in 1918-19, including mobile cavalry sweeps, were carried out using irregular or guerrilla warfare tactics.[5] Eventually, as the civil war progressed, the Red Army defeated the Whites, and increasingly developed into a largely regular force with an established military hierarchy and organisation.

However, the revolutionary atmosphere of the time gave birth to internal risings in Russia whose opposition to the regime involved a degree of guerrilla warfare. One was the rebellion in 1921 of the naval garrison at Kronstadt outside St Petersburg, a rebellion suppressed with great brutality by the Red Army – though this was restricted to the fortress garrison and lacked the characteristics of guerrilla or partisan warfare. Another more genuine guerrilla effort was the 'peasant-anarchist' republic set up in Ukraine in 1919 by Nestor Makhno. He had collaborated with the Red Army against the Whites and the Poles in 1920, but turned against the Government in a partisan-type campaign in defence of his 'anarchist' republic. His forces were crushed by the Red Army and Makhno himself escaped abroad.[6] The other guerrilla action against the Soviet government took place in Tambov province in central Russia, led by a former Communist policechief, V. A. Antonov-Ovseyenko. Under his leadership the peasants of the province rose against the Government in late 1920. So successful were the insurgents, who held out until the summer of 1921, that over 12 Red Army divisions were required to suppress the rising and put an end to their guerrilla operations.[7]

The Second World War

Guerrilla and partisan warfare re-appeared in Europe during the Second World War, and nowhere more intensely than in the Balkan peninsula. There are several reasons for this, mainly concerned with geography and history – the terrain of the region and the centuries of foreign rule and occupation against which the indigenous populations struggled and sometimes rose in armed revolt. The Balkan peninsula from the Alps to the Aegean Sea is dominated by ranges of mountains, some rising to over 9,000 feet, running mainly from west to east, which cut off the central European plains and the Danube valley from the Adriatic, Mediterranean and Aegean Seas, intersected by only a few valleys and gorges. Access to these warm waters was limited by these geographical features to the main invaders from the east, especially those from Central Asia whose main mode of advance was on horseback. Many of these 'Hordes' (as they came to be called) turned away from the inhospitable mountain terrain to more favourable pastures, leaving smaller groups of agricultural workers to settle in the valleys. Among these were the Slavs, primarily farmers, who conquered or merged with earlier inhabitants.

The combination of geography and history also meant that these settlers had little contact with their neighbours in the next valley – even if they were of the same ethnic origin and spoke the same language. Few regional states of any size or duration emerged in the Balkans in the early Middle Ages; in their place small individual kingdoms or principalities tended to appear in the area. The influence of Rome and its Church was predominant in the west of the Balkans, and that of Greece, Byzantium and the Orthodox Church in the east, until the all-conquering armies of the Ottoman Sultans overran the whole peninsula and beyond by the 15th century. During Turkish rule the only feasible method of warfare against them – and amongst themselves – was guerrilla or partisan struggle. This was the origin of the tradition that after many decades of armed conflict burst into flames in the Balkans during the Second World War.

Yugoslavia

The spark that lit guerrilla war in the Balkans was the coup d'état in Yugoslavia on the night of 26-27 March 1941, when a group of officers of the Royal Yugoslav Army, mostly Serbs and led by an Air Force General Simovic, seized power in Belgrade and overthrew the Government of the Yugoslav Regency under Prince Paul, the uncle of the young King, Petar II. The Regency had signed a treaty with the Germans and their Axis allies allowing their Army to cross Yugoslav territory on their way to Greece and the Mediterranean on 25 March, two days before the coup. The German response was a massive air attack on Belgrade on 6 April and a land invasion, mainly against Serbia, which crushed the Royal Yugoslav Army and drove it to surrender on 22 April 1941. German forces, together with troops already deployed in Bulgaria, pushed southwards into Greece, defeating a small British and New Zealand force in Thessaly, and occupying the whole of Yugoslavia and Greece, including Crete, by the end of May 1941.

Germany and the other Axis powers divided Yugoslav territory among themselves, with substantial garrisons located in the main towns and communication centres. Germany (including Austria) and Italy annexed Slovenia; Hungary was given part of Croatia and the Vojvodina, which she shared with Germany; and Bulgaria received most of Macedonia, though its western lands were incorporated into a 'Greater Albania', then under Italian colonial rule, together with the province of Kosovo. Italy also annexed two enclaves on the Yugoslav Adriatic coast – Dalmatia and Cattaro (Kotor) – and garrisoned Montenegro, though without annexing it. Germany established a 'Protectorate' over the rest of Serbia, placing it under a Yugoslav General called Milan Nedic, formerly a Chief of the Yugoslav General Staff. Most significant of all, the Germans supported the creation of a Croatian State, under a fascist ruler, Ante Pavelic, which included the historic territory of Croatia together with Bosnia and Herzegovina. Croatia joined the Axis and sent troops to serve with the German Army on the Russian front.

With the collapse of the anti-Nazi campaign in the Balkans in the summer of 1941 it became very difficult for the Western Allies to obtain reliable and up-to-date information on events in Yugoslavia and, indeed, in Albania and Greece. Some reports that reached General Headquarters in Cairo in August 1941 via sources in Turkey talked of risings against the Germans and their allies, especially in mountainous and wooded areas of the country. One of these mentioned a local rising – probably the first – on 13 June 1941 in Montenegro, in which two groups of fighters took part, later to be identified as political and ideological opponents; these were the 'nationalists' or 'Chetniks', loyal to the exiled Royal Yugoslav Army and commanded by a Colonel (later General) Draga Mihailovic, and the 'Partisans', organised by the illegal Yugoslav Communist Party under its leader Josip Broz – later to be known to the world by his guerrilla pseudonym 'Tito'. Mihailovich's forces were drawn mainly from Serbs and regular soldiers of the Royal Army; while Tito's colleagues were Communist Party members, but he recruited adherents from all parts of the country – Slovenia, Croatia, Bosnia, Montenegro and, to a lesser extent, Serbia.

The June 1941 rising was put down by the Italian Army, and the two groups of guerrillas transferred their operations to western Serbia and eastern Bosnia, where they both came under German attack. But the Partisans captured an important town in western Serbia, Uzice, and actually proclaimed a 'Free Republic' there. Attempts were made by both movements to co-ordinate their operations – encouraged by Britain and the Soviet Union and the Yugoslav Government in exile. Tito and Mihailovich actually met twice in Serbia, once on 19 September and again on 26-27 October 1941. A momentary provisional agreement was reached on joint staff collaboration, but overall operational co-operation was rejected. Tito refused to place his all-Yugoslav Communist-led Partisans under Mihailovich's command, and Mihailovich refused to take part in Tito's plan for an immediate nationwide uprising that could lead to massive German reprisals – particularly against the rural population of the Serbian lowlands. The Chetniks (who took their name from the old Serbian title of a 'warlike band' fighting against the Turks) were willing to attack German targets individually, but wanted to husband their forces until full-scale operations could be undertaken more effectively. The Partisans wanted all-out guerrilla war regardless of casualties, military or civilian. The two leaders parted on 27 October 1941, never to meet again.[8]

A month later, in November 1941, the German Army in Serbia launched the first of a series of offensives against the Partisans and the Chetniks, driving the former out of Uzice and the latter towards the Bulgarian border. These offensives became known by their numerical order and lasted until the summer of 1944. The First Offensive forced the Partisans to retreat into Montenegro, then garrisoned by the Italians, who proved to be a less formidable opponent than the Germans. There Tito began to organise his supporters into something like military units, including companies, battalions and brigades (the brigades from 800 to 1,000 men and women each) and, by June 1942, divisions. The German-Italian Second Offensive aimed to clear all resistance fighters out of Bosnia, and the Third was directed against the units in Montenegro – who promptly retraced their steps into Bosnia in June 1942. In November 1942 the Partisans were sufficiently well established in the town of Bihac to hold their first political meeting at which the Yugoslav National Anti-Fascist Liberation Council (or AVNOJ) was set up; this became the precursor of the eventual Federal Republic of Yugoslavia. The Council met whenever the military situation permitted, and became the forum at which the movement's political, ideological and administrative policies and structures were decided.

What kind of guerrilla war were these two resistance forces fighting? Observers on the scene reported a motley army, often dressed in captured German or Italian uniforms, lightly armed with rifles or light sub-machine guns with bandoliers of ammunition or Italian hand-grenades attached to their belts. The generations blended, ranging from veterans of earlier campaigns of Balkan wars to boys and girls in their teens. Some units grouped the young into special battalions and companies.[9] Once the fighting had got under way, its conduct was both savage and confused. The wild terrain, the poor roads, rough tracks, few railways, the complex mix of populations and the varied motivation of all sides made sustained and well-controlled campaigning virtually impossible. Strategically this situation was at least suitable for irregular operations. Everything in Yugoslavia favoured the guerrilla: the enemy's long-drawn-out lines of communications, his isolated garrisons and installations. In the hills and the woods Partisans had a background for their operations that could be made to serve at will as a base, as a jumping-off ground, as space in which to manoeuvre, and as a place in which to hide. By emerging unexpectedly from such bases the Partisans were able to achieve the surprise that is the essence of irregular operations. By fading back into it once their immediate task was completed, they could deny the enemy any solid target at which to strike back. They enjoyed, too, the support of a civilian population deeply imbued with centuries of resistance to any foreign invader from wherever he came.[10]

To return now to the actual guerrilla operations in Yugoslavia. In January 1943 the Germans (reinforced by the 1st Mountain Division from the 22nd Mountain Corps in north-west Greece) launched the Fourth Offensive, sweeping through Bosnia, Herzegovina and the Dalmatian hinterland, driving the Partisans into a trap in the mountains of Montenegro. By early May it became clear to Tito that if his movement was to survive it must break out northwards and try to re-establish itself in Bosnia. By co-incidence, May 1943 was chosen by the British Government as an appropriate time to send an official military mission to the Partisans; and, with their agreement, the officer selected to lead it was Captain (later Colonel Sir William) F. W. D. Deakin, an Oxford University don then serving in the Army in the Middle East. Deakin was parachuted into Montenegro on 27 May 1943, where he presented himself to Tito.[11] Deakin's instructions were to assess the Partisans' situation, their record in fighting the Germans and Italians, and their requests for the supply of arms – and report back to Cairo. His assessment of the nationwide struggle of the Partisans against all the occupying powers impressed the British military leadership in the Middle East and the British Government, and led to the launching of a major British, and later American, effort not only to supply the Partisans with arms, but also to collaborate with them on land, sea and in the air as the Allied forces approached the Italian mainland and the Balkan peninsula.

As it happened, the arrival in Yugoslavia of Bill Deakin, now a Major, coincided with the opening of Tito's counter-offensive to escape from the Fifth Offensive encirclement in Montenegro, and Deakin was able to witness at first hand a major Partisan operation against much superior enemy forces. The Partisans had to reach the valley of the river Sutjeska and pass through its main northbound gorge in order to reach the Bosnian plain, fighting hard to dislodge German and Italian troops holding the precipitous mountain ridges surrounding the valley. Major Deakin takes up the story in his invaluable book *The Embattled Mountain*:

'The Partisans were moving on inner lines within a tightening ring. Lightly armed and familiar with the terrain, trained to operate instinctively in small and isolated parties, their units could evade encircling thrusts of the enemy. Skilled in ambush and experts in night fighting at close quarters – for which the Germans showed peculiar reluctance – the Yugoslav troops could often gain brief but vital local superiority. The protection of the general movements of their columns was decisive to the outcome of the battle. This narrowed to a race for the mountain crests; each height was the scene of hand-to-hand clashes without quarter, to be held at all costs in unison with the moving columns of the main group of Tito's forces with their sick and wounded.

By 6 June the Partisans had reached the edge of the Sutjeska valley and had begun the march up the gorge. On 13 June the German positions there were forced and on the 22nd advance guard units left the gorge and entered a Bosnian village on the plateau. The remaining Partisan forces followed and spread out northwards, entering the key town of Jajce in which, on their arrival, Tito established his headquarters. On this Yugoslav success, the German Army called off the Fifth Offensive on 16 June.'[12]

The Partisan break-out through the Sutjeska gorge was an outstanding strategic and tactical success, and not only greatly improved the morale of the Partisans but also their reputation with the Western Allies and with the Soviet Union. Shortly after this victory the shape of the war in Europe changed significantly with the surrender of Italy to the Allies on 8 September 1943 following the first landings of Allied troops on the Italian mainland. The eight Italian divisions in Yugoslavia – mostly in Dalmatia and Montenegro – agreed to surrender to the Allies, including the Partisans, and Tito's 1st Proletarian division, accompanied by Major Deakin, arrived at the port of Split on the Adriatic coast, and was quickly on the scene to accept the Italians as prisoners-of-war. This also enabled the Partisans to gain access to some of the Dalmatian Islands, which later figured in joint British-

American-Partisan operations and naval contacts. The Germans, however, reacted to the new situation with characteristic speed and determination. Two divisions took over the Italian garrisons in Dalmatia, two marched into Herzegovina and one into Montenegro with the aim of cutting off the main Partisan forces in Bosnia from the Adriatic coast. In fact, Partisan access to the islands there, Korcula, Vis and Hvar, remained effective and became a direct link with Allied forces operating in the Adriatic Sea.

Once the Germans had settled accounts with the Italians, they established their own forces in key positions from which they could resume the campaign against the Partisans. They launched the Sixth Offensive in early 1944 aimed at Bosnia, and after hard fighting they captured the town of Jajce where Tito's Headquarters was located. Partisan HQ had, however, already been moved westwards to the town of Drvar in the Dinaric Alps. Yugoslav intelligence indicated that a German attack on Drvar was being planned with the aim of killing or capturing Tito and all his staff, including the new British Liaison Officer with the Partisans, Brigadier (Sir) Fitzroy Maclean, who had arrived to take over from Major Deakin on 17 September 1943. This was the Seventh German Offensive. On 26 May 1944 a German airborne and glider assault was carried out on Drvar; the town was captured and sacked and Tito's Headquarters seized, but he and most of his staff escaped up a precipitous cliff into woods and mountains, pursued by elite German troops.[13] A rearguard action by the 5th Yugoslav Corps held them off; both Yugoslav and British advisers decided to relieve Tito of the onslaught of the Seventh Offensive, and he was flown to Italy by the Royal Air Force, where he had an opportunity to meet and discuss the war in Yugoslavia with Allied leaders, including the British Prime Minister, Winston Churchill.

By the summer of 1944 the Germans' Seventh Offensive had petered out, and with it the fully guerrilla element of the patriotic rising of the peoples of Yugoslavia against the Axis. From that time the Partisans and their political leadership became in effect an Allied Government, a member of the Alliance against Germany fielding virtually full-scale armies waging almost regular operations. In addition, the strategic situation of Yugoslavia in South East Europe was changing rapidly. The Soviet Army entered the peninsula in August 1944, occupying Romania and Bulgaria and taking part in the liberation of Belgrade in October 1944 on its way up the Danube valley to Budapest and Vienna in 1945. Communist-led partisans were campaigning successfully (with British help) in Albania and Greece (see below), and the German Army was withdrawing northwards from the Greek mainland through Albania, Macedonia, Serbia and Bosnia under severe pressure from Partisan and some regular forces – the Chetniks and the Bulgarian Army, which had changed over to the Allied side. The main effort, however, was in the hands of the Yugoslav People's Liberation Army commanded by Tito, now a Marshal of Yugoslavia. These forces pursued the Germans and their surviving Croat allies through Bosnia, Croatia and Slovenia (re-capturing at last the Party's earlier capital of Bihac on 20 March 1945) until they reached the Italian and Austrian frontiers. Yugoslavia was liberated, and many observers agree that this was achieved almost single-handedly by the Yugoslav Partisans under Marshal Tito's leadership.

Albania

The Albanians are one of the oldest peoples in Europe who still exist as a nation state today. Recent research claims that they are descended from the ancient Illyrians, an Indo-European people who migrated to the shores of the Adriatic Sea from central Europe in the Iron Age – about 1000BC.[14] They were conquered successively by the Romans, the Byzantine Greeks and later the Ottoman Turks, from whom, in spite of national risings, they gained their independence and acceptance as a nation state only in 1913. After the First World War the state existed largely as a tribal society divided mainly in Gheg clans in the north and the Tosks in the south, with Tirana, the country's nominal capital, in the centre. Such industry as there was existed in the south; the north tended to be ruled by mountain chieftains to whom peasant herdsmen owed allegiance. Under Turkish rule about 75 per cent of Albanians became converted to Islam, though areas in both north and south remained Christian – either Roman Catholic or Greek Orthodox in faith.

In the 1920s a rising among northern chiefs brought a powerful landowner from central Albania to power in Tirana; he was Ahmad Bey Zogu, who proclaimed himself King as Zog I in 1928.[15] King Zog attempted to modernise the country and establish trade relations with other European states. On 7 April 1939, however, Italy invaded Albania, met little resistance, and established a colonial administration with a large Italian Army at its disposal. King Zog fled to Greece, then to Paris and London, and although he never returned to Albania, his supporters there played a major role in the guerrilla movements that grew up in that country during the Second World War.

Towards the end of 1941 some evidence of guerrilla activity appeared in Albania, particularly in the south. Here Italian troops that had invaded Greece on 28 October 1940 were driven back by the Greeks into Albania, and Albanian partisans began to harass Italian lines of communication.[16] Three political groups identified by their leaders' names took up arms to fight the Italians and pro-Italian 'collaborationists' in 1942. In the north a royalist chieftain, Abas Kupi, raised support for a guerrilla struggle among the Gheg tribes, some of whom had welcomed, under German orders, the incorporation of the Yugoslav province of Kosovo into Albania, but proclaimed their readiness to fight the Italian Army of occupation. In the south, two resistance movements emerged: the Communist-led Partisans (especially after the German invasion of the Soviet Union in June 1941 – the Albanian Party was only founded in November of that year) under Enver Hoxha, and a republican conservative movement in the Tosk region known as Balli Kombetar (or National Union) led, among others, by Midhat Frasheri. Of these the Communist-dominated group, though small, was the driving force; it operated under the guidance of the Yugoslav Communist Party with Yugoslav Partisan leaders in its headquarters.[17] Early in 1943 plans were made to unite the three resistance groups in a 'National Liberation Movement' (or LNC). Agreement was reached at a conference held at Mukë near Tirana in July 1943, and joint action against the Italians – who had five divisions in Albania – was undertaken.[18] A British military mission under Lieutenant-Colonel Bill Maclean of Special Operations Executive (SOE) entered Albania by land from

Greece, contacted all three movements, and worked hard to encourage their
mutual co-operation in a guerrilla war against the Italians and their Albanian
collaborators. In order to carry out this difficult task the British mission detached
officers to all the relevant groups, and, wherever possible, arranged supplies of
arms and equipment to those who were genuinely up in arms against the Axis
forces.

The Mukë agreement, however, did not last long. Enver Hoxha's Yugoslav
advisers urged its rejection, and this he did soon after it was signed.[19] When Italy
surrendered to the Allies in September 1943, the Italian Army in Albania
disintegrated, and the guerrilla forces helped themselves to their weapons and
captured many of their bases. A premature national rising led by the LNC was
frustrated by the arrival of significant numbers of German troops, mostly from the
21st Mountain Corps from north-west Greece, comprising the 181 Mountain and
297 Infantry divisions, who took over Tirana, Durazzo (Durres), Scutari and
Valona, and drove the Partisans, Balli Kombetar and Abas Kupi's forces into the
mountains and forests of northern, central and southern Albania. The Germans,
however, then decided to adopt a defensive strategy, concentrating on holding on
to their garrisons; this gave the Communists a free hand to assume total control
of LNC and to prepare for guerrilla warfare against the Germans and also against
the Abas Kupi royalists and Balli Kombetar, both of whom used the winter
months of 1943-44 to recruit fighting men and to anticipate external and internal
conflicts.

In fact, the Albanian guerrillas faced a 'war on two fronts'. With British support
Abas Kupi opened the 1944 campaigning season against the Germans by blowing
up a vital road bridge at Gyoles, north-west of Tirana, on 21 June, and on the 26th
the Communists' 1st Proletarian division crossed the Shkumbi river, which
divides north Albania from the south, capturing the key German-held town of
Dibra on the Albanian-Macedonian frontier.[20] In early July, however, the
Communists (ie the LNC) launched an offensive north-westwards against the
royalists, driving them back into the Mati valley, one of Abas Kupi's home bases.
He counter-attacked, defeated the LNC and brought what came to be called the
LNC's first offensive to a halt. British efforts to bring about a truce failed, and the
Communists' second offensive northwards on 10 August 1944 opened with 20,000
men pushing the royalists towards Scutari and the Yugoslav border. By mid-
September 1944, as the German Army began to pull out of Albania, the non-
Communist Albanian leaders (and their British military advisers) decided to give
up the guerrilla war and concluded that they could not rival the LNC in the power
struggle for the future of Albania. Plans were therefore made by the British
(primarily their SOE headquarters in Bari) to evacuate the royalist and the Balli
Kombetar chiefs, including Abas Kupi and Midhat Frasheri, by sea to Italy. On 4
October 1944 the British missions with the northern resistance groups set sail, and
on 24 October their Albanian colleagues joined them in Italy.[21] The guerrilla war
had been won in Albania by the Communist-led forces, and Enver Hoxha became
the leader of the new Albania.

Greece

Of all the countries of Europe in which guerrilla and partisan warfare developed during the Second World War, Greece was probably the best known to the outside world because of its history, geography and the importance of the sea and seaborne trade to her existence. Greece's classical civilisation had been at the heart of much of Europe's advance into the modern era, and by the 20th century a Greek diaspora of considerable dimensions existed right across the world. But Greece had also been subjected to Ottoman Turkish rule for several centuries, and thus shared the effects of foreign rule with her neighbours to the north – Albania, Bulgaria and much of Yugoslavia. This historical fact influenced Greek thinking at all levels during the wars of the 19th and 20th centuries – especially when Greece was once again occupied by a foreign invader during the Second World War.

Involvement in the Second World War was forced on Greece on 28 October 1940 when Italy sent its large army to Albania, seized on 7 April 1939, across the Greek frontier into north-western Greece (Epirus) with the intention of annexing that province to Italy. The Greek armed forces resisted stoutly, and during the winter campaign drove the Italians back into Albania.[22] In March 1941 British and Commonwealth troops from the Middle East were deployed in Greece to help to defend her northern frontier, but Germany's attack on Yugoslavia on 6 April and Yugoslavia's subsequent surrender led the Germans to invade Greece and occupy, along with the Italians, the whole country – including Crete. The British and Commonwealth troops, together with parts of the Greek regular forces, were evacuated to Egypt and North Africa.

Sporadic resistance by the Greeks began almost immediately, and in September 1941 a skeleton Greek resistance movement came into being. Motivation was clearly remembered by Christos Jecchinis:

'When you see people being rounded up and taken to concentration camps. When you see people being shot. When you see people starving in the streets as a result of the German forces taking everything and leaving very little. When you see the loss of your home; your mother suffering. When you see the Germans collaborating with the Right Wing Greeks to suppress the Greek people and supporting all the claims that the Bulgarians and Italians had at the time on Greece, that creates a certain amount of hatred.'[23]

The Greek Communist Party (known by its initials KKE) set up a National Liberation Front (or EAM) on 27 September, which patriots of all political affiliations were invited to join – significantly concealing its connections with the KKE.[24] Another group, the National Republican Greek League (or EDES), came into existence at the same time; a politically middle-of-the-road group officially under a retired General Nicholas Plastiras, then in exile in France, it was militarily in the hands of two former Generals, Stylianos Gonotas and Napoleon Zervas. EAM, meanwhile, had also created a military wing, the National Popular Liberation Army (or ELAS), which, because of its identical subordination, is usually referred to as EAM/ELAS. Both organisations claimed to have active support in the mountain areas of Greece, from the Peloponnese in the south to Roumeli, north-west of Athens, Thessaly, Epirus and Macedonia.

The first recorded guerrilla operations took place in May 1942 in Roumeli, carried out by ELAS under its most militant and effective leader, Aris Veloukhiotis (a code-name for the Communist leader Athanasias Klaras). In July 1942 General Zervas left Athens for his home territory of Epirus, where he established a guerrilla force that undertook successful operations against German garrisons – primarily the 22nd Mountain Corps in Yanina – and Italian road and rail communications with the Gulf of Corinth and into the Pindus mountains. ELAS also extended its operations against Italian troops in Thessaly and tried to enter Macedonia, where military activities were complicated by a large German presence in Salonika and a Bulgarian occupation force to the north-east.

Undoubtedly the most spectacular guerrilla or partisan operation at this stage of the war was the destruction of the Gorgopotamos rail viaduct on the main line between Salonika and Athens on 25 November 1942 by British Special Forces and both Greek resistance movements – ELAS and EDES – acting together for the only time during the war in Greece. Originally planned by British GHQ in Cairo to delay the dispatch by sea from Greece of reinforcements for the German Afrika Corps, the operation was carried out by a team of 12 British SOE personnel under the command of Brigadier E. C. W. Myers, who parachuted into Roumeli on 30 September 1942. Partisans from EDES and ELAS were recruited into the force, and led by Brigadier Myers and his second-in-command Major (later Colonel) C. M. Woodhouse, destroyed the viaduct, which the Germans were unable to use for several months. The success of this joint operation demonstrated that if the Greek resistance movements could, even temporarily, abandon their political and ideological ambitions, combined Greek and British guerrilla operations would contribute significantly to the success of the Allied war effort.[25]

Unhappily, this was not to be. Certainly the Gorgopotamos operation increased the enthusiasm of the Greeks for fighting the enemy across the country, and led, in February 1943, to the creation of two new Partisan groups. These were set up by Republican army officers, Colonel Stephanos Saraphis in Thessaly and Colonel Dimitrios Psarros in the Roumeli-Mount Parnassos region. Both bands were regarded by EAM/ELAS as politically hostile, and in March 1943 ELAS attacked and wiped out Saraphis's group, taking the Colonel prisoner. ELAS persuaded him, however, as a professional soldier, to join them, and appointed him their Commander-in-Chief – a post he held until the end of the war. Psarros's group, however, managed to hold its ground under their title of National and Social Liberation (EKKA) until 1944, when ELAS finally destroyed it.

In spite of these internecine conflicts the Greek resistance movements increased their guerrilla attacks on German and Italian military targets on a nationwide basis in 1943 and 1944. Indeed, the mainly mountainous areas of Epirus, Thessaly, Roumeli and the Peloponnese were effectively in guerrilla hands in this period. In June 1943 British SOE personnel destroyed another important viaduct on the Salonika-Athens railway at Asopos; although no Greek partisans took part in this operation, it was carried out in an area largely controlled by EAM/ELAS, and isolated a German Panzer division in the Peloponnese for four months.

Partly as a result of British efforts a Joint Headquarters was set up in Greece for the main resistance movements under an organisation known as the 'National Bands of Greek Guerrillas', to which EAM/ELAS, EDES and EKKA agreed to adhere. On 9 August 1943 leaders of the three movements flew to Cairo accompanied by Brigadier Myers and Colonel Woodhouse for further talks on collaboration; unfortunately the discussions got nowhere as the Greek representatives used the occasion to engage in internal political disputes, for example on the post-war government of Greece, and the delegates returned to their country without substantial agreement on how to proceed.[26]

At this point external affairs began to influence the guerrilla war in Greece. The Western Allies' forces landed in Sicily on 10 July 1943, then on the Italian mainland, and Italy surrendered on 8 September. EAM/ELAS interpreted these developments as indicating the imminent withdrawal of German troops from Greece, and, raiding all the relevant Italian Army garrisons, seized as many of their weapons as they could in preparation for an all-out assault on centres of power in Greece – including those of their own allies in the 'National Bands'. One of the Italian divisions, the Pinerola division in Thessaly, formally surrendered to the British element of the Joint Headquarters, but this did not stop ELAS and EDES carrying off their weapons.[27] In fact, the surrender of Italy continued to affect the resistance struggle in Greece. The Germans brought in fresh forces to replace the Italians, but deployed them very skilfully in a manner intended to deceive the 'National Bands' and persuade them to believe that the Germans were indeed about to evacuate Greece. ELAS in particular launched its planned offensive against its rivals in the central mountains, unaware that the Germans were ready to strike back. In a series of counter-insurgency attacks the reinforced German Army crushed a number of ELAS units in Thessaly and Macedonia and drove EDES back into the centre of Epirus. It left the resistance at what one observer on the spot called 'their lowest ebb'.

Relatively little guerrilla fighting took place in the winter of 1943-44, given the strong military position of the Germans. But some political contacts were renewed between EAM/ELAS, EKKA and EDES in January 1944, leading to a cease-fire agreed on 19 February. This armistice led, with the approval of the British Mission (now expanded to an Allied Mission by the addition of an American officer, Major G. K. Wines) to an agreement known as the Plaka Bridge accord, signed on 29 February, in which all three parties committed themselves again to ending hostilities between them. The Allied Military Mission hoped that this agreement could be honoured by all its signatories.

The first decision taken following the Plaka accord was promising. On 26 March 1944 EAM/ELAS announced the formation of, in effect, a Provisional Government known as the 'Political Committee of National Liberation' (or PEEA) in the mountains, which announced its readiness to talk to other resistance organisations – including the Greek Government in exile. A month later, however, ELAS switched once again to military action. On 17 April 1944 it attacked EKKA in Roumeli, destroyed its forces and killed its leader, Colonel Psarros.[28] In May 1944 Andreas Papandreou became leader of the Greek Government in exile, but relations between PEEA and the exiles deteriorated.

Meanwhile, the Germans continued to hold on to their hard-won positions of the winter campaign against guerrilla actions by both ELAS and EDES who were, as before, also facing each other in mountain partisan warfare.

Nevertheless, by August-September 1944 the whole scene in the Balkans was undergoing major changes that affected Greece as well as Yugoslavia and Albania, as described above. Romania and Bulgaria surrendered to the Allies and were occupied by the Soviet Army, which was preparing to advance up the Danube Valley and beyond. British and Allied troops were in central and northern Italy, and much of Yugoslavia was in Partisan hands. The Twelfth German Army finally decided to leave Greece in September, mainly through Albania, and the territories they had occupied were filled as they went by either ELAS or EDES units. A decision was taken by the Allies that the main vacuum – that is, the Greek cities, including Athens – should be filled by British troops dispatched from Italy under General Robert Scobie. The two senior guerrilla commanders, General Saraphis for ELAS and General Zervas for EDES, were flown out of Greece to Caserta in Italy on 26 September 1944, where they signed an agreement placing all Partisan forces under Government command and defining the areas of their respective liberated territories. British troops entered Athens under this agreement on 18 October, and the last German soldier left Greece on 1 November 1944.[29]

An indication of the miseries visited upon the Germans in their last months in Greece is provided by both official documents and personal memories of men charged with the harassment of the occupying forces. The stern commitment of the partisans is evidenced by Colonel Papathanasiou of the 3rd Division 'Free Mountains of Greece, National Squads of Greek Andartes', and his order that '20 of the most courageous men following rigorous selection', with an appropriate number of officers, were to help the 'English Lieutenant Bill to lay 80 landmines along the Ioanina-Metsovon route.' Five of the men were to remain to watch for the explosion of the mines.[30]

Train derailment was the speciality of another group, in which 17-year-old Christos Jecchinis played his part. His first derailment was not of the ammunition train expected but a train-load of oranges en route for Germany. However, many more materially successful exploits were to follow, and Jecchinis remembers the confidence instilled when a large band of guerrillas, more than 50, was strengthened by the increased firepower available after an American officer was assigned to their group: 'You don't feel the same fear as you do when you are alone.'[31]

With the final departure of German forces this account of the Greek guerrilla and partisan war also comes to a close. The political and military history of Greece took on a turbulent and even blood-thirsty character in the next few months, involving an all-out ELAS assault on Athens, then defended by British troops, the destruction of ELAS in further civil wars, and the re-establishment of elected governments in Greece – all outside the subject of this chapter. But to conclude, there follows a quotation from a Western participant about the guerrilla war in Greece:

'The real heroes of the Greek war of resistance were the common people of the hills. It was on them, with their bitter, uncomplaining endurance, that the German terror broke. They produced no traitors. We moved freely among them and were guided by them into German-held villages by night without fear. They never surrendered or compromised, and as a result the Germans kept five divisions guarding Greece all through the war. The Greek people paid a terrible and disproportionate price for this resistance.'[32]

The Soviet Union

Partisan and guerrilla warfare came to the Soviet Army of the Second World War from the earliest roots of Russian history, and also from the Civil War of 1918-22, which led to the foundation of the Soviet State. Since, as has already been noted, the Civil War was fought over immense distances in European and Far Eastern Russian territory by remnants of a disciplined and well-armed Imperial Army and Navy (the White Forces) against a mass-mobilisation force of reluctant peasant soldiers commanded by dedicated Communist political ideologists (the Red Army and Navy), it was inevitable that large gaps in the theatres of war were filled by bands of guerrilla fighters on both sides. This was especially true of the Far East.[33]

With the end of the Civil War and the formation of a peacetime regular Red Army and Navy, it was logical that some degree of attention should be paid by both political and military leaders to the need to prepare, train and indoctrinate fighting units that could operate behind enemy lines in the event of war and invasion. Most of these troops were drawn from the ranks of the Army of the People's Commissariat of Internal Affairs (the NKVD), the predecessors of the KGB, and were commanded by Party-approved Communist officials with minimal subordination to the Armed Forces. As the Soviet Union developed its political, industrial and military might in the 1930s, new military doctrines emerged based on 'carrying the war into the enemy's territory', which led to the virtual abandonment of plans for partisan warfare. Stalin apparently believed that Soviet territory was 'inviolable' and that the Soviet State was 'invincible', especially as the Red Army grew in size in 1941 to 303 divisions and 61 air force divisions.[34] Five Airborne Corps (one in the Far East) were established to act as an advance guard as the Army entered hostile territory with the aim of seizing vital targets and installations in the enemy's rear.

When the German invasion came, however, in June 1941, the Red Army, including its Airborne Corps, fell back eastwards in total disorder; the Communist Party leadership returned to partisan warfare concepts, and issued instructions for guerrilla actions to be undertaken in the rear of the advancing German columns – but clearly under Party and not Army control. As early as 29 June 1941 the Central Committees of the Republican Parties in the line of fire, especially in Belorussia, Ukraine and the Leningrad area, ordered Party members to organise units to 'blow up bridges, railway tracks and enemy ammunition dumps' and to recruit citizens to carry out these tasks. In fact, such partisan groups that did appear at this time were mainly drawn from soldiers from the frontier armies in the process of disintegration under the first German attacks, who could not, or dared not, rejoin their shattered formations. In the Ukraine the First Party Secretary, Nikita Khrushchev, took charge of trying to organise partisan units, as did his opposite number in Belorussia, P. K. Ponomarenko. But the collapse of morale among the population and the success of the German armies in the field, as well as their counter-insurgency operations, hampered recruitment and led to meagre and scattered military results.[35]

It was not until the end of 1941 that, coincidental with the victory of the Red Army at Moscow, a more systematic attempt by the Soviet Party and military leadership raised the effectiveness of the partisan movement. On 20 January 1942 a task force from the surviving Airborne Corps – the Fourth – was parachuted into the Vyazma area west of Moscow, linking up with elements of a Cavalry Corps operating behind German lines (in the depth of winter) and with partisan units to strike at German rear communications – and to expand the partisan movement itself.[36] Indeed, the Partisan Movement was formalised in a decree of 30 May 1942 establishing a Partisan Central Staff in Moscow attached to the State Defence Committee under Stalin, and subordinate to the Supreme High Command (the STAVKA). The Chief of Staff was P. K. Ponomarenko. Partisan staffs were also set up at Front Headquarters, especially in Ukraine and the Bryansk, Leningrad and central Russian areas. Units and formations were designated as divisions, brigades and regiments, and given the task – in a decree signed by Stalin on 5 September 1942 – of 'developing the struggle against the enemy behind his lines on a wide and deep front ... this is the most valuable assistance that the Partisan movement can give to the Armed Forces. Joint action by the Red Army and the Partisan movement will lead to the destruction of the enemy...' On the next day, Stalin appointed his unemployed friend and colleague, Marshal Klimenti Voroshilov, as Commander-in-Chief of the Partisan Movement.

The creation of a Central Staff of the Partisan Movement in mid-1942 is clearly linked to the fact that it was at this time that the German Army occupied most of the territory that it had seized in the first year of the Soviet-German war, much of it wooded and marshy, and suitable for the operations of partisan and guerrilla formations. These military partisans acted in co-operation with underground organisations and genuine local guerrillas who came into the field as a result of the harsh treatment of the people meted out by some German units – especially the SS formations. While the underground organisations' task was to maintain a skeleton Communist Party structure in being in the occupied areas, the military partisans acted in support of the Red Army in destroying German bases and communications. On 14 July 1943 the STAVKA proclaimed a 'rail war', switching the main targeting of the partisans to the rail network throughout Russian territory in the hands of the Axis troops. At the height of the partisan movement in 1943, according to Soviet statistics, 260,000 Partisans were active in Russia, and 220,000 in Ukraine; 10,000 of these were commanded by a famous Partisan leader, Sidor Kovpak, others by A. N. Saburov and A. F. Fedorov. In Belorussia some 374,000 Partisans were in the field; all of these units made up an Order of Battle of 199 Brigades.[37] Even when German troops were at the gates of Leningrad, Moscow and Stalingrad, partisan units centrally commanded were engaged in operations as far west as Minsk, Kiev and Odessa.

On the German side, the growth in the activity of Soviet partisans was causing increasing alarm. Army-Group Centre's Report for 21-31 March 1943 stated that 2,466 Soviet prisoners were taken, 452 of whom were executed as 'Banditen' (Partisans). One German Colonel stationed in Minsk in August 1944 wrote:

'We hear booming every day and night: there is firing just like in the trenches. Sometimes gun fire, sometimes it's land-mines. There are plenty of them here. The power station was blown up and we had no electricity for a week. On Sunday a car blew up at the officers' club and a locomotive beside the water-tower. Many Germans have been shot in the streets from behind corners: I'm cracking up.'

Even in 1942 the Wehrmacht diverted up to 24 divisions of its regular Army to fight the Partisans; according to one Soviet military historian, partisans accounted for 460,000 German troops in the Ukraine.[38]

Towards the end of 1943 the Red Army, having won the battle of Kursk and crossed the Dniepr River, was approaching the western frontier of the Soviet Union. By September the whole of the line was on the move, with increasing co-operation from effective partisan units – especially those 'creating diversions and carrying out well-planned acts of sabotage'.[39] On 13 January 1944 the Soviet State Defence Committee issued a decree disbanding the Central Staff of the Partisan Movement, mainly because, as the Red Army advanced, the areas in which the partisans could operate were rapidly diminishing.[40] Partisan divisions, brigades and regiments under the political and military authority of the Central Staff were re-assigned to Red Army Fronts and armies as regular formations – often under new titles and designations. Officially, therefore, the Partisan Movement ceased to exist on that day; though it is said that some units reverted to the NKVD and carried out intelligence, counter-subversion and punishment roles, for example in the arrest and execution of real or alleged collaborators with the Axis forces, using their knowledge of the country to track down suspects and hand them over to the authorities.

On the basis of the somewhat controversial evidence available, it is difficult to assess the value of the Partisan Movement in helping to create the ultimate victory achieved by the Soviet forces on the eastern front. There can be no doubt that the German invasion inspired something of a nationwide and patriotic resistance movement among the peoples of the Soviet Union, and effective acts of warfare were carried out by groups of partisans, especially in 1942-43. Nevertheless, the evidence suggests that partisan operations were, in the eyes of the Soviet leadership, primarily intended to give active support to the Red Army, both as sabotage units behind German lines and as advance guards preparing territory ahead of the Army for successful operations, both strategic and tactical on the ground. In this they clearly played a valuable role; but it was a different role from those already examined in the Balkan countries, where most partisan operations were carried out by independently formed guerrilla detachments raised in popular risings.

Italy

Finally in this summary of guerrilla and partisan warfare, recognition must be given to the role of pro-Allied partisans in northern Italy as the war in Europe approached its close in April-May 1945. Italy had entered the war as an ally of Germany in June 1940 with considerable forces on the French frontier, in Albania, in North Africa and in Ethiopia, and attempted to use them not only against

Britain but also France, and, in 1941, Greece and Yugoslavia. All these Italian campaigns came to grief on the battlefield – including costly counter-insurgency warfare. By mid-1943 Italy was itself the target of Allied landings, first in Sicily on 11 July, then on the Italian mainland. Anti-fascist left-wing and radical anti-war and anti-German movements that had been active in Italian politics since 1942 found themselves in the same camp as the King, Victor Emmanuel III, and certain leaders of the armed forces. The latter had overthrown the Government of Benito Mussolini on 25 July 1943, and appointed a politico-military administration under Marshal Pietro Badoglio, who proceeded to offer an armistice to the Allies on 8 September, and later a surrender to the Western alliance. The new Government declared war on Germany in October 1943 and was accorded the status of a 'co-belligerent' by the Allies. However, German troops quickly occupied northern and central Italy in late 1943, and the Allies, including some Italian troops, faced 18 months of hard fighting as they advanced north until the final battles in Italy in the valley of the River Po and the end of the war in April-May 1945.

Meanwhile, the anti-fascist and pro-Allied movements combined to form a political grouping on the basis of which an Italian resistance force could be created and take the field as partisans or guerrillas. On 9 September 1943 a Committee of National Liberation (CNL) was set up in Rome to operate underground while the Germans occupied the city. A Congress of these political parties was held in Bari in January 1944 attended by the Communist Party of Italy (PCI), the Christian Democrat Party (CD), Socialist and Liberal Parties, a new Party of Action, the Justice and Liberty Party (in exile in France) and a Democratic Labour Group – none of whom would serve under the King or Marshal Badoglio, even when the King abdicated in favour of his son, Prince Umberto, in June 1944. The deadlock was solved when, on 27 March 1944, the General Secretary of the PCI, Palmiro Togliatti, arrived in Italy from a 20-year exile in Moscow and immediately agreed to serve in the Badoglio Government – to the consternation of the Communists and the non-Communist anti-fascists.[41] Togliatti's return and decision to serve has been attributed to Stalin's desire to give priority to fighting the Germans on every front; and Moscow's recognition of the Badoglio Government tends to support this interpretation. Under Togliatti's direction the PCI turned its attention to a guerrilla warfare struggle in northern Italy under a clandestinely organised Committee of National Liberation of Upper Italy (CNLAI) with headquarters in Milan. The Partisan forces were organised in 'Garibaldi' Brigades throughout the occupied territories; strikes took place in armaments factories led by PCI members, and raids were carried out on targets in the routes of planned Allied advances – especially in the Florence-Bologna-River Po area. A Partisan unit accompanied British forces in their liberation of Florence on 22 August 1944. At the same time, wherever possible, the CNL took over the administration of towns and country areas evacuated by the Germans or no longer administered by their armed forces, in effect forming a new Italian local government system. In this activity all six members of the Bari Committee collaborated fully.

At the end of 1943 it was calculated that active Italian partisans numbered about 9,000, and some air drops of weapons and supplies were made to those in northern Italy. A year later the Resistance forces numbered at least 80,000; of these

50,000 were Communists, 20,000 were Christian Democrats, Socialists and Liberals, and the remainder belonged to the Party of Action. Most of the Partisans who joined CNLAI were either former soldiers (with their arms), escapees from conscription, ex-prisoners-of-war or urban workers, and thus many of them had military training or experience of war. In the period 1944-45 most of the 'Garibaldi' Brigades were active in the hills and mountains – the Apennines and the Alps – where they tied down German troops and assisted the Allies in their slow but inexorable advance northwards.

The final battle of the Italian campaign began on 9 April 1945 south of the River Po. In the British Eighth Army's advance near Argenta and Lake Commachio a Partisan unit participated with distinction.[42] On 23 April the Resistance headquarters in Milan gave the order for a general rising of the Partisans throughout northern Italy, beginning in Genoa[43]; all the major cities were taken by the Partisans, including Milan, Turin, Padua, Verona and Venice before the arrival of Allied troops, and they installed CLN administrations – with the exception of Trieste, which became a bone of contention between the Allies, the Italian Partisans and the Yugoslavs, a problem that was solved only much later. Mussolini was captured at the village of Dongo on Lake Garda on 27 April 1945 and summarily executed in Milan the next day.[44]

Although the main uprising and operations by the Italian Partisans in northern Italy was brief, its preparation and planning beginning in 1943 were lengthy, and the final seizure of the cities and other targets was successful. Partisan Brigade numbers were considerable and the aid they gave to the advancing Allied armies from 1944 onwards was very effective. There can be no doubt that the military effort was largely in the hands of the PCI, and that the key event was the arrival in liberated Italy of Palmiro Togliatti, clearly carrying out the instructions of Stalin to serve in the Badoglio Government and avoid the outbreak of a Communist/non-Communist civil war – as long as the war lasted. Togliatti's status and prestige carried the day among Italian Communists (though a militant section of the Party rejected his decision – especially in the factories) and turned the main Partisan movement into a loyal and disciplined element of the national resistance efforts discussed in this chapter, which contributed significantly to Allied victory on the Italian front.

Notes on contributors

Malcolm Mackintosh CMG, Independent Historian and Author, London, UK. Malcolm Mackintosh saw service in Middle East, Italy and the Balkans during the Second World War, latterly as a British Liaison Officer with the Soviet Army in Bulgaria. He later worked for the BBC overseas service, then the Foreign and Commonwealth Office and finally the Cabinet Office, specialising in Soviet and East European affairs. He is a graduate of Glasgow University and the author of books on the foreign policy of the Soviet Union and the Soviet armed forces.

Recommended reading

Amery, Julian, *Sons of the Eagle: A Study in Guerrilla War* (London: Macmillan & Co Ltd, 1948)

Bennett, Gill (ed), *The End of the War in Europe* (London: HMSO, 1996)

Clive, Nigel, *A Greek Experience, 1943-1948* (London: Michael Russell, 1985)

Deakin, F. W. D., *The Embattled Mountain* (London: Oxford University Press, 1971)

Erickson, John, *The Soviet High Command: A Military-Political History* (London: Macmillan & Co Ltd, 1962)

    The Road to Stalingrad: Stalin's War with Germany (London: Weidenfeld & Nicolson, 1975)

Foot, M. R. D. Foot, *Resistance: An Analysis of European Resistance to Nazism 1940-1945* (London: Eyre Methuen, 1976)0

Karpov, Vladimir, *Russia at War, 1941-1945* (London, Melbourne, Auckland, Johannesburg: Stanley Paul, 1987)

Lawrence, T. E., *Seven Pillars of Wisdom* (Oxford: Oxford University Press, 1935)

Woodhouse, C. M., *Apple of Discord: A Survey of Recent Greek Politics in Their International Setting* (London: Hutchinson & Co Ltd, 1948)

Stafford, David, *Britain and European Resistance 1940-1945: A Survey of the Special Operations Executive, with Documents* (London: The Macmillan Press Ltd, 1980, in associations with St Antony's College, Oxford)

Notes

[1] *The New Encyclopaedia Britannica*, Vol 29 Micropaedia (Chicago, London, Paris: Encyclopaedia Britannica Inc, 1998) p689

[2] Ibid, p691

[3] Dispatches sent by General Sir Edmund H. H. Allenby, 31 October 1918, quoted in 'A Brief Record of the Advance of the Egyptian Expeditionary Force, July 1917 to October 1918' (Government Press and Survey of Egypt, 1919) p36

[4] *Official History of the Great War: Military Operations, Egypt and Palestine, from June 1917 to the end of the War*, Vol II (London: HMSO, 1930)

[5] John Erickson, *The Soviet High Command: A Military-Political History* (London: Macmillan & Co Ltd, 1962) pp64-5

[6] Ibid, p87 (f)

[7] Ibid, p127

[8] F. W. D. Deakin, *The Embattled Mountain* (London: Oxford University Press, 1971) pp75-6, 136

[9] Ibid, p95

[10] *The New Encyclopaedia Britannica*, op cit, Vol 5, p545; Vol 29, p689

[11] F. W. D. Deakin, op cit, pp6-7

[12] Ibid, p96

[13] Fitzroy Maclean, *Eastern Approaches* (London: Jonathan Cape, 1949) pp450-4

[14] *The New Encyclopaedia Britannica*, op cit, Vol 1, p207

[15] Julian Amery, *Sons of the Eagle: A Study in Guerrilla War* (London: Macmillan & Co Ltd, 1948) p20

[16] M. R. D. Foot, *Resistance: An Analysis of European Resistance to Nazism 1940-1945* (London: Eyre Methuen, 1976) p183

[17] Svetozar Vukmanovic, *Struggle for the Balkans* (London: Media Press, 1980; translated by Charles Bartlett in English edition in 1990), pp126-33

[18] Julian Amery, op cit, p189

[19] Svetozar Vukmanovic, op cit, pp126-33

[20] Julian Amery, op cit, pp200-1

[21] Ibid, pp326-30

22 Ibid, pp39-40
23 Professor Christos Jecchinis, tape-recorded interview (Second World War Experience Centre, Leeds)
24 M. R. D. Foot, op cit, p179
25 C. M. Woodhouse, *Apple of Discord: A Survey of Recent Greek Politics in Their International Setting* (London: Hutchinson & Co Ltd, 1948) p26
26 Ibid, pp149-50
27 Ibid, pp161, 166-7 and 301 (the Italian Armistice terms)
28 Nigel Clive, *A Greek Experience, 1943-1948* (London: Michael Russell, 1985) p100
29 C. M. Woodhouse, op cit, p204
30 From the papers of G. A. W. Heppell (Second World War Experience Centre, Leeds)
31 Professor Christos Jecchinis, tape-recorded interview (Second World War Experience Centre, Leeds)
32 M. R. D. Foot, op cit, p182; quoting John Mulgan, *Report on Experience* (Oxford University Press, 1947) p99
33 John Erickson, op cit, pp218-25
34 David M. Glantz, *Stumbling Colossus: The Red Army on the Eve of World War* (University Press of Kansas, 1998) pp11-23
35 John Erickson, *The Road to Stalingrad: Stalin's War with Germany*, Vol 1 (London: Weidenfeld & Nicolson, 1975) p246
36 Malcolm Mackintosh, *Juggernaut: A History of the Soviet Armed Forces* (London: Secker & Warburg, 1967) p173
37 *Istoria Velikoi Otechestvennoi Voiny* (*History of the Great Fatherland War, 1941-1945*), Vol 2 (Moscow: Military Publishing House of the Ministry of Defence, 1961) pp476-86 (in Russian)
38 Vladimir Karpov, edited by Carey Schofield *Russia at War, 1941-1945* (London, Melbourne, Auckland, Johannesburg: Stanley Paul, 1987) p139
39 *Istoria Velikoi Otechestvennoi Voiny*, op cit, Vol 6, pp253-5
40 Ibid, Vol 4, p469
41 Gill Bennett (ed), 'Italy: from Fascism to Democracy' by Christopher Seton-Watson, Chap 8 in *The End of the War in Europe* (London: HMSO, 1996) p108
42 Ibid, p109
43 Ibid, Chap 3, 'The Defeat of the German Southern Armies' by Sir David Hunt, p51
44 Ibid, Chap 8, p111

Chapter 13

The experience of being abroad: doughboys and GIs in Europe

James J. Cooke

Nine years after the guns fell silent on the Western Front a New York publisher issued sheet music for a popular ballad, 'Memories of France'. Published for piano, ukulele and voice, the song recounted what Tin Pan Alley writers believed American soldiers remembered of their time in France during the Great War:

'Someone whispers to me, I love you mon chéri
In my memories of France
And we stroll once again by the old River Seine
In my memories of France
And I see her still placing roses
Where many an old pal reposes
And we laugh and we cry, then a kiss goodbye
In my memories of France.[1]

For the American soldier, the 'doughboy', the reality of war had faded into fond thoughts of good times in France that never really existed. Precious few soldiers ever saw the Seine River. They saw the Meuse through the haze of powder, smoke and gas. The Americans went into the Great War with lofty ideals of 'making the world safe for democracy'. It was a moral crusade that turned into the cold, miserable truth of the Meuse-Argonne. Those rows upon rows of white crosses haunted them for years. They returned home often jobless and alienated from those who could not comprehend that France was not flowing red wine, the dark flashing eyes of a mademoiselle. A quarter-century later their sons would return to Europe in another war inspired by, as General Eisenhower called it, a Crusade in Europe.

The experiences of the doughboy of 1917-18 and the GI of 1941-45 were very different, not because Europe or the battlefields bore no similarity, but that a little over 25 years had produced very distinct generational differences. The soldier of the Great War had his concepts firmly rooted in the American Civil War and the Spanish-American War of 1898, while the GI was the product of a great technological revolution and looked ahead more than behind. The soldier of the Great War came from an America that had just experienced a great reform period under Presidents Theodore Roosevelt and Woodrow Wilson. The United States had recently emerged on to the world stage as a giant, clumsy, youthfully arrogant nation, which often saw itself as morally superior to the Old World. The soldier of 1917-18 came from a slow, rural world where the railroad was the fastest mode of transportation. The great frontier that had moulded so much of the American character had just closed by the census of 1890. A vast continent, stretching from the shores of the Atlantic to the Pacific, had been conquered; not really civilised, but subdued.

The GI of 1941-45 came from towns, many just as small as they had been in 1898 or 1914, but now linked by concrete roads and automobiles. The movies, talking, and now often in colour, showed them the cities of America in motion. The soldiers of the second Great War were the products not of a Victorian world, but an Art Deco and Modernist time. Most of the soldiers of the First World War were born while Victoria was Queen, and they were the products of that age. By America's entry into the Second War the Roaring Twenties had passed into history, the Depression had occurred, and the big bands of Harry James and Glenn Miller and the frenetic jitterbugging dances had altered the recreational relationship between the sexes.

Stephen E. Ambrose stated the great differences and similarities when he wrote, '…I think cause and country were as critical to GIs as to the Civil War soldiers. The differences between them were not of feeling, but of expression. Civil War soldiers were accustomed to using words like duty, honor, cause and country. The GIs didn't like to talk about country or flag and were embarrassed by patriotic bombast.'[2] What had happened, then, in less than a quarter-century to reshape thought and expression? The soldiers of the Second World War fought as hard as their grandfathers in blue and grey, and they suffered just as many horrible wounds and endured many of the same hardships. Ambrose states it succinctly. Between the Civil War and The Second World War came the Great War. It did not change courage or sense of duty by any means. The war of 1917-18 was a bridge over which much American history passed.[3]

But the Great War alone did not create those differences between 1918 and 1941; other alterations drew distinct lines between the two groups. Even their names were different. The 'doughboy' of 1917-18 got his name from the adobe dust of the Mexican Border and Punitive Expedition of 1916-17 – the dust from adobe buildings covered their uniforms – but by the entry of America into the Great War 'adobe' had become 'dough'. The origins of the term 'GI' most probably came from the ever-present 'government issue' that was printed or stencilled on uniforms and equipment given to recruits of the Second World War. In 1941 there were attempts to resurrect the doughboy sobriquet, but that was quickly eclipsed by GI, and GIs they remained for the duration of the conflict.

There was, of course, new technology that produced life-changing inventions during the 1920s and 1930s. Private Everett Scott of the 168th Infantry, from rural Iowa, saw his first airplane at Camp Mills, New York, in 1917. He was so amazed that he stopped all of his duties to see this phenomenon in the sky.[4] Very few GIs of the next conflict would have given a massive formation of bombers flying to destroy German industries and cities a second glance. The length of the American involvement in the First War was a little over a year and a half, while the Second lasted almost four years, and some soldiers had been training for a year before Pearl Harbor. This allowed the GIs to travel more and often, especially during training or on air bases, to get to see more of Europe.

Training itself was different. Many Great War soldiers went to France, hopefully trained for a month or two, then went into combat. The 82nd Division trained for two months in France before the St Mihiel Offensive of September 1918. Some American divisions were sent into the Meuse-Argonne fight in September 1918 with little or no training. On the other hand, the 45th Division, made up of Western National Guard units, was mustered into service in February 1940, trained as a division in the Texas and Louisiana manoeuvres, deployed to North Africa in June 1943, then committed to battle in Sicily in July 1943. Both the 82nd Division and the 45th Division became good, reliable combat units. The differences in training time and unit preparation are indeed telling. The type of tactical training was very different in that the doughboys trained for a while in the trenches and were then expected to fight in what General John Pershing called 'open' or manoeuvre warfare. The GIs, however, began tactical training as small units, then prepared to fight as integral parts of divisions, corps and armies. In spite of the stark lessons of the Great War, foolish errors were made in the Second World War. The 106th Division was sent to Europe in 1944 with little training and unit cohesion, and was swamped and humiliated in the last great German offensive in December 1944. The anticipation of a Nazi capitulation by Christmas 1944 had thrown lessons learned in 1918 and caution to the winds with tragic results.

General John J. Pershing had led an expeditionary force into Mexico in 1916-17 with little success, but the future General of the Armies learned valuable lessons there. It fell to Pershing to find a way to build the American Expeditionary Forces in Europe, then to fight less than a year later. The Army Chief of Staff, General George C. Marshall, was determined that when the United States entered the Second War the errors of unpreparedness and confusion of doctrine that prevailed in 1917 and 1918 would not be repeated. There is a day-night quality in comparing the two armies that came to Europe, though neither surpassed the other in courage and commitment.

The GIs who arrived in Europe in the 1940s came from a different America, an America sobered by a great Depression. The business of America was business, proclaimed an American President, but that dream had ended on Wall Street in October 1929. Most GIs had grown up with memories of the exuberant, often excessive, 1920s on the one hand and the grim Depression on the other. The naive energy of the turn of the century was matured by the difficult task of reconstructing a battered United States. Under the guiding hand of President Franklin Roosevelt recovery began, but it was exactly that – recovery. It was a task that forced American to turn inward, seeking reassurance that the United States was still a viable democracy that could weather the storm.

One can dwell on the Depression and its results, but one cannot overlook the huge technological changes that differentiated the two generations. The vast majority of the doughboys who reported for service in 1917 and 1918 had never driven an automobile. The GIs who went into service in 1941 were part of a driving generation. Transportation and speed occupied a great deal of the world in which they lived. Letters could be sent air mail, and people could travel in relative comfort by air as well as by train across the nation. This love affair with movement was reflected in the designs of automobiles, radios and furniture. Most GIs of the Second World War would never have known that they were part of the 'modernist movement', but the world around them was certainly a world of lines and movement based on motion and speed. The United States in the 1920s and into the 1930s came face to face with the question of air power. The humble Charles Lindberg, the daring Amelia Earhart and the aggravating William 'Billy' Mitchell preached a new gospel of further, faster, higher. It was a sermon well guarded to a vast continent supposedly geared by two great ocean barriers.

While technological changes shaped the soldier of the Second World War, so did place and time. The doughboys of the Great War began to arrive in France in the summer and early fall of 1917. By the Christmas season of that year General John J. Pershing had only four combat divisions. American troops in large numbers would not see combat until the late spring of 1918, and by November the Armistice was signed. The actual war experience for the vast majority of doughboys was less than one year. During the Second War the majority of American soldiers served from three to four years. Most First World War soldiers, unless training briefly in England or assigned to a very small combat force in Italy, saw their service in France. It was not unusual for American troops during the Second War to see service in North Africa, Italy, England, France, Belgium, Holland, Germany, Austria and Czechoslovakia before the war ended in 1945.

The lucky (or unlucky, depending on one's perspective) who did stay in one place for a length of time were in Britain during the Second World War. In 1917 and 1918 US ground troops often disembarked in England, paraded through the streets, then moved quickly to ships that would take them to training or to combat on the Western Front. Private Thurmond Baccus of the 307th Field Signal Battalion marched through the streets of Winchester in the morning, saw a few sights and visited a British hospital in the afternoon; the next day he was on a train bound for the South Coast of England for transport to France.[5] Paul N. Chase of the 2nd Maintenance Regiment was from Aurora, Illinois, a town 35 miles west of Chicago, which he had visited numerous times. He landed at Liverpool and moved by train to his port of embarkation. Fairly well educated, no stranger to large cities, Chase wrote to his mother, 'I had no idea that England was so beautiful. All of the buildings [are] of brick of different colors and roofs of slates of different colors... Everything was kept up so nice. No dirty fence corners or waste places. You have seen a good many pictures of the country houses, well I thought they picked them out but not so for they are all that way...'[6] After seeing things he had only read about, Chase told his mother that, '[I] would not take a whole lot for my trip.'

On the other hand, American flyers to be trained in England spent three months under the guidance of the Royal Flying Corps before moving on to airfields in France. It was just enough time for the flying cadets to see a few sights and to complain loudly about the differences in the American and the British diet. Except for a select few, time spent in England was limited to three months, and most of that time was taken up with intensive training.[7] There was no feeling that their war would be spent on British soil. Combat in the air would begin when they reached airfields in France. The thought of conducting any air campaign against the Germans from England was preposterous, and just the flight across the English Channel was filled with danger. Most American aviators in the Great War left their training aircraft in Britain, boarded trains, then crossed the Channel in troop ferries just as the infantrymen were doing. There were no sentimental songs about Britain, and the memories of the First World War were made almost exclusively on the soil of France. Two decades and vast technological changes would alter the landscape of Britain and the perceptions of Americans about the island nation a great deal indeed. American aviators and soldiers who passed through Britain on the way to the Western Front recalled the cheering crowds and friendly faces in pubs and theatres, but by the Second War, when there were so many Americans on the island, feelings would change considerably for both Britons and for their 'American cousins'.

The ultimate destination for the Great War American doughboy was France and the Western Front. Only a very few went to Italy: an infantry regiment, some flyers, support troops, and a small staff. Unlike their military descendants, they did not have to storm beaches, nor did they have to face huge mounds of rubble that had once been picturesque French villages. Once off the boats they were packed into boxcars – the famed 40 and 8s– and, if lucky, were sent to some training camps before combat. However, like their later counterparts, they were thirsty and found the French red wine available, cheap, hearty, and heady.

Leslie Langille of the 149th Field Artillery Regiment of the Illinois National Guard had his first view of France at the vast French artillery training centre known as Camp Coetquidan in Brittany. While learning, for the first time, to fire his 105mm French artillery piece (the Americans could provide no modern guns for their artillery units), Langille explored the area around the camp:

> 'Wooden shacks sprung up as far as the eye can see, and they all offer thirst-quenching possibilities. Every shack is a saloon and they vie with each other in capturing our trade. They assume trade-catching names, such as "The Stars and Stripes Bar", "The Franco-American Bar", etc. There is plenty of business for all, and they gather in the shekels and thank fate for bringing America into the war.'[8]

Private Burt A. Hunt, serving in the 114th Field Signal Battalion, was from West Point, Mississippi. Prior to the war he had never travelled out of his native state. Now he was seeing France. He wrote: 'We have been just like country people when they came to town. Every one with his eyes "peeled" back trying to see more than the other fellow. Everything seems awfully funny over here, every thing is so different from the US, but think we will like it all ok when we get so we can count our money.'[9] After a few weeks' training in France Hunt was still overcome with wonder at being so far from a very small town in a very rural state. He told his father: 'Don't think I have seen a wooden building any where, every thing is stone or cement. It don't look like America at all and their ideas about farming and building seem awfully old timey but, when they get anything done it is there to stay for about a century.'[10]

Due to a very strict censorship imposed by General Pershing, the horrors experienced by the doughboys of 1917-18 were largely unknown to the American people.[11] The prevailing view, until a telegram arrived from the War Department announcing the death or wounding of a soldier, was that the soldier was a tourist enjoying the supposed pleasures of being in La Belle France. In 1917 a popular song entitled 'When Yankee Doodle Learns to Parlez Vous Francais' stated that, 'When Yankee Doodle came to Paris town, upon his face he wore a little frown, to those he'd meet upon the street he couldn't speak a word, To find a miss he could kiss it seemed to be absurd…'[12] The soldier of the Great War came from an America that was mainly small-town, church-attending, and wedded to Victorian values, especially concerning sex. The family back home assumed that their 'laddie in Khaki' danced with pretty French girls and, if fortunate, got a goodnight kiss.

The doughboy, despite his background, came into contact with very available, negotiable sex. French styles were several years ahead of what was current in America. The shortening of dresses to mid-calf was *très chic* in Paris to be sure, but in the areas where the doughboys trained and fought the prevailing colour was the black of mourning. Close to the front very few Americans met French girls from local families. Most often they were protected by local customs and guardian mothers and aunts. Sergeant Eustace Fielder from Vicksburg, Mississippi, who was in a support unit, responded to his friends back in the United States: '…there are plenty of pretty girls in France, but none to come up to [American girls], and if I stay over here six years I would never learn how to talk French and understand what they say, but they think the world of the American soldiers.'[13]

Behind the trenches, in towns and villages ravaged by war, the doughboys found the prostitutes and the cheap saloons that catered to soldiers fresh from the dangers of the front. Sergeant Albert M. Ettinger, from New York City and a member of the hard-fighting 165th Infantry, recalled that it was in the town of Lunéville, close to the trenches, that he had his first encounter with a prostitute, a woman who claimed that her husband had been killed in the war and her widow's pension was too meagre to exist on.[14] True tale or not, Ettinger, from the largest, most sophisticated city in the United States, visited her a number of times while at Lunéville. The words of a popular song, 'Willie Earl met a sweet young girl one day in France, her naughty little glance put Willie in a trance; Willie Earl couldn't understand her talk you see, He only knew two words in French, that he learned in the trench, They were oo-la-la and wee-wee…,'[15] was the myth. The reality was prostitution, cheap bars, and venereal disease. The First World War produced very few European 'war brides'.

Not even women serving with the American Expeditionary Forces in France were immune from the hints of possible misbehaviour. Women served in France in large numbers with the Army and as military nurses.[16] For the nurses, the picture was one of horror as the wounded and gassed poured into the field hospitals, then into the base hospitals, but a public fed a steady diet depicting France as the land of wine and song believed that it was just possible that those women who chose to serve 'Over There' had as many opportunities to enjoy themselves as did the soldiers. Few civilians would have believed what Lieutenant William W. Van Dolsen of the First Field Hospital of the 17th Sanitary Train saw. A German artillery shell landed near a slightly built nurse, exploded, and tossed her through the air. To Van Dolsen's utter amazement he saw the diminutive woman pick herself up, brush the dirt from her uniform, adjust her steel helmet, and proceed with her duties.[17]

With the battle-tough 82nd Division there were a number of women who served in the YMCA at the front. Under German fire Mary and Sunshine Sweeny and Bernetta Miller heated coffee and hot cocoa, filled bags with candy and cigarettes and went into the trenches to help the troops. The division commander cited them for 'exceptional meritorious service' under fire, and the French awarded Mary Sweeny and Bernetta Miller the Croix de Guerre for valour.[18] Women served all across the front with the American forces, and the closest many ever came to French champagne was the bitter fighting in that region. Some were killed and wounded in the conduct of their duties. Female soldiers served at the large headquarters in the telephone exchanges, and these 'hello girls' performed valuable service.

When the United States entered the war it was assumed that this would be a 'white man's fight'. The American Civil War had seen the first large number of black troops on the battlefield, and after the war the Army retained a few black infantry and cavalry regiments, normally officered by whites. The initial conscript law of 1917 called for only whites to be registered and drafted, but this was amended later to include 'colored' as well. The Army remained segregated and formed their white divisions first, which meant that many blacks who enrolled stood little chance of service. The Selective Service, the American conscript system, noted after the war that it was obvious that blacks were eager to enrol, be called, and render service at the front.[19] That was not to be the case, however, because most blacks sent to France remained in labouring units in the rear areas.

When the black 15th Infantry Regiment of the New York National Guard arrived at Camp Mills, New York, it was greeted with hostility by other, all-white, national guardsmen.[20] One black regiment made application to join a number of divisions, but was turned down. Finally they were assigned to the French Army and did exceptional service at the front. The 92nd Division was formed and sent to France, but remained poorly trained and equipped. When it was committed to battle the division did not have their allotted three artillery regiments. What had started out as eagerness to participate in the war turned into an opportunity lost for the United States, which claimed that it went to war to 'make the world safe for democracy'. This situation would continue into the next war as well: the Great War for black Americans was a harsh lesson that would be perpetuated during the next great conflict.

As the troops returned home from France, bitterness set in that would shape their views of foreign involvement for decades to come. The failure of the United States to ratify the Versailles Treaty and to join the League of Nations coupled with deteriorating conditions in both Europe and the Orient made veterans of the Great War sceptical of any American commitment. Officers such as George C. Marshall, as Chief of Staff of the Army, recognised early that if war came again the United States would be drawn into the conflict. In 1940 President Roosevelt and General Marshall took steps to bolster the Army in the name of national defence.

When war did come in December 1941, there were no flowery, idealistic slogans to energise the American soldiers. Idealism had been left behind on battlefields of France in the Great War. It was, as Stephen Ambrose has pointed out, a very different American soldier who went to Europe in the Second World War. He did not want to hear high-blown ideas; he was more sophisticated, and he was better educated than his Great War ancestor.

Before the entry of the United States into the Great War the most popular song in America had been 'I Didn't Raise My Boy to be a Soldier'. Almost overnight Americans experienced an explosion of patriotism without really knowing much about the implications of the war. The Second World War was different in that the Japanese had attacked without a declaration of war, and Germany declared war on the United States a few weeks later. There appeared a sense of grim determination to expunge evil, and it was expressed in workplace terms – get the job done. There were patriotic reminders of the war everywhere, rationing was strict, men were drafted in huge numbers, women went to work in the factories, and there was a feeling that this would not be a short war. The United States did not stumble and stagger into battle as it had in 1917-18. It would send US-trained troops to combat or to further training in Europe, and these forces would be supported by a vast, complex logistical system. There were growing pains to be sure, and often the GIs and their leaders seemed naive and childlike, unaware of many of the greater issues of this global conflict; however, in this war America was not an associate, but an ally.

Women were recruited into the service in unprecedented numbers. One recruiting pamphlet stated, 'This is our war … Join the WAAC'. The Women's Army Auxiliary Corps had strict standards requiring two character references, and offered service in the United States and in combat theatres in 34 areas, but not combat. So great was the outpouring of support that on 20 November 1942 President Roosevelt issued an executive order that enlarged the WAAC to almost half a million.[21] There were no more 'hello girls' of the AEF; now there were captains and sergeants in skirts. Of course, the US Navy and Marines were quick to see the benefits of large numbers of women who could free men for the combat that lay ahead.

American forces landed in North Africa in November 1942, and GIs began pouring into Britain to train for a future cross-Channel operation. Britain became the focus of the GI just as France had been for the doughboys, and pretty soon Britons would say of the Americans that they were 'overpaid, oversexed, and over here'. In contrast to the First World War, the number of overseas marriages was quite large, and the term 'war bride' first began in England. In the United States postcards began to appear with the not-so-funny inscription, 'A modern maiden's prayer: Dear Lord, bring him back safe, sound, and single'.[22] Being stationed in England for training or for air missions gave young men the time to meet local girls who were quite like those they knew back home and who spoke the same language, after a fashion.

The GIs in Britain realised that they were not there as suitors or as tourists. As they trained, other Americans were fighting in North Africa, Sicily, and in Italy. There was a certain grim awareness that Britain had suffered greatly before the

United States came into the war. Sergeant Charles B. Linzy, from Little Rock, Arkansas, had trained for over a year in Texas before arriving in England with the 459th Mobile Anti-Aircraft Battalion. Before he returned home in 1945 he had fought from Normandy into North West Europe and into Germany. On 11 November 1943 he wrote his wife, 'Well, honey this day was certainly not a holiday in this war torn gloomy country. But at that I wonder sometimes if we would have stood up to the Blitz as this country has done.' In the same letter Linzy told his wife, who had gone to work in a local war production plant, 'They do not have beer over here. They have what they call bitters. It is.'[23] On 23 December, while on duty in London, Linzy experienced his first air raid, his introduction to the totality of modern war.[24] By the time Linzy left England on 8 June 1944 he had been in the Army longer than the American presence in the First World War, and he had yet to be committed to combat.

Unlike the doughboys of the First War, the GIs often moved from one country to another. For most American soldiers this was the first time that they had been out of the United States, and they found, when not in battle, time to compare cultures. Private First Class Hugh K. Wiltshire from New York, serving in the 351st Infantry Regiment, wrote to his friend who was training in England: 'I've moved around so much since I left you guys, that I'm not satisfied in one place. I'm ready to go some other place now [he was in Italy]. Not back to Africa tho. ...It was nice in Casablanca and Oran.'[25] Wiltshire's sense of geography was not too exact.

Sergeant William E. George of the 415th Night Fighter Squadron illustrates the travels of the American soldier and his reactions. George served from North Africa to Sicily, Italy, England and France from 1943 to 1945, and was in each place long enough to observe local customs and make comparisons between peoples. He wrote:

> 'These natives [Sicilians] are much different to the Arabs, they are so nice and kind and some of them are usually on the camp site with lemons, peaches, or some kind of fruit ... had a nice time picking up almonds..., but it is so much fun to pick them up and then sit down and eat them, just "hunker" down like the Arabs did...'[26]

Sergeant George, from a middle-class family in Little Rock, Arkansas, while serving in England became an anglophile who described with great pleasure his love for afternoon tea, a practice obviously very foreign to a young man from the American South.[27] With his mother's cooking now a memory, George found 'bean pies' in the local RAF canteen to be a very fine meal. Not every American became an anglophile, however. Technical Sergeant Elmer Franzen of Indiana served in the 329th Service Group, which saw action from North Africa to Sicily, to Egypt, and finally India. While in North Africa he made friends with local French families, and on his 23rd birthday they presented him with '...a bouquet of roses... My French friends are responsible for it all. They do my laundry for a moderate price, then iron and press them. I do give the kids candy and gum occasionally.'[28] Like most of his comrades, Franzen continually marvelled at the sights and sounds of each place the war took him.

Charles B. Linzy's anti-aircraft battalion, by some chance of war, found itself attached to General Leclerc's 2nd French Armoured Division speeding toward Paris in August 1944. The French, being short of anti-aircraft artillery, needed security on every Paris bridge. No one in Linzy's battalion complained, and Linzy wrote in his diary, 'Boy what an entry into the town.'[29] Once in Germany Linzy wrote:

'When we came across France, Belgium, and Holland the people would have their own flags and American flags sticking all over. Now then the only flag you see is a white cloth nailed onto a stick. Boy they believe in making them that way before you get to them or otherwise it means a grenade tossed through the window or a round of artillery thru the wall. Even then you have to watch them as they are treacherous as hell. Will be so glad to get out of this darn country.'[30]

In the same letter Linzy touched on a great difference between the combat GI and the doughboy when he wrote, 'Gee but these Heinie towns are taking a beating and I am really glad to see them destroyed.' Linzy was seeing total war, war waged on civilians as well as the enemy military.

The American soldier of the Great War saw battlefields, trenches and no-man's-land. German bombing raids on British or French cities were not common occurrences. When presented with a possible plan for a strategic bombing campaign in late 1917 both Pershing and Secretary of War Newton Baker had grave doubts about hitting civilian targets inside Germany. For a generation thereafter air power strategists urged such operations, arguing that to break enemy civilian morale and destroy industry would shorten a war and would lessen battlefield casualties. Events leading up to the outbreak of war in 1939 – Spain, Ethiopia, China – foretold war with no safe haven.

Americans were well aware of the Blitz through reporters such as Edward R. Morrow, and they knew that the British were being pounded by the Luftwaffe. The GI's mind was conditioned to accept the concept of total war. How they would react, however, when face to face with it was a different matter. The vast destruction of French cities in the Normandy area and across Northern France was a visual reminder of the type of war in which they were now engaged. Troops arriving in England were greeted by modern war. Sergeant James A. Jacques, from Evansville, Indiana, serving with the 843 Engineer Aviation Battalion, was greeted with bombs hitting Liverpool the day he disembarked. He told his parents that they continued to hit England the entire two weeks he was there.[31]

Just before his wild ride to Paris, Sergeant Linzy wrote to his wife: 'These refugees coming back into the liberated ports get me. Some walking, carrying their stuff on their shoulders, some use bicycles, baby buggies, wheelbarrows, and horse carts. From tiny kids to real old men and women... One thing will make you wonder, I have seen churches completely destroyed by bombs and shells and a statue of Christ maybe at the entrance not even touched.'[32] As GIs moved toward Germany scenes would get worse as far as civilians were concerned, and precious few Americans had ever heard about concentration camps at that time.

As US troops crossed the Rhine River they came face to face with the terrible destruction of total war. When doughboys reached the west bank of the Rhine in November and December 1918, they found Germany unscathed, but in 1945 the landscape had changed, as had their concepts of waging war. Sergeant Kenneth Lummer, from York, Pennsylvania, served in General George S. Patton's hard-driving 3rd Army as a tank commander in the 482nd Tank Battalion. Tired from combat, he confided to his diary on 2 April 1945:

'We have been driving all day again today and passed through quite a few towns two of which were nearly burned to the ground. I don't know exactly how much ground we have covered but we must have drove about seventy miles today.'[33]

Eight days later Lummer wrote:

'...And then we got a fire mission and pulled off the road and really laid another town to the ground. We went through it nearly a half-hour later and darned near roasted ourselves. The people are getting a taste of their own medicine...'[34]

In 1945 GIs faced masses of rubble on one hand and the spectre of Nazism and Hitler on the other. First Sergeant Will C. Johnson of Nettleton, Mississippi, fought across Germany with the 104th Infantry Regiment. He was shocked at the resistance of the Germans, and told his parents:

'The other day we took about 80 prisoners in one little town and they were all above 45. The day before, you won't believe this but it is true, we got around 15 that were from 8 to 14. Then there are those SS that keep them going.'[35]

As Johnson wrote this letter he was sitting in the living room of a German home he had occupied. An old German man watched him as he wrote, and Johnson knew, 'He had a son killed in Russia, big picture of him here on the wall.'[36]

An exhausted Sergeant Kenneth Lummer pulled his tank to the side of the road to watch a strange procession moving to the west from a town he called 'Eisheinbach'. He wrote in his diary, 'It really is a pleasant sight to see all of the slave labourers from France, Belgium, Poland and Russia being set free after about five years of slavery. They are really a happy crowd.'[37] For many a GI during that spring of 1945 the war had taken on a very human face. There were no vague slogans when looking at the faces of forced labourers going home. The reasons for the war came late for the Americans. They had not been propagandised, and, as Stephen Ambrose has written, they behaved correctly and with honour.[38] Much of this was due to the GIs figuring out, in their own terms, why they were fighting. Tank commander Lummer did not need slogans to tell him why he had fought. He wrote in his diary after seeing concentration camp survivors:

'They cheered us, shook our hands, and even hugged and kissed us they were so happy to see us. They were nearly starved to death and when we stopped on the road and would give them cigarettes and rations they could not thank us enough even if it was only a small amount.'[39]

At the end of the Great War General Pershing was ordered to send American forces home as quickly as possible. But at the end of the Second War Americans settled into being a military government. Most of the GIs who had served for three or four years were ready to go home, to be sure, but like Sergeant Linzy they were more worried about being sent to the Pacific Theatre of Operations to fight against Japan.[40] To Linzy and to most fellow soldiers their war of liberation was over. He wrote to his wife, '…you cannot imagine the number or the truth about all of these people who were slaves for the Nazis. As good and as pretty a country as this is I do not understand why they ever wanted to start a war, and get it laid in ruins the way it is.'[41]

In 1944 the Congress of the United States began passing a series of laws that provided unprecedented benefits for veterans. Of great importance was the 'GI Bill', which guaranteed Government assistance for veterans who wished to attend colleges, universities and technical training schools. After the Great War veterans faced a dismal future with few benefits and almost no guarantee of re-employment. With these new laws, returning veterans could look forward to a much brighter future than their First World War counterparts. The situation in Europe, however, dictated that the United States remain in force on the continent. While the US maintained a small occupation force on the Rhine from 1918 to 1923, the current situation, with widespread destruction, severe hunger, displaced persons, demanded a more specific involvement. Combat forces would remain in place until relieved by new forces from the United States, usually in the late autumn of 1945 or early 1946.

It is safe to say that most American soldiers who served in the European Theatre wanted to go home. There were those who realised that momentous events were taking place. Sergeant Jacques, whose aviation engineer battalion was really needed in reconstruction in the Munich area, took time to travel to Nuremberg to watch the War Crime Trials. 'Yesterday I went to Nernberg,' he wrote to his parents, 'and while there I looked on the court proceedings at the war crimes you have been reading about. I was in the court after the trials and was told seven would be hung, the rest received fifteen years. I saw four of the prisoners who will be hung, boy they really had a MP escort.'[42]

There were a number of units that became engaged in tackling immediate and problematical post-war problems and in so doing came into contact with the Russians. Will C. Johnson's 104th Infantry Regiment was part of the 26th Infantry Division, which had driven into Austria and Czechoslovakia by the end of the war. They had the difficult task of dealing with displaced persons, concentration camp survivors, and liaison with Russian forces in Czechoslovakia.[43] Johnson, who was highly educated, detected very quickly a growing antagonism between the Americans and Russians, especially over the treatment of Austrian and German civilians. In a letter to his parents, Johnson wrote:

'…to take care of the aftermath of war is quite a job… Met some more Russian soldiers yesterday and I honestly believe that they are the roughest looking and acting characters that I have ever seen. They don't care what they do or how they act and it is very plain to see how and why the Germans are afraid of them… If we would let them, they would take the whole country away.

They have no mercy on the Germans at all, not even now that the war is over. They still don't think they have paid dear enough.'[44]

For those who remained behind there was a grudging acceptance of their fate. Sergeant George found himself in Darmstadt, Germany, where his 415th Night Fighter Squadron would remain until 1946. He wrote to his parents in Little Rock, 'I'm sitting here with a mouth full of beer (do you mind, the beer I mean)... I do love salted peanuts, we got an 8oz can in our rations this week.'[45] After recounting some of his experiences and travels he added, 'I am happy.'

With the war over, veterans returned to begin their lives again, many with educational opportunities that would have been unthinkable when the war broke out. There were marriages resulting from war and post-war occupation service, and in 1946 and 1947 the United States would experience a 'baby boom' that would shape the nation for decades to come. However, there still remained the stark contrasts between doughboy and GI. The doughboys had come from a nation that was closer to the tribulations of the Civil War, and this was reflected in how they viewed their role in the war. When the patriotic slogans and martial ardour turned sour by 1919 and 1920 the veteran turned inward. They were grieved that, due to censorship and the short duration of the war, no one really knew of their sacrifice and hardship. The soldier of the Great War marvelled at the airplane, the silent movie, the automobile.

By 1941 the GI was a product of motion, with the automobile, railway and air transportation that linked the nation from shore to shore. Charles A. Lindberg's solo trans-Atlantic flight in 1927 meant that the ocean was no longer a barrier protecting the eastern United States. On 7 December 1941 the Japanese Navy made it painfully clear that the Pacific was no longer a protective wall.

The GI's relationship with women had changed. Through the excesses of the Roaring Twenties into the Big Band jitterbug era of the late 1930s, men and women were associating without the restrains that bound the doughboys of the Great War. The massive nature of the Second War dictated that women went into the factories and into the services in unprecedented numbers. Gender roles, shaken during the First War, would be forever changed by the magnitude of the Second. However, hanging over both wars was the unsettled question of race. There were black units in the Second World War, and many turned in fine combat records, but the United States emerged from that war still unable to cope with a question that would haunt the nation.

The experience of being abroad in the two wars was quite different in time and location. The First War was, for the Americans, short, and the doughboys focused their minds on France and the Western Front. During the next war the term 'in for the duration' could mean four or five years, and soldiers would move from North Africa to Sicily to France, and then beyond. Britain, not France, held the fascination of the GI because so many trained there or flew their combat missions from there. There were attempts to propagandise GIs, to build up the martial spirit, but those men and women of the 'modern' period had to find their own reasons to fight. Sergeant Lummer of York, Pennsylvania, found his reasons in the smiles and tears of concentration camp survivors. Sergeant Linzy found his reason to fight to be his buddies, the men he trained with. They all came to realise eventually that Hitler and Nazism were evil.

Did then Lightning Strike Twice? In a sense it did, because Americans were again sent to fight on foreign shores. In a broader context it did not, because of the great cultural and material differences between the generations. The popular 1918 song 'How You Gonna Keep 'Em Down on the Farm After They've Seen Paree?' would have made no sense to a GI. 'Don't Sit Under the Apple Tree With Anyone Else But Me' more represented the feelings of the GI. If lightning did indeed strike twice it must be seen as the differing bolts of a mid-spring rain and a great raging tempest, so great was the gulf between the two.

Notes on contributors

Professor Emeritus James J. Cooke, University of Mississippi, Oxford, Mississippi, USA.

Professor Cooke is the author of The Rainbow Division in the Great War (1994), The US Air Service in the Great War (1996), Pershing and His Generals (1997), and The All-Americans at War (1999). He contributed to Facing Armageddon (1996) and At the Eleventh Hour (1998). He is a Fellow of the Royal Historical Society

Recommended reading

Ambrose, Stephen E., *Citizen Soldier* (New York: Simon & Schuster, 1997)
 The Supreme Commander: The War Years of General Dwight D. Eisenhower (Garden City, NY: Doubleday, 1970)
Astor, Gerald, *The Mighty Eighth* (New York: Donald Fine Books, 1997)
Braim, Paul F. *The Test of Battle: The American Expeditionary Force in the Meuse-Argonne Campaign* (Newark, DE: University of Delaware Press, 1987)
Cooke, James J. *Pershing and his Generals: Command and Staff in the AEF* (Westport, CT: Praeger Publishing, 1997)
Doubler, Michael D., *Closing with the Enemy: How the GIs Fought the War in Europe, 1944-1945* (Lawrence, KS: University of Kansas Press, 1994)
Hallas, James H., *The Doughboy War: The American Expeditionary Force in World War I* (Boulder, CO: Lynne Rienner Publishers, 1999)
 Squandered Victory: The American First Army at St Mihiel (Westport, CT: Praeger Publishing, 1995)

Notes

1 Al Durbin and J. Russel Robinson, 'Memories of France' (New York: Waterson, Berlin & Snyder Co, 1928)
2 Stephen E. Ambrose, *Citizen Soldier* (New York: Simon & Schuster, 1977) p14
3 Ibid
4 Scott to his Mother, Camp Mills, NY, 13 September 1917 (Everett Scott correspondence: author's personal collection)
5 Memoir by Private Thurmond J. Baccus (US Army Military History Institute Archives, World War One Survey, Carlisle Barracks, Pennsylvania)
6 Chase to his Mother, Camp Mills, NY, 13 September 1917 (Everett Scott correspondence: author's personal collection)
7 Typescript copy, 'A History of the American Air Service in Great Britain, September 2, 1917-December 2, 1918' in The General William D. Mitchell Papers, The Library of Congress,

Washington DC, Carton 34
8   Leslie Langille, *Men of the Rainbow* (Chicago: The O'Sullivan Publishing House, 1933) p46
9   Hunt to his Mother, France, 6 September 1918 (Burt A. Hunt correspondence: author's personal collection
10 Hunt to his Father, France, 20 September 1918, ibid
11 See James J. Cooke, 'The Americans' in Hugh Cecil and Peter Liddle (eds) *At the Eleventh Hour* (London: Leo Cooper, 1998) pp142-56
12 Will Hart and Edward Nelson, 'When Yankee Doodle Learns to Parlez Vous Francais' (New York: Stasny Music Co, 1917)
13 Fielder to his Parents, France, 6 September 1918 (Eustace Fielder correspondence, courtesy of Mrs Gail Fielder Andrews)
14 Albert M. Ettinger and A. Churchill Ettinger, *A Doughboy With the Fighting 69th* (Shippensburg: White Mane Publishing 1992) p61
15 Harry Ruby and George Jessell, 'And he's Say OO-LA-LA, WEE-WEE' (New York: Waterson, Berlin & Snyder, 1919)
16 For just such a view of women in service, see Ed Rose and Abe Oldman, *Oh, Susie Behave* (New York: McCarthy & Fisher, Inc, 1918) See also Lottie Gavin, *American Women in World War I: They Also Served* (Boulder: University of Colorado Press, 1997)
17 Van Dolsen to Sister, np, 17 March 1918 (Van Dosen correspondence, US Army Military History Institute Archives, Carlisle Barracks, Pennsylvania)
18 HQ, 82nd Division, General Orders No 1, 13 January 1919 (Records Group 120, 82nd Division, National Archives, Washington, DC, Carton 85). See also Gavin, op cit, pp152, 272, 273
19 'Second Report of the Provost Marshal General to the Secretary of War' (Washington: Government Printing Office, 1919) pp194-5
20 Albert M. Ettinger, op cit, p7
21 Extract from numerous pieces of recruiting material (Alice Whitaker papers: author's personal collection)
22 From the Clarice F. Clark scrapbooks and papers (author's personal collection). Clark maintained scrapbooks that pertained to her and her fiancé, a pilot in the 585th Bomb Squadron in England. He was killed in action over Germany in 1945, and Clark became an army nurse soon thereafter.
23 Linzy to Wife, England, 11 November 1943 (Charles B. Linzy diaries and correspondence: author's personal collection)
24 Diary entry, 23 December 1943, ibid
25 Wiltshire to Cpl Jack Wilson, Italy, 25 March 1943 (Hugh Wiltshire correspondence: author's personal collection)
26 George to his Mother, Sicily, 10 September 1943 (William E. George correspondence: author's personal collection)
27 George to his Mother, Scotland, 23 May 1943, ibid
28 Franzen to his Parents, North Africa, 22 April 1943 (Elmer Franzen correspondence: author's personal collection)
29 Diary entry, Paris, 27 August 1944, Linzy diaries, op cit
30 Linzy to his Wife, Germany, 5 March 1945, Linzy correspondence, op cit
31 Jacques to his Parents, France, May 1945 (James A. Jacques correspondence: author's personal collection)
32 Linzy to his Wife, France, 16 August 1944, Linzy correspondence, op cit
33 Diary entry, Germany, 2 April 1945 (Kenneth C. Lummer Diary: author's personal collection)
34 Diary entry, Germany, 10 April 1945, ibid
35 Johnson to his Parents, Germany, 16 April 1945 (Will C. Johnson correspondence: author's personal collection)
36 Ibid
37 Diary entry, Germany, 19 April 1945, Lummer Diary, op cit
38 Stephen E. Ambrose, op cit, pp449-50
39 Diary entry, Germany, 19 April 1945, Lummer Diary, op cit
40 Linzy to his Wife, Lauterbach, Germany, 18 May 1945, Linzy correspondence, op cit
41 Ibid
42 Jacques to his Parents, Munich, Germany, 17 November 1945, Jacques correspondence, op cit
43 'History of a Combat Regiment, 1639-1945' (Printed in Germany, 1945) pp125-30
44 Johnson to his Parents, Krummau, Czechoslovakia, 18 May 1945, Johnson correspondence, op cit
45 George to his Parents, Darmstadt, Germany, 30 July 1945, George correspondence, op cit

Chapter 14

German soldiers in victory, 1914 and 1940

Benjamin Ziemann (1914) and Klaus Latzel (1940)

1914

On 19 August 1914, just a few days after the beginning of the First World War, Wilhelm Muehlon, Director of the Krupp Works in Essen and a critical observer of German politics, wrote in his diary:

> 'The way in which our newspapers allow no criticism to appear in the letters they publish from our soldiers on campaign has become a real nuisance with regard to public opinion. Boasting, excited, ignorant soldiers of course write the most inconsistent stuff, no matter if about conquests, no matter if about cruelties. Carelessly they mix up things that they only have heard as rumours and even things which they have only read in newspapers.'[1]

With such an assessment of what it was like to be at the front and its depiction 'at home' at the time, Muehlon takes the position of an outsider. That was because since the summer of 1914 unreal descriptions of the advance of German troops through Belgium and France and their victories dominated public opinion, or, to be more exact, dominated published opinion in Germany. In particular the war experience of the volunteers became a symbol of the enthusiastic response of the German nation. Politicians and the people of Germany expected a campaign that would end after a few months and would free Germany from the clutch of its enemies. Since the beginning of the war, letters from volunteer soldiers had been published in the newspapers. They had provided a pattern in which hopes regarding the war, as well as the cruel reality experienced in the fighting, were now elevated into sublime sentiment. This idealistic and imaginative expression, flowing mostly from Protestant academics, linked two contradictory impressions: the expectation of swift victory and the shattering experience of what destruction was being done. This was drawn together as the German soldier's altruistic sacrifice for the nation and of his being purified by the war. A classic example for these ideas and impressions can be found in the edition of *War Letters from German Soldiers*, which was edited by the Professor of German Studies, Philipp Witkop, in 1916, and republished in larger editions during the 1920s and '30s.[2]

These student letters about the beginning of war had long-term effects on the popular and historiographical perception of the experiences of German soldiers during 1914. Generations of readers memorised these images of the enthusiastic leap into war and the first victorious battles. The descriptions seemed to be as credible as the inner attitude of 'exalted seriousness' that enabled German people to bear the immense loss of life in their Armies during the first months of war. It has only been in the last ten years that the interpretation of those documents has changed radically. Up until then, those letters published during 1914-18, especially those written by students, were not read and interpreted as authentic and representative testimony of the experience of war. Modern scholarly criticism regards them as cultural and political constructions, as Wilhelm Muehlon already did in the year they were written. Those letters were a symbolic fragment of a public description of war experience that clearly demonstrated the nation's inner unity at the beginning of the First World War.[3]

In relation to today's interest in soldiers' letters, historians concern themselves in the main with two related perspectives. Their analysis focuses upon those field-post letters and war diaries that are to be found in archives or in private property. It is important to appreciate that the writers themselves never expected this. Second, scholars occupy themselves with the description of immediate impressions of the front, and the multitude of contradictions in the soldiers' moods resulting from their front-line experience. Scientific interest primarily focuses on the soldiers' motivation and on the frequently immense differences that existed, even at the same time, in a universal conscript army, with its soldiers of different social and regional backgrounds and different ages. The second perspective focuses on long-term continuities in the forming and changing patterns of human reaction, patterns that can be analysed through the linguistic descriptions in the letters. In this perspective, two dimensions – expectations concerning the future and experiences made by looking back on the past – are linked continuously. General impressions can then be drawn, impressions consistently evidenced throughout the war. From all this, some conclusions can be drawn about the universal experience of German soldiers on this front at that time.[4]

The following remarks about German soldiers in 1914 attempt to link both perspectives as closely as possible. The intention is to demonstrate the contradictory expectations and experiences of soldiers when advancing into hostile country, as well as the ambivalence between being cheerful and disillusioned. Another question is how ordinary soldiers experienced physical violence as victims and perpetrators. It should also be shown how men in the ranks regarded the way of life of the people of the conquered countries and their attitude towards the war.

So far there has been no systematic research on this topic, but we can see how it might be done through looking systematically at sets of letters, and here we shall quote from three eyewitnesses who describe events during the first weeks of the war. The first source is that of Georg Schenk, born in 1888, who worked and lived as a carpenter in Nuremburg. Schenk was drafted on 4 August 1914 and became a Private First Class in the 21st Bavarian Infantry Regiment, in which he experienced the German advance into Lotharingia and Northern France. The notes in his diary start on 1 August 1914 when mobilisation in Germany was declared:

'Finally at six o'clock in the evening of August 1st it became known that mobilisation has been ordered and everything has been stepped up to its maximum. Many a tear fell and many an eye that had been dry for ten years became wet. They were especially from women and girls because a lot of men and boys had to leave their homes to fight for their fatherland, endangered by Russia and France. In the first night only a few slept; the worry about the wife of a husband, the bride of a bridegroom, was deep because everybody knew that hard war was imminent...

[20 August:] We were lucky to escape with our lives because it was a hard day and we received our baptism of fire. Trust in God, he will help in the nick of time, that is my comfort... When I laid in the line of fire I thought, what will my Gretl [his bride] do and think, and a few thoughts flashed through me, what she would say if I would remain lying down wounded or dead... Now, God be thanked, the first battle is over, how many shall we have to take part in? We don't know...

[25 August – there is heavy fighting at Serres:] For the rest of our entire lives we will remember August 25th, it cost a lot of human lives on both sides, without even considering the wounded. I promised that I would pray or get a prayer said for me in my family every day if I were to return safely from this campaign...

[31 August:] Life in war is quite nice if there are not any battles, but we have an officer who should have remained at home because he made our life even more difficult than it should be. We don't get a minute's rest, because none of the officers and NCOs like to see us unoccupied.

[3 September:] This afternoon I was put on patrol with Lieutenant Merz but we did not see anything and got some rest again. Our First Lieutenant has made a mess in his pants; when he hears something caused by the enemy he is frightened and when the enemy is not close by he is terribly harsh and fairly stupid. We have got a company leader who knows less than a recruit and is more frightened than a scaredy-cat.

[7 September:] At four o'clock the infantry's shooting started and attacking began, the 8th company was at the very front and was shot at by our own artillery in such a serious way that probably not a single man in the first squad survived unscathed and of the ones who were not dead or wounded the rest pulled back of their own accord. It was a terrible sight to see the wounded coming back, often three, four or five together... During this night from [September] 6th to [September] 7th Remereville was ablaze. Four other villages have been set on fire and the whole area was illuminated. Now Remereville is a place of devastation, there is scarcely a single house left – I have not received mail for five days, otherwise I would have written. In the trenches I had no other occupation than writing down my notes and talking to my colleagues. Well, when observing the war this way, everybody has to admit that there is nothing more terrible than war. About 300 metres in front of us the dead of yesterday are lying, most of them killed by our own artillery.'[5]

When reading this description of the first weeks of war the reader can see clearly that Schenk confirms the argument established by recent research: in the German population exaggerated joy over the beginning of the First World War was not the prevalent reaction. Especially among the working classes of the cities, and Schenk belonged to them, but also in the more rural areas, the prevalent emotions in August 1914 were dejection and desperation. This suggests that most soldiers did not march off to war with a feeling of patriotic élan, but with an inkling of the scares and fatigues that were yet to come.[6] However, Schenk believed too that the threat to Germany offered by Russia and France justified the sudden separation from home and family. In Schenk's thoughts the baptism of fire on 20 August 1914 caused him to reflect upon his relationship with his girlfriend Gretl. However, just over two years later, on 1 January 1916, he married her. To the extremely grim fighting on 25 August, Schenk reacted in a traditional pattern of interpreting and overcoming his personal problems. This pattern arose from the Catholic faith in which he believed deeply, as most Catholic soldiers did, a pattern that was most probably well-rooted in his personal make-up.[7] A clear device for this philosophical approach was the fact that he sought consolation in good days before his terrible experience. It is also obvious that the battle was not the first situation of crisis in which he had resort to a rosary.

Up to this time only the harassing and cowardly behaviour of his superiors prevented Schenk from enjoying the experience of war. At first he saw the campaign as a quick advance into an unknown country, a journey of adventure and discovery. But the battles of 6 and 7 September seem abruptly to have changed Schenk's mind. The sight of casualties of his own side, killed by 'friendly fire', may have caused serious doubts in his belief that a defensive war was justified. But even towards the victims of the other side Schenk behaved sensitively and found the sight of them distressing, as indeed he did the sight of some destroyed villages. He was undergoing an experience that was the reflexive process of learning common to his comrades. It seems that he was no longer able to find support in family feelings or religious traditions. Because of technical problems the Field Post as a medium of communication between him and his family was not effective.[8] Instead of writing letters Schenk expressed his concerns to other soldiers. These talks seem to have been generally an important medium for drawing together the essence of the front-line experience. However, only in a very few cases can we examine the essence of those talks from written sources. In connection with this it is interesting that Schenk used the neutral word 'colleague' but not the more 'loaded' term 'comrade' when he talked about the other soldiers of his squad.

The outcome of such a collective opinion-making process in the trenches in France was unmistakable. It was contradictory to Schenk's opinion a week before, when he wrote about a 'comfortable' life in war, and it was also contradictory to the theology of a 'justified war' that was preached by many well-known representatives of the Catholic confession from the beginning of the war, a confession in which

Schenk had found comfort only two weeks before. ('There can not be anything more terrible than war.') Apparently this statement was the smallest common denominator that all soldiers of the 21st Infantry Regiment agreed to in the first four weeks as they grasped the reality of war on the Western Front and tried to interpret it in an appropriate way.

This does not say anything about any changes that Schenk made in his interpretation of the war before he died on 24 October 1917. Furthermore, he did not continue his entries in his diary after 7 October 1914. This fact could be a hint that, after the first four weeks of war, he had found a satisfactory interpretation of war. In 1917 Schenk resumed writing in his diary for a short period of time. In these entries it can be seen that he continued to believe in his subtly differentiated opinion concerning the enemy. On a patrol in April 1917, the French unit opposite Schenk's took a German prisoner who was not very popular in Schenk's unit. Schenk evaluated it as 'very reasonable' that the French did not open fire when the German patrol advanced.[9]

When Schenk wrote down his statement that 'there is nothing more terrible than war' he had not yet considered how it might be brought to an end. Clearly he had no firmly established political views that would have led him to interpret the war in a particular way. Soldiers who had been members of the Social Democratic Party (SPD) before the war were drawing their own conclusions by the end of 1914. An important event for the formulation of such conclusions was the Reichstag speech delivered by Karl Liebknecht, a leftist SPD politician, on 2 December. He was the only member of the parliament who spoke up against the granting of further war-loans. After that speech Karl Liebknecht was to receive a lot of letters from ordinary soldiers at the front, most of them industrial workers, congratulating him on his courageous stand and expressing their support. Many of these field-post letters showed that the authors did not simply think that the war was a terrible and faceless cruelty, but they also maintained that the 'big capitalists' were the ones responsible for the outbreak of the war and were the ones who were interested in continuing it for their profit. Even at this early stage of the war such soldiers expressed their conviction that only a united and determined act of the whole population could bring the war to an end.[10]

The second eyewitness whose diary offers information about the patterns of interpretations developed by ordinary soldiers was 24-year-old David Pfaff, a volunteer soldier serving in the German advance through Belgium and France. His diary is maintained until he was killed on 4 November 1914:

'11 August: Dug trenches and drill.

12 August: Drill.

14 August: Drill and training at night. A lot of harassment by our superiors. Everybody wishes that we are at last going to march against the enemy. In the morning the artillery fired at a plane. Later we found out that the plane was one of ours.

15 August: Drill. In the afternoon at the swimming pool in the town of Luxembourg. Great swimming pool. Never seen such a beautiful one in all my life before.

16 August: The square-bashing is getting out of control. Someone who feels like me tells me that only the inborn patriotism of the Germans enables us to put up with these monotonous drills without grumbling.

30 August: In the morning a field service in intense heat. We sang "We stand in prayer before God the Almighty", deeply affected every one of us. Many of them who turned away from God have found their Saviour again. I myself too.

8 October: In the trench, "standing to". I was very sick. But the doctor has not helped me.

2 November: Our Lieutenant has beaten Paul and Jakob because they wanted to get wood and material for entrenching without their rifles. Surely it cannot be right that a young lieutenant can beat an experienced soldier and reservist who fights for his Fatherland. Of course resentment is strong and such events are as shameful as when young officers use their pistols to force their soldiers to advance while they themselves remain under cover. That's something I experienced on the first of October.'[11]

Compared with Schenk's diary there are a lot of differences in Pfaff's notes, but also some similarities. To the Protestant Pfaff, the identification with the 'Fatherland' as a political and moral value was more important than to the Catholic Schenk. This is proved by the way he writes about the officer's harassing behaviour towards ordinary soldiers, something that caused Pfaff as well as Schenk to find fault with certain disgraceful incidents as early as during the first weeks of war. Schenk itemised these incidents. He interpreted them as a consequence of a lack of character in certain officers. But Pfaff interpreted the behaviour of one of them as being much more than an individual disgrace and so, for him, such persons were a threat to the readiness of the Germans to serve effectively in the war. By referring to 'Russian conditions', he does not mean what was a popular opinion of many Social Democrats, that this war was a campaign against the 'enemy of all civilisation', as August Bebel referred to Russia in 1907. For Pfaff the use of physical force against veteran soldiers was a moral outrage that endangered the inner Teutonic values on which the German nation was built. So, as also with Schenk, the war meant that those values were under trial. By trusting in God this feeling was strengthened even more.[12] When referring to his newly acquired spiritual attitude on 30 August, Pfaff had most probably not yet participated in a battle. As far as he was concerned this certified to him that religion was not a last resort when danger was being faced. Georg Schenk, however, only prayed to God in a moment of danger. Maybe his reference to his Protestant image of the German nation prevented him from writing down his opinions about the French or Belgian people as well as about their soldiers.

The indoor pool in Luxembourg was described as an architectural sensation. This impression bears out the statement of Georg Schenk that when advancing through Belgium and France they revealed the tourist in them as well as the soldier.

More facets of the experience of the ordinary soldier become obvious when one reads the letters of the German farmer and Territorial Army soldier, Stefan Schimmer. Nearly every day he wrote a letter to his wife Katharina who was at home on their farm in Oellingen in Lower Franconia. At first Schimmer wrote from Herxheim, in the Bavarian Palatinate, where his regiment was garrisoned. As late as 2 October 1914 he crossed the border into France and during the following weeks he was garrisoned in Senones, a village in the French Vosges. His letters record:

'[11 August 1914:] 'I would like it best, if there were an armistice by now.'

[24 August:] 'Four villages in Lotharingia were set on fire, because they harassed the German troops. On the German side up till now every battle has been won. The Bavarian army fights like fury. Those whom the bullet spares are slaughtered with the bayonet or the rifle butt.'

[25 August:] 'Had to go to church, after that our captain read war history to us. We took an enormous number of prisoners, more than 150 guns, a lot of machine-guns and an enormous number of rifles and ammunition. The war will and must be won by the Germans. The French have never won the tiniest engagement... On August 25th, on my birthday, I went to confession again early, well, because we were off duty. Maybe I'll not get another chance, because nobody knows where we will go to. If I should not return, you will marry Michael. You will get out of this war anyway. As I mentioned before, the Germans are winning the war, there can not be any doubt. The Belgian fortress of Liège is now in German hands after 14 days being besieged by the German artillery. But the war costs lives, and it can last till spring. With the French the Germans would be finished by winter. They run away if the Germans go after them or they surrender.'

[1 September:] 'The blockade of Paris will be achieved in a few days. The poor people already are having to leave there.'

[3 September:] 'Leuven is a town in France [sic] of 7,000 inhabitants. It has been battered as well, because the inhabitants shot at the German troops.'

[4 September:] 'The German cavalry is at the gates of Paris. The Bavarian army is in battle in the Vosges. It is reasonable to expect that Paris will capitulate within 8 days.'

[27 September:] 'Please celebrate two masses to gain divine providence (in our village church). Today I was at confession again and at two masses and in one service.'

[2 October:] 'I am telling you that we crossed the border on October 2nd at 7am. One saw battered waggons lying there as well, a shattered custom-house. The air smells of burning because of the ruined villages. We have just rested in a French village. It is mostly abandoned. One can only see the sky and the troops. (No sign of French troops in the villages.)'

[9 October:] 'Write to tell me how the war is going. We know absolutely nothing. Is not there going to be a peace settlement very soon?'

[14 October:] 'Is there no news of the war coming to an end soon? Pray for me often… Where we are now doesn't look beautiful because there has been a battle. There are lots of soldiers' graves.'

[18 October:] 'Often I do not sleep two hours the whole day long because I am so afraid. I only hope because of you and the children I don't have to be killed… Where we are now was a battlefield as well as the other place. It is a horror of devastation.'

[20 October:] 'What the Kaiser tells we don't believe here. There seems to be no attempt to achieve a peace settlement.'

[29 October:] 'What the Kaiser says, in my opinion, is intended to calm down the troops.'

[17 December:] 'There is no sense in thinking of peace before March. Now it's a siege war. The nation which is going to hold out longest with its money and food is going to win the war.'[13]

When reading these letters there is a striking fact – the difference between the expectations concerning the war when the men were garrisoned on German soil and then when they were in France. In Herxheim, Schimmer believed in rumours and statements spread by officers who told their soldiers about quick and decisive victories achieved by the German Army. But this expectation of a victory was neither loaded with patriotic feelings nor with euphoric emotions because Schimmer knew very well how many victims the war demanded. From the very beginning of the war he expected the very worst for himself. So he gave his wife advice that she should marry again if he should die. Thus the continuation of their farm would be ensured. Even when the truth about the propagandist reports about German successes became known (as was the case with the report that Paris had been captured, a report that first had to be corrected and finally had to be dropped) Schimmer continued to believe such news during the first weeks of war.[14]

At the front, Schimmer's attitude suddenly changed. Now, as a result of experiencing the reality of war, the scenes of destruction replaced his fanciful images of the first weeks. Also, when seeing what war was like, the feeling that he had been properly informed about the whole context of the war soon disappeared. Schimmer was no longer observing the war from a higher level. Now he exercised the worm's-eye perspective of the ordinary soldier. He gained insight into the aims of the High Command as it spread official statements about the war. As with Georg Schenk, the start of Stefan Schimmer's process of learning came from talking with other soldiers. The expectation of a quick victory was replaced by a strong desire for peace. By the end of the year, Schimmer had clearly got an insight into the stalemate character of war. He now believed that the progress of the war would be dominated by the fullest economic mobilisation of the participating countries. Schimmer's serious reference to Confession and the Holy Mass confirm again the significance of religion for Catholic soldiers when trying to assimilate the experiences of war.

In his letters Schimmer mentioned atrocities by the German Army in Belgium and France. As is well-established, 6,000 French and Belgian civilians lost their lives as a result of undisciplined savagery, or 'official' executions of civilians by German troops. Over more recent years the reasons that led to this escalation of violence have been researched carefully. In particular, there has been consideration of the reasoning of the middle-ranking and more senior officers when ordering or endorsing the atrocities committed against civilians. We have to realise that there were heavy pressures weighing upon the officers concerned, in particular pressures of time because of the constraints of the Schlieffen Plan. There were also other factors – social-Darwinistic and anti-Catholic resentment, which, in the opinion of the officers, justified such measures 'against the Belgian state and its inhabitants'.[15]

The reports of atrocities seem to have reached Stefan Schimmer as rumours. This enables us to understand the ordinary soldier's interpretation and evaluation of them. The entries of 24 August report in one sentence about the devastation of a village and the popular myth of fighting like a brave and belligerent lion, as the Bavarian soldiers were often referred to. So Schimmer maintained the stereotype of the extremely belligerent Bavarian, with which, of course, the Bavarians used to characterise themselves. Referring to the atrocities committed in Leuven, the report was completely wrong. The town was situated in Belgium, not in France, and was larger than described. Furthermore, the reason for the confusion and the judgement that they were attacked by *francs tireurs* ('free-shooters')was that two German units shot at each other. Schimmer did not seem to realise that the killing of civilians was an injustice. There are some reasons to believe that most of the German soldiers in 1914 shared this attitude. Because it was a rumour that the supposed *francs tireurs* fought by preparing ambushes, the German soldiers seemed to be nervously apprehensive of them, so, for them, a violent reprisal seemed justified. There is a decisive difference in the way the German soldiers of the First World War and those of the Second refer linguistically to the 'irregular' enemy. In 1914 'civilians', or, as in Schimmer's text, 'villagers', were the ones who fought a guerrilla war. So here the soldiers used quite neutral terms to describe those guerrillas. The soldiers of the Wehrmacht used a large variety of swear-words like 'scoundrels', 'scum', 'vermin' or 'sub-human' to describe the Partisans. So the soldiers not only expressed their outrage about this kind of warfare but, as we know from irrefutable evidence, never mind their use of pejorative words, they behaved more brutally still than did the German soldiers of the First World War.[16]

In an endeavour to show the way in which German soldiers recorded and reacted to their service experience in the First World War we have looked at and analysed in detail the letters and war-diary entries of three soldiers. It should be added that there are other personal testimonies that are similar to those discussed here.[17] The war could at first be interpreted as a touristic adventure that took soldiers from their usual surroundings at home into an unknown country. However, this optimistic point of view was often destroyed by the bullying behaviour of the officers, often even before the unit reached the front or participated in a battle. The 'baptism of fire' and the battles thereafter increased the speed of disillusionment. Catholic soldiers in particular used a religious formula to assimilate their service experience. As early as the first battles in the initial phase of the war, many soldiers saw themselves not as soldiers who were advancing full of pride and confidence but as victims who were advancing because they had to. A good example is the German soldier Dominik Richert, a farmer's son from Alsace, who deserted to the French by the end of the war in 1918. From 1914 he stuck to the conviction that he formed after the first battles:

> 'Courage, heroism, is there really anything like this? I really do doubt this because in the battle I see nothing but fear, worry and despair in everyone's face. Of course, of bravery and such things [I saw] nothing because in reality it is only the cruel discipline, the coercion, which forces the soldier to advance and [forces him] towards death.'[18]

It is necessary to remark that this attitude in its certainty and straightforwardness does not represent the attitude of the majority of the German soldiers in 1914. Referring only to Richert's memoirs of war it seems that he had a dislike for the war before he was even involved in it. The most important reason for this attitude was probably because he came from Alsace. Because of that he was a member of a group of 'inner enemies' of the Prussian-German Government, and when he had just been drafted into the army he was always being confronted with prejudices and prejudiced action against him by officers and NCOs.[19]

Documents written by other soldiers make it obvious that the quick advance through hostile territory was not sufficient to make the soldiers confident of victory. The immense loss of life during the first weeks of war was too great for this to be the case. This can be seen when reading the diary entries of Ernst Nopper, a painter from Württemberg, born in 1877. He wrote on 23 August 1914, the date of the battle of Longwy:

> 'We are walking over much of the battlefield and we can see what a colossal number of victims this battle has cost us. There are whole rows of our fellows lying there, especially in the village which is totally burned out... I don't want to record these shameful horrors here but I have not seen anything as sad as this battlefield with so many victims who are dead or wounded and in spite of our victory this makes us all feel dejected.'[20]

In the main it was the victims of one's own side that everyone took notice of. Only a very few soldiers felt any affinity with the other side's sufferings, as Georg Schenk did in his diary. Remarkably, there are only a very few letters in which the German soldiers talk of the inhabitants of the enemy territory and of their soldiers in a scornful way and denounce the civilians as 'enemies'. This is the case for letters from the Western Front, though from the Eastern Front there are in fact some particularly negative descriptions of the enemy, referring to the population's poor living conditions and the absence of culture in Russia as perceived by the German observer. It is quite striking that no such judgements were made of the French and Belgians. In 1940, but not in 1914, an attitude became prevalent whereby the inhabitants of a conquered country were seen as inferior, and were thus deprived of human dignity. The young volunteer, Reinhold Maier, wrote from Kowal in Russian Poland on 4 December 1914: 'Most of the civilians we see primarily are Polish Jews; friendly people and interesting characters.'[21] Even during the First World War such a positive remark about the Jewish population in the East was exceptional. However, in the letters from soldiers during the Second World War, a search for such a positive remark without any racial stereotypes would be in vain.[22] There are also letters written by soldiers in 1914 aggressively 'imploring' victory. A good example is one written by a teacher from Hesse on 16 September:

'For 14 days we have been here in Eastern Prussia. Close to Allenstein we met the enemy on September 8th. The battle lasted from Tuesday to Friday. I am not able to tell you what we had to bear during those days. There was no possibility of sleep, the kitchen cars were not able to follow and food became short. Above all there were those huge marches! But we were victorious. In wild flight we chased those hordes of robbers back into their country. 120,000 prisoners, an immense amount of ammunition and waggons and horses fell into our hands. The Russians ravaged here in a cruel manner. They did not spare anything. The Huns could not have behaved worse... You can imagine that we went at those fellows ferociously. In a village close to Gumbinnen 500 Russians and 30 Germans have been buried: that seems, in general to be the proportion... We do not get any newspapers and hear of only a very few. Now they tell us that the Germans are in Paris. Anyway, France will be finished soon and after that Russia has to go down too. I do not believe that the war is going to last long. In fact it must not last much longer.'[23]

Surely it is no accident that this letter comes from the Eastern Front and, to be more precise, from the only section of the front in 1914 where Germans had to defend their country on their own soil. By the middle of August Russian troops advanced into Eastern Prussia and occupied the Eastern part of this Prussian province. After only two battles, at Neidenburg (23-31 August) and the Masurian Lakes (8-15 September), the Germans were able to defeat the Russians and force them to withdraw from Eastern Prussia. The first battle to 'free' German soil, Tannenberg, went into the cultural history of the region and into folklore as a celebration of German strength among the nationalist political camp in the period of the Weimar Republic.[24] But the short period of time during which Eastern Prussia was occupied by the Russians was not only important for the myth of 'Tannenberg', which Paul von Hindenburg used later to gain military and political popularity. Reports about deliberate destruction, pillage and atrocities committed against civilians were spreading rapidly on the Home Front and were treated with a high intensity of emotion.[25] Thus a German soldier, by fighting against the Russians, could not only enter into the propagandist image and stereotypes referring to the inferior Russians, but at the same time this soldier was helping to free his Fatherland from the fears of war in its most immediate form: occupation of one's own country by the enemy. This drawing together of perspectives accounts for soldiers on the Eastern Front being filled by an illusory expectation of victory, and, showing the self-confidence of a perpetrator, they committed acts of harsh reprisals immune from any reflective considerations, only the horror of battle. Displaying this attitude they were less like the German soldier on the Western front in 1914 than to the 'Landsers' of the German Wehrmacht in the Second World War.

<h2 style="text-align:center">1940</h2>

On 14 September 1914, six weeks after the beginning of the First World War, the Chief of the General Staff of the German Army, General Colonel Helmuth von Moltke, was replaced by General Erich von Falkenhayn after the German defeat on the Marne. This change in German military leadership not only symbolised the ultimate failure of the German offensive, but at the same time represented the transition to a new type of warfare. Following autumn 1914, when the great armies in the West had got bogged down in trench warfare, the front extended over a length of more than 700 kilometres from the Alps to the Channel. It was on this Western Front where most soldiers were deployed, wounded and killed. The war developed its well-known character there and was ultimately decided there. Even today, the experiences of the Western Front continue to shape most perceptions of the First World War. However true it may or not be, it is generally considered that the generals of the First World War, over the course of its years, produced ever bloodier and more absurd materiel battles in which the penetration of the front lines could not decisively be achieved, even with the employment of the most modern methods of destruction. The enemy was thus to be 'bled white' instead. This – never worked-out – strategic calculus came down to the 'satanic willingness' to sacrifice 'hundreds of thousands of one's own soldiers in order to kill or maim twice the number of opposing soldiers'.[26] In the 'bloodmill', in the 'hell' of Verdun, this type of warfare found a symbol that is indelibly burned into the memory of the peoples of Europe.

On 22 June 1940, six weeks after the Wehrmacht's invasion of France, Belgium and the Netherlands, the Franco-German Armistice was signed in the forest of Compiègne by General Keitel and General Huntziger. If the German troops of the First World War had tried in vain to penetrate the Western Front during four years, the Wehrmacht was able to achieve this success in four days near Sedan. The massive operational employment of tanks and aircraft led to the fact that, compared with the years of slaughter on the Western Front in the Great War, the battle with France was merely a quick episode for the Wehrmacht of 1940. The number of German dead it had cost – 27,000 – was far fewer than the cost of First World War offensives, which had been without profit. Correspondingly, the 'western campaign' produced a completely different significance in the collective memory. The myth of the Blitzkrieg[27] developed its persistent and still influential effect, and pushed Hitler for a short period in 1940/41 to the high point of his power and reputation among the German people.

In the soldiers' letters from the field of both the World Wars, we can see this fundamental difference between four years of trench warfare and six weeks of Blitzkrieg. Investigation of these letters yields both insights into the soldiers' changing moods and into the long-term orientations and patterns of reaction by which the soldiers tried to understand war as well as their own position therein.[28] We cannot simply deduce these different levels one from another. From the Kriegsbegeisterung of August 1914, which has been put into a less strong perspective in recent research[29], one cannot conclude deeper-rooted attitudes towards the war. The same is valid to the often-stated lack of Kriegsbegeisterung in September 1939; this does not necessarily mean a fundamental detachment from the war either, as rather the opposite seems to have been the case. The inherent tie to the national project of war was clearly stronger and more persistent in the Second World War than the First. In the widely used historical assessment of a 'reluctant loyalty' in September 1939, it can be more accurately summarised as reluctance at the beginning, soon to be followed by thorough enthusiasm, ending in fatalism and doubt. Regardless of these changes in mood, the loyalty of the Wehrmacht's soldiers, a kind of bond to the National Socialist war and to its Führer, remained amazingly constant and effective on a long-term basis.

In the following I will examine both the impressions and feelings of the Wehrmacht's soldiers in the victorious war of 1940 and the way in which they viewed the war. These aspects will be investigated from personal experience documentation, the soldiers' letters. Since the letters are always socially influenced, they yield insights into national and political consciousness. The nature of archive sources available means that the largest proportion of the letters cited in the following comes from members of the old middle classes (farmers, craftsmen, small merchants) and the new middle classes (employees, lower and mid-level officials) as well as the educated middle classes (priests, teachers), while the lower classes, especially workers, are little represented. The authors of the letters are soldiers in the ranks, NCOs and junior officers.

The letters are examined with regard to the reaction to experience. They are not classified on the basis of already defined large socio-economic groups, but they are used as if they can group soldiers around these reactions. The war appears to offer an experience where differences are minimised, where men primarily become members of a 'non-class specific community of military men'[30], which not least defines its cohesion by dissociation from the enemy and the people in the occupied countries. How did the soldiers view the western countries that they had conquered, and their inhabitants? How did they view enemy soldiers? For what and against whom did they believe they were fighting in 1940? What meaning did their war experiences and, ultimately, what meaning did death entail regarding their feelings and basic values?

Conquerors in a foreign country

First of all, in addition to the fundamental difference between the western battles of the two World Wars mentioned above, a further but no less fundamental difference between the theatres of war in the Second World War has to be emphasised, which the soldiers themselves immediately expressed. 'Here,' a private lamented on 14 July 1941 after three weeks of participation in the 'Russia campaign', 'it is not as in France. There, there was everything that we could have wanted and here is absolutely nothing.' Others voiced similar complaints: 'Here, in comparison with France, one has absolutely nothing.' (14 March 1943) One could summarise this easily: namely that indeed 'life [in the Soviet Union] is not as cultivated as it was on other campaigns' (12 October 1941), which always meant the same: 'The war here,' as someone could sum up, 'is simply poverty-stricken and offers no joy.' (17 July1941)

The formulation 'war makes joy' should not be taken completely literally, but one should not ignore its central signification either. What 'made joy' in war was the compensations the war offered for what the soldiers missed and for what they had to suffer. In this regard the theatre of war in the West was without competition. Plundering in the occupied countries had an official and a private side as well. The former, with the hunger strikes of the First World War in mind, pertained to the systematic exploitation of human and economic resources in the occupied areas, organised by the military or civil administration of the occupying power in order to maintain the supply situation in Germany at a bearable level. Additionally, meeting the needs of the troops from the occupied country was done by 'requisitioning' and 'organising'. While requisitioned goods were at least officially certified and recompensed later, the concept of 'organising' had a meaning for the soldiers' minds that spreads across the wide grey area between 'legally, illegally and completely equal!'[31] In their letters the soldiers did not always state clearly under what circumstances this or that 'booty' had been acquired. One thing, however, is certain: whatever came into their hands in Holland, Belgium and France, it was adequate to reconcile at least partially their sufferings and strains, without which even so-called Blitzkriege could not be conducted. The beneficiaries of the plundering spoke thus:

'Otherwise we live very well here, a good many things from the Frenchmen have fallen in our hands. We already drank much wine in Baden, but what we consume here is enormous. Our division is slowly becoming motorised, everywhere abandoned cars and motorcycles are standing about, which anyone who desires can ride around on. Additionally one sees discarded French weapons, gadgets and clothing lying about everywhere. Everyone takes what pleases him.' (20 June 1940)

'We made ourselves healthy at Boulogne ... two crates of genuine Benedictiner Cointreau, many [?], jam, canned fruit, coffee with Cognac, goose liver pâté, cooked ham and thousands other wonderful things.' (27 May 1940)

'We have been taking very good care of ourselves the few days that we have been here. There is champagne and wine in each house too. We have already emptied quite a few bottles.' (31 May 1940)

The compensatory character of the appropriation of the country's pleasures for the soldiers is reflected linguistically in phrases such as 'to make healthy' or 'take good care of oneself'. The soldiers' force of habit on organised or anarchic plundering of conquered peoples had a centuries-old tradition in which preserving attempts like the Haager Landkriegsordnung of 1907, which placed private property under strict protection, could modify things formally rather than factually. That does not mean that the German soldiers proceeded like marauding Landsknechte through France, which would already have interfered with the goals of the military leadership, the so-called Manneszucht. At least during fighting the various practices of 'organising' seem to have been tolerated; later they changed into more regulated forms of 'self-service'. '...Now we don't have the permission to steal, but to buy' was said in plain language after the signing of the Armistice at the end of June 1940. 'If we could only send, because it is cheap for us.' (24 June 1940) The extreme devaluation of the franc, with an exchange rate of 1 franc to 5 pfennig imposed by Germany, made the entire French range of goods ridiculously cheap for the German soldiers, who took advantage of this source of goods so readily that the military commander of Belgium and Northern France warned of a sell-out of the country and an endangering of the general supply situation. This was the second side of plundering, personal 'booty-making' for oneself and the 'beloved ones at home'. In the beginning the army postal service packages from Belgium and France were permitted in any number; the final restrictions were cancelled in August 1942. On business or vacation trips home, everyone could take as much as he could carry.[32]

'Of course I haven't forgotten,' a private reassured his parents regarding their shopping list for him, 'a coffee filter and a shoe brush; ideally I would like to buy everything which pleases me... I bought something again, a silk shirt and 3 ties. You will save it for me, won't you, dear Mama...' (21 September 1940) Another sent his wife from Netherlands '...an apron for 1.50 M, hopefully a good one. The coffee, which is on the way, is the best kind, and will most likely taste good, Prost.' (7 July 1940) He was also '... under way again because of Kurts' suit. There is no more way, even with the best will, that I can get a wool suit... I sent 3 packages again, one with tea, one with soap.' (20 July 1940)

Of course the purchasing power for a soldier in war, with an income of 75 Marks per month, was limited, even if the goods were cheap. In consequence, one soldier let his wife occasionally send him small amounts of money to France, one time 5 Marks, another time 10, another time again 35. He bought dresses, materials, wool, rompers for the child he wanted to have, he bought silk, satin and lace for his wife, and he tried to calm her down because of the ever-increasing amounts: 'What do we need money for? There is still a war on!' At the same time, however, he was too much of a businessman to think only of consumption. He sent cheaply purchased goods from France to his wife, so that she could profitably sell them in their joint small business she now managed alone. For instance, pillows made of velvet and silk, '...just don't say that they are from here', or cigarette papers, '...however only to customers that can keep their mouths shut... Be careful, no one needs to know.' (12 November, 24 September and 23 October 1940)

The western theatres of war obviously had something to offer, and of course that was not limited to good shopping opportunities. For the majority of soldiers the war offered, for the first time, the opportunity to see beyond the boundaries of their own country. The letters document the view of the victors on the defeated country and its inhabitants. Writing about these topics, the soldiers always wrote comparatively. The criteria by which the soldiers judged what they saw originated from the context of German life, the sphere of everyday normality, with which the other country was compared. This 'war as a journey' led through unknown areas and landscapes that were described positively almost throughout: '...the area is simply wonderful.' (20 June 1940); the '...Belgian countryside is nevertheless more beautiful than France.' (31 May 1940); 'the region is quite nice' (9 July 1940). Thus the writers ranged between restraint and excess.

When they approached the local inhabitants or their cities and villages, opinions became clearly more divided. Certainly 'one must have seen' Paris (31 October 1940), but whole villages gave the 'impression of decline' (16 June 1940). Also sympathy for the suffering inhabitants was present: 'The people are now very poor. Imagine..., everything devastated and destroyed.' (29 August 1940) 'We have seen some villages and a city that were completely burned. We hope that the same thing doesn't happen at home. Because something like this is terrible.' (31 May 1940) To one person, the population was considered 'nice and kind', even if 'we are always treated as enemies here.' (11 July 1940) 'The population doesn't want to have anything to do with us,' complained a private. (9 July 1940) They apparently have 'no interest' in the 'development' of the country, wrote a lieutenant. Another noticed 'that the French people are dying out', a strong theme of National Socialist propaganda. (16 June 1940). 'And besides,' again wrote the soldier quoted above, 'the French women, yes, no comment. One reason more to feel and to think proudly about Germany.' (3 July 1940) These are the only comments about German soldiers' relationships with French women in my body of letters, and it seems not surprising since sons or married men would be unlikely to write to their parents or wives, for instance, about the Wehrmacht's brothels. Above all, however, one criterion focused the attention: 'I don't think there is a people as dirty as the French anywhere; comparatively, the Belgians are clean in all respects.' (13 June 1940)

> '...we are situated ... in an old hospital, but do not ask what it looked like. One cannot describe it. In a word: terrible [?] the blacks wreaked destruction in this place in a gruesome way. The dirt is metre-high in the rooms. It simply cannot be described ... it looks like this in almost every home. We are sleeping on straw, we have no light and water only the last few days. And France called this culture. The newspapers don't describe it sufficiently. The soldiers say Poland looked better than it does here. We have got a wonderful idea of the civilisation of the blacks here.'[33] (21 August 1940)

Here, after the first surprise, the experiences became confirmation of what one 'already knew'. The devastation the French troops had caused in the partially evacuated Alsace[34] was projected as the culture of France or of the 'blacks' in order to be able thereby, as German and white, to distinguish from them the boundary between 'dirt' and 'cleanness'. A further criterion was stated – 'One does not know a social welfare service in France' – in order then to assess: 'I must always say, there is in fact only one Germany. Everything else stays far below it.' (4 July 1940)

But particularly one distinguished oneself from the French 'dirt'. This line of separation was located in the centre of the perception of the Wehrmacht's soldiers. The identification with their own country occurred less often on the political than on the everyday-life level. What did not correspond to the norm at home was detested by the soldiers. That was not primarily an effect of propaganda. The middle class's fundamental norm of 'cleanness', deeply established a long time ago, sufficed completely. To what extent this norm was bound with a specific social-racism of the soldiers is what the letters from the Soviet Union should show explicitly later on. Here, from the East, the soldiers perceived the miserable circumstances of life of the population as 'properties of their character' and tended to perceive humans itself as 'dirt'[35]. This was one of the prerequisites that, radicalised by propaganda, made possible the extension of the war of extermination on the civil population in the Soviet Union.

Enemy soldiers

How did the Wehrmacht's soldiers look on their opponents? First they got only a few direct impressions of them. Already in the First World War firepower and destructive capacities of weapons had made covering and camouflage the highest requirement and had already driven the surviving soldiers under the earth. Between the opposing trench systems extended no-man's-land, a deserted zone full of deadly dangers for anyone who found himself there. Even if in some places the nearest trenches were no more distant than 50 metres apart, the opponents remained invisible from each other. In the Second World War the fronts turned out to be moving boundaries, and the use of tanks, combat aircraft and the increasingly destructive power of the weapons strengthened the expansion of the battlefield again, where the soldiers hardly ever came face to face. Rarely were they in close combat; predominantly they slaughtered one another from a distance. Usually the adversaries faced each other only at the time of capture, a circumstance that did not make these moments less dangerous, because the soldiers suddenly had to switch from deception and destruction of the enemy to a relationship requiring co-operation. This not uncommonly led to deadly misunderstandings. If this moment passed without summary execution, one could regard one's opponent in a more relaxed way.

'All people of all nations were represented' we can read about a camp of French prisoners at the end of May 1940. Here a classification was formulated that was usually expressed by other soldiers in France: 'Black ones, brown ones, yellow ones, I tell you all colours are represented.' (6 September 1940) Apart from this stress of the exotic and strange, the opponent in soldiers' letters remained largely without a face, because most remarks related to his equipment, his battle performances and his fighting spirit. Even before any combat, a lieutenant revealed symbolically how he generally assessed the Frenchmen: 'Since 15.00 hours, we are fighting also with France,' he wrote on 3 September 1939. 'I have just interrupted the work around this historical moment, let my section line up with their front to Germany, let them deeply bow and told them that one greets the Frenchmen in this way.'

Judging by the few further voices, the French soldiers were unable to raise their reputation, neither in the Phoney War nor in the Blitzkrieg in May and June 1940. Already on 24 September 1939 the same lieutenant wrote: 'He [the Frenchman] is however apparently fed up.' One month later: 'Our guys have perfectly proved themselves and shown again their unique superiority over the Frenchmen… Their weapons are far less effective than ours… Our people now have a great moral superiority.'

Then, when the fighting really started, Frenchmen, in the view of a different lieutenant, soon made 'a completely indifferent impression' (27 May 1940), which another confirmed later: 'To an extent the Frenchmen simply run away from their units. Everything is in dissolution. The French soldiers simply run into our arms without weapons. They sometimes dress in civil clothes and take their wives with them.' (20 June 1940) Finally, from a private soldier: 'No Frenchman still desires to fight against us.' (22 June 1940) Another expressed on 30 May 1940 the feeling of a basic superiority of the German soldiers, which inspired them considerably:

> 'You will not believe it at all, if we pass through a city or a village, the people look at us as if we were celestial beings. On certain questions, they say again and again, they would not have thought that their proud armed forces could be destroyed and partly wiped out in a time so short. Certainly the performance was superhuman and we exemplify it.'[36]

Already on 26 May 1940, after only two weeks of Blitzkrieg against the west, Goebbels had said that 'today the German Army, which is something of great psychological importance, carries with it the magic of being invincible and of a revolutionary quality.'[37] Even if the Minister of propaganda always liked to exaggerate unscrupulously, he accurately characterised the soldiers' self-confidence. Even in the Soviet Union the conviction of the German soldiers' basic superiority did not decline for a long time, despite an appreciation of the worth of their own troops.

War aims

Identification with political-military aims of a war can have different meanings. These aims can be defined in a positive ('for our good cause') or negative ('against Bolshevism') manner, as temporary ('to get the other side of the river') or definite ('to secure the liberty of Germany'). At any rate they integrate, by dissociation or by identification, the participants that gather around these aims. Let us ask first against what the Wehrmacht's soldiers thought they were fighting in 1940 and what damage their opponents had deserved, in their view.

On 16 May 1940, a short week after the beginning of the German offensive, a lieutenant reported breathlessly: 'We are always afraid of coming too late, because everything happens enormously fast… Perhaps in Belgium there will be a real battle, that would be very favourable for us; then we would beat the shop over there completely.' This had already occurred with the old town of Rotterdam two days before; eight days later, the same man announced: 'For the moment it is necessary to destroy the English, Belgian and French armies in Flanders.' On 30 May a private wrote: 'We have contributed to the proud success that will end with the whole destruction of England, and, if France does not become reasonable at the last moment, also with the total destruction of France.'[38]

On 31 May another soldier wrote that the destruction did not remain limited to the military: 'We have already seen some villages and a city completely burned down … no doubt that is terrible. But the Frenchmen wanted to have it like this. And we also hope that the French collapse soon.' They did three weeks later. 'Yesterday France signed,' a lieutenant expressed happily. 'Heil! Now the Tommy is next!' (23 June 1940) He had named the enemy who for the next months would occupy the fantasy of the soldiers in their feeling of victory over France: 'After all that has happened here it seems that we will remain here for longer and either stagnate or, which we hope urgently, we will be fit for the big strike against England.' (26 June 1940) 'All of us feel the pain that we may not help to chase away the Englishmen. We would have done it too willingly.' (2 July 1940)

The regular air raids of the Royal Air Force on cities in the north and west of Germany prompted the prophecy: 'It will not take a long time until they will get a terrible kick in the ass. I believe there will be murder and homicide over there… It will look more badly than in Poland and not a stone will be left standing.' (23 June 1940) On 8 September 1940 a private promised, 'If we can get things straightened out in England, then I will come home to my darling,' and in November another soldier took the same line: 'It would be more than strange if the scoundrels get through winter. Not a stone will be left standing there, there will be no rest for them.' (30 November 1940)

The voices quoted above identified with the violence of war by sharing the official definition of the opponent for whom this violence was meant. This identification usually was done ad hoc, depending on the war situation, and it largely amounted to nothing more than the current definition of the enemy and the next war aims, while fundamental or political statements about the reasons to fight in the west rarely occurred. If the latter was the case, a private soldier, for instance, propagated on 24 July 1940 the 'fight for German liberty', a typical idiom of numerous Hitler speeches that in 1940 above all meant 'liberation … from the chains of the Versailles dictation'.[39]

It was in particular identification with the Führer that made the war in the west seem plausible to the soldiers. Their expressions in letters referring to Hitler enable us to find out something about his effect on the soldiers' minds, and of the importance they attached to him:

'The Führer now is really great again in his resolutions. After his current speech it seems that he wants to be finished in Poland within 14 days.' (3 September 1939)

'Otherwise, [we] hope … that the Englishman will still come to his senses, even [if] the chances of that are quite small. The Führer has told them again, in fact completely clearly.' (20 July 1940)

'Yesterday evening the Führer spoke… And the speech has livened us up a bit again. It will not take a long time, then it will start. And will be real.' (5 September 1940)

It is obvious that the soldiers were uplifted by and aligned themselves with Hitler's speeches. In these letters Hitler appears not only as a propagandist influencing the soldiers, but also as their spokesman. On the one hand Hitler had the effect of a guide raising their hopes, on the other, in some expressions, he was someone who provided the experiences of the soldiers with publicity and respect. One can speak here of a mutual identification: these soldiers identified themselves with the Führer, and in their view the Führer identified himself with their fate, a constellation that Hitler constructed in many of his speeches. In this constellation we can see something of the way 'charismatic power' works.[40]

Next to faith in the Führer, another pattern of awareness showed in its special impact on the soldiers' minds, the idea of a permanent struggle-for-life in which one has to prove one's value. In May 1940 a private intended to fight for 'the victory of Germany', and this would be a fight 'to be or not to be' that he would like to carry out 'with even more fanaticism.' (11 May 1940) Another soldier interpreted the fight for the 'Fatherland', in connection with the ideology of struggle-for-life, as follows: 'A man always has a hard time, he not only has to fight for his Fatherland, but also for his woman and for his own life. And that is just life as man has known for centuries.' (15 November 1940) The struggle-for-life was also transferred into the private sphere, as an author of a letter tried to explain to his wife: 'You may be proud of having taken up the struggle for life from your youth and of having fought your way through, not like these little ladies who live at the expense of others and who don't know at all what it means to stand on one's own two feet in life.' (22 August 1940) If the struggle-for-life takes the form of war, then, as a soldier expressed, 'we men have to be out there in order to protect our own good. It is just a hard law that determines the fight for life. That is to say: do your utmost.' (26 September 1940) In this fight there was only the unattractive alternative already mentioned – victory or decline: 'What is forthcoming for us is the great decision of to be or not to be, of millions of people, and we want to take part in it as well…' (11 May 1940)

Already in the First World War the alternative between 'to be or not to be' was not unfamiliar to the soldiers, but did not have the status it held in the Second War. For the expressions from the Second World War it has to remain undecided, even taking into account every affinity to the National Socialist struggle-for-life ideology, whether the racist core of National Socialism is present by implication. Social-Darwinism and racism are kindred with regard to their evolution and contents, but they don't coincide[41]; whether the letters' authors comprehended their National Socialist fusion or not, we can suspect that it is justified in individual cases but can hardly prove it.

In the First World War, traditional, which means Christian, monarchist, authoritarian state and national values predominated in the soldiers' minds, increasingly accompanied and also challenged by socialist ideas. In 1940 the soldiers were occupied by new objects of identification: the Führer and the soldier in a struggle-for-life. Concepts like 'Germany' or 'Fatherland' were promoted and upheld, impregnated with Social-Darwinism and racism. Christian beliefs ('God will help us') were secondary to the new belief in the Führer, and this could extend to fanaticism.

Death

But even if the war was often described under the 'tourist' point of view in 1940, if the consciousness of their own military superiority were to prevail, if the certifications of a basic identification with this war and its Führer were clear, the six weeks' war in the west also meant fighting, destruction, blood, wounds, killing and death. Before 'booty making', the risk was one's own life. In the following letter, an exceptional case, a man wrote frankly about the violence exercised by himself: 'After 1½ hours of dreadful fire the first combat patrols of the infantry already crossed the Rhine in boats and finished off the hostile bunkers right on the waterfront with flame-throwers, hand grenades and other things...' (20 June 1940). The consequences for the opponents are overlooked in the letters. Also, the consequences for the civilians of the destruction around them were mentioned only rarely: 'One gets to see clearly, above all, the devastation and misery and it will take years to repair the damage of these couple of days.' (24 July 1940) 'The accumulations of refugees increase still, a hopeless picture.' (20 June 1940) 'We are located on the Seine ... the fishes all dead, they have blown up all oil and gasoline and drained it into the Seine.' (15 June 1940) 'The place where we got so much opposition is totally broken.' (29 May 1940)

In particular, the death of their own comrades again and again took the soldiers to the edge of their capacity to communicate. In 1940 the soldiers presented themselves, as also later in the Soviet Union, with noticeable restraint on this subject. The image of a soldier dominating in the Second World War, above all accepting hardness himself, considerably contributed to this restraint. Expressions like the following appear rarely:

'We are humans here no more. We had to attack a large village in France [without artillery] preparation, our regiment's commander is a dog. We again, the 4th section, and me at the 1st gun were the first to go forward and we got such a fire that every moment I thought it is over. Marksman 1 was wounded, and shots passed by close to my legs and my head, everywhere.' (29 May 1940)

'Pride in mourning' the Nazis had required in the face of death, a slogan that took up the feeling of mourning only in order to go into renewed action and readiness to make sacrifices. 'You are nothing, your people are everything', to die for 'Großdeutschland' or for 'Führer, Volk und Vaterland' – these values were seldom expressed by soldiers. However strong their identification with the war may have been, if death was at stake, these identifications obviously had their limits. Also the formulation of such ideas as the following are hard to find: 'And now we have to go again, sure it's hard to go, but as God wants it. If I really have to lose my life, God will forgive me everything, and so will you ... pray for me as well as you can.' (May 1940) If one wrote about death, then not only the Führer, but also God,

Christian beliefs, the hereafter, usually were left unrecorded. Some referred to 'fate' in order to come to terms with death: 'It is very sad that Wagner had to die so young, but one doesn't know what fate has left over for us. Everyone will be for it, whether rich or poor.' (15 July 1940) However, one cannot record any positive response to the question 'What value accrued from the death of "a" Wagner?'

Nevertheless, on the whole in 1940 there is no sense of any general disillusionment caused by the experience of death, as is often testified for the First World War, nor the breaking of fundamental identification with the war. Too strong was the euphoric certainty of victory and comparatively short the emotional strain of the six weeks' campaign. Even for the war to follow, that against the Soviet Union, there is no documentary evidence that could indicate a revolutionary development among the troops as had obviously been the case in 1918.

Coping with the consequences of the overwhelming experience of death in the First World War had been an enormous challenge in the post-war era, and this challenge could never be answered in a bearable manner. This became a major factor in achieving the later extensive consent between the Wehrmacht's soldiers and the National Socialist war. The transferred experience of violence in the First War remained in the consciousness of many and could not simply be incorporated into the individual nor the collective stock of actual experience. The Nazis fled from this supremacy of death while trying to seize hold of its compelling power: they fled from death into killing, into the black utopia of extermination. For this utopia the war of 1940 was still atypical – it showed its core in the following years in the war of extermination against the Soviet Union.[42] The Wehrmacht's soldiers followed this vision in a way that the comparatively easy victories of 1940 hardly even indicated. In fact, death left them without words, already in the campaign in the West, and later in the Soviet Union, again and again. But the National Socialist's favourite virtue of aggressive ruthlessness was familiar to them and was a weapon against the armed and unarmed opponents of the German will to conquer and destroy the obviously provocative challenge of German middle class conceptions of 'normality' by 'primitive' forms of life, in particular with regard to the Slavish people. In this respect and against the background of the First World War, the letters of German soldiers, particularly after 1940, can be seen as an unfailing seismograph of a comparatively unlimited readiness for violence.

Notes on contributors

Dr Benjamin Ziemann, Ruhr University, Bochum, Germany
Dr Ziemann's main fields of research are the social history of German Catholicism in the Twentieth Century, German military history and the social history of the two world wars.

Dr Klaus Latzel, University of Bielefeld, Germany
Klaus Latzel is a member of the Faculty of Sociology at the University of

Bielefeld. His main areas of research are the history of the First and Second World Wars, and the history and theory of sociology. His most recent books are: Deutsche Soldaten – nationalsozialistischer Krieg? Kriegserlebnis – Kriegserfahrung 1939-1945 (Paderborn: Schoeningh, 1998); (ed) Georg Simmel, Aufsätze und Abhandlungen 1908-1918, Vol. 1 (Frankfort/M: Suhrkamp, 2000). He is co-editor-in-chief of Simmel Studies.

Recommended reading

1914

Geinitz, Christian, *Kriegsfurcht und Kampfbereitschaft: Das Augusterlebnis in Freiburg: Eine Studie zum Kriegsbeginn 1914* (Essen: 1998)

Raithel, Thomas, *Das 'Wunder' der inneren Einheit: Studien zur deutschen und französischen Öffentlichkeit bei beginn der Ersten Weltkrieges* (Bonn: 1996)

Ulrich, Bernd and Ziemann, Benjamin (eds), *Frontalltag im Ersten Weltkrieg: Wahn und Wirklichkeit: Quellen und Dokumente* (Frankfurt/M: 1994)

Ziemann, Benjamin, *Front und Heimat. Ländliche Kriegserfahrungen im südlichen Bayern 1914-1923* (Essen: 1997)

1940

Buchbender, Ortwin and Sterz, Reinhold (eds), *Das andere Gesicht des Krieges: Deutsche Feldpostbriefe 1939-1945* (München: Beck, 1982)

Latzel, Klaus, *Deutsche Soldaten – nationalsozialistischer Krieg? Kriegserlebnis-Kriegserfahrung 1939-1945* (Paderhorn: Schöningh, 1998)

Müller, Rolf-Dieter and Volkmann, Hans-Erich (eds), *Die Wehrmacht: Mythos und Realität* (München: Oldenbourg, 1999)

Notes

1   Wilhelm, Muehlon, (ed Wolfgang Benz), *Ein Fremder im eigenen Land: Erinnerungen und Tagebuchaufzeichnungen eines Krupp Direktors 1908-1914* (Bremen: Donat) p143

2   Philipp, Witkop, (ed), *Kriegsbriefe gefallener Studenten* (München: Georg Müller, 1928; first edition, Gotha, 1916)

3   See the groundbreaking study by Bernd, Ulrich, *Die Augenzeugen: Deutsche Feldpostbriefe in Kriegs- und Nachkriegszeit 1914-1933* (Essen: Klartext, 1997)

4   See Latzel, Klaus, 'Vom Kriegserlebnis zur Kriegserfahrung: Theoretische und methodische Überlegungen zur erfahrungsgeschichtlichen Untersuchung von Feldpostbriefen' in 'Militärgeschichtliche Mitteilungen' 56 (1997), pp1-29

5   War diary of Georg Schenk (Bayerisches Hauptstaatsarchiv München, Abt IV (BHStA/IV), HS 3410

6   See Jeffrey T., Verhey, *The Myth of the 'Spirit of 1914' in Germany, 1914-1945* (Cambridge: Cambridge University Press, 2000) and Geinitz, Christian, Kriegsfurcht und Kampfbereitschaft, *Das Augusterlebnis in Freiburg: Eine Studie zum Kriegsbeginn 1914* (Essen: Klartext, 1998)

7   Benjamin, Ziemann, 'Katholische Religiosität und die Bewältigung des Krieges: Soldaten und Militärseelsorger in der deutschen Armee 1914-1918' in 'Jahrbuch für Historische Friedensforschung' 6 (1997) pp116-36

8   For this interpretation see Klaus, Latzel, *Deutsche Soldaten – nationalsozialistischer Krieg?*

Kriegserlebnis-Kriegserfahrung 1939-1945 (Paderborn: Ferdinand Schöningh, 1998) pp31ff, 129ff

9 War diary of Georg Schenk, op cit

10 See the letters in Walter, Bartel, 'Unbekannte Briefe an Karl Liebknecht anläßlich seiner Ablehnung der Kriegskredite im Deutschen Reichstag am 2 Dezember 1914' in 'Zeitschrift für Geschichtswissenschaft' 7 (1959) pp597-629

11 Ibid

12 See also the letter of a German soldier, dated 27 September1914, cited in Knoch, Peter, 'Erleben und Nacherleben: Das Kriegserlebnis im Augenzeugenbericht und im Geschichtsunterricht' in Gerhard, Hirschfeld, Gerd, Krumeich, and Irina, Renz, (eds), *Keiner fühlt sich hier mehr als Mensch...': Erlebnis und Wirkung des Ersten Weltkriegs* (Frankfurt/M: Fischer Taschenbuch Verlag, 1996) pp235-59, 246

13 Letters of Stefan Schimmer, born 1876, farmer in Oellingen (Lower Franconia), to his wife (BHStA/IV, Amtsbibliothek 9584)

14 For the treatment of military operations in the German press during 1914 see Raithel, Thomas, *Das 'Wunder' der inneren Einheit: Studien zur deutschen und französischen Öffentlichkeit bei Beginn der Ersten Weltkrieges* (Bonn: Bouvier, 1996) pp311ff

15 John, Horne, and Alan,Kramer, 'German "Atrocities" and Franco-German Opinion, 1914: The Evidence of German Soldiers' Diaries' in *Journal of Modern History* 66 (1994), pp1-33; John, Horne, and Alan,Kramer, *German Atrocities in Belgium and North-Western France during the First World War* (Oxford: Berghahn Books, 2000)

16 Latzel, *Deutsche Soldaten*, op cit, pp164, 191-6

17 See especially the documents in Ulrich, Bernd and Ziemann, Benjamin (eds), *Frontalltag im Ersten Weltkrieg: Wahn und Wirklichkeit: Quellen und Dokumente* (Frankfurt/M: Fischer Taschenbuch Verlag, 1994) pp42ff, 50ff; Kruse, Wolfgang, *Krieg und nationale Integration: Eine Neuinterpretation des sozialdemokratischen Burgfriedensschlusses 1914/15* (Essen: Klartext, 1993) pp185ff; idem, 'Die Kriegsbegeisterung im Deutschen Reich zu Beginn des Ersten Weltkrieges: Entstehungszusammenhänge, Grenzen und ideologische Strukturen' in Marcel van der Linden and Gottfried Mergner (eds), *Kriegsbegeisterung und mentale Kriegsvorbereitung. Interdisziplinäre Studien* (Berlin: Duncker & Humblot, 1991) pp73-87, pp80ff Edith, Hagener, *'Es lief sich so sicher an Deinem Arm': Briefe einer Soldatenfrau 1914* (Weinheim, Basel: Beltz, 1986) p53

18 Dominik,Richert, edited by Bernd Ulrich and Angelika Tramitz, *Beste Gelegenheit zum Sterben: Meine Erlebnisse im Kriege 1914-1918* (München: Knesebeck & Schuler, 1989) p29

19 See Alan,Kramer, 'Wackes at War: Alsace-Lorraine and the failure of German National Mobilization, 1914-1918' in Horne, John (Hg), *State, Society and Mobilization in Europe during the First World War* (Cambridge: Cambridge University Press, 1997) pp105-21

20 Cited in Peter,Knoch, 'Die Kriegsverarbeitung der "kleinen Leute" – eine empirische Gegenprobe' in Wolfgang Greive (ed), *Der Geist von 1914: Zerstörung des universalen Humanismus?* (Loccum: Evangelische Akademie, 1990) pp151-93, 186

21 Reinhold, Maier, *Feldpostbriefe aus dem Ersten Weltkrieg 1914-1918* (Stuttgart: W. Kohlhammer, 1966) p38

22 See Latzel, *Deutsche Soldaten*, op cit, pp156-82

23 Cited in Knoch, *Kriegsverarbeitung*, op cit, pp188ff

24 For the operational aspects of this battle (and much more!) see Dennis E.,Showalter, *Tannenberg: Clash of Empires* (Hamden, 1991; for the remembrance of this battle see Robert Traba, 'Kriegssyndrom in Ostpreußen: Ein Beitrag zum kollektiven Bewußtsein der Weimarer Zeit' in Thomas F. Schneider (ed), *Kriegserlebnis und Legendenbildung: Das Bild des 'modernen' Krieges in Literatur, Theater, Photographie und Film*, Vol 1 (Osnabrück: Universitätsverlag Rasch, 1999) pp399-412

25 See Peter, Jahn, '"Zarendreck, Barbarenndreck – Peitscht sie weg!": Die russische Besetzung Ostpreußens und die deutsche Öffentlichkeit' in Berliner Geschichtswerkstatt (ed), *August 1914: Ein Volk zieht in den Krieg* (Berlin: Dirk Nishen, 1989) pp147-55

26 Jehuda L. Wallach, *Das Dogma der Vernichtungsschlacht: Die Lehren von Clausewitz und Schlieffen und ihre Wirkungen in zwei Weltkriegen* (Frankfurt/M: 1967) p268

27 Karl-Heinz Frieser, 'Die deutschen Blitzkriege: Operativer Triumph – strategische Tragödie' in Rolf-Dieter Müller and Hans-Erich Volkmann (eds), *Die Wehrmacht: Mythos und Realität* (München:

Oldenbourg, 1999) pp182-96

[28] In this article I refer again and again to the results of my work *Deutsche Soldaten – nationalsozialistischer Krieg? Kriegserlebnis-Kriegserfahrung 1939-1945* (Paderborn: Schöningh, 1998). All references for quoted letters ibid. For the problem of representativity and for other theoretical and methodological problems see also Klaus Latzel, 'Vom Kriegserlebnis zur Kriegserfahrung: Theroetische und methodische Überlegungen zur erfahrungsgeschichtlichen Untersuchung von Feldpostbriefen' in *Militärgeschichtliche Mitteilungen* 1997, Vol 56, pp1-30

[29] See Bernd Ulrich, *Die Augenzeugen: Deutsche Feldpostbriefe in Kriegs- und Nachkriegszeit 1914-1933* (Essen: Klartext ,1997); Benjamin Ziemann, *Front und Heimat: Ländliche Kriegserfahrungen im südlichen Bayern 1914-1923* (Essen: Klartext, 1997)

[30] Ulrich Herbert, 'Arbeiterschaft im "Dritten Reich": Zwischenbilanz und offene Fragen' in *Geschichte und Gesellschaft*, 1989, Vol 15, pp320-60, particularly p353

[31] See Albrecht Lehmann, '"Organisieren": Über Erzählen aus der Kriegs- und Nachkriegszeit' in *Der Deutschunterricht*, 1987, Vol 39, No 6, pp51-63; Militärgeschichtliches Forschungsamt (ed), *Das Deutsche Reich und der Zweite Weltkrieg*, Vol 5/1 (Stuttgart: Deutsche Verlagsanstalt, 1988) pp216-35 (contribution by Hans Umbreit)

[32] Ibid, pp236ff

[33] See endnote 28

[34] Lothar Kettenacker, *Nationalsozialistische Volkstumpolitik im Elsaß* (Stuttgart: Deutsche Verlagsanstalt, 1973) pp131-5

[35] See Klaus Latzel, 'Wehrmachtsoldaten zwischen "Normalität" und NS-Ideologie, oder: Was sucht die Forschung in der Feldpost?' in Rolf-Dieter Müller and Hans-Erich Volkmann (eds), *Die Wehrmacht: Mythos und Realität* (München: Oldenbourg, 1999) pp573-88

[36] Ortwin Buchbender and Reinhold Sterz (eds), *Das andere Gesicht des Krieges: Deutsche Feldpostbriefe 1939-1945* (München: Beck, 1982) p57

[37] Ernst H. Gombrich, 'Mythos und Wirklichkeit in den deutschen Rundfunksendungen der Kriegszeit' in *Die Krise der Kulturgeschichte: Gedanken zum Wertproblem in den Geisteswissenschaften* (München: Deutscher Taschenbuch Verlag, 1991) pp144-73, particularly p150

[38] Ortwin Buchbender/Reinhold Sterz (eds), op cit, p57

[39] See, eg, Max Domarus, *Hitler, Reden und Proklamationen 1932-1945: Kommentiert von einem deutschen Zeitgenossen* (München: Süddeutscher Verlag, 1965) pp1,540ff

[40] See Ian Kershaw, *Hitlers Macht: Das Profil der NS-Herrschaft* (München: Deutscher Taschenbuch Verlag, 1992)

[41] Hans-Walter Schmuhl, *Rassenhygiene, Nationalsozialismus, Euthanasie: Von der Verhütung zur Vernichtung "lebensunwerten Lebens", 1890-1945* (Göttingen: Vandenhoek & Ruprecht, 1992) pp29ff

[42] Hannes Heer and Klaus Naumann (eds), *Vernichtungskrieg: Verbrechen der Wehrmacht 1941-1944* (Hamburg: Hamburger Edition, 1995)

Chapter 15

The experience of defeat: Kut (1916) and Singapore (1942)

Robin Neillands

'But, in the end, it is not the Flag, or the Cause.
In the end it is simply those of us here in this regiment.
In the end, we are fighting for each other.'

Lt-Colonel Joshua Chamberlain, Colonel, The 20th Maine, 1863

The theme of this chapter is a comparison of armies in defeat, illustrated by short accounts from the men present at two British disasters, Kut-al-Amara in Mesopotamia in 1916 and Singapore in 1942. The most noticeable points of difference between these two events lie in the lengths of the sieges and the reasons for resistance or collapse. The garrison of Kut held out for months and only surrendered when men were dying of starvation, and the troops were out of food and ammunition. The garrison of Singapore, on the other hand, surrendered after ten days because, although they outnumbered the attacking force and were amply supplied, a significant number of men simply refused to fight. A close examination of both defeats reveals that in the tenacity at Kut and the collapse at Singapore, unit morale – or the lack of it – played a considerable part.

But what is morale? How is it defined? Can it be created and how is it maintained? If soldiers can be forced to fight, by fear of the enemy or the firing squad, is morale even important? Does morale actually matter in military affairs, or is good morale simply a bonus, something worth having but well down the list of military essentials, ranking well below discipline, leadership or training in the order of priority?

The answer to the last question can be made unequivocally. Anyone with experience in military affairs knows that the creation and maintenance of morale are vital to the success of military operations. Morale is the most important aspect of military life and the assets listed above, discipline, leadership, training – and many more to be listed shortly – have the creation of unit morale as a large part of their purpose; discipline, leadership and training are important largely because they contribute to high morale. Without discipline, a military unit is an armed mob; without high morale even the most disciplined unit will never achieve its full potential, and it is with this aspect – unit morale – that any account of Kut or Singapore must be chiefly concerned.

Even the 'Great Captains' could achieve little without creating high morale. Speaking to an audience of Sandhurst cadets in 1938, General Wavell said, 'To learn that Napoleon won the campaign of 1796 by manoeuvring on interior lines is of little value. But if you can discover how a young, unknown man inspired a ragged, mutinous, half-starved army and made it fight, then you will have learned something.'

But if morale is so important, what is it? In 1946 Field Marshal Montgomery defined morale like this:

'Morale is a mental and moral quality. Morale is that which develops a man's latent heroism so that he will overcome his desire to take the easy way out and surrender to fear; leadership, discipline, comradeship, self respect and devotion to a cause are the components of morale.'[1]

Morale is intangible but can be defined as the spirit, the ethos, the collective will and comradeship of the group. Morale is essentially a group or unit asset – and the word 'unit' can cover everything from a section to an army, from an aircrew to a ship's company. This ethos is one to which every member of the unit must make a contribution. In this it cuts both ways; the individual adds value to the unit and in return becomes imbued with the belief that he must not let the unit down. In military affairs, high morale is a product of self-respect and unit pride; it arises from the sense that it is important to stand for something, not least at a time when that something matters.

Since morale is important, what elements combine to create it? The list is long but the following are essential: sound training, good leadership and sensible handling in the field. Then comes the prospect or experience of action, a chance to fight. Recognition, medals, professional respect have to be provided, but comradeship and good administration, the regular provision of supplies, especially food, mail and – in earlier times – tobacco are extremely important, not just because they are important in themselves but because they indicate, even to the lowest private soldier, that matters up above are well in hand. It also helps to have a cause, or a clear objective, something to achieve while advancing, or reach while retreating, or hold if defending. Regimental tradition, a sense of community among the members of the unit, be it battalion, ship or aircraft, all this and much more contributes to morale – and morale will decline as these assets disappear or are not provided. Examples of this harsh fact will be found in the accounts that follow.

Morale can also be created and the fighting spirit of a unit transformed by the actions of one man, often, but not always, the commander. None of these factors are absolutes – morale remains intangible. Self-respect comes into it but must be enhanced by the assets listed above, which combine to make a man do more than he might do otherwise. A sensible man avoids danger or, when confronted with it, wisely takes shelter or runs away. A good soldier faces up to danger and privation, because to do otherwise would let down his friends or his regiment. As for regimental tradition, that has a part to play, but again there are few absolutes. The ethos of 'elite' units – the Guards, the Royal Marines, the USMC, the Foreign Legion – is well known and some units have established a well-deserved reputation as 'elite' units, based on a long-established – and carefully-maintained – performance on the battlefield; but simply being an established 'elite' is not enough.

It is worth remembering that during the Gulf War of 1990-91, Iraq's 'elite' Republican Guard – that adjective was never missing from accounts in the Western media – was the first to run away. It could even be argued that elitism is dangerous, unless it is constantly backed up with those other essential assets – discipline, training, leadership, etc. Simply to claim 'elite' status on the basis of past performance or that of another national force elsewhere is simply 'bullshit' – and when push comes to shove on the battlefield, 'bullshit' is not enough.

With the centrality of morale and the elements in its composition at least aired, it is now time to consider how the morale factor among the officers and men affected the outcome in the defeats at Kut and Singapore. As a first point for consideration, it should be noted that in both cases the siege began after a retreat.

Kut-al-Amara

British military involvement in Mesopotamia in 1915 has similarities with the British Army's involvement in Malaya 25 years later. In both cases it was necessary to secure the supply of vital strategic commodities; in Mesopotamia, oil, in Malaya, rubber and tin. In October 1914 a brigade of the Indian Army was sent to secure the refinery at Abadan, protect the pipeline from the wells in Persia and deter the Turks. The aims of this force – Indian Expeditionary Force 'D' – then expanded. The security of Abadan was believed to lie in further advances up the Tigris, and so began a process that led inexorably to the disastrous siege of Kut.

To understand what happened at Kut it is necessary to understand the ground.[2] Ground is a vital consideration in military operations, but ground is in limited supply in the Shatt-el-Arab delta, which is at best a swamp and under water for much of the year. To move up the Tigris to Kut and Baghdad requires boats, to supply an army requires a fleet of craft, and the operations of the Indian Army in this part of Mesopotamia in 1915-16 are best imagined as an amphibious campaign; it is fair to say that the British and Indian forces were woefully ill-prepared for this kind of operation.

Nevertheless, a British force under Major-General Charles Townshend advanced up the river until checked by the Turks at Ctesiphon on 22 November 1915. Ctesiphon, though a victory, was a Pyrrhic one. The Turks left the British in possession of the field, but British losses were heavy – almost 4,000 men killed and wounded, more than 40 per cent of the force committed. Townshend could not stay where he was, at the end of a tenuous supply line clogged with wounded men. A withdrawal was inevitable, and Townshend fell back to Kut-al-Amara, entering the town on 3 December 1915. The retreat was well-conducted and the enemy recognised as worthy opponents. 'There are a lot of hardships ahead before we get to Kut. He is a good and stubborn fighter, the Turk,' recorded Lt M. M. Thorburn MC of the Black Watch, during the retreat from Ctesiphon.[3]

The troops were in good fettle when they entered Kut. 'The troops were in high praise of their leader and to all it seemed a marvel how he had extricated them,' wrote Gunner W. D. Lee[4] – though he was glad to be inside the defences. Having picked up troops along the line of communications as he fell back from Ctesiphon, Townshend had about 12,000 men to defend the town and occupy a mile and a half of trenches. To feed them he had 60 days' supply of food for the soldiers and three months' supply for the Arab inhabitants.

Townshend had made his name as a captain in 1895, defending a fort in Chitral, a small buffer state between India and Afghanistan, for 46 days, and he was determined to repeat this feat at Kut. The first note in his diary declared an intention, 'To defend Kut as I did Chitral'[5], buying time for his superiors to assemble more forces and come to his relief. This prospect clearly enthused his officers, for Lt-Colonel J. S. Barker wrote on 7 December 1915, 'The Force is very cheerful as we are confident we can keep the enemy off as long as ammunition and food supplies hold out and this I believe is quite a long time'[6], a prediction that turned out to be entirely accurate.

Townshend's decision was supported by his superior, Lt-General Nixon, and the General Staff in Delhi, and he held Kut for almost five months, until 28 April 1916, beating off a series of Turkish assaults, carefully conserving food and ammunition. Morale remained high, for, according to Gunner Lee, 'General Townshend created an optimistic feeling by saying we should soon be relieved ... he implored the men to save their ammunition as if it were gold, and would visit certain points of the defences and always had a cheery word.'[7] As the siege wore on Lee complained of a shortage of tobacco and food, mourned the loss of two officers – 'the loss of these officers was keenly felt in the ranks of the artillery'[8] – and mentioned that there were desertions among the Indian units: 'Several times groups of Indians, Muslims, who had tried to desert to the Turks were caught and shot before their regiments.'[9]

Morale in the Indian battalions suffered from the death or wounding of their British officers, men to whom the sepoys were devoted and who understood their needs, and from the fact that, as rations ran out, the Muslim sepoys refused for religious reasons to eat horse or mule flesh, the only commodity in adequate supply. They were also put under pressure by propaganda from the Turks, urging them to leave the British lines and come over to their co-religionists. In the circumstances it is hardly surprising that some of them succumbed. Writing on 9 April 1916, Captain Rogers of the 76th Punjab Regt recorded: 'The poor sepoy, how I do feel for him; what is seven ounces of food a day for a grown man?'[10] The sepoys were eventually reduced to about 5 ounces of atta – grain – a day, and were soon starving, while the British soldiers, even with the horseflesh, had very little more. 'God only knows how poor Tommy Atkins keeps body and soul together,' wrote Colonel Barker of the Royal Engineers[11], adding on 20 April that, 'One is awfully hungry all day.'

Several attempts to relieve Kut were made by the new commander at Basrah, General Aylmer, who had assembled two divisions and a cavalry force for this purpose, but Aylmer's command was too small for the number of Turks now in the field and the Tigris was in flood, making any advance extremely difficult. At the end of January, two months into the siege, Gunner Lee wrote: 'I must say the troops are still in good spirits and certain that our relieving force will soon break through'[12], but six weeks later, on 3 March, Colonel Barker noted, 'I am afraid Aylmer has failed again and has had to go back.'[13]

In spite of these disappointments, Townshend held out for another seven weeks, surrendering on the promise of favourable treatment for his starving men, especially the sick and wounded; this promise was not kept and more than half the troops taken prisoner died of ill-treatment in captivity. Unlike later historians, the men did not blame Townshend for this defeat. 'General Townshend had played his part and all his force was sorry at the way he had been let down,' wrote Gunner Lee[14], a point taken up by Captain Rogers[15]: 'Well, the end has come at last and although it is not what we want or what we deserve after a gallant stand, still I thank God for it.'

Surrender was inevitable. By the time Kut fell, men were dying of starvation every day and stocks of ammunition were almost exhausted. What was still available, and in adequate supply, was good morale. Private J. E. Sporle wrote in his diary that, 'During the siege things were very unhappy for us for we were living like rats in the ground and rations were cut until we were living on horseflesh'[16], but nowhere does he mention any failure in morale or any unwillingness to fight on. Nor do any other accounts.

This is not to say that the men were happy. It is too much to expect that starving men, ravaged with sickness, surrounded by the enemy and with little hope of relief, will remain cheerful and crack jokes – though a surprising number managed to achieve both feats. The point is that they remained willing to fight and continued to do so – and worked hard when not fighting, to maintain and improve their defences. Comforts were non-existent, no mail arrived – a failure, since mail could have been dropped in from aircraft – and the men endured terrible weather and constant bombardment without flinching. What brought the siege of Kut to an end was not a failure of morale, but starvation. The surrender at Singapore is far less easy to excuse or explain.

Singapore

Among the many differences between the siege of Kut and the fall of Singapore, one is particularly outstanding – time. The situation at Kut developed quickly, the defences were ad hoc and the defenders outnumbered, yet Kut held out for months. The state of Singapore's defences had been under review for years, the force available exceeded that of the attackers, and yet the Malayan peninsula and Singapore fell in a matter of weeks – just two weeks in the case of Singapore. To trace the reasons for the sudden fall of 'Fortress Singapore', it is necessary to examine the assumptions on which the defence of Singapore were based, assumptions that led directly to the final defeat.

The problems affecting the defence of Singapore pre-date by many years the arrival of General A. E. Percival, GOC Malaya, in 1941-42. To defend Singapore meant the creation of forward defences in Malaya in the pre-war years, but the money to construct them was simply not available in the 1920s and 1930s. Indeed, the proposal to build the Singapore Naval Base was shelved in 1924 and work did not recommence until 1926. This gave the three services time to argue about how the base should be defended; the Army and Navy held out for fixed local defences and 15-inch guns, while the RAF suggested that the only sure safeguard was the stationing of torpedo-bombers on Singapore and on bases in Malaya.

The Anglo-German Naval Agreement of June 1935, allowing the development of a German Fleet, meant that the Royal Navy would be kept in the Atlantic to protect the sea routes to Britain, and unable to deploy sufficient strength in the Far East to deter the ambitions of an expansionist and aggressive Japan. Without a Fleet, the Singapore Naval Base was a white elephant, but Malaya and Singapore had those vital strategic and economic assets that had to be defended, and that defence now rested on the Army and the RAF. Posterity, however, has placed the blame for all that happened at Singapore on the shoulders of the Army Commander, Lieutenant-General Percival.

When Percival arrived in Malaya in 1941, no steps of any kind had been taken to prepare defences, though Intelligence reports recorded that the Japanese were developing an amphibious capability based on aircraft carriers and landing ships and their war in China was providing the Japanese commanders with a quantity of experienced, battle-hardened soldiers. Having reviewed all these factors, Percival decreed, correctly, that the defence of Singapore must begin further out, offshore and in the north of Malaya. Actually providing such defence was another matter.

Apart from defensive preparations, fortifications, minefields, ammunition and supply dumps, Malaya Command also needed more troops, artillery, transport and tanks. The equipment available was either obsolescent or in short supply, or, in the case of tanks, unavailable, not least because the powers-that-be in Britain had decided that tanks could not operate in the 'jungles' of Malaya, a point that ignored the fact that the coasts of Malaya are often free of jungle – as are the numerous rubber plantations. These same powers had also made the fundamental mistake of underestimating the enemy. Captain A. K. Butterworth of the 2/16th Punjab Regiment in the 11th Indian Division wrote, 'We were told that the Japs were small, wore glasses, had buck teeth, were unable to see in the dark, were poor soldiers and had aircraft that fell out of the sky if they went too fast. None of this was true; the Japanese were superbly equipped and trained.'[17]

To oppose the Japanese, Percival had a motley range of forces, and a plan. His chief subordinate was Lt-General Lewis Heath, commanding III Indian Corps, which consisted of the 9th and 11th Indian Divisions; these divisions were understrength, with just two brigades each. The Australian contingent was a small division commanded by Major-General Gordon Bennett; this division also had two brigades, one recently arrived. In addition there were a number of unbrigaded battalions and local volunteer units. All these troops were in urgent need of jungle training, and some of the Australian units were in need of basic training and an injection of discipline. There were no tanks, no heavy artillery, and a shortage of transport and anti-aircraft guns. As for the plan – 'Operation Matador' – that called for a rapid advance into neutral Siam – now Thailand – and the north-east coast of Malaya immediately the Japanese were seen to be attacking.

Heath's Corps was deployed in the north, close to the Siam border, most of it in brigade groups between Alor Star in the west and Kota Bharu in the east, with the

28th Indian Brigade around Ipoh. The Australians were further south, in Johore, organised in two brigade groups with the AIF HQ in Johore Bharu. Neither of his two subordinate commanders was of much help to General Percival. Heath was senior to Percival – on the Indian Army list – and nursed a chip on his shoulder, resenting the appointment of his newly promoted commander.

Gordon Bennett, an archetypal Australian, had a chip on both shoulders, one about the British and one about the Indians; he was reluctant to accept instructions from Percival and kept a direct line open to the Australian Government in Canberra. He also spent a great deal of time telling his troops and the media that his men were superb and, if only by implication, that the Indian and British troops were rubbish. This time might have been better employed improving the training and discipline of the Australian contingent, which stood in need of such improvement. Nor did Gordon Bennett get on with Heath and clearly both men should have been replaced. Though sacking Gordon Bennett would have been difficult, Percival's failure to get a grip on both his generals, insisting that they followed his orders with less carping and more enthusiasm, was a clear failure in command.

This sets the scene for what followed, and it should now be clear that the defence of Malaya and Singapore was flawed from the start. Not even a Marlborough or a Wellington could have held Malaya in 1941; it was a matter of too little, too late. If Malaya and Singapore were to be defended, steps to that end, from fortifications to the provision of an adequate garrison, with suitable, modern air and naval support, should have been taken years before. When war came, there were not enough troops – on infantry alone Percival was short by 17 battalions – the troops were not well-trained, they lacked every kind of support, their commanders were at odds on many points, and some of the units were badly disciplined. When the defenders were confronted by a well-equipped, skilled and resourceful enemy, the issue could not long be in doubt.

Major Phillip Parker, a Staff officer with the 11th Indian Division, recalled that even the demolitions hurriedly placed to slow or stem the Japanese advance after they landed were not deployed correctly. 'Many demolitions failed; others went up when they should not have done. Several casualties were caused by friendly fire and there were chaotic conditions as the men retreated south.'[18] The word 'chaos' appears in many accounts of the Malayan campaign.

Japan attacked Malaya on the night of 7/8 December, with landings on the east coast of Thailand and around Kota Bharu in the north of Malaya; as at Pearl Harbor, the attack came without a declaration of war. General Yamashita's 25th Army had just four divisions for this assault. Two of these, the 5th and 18th, were battle-hardened and well-trained in infiltration tactics. The third was from the Imperial Guard, as yet unblooded but full of superb troops, and such was the speed of Yamashita's advance that his fourth division, the 56th, never saw action at all. Yamashita also had a quantity of tanks, and plenty of air support from bombers and Zero fighters. His troops surged forward with great speed, using everything from bicycles to captured transport.

C. R. Boyton, an officer on the Staff of the 9th Indian Division, described the Malayan campaign as one of 'skirmishing, scrapping and scarpering' in which 'the troops were completely bewildered by [Japanese] infiltration tactics', adding later that 'incompetence characterised the whole campaign' and the troops were not fired with zealous old time patriotism and were 'very jittery'.[19] Captain Butterworth, of the 3/16th Punjab Regiment, recorded that the battalion routine became one of, 'Defend by day, retreat by night, one retreat after another. Rumours that the RAF had left us and flown out to Sumatra caused many a rude comment and morale was at an all time low. We all regarded arriving at Singapore as a blessing.'[20]

What happened after the Japanese invaded Malaya can be quickly told. The campaign was a shambles and there is no space to cover all the details here. The invasion fleet was spotted off the East Coast on Saturday, 6 December. Percival put his forces on full alert for 'Matador' but the Commander in Chief, Air Marshal Brooke Popham, did not give the order to move. As a result, the Japanese got ashore completely unopposed and struck south and west from the east coast, down the roads towards Alor Star and Penang, surging over the Malayan frontier with both speed and force.

Heath blamed Percival for the failure to implement 'Matador', and his attitude towards his commander rapidly went from anger to contempt. This did not help, but the situation was already beyond redemption. On 8 December strong Japanese air forces attacked from bases in Indo-China and caught many British aircraft on the ground. Some Japanese ships were sunk or damaged by RAF sorties, but the troops were now ashore and 8 December was the only day that the RAF was able to mount any meaningful opposition. By 9 December more than half of the 150 aircraft deployed to defend northern Malaya had been destroyed.

On 10 December came another disaster. The two capital ships of Force Z, HMS *Prince of Wales* and HMS *Repulse*, sailing north from Singapore to attack Japanese shipping in the Gulf of Siam, were attacked by strong forces of Japanese bombers. The air attacks started at 1100hrs, and by 1300hrs both ships were at the bottom of the sea. The RAF and the Royal Navy had shot their bolt; now it all depended on the Army.

The Army had been caught on the back foot by the failure to implement 'Matador', and it stayed that way. On the second day of the campaign Kota Bharu fell to the Japanese and General Heath proposed pulling the troops back to Kuala Lipis, a distance of 100 miles, before making a stand, a proposal that provoked a row with Percival. The Jitra position, on the Kedah River north of Alor Star, was attacked with tanks and infantry on the night of 11/12 December and rapidly reduced, the defenders falling back to Kroh and beyond. The defeat at Jitra spelt the end of serious resistance in Malaya, and another position on the Slim River, south of Kuala Lipis, fell in a day, on 7 January. From then on the Japanese had the British forces on the run and stayed hard on their heels, either overwhelming positions by direct assault or outflanking them with infiltration tactics or seaborne landings.

Major S. P. Fearon of the 5/14th Punjab Regt, but serving with the 1st Independent Infantry Battalion, recorded that: 'One of the most exhausting features of the campaign was the almost continual movement by night without proper lighting. Drivers fell asleep driving and ditched vehicles were a common sight. It was necessary to have three drivers for every vehicle, one for day running and two for night.'[21] It is good to notice that there are several accounts in which the Australian drivers of the Transport Companies have been singled out for praise after their work during the retreat through Malaya – a fact that illustrates the point that high morale and efficient soldiering are not the preserve of 'elite' units.

Singapore – 'Fortress Singapore' – soon became a Mecca to the men retreating south through the Malayan peninsula. The notion had spread that once they got to Singapore, they would be all right, the Japanese advance could be halted and the real fight back would begin. When this belief was seen to be false, morale plummeted. 'Hooray! Singapore and safety,' wrote C. R. Boyton of the 9th Indian Division. 'We arrived in high spirits but once again the old chaos took command.'[22]

No military operation is more difficult to execute or more deleterious to morale than a withdrawal. The withdrawal to Singapore never became a rout and, where the troops stood and fought, they did well – the Australian ambush at Gemas on 14 January was particularly well-handled – but the Japanese were better trained and better equipped and they kept pushing back the British – and the Indians and Australians. This process produced another dispute between Heath and Percival. Percival wanted the front-line troops to stand and fight, whatever the cost, so that an adequate defence line could be prepared in the rear. Heath was attempting to keep his forces intact, pulling them back before they were surrounded, perhaps to a defence line manned by the AIF in Johore.

Both ideas had merit, but neither was actually possible; the Japanese had the upper hand – they would dictate how the campaign was fought – and their tactics are summed up in this account of a Japanese attack from Lt-Colonel C. C. Deakin of the 5/2nd Punjab Regiment:

> 'The din defies description. The [Japanese] tanks were nose to tail with their engines running, their crews yelling, their machine-guns spitting tracer, and their mortars and cannon firing all out. The noise of exploding mines, Molotov cocktails [petrol bombs] and anti-tank fire added to the din ... how many men of the battalion were killed or wounded and how many took to the jungle was not known and perhaps will never be known. Be what it may, the battalion had disintegrated and had failed to stand and fight to the last man.'[23]

It would be some years before the British learned that the answer to Japanese infiltration was to form 'boxes' for all-round defence, then stand and fight. In 1941 all this was new, so the British, Indian and Australian troops were forced back down the peninsula. The last troops crossed the Johore causeway on to Singapore Island on 31 January, when the Malayan campaign had lasted exactly 55 days. The battle for Singapore would be equally brief.

Morale had suffered from this retreat and morale was not high in Singapore. Writing in his diary on Christmas Day, 1941, the Rev Captain G. V. Chambers, serving with the 35 LAA Regiment, commented, 'Somebody ought to be hung for the state of affairs here. Not enough of anything and the poor old RAF saddled with ancient and wrong type machines. It's plain murder.'[24] Captain Chambers also came to dislike the local civilians – the 'expats' – writing on 20 January 1942, 'If we were not here with hundreds of good soldiers I would say it [Singapore] deserved to fall.'[25]

During January more troops arrived in Singapore, including more Australians, the British 18th Division, and 50 Hurricane fighters, which alas proved no match for the Japanese Zero. General Wavell, the Supreme Commander for the South West Pacific, made a number of visits and seemed to believe that the island could be held. Some of the new arrivals were more than willing to fight, and Lt Owen Eva of the Royal Northumberland Fusiliers recorded on 6 February that, 'Morale in the battalion high when we landed here last evening,'[26] a comment written just nine days before the island fell.

It took just two weeks to reduce the defences of Singapore. The Japanese crossed the Johore Straits on 8 February, coming ashore on a part of the island held by the Australians, who promptly gave way. By this time Japanese guns were pounding Singapore City, which was also under attack by Japanese aircraft, and a general leakage of men from the front line was soon apparent. The fight for Singapore Island lasted seven days, most of the surviving RAF fighters and the last Hurricane squadron being shot down on the first day, the shore defences being overwhelmed or outflanked within hours. Compounding these calamities was the fact that many of the defending troops declined to fight.

It should have been possible for resolute troops to hold Singapore Island for longer than a week, or at least to make a better fight for it. As the Japanese were to demonstrate later in the Pacific War, at Tarawa, Saipan, Iwo Jima, Okinawa and other places, even if the outcome is inevitable, a resolute defending force can take a heavy toll of the attacker – and on these Japanese-held islands the defenders were always heavily outnumbered. At Singapore, Percival had over 100,000 troops and actually outnumbered the Japanese invaders. Certainly he lacked air cover, heavy artillery and tanks, but he was fighting on the defensive and could have done better, held out longer and charged the Japanese a heavy price for their victory. The reason he failed to do so was that – quite apart from a lack of prepared defences – he had problems with his men.

The fundamental problem was a lack of discipline and training and – above all – poor morale. The newly arrived troops were not fully trained and were flung directly into combat, while the troops that had retreated from Malaya were already discouraged by weeks of retreat. By 10 February positions were being abandoned, and there are particular reports of Australian troops 'streaming back towards the harbour, shouting that the fighting was over and they were clearing out'.[27] Groups of Australian soldiers, having deserted from their units, were soon roaming the city, looting and looking for drink or ways of escape. The prevailing mood was one of hopelessness. With Malaya lost, Singapore under heavy attack, the Japanese ashore and the defences collapsing, what was the point of fighting on? The Naval Base, the main reason for holding Singapore, had no ships, and a Japanese victory was inevitable, so why not surrender now and save further suffering?

Captain Butterworth of the Punjab Regiment recalled the situation after the Japanese crossed to the island: 'The Australians had broken and were running back, many of them throwing away their equipment. We were ordered to stop them and make them turn back and shoot them if they refused to comply. Can anyone imagine the shame of British officers explaining the position to Indian soldiers? The whole world was collapsing.'[28]

Not all the Australians ran away. Captain Chambers, the padre, recalls one lightly wounded Australian turning up at the hospital and accounting for his desertion by saying, 'No fucking Australian could stand it,' to which an Australian padre replied, 'You are a fucking Australian. Others did stand it and are there now.'[29] There was leakage of men from many units, but many soldiers, Australian, British and Indian, stayed in the line and fought on, partly because there was nowhere to go, partly to stay with their friends. The Argyll & Sutherland Highlanders made a very fine showing, as did the Loyals and a detachment of the Royal Marines attached to the Highlanders and later known as 'The Plymouth Argylls'.

There were good reasons for fighting on, not least the effect that a British collapse and defeat might have in India and throughout the Far East, but fighting on in the present situation was regarded as impossible. This was partly because the Japanese had command of the air so that reinforcement or a general evacuation were impossible, and partly because it could only lead to the total destruction of the city and the loss of many civilian lives. General Heath, for one, felt that further resistance was useless, and when Percival remarked on 13 February that, 'I have my honour to consider and there is also the question of what posterity will think of us if we surrender this large Army and valuable fortress,' Heath sneered that, 'You need not bother about your honour. You lost that a long time ago, up in the north.'[30] Percival still decided to fight on, for as long as possible, but that was only for another two days. At 2030hrs on Sunday, 15 February 1942, Singapore fell, and over 100,000 Australian, British and Indian soldiers went into a long and brutal captivity.

Major-General Gordon Bennett did not go with them. Reluctant to share the fate of his soldiers, he vanished shortly after the surrender and made his way back to Australia, where his account of the campaign established the now-popular Australian myth that the British had let Australia down. Percival, who went into captivity with his men, judged in his memoirs that, 'The right place for an officer, especially a senior officer, is with his men ... that may mean the ruin of a career and personal ambitions, but one of the corner stones of our tradition is that an officer stands by his men.'[31]

Regarding the commanders, the wonderful gift of hindsight makes it easy to see that Percival was not the right man for Malaya and should have immediately got a stronger grip on his immediate subordinates, Heath and Gordon Bennett – or sacked them. What Malaya Command needed in 1941 was a ruthless commander, one who could sum up the situation, see what was needed, order it done and sack anyone who did not instantly comply. Such a person might also have been able to insist on the rapid supply of tanks, bombers, fighter aircraft and more troops, from Australia, India or the UK, demand more training for his troops in Malaya, and have extracted a supply of civilian labour from the local authorities for the construction of defence lines in Johore and Singapore. Was there such a man available at the time?

Someone like Montgomery springs to mind, but a hard-driving general alone was not enough. Without the long preparation of defensive assets, Singapore, an island the size of the Isle of Wight, was doomed, and had been doomed since at least

1935. Less easy to fathom once the issue came to be tested is the matter of morale, but a comparison of Kut and Singapore does provide some useful lessons.

Kut was a smaller affair, small enough for the commander to imprint his personality on the troops. The retreat to Kut was well-handled and followed a battle that, in spite of the outcome, was regarded by the British and Indian troops as a clear victory. In fact, morale never became an issue at Kut-al-Amara. The morale of the troops, though frequently tested, never faltered, and they held out until starvation forced a surrender.

In Malaya and Singapore morale was a factor from the start, not merely at the end, and many of the essential principles outlined at the start of this chapter were either not observed or promptly broken. The men were not well or properly trained, leadership was poor, and their equipment and support were inadequate, not least in aircraft and in an absence of tanks. They had also been taught to undervalue the enemy, which even Shakespeare's Dauphin – no soldier he – knew to be unwise:

> 'In cases of defence 'tis best to weigh
> The enemy more mighty than he seems'[32]

There was failure at all levels, civil and military, and the end result was a collapse of morale, civil and military. Singapore would probably have fallen anyway, but the defeat would have been far less crushing if the defence had been properly handled and the surrender not accompanied by disgraceful scenes of panic and disorder.

As for Major-General Gordon Bennett, he despised not only the enemy, but also his allies. The result of this attitude was two-fold, and tragic. First of all, it made the Australians arrogant and careless of the enemy, but when the enemy was found to be formidable, it also made them nervous of their flanks. They had been told that the British and Indians were inferior soldiers who would leave them in the lurch, so, to prevent being left in the lurch, they gave way to the Japanese – and left their allies in the lurch.

In failing to train or discipline his men, in spreading slanders about their British and Indian comrades, in encouraging a belief in their military prowess based on arrogance, 'bullshit' and chippiness rather than on sound training and discipline, Gordon Bennett did his men great harm. In failing to co-operate with his peers or superior officer, even to the extent of ignoring the chain of command and telling Canberra – without telling Percival – that he intended to pull his men out of the line if the Japanese looked like overwhelming them, Gordon Bennett was a two-star disaster, who did little for his men apart from delivering them to a harsh captivity he was careful not to share.

This is not a popular thing to say, but the facts are supported by the following extracts from a long and condemnatory article published in Australia shortly after the Singapore debacle, written by Sir Keith Murdoch, father of the now more famous Rupert, and no lover of the 'Poms':

> 'Why the island passed so quickly into Japanese hands is explicable only by researches into the intricate subjects of morale, tactics and leadership. From

the first the garrison had few chances and, except for some sections of officers who maintain that if the Australians had held on the north-western beaches we would still have the island, the feeling of hopelessness seems to have been general...

We were overwhelmed in our forward positions, particularly where the 19th Bn, with its 60 per cent reinforcements stood. The Japanese came straight through the middle of the Australian positions ... the only landing for the first two days was against the Australians, and Singapore was lost on the first day. There were, of course, many heroic incidents and much brave fighting worthy of the best tradition. We had sad defections and it was notable that the men who did not stand were the boozy "tough" men, who had always had the wrong ideas of discipline and were noisy and boastful...

Our own part [in the pre-war preparations] was marred by a constant belittlement of our British and Indian comrades, by inadequate discipline and by the percentage of weak and undisciplined soldiers breaking down under the strain of battle.'[33]

Lessons in how not to do it abound in the Malayan campaign and in the fall of Singapore, but they are the old lessons, ones that should not need retelling to every generation. And yet, as recently as 1999, we hear of Australian soldiers in East Timor saying they won't serve under a British Commander 'after what happened in Singapore', so clearly the Gordon Bennett version of the facts about Singapore still flourishes in the Antipodes. Australia produces fine soldiers, but they need discipline and training – and high morale – just as much as any other.

So, what was the experience of defeat like in these two places, Kut and Singapore? 'Very different' is the short answer. At Kut the men could surrender with their pride intact, knowing that they had done their utmost and could do no more. The experience of Singapore, on the other hand, is summed up by the words that appear in many accounts, words like 'chaos', 'failure', 'shambles', feelings of hopelessness, and 'shame'. Many men and some units fought well in the battle for Singapore, but unit morale frequently failed and the end result of that was a terrible defeat.

Morale is an intangible dish, made up of many ingredients, but its essence is composed of unit pride and self-respect. These elements will make a soldier fight, whatever the odds and in spite of the outcome; without these assets, units – and soldiers – simply cannot function. This fact has been well summed up by the distinguished American writer, William Manchester, a man who takes pride in the fact that in the last year of the Second World War he was a Sergeant in the United States Marine Corps. Manchester fought in the Pacific campaign and was wounded in the fighting for another island, Okinawa. At heart Manchester remains a United States Marine, and he sums up what that means to him like this:

'There is a seed; unit pride. It is planted in every man during training and it grows to be tougher than he is. He may want it gone but he can't shuck it. He may jeer at all heroes as "Gung ho", and call the Sergeant "Daddy-O", but this thing stays inside him until he finds himself in the line. He may never have heard the Marine Band, may not know who the Montezumans were or where Tripoli is.[34] Still he'll jump up and go forward when "Daddy-O" pumps his arm for the assault, because someone once told him it was better to die than let the Marine Corps down, and he believed it then, and part of him always will.'[35]

If even a little of that spirit had been more widely present at Singapore, the defeat might not have been a disaster.

Notes on contributors

Robin Neillands, Independent Historian and Author, Marlborough, UK. Robin Neillands is a journalist, writer and popular historian. His books include A Fighting Retreat: Military Campaigns in the British Empire 1947-1997 (1997), The Conquest of the Reich, 1945 (1995) and The Great War Generals on the Western Front (1998). His next book concerns Sir Arthur Harris and the combined bomber offensive.

Recommended reading

Barker, Arthur J., *Townshend of Kut* (London: Cassell, 1967)

Bennett, H. Gordon, *Why Singapore Fell* (Sydney: Angus & Robertson, 1944)

Callahan, *The Worst Disaster: The Fall of Singapore* (University of Delaware Press, 1977)

Elphick, Peter, *Singapore, the Pregnable Fortress* (London: Hodder & Stoughton, 1995)

Dixon, Norman F., *On the Psychology of Military Incompetence* (London: Jonathan Cape, 1976)

Kinvig, Clifford, *Scapegoat: General Percival of Singapore* (London: Brassey's, 1997)

Liddle, Peter, *The Soldier's War, 1914-1918* (Blandford Press, 1988)

Moberley, Brigadier-General F. J., CB, CSI, DSO, *History of the Great War: The Campaign In Mesopotamia*, Vol 1 (London: HMSO, 1923); Vol 2 (London: HMSO, 1924)

Moran, Lord, *The Anatomy of Courage* (London: Constable, 1945)

Percival, Lt-Gen A. E. C. B., DSO, OBE, MC, *The War in Malaya* (London: Eyre & Spottiswoode, 1949)

   Operations of Malaya Command, 8 Dec 1941-15 February 1942 (London: HMSO, 1948)

Regan, Geoffrey, *Great Military Blunders* (London: Channel 4 Books (Macmillan), 2000)

Sherson, Erroll, *Townshend of Chitral and Kut* (London: Heinemann, 1928)

Notes

1   Field Marshal Viscount Montgomery of Alamein, *Morale in Battle: An analysis* (1946)
2   Kut-al-Amara papers, Imperial War Museum (IWM) 88/56/1P
3   Lt M. M. Thorburn papers, IWM 99/56/1P
4   Gunner W. D. Lee papers, IWM 91/25/1
5   Townshend diaries, quoted in Sherson, Erroll, *Townshend of Chitral and Kut* (London: Heinemann, 1928) p297
6   Letters of Lt-Colonel J. S. Barker, MVO, IWM 96/36/1
7   Gunner W. D. Lee, 86th Heavy Battery RGA, memoir written in the 1930s, IWM 91/25/1

8   Ibid
9   Ibid
10 MS diary on the siege of Kut by Captain G. N. Rogers, IWM 92/36/1
11 Lt Colonel J. S. Barker, op cit
12 Gunner W. D. Lee, op cit
13 Lt Colonel J. S. Barker, op cit
14 Gunner W. D. Lee, op cit
15 Captain G. N. Rogers, 76th Punjab Regt, op cit
16 MS account from Private J. E. Sporle, Royal West Kent Regt, IWM 82/1/1
17 Capt A. K. Butterworth memoir, Department of Documents, IWM 95/17/1
18 Family history, recorded in Elphick, Peter, *Singapore, the Pregnable Fortress* (London: Hodder & Stoughton, 1995) p217
19 Capt Boynton account of Malaya Campaign, Department of Documents, IWM
20 Capt A. K. Butterworth, op cit
21 Quoted in *Singapore, the Pregnable Fortress*, op cit, p254
22 Capt Boynton, 9th Indian Division, op cit
23 War Diary, 5/2nd Punjab Regt, National Army Museum, London
24 Capt Rev G. J. Chambers, memoir of Singapore, Dec 1941-Feb 1942, Department of Documents, IWM
25 Ibid
26 Lt Owen Eva, Royal Northumberland Fusiliers, 5 February 1942, IWM 93/17/1
27 Quoted extensively, but noted in Kinvig, Clifford, *Scapegoat: General Percival of Singapore* (London: Brassey's, 1997) p213
28 Capt A. K. Butterworth, 3/16th Punjab Regt, 11 Indian Div, op cit
29 Capt Rev G. J. Chambers, op cit
30 Percival, Lt-Gen A. E. C. B., DSO, OBE, MC, *The War in Malaya* (London: Eyre & Spottiswoode, 1949) p285
31 Percival, Lt-Gen A. E. C. B., op cit
32 William Shakespeare, *Henry V*, Act II, Scene 4
33 Article in the *Adelaide Advertiser*, 17 March 1942, widely reproduced and quoted in *Singapore: the Pregnable Fortress*, op cit, pp336-7
34 'From the Halls of Montezuma, to the Shores of Tripoli' are the first two lines of the USMC Hymn, and recount the range and scope of USMC engagements since the Corps's foundation in the War of Independence
35 Article by William Manchester for the Marine Corps League, 1965

Chapter 16

The experience of killing

Joanna Bourke

'I shot him, and it had to be
One of us! 'Twas him or me.
Couldn't be helped, and none can blame
Me, for you would do the same.'[1]

With these words, the First World War poet Ivor Gurney encapsulates the decisive distinction between human interaction in wartime compared with normal expectations of interaction in times of peace: in many instances during war, people are required to kill each other. It is not a popular topic of debate and discussion either within the military or in civilian contexts. As a recruiting tool, an emphasis on the most aggressive aspects of military life has a negative rather than a positive value, particularly in times when plummeting enlistment figures increase the need to attract women and ethnic minorities to the services. Consequently, recruitment posters generally emphasise either the sophisticated technology enabling combatants to locate and destroy 'hardware', or the role of service personnel as 'peace-keepers'. Furthermore, very few service personnel welcome emphasis upon this aspect of their job. Indeed, the question 'How many men did you kill?' is frequently dreaded by ex-servicemen. On active service their letters back home may be replete with high-blown stories of murderous violence, but once on home soil such things seem distinctly out of place. As one soldier insisted in 1915, memories of killing are 'best forgotten'.[2] It is 'not a thing you like to talk about, or think about either', agreed a member of the French Foreign Legion and former gunner in the US Navy in 1918.[3] While pacifist organisations might have a rationale for drawing attention to the more sordid aspects of combat, for most civilians the actions of their friends and loved ones in combat are best forgotten.

In this chapter, however, it is argued that the ways in which British, American, Canadian and Australian men and women experienced the act of killing (as opposed to being killed) in wartime cannot be ignored. Too often, military history reads as though soldiers were only on the battlefields to die for their country, rather than to attempt to kill for it as well. Combatants could not erase their memories. When least expected, recollections of killing flared up, often, as one infantry captain complained, 'right in the middle of an ordinary conversation' when 'the face of a Boche that I have bayoneted, with its horrible gurgle and grimace, comes sharply into view.'[4] During the Second World War in particular, the problem of guilty consciences was exacerbated by the fact that it was increasingly civilians at risk of being killed. As a radio operator, engaged in a mass raid on Hamburg, wrote to Canon Collins:

'It was a nightmare experience looking down on the flaming city beneath. I felt sick as I thought of the women and children down there being mutilated, burned, killed, terror-stricken in that dreadful inferno – and I was partly responsible. Why, Padre John, do the Churches not tell us that we are doing an evil job? Why do chaplains persist in telling us that we are performing a noble task in defence of Christian civilisation? I believe that Hitler must be defeated; I am prepared to do my bit to that end. But don't let anyone tell us that what we are doing is noble. What we are doing is evil, a necessary evil perhaps, but evil all the same.'[5]

Emotional and psychological survival depended upon combatants being able to justify their actions to their consciences. The difficulties many combatants experienced in coming to terms with the fact of having killed another human being led some influential officers – including powerful men such as S. L. A. Marshall, author of *Men Against Fire* (1947) – to argue that 'fear of killing' was actually a more common cause of battle fatigue than 'fear of dying'.[6] Furthermore, those psychiatric casualties who experienced guilt over killing were particularly resistant to treatment.[7]

As implied above, there were certain events in combat that were especially difficult to cope with. The experience of killing that was often most recalled in tortuous passages in letters and diaries involved killing one's own comrades. In terse prose in his diary on 29 April 1915 Lieutenant Colonel J. W. Barnett described one such event:

'Shelling continues… Have lost good men doing nothing. St Jean church blazing & whole village smashed to pieces. Gurkha jammed under beams in burning house. Had to shoot him in head as could not be got out. Horrible. Curse this war – it is murder. All fellows look done – drawn faces.'[8]

The 'first time' was often a most traumatic occasion. One young soldier during the First World War described how in his first action he 'went silly and cried for mother ten times'. Once the 'action' had begun, however, 'courage loomed up in me. I thought I could not have enough nerve to stick a man with a bayonet, but during a charge one goes mad'.[9] Albert N. Depew was tormented for a long time after bayoneting a man during the First World War. He described the event, and its aftermath, in the following words:

'…when we got to the German trench I fell on top of a young fellow, and my bayonet went right through him. It was a crime to get him, at that. He was as delicate as a pencil. When I returned to our trenches after my first charge, I could not sleep for a long time afterwards for remembering what that fellow looked like and how my bayonet slipped into him and how he screamed when he fell. He had his legs and his neck twisted under him after he got it. I thought about it a lot, and it grew to be almost a habit that whenever I was going to sleep I would think about him, and then all hope of sleeping was gone.'[10]

While the enemy was often dehumanised (as we shall see later), it was ironic that combatants were often particularly upset by those occasions of killing when the enemy could not be seen or when the opponent was regarded as being denied a 'fair chance'. An Australian soldier fighting in New Guinea during the Second World War expressed the first of these fears:

'There are mists creeping over the trees all day, and sometimes you can't see your hand in front of your face under the cover of the jungle. Most of our chaps haven't seen a Jap! You don't even see the Jap who gets you! It's like fighting the invisible man. Those Japs are tough, hard fighters and their camouflage is perfect. They can move through scrub or tall grass without making a sound and without showing a sign except – if your eyes are good – an occasional stirring in the vegetation.'[11]

Such forms of warfare were particularly difficult for combatants. The terror that it inspired not only encouraged dehumanising of the enemy but also rough treatment – 'take no prisoners, show no mercy'.

High levels of seeming lawlessness in combat could also make it particularly terrifying. Time and time again British, American and Australian servicemen expressed dismay at the patently 'unequal' nature of the fray. The legitimacy of aiming at an unsuspecting man through a periscope and firing was frequently questioned. For instance, during the Second World War John Guest served in an AA Battery in Italy. He was generally a squeamish killer who could scarcely bring himself to fire guns into the anonymous no-man's-land, but his attitude towards snipers was uncompromising; the idea of firing at an 'unsuspecting man that I could see' seemed to be so unfair and beastly to him that he 'tried not to think about it'.[12] It was a 'dirty' and dishonourable trade, admitted Colonel Rowland Feilding in letters to his wife during the First World War (although he ordered others to do it).[13] Even snipers admitted that their business was 'little better than murder' and 'a filthy sort of business.' 'Every bit as bad as Jerry,' lamented the sniper Victor G. Ricketts.[14] As one Irish combatant described it from the trenches:

'You can't talk of fighting cleanly. There is no cleanliness in warfare. It isn't clean to live in the earth. It isn't clean to batter men's heads in... You have no idea how ridiculous this war is. You sit in a trench and wait, and fire, and send bombs over, and shell, and wait again, and bury a few men, and wait again, and fire, sleep – possibly – and wake, and wait and shell and wait, and that's all! It is not warfare; to use an impossible expression, it's civilised savagery and barbarous civilisation.'[15]

This combination of extreme fear, numbing boredom, and the sudden outpouring of murderous aggression did create psychological problems. It is important to recognise, however, that it was not only fear of being killed or killing that led to emotional conflicts. The environment of the military was profoundly upsetting to some men, and the day-to-day anxieties experienced in civilian contexts did not simply 'go away' in the camps. Indeed, there is some American evidence to suggest that the strain of killing (as opposed to the other strains of wartime) had a strong religious component. Statistical evidence from the Second World War clearly indicates that Catholics experienced more stress in combat than others. In one major study of ex-servicemen who had broken down during the Second World War, 51 per cent of Catholics, 39 per cent of Protestants, and only 25 per cent of Jews declared that combat itself had been their main area of stress. Protestants and Jews were much more liable to point to environmental and civilian forms of stress to explain their breakdown.[16]

This said, the act of killing, combined with the need to repress feelings of disgust or nausea about the sights, were traumatic for combatants. Men were not prepared for the horror of being unable to remove their bayonets from the bodies of their foe. Or for the stench of blood. Even that most romanticised form of killing – in aerial combat – could be disillusioning. For pilots, the disjunction between their chivalrous imaginings of aerial combat and their subjective experiences of it, sometimes caused them to vomit every time they shot down another pilot.[17] Airmen interviewed by Roy R. Grinker and John P. Spiegel in *Men Under Stress* (1945) might have expressed 'eager-beaver' reactions prior to going overseas, but their keenness lacked any sense of reality. 'The men seldom have any real, concrete notions of what combat is like,' Grinker and Spiegel continued, 'their minds are full of romanticised, Hollywood versions of their future activity in combat, colored with vague ideas of being a hero and winning ribbons and decorations.' If they were told more realistic stories about what to expect 'they would not believe them.'[18] Actual aerial combat could be 'a cruel awakening'[19], particularly when forced to kill people on the ground. For instance, in 1942 Commander B. W. Hogan observed the difficulties experienced by pilots during an attack on Guadalcanal. Men experienced 'elation' after shooting down Japanese planes, but were profoundly shaken when forced to fly down 'on running human beings, opening up all the guns, and bullets spraying, killing and maiming many of those unknown individuals.'[20] In fact, by this stage in modern aerial warfare, chivalry had long departed. Indeed, what little chivalry might have existed in aerial warfare had evaporated as early as 1917. It was a painful lesson that combatants in all branches of the military had to learn: there was no role for the 'gentlemanly ethos' in modern warfare. In the words of Stanley Johnson in 1945, 'under no circumstances must an enemy, caught at a disadvantage, be allowed to escape… There is no chivalry in this war and no place for it.'[21]

Acts of vicious killing were traumatising. As the renowned psychologist, Therese Benedek, argued in *Insight and Personality Adjustment: A Study of the Psychological Effects of War* (1946), in the aftermath of war combatants were reluctant to speak about killing not out of modesty but because they wanted to avoid facing a 'humiliating memory'. She continued: 'With the killing he has to remember the fear he experienced and the threatening depth of his own emotions, so different from what he had been taught all his life.' While in danger, and in the presence of other men who 'did as he did' and 'know all about it', anxiety about one's brutal actions did not rise to the surface:

> 'However, when the soldier is released from his group and stands alone among civilians, the memories of the inhuman hatred and humiliating fear which he felt and the recollection of what he did, or felt capable of doing, separates him, like a wall, from civilians. People who do not know about fear and killing appear to the combat soldier like his past world of the Sunday-school. He tries not to take it too seriously, yet it affects him in such a way that his guilt-feelings creep up on him.'[22]

It would be wrong to assume, however, that all acts of killing in wartime elicited such painful responses. On the contrary, many ordinary service personnel found that they could generate pleasure out of acts of extreme violence against other human beings. Combatants were often unabashed about their eagerness to kill. In a letter to his wife on 30 January 1916 from France, Alfred E. Bland wrote:

> 'I am still absolutely buoyant and I love my Company, and all is very well with us, and I am welcoming the change about to come – real business with real Germans in front of us. Oh! I do hope I shall visibly kill a few.'[23]

Without the threat of being killed, killing was even more fun. The Australian, William Nagle, described killing German paratroopers who were trapped inside their planes on Crete:

> 'Not one man jumped from any of the planes that I fired at. I had a feeling of complete exhilaration, full of the hate to kill. I wanted to go on and on. I used up all twenty-four magazines quickly and the rest of the section were filling the empty ones as fast as I emptied them. I could have kissed the Bren with sheer delight but it was too dammed hot to touch.'[24]

Under what circumstances could killing be experienced as exciting, exhilarating even? Clearly the 'outcome' was important. In the aftermath of battle, men were less liable to recall their sense of glee if it was clear that they were on the losing side. Unquestionably, the ultimate failure to protect one's comrades placed a powerful damper on celebrations and giddy bragging. For the victors, however, a certain amount of pleasure could be generated from acts of killing. Excitement did vary according to the branch of service. Air force personnel were most liable to express pleasure in combat. According to one American survey conducted during the Second World War, three-quarters of combat aircrew expressed a willingness to perform further combat duty compared with only two-fifths of combat infantrymen. The more 'personal' the fight, the more combat aircrew enjoyed their job. Thus, when American aerial combat personnel were asked during the Second World War, 'If you were doing it over again, do you think you would choose to sign up for combat flying', 93 per cent of fighter pilots, 91 per cent of pilots of light bombers, 81 per cent of pilots of medium bombers, and 70 per cent of heavy bomber pilots replied 'Yes'.[25] It 'amused' one light bomber to 'see the people running away from under the machine', even though he 'felt sorry when I saw the remains of an ancient city being blown up by my bombs.'[26] Aerial fighters enjoyed 'stalking' their prey. In the words of James Byford McCudden, after shooting down a 'Hun':

> 'I think that this was one of the best stalks that I ever had. I cannot describe the satisfaction which one experiences after bringing a good stalk to a successful conclusion.'[27]

Roderick Chrisholm was a night-fighter in the Royal Air Force during the Second World War. On 13 March 1941 he destroyed two enemy aircraft. The experience (he wrote) could 'never be equalled':

> 'For the rest of that night it was impossible to sleep; there was nothing else I could talk about for days after; there was nothing else I could think about for weeks after … it was sweet and very intoxicating.'[28]

Equally, the Spitfire pilot Flight-Lieutenant D. M. Crook described the 'moments just before the clash' as 'the most gloriously exciting moments of life.' He was 'absolutely fascinated' by the sight of a plane going down and could not pull his eyes away from the sight. The day after shooting down his first plane, he bragged about it to his wife (readers are told that 'she was delighted') and 'with considerable pride' also informed his family of his success.[29]

The metaphors used to express joy in the prowess of killing were different for infantrymen. For them, killing was frequently conceptualised as a sport. Indeed, such myths seemed to legitimate it. Recourse to the gleeful language of adolescent play was coupled with a sense of unreality. The War Office's training manual, *Sniping, Scouting and Patrolling*, described combatants crawling into no-man's-land as 'spend[ing] a jolly evening playing with the enemy working parties'.[30] It was a schoolboys' outing, a 'glorious game' to be wildly cheered as if on some playing field.[31] Or it was like spending time on a shooting range (in the words of C. J. Lodge Patch, 'the killing was good… The rifles and Lewis Guns were hot after the slaughter they had effected; but the men were as cool as if they were on a tactical range, with disappearing targets in front of them. Every Hun head that bobbed up got a bullet through it.'[32] The act of killing was described as 'like cowboys shooting at Indians through the wagon wheels.'[33] Men performed war dances after scoring a hit.[34] In preparing for a raid they would blacken their faces and place feathers in their helmets.[35] This ritual was 'minstrel entertainment' and men vied with each other in their artistry.[36]

More than any other sport, however, battle was conceptualised as similar to game hunting.[37] Souvenirs were portrayed as hunting trophies, generously distributed to wives, girlfriends, sisters or mothers. The words used to describe their actions were carefully chosen from sport: the enemy was not 'killed', but 'had', 'disposed of', or 'exterminated'.[38] The 'enemy' were animals or 'beasts'.[39] When a German was hit, he 'jumped like a shot rabbit'.[40] The enemy were 'specimens' to be 'bagged'.[41] Even more 'personal' forms of killing, such as by the rifle, might be 'as easy as shooting a fox' because 'when you shoot a man you never see his face'.[42] Going to war was the equivalent of being 'blooded'.[43] According to Neil Tytler, gunnery was like stalking, with the exception that when stalking animals the 'head of heads' might be feeding just outside of the guns' range, while in war a 'glorious target' could be only a few hundred yards away and Huns were 'always in season'.[44] Lieutenant Colonel John Campbell led his troops over the top during the Battle of the Somme by sounding his hunting horn. As he explained it: 'I carried my hunting horn because I had always used it for training my men... I don't think that without the help of the horn I could have pulled that attack out of the fire.'[45] In both wars, the ideal infantryman was portrayed as a poacher.[46] For such combatants, the game-hunting metaphor held certain attractions. It ennobled bloody fighters by linking it with traditionally upper-class activities, and could enable a certain degree of emotional distancing. Furthermore, it tied into ideas in common circulation about human nature and warfare: it was in man's instincts to kill. There was no point in feeling guilty for what was inherent in human nature.

Furthermore, servicemen who admitted to wanting to kill, expecting it to be exciting and enjoyable, performed more effectively in the field than their less enthusiastic comrades. Good statistical evidence exists telling us about the way American soldiers in the Second World War experienced the act of killing. During the Second World War, Samuel A. Stouffer and his team of researchers carried out the most comprehensive study of the attitude of American soldiers to combat. His study of their attitude to killing German or Japanese soldiers is particularly enlightening. A year prior to going into combat 309 infantrymen were asked how they would feel about killing a Japanese or a German soldier. A year later, after having experienced combat, their performance in the fray was noted – they were rated as performing 'below average', 'average' or 'above average'. The results can be seen in Table 1 overleaf.

As the table shows, those men who performed particularly well during combat had tended to show, in their training period, attitudes which were 'superior from the Army point of view', as compared with the other men. In other words, they were more likely to regard killing as simply 'part of the job'. The racial element was also prominent. Soldiers were especially keen to kill Japanese soldiers and much less likely to 'feel bad' about it afterwards. The results of this survey were conservative because factors such as education, AGCT scores, mechanical aptitude scores, age and marital condition were held constant in the survey, yet these factors had a major impact on attitudes to killing and combat performance. As Stouffer explained it, 'the more intelligent tend to have the "better" attitudes toward combat, and the more intelligent also get the better ratings on combat performance. If the background factors, therefore, are not held constant, the differences in attitudes between the above average and below average performance groups are somewhat greater.'[47]

A distinction has to be made, however, between these expressions of eagerness for the bloody fray and other rationalisations for killing that combatants adhered to. Irrespective of their emotions upon killing someone, most men claimed to be capable of carrying out this act when faced with the terrifying option: 'kill or be

Table 1
'How Do You Think You Would Feel About Killing a Japanese Soldier?'
Distinguished by their Combat Performance During Training Period
(Percentage Giving Indicated Responses)

Combat Performance Group	Below Average	Average	Above Average
'I would really like to kill a Japanese soldier'	38%	44%	48%
'I would feel that it was just part of the job, without either liking or disliking it'	35%	32%	34%
Some other idea or no answer	7%	2%	0%
'I would feel that it was part of the job, but would still feel bad about killing a man even if he was a Japanese soldier'	16%	18%	17%
'I would feel I should not kill anyone, even a Japanese soldier'	4%	4%	1%
Total Percentage	100%	100%	100%
Total Number Asked	94	120	95

'How Do You Think You Would Feel About Killing a German Soldier?'
Distinguished by their Combat Performance During Training Period
(Percentage Giving Indicated Responses)

Combat Performance Group	Below Average	Average	Above Average
'I would really like to kill a German soldier'	5%	6%	9%
'I would feel that it was just part of the job, without either liking or disliking it'	45%	52%	55%
Some other idea or no answer	4%	2%	3%
'I would feel that it was part of the job, but would still feel bad about killing a man even if he was a German soldier'	41%	34%	32%
'I would feel I should not kill anyone, even a German soldier'	5%	6%	1%
Total Percentage	100%	100%	100%
Total Number Asked	94	120	95

killed'. This rationale was applied, in varying levels of intensity, from the nation to identified strangers ('women and the weak'), to friends, and finally to oneself. As the level of abstraction decreased, the legitimacy of killing increased. Thus, for soldiers on active service, the legitimacy of killing was least convincing when the threat was the nation. This is not to argue that belief in the cause was completely ineffective in justified actions that, in any other context, they would have regarded as abhorrent. In 1918, Coningsby Dawson tried to explain this feeling:

> 'I do not mean to glorify war; war can never be anything but beastly and damnable. It dates back to the jungle. But there are two kinds of war. There's the kind that a highwayman wages when he pounces from the bushes and assaults a defenceless woman; there's the kind you wage when you go to her rescue. The highwayman can't expect to come out of the fight with a loftier morality – you can. Our chaps never wanted to fight. They hate fighting... They entered the war to defend rather than to destroy.'[48]

At all stages of military training and during manoeuvres, officers insisted on the rightness of the cause and emphasised the fact that men were 'just obeying orders'. The 'simple Army conscience' depended upon leaving 'all responsibility on the shoulders of his superior officers' enabling the combatant to 'sleep like a child and awaken refreshed – to kill and fear not.'[49]

The rightness of the cause as an incentive to kill should not be exaggerated. It was the weakest of the rationalisations employed by combatants. It worked very well in getting people to enlist, and it shored up people behind the lines, but in the front lines it had limited usefulness. The efficacy of 'calls to arms' by senior personnel was particularly limited once the gulf between experienced troops and Staff Officers perceived as not having experienced the realities of war had widened. H. S. Taylor described one such occasion when, after two months of duty on the Somme, a new and very senior Staff Officer came to address the battalion. He began his talk with the words, 'I am your new "——" and my motto is "Kill Bosch!"'. The men were not impressed. As Taylor dryly commented: 'This remark was no doubt suitable in other circumstances but it fell rather flat when addressed to remnants of a fine Battalion which had lost virtually all its officers, sergeants and about 300 men.'[50]

More effective was the appeal to the sufferings of 'innocents' – persecuted minorities, woman, and children. The lightly clad corpses of women drowned from the *Lusitania* gave C. A. Brett 'a bitter dislike for all Germans and a desire to kill as many as possible.'[51] The Second World War Spitfire pilot nicknamed 'Bogle' could not decide whether or not to fire at a German gunner who was attempting to bale out of his pilot-less plane. 'Good God, he's stuck!,' Bogle realised, suddenly becoming overwhelmed with nauseous guilt – that is, until he conjured up a vision of 'the people down below, wives, young mothers, kiddies, huddled in their shelters, waiting for the "All Clear",' so he killed the man.[52] The extermination camps of the Second World War had an even greater impact. The black soldier, Captain John Long of an American tank division, recalled 'liberating' one of these camps:

'From this incidence on Jerry was no longer an impersonal foe. The Germans were monsters! I have never found any way to find an excuse for them or any man who would do to people what I saw when we opened the gate to that camp and two others. We had just mopped them up before but we stomped the shit out of them after the camps.'[53]

Chicago schoolteacher Timuel Black agreed. In 1945 his unit arrived at Buchenwald and, appalled by the stench, he roared: 'Let's kill all the son-of-a-bitches. Kill all the goddam Germans. Anyone who would do this to people, they're not worth living.'[54]

More than any other experience, though, witnessing the death of a comrade was guaranteed to cause a welling-up of murderous hatred. W. R. Kirkby was one such soldier. During the Battle of Cambrai in 1917 he saw his closest friend killed. As he put it:

'I was unable to move, so great was the blow his sudden passing inflicted upon me... At long last, so it seemed to me, I snapped into action, my whole being bent upon avenging his death and the deaths and wounds inflicted upon my gallant pals of the 2nd/6th West Yorks. Standing upright I fired round after round through the windowless openings of the houses facing us, my one aim and purpose to destroy the killers within those houses.'[55]

In Burma, during the Second World War, George MacDonald Fraser put it even more strongly. For him, any 'higher thoughts' became irrelevant once the fighting started:

'Putting a grenade into a bunker had the satisfaction of doing grievous bodily harm to an enemy for whom I felt real hatred, and still do. Seeing Gale [a friend] killed shocked me as our first casualties had done, and I think enraged me. I wanted a Jap then, mostly for my own animal pride, no doubt, but seeing Gale go down sparked something which I felt in the instant when I hung on my aim at the Jap with the sword, because I wanted to be sure. The joy of hitting him was the strongest emotion I felt that day.'[56]

Finally, the rage that came with the realisation that 'they' were trying to kill 'me' stung men out of their lethargy. As a man with a bayonet wound below his left groin described it:

'When I finished with him, sir, he wasn't goin' to do any more bayoneting; and he wasn't goin' to shout "kamerado" no more same as he did before he got me. Served me right for trusting a dirty Boche. But after he stuck me I fairly cut him up. Oh, I made sure of him alright.'[57]

With equal fervour, the Rev Harold Augustine Thomas recalled one man who had been wounded 'in a tender part of the body' while visiting the latrine. This wounding transformed a man who had been extremely mild and one who could 'wax elequently [sic] on the brotherhood of man and the iniquity of an appeal to Arms' into a 'revengeful militarist'. He wanted 'blood, rivers of blood, the blood of every Turk on the Peninsula, but particularly the blood of that sniper, his ancestors and progeny to sanguinarily [sic] specified generations.'[58]

Apart from these rationalisations, there was one further element that enabled men to kill: dehumanisation of the enemy. This took two forms. On the one hand, as we saw in the discussion about killing as a sport, there was the simple refusal to regard the enemy as anything 'living'. During the First World War artilleryman Kenneth H. Cousland expressed this view:

'I never thought in terms of killing others ... artillerymen were rarely in personal touch with enemy soldiers. I never came face to face with living Germans except those who had been captured. Sometimes from an OP [Observation Post] we saw moving figures but I never seem to have thought of them as human beings. It was a strange impersonal feeling; they were merely targets.'[59]

The shadowy figure of the enemy running towards you was no more than a 'target figure of the musketry course' or 'tactical range'.[60] Dehumanisation enabled desensitisation.

On the other hand, some soldiers explicitly depersonalised enemy troops as lesser humans or animals. As the historian John W. Dower has shown in his classic *War Without Mercy: Race and Power in the Pacific War* (1986), this was particularly true when the enemy was a racial 'other'.[61] Jo Gullett, for example, fought with the Australian Army during the Second World War. For him, the Japanese soldiers were 'clever animals with certain human characteristics, but by no means the full range.'[62] Such attitudes were deliberately fostered by senior officers keen to stimulate the 'offensive spirit' in their men. Thus General Sir Thomas Blamey encouraged men in an AIF battalion near Port Moresby with the following words:

'You are fighting a shrewd, cruel, merciless enemy, who knows how to kill and who knows how to die. Beneath the thin veneer of a few generations of civilisation he is a sub-human beast who has brought warfare back to the primeval, who fights by the jungle rule of tooth and claw, who must be beaten by the jungle rule of tooth and claw. Kill him or he will kill you.'[63]

It is important not to exaggerate either the extent of dehumanisation or its efficacy in enabling men to kill without guilt. In the front lines (as opposed to training camps) it was often impossible to believe notions of a dehumanised enemy. Even Kenneth Cousland, quoted above, admitted that his comrades did not harbour any 'hard feelings' against the Germans. 'In fact,' he admitted, 'we respected them as brave soldiers, but our job was to defeat and win the war.'[64] Time and time again, combatants recalled that the enemy 'came from families like we came from and that they had loved ones and there were good guys and they were bad guys'.[65] Furthermore, dehumanisation could be counter-productive, as the philosopher, William Hocking, noted in 1918:

'...it is never wise to make him out less than human. For anger ... runs in the opposite direction; it personifies and attributes conscience to even inanimate things. If we dehumanise the foe we remove him from the reach of instinctive indignation.'[66]

In other words, portraying the enemy as a different species diminished any sense that the enemy should be held accountable for his actions, yet it was precisely this accountability that sustained condemnation. During the war against the Japanese in the Second World War, excessive dehumanisation of the enemy ended up being questioned by certain sections of military command. In a report in 1944 on morale in the Far East, Major General Lethbridge warned that atrocity stories might merely make combatants frightened of combat or of having to bale out of hit aeroplanes.[67] Dehumanising the enemy could increase levels of fear by transforming the enemy into 'mysterious wraiths'; men yearned for the reassurance that they were 'flesh and blood', even if this induced feelings of remorse.[68]

Finally, it must be recognised that combatants who admitted to pleasure in combat were not 'aberrant', and their violent fantasies were shared by a wide group of men and women who never got near the killing fields. Only a minuscule proportion of combatants could be classified as psychopaths. Of course, there were some particularly brutal killers who wallowed in the slaughter for its own sake. The British pilot, 'Little Butcher', was one such combatant, but it was precisely his bloodthirsty 'haste to get to his kill' and his 'gloating' over successful hits that repelled his comrades and made them regard him as 'sinister' and 'unpleasant'.[69] Such men were not welcomed in any of the services. As the military psychiatrist William C. Porter argued in *War Medicine* (1941), the 'aggressive type of psychopath is one which the Army can make a good deal of use under certain circumstances'. The problem lay in the fact that a psychopathic serviceman 'stands retreat poorly; he stands monotony very poorly; he stands discipline and teamwork very poorly'.[70] Fundamentally, he was bad for morale. The best men in combat were unexceptional in civilian life.

Furthermore, although the actual act of killing was done by combatants, killing was legitimated and experienced vicariously by civilians as well. H. R. L. Sheppard was converted to pacifism after observing the 'satisfaction' of civilians as they read about enemy losses in the newspapers during the First World War. Their 'delight in vicarious slaughter' profoundly shocked him.[71] Indeed, during both World Wars it was widely feared that women were taking more pleasure in the bloodshed than male combatants. Even the feminist and pacifist Helen Mana Lucy Swanwick ruefully admitted that although men made war, they could not have done so had women not been so adoring of their efforts.[72] Caroline Playne agreed, writing in the early 1930s that the 'souls of women were as much possessed by [military] passion as the souls of men'.[73] The popular press highlighted feminine fondness for the gun. During the Second World War, Miss Marjorie Stevens, a 17-year-old member of the Australian Women's Army Service, begged to be allowed to go overseas: 'I would just like to have a go at the enemy,' she pleaded. 'Give me a rifle and I would be satisfied if I only got one of them!' Similarly, Miss June Buckley of Kings Cross (Sydney) argued, 'Why should women always be asked to be the cooks? I want to go overseas and take my part with the men. Girls in Russia have proved capable fighters and Australian girls could do the same as they have!'[74] Or, in the words of Patricia Pitman, musing on her service during the Second World War in the Auxiliary Territorial Service, 'I'd joined to kill Germans.'[75] Furthermore, the autobiographies of women such as Flora Sandes (an Englishwoman who served in the Serbian Army) and Vee Robinson (an Auxiliary Territorial Service soldier who fired guns at anti-aircraft gun sites) testified to the joy of being a warrior.[76] Peggy Hill, a member of the Women's Royal Navy Service during the Second World War, never got to shoot at anyone, but would have. She volunteered to do rifle training: 'I was quite a good shot,' she recalled. 'It was like playing darts, I thought! And I didn't give it a thought that there might be a person at the other end.'[77] They could also be more bellicose than their husbands. Joyce Carr worked on an AA gun site during the Second World War. She later admitted:

'I never worried about killing when I was on the guns: I wasn't actually killing the Germans, I was killing those that were flying with their bombs. I thought that was good, I really felt that. The only thing Tom [her husband, a bomber pilot] worried about later on was when he saw how much damage he'd done, and how many people were killed. But in war the innocent do suffer, don't they?'[78]

In conclusion, during both World Wars British, American, Canadian and Australian men and women proved themselves capable of degrees of violence that would have been unimaginable in other contexts. There were particular circumstances that made killing easier (such as when the foe was considered to be racially distinctive) and other circumstances that made it more pleasurable (such as when it could be interpreted according to chivalrous codes). However, the ease with which such sentiments could be stimulated, and the complacency with which their experiences of killing were internalised after each conflict are notable. Of course, there were variations between the two wars examined in this chapter. It is probably the case that ideological factors loomed larger in the minds of combatants during the Second World War and were less liable to diminish rapidly as they did in the 1914-18 conflict. Contrary to common belief, it is also the case that face-to-face killing (and the traumas involved in such a fight) was more common during the Second World War than in the First World War, particularly (for Americans) in the War in the Pacific. Those combatants who failed to cope with the aggressive demands being placed upon them were more liable to receive effective help from 1942 onwards than they would have done before this time.

Finally, the greater requirement to kill civilians in the latter war distinguished it from the entrenched battles of the First World War. Such comparisons aside, it is clear that there was considerable continuity in the emotional responses of people to killing during the two World Wars, especially when contrasted with the vast shifts in technology, for instance. Although a majority of combatants may have found military life uncongenial, and a large minority suffered some degree of emotional collapse as a consequence, what is interesting is the ways in which combatants attempted to 'make sense' of the many sudden shifts in their lives and the roles they were expected to play. The slaughter of fellow human beings could elicit feelings of satisfaction and pleasure; that was the dirty secret that dared not be uttered after the war if combatants were to settle back to their calm civilian lives, unbrutalised.

Notes on contributors

Professor Joanna Bourke, Birkbeck College, University of London, UK. Professor Bourke is the author of Dismembering the Male: Men's Bodies, Britain and the Great War (1997), An Intimate History of Killing (1999) as well as books on Irish history and the British working-classes. She is currently writing a history of Fear in the nineteenth and twentieth centuries.

Recommended reading

Bourke, Joanna, *Dismembering the Male: Men's Bodies, Britain, and the Great War* (London and Chicago: Reaktion Books and University of Chicago, 1997)

An Intimate History of Killing: Face-to-Face Killing in Twentieth Century History, London and New York: Granta and Basic Books, 1999)

Caputo, Philip, *A Rumor of War* (London: Macmillan, 1977)

Fussell, Paul, *Killing in Verse and Prose, and Other Essays* (London: Bellew, 1990)

Wartime: Understanding and Behaviour in the Second World War (Oxford: Oxford University Press, 1989)

Glover, Jonathan, *Humanity: A Moral History of the Twentieth Century* (London: Jonathan Cape, 1999)

Keegan, John, *Face of Battle* (London: Cape, 1976)

Travers, Tim, *The Killing Ground: The British Army, the Western Front, and the Emergence of Modern Warfare, 1914-1918* (London: Allen & Unwin, 1987)

Notes

[1] Ivor Gurney, 'The Target', first published in 1919

[2] Entry by Corporal Frederick W., of the 7th Northumberland Fusiliers (The Fighting Fifth), 13 July 1915, in Clifford Nixon, 'A Touch of Memory', p23, in the Imperial War Museum (IWM), Misc 163, Item 2508; a reproduction of a 1915 autograph book belonging to Miss Mabel King, Commandant of the British Red Cross Convalescent Hospital at Halloughton Hall at Whitacre.

[3] Albert N. Depew, *Gunner Depew* (London: Cassell & Co, 1918) p145

[4] Quoted by Harvey Cushing, *From a Surgeon's Journal 1915-1918* (London: Constable & Co, 1936) p489

[5] This unnamed radio operator was killed on his next operational flight; quoted by Canon L. Collins, *Faith Under Fire* (London: Leslie Frewin, 1965) pp85-6

[6] Samuel Lyman Atwood Marshall, 'Men Against Fire: The Problem of Battle Command in Future War' (Washington DC: *Infantry Journal*, 1947) p78

[7] Lieutenant Commander R. A. Cohen and Lieutenant J. G. Delano, 'Subacute Emotional Disturbances Induced by Combat', *War Medicine* 7.5 (May 1945) p286

[8] Lieutenant Colonel J. W. Barnett, 'War Diary', entry for 29 April 1915, IWM 90/37/1

[9] Unnamed young soldier quoted by Rev E. J. Hardy, *The British Soldier: His Courage and Humour* (London: T. Fisher Unwin, 1915) p120

10 Albert N. Depew, op cit, p61

11 Australian soldier, quoted in George H. Johnston, *The Toughest Fight in the World* (New York: Duell, Sloan & Pearce, 1944) p127

12 John Guest, *Broken Images: A Journal* (London: Leo Cooper, 1949) p214

13 Colonel Rowland Feilding, *War Letters to a Wife: France and Flanders, 1915-1919* (London: The Medici Society, 1929) pp45 and 212, letters written on 2 October 1915 and 8 October 1917

14 Letter from an unnamed British officer, dated 19 November 1914, after sniping at four men (and hitting two), in Amy Gordon Grant, *Letters from Armageddon: A Collection Made During the World War* (Boston: Houghton Mifflin Co, 1930) p37, and Victor G. Ricketts, 'Account of his Service', p34, IWM 68/14/1. See also A. J. Turner, 'Zero Hour', p51, IWM 81/21/1

15 Anonymous letter quoted in James J. Fisher, 'The Immortal Deeds of Our Irish Regiments in Flinders and the Dardanelles', No 1, unpaginated (Dublin: Irish Regiments, 1916)

16 Norman Q. Brill and Gilbert W. Beebe, *A Follow-Up Study of War Neuroses* (Washington, DC: US Government Printing Office, 1956) pp222-3

17 For example, see 'A Flying Corps Pilot', *Death in the Air: The War Diary and Photographs of a Flying Corps Pilot* (London: William Heinemann Ltd, 1933) p75, and James Byford McCudden, *Flying Fury* (London: John Hamilton Ltd, 1930; first published 1918) p170

18 Roy R. Grinker and John P. Spiegel, *Men Under Stress* (London: J. & A. Churchill, 1945) p44

19 Samuel A. Stouffer et al, *The American Soldier: Combat and Its Aftermath* Vol II (Princeton: Princeton University Press, 1949) p332

20 Commander B. W. Hogan, 'Psychiatric Observations of Senior Medical Officer on Board Aircraft Carrier USS *Wasp* During Action in Combat Areas, at Time of Torpedoing, and Survivors' Reaction' in *The American Journal of Psychiatry*, 100 (1943-44) p91. He also noted, however, that it was not long before they took this form of killing in their stride.

21 Stanley Johnston, *The Grim Reapers* (London: Jarrolds Publishers, 1945) p39

22 Therese Benedek, *Insight and Personality Adjustment: A Study of the Psychological Effects of War* (New York: The Ronald Press Co, 1946) pp55-6

23 Letter to his wife, 30 January 1916, in Captain Alfred E. Bland, 'Letters to His Wife', IWM 80/1/1

24 William Nagle, 'Do You Remember When?', p7, AWM PR89/148

25 Samuel A. Stouffer et al, op cit, pp333 and 335. The numbers involved in the questions to pilots were 351, 242, 200 and 654 for pilots of heavy bombers, medium bombers, light bombers and fighter planes respectively.

26 Second Lieutenant Harold Warnica Price, 'Diary', in Brereton Greenhous (ed), *A Rattle of Pebbles: The First World War Diaries of Two Canadian Airmen* (Ottawa: Canadian Government Publishing Centre, 1987) p250; diary entry for 17 December 1917

27 James Byford McCudden, op cit, p203. He also admitted, however, to feeling 'very sorry indeed' when seeing the dead pilot. He preferred shooting down planes in 'Hunland' where he could not see 'the results'.

28 Roderick Chrisholm, *Cover of Darkness* (London: Chatto & Windus, 1953) p71

29 Flight-Lieutenant D. M. Crook, *Spitfire Pilot* (London: Faber & Faber Ltd, 1942) pp28, 30-1 and 75

30 *Sniping, Scouting and Patrolling* (Aldershot: HMSO, no date) p23. See also War Office, *The Training and Employment of Bombers* (London: HMSO, 1916) p3

31 W. R. H. Brown, 'The Great War. Descriptive Diary', pp14-15, IWM 81/14/1; Dixon Scott, 'Letters', letter to A. N. Monkhouse, 6 January 1915, in Manchester City Council Local Studies Unit; Sir Geoffrey Vickers, 'Papers', diary of his brother Willie Vickers, 24 November 1916, in Liddell Hart Centre for Military Archives

32 Charles James Lodge Patch, 'Memoir', pp37-38, IWM 66/304/1. See also Kenneth H. Cousland, 'The Great War', p61, Liddell Hart Centre for Military Archives, and E. Gardiner Williams, 'The Last Chapter', p8, Liverpool Records Office, Acc 2175

33 William F. Pressey, 'All for a Shilling a Day', pp132-3, IWM 77/84/1

34 Victor G. Ricketts, op cit

35 Frederick Hunt, 'And Truly Serve', 1980, p22, IWM 88/52/1

36 Alfred Richard Williams, 'Letters from the West [sic] Front', letter to his brother, 10 July 1916, pp68-9, IWM 82/26/1

37 Alexander Catto, *With The Scottish Troops in France* (Aberdeen: Aberdeen Daily Journal Office,

1918) p35; Coningsby Dawson, *The Glory of the Trenches* (London: John Lane, 1918) p12; H. Hesketh-Prichard, *Sniping in France* (London: Hutchinson & Co, 1920, p37; *Sniping, Scouting and Patrolling* (Aldershot: HMSO, no date) p1; A. Douglas Thorburn, *Amateur Gunner: The Adventures of an Amateur Soldier in France, Salonica and Palestine in The Royal Field Artillery* (Liverpool: William Potter, 1933) p155-7; Lieutenant Colonel Neil Fraser Tytler, *Field Guns in France* (London: Hutchinson & Co, 1922) p90, letter on 17 July 1916

38   K. S. Dance, 'Diary', 6 March 1916, IWM 84/58/1; Norman Shaw, 'Papers', letter on 14 July 1916, IWM 84/9/1; Harold Stainton, 'A Personal Narrative of the War', p28, IWM 78/11/1

39   W. R. H. Brown, 'The Great War. Descriptive Diary', pp14-15, IWM 81/14/1, and Gerald V. Dennis, 'A Kitchener Man's Bit', p67, IWM 78/58/1

40   Charles Gordon Templer, 'Autobiography of an Old Soldier', p25, IWM 86/30/1. See also Harold Dearden, *Medicine and Duty: A War Diary* (London: William Heinemann Ltd, 1928) pp60-1

41   Sir Edward Hulse, 'Letters', letter to 'Uncle Mi', 2 February 1915, p3, IWM 86/30/1, and Charles Gordon Templer, op cit, p25

42   Philip Orr, *The Road to the Somme: Men of the Ulster Division Tell Their Story* (Belfast: Blackstaff Press, 1987) p155, quoting R. H. Stewart's reaction to killing during the Battle of the Somme.

43   Harold Stainton, op cit, p12

44   Lieutenant Colonel Neil Fraser Tytler, *Field Guns in France*, op cit, pp131-2, letters dated 10 November 1916 and 8 May 1917

45   Quoted by Captain Lionel Dawson, *Sport in War* (London: Collins, 1936) pp14-6

46   Major Gordon Casserly, *The Training of the Volunteers for War* (London: Hodder & Stoughton, 1915) p75; A. T. Walker, *Field Craft for the Home Guard* (Glasgow: John Menzies & Co Ltd, 1940) p13; General Sir Archibald Wavell, 'Rules and Stratagems of War', in *Wavell, Speaking Generally: Broadcasts, Orders and Addresses in Time of War (1939-43)* (London: Macmillan & Co, 1946) p80, issued July 1942

47   Samuel A. Stouffer et al, op cit, pp34-5

48   Coningsby Dawson, *The Glory of the Trenches* (London: John Lane, 1918) pp119-20

49   Stephen Graham, *A Private in the Guards* (London: Macmillan & Co, 1919) p3

50   H. S. Taylor, 'Reminiscences of the Great War 1914/1918', p9, IWM 80/19/1

51   C. A. Brett, 'Recollections', p3, IWM 78/42/1

52   'Bogle', interviewed in Wing Commander Athol Forbes and Squadron Leader Hubert Allen, *The Fighter Boys* (London: Collins, 1942) p72

53   Captain John Long of the 761st (Tank Division), interviewed in Mary Penick Motley (ed), *The Invisible Soldier: The Experience of the Black Soldier, World War II* (Detroit: Wayne State University Press, 1975) p155

54   Interview with Timuel Black, in Studs Terkel, *'The Good War': An Oral History of World War Two* (London: Hamish Hamilton, 1985) p281

55   W. R. Kirkby, 'The Battle of Cambrai, 1917: I was There', p104, IWM 78/51/1

56   George MacDonald Fraser, *Quartered Safe Out Here: A Recollection of the War in Burma* (London: Harvill, 1992) p86

57   *Great Advance: Tales from the Somme Battlefield* (London: Cassell & Co, 1916) p2. See also R. P. Harker, 'Letters', letter to Freddy, 6 November 1914, IWM Con Shelf

58   Rev Harold Augustine Thomas, 'A Parson-Private with an Aspect of Gallipoli', p43, IWM Con Shelf

59   Kenneth H. Cousland, 'The Great War', p61, Liddell Hart Centre for Military Archives

60   Charles James Lodge Patch, 'Memoir', op cit, p38, and E. Gardiner Williams, 'The Last Chapter', op cit, p8

61   John W. Dower, *War Without Mercy: Race and Power in the Pacific War* (New York: Faber & Faber, 1986)

62   Henry ('Jo') Gullett, *Not as a Duty Only: An Infantryman's War* (Melbourne: Melbourne University Press, 1976) p127

63   General Sir Thomas Blamey, quoted in George H. Johnston, *The Toughest Fight in the World*, op cit, p207

64   Kenneth H. Cousland, 'The Great War', op cit

65   Elliott Johnson interviewed in Studs Terkel, *The Good War*, op cit, p259

66   William Ernest Hocking, *Morale and Its Enemies* (New Haven: Yale University Press, 1918) pp56-

8. See also Professor H. J. Laski, *The Germans – Are They Human? A Reply to Sir Robert Vansittart* (London: Victor Gallancz, 1941) pp3-6

67 'Morale (Far Eastern) Inter-Services Committee: Interim Report: Second Draft', 1944, p4, in PRO WO32/11195. See also 'Morale (Far Eastern) Inter-Services Committee: Minutes of the Eighth Meeting Held in Room 433, Hobart House, on Wednesday, 16th August, 1944', pp4 and 7, PRO WO32/11195

68 Philip Caputo, *A Rumor of War* (London: Macmillan, 1977) p124. See also p109

69 Boyd Cable, *Air Men O' War* (London: John Murray, 1918) pp165 and 176

70 William C. Porter, 'Military Psychiatry and the Selective Services', *War Medicine* 1.3 (May 1941) p370

71 H. R. L. Sheppard, *We Say 'No': The Plain Man's Guide to Pacifism* (London: John Murray, 1935) p74

72 Helen Mana Lucy Swanwick, *I Have Been Young* (London: Victor Gollancz Ltd, 1935) p246

73 Caroline Playne, *Society at War 1914-1916* (London: George Allen & Unwin Ltd, 1931) p143

74 Both cited by Ann Howard, *You'll Be Sorry!* (Sydney: Tarka Publishing, 1990) p155

75 Patricia Pitman, 'Private Hatred', in Mavis Nicholson, *What Did You Do in the War, Mummy? Women in World War II* (London: Chatto & Windus, 1995) p172. She was disappointed that she was only able to 'kill them through my Morse Code'. She had wanted a more intimate aggressive role on AA guns but did not have sufficient knowledge of mathematics.

76 Vee Robinson, *On Target* (Wakefield, West Yorkshire: Verity Press, 1991) p44. She was also anxious to be allowed to do more rifle training (p40); Flora Sandes, *The Autobiography of a Woman Soldier* (London: H. F. & G. Witherby, 1927); Flora Sandes, *An English Woman-sergeant in the Serbian Army* (London: Hodder & Stoughton, 1916)

77 Peggy Hill, 'Wartime Bride', in Mavis Nicholson, op cit, p131

78 Joyce Carr, 'Just Like William', in Mavis Nicholson, op cit, p112

Chapter 17

The experience of captivity: British and Commonwealth prisoners in Germany

Peter H. Liddle and S. P. Mackenzie

In both World Wars large numbers of men taken prisoner endured ill-treatment; but making legitimate comparisons on the experience of that treatment is fraught with difficulty. From one war to the next, frequently the captor was different, the circumstance and location too, so that only the degree of harshness remains for evaluation. Yet can one fairly compare what British and Indian Army other ranks suffered after the fall of Kut to the Turks with what servicemen from all arms, all ranks and many countries, underwent following captivity by Japanese forces? Even for Germans and Russians captured by their opposite numbers, the Second World War's ideological base marks off as distinct a captivity that, in any case, given the sheer scale of numbers involved and seasonal and supply logistics, was unlikely to be anything better than grim. However, for British and Commonwealth servicemen captured by Germans, several factors legitimise comparative study. The numbers of men involved are similar, just over 170,000 for the First War and just over 192,000 for the Second; we have the same nationality of captor, and, of great significance, there is an abundance of evidence for both wars. Accordingly, in this chapter an attempt will be made through an examination of this evidence to determine to what extent there were similarities and dissimilarities in the experience of British and Empire/Commonwealth prisoners of the Germans in the First and Second World Wars.

What, though, do we mean by 'experience'? The answer offered here is what impinged on the body and mind of the prisoner of war at capture, during interrogation, the journey towards incarceration, in camps with regard to food, work, recreation and exercise, parole, escape, the possibility of neutral country internment and repatriation, medical care, morale, collaboration, German reprisal action, relations with the Germans (both military and civilian), and the circumstances of final release.

Perhaps the most dangerous moment for a man seeking to surrender is the point at which he offers the white flag or raises his hands, thereby putting himself entirely at the mercy of the enemy. If the fighting were to have been particularly close and intense, if it were to have seemed dangerous or impractical to take prisoners, or if the enemy were under the impression that the other side has not been 'fighting fair', then on occasion prisoners, if taken at all, might not live long.[1] However, with some atrocious collective exceptions – the slaughter of men of the Royal Warwickshire Regiment in 1940 and some Canadians in Normandy in 1944 – in both wars the majority of British POWs survived the first few crucial hours of captivity, even if bullied and robbed of personal possessions.

'The ever-gallant Huns,' Corporal C. E. Green, Scots Guards, wrote in a secret diary shortly after his capture in October 1914, 'made us go on our knees, and proceeded to take our money, tobacco, cigarettes etc from us.' Those found with German money on them 'were very roughly handled'. Yet it was often noted that front-line troops, men who had shared the rigours of combat, tended to have more sympathy for the plight of the prisoner than blustering rear-area types. Donald Laird, a trooper in the 7th Canadian Mounted Rifles, after being wounded in the leg in June 1916, found himself on a stretcher in a German communication trench. A 'German soldier, a lad of not more than seventeen, came up to the side of my stretcher,' he remembered, 'and … dropped a couple of cigarettes and several pieces of loaf sugar on the blanket which covered me.' Private E. Ayling, Sussex Regiment, captured by a panzer unit in October 1942 at El Alamein, recalled that the 'German was quite decent, and offered us cigarettes, and a little water, an unexpected gesture'. Even more unexpected – indeed exceptional – were the actions of the German NCO who captured Lieutenant J. A. Brewster, Royal Fusiliers, in May 1915 near Ypres. Having struck up a friendship with the wounded lieutenant while they were both stranded in a shell-hole, Egbert Wagner carried out a promise he made to send a letter to Brewster's father via a contact in Denmark, informing him of his son's 'deliverance' into captivity. Such small acts of kindness, though, tended to disappear as prisoners were moved rearward. 'I found that the further we got behind the line,' Captain L. McNaught-Davis of the Lincolnshire Regiment remembered of his capture near Loos in September 1915, 'and away from the scenes of war and strife, so the enmity and hostility against us increased.'[2]

The interrogation experience, usually the next rite of passage, varied a lot. When the German Army was advancing quickly, such as in March 1918 and May 1940, the questioning of soldiers could be cursory or non-existent, any knowledge of dispositions they might possess being rendered useless by the rapidly changing tactical situation. When the front was more static, intelligence officers often wanted to know as much as possible about the units they faced. Those prisoners with technical knowledge, such as airmen, were subject to close questioning. Interrogation usually took place at formation HQs from brigade to divisional level or at naval bases, with the Luftwaffe centralising the process for Allied airmen by creating a special interrogation transit camp (Dulag Luft) just outside Frankfurt am Main in the Second World War.

There were a few instances of threats, and quarters being made uncomfortable in a bid to obtain information[3], but the main weapon in the German arsenal appears to have been guile and unsettling displays of background knowledge. N. A. Birks, an RFC officer wounded and shot down in April 1917, was questioned by an elderly major in Douai hospital. 'He asked me the number of my squadron and its location, and when I would not tell him he said he knew and showed me an aerial photo of our field which must have been taken during the last four weeks as our new firing range was shown on it.' The rationale for this approach was spotted by Pilot Officer George Atkinson, whose interrogator at Dulag Luft in August 1943 'tried to give the impression that they knew a great deal and there was no use my withholding further information as they knew so much.'[4]

Such efforts, however, were mostly in vain and occasionally self-defeating. E. N. Allan, an infantry officer captured in April 1917, recalled how he misled his interrogator about the location of his unit, using a map provided at divisional HQ 'to lead him well away in the wrong direction'. More consequential were the successful efforts of an RAF prisoner to convince his interrogators that Allied success in sinking U-boats in 1943 was due to a spurious ability to home in on a radar warning device rather than – as was actually the case – success in codebreaking.[5]

In both wars the journey from the battlefield to camps in Germany ranked among the worst periods of captivity. When the front was relatively stable and close to Germany, and when limited numbers of prisoners were being taken with a well-developed system worked out for their disposal, travel on foot and by rail to POW camps could be uncomfortable but bearable. For the majority of prisoners, though, the thousands of soldiers taken in big offensives, the journey into Germany was usually a gruelling experience.

Prisoners were sometimes on the march for weeks, food and water being extremely short, shelter inadequate, and the escorting guards occasionally brutal. 'As the days went by,' Private R. P. Evans of the Worcestershire Regiment remembered of the march from Dunkirk in 1940, 'some men began to weaken, and I saw one man shot by the roadside because he had collapsed and could not get up again.'[6] Efforts to provide British prisoners with food and drink by sympathetic civilians in the occupied countries were almost always blocked. 'Uhlans formed the escort,' Lieutenant M. H. Abram, Royal Field Artillery, wrote of his experience in November 1914, 'and employed their lances for beating off Belgian or French women who tried to give us food, hitting them anywhere.'[7] Private E. B. Davis, King's Own Royal Regiment, remembered how near Maastricht in June 1940 local nuns set out tables with sandwiches. 'To our helpless disgust the guards forced us at rifle point to pass by on the other side of the road while they loaded up on "our" sandwiches.'[8]

Once POW columns reached a railhead or port, conditions grew, if anything, tougher. Other ranks prisoners, including the wounded, and often officers as well, were packed into enclosed cattle-type trucks, river barges or ships, and sent off on journeys that could last a week or more. 'There was no room to lie down, or even for nearly all the men to sit down,' Lance-Corporal J. Abbott of the Dorset Regiment, captured in the autumn of 1914, recalled of an experience in a cattle truck matched by thousands of others in both wars.[9] Almost suffocated or frozen, depending on the season, still only receiving sporadic nourishment, and usually without sanitary facilities, POWs in these trucks were in a state of misery and degradation. 'Several men with diarrhea [sic] relieved themselves as best they could,' Sergeant John Brown, Royal Artillery, later wrote of his unfortunately quite typical experience in 1940. 'The stench was unbelievable.'[10]

The ultimate destination for prisoners was one of many dozens of established POW camps in German territory; one set for the officers, the other – usually larger and more spartan – for the men. As well as purpose-built hutted camps complete with floodlights, guard towers and wire fences, the German authorities pressed into service old fortresses, castles, barracks, schools, and a variety of other structures as Kriegsgefangelageren.

Camp conditions varied, though practically all camps became overcrowded. In the 1914-18 war, high standards at Friedrichsfeld distinctly impressed a neutral observer. Conversely, conditions at Minden justified its poor reputation among other ranks prisoners.[11] Officer camps also varied. Augustabad, for example, was rated one of the best places to be in 1915. 'The camp was a hotel which had been converted,' Captain J. L. Hardy of the Connaught Rangers later wrote, a lager where 'our rooms were clean and comfortable.'[12] The camp at Ingolstadt, on the other hand, an old semi-underground fort, was described by a neutral visitor as 'poorly lighted and damp' and as having 'a gloomy, cheerless, depressing atmosphere.'[14] Twenty years on there was still the same variation. The other ranks camp at Lamsdorf (Stalag VIIIB) had the reputation of being 'the worst camp in Germany.'[15] One inmate described it as 'dirty' and 'depressing', another as 'a terrible place'.[16] For army officers, the worst regular camp was probably Warburg (Oflag VIB) in 1941-42, vermin-ridden and short of facilities (though one officer remembered it as being not 'all that bad'[17]). The small and well-run Navy camp at Westertimke (Marlag Nord) had a very positive reputation – 'the best camp in Germany'[18] – while conditions in the Luftwaffe camps were often better than in their Army equivalents. Sergeant Albert Jones, transferred from Lamsdorf to Stalag Luft III at Sagan, recalled that it 'was like moving off the gutters into a luxurious hotel.'[19]

Among the worst places in both wars were reprisal camps, created in response to supposed Allied mistreatment of German POWs. In 1917 hundreds of British soldiers were kept under very harsh conditions in working camps within range of Allied guns after reports appeared of German prisoners being kept too near the front in France. When one such party was sent back to Germany, an observer remembered that 'they were in a shocking state, literally skin and bone, hardly able to walk, and quite worn out physically and mentally.'[20] There were also strafe camps for officers, such as an underground fort at Thorn, a dark and dank place alive with vermin in which 500 officers were confined for six weeks in 1941 in retaliation for the supposedly primitive conditions endured by German prisoners in Fort Henry, Ontario. 'The living conditions were appalling,' one inmate remembered.[21]

Those in regular camps could also suffer from retaliatory moves, such as the withdrawal of certain privileges and amenities at Holzminden in 1917 and Oflag VIIB (Eichstätt) in 1945 due to adverse reports on certain British camps, or the large-scale shackling of Canadian and British prisoners in various camps that occurred in 1942-43 in response to the tying of German prisoners' hands after capture. As Captain H. C. Durnford, a Royal Artillery officer subject to the Holzminden strafe later wrote, 'reprisals as a means for one belligerent to stop the malpractices of another' seemed to him and other POWs concerned 'a poor arrangement at best.'[22]

The single most important factor in the life of a POW in both World Wars was food. The rations provided by the Germans – usually involving cups of acorn coffee, bowls of watery soup, thin slices of black bread, small jacket potatoes and other root vegetables, along with the occasional issue of unidentified bits of meat or preserved fish, cheese, and dabs of margarine and synthetic jam – were both minuscule in quantity and nasty in taste. At points when this was the only sustenance available for any length of time, vitamin deficiencies and semi-starvation set in. 'Anyone who heedlessly got up from his bunk,' Sergeant Richard Passmore wrote of such a time in the winter of 1940-41 at Stalag Luft I (Barth), 'was likely to black out and find himself lying on the floor.'[23] Luckily, as long as the routes were open and no recent moves had taken place, registered British prisoners would usually receive Red Cross and other parcels from home after several months. The parcels contained enough condensed milk, sugar, tea, biscuits and sundry tins of food to keep body and soul together. 'We depended on the parcels, could hardly have survived without them,' Private Maxwell Bates, Middlesex Regiment, later reflected, 'and it would be difficult to over-estimate their value to us.'[24] One Red Cross parcel per week, according to Leading Seaman James Laurie, incarcerated in the seamen's compound at Marlag Nord, was enough 'to live reasonably well', and at certain junctures parcels might be plentiful enough for the more discriminating to dispense with German rations altogether.

'We didn't bother about the German food at all,' Corporal J. E. Draper, Royal Fusiliers, remembered of his life as a Kriegsgefanger in the summer of 1917, 'except there were times when we had to when there was a hold-up in parcels for some reason or other.' Most of the time parcels were not available on a scale to allow this, and food always remained at the forefront of prisoners' thoughts in both wars.[25]

POWs might also on occasion seek solace in alcohol or at least the excitement of its association with freedom. At times, in both wars, weak beer and wine could sometimes be purchased from the camp canteen, but hard liquor could only be obtained through illicit stills built out of everything from musical instruments to lavatory pipes. The resulting alcohol, made from ingredients as diverse as shoe polish and dried fruit, was often tremendously potent – 'like drinking TNT' was how one sailor characterised it – and could sometimes cause blindness or even death.[26] In 1944 Sergeant H. E. Wooley and some friends at Stalag Luft IV attempted to create a form of vodka, the final product being poured into a metal basin and left overnight. The next morning, 'The whole area around bed was damp and smelled vaguely of disinfectant. I picked up the basin. It was pitted and corroded, full of tiny pinprick-sized holes.'[27]

In both wars it was accepted that other ranks POWs could be legitimately utilised as labour within the captor state, with NCOs able to volunteer if they so wished. The result was a host of large and small working parties, administered from the main camps but paid for and housed by civilian contractors, in which prisoners served as manual labourers of one kind or another six days a week. Prisoners of war were not, needless to say, the most motivated of workers, and tried to do as little as possible. Sir Frederick Corfield, Royal Artillery, out on a parole walk in 1944, witnessed a favoured tactic:

'I vividly recall … when we passed a party of British other ranks supposedly working on a drainage project but in fact giving a splendid example of typical British bloody-mindedness when in a difficult situation by studiously playing the "idiot boy". Whatever efforts the Germans made to explain what was required they were greeted by a row of totally blank faces murmuring "nicht verstehen" (don't understand) until in desperation the Germans themselves took off their jackets, rolled up their sleeves and leapt into the trench to demonstrate – a wag amongst our troops commenting, "That's right; you are the master race; you do it"! Although we were hurried on by our escort, it must have been a further twenty minutes or so before our "working party" was out of sight. They were still standing, arms folded, watching the Germans hard at work with pick and shovel.' [28]

Illnesses were faked, strikes organised, and furtive sabotage missions undertaken. Sometimes such manoeuvres were successful, but there were real risks. Prisoners refusing to work, seen malingering, or caught in acts of sabotage, risked being beaten up, starved, and court-martialled. 'If we tried to protest,' remembered Private F. Cunnington, captured in March 1918 and put to work on a party unloading shells behind the lines, 'we were told to get on with it and if we didn't we got the butt end of a rifle.' Private William Walsh was given six years' penal servitude in November 1942 by a military court at Danzig for 'destruction to an important public supply undertaking.' [29]

The best Arbeitskommandos were generally those on farms, where more food was usually available and an acceptable modus vivendi could be established with the farmer and his family. The working parties that everyone tried to avoid were coal- or salt-mine gangs, where the work was hard and dangerous and employers often vindictive. In January 1917, for example, Corporal Green witnessed a far from rare incident in which pickaxe-handle-wielding overseers beat two prisoners senseless for daring to argue. 'When a prisoner became a miner,' a New Zealander concluded after being posted to a Silesian pithead in 1944, 'he had reached the end of the line.' [30] Self-inflicted wounds were sometimes resorted to as a means of avoiding mine work. [31]

The edict against officers being made to work was a mixed blessing, as it greatly magnified a problem that all prisoners faced: how to make time hang less heavily. The routines of camp existence were inherently dull and repetitive, with all the important decisions being made by the captors. Prisoners therefore looked for individual and organised diversion.

One way for POWs to pass the time was to read, and camp libraries – made up largely of volumes obtained through aid societies – were popular. Linked to this was the opportunity to study. Starting with ad hoc lectures on whatever subjects individual prisoners knew something about, the intellectual side of POW life eventually became highly elaborate, with prisoners able through correspondence courses to read and sit for exams for a variety of educational and professional certificates by the latter years of the Second World War. The only large-scale First War parallel for this was in the civilian internment camp at Ruhleben near Berlin. Foreign languages were particularly popular among officers with time on their hands. Study, though, had its limitations. Camps were crowded places, and the necessary peace and quiet difficult to obtain. 'Let the reader imagine if he can,' Captain Gilliland wrote concerning study at Minden in 1915, 'trying to learn a foreign tongue with the whole of the rest of the people in his room babbling aloud other languages.' It also took willpower, and in most cases only the exceptionally self-motivated would stay the course.[32]

Music and the theatre also offered scope for distraction in the main camps. Gramophones and records, together with musical instruments, all purchased from the Germans or obtained through the YMCA or Red Cross from home, allowed for music appreciation and performance groups of all kinds. Where there was space to develop some sort of stage, theatrical performances were also popular, with light comedy and musical revues usually taking pride of place. 'After you get used to the big feet, hands and deep voices of the "females",' Flight Lieutenant Geoffrey Willatt noted in his Stalag Luft III diary in November 1943, 'the theatre shows are the brightest spot in the camp, and it is possible to forget for a bit.'[33] There is no doubt whatsoever that preoccupation with dramatic or musical productions of one sort or another did not just ease away idle hours but also stimulated creativity that for some had life-lasting significance. A superb example of this was piano-playing Gordon Jacob, First War officer POW, for whom responsibility for entertaining his fellow prisoners fixed him upon a career of the utmost distinction in musical composition and teaching.[34] Relatedly it should not be presumed that it was exclusively in officers' camps where dramatic productions of excellence were achieved. Photographs surviving of the sets for the plays and shows in Stalag 344 indicate the high standards consistently reached. In the photograph of the cast, incidentally, at least one actor of later fame can be discerned – Denholm Elliott.[35]

Other activities also provided satisfaction, notably card games, with bridge being especially popular among officers. Commander Peter Buckley, thinking about his time at Westertimke, recalled that 'most of the day was [spent] playing cards.'[36] Hobbies of various other kinds were also pursued, including painting, wood carving and gardening. Team sports were very popular when men were fit enough to undertake them. 'We had as much sporting activity as we could arrange,' Sergeant James 'Dixie' Deans, a leading figure at Stalag Luft I in early 1941, remembered.[37] The games played varied according to nationality and class. Football, needless to say, was commonly the sport of choice in the men's camps. Materials for these and other diversions were either home-made, purchased from the Germans through the canteen (where pencils, combs and other personal items could be bought) or obtained through the YMCA. Perhaps the most common form of exercise involved walking circuits around the inside of the camp perimeter.

Officers were also on occasion offered the opportunity to take escorted walks beyond the confines of their camps if they were willing to give their parole – that is, promise not to use the opportunity to make a break for it. In the Great War such walks were not uncommon. The frequency of such walks varied and if the terms laid out seemed unduly humiliating, officers might refuse to sign, as was the case at Holzminden for a time.[38] At Augustabad, Captain J. C. Thorn of the 1st Canadian Contingent remembered, 'nearly every day, by giving their word of honour they would not escape, [officers] were permitted to play in the morning outside the camp for two hours, and when the weather permitted, one could go for a walk of two hours in the surrounding country.' Captain Douglas Lyall Grant of the London Scottish reported that batches of 40 POWs were allowed out twice a week from Gütersloh, while Lieutenant Douglas Harvey, 4th Canadian Mounted Rifles, remembered only four parole walks over seven months at a military hospital in Cologne.[39] Such activity was much appreciated, as in Thorn's words it 'helped very much to keep the officers in fairly good health, and to pass a little time.'[40] Parole in the Second World War was more problematic, with frequent arguments about the precise terms of the agreements prisoners were to sign and many officers refusing to do so.[41] There were, however, still instances of such excursions, as at Oflag IXA/H, where Captain John Phillips, Argyll & Sutherland Highlanders, recalled limited parole being given to allow for games and other activities beyond the confines of Spangenberg Castle.[42]

In both wars there were those determined to break out and get home. 'I was getting restless,' wrote Captain Thorn of life after a short time at Bischofswerda in 1915. 'For a man full of energy this kind of life did not suit, and I set about thinking how I could best get out of the camp.' Flight Lieutenant John Wilson, also an inveterate escaper, could not explain why he did what he did in the Second World War – 'I don't have a bloody clue' – except to say, 'It just seemed to me something that one had to do.'[43] But, given the odds against making a home run, the difficulties and risks involved, such dedicated escapers were in a minority in most camps. 'I don't think many people contemplated escape, quite frankly,' reflected a Royal Marine, Edward Marshall, on his years on working parties attached to Stalag IVA. Officially it was considered a prisoner's duty to try to escape. 'As against this,' Sergeant Richard Passmore (Stalag Luft I) explained, 'many of us felt that we had already taken enough risks for our country.' Indeed, since attempts at getting away were invariably followed by the withdrawal of privileges, they sometimes struck more sedate POWs as acts of juvenile selfishness. Captain Hardy, trying to break out of Magdeburg in 1916, found that 'one was made to feel not quite a gentleman. It simply was not done to break out of camps.' Corporal Graham Palmer, sent to Lamsdorf after an escape bid from an Arbeitskommando in 1941, was upbraided by a British CSM for having made things worse for his fellows. Lieutenant Hugh Bruce, Royal Marines, later claimed that no less a person than the Senior British Officer at Marlag warned him when he planned to make a break in 1941 that 'the camp was very stable, and he didn't want anything to disturb that situation'.[44]

It should be pointed out that however much they may have resented the hard-core escapers, other POWs rarely tried actively to interfere. Sergeant Derek Thrower, planning to make a break from a quarrying party in 1941, found that his fellow workers from the 51st Highland Division were 'unsettled' by his determination; but, significantly, 'nobody tried to dissuade me.'[45] Moreover, beyond the hard-core types was a much larger group of prisoners for whom digging tunnels, dispersing sand, forging passes, making civilian clothes, constructing wire-cutters, and keeping an eye out for guards while others worked, were yet other means of making time pass more quickly. At Stalag Luft III it was calculated that while half the prisoners were not themselves interested in escaping at all, and only 5 per cent were hard-core types, 95 per cent were willing to stooge or perform other escape-related tasks.[46] Even though he correctly guessed 'it would never come to fruition', Hugh Bruce was willing to work on a tunnel scheme at Oflag VIIC (Laufen) in the spring of 1941, because it 'was something that I quite enjoyed.'[47] Escape attempts therefore did take place in most camps, and were indeed a dominant influence at Ingolstadt in the First World War and Colditz in the Second, where the Germans sent their most rambunctious charges. Everywhere, however, the principal factor in escaping was the ingenuity and bravery of the men involved in carrying through tunnel projects, wire jobs, gate schemes, train jumps, and sundry variations. Getting out and, especially, getting home, however, required, in addition, an enormous amount of luck. Of the 15,000 RAF aircrew held in Germany during the Second World War, less than 30 made it to a neutral country.[48]

There was also the possibility of neutral internment and repatriation through international negotiation. Following on from a 1916 agreement, several thousand seriously ill and disabled British POWs were allowed to spend the remainder of the Great War in the far more congenial atmosphere of Switzerland. Those clearly unable to fight again were eventually repatriated, and in 1918 prisoners who had been more than three years in captivity were offered the chance of internment in Holland. The equivalent in the Second World War involved exchanges of the most sick or disabled cases through neutral ports, beginning in October 1943, during which several thousand such British prisoners made their way home.[49]

For such men, hopes, naturally enough, ran high – and were all too often dashed. 'I cannot describe the change that took place in our hut,' wrote Trooper Harry Laird of the mood at Stendal in October 1916 when a Swiss medical commission came to determine who was eligible for neutral internment. 'There were but few who could hope to be passed for exchange, or even hope for the consideration of the Commission, but every man tried to make himself believe that he would be passed, that he was as good as passed already, and nothing could shake that faith.' Some prisoners took a more active approach. 'One or two were included,' Sergeant Moreton recalled after a commission visit to Stalag VIIIB in 1944, 'who pretended to be insane. Their acts were most convincing, so they were passed.' Hard-core escapers, however, were not enthusiastic about internment in Holland. Captain Hardy related that 'not a few of us regarded the prospect with horror', the problem being that 'once in Holland one lost all right to attempt to escape, and we felt that our only hope of future happiness lay in freeing ourselves before the end.'[50]

The medical treatment afforded POWs in both wars – some recovering from wounds, a few developing barbed-wire psychosis, all vulnerable to disease through crowding and lack of food – was mixed. German doctors did not always appear particularly competent to British patients, such as Captain Gilliland, who eventually learned that the civilian doctor who made bi-weekly visits to Bischofswerda in 1915-16 had consistently mis-diagnosed his chest complaint. Working POWs who reported sick often received short shrift from German doctors who suspected they were shirking, even in cases where men were really quite ill. 'Young Davis was a bad case,' Corporal Green noted in his secret diary of a fellow POW working in the mines. 'He was in Beuthen hospital for three weeks, and was only out for a few days when he had to return. On January 3 1916 we had a surprise to hear he was dead on New Year's Day. He was only a youngster.' Private

McGowan, Black Watch, remembered the POW hospital in West Prussia in which he found himself in the spring of 1918 as 'an awful place. The prisoners were starved; I had nearly two months in the place and I nearly died with hunger.'[51] Yet Gilliland admitted that once his problem was correctly identified – shell splinters lodged in the lung – the operative treatment he received at a Dresden hospital 'was of the very best'. There were at least some German doctors willing to give working prisoners the benefit of the doubt, and Captain McNaught-Davis found that for the most part German physicians 'earned the respect of their patients'.[52] Camp hospitals, largely run by British medical personnel, were usually good but suffered acutely from shortages of medicine and other essentials.[53]

British POW doctors had mixed opinions of enemy medical personnel in the Second World War, as did many prisoners. Many German doctors, however, were second to none. As Herbie Pennock has written: 'I still had septic sores on my legs from Italy. I got first class treatment by the German doctor [ie Army Doctor]. He took thirty-two pieces of shrapnel and one spent bullet from my legs, and after two weeks I was able to go without bandages at all.' Later, having been struck by a camp guard, Pennock arrived at the coal pit where he was labouring, his right ear bleeding badly. He was ordered by the pit boss to go to the industrial concern's medical officer. 'The German doctor pumped all the blood from my ear, sent for a mug of tea for me, then we had an hour's chat. The doctor had been at Oxford University before the war.'[54]

Despite every effort to keep mind and body occupied, being a POW could scarcely be an uplifting experience and was sometimes utterly dispiriting. Harsh conditions at various points, combined with uncertainty about the duration of the war, could have a negative effect on morale. Lack of information only tended to feed the rumour mill. 'We knew nothing,' Corporal Edwards wrote of life at Giessen in 1915, 'and could only speculate on the outcome of the commonest events which came to us on the tongue of rumour or arose from our own sad thoughts.' As Martin Lidbetter, an ambulance unit member, reported in a letter from Lamsdorf in 1943, 'Somebody overhears a chance remark … immediately two-million soldiers are in France, or the Russians are shelling Warsaw, or Turkey declared war on Germany … and everyone in camp knows about it within an hour.'[55] Newly arrived POWs found themselves deluged with questions about outside events.[56]

Aware of the significance of war news to prisoners, the Germans, in both wars, attempted to undermine morale through specially produced English-language newspapers, respectively *The Continental Times* and *The Camp*, in which German victories and Allied defeats were disproportionately magnified. Neither paper was particularly effective as propaganda, though issues did have their uses. As Sergeant Passmore noted: 'The texture [of *The Camp*], at least, was excellent.'[57] A better picture of events could be gleaned from German newspapers, though 'you had to read between the lines' as Second Lieutenant J. H. Birkinshaw unsurprisingly pointed out.[58] While the press was much more tightly controlled during the Second World War, POWs in permanent camps usually had a better source of information: the BBC news, taken from illicit radio sets (built from bits and pieces bought from guards) and passed on.[59]

Perhaps even more important to morale were personal letters received from loved ones. 'The immediate impulse,' Lieutenant Joseph Lee wrote of receiving his first letter at Karlsruhe in 1917, 'was to retire with it ... [and] devour it, and for days one was continually impelled to a re-perusal.' Sergeant H. E. Wooley, who spent the years 1941-45 in a variety of camps, explained that such letters 'were all-important in reassuring men that some sort of normal life still existed'.[60] The inevitable 'Dear John' letters were of course devastating, though in the RAF camps the practice was to pin the offending item on a notice-board. 'The effect was oddly therapeutic,' Richard Passmore wrote, 'all your friends understood and sympathised.'[61] Though letters were censored, writing home was also important, the use of codes allowing some to pass on information and requests that would otherwise have been blocked.[62]

War news, however it was obtained, could either depress or help boost morale. The death of Lord Kitchener in 1916, for instance, struck Corporal Edwards as a 'terrible blow' as it did Lieutenant Hardy. The late summer and autumn of 1940 was a 'low period' at Oflag VIIC (Laufen) according to Lieutenant Jim Rogers, in part because it looked as if Britain might lose the war. Signs of Allied progress, however, such as D-Day, lifted spirits. As Sergeant Geoff Taylor, incarcerated at Stalag IVB (Muhlberg) in 1944 summed up, 'Morale fluctuates with the tempo of the fighting in France.'[63]

Of some importance in maintaining morale, especially in tough times, were well-led religious services. During the Great War the periodic visits paid to camps by the cheerful Mr Williams, a civilian chaplain resident in Germany, were noted by Captain Gilliland as 'one of the few bright spots', a sentiment echoed by Lieutenant Douglas. 'The Psalms are a great comfort in captivity,' Private A. Beaumont remembered of lay readings on an Arbeitskommando in 1918. It was the same 20 years later. 'I cannot find words to express what these services meant to us,' wrote Private James Stedman of his time at Stalag XXIA (Schedberg) in 1942.[64] Attending, however, was not always a sign of deepening spirituality. Without church on Sundays to end the week, Captain McNaught-Davis explained, 'captivity [at Rosenberg] would have proved a very monotonous existence – not knowing one day from another.' While being 'very conscious of our attendance at religious gatherings', Padre David Read recalled that, as soon as Red Cross parcels began to arrive, attendance dropped off. Cyril Scarborough, also a padre at Oflag VIIC, later stressed that 'it's a mistake to think that POWs are good at practising their religion – they're not.'[65] In both World Wars it seems that while there were men who consistently held to their faith, in the main the prisoner, like the fighting soldier, took his religion as and when he needed it.

In both wars the Germans made efforts to persuade POWs to collaborate, either en masse or as individuals. Very few chose to do so. At Giessen, for example, thousands of POWs were offered various incentives in 1916 to join an Irish Brigade, but only 17 volunteered. 'About a week afterward,' Sergeant Arthur Gibbons recalled, 'these 17 men were called out, but in the meantime the other Irish prisoners had heard all about it, so it was not surprising that the 17 were unfit for service in the "Kaiser's Own" or for that matter anyone else's own. The other Irishmen in the camp had seen to that.'[66] Efforts to obtain men for the British Free

Corps in 1944 were equally ineffective; the reaction of POWs on a working party from Stalag IVA to the arrival of two recruiters, as recalled by Edward Mine, being quite typical: 'They were told to clear off in no uncertain terms.'[67]

In betraying escape plans, individual collaborators could be a problem, but once identified they became marked men. Private Steve Mitchell remembered how at Stalag IXC (Molsdorf) one such traitor had to be removed quickly by his handlers: 'By that time he was half dead from the beating the French Canadians gave him.' At Lamsdorf in 1944 an informer gave a tunnel away. 'One morning, some time later,' Sergeant Bill Jackson wrote, 'a khaki-clad body was found floating in the emergency water pool.'[68] Equally insidious were the small numbers of NCOs in positions of authority who co-operated rather too zealously with their captors in return for better treatment. Corporal Edwards remembered one such sergeant at a camp near Hanover in 1916: 'He assumed the authority of his rank with us, he reported the slightest of misdemeanours amongst us to the guards and was instrumental in having many punished.'[69] A Royal Armoured Corps sergeant-major, widely thought by those under him to have been overactive in enforcing the enemy's will at Salonika in 1941, was later – in the words of a British Medical Officer – 'beaten up by our men in Lamsdorf and had to be put under protective arrest.'[70]

Confined as they were to camps, the contact of officer prisoners and non-working NCOs with the civilian population was limited to journeys to and between camps and on parole walks. Sometimes this could produce only mutual hostility, especially if the civilians in question believed the war and its depressing consequences were the fault of the Allies. Major Arthur Peebles, Suffolk Regiment, was disgusted, like many others, by the behaviour of enraged Germans in the autumn of 1914: 'At every stop, everywhere there were enormous crowds of people singing, shouting, spitting, cursing.' RAF Sergeant David Hawkins admitted that standing on a railway platform next to seething civilians in Hamburg on his way to hospital just after a big bombing raid in 1942 was not a pleasant experience: 'That was a little bit dodgy, a bit frightening.' Yet such brief contacts could also engender a more positive attitude. Captain Waugh, expecting abuse from German civilians when he was taken into Germany in March 1918, was pleasantly surprised to find that 'they regarded us with friendly curiosity.'[71]

Working prisoners had much more contact with German civilians. Attitudes to foremen and other German workers encountered on the job depended to a considerable degree on the working conditions. First World War Canadian Private John O'Brien remembered with great bitterness that if he and his fellows did not meet their production quota down a particular coal mine they were forced to 'run a gauntlet of German miners' wielding shovels and pick handles.[72] Conversely, much goodwill was produced among prisoners at a sugar-beet factory in 1944 when the foreman agreed to allow them to negotiate shorter shifts. 'Our guards were not very pleased,' James Stedman recalled, 'but the civvy boss said that he did not mind so long as the work was done.'[73] A willingness to trade also tended to produce friendlier attitudes. 'Many [POWs] had found that they could barter with German civilians using cigarettes and chocolate from their parcels,' Sergeant John Brown wrote about a working party at a petroleum plant in the summer of 1941. Relations with German women could be even closer, though the penalties for getting caught were so draconian that liaisons with foreign women workers were preferred. One British soldier received a three-year sentence for 'having sexual intercourse four times with a German married woman.'[74]

Attitudes towards guards and other camp staff varied too. In the regular camps, especially the big ones, interaction with ordinary guards was usually quite limited. 'They did not interfere or trouble us very much,' Sergeant Gibbons said of the sentries at Giessen, 'and as long as the prisoners behaved they did not mind what happened.' It was very much the same 20 years later, Flight Lieutenant William Reid remembering that at Sagan, 'You seldom came in touch with them.' Contacts were established, however, in order to trade, Geoff Taylor writing that at Stalag IVB in 1944 'when they come on duty after dusk their gas-mask containers and greatcoat pockets are filled with hunks of bread which they barter for [parcel-delivered English] cigarettes.[75]

On working parties there was greater contact, with variable results. 'Our escort was a decent chap who never bothered us,' Corporal G. Kenworthy, Duke of Wellington's Regiment, remembered of his time working in Mecklenburg in 1917-18, noting that other guards could 'bite'.[76] A tolerant guard was much appreciated, such as on a 1944 tree-felling stint that Private Frank Pannett remembered in which a piecework quota was negotiated that allowed prisoners half the day off.[77] At the opposite end of the spectrum were those German soldiers who enforced their will by physical means. For a POW this could mean anything from being forced to stand at attention, hour after hour, to being knocked out. An English private repatriated in 1918 recalled that at a coal mine at Lunen anyone who fell down on the job 'was beaten with rifles and bayonets until he began again'.[78] There was, too, a particularly gratuitous collective beating given to RAF (and American) other ranks prisoners in July 1944 after an overcrowded ship and rail journey during which some had been chained and all had had to remove their boots. At a rail wayside halt they were herded into columns to be marched to a camp, their guards supplemented by armed Kriegsmarine youths and Alsatian dogs. The prisoners, carrying their kit, were ordered to run. This caused a concertina effect infuriating the officers in charge. Prisoners, falling, were set upon by the dogs. Some of the men were wounded by bayonets. 'All of us were scared we would be shot if we fell out of line. I can remember jumping over a fallen prisoner chained to another who was trying to help him up.' They eventually reached the camp: 'Nobody had any serious wounds but all had suffered fear, humiliation and the loss of necessary food and clothing in our abandoned kit.'[79]

What held true here also held true in the camps for the NCOs and the Lager officers with whom there was constant contact. As Sergeant Prouse put it, 'there were the good, the bad, and the absolutely rotten.'[80] Among the most respected was Lagerfeldwebel Hermann Glemnitz at Sagan, summed up by one of his charges as 'a loyal German soldier, an incorruptible guard, a man of good humour'.[81] A more sinister reputation surrounded Joseph Kussell, also known as 'Ukraine Joe', the NCO in charge of the RAF compound at Lamsdorf, about whom Bill Jackson was told, 'he doesn't bother us much, but if you cross him, he's a bastard.'[82]

Encounters with physical brutality were rare among officer prisoners. In their camps opinion tended to be shaped by the attitude and behaviour of the more senior Lager staff, not least the Kommandant. At Crefeld in 1917 Captain McNaught-Davis attributed good relations to the Kommandant, 'one of the few gentlemen that I came in contact with in Germany.' Similarly, Oberst Freiherr Franz von Linderer was generally admired for what one Flight Lieutenant called his 'gentlemanly approach', the dignified and correct way in which he dealt with officers in Stalag Luft III. By way of contrast, '[Hauptmann Charles] Niemeyer,' according to Captain Durnford, 'succeeded in impregnating the entire camp [at Holzminden] with an atmosphere of acute discontent and jumpiness.'[83]

News that the fighting was over came none too soon for POWs in both wars. They were seriously short of food and subject to new dangers. In the autumn of 1918 the influenza pandemic added to the miseries of working POWs: 'You can imagine what a clean sweep it made amongst us in our miserable condition,' wrote Corporal Arthur Speight, then working on railway repairs.[84] In 1945 tens of thousands of POWs were marched westward to keep them from falling into the hands of the Red Army. On the road there were several instances of Allied pilots mistaking columns of prisoners for the enemy. Flight Lieutenant Robert Buckman, RCAF, on the road from Sagan since January 1945, noted in his diary on 12 April 'the news that two men were killed and seven wounded yesterday afternoon, when the Navy column which is trailing us was strafed by an Allied fighter.'[85] When the end finally came, reactions varied from rioting to numbness, but one desire was paramount. 'Let's get home as quickly as possible,' as Peter Buckley put it; 'I wonder what it'll be like at home?'[86]

The immediate consequences of being at liberty included anxiety over resuming private lives and work and a natural resentment of authority. Though some bore long-term physical and emotional scars, most seem to have been able to adjust to their new circumstances. Corporal Arthur Topliss, Royal Tank Regiment, remembered that he suffered from 'barbed wire phobia' on returning to Britain in 1945, but that this went away after about six months.[87] This did not mean, however, that there were no lingering effects even among the better adjusted. 'For a long time after the war,' actor and ex-Lamsdorf prisoner Denholm Elliott remembered, 'I got terribly irritated with people who complained about food. When you have been extremely hungry you get down to basics and learn the real value of a humble piece of bread.'[88]

How then does the experience of captivity in the two World Wars compare? There are many points of convergence and there are some interesting contrasts.

In the First World War prisoners from all nations were usually mixed together. There was more segregation in the Second, but not always for airmen and not at Colditz in the early years. The relative absence of segregation had potential advantages for prisoners in the Great War, in that it widened the possibilities for trading and obtaining knowledge in everything from languages to escape techniques. It also had potential disadvantages, since it was sometimes difficult to judge the trustworthiness of foreigners, and – in the case of Russian soldiers who acted as carriers – there was greater risk of catching virulent strains of typhus and other dangerous communicable diseases.[89]

Enemy handling of Red Cross parcels also differed, being better overall in the Second War than in the First. In the midst of the food blockade imposed in the

Great War, German civilians and corrupt camp personnel were not above stealing from parcels on a regular basis.[90] During the Second World War, when the food situation was usually better and policing more stringent, Allied POWs were often struck by the general absence of pilfering.[91]

Other differences related to escape. Though the basic choices for break-out attempts remained the same, there were differences in terms of where to go from there, due to changed fighting fronts and the differing patterns of German conquest. The Swiss frontier was an option in both wars, but distance and military geography made the odds of getting to the Dutch frontier in the First World War better than reaching Sweden or getting to the Spanish border in the Second. On the other hand escapers in the Great War did not have the chance of aid from externally or internally organised networks of escape routes in Occupied Europe. Well-structured escape committees from 1940 became *de rigueur* in Oflags and many Stalags, while escape aids – principally maps and money – were sent in games and other parcels not bearing the Red Cross symbol by a special escape and evasion unit, MI9. Though the military authorities in both wars more or less abided by the terms of the 1907 Hague and 1929 Geneva rules governing the correct treatment of POWs[92], under Nazi rule there was also the risk that an escapee might be 'done away with' on recapture rather than returned to a camp. The most notorious instance of this happening was the murder by the Gestapo of 50 RAF officers from a mass tunnel escape from Stalag Luft III in March 1944.[93] Nevertheless it should be reemphasised that the increased danger and difficulty of getting home in the Second War was somewhat counterbalanced by the higher degree of organised support in making the attempt.[94]

The pattern of release also varied. Many prisoners remained in Germany for some weeks after the 1918 Armistice while arrangements were made for their return amidst the political chaos in Germany. Matters were better handled in 1945 with the Allied authorities fully in charge, ex-kriegies being flown home as part of a prearranged plan within days of coming into contact with British and American forces (though admittedly those in eastern camps overrun by the Red Army had to wait considerably longer while negotiations for their transfer to the west took place).[95] In the aftermath of the Second World War, moreover, officers did not have to justify before a War Office panel their decision to surrender as they had in the wake of the Great War.[96]

Overall, both for officers and men, the POW experience in the World Wars appears remarkably similar. In this chapter on several occasions reference has been made to factors that sustained morale in the camps. The universal qualities held by the individual in some measure also helped. Stoicism, resilience, strength through collective experience, comradeship, self-respect, a sense of humour, all played their part in limiting the degrading influence of captivity; but we should not fail to recognise that the experience was a searching test of endurance.

In the words of Major E. R. Collins, East Lancashire Regiment, being a prisoner for four or more years was a 'shocking waste of time, such a lump out of a short life.'[97] Mental and physical frustration are burdens and carry effects difficult to quantify, but in this respect singularly unlucky were those for whom lightning did literally strike twice: men like Jack Poole, who found himself a prisoner of the Third Reich having earlier been a prisoner of the Kaiser.[98]

Notes on contributors

Dr Peter H. Liddle, Director of the Second World War Experience Centre, Leeds, UK.
Peter Liddle was appointed Director of the Second World War Experience Centre in 1999, having been founder and Keeper of the Liddle Collection in the University of Leeds. The Centre's mission is to save and make available evidence of personal experience in the 1939-45 war. Dr Liddle, a Fellow of the Royal Historial Society, has written or edited many books on the Great War, including studies of Gallipoli, the Somme and Third Ypres. His most recent book, with Richard Campbell Begg, is on the Second World War, All for Five Shillings a Day.

Dr S.P. MacKenzie, The University of South Carolina, Columbia, USA
Paul Mackenzie is Associate Professor of History at the University of South Carolina. He is the author of several war-related books, among them The Home Guard (1995) and British War Films (2000), as well as a number of articles on POW affairs. He is currently examining the development of the Colditz phenomenon.

Recommended reading

Crawley, Aidan, *Escape from Germany* (London: HMSO, 1985 edn)

Barker, A. J., *Behind Barbed Wire* (London: Batsford, 1974)

Garrett, Richard, *P.O.W.* (Newton Abbot: David & Charles, 1981)

Jackson, Robert, *The Prisoners, 1914-18* (London: Routledge, 1989)

Moore, Bob and Fedorowich, Kent (eds), *Prisoners of War and their Captors in World War II* (Oxford: Berg, 1996)

Morton, Desmond, *Silent Battle: Canadian prisoners of war in Germany, 1914-1919* (Toronto: Lester, 1992)

Rolf, David, *Prisoners of the Reich: Germany's Captives, 1939-1945* (London: Leo Cooper, 1988)

Speed, Eric B. III, *Prisoners, Diplomats, and the Great War* (Westport, CT: Greenwood, 1990)

Vance, Jonathan F., *Objects of Concern: Canadian Prisoners of War through the Twentieth Century* (Vancouver: UBC Press, 1994)

Wynne-Mason, W., *Official History of New Zealand in the Second World War: Prisoners of War* (Wellington: Internal Affairs, 1954)

Notes

The quotations given in this chapter are, unless otherwise noted, typical. Statements are made on the basis of the existing secondary literature and – above all – on analysis of several hundred published and unpublished accounts, the latter held in the Liddle Collection (LC), The University of Leeds, The Second World War Experience Centre, Leeds (SWWEC), the Imperial War Museum (IWM) Sound

Archive (SA), and the Imperial War Museum Department of Documents.

1   For evidence of such cases see, eg, Cd 9106, Misc No 19 (1918), p8; H. G. Gilliland, *My German Prisons* (London: Hodder & Stoughton, 1918) pp23, 29; George Pearson (as told to Edward Edwards), *The Escape of a Princess Pat* (New York: George H. Doran, 1918) pp42-3, 68; Liddle Collection (hereafter LC), A. Beaumont interviews, TS, p4; Public Records Office (hereafter PRO), WO 309, BOAR war crimes investigation files

2   LC, J. A. Brewster file, E. Wagner to L. Brewster, 1915; LC, McNaught-Davis, IS, p8; IWM, 78/35/1, p3; LC, C. E. Green Diary, 29 October 1914; Donald Harry Laird, *Prisoner Five-One-Eleven* (Toronto: Ontario Press, 1918) p35. See also, eg, LC, N. A. Birks, TS, p7; Graham Palmer, *Prisoner of Death* (Wellingborough: Patrick Stephens, 1990) p44; David H. C. Read, *This Grace Given* (Grand Rapids, MI: Eermans, 1984) p100; PRO, ADM 1/118695, p9

3   See Eric Cuddon, ed, 'The Trial of Erich Killinger... (The Dulag Luft Trial)', War Crimes Trials Series, Vol IX (London: Hodge, 1952)

4   Imperial War Museum Sound Archive (hereafter IWM SA), 6 176/1, G. Atkinson; LC, E. N. Allen interview, TS; see also Pat O'Brien, *Outwitting the Hun* (New York: Harper, 1918) p51; IWM SA, 13296/1, R. Churchill; IWM SA, 15247/1, D. Hawkins; George Moreton, *Doctor in Chains* (London: Corgi, 1980 edn) pp66-70; Richard Passmore, *Moving Tent* (London: Harmsworth, 1982) pp36-8; Alec Waugh, *The Prisoners of Mainz* (London: Chapman & Hall, 1919) p21

5   F. H. Hinsley, et al, *British Intelligence in the Second World War: Its Influence on Strategy and Operations*, Vol 3, Part I (London: HMSO, 1984) p516 ; LC, E. N. Allen, TS

6   IWM, 90/18/1, R. P. Evans

7   Parliamentary Command Paper Cd 8984, Misc 3 (1918), p25; see also, eg, LC, L. McNaught-Davis, p8

8   IWM, 67/356/2, Rolf Collection, No 132

9   Parliamentary Command Paper Cd 8984, Misc 3 (1918), p45

10 John Brown, *In Durance Vile* (London: Hale, 1981) p29

11 Daniel J. McCarthy, *The Prisoner of War in Germany* (New York: Moffat, Yard, 1918) pp63-72, 76-93

12 J. L. Hardy, *I Escape!* (London: Bodley Head, 1928) p23

14 Daniel J. McCarthy, op cit, pp191-2

15 PRO, ADM 1/18695, p57

16 Kingsley Brown, *Bonds of Wire* (Toronto: Collins, 1989) p155; IWM SA, 13573/2, A. Jones. See W. Wynne Mason, *Official History of New Zealand in the Second World War: Prisoners of War* (Wellington: Internal Affairs, 1954) p130

17 IWM SA, 1137/2, H. Bracken; see PRO, WO 208/3290; W. Wynne Mason, op cit, p126

18 Barbara Broom, ed, *Geoffrey Broom's War* (Edinburgh: Portland, 1993) p98. See PRO, WO 208/3270

19 IWM SA, 1357/2, A. Jones

20 Cd 8988, Misc No 7 (1918), p9

21 Michael Duncan, *Underground from Posen* (London: William Kimber, 1954) p74

22 H. G. Durnford, *The Tunnellers of Holzminden* (Cambridge: Cambridge University Press, 1920) p107; PRO, WO208/3291, p1; see S. P. MacKenzie, 'The Shackling Crisis', *International History Review* 17 (1995), pp78-98; J. M. Vance, 'Men in Manacles', *Journal of Military History* 59 (1995), pp483-504

23 Richard Passmore, op cit, p70

24 Maxwell Bates, *A Wilderness of Days* (Victoria, BC: Sono Nis, 1978) p73

25 LC, J. E. Draper, p9; IWM SA, 5 194/2, J. Laurie; see, eg, IWM SA, 4933/2, W. Reid; LC, G. Kenworthy, p10

26 IWM SA, 5 194/2; see, eg, IWM SA, 4759/4, P. Buckley; John Brown, op cit, pp49-50; Adrian Vincent, *The Long Road Home* (London: Allen & Unwin, 1956) p115

27 H. E. Wooley, *No Time Off for Good Behaviour* (Burnstown, ON: GSPH, 1990) pp141-2

28 Second World War Experience Centre, Leeds (hereafter SWWEC), F. Corfield memoir, p41

29 PRO, WO 32/15294; LC, F. Cunnington, p7; see E. S. Dane in Michael Moynihan, *Black Bread and Barbed Wire* (London: Leo Cooper, 1978) chap 2; Robert Jackson, *The Prisoners, 1914-18*

(Routledge: London, 1989) pp29-31, 41; David Rolf, *Prisoners of the Reich: Germany's Captives, 1939-1945* (London: Leo Cooper, 1988) pp70-2

30 Peter Winter, *Free Lodgings* (Auckland: Reed, 1993) p116; LC, C. E. Green Diary, 12 January 1917
31 See George Moreton, op cit, p100; Lee, pp182-3
32 H. G. Gilliland, op cit, p51; see, eg, Alec Waugh, *Prisoners of Mainz* (London: Chapman & Hall, 1919) p67
33 Geoffrey Willatt, *Bombs and Barbed Wire* (Tunbridge Wells: Parapress, 1995) p56; see, eg, IWM SA, 4827/3, R. Loder; Frank Taylor, *Barbed Wire and Footlights* (Braunton: Merlin, 1988)
34 LC, G. Jacob, tape-recorded recollections
35 SWWEC, P. M. Peel, photographs, artwork and tape-recorded recollections
36 IWM SA, 4759/4, P. Buckley
37 IWM SA, 6142/3, J. Deans
38 H. G. Durnford, op cit, pp29-31; LC, McNaught-Davis, pp48-49
39 J. Harvey Douglas, *Captured* (Toronto: McClelland, Goodchild & Stewart, 1918) p106; Grant in Michael Moynihan, op cit, p87; J. C. Thorn, *Three Years a Prisoner in Germany* (Vancouver: Cowan & Brookhouse,1919) p31
40 J. C. Thorn, op cit, p106
41 See, eg, IWM SA, 4759/5, P. Buckley; also PRO, WO 32/9912, encl 111A
42 IWM SA, 4769/2, J. Phillips; see PRO, WO 208/3293, pp1-2
43 IWM SA, 15336/3, J. Wilson; J. C. Thorn, op cit, p9
44 IWM SA, 16797/2, H. Bruce; Graham Palmer, op cit, p124; J. L. Hardy, op cit, p100; IWM SA, 4747/6, E. Mine; see, eg, Richard Passmore, op cit, p139; J. C. Thorn, op cit, pp40-1; Alec Waugh, op cit, p165; IWM SA, 4769/2, J. Philipps; Jim Rogers, *Tunnelling into Colditz* (London: Hale, 1986) p143; Peter Winter, op cit, pp10, 36; see also Aidan Crawley, *Escape from Germany* (London: Collins, 1956) p19
45 Derek Thrower, *The Lonely Path to Freedom* (London: Hale, 1980) p66
46 Allan Burgess, *The Longest Tunnel* (New York: Grove Weidenfeld, 1990) p16
47 IWM SA, 16797/2, H. Bruce
48 Aidan Crawley, op cit, p23
49 See *Report of the International Committee of the Red Cross on its activities during the Second World War (September 1, 1939-June 30, 1947)* Vol I, General Activities (Geneva: ICRC, 1948) Chap 9; Richard B. Speed III, *Prisoners, Diplomats, and the Great War* (Westport, CT: Greenwood, 1990) Chap 2; André Durand, *From Sarajevo to Hiroshima: History of the International Committee of the Red Cross* (Geneva: Henry Dunant Institute, 1978) p75
50 J. L. Hardy, op cit, p224; George Moreton, op cit, p195; Arthur Gibbons, *A Guest of the Kaiser* (Toronto: Dent, 1919) p179; Donald Harry Laird, op cit, p77; see also J. C. Thorn, op cit, p125
51 LC, McGowan, p8; LC, C. E. Green, 3 January 1916; see, eg, IWM, Rolf Collection, 67/356/2, No 207, F. Ayres; IWM SA, 4830, F. Pannett; A. Robert Prouse, *Ticket to Hell via Dieppe* (Toronto: Van Norstrand Rhiehold, 1982) p86
52 LC, L. McNaught-Davis, p50; Maxwell Bates, op cit, p64; H. G. Gilliland, op cit, pp182, 126-7, 79-81; LC, N. A. Birks, p7
53 See, eg, John Borne, *Despite Captivity* (London: William Kimber, 1975)
54 SWWEC, H. Pennock, typescript recollections; for doctors' opinions see George Moreton, op cit, passim; Ion Ferguson, *Doctor at War* (London: Christopher Johnson, 1955)
55 Martin H. Lidbetter, *The Friends Ambulance Unit 1939-1943* (York: Sessions Book Trust, 1993) p99; George Pearson, op cit, pp101-2
56 See, eg, H. G. Gilliland, op cit, p92; IWM SA, 5 194/4, J. Laurie
57 Richard Passmore, op cit, p84; see IWM SA, 4694/4, E. Ayling; George Pearson, op cit, p95; Alec Waugh, p222; LC, McNaught-Davis, pp58-59
58 LC, J. H. Birkinshaw, p4; see Alec Waugh, op cit, p223; IWM SA, 4830/2, F. Pannett
59 See PRO, WO 208, camp histories, passim
60 H. E. Wooley, op cit, p41; Joseph Lee, *A Captive at Carlsruhe* (London; John Lane, 1920) p35
61 Richard Passmore, op cit, p162; see H. E. Wooley, pp42-5; IWM SA 13573/2, A. Jones
62 On code letters, which became regularised through MI9 in the Second World War, see, eg, A. J. Evans, *The Escaping Club* (London: John Lane, 1921) p48; J. M. Green, *From Colditz in Code*

(London: Hale, 1971)

63 Geoff Taylor, *Piece of Cake* (London: Corgi edn, 1980) p184; Jim Rogers, op cit, p41; J. L. Hardy, op cit, p115; George Pearson, op cit, pp157-8

64 James Stedman, *Life of a British POW in Poland* (Braunton: Merlin, 1992) p15; LC, A. Beaumont, p9; J. Harvey Douglas, op cit, p90; H. G. Gilliland, op cit, p105

65 IWM SA, 4820/1, C. Scarborough; David H. C. Read, *This Grace Given* (Grand Rapids, MI: Eerdmans,1984) p106; IWM SA, 4827/2, R. Loder; LC, L. McNaught-Davis, p26

66 Arthur Gibbons, op cit, pp173-4; see George Pearson, op cit, p93

67 IWM SA, 4747/6, E. Mine

68 Bill Jackson, *The Lone Survivor* (North Battleford, SK: Turner-Warwick, 1972) p72; see Steve Mitchell, *They Were Invincible* (Bracebridge, AL: Herald-Gazette, 1979) p45; see also James Stedman, op cit, p22; A. Robert Prouse, op cit, p124

69 George Pearson, op cit, pp119-20

70 PRO, ADM 1/1 8695, p20; see Ed Annetts, *Campaign Without Medals* (Lewes: Book Guild, 1990) p59; Graham Palmer, op cit, p124

71 Alec Waugh, op cit, p35; IWM SA, 15247/2, D. Hawkins; Cd 8984, Misc 3 (1918), p7; see LC, McNaught-Davis, p26

72 Desmond Morton, *Silent Battle* (Toronto: Lester, 1992) p84

73 James Stedman, op cit, p24; see Ed Annetts, op cit, p148-9

74 PRO, WO 32/15294; see John Brown, p55. Homosexual encounters also took place between prisoners and with civilians, but were quite rare to judge by statements made in memoirs and answers given to questions about such activity by IWM interviewers.

75 Taylor, op cit, p178; IWM SA, 4933/2, W. Reid; Arthur Gibbons, op cit, p162

76 LC, G. Kenworthy, p35

77 IWM SA, 4830/4, F. Pannett

78 Cd 9150, Misc No 23 (1918), p5; see Arthur Gibbons, p168

79 SWWEC, S. Hope, manuscript and tape-recorded recollections

80 A. Robert Prouse, op cit, p105

81 Brown, op cit, p96

82 Bill Jackson, op cit, p33; see John McMahon, *Almost a Lifetime* Lantzville, BC: Oolichan, 1995) p57

83 H. G. Durnford, op cit, p34; LC, McNaught-Davis, p27; IWM, 88/47/1, U. A. Atkinson

84 Robert Jackson, op cit, p110

85 Robert Buckman, *Forced March to Freedom* (Sttitsville, ON: Canada's Wings, 1984) p66

86 IWM SA, 4759/6, P. Buckley; see Robert Jackson, op cit, Chap 9; David Rolf, op cit, Chap 9

87 IWM SA, 12093/4, A. Topliss; see IWM SA, POW interviews, passim; David Rolf, op cit, chap 10

88 Susan Elliott with Barry Turner, *Denholm Elliott* (London: Headline, 1994) p28; see IWM SA, 4747/7, E. Mine

89 See, eg, Daniel J. McCarthy, op cit, p50; Cd 8224, Misc No 10 (1916)

90 See, eg, LC, McNaught-Davis, p48

91 See, eg, Richard Passmore, op cit, p104

92 On the 1907 Hague and 1929 Geneva rules governing POWs, which Germany claimed to abide by with respect to British POWs, see André Durand, op cit, pp66-75, 255-56. British civilians interned in Germany in the two wars were in a less well-defined legal position, which makes comparison more problematic than with service personnel.

93 See Allan Burgess, op cit. The presence of the Waffen-SS could also make life short for newly surrendered personnel. See, eg, Howard Margolian, *Conduct Unbecoming: The Story of the Murder of Canadian Prisoners of War in Normandy* (Toronto: University of Toronto Press, 1998); Leslie Aitkin, *Massacre on the Road to Dunkirk: Wormhout 1940* (London: Kimber, 1977); Cyril Jolly, *The Vengeance of Private Pooley* (London: Heinemann, 1956)

94 See M. R. D. Foot and J. M. Langley, *MI9* (London: Bodley Head, 1979); PRO, WO 208, camp histories, passim

95 David Rolf, op cit, chap 9; Jackson, op cit, chap 9

96 See, eg, LC, War Office letter to F. O. Lane, 8 May 1919

97 LC, E. R. Collins, f281, letter of September 1918

98 See, eg, SWWEC, Roger Mortimer, TS

Chapter 18

Casualties and British medical services

Nick Bosanquet and Ian Whitehead

T he result of much recent research on military medicine has been to demonstrate its centrality in the prosecution of modern warfare.[1] Indeed, in 1914-18, and again in 1939-45, the existence of efficient systems for the rapid treatment of the sick and wounded became a vital component of the wider military machine. The science of medicine, rooted in humanitarian concern for the patient, had become an essential weapon of war. This chapter examines the response of the British medical services to the challenges of modern warfare, comparing the arrangements for evacuating the sick and wounded in the two World Wars, and revealing how surgeons and physicians responded to the demands of war medicine.

According to Lieutenant-Colonel J. C. Watts, the role of the surgeon in warfare ought not to be seen as being fundamentally different from his work in civilian life: 'A great deal of claptrap has been written about the principles of war surgery, which are in reality the same as those governing all surgery – that is to say, saving life and restoring health and function.'[2] On the other hand, the war surgeon does not enjoy the degree of autonomy and control that would be his in a civilian context. In particular, he has to recognise that surgery is only a part, albeit a vital part, of a wider military machine. Thus the location of surgical units and the nature of surgical treatments have to take account of the military situation. As one doctor observed, this meant that Medical Officers had to accept 'the incongruity of medicine and war' and recognise 'that first and foremost we are soldiers'.[3] Major-General W. H. Ogilvie, a consultant surgeon, warned of the necessity 'to temper surgical idealism with military realism,' and highlighted the four principal aims of military surgery: '(1) to win the war; (2) to save life; (3) to prevent suffering; (4) to preserve function'.[4] The conditions of battle would inevitably dictate the surgeon's ability to meet these goals. He had to recognise that war surgery simply meant giving the best possible treatment that these conditions would allow:

'The surgery of any campaign will depend on very many things besides the surgical knowledge of the time; on the terrain, on the climate hot or cold, the weather wet or dry, on the fitness of the troops, the adequacy of their supplies of food and water, the hygiene of the army and the prevalence of endemic or epidemic diseases at the time, on the weapons in use, on the quantity of supplies and the adequacy of their supply lines, on the liability to air attack, on the severity of the fighting, on the time-lag between wounding and primary surgery and between primary and secondary surgery, on the lines of evacuation, the distance to the base, the quality of the transport, and the opportunities for staffing and supervision en route, above all on whether the force is fighting a winning or losing battle.'[5]

Variations in such conditions meant that the military surgical organisation had to be flexible, with a staff sufficiently adaptable to recognise those methods for evacuating and treating the wounded that were most appropriate in the prevailing circumstances. Aside from these variables, however, the principal concerns of military surgery remained consistent: the need to provide basic first aid as soon as possible after wounding; the necessity for an evacuation and triage system that rapidly delivered the wounded to appropriate surgical treatment, whilst avoiding delays in their return to duty; the importance of early surgery; the significance of measures to combat shock and wound infection; and the need to ensure that surgical treatment provided the best specialist care, based on the latest techniques.

The way of the wounded on the Western Front, in 1914, began at a Regimental Aid Post, where they received basic first aid treatment. They then proceeded by stretcher-bearer to an Advanced Dressing Station (ADS) and by ambulance car to a Main Dressing Station (MDS). The ADS and the MDS were both operated by the divisional Field Ambulance (FA), from whence the wounded were transported to a Casualty Clearing Station (CCS). The next stage of their journey was by ambulance train to a general hospital at the base, then finally by ship to a hospital in the UK.

The overriding concern of the system was to ensure that the wounded received appropriate treatment at the earliest opportunity, then to return them quickly to active duty. The adoption of triage, and the establishment of convalescent depots in the corps and army areas, ensured that men were treated as near to the front as possible, thus avoiding the delays that occurred, early in the war, due to unnecessary evacuation to the base or UK hospitals. The increasing focus on treatment near the front reflected the largely static nature of the fighting, and the relatively short lines of communication that characterised the campaigns in France and Flanders after the opening months of the war. These conditions enabled the CCS, originally envisioned as a mobile unit, to be transformed into a large, permanent hospital. The development of the Motor Ambulance Convoys ensured that the wounded were rapidly transported from the FAs to the CCSs, which were sited in increasing proximity to the front line, but at sufficient distance to provide the stable conditions required for major surgery. By 1917 the CCSs were undertaking more surgical work than the general hospitals, completing 61,423 operations throughout the course of the Passchendaele campaign.[6]

The growth of the CCSs, however, meant that they could no longer keep pace with the advance or retirement of the troops. It became the practice to form Advanced Operating Centres, in order to meet the need for surgery to stay in touch with the fighting. The problem of mobility became even more acute in 1918, with the collapse of stable trench warfare. The size of the CCSs hampered their ability to retreat, and meant that they were slow to reassemble elsewhere. Thus, during the course of the German offensive surgical work at the CCSs rapidly diminished, as they reverted to their originally intended function of clearing wounded from the FAs on to the base hospitals. Not until June 1918, with a lighter scale of organisation, were the CCSs able to resume their work as centres for forward surgery.[7]

Such difficulties presaged the problems that were to confront the RAMC in 1939-45, as increased mechanisation ensured that this was predominantly a war of movement. In the inter-war years, however, little consideration appears to have been given to technological advances in the conduct of warfare and their implications for the medical organisation. The RAMC entered the Second World War with an organisation for evacuating the wounded that was based on the trench warfare of the previous conflict.

The medical situation in France, in 1940, closely resembled that in the opening months of 1914. In the context of retreat, stable lines of evacuation proved difficult to maintain and communications between medical units were often poor. The Regimental Medical Officer (RMO) of the Second Battalion Royal Warwickshire Regiment recalled the chaotic position between 10 and 20 May 1940:

> 'My contact with the Fd. Amb. during this time was extremely tenuous, my impression ... is that they were overwhelmed by the difficulties of moving the Fd. Amb. and had no time to spare to link up with their R[egimental] A[id] P[osts] even if they knew where we were... I used to go back on a motor bicycle to find them and rarely had much success as they were always on the move. When I did find them they usually wanted to know if I had seen their section.'[8]

Fortunately, he recalled that the pressure of casualties was not too great. The RAP was well supplied with morphia and shell dressings, while his staff of 20 stretcher-bearers (an increase from the 16 that had been standard in 1914-18) coped well with the collection of wounded. However, the experience taught him that in a retreat 'normal rules' did not hold good; flexibility and initiative were the watchwords, as the unit needed to take responsibility for evacuating its own wounded:

> 'It at times happens that all the [transport] must be sent back some distance, say 15-20 miles, and the battalion, if it is in contact, will, when the time comes, thin out and break contact by forced marches. You must decide what [medical equipment] you must carry and divide the loads between your staff, but only let your truck go at the last possible moment – naturally, a 3-tonner and an ambulance car must go before a 15cwt and that before a jeep; if you have a jeep you are lucky – it may well be your only way of getting wounded quickly back.'[9]

The really difficult time for an RMO was when the speed of retreat necessitated wounded men being left behind. In both World Wars, the RAMC command was concerned to prevent Medical Officers from placing themselves in too much danger. On 27 May 1940, with his RAP at Wormhoudt, 15 miles south of Dunkirk, soon to be overrun by the battle, the Second Battalion Royal Warwickshire's RMO recognised that the moment to withdraw had arrived:

> 'We have been told that it is only lack of guts which prevents one escaping at this time. That is agreed and this is the time of selection for escape. But it is not only guts, if you have wounded officers and men of your bn. around you, all friends of yours, I defy anyone of any spirit to make the decision to go. The argument is simple, it takes five years to train a doctor, therefore put a medical orderly in charge and clear out.'[10]

During the First World War, the role of FAs, which operated the Advanced and Main Dressing Stations (ADSs and MDSs), had been brought into question. The growth of the CCSs and the relatively short lines of evacuation on the Western Front meant that by 1917 the MDSs were increasingly being bypassed. This led to claims that the FAs had become largely redundant; that they offered little work for Medical Officers, much needed elsewhere; and that they acted as an obstacle to early surgical treatment of the wounded. Such criticisms, however, failed to appreciate the vital work undertaken by the FAs in the mobile warfare of 1914, and which they were to perform again in 1918. After the war the RAMC authorities concluded that FAs could not be dispensed with.[11] This decision was justified in 1940 when they played an important part in the evacuation and treatment of wounded from the Dunkirk retreat. On 23 May 1940 the war diary of the 10th Field Ambulance recorded that its MDS, situated in a crèche at La Vignette, was taking in casualties 'in fair numbers, including a high proportion of seriously wounded cases'.[12] Moreover, the distance to the nearest CCS, at Bailleul, was such that the FA was undertaking surgery. Six days later the unit took over the Grand Hotel Regina, in Coxyde-Les-Bains, where its surgical work expanded further, owing to pressure on the CCSs:

> 'From this moment on the unit was called upon to play the role of a CCS. All cases on arrival were taken into a large room on the ground floor, which was also used as a ward capable of holding eighty stretcher cases. In this room, they were sorted, those requiring immediate and urgent treatment being taken into a large M[edical] I[nspection] Room, where three M[edical] O[fficer]s were continuously at work. From this room cases requiring operation were taken to the kitchen of the hotel, where a surgical team was at work all night.'[13]

Ian Samuel's experiences with the 6th Field Ambulance paint a similar picture. He found himself undertaking serious surgery on several cases, including resecting a small bowel, closing an open pneumothorax and plugging liver wounds. The unit had to improvise an operating theatre in the kitchen of a farmhouse, at Le Doulieu, where Samuel got further unexpected opportunities to bring his civilian surgical experience to bear:

'...one doesn't expect when working normally with a field ambulance to have to undertake major surgery. In the normal course of events, these cases would have been sent back behind the lines to a Casualty Clearing Station where they would have received expert surgical attention. But alas we were not in contact with one. In all, in the 24 hours at Le Doulieu we received some 400-500 casualties and throughout the day and night we operated continuously in atrocious conditions.'[14]

These conditions included having to work with inadequate surgical equipment. Samuel did not possess a scalpel large enough for major amputations, so he borrowed a carpentry saw. Thick rubber tubing with a tape through one end provided makeshift airways, but he had to dispense with other luxuries, such as curved forceps and needle holders. All cases were, however, given a dose of anti-tetanic serum.[15]

Early in 1940 the commander of Number 8 CCS recorded far less chaotic scenes. The medical organisation was operating 'according to the text-books'. The CCSs were treating all the emergency and acute cases in the forward area, and were well served by ambulance trains to the general hospitals. Although the distance to these base hospitals was longer than in the Great War, the journey of the wounded was a comfortable one:

'It was a fascinating experience to see how excellently the Ambulance Train tackles its job. There are six of them, all superbly appointed, and one calls at the local siding twice a week. I well remember my own journey from Ypres to Camiers in the first war, when I was wounded at Passchendaele. I felt that I had reached civilisation at last. The patients must feel the same way today.'[16]

In other theatres of operations, the contrast with the short lines of evacuation on the Western Front during 1914-18 was even more pronounced. Number 20 Indian Ambulance Train, in 1944, was covering nearly 300 miles between Chittagong and Sylhet. Major T. R. Maurice, the officer commanding this unit, recognised the importance of maintaining the wounded in comfort and good spirits, and found that this often placed him in the position of hotel manager rather than doctor:

'I have a loud speaker attached to my wireless set and a point to which I can plug it in in the first ward car in which we carry British troops and officers. I usually keep this up my sleeve and then if the train stops, as it often does ... I get someone to plug it in and give them some light music from London. To people fresh from the Burma and Assam jungle, and those are the people we carry very largely, the whole outfit makes a big impression. One officer fresh from Burma told me it was the best organised show he'd found in India yet and a colonel yesterday complained there were no dancing girls, he said we had thought of everything else.'[17]

At Rouvroy, in March 1940, Number 8 CCS was operating a smoothly functioning hospital, admitting routine cases. Beneath this tranquil surface, however, the commander had worries about the unit's lack of mobility if a move were to prove necessary. During the retreat to Dunkirk his fears proved justified, and the CCS was seriously hampered by a lack of transport. Meanwhile, the text-book evacuation schemes that had operated in less testing times began to break down under the pressure of the German advance, as is clear from this account of the CCS's experiences at Wormhoudt:

'The tale of Wormhoudt is one of stench and filth and gore. And superhuman efforts on our part to succour the wounded as best we could. We remained three days there from Thursday until yesterday (Sunday). We admitted about 900 wounded, we fed them, operated on a hundred men and buried nearly fifty. Then we evacuated all our patients to a hospital ship at Dunkirk. Let us hope that they are all back in Blighty by this time and that they soon forget the horrors of the last few days. What calls most for remark was the courage and endurance of the men. I never heard a word of complaint. Perhaps the sight most depressing to me was the long queue of ambulances waiting to come in. Many of the plastered limbs were swarming with maggots and the stench was dreadful. Yet never a word of complaint... The theatre worked night and day and my job was to select cases for immediate operation. X-rays and transfusions were judged impossible. Many plasters were applied and reapplied and it was quite noticeable that the maggots seemed to have done no harm, except for the smell... The worst rush was on Thursday when patients arrived very soon after we did. Still, I suppose this is the biggest challenge of army medicine. We must be prepared to function under any circumstances and to improvise... One can well view with a macabre sense of humour the elaborate medical scheme for evacuation of casualties. It worked excellently at Rouvroy. Now, as our lines of communication are cut, it has proved to be useless. A few days more at Wormhoudt and we should be nothing but a mortuary.'[18]

The limitations of the 1914-18 medical organisation became equally apparent on other fronts. In February 1941 Major General P. S. Tomlinson wrote an assessment of the problems of casualty evacuation and treatment that had occurred during the operations in Libya. The cumbersome CCS proved unable to keep pace with the advancing troops, and the wounded faced increasingly long and uncomfortable journeys as the line of evacuation extended. Tomlinson noted that the 'road surface between Sidi Barani and Mersa Matruh was universally described as appalling and, as soon as possible after the capture of Sollum, evacuation from that port was initiated.'[19] Evacuation by ship also took the strain off the motor ambulance cars. The establishment of eight ambulance cars per FA was found to be too few to cope with the long distances over which the wounded had to be transported.[20] In order to minimise the suffering of the wounded staging posts were established. The importance of the latter was acknowledged by Major P. T. S. Morrison: 'Patients are apt to get uncomfortable during long journeys over bad going and a tactful competent senior NCO in a staging post can make all the difference – adjusting bandages etc, with perhaps hot soup or tea which are always on tap in all the divisional medical units; a little sustenance puts a patient in a happy frame of mind automatically.'[21]

The transportation of the wounded in Libya, in 1940, therefore offered a complete contrast to the experience that was common on the Western Front in the First World War. By 1917 CCSs were sited within a few miles of the fighting, providing immediate surgery, whereas in 1940 the wounded man probably faced a much more arduous journey:

'50 miles back to his own RAP (Going bad)
25 " " " Brigade ADS (Going bad)
30 " " " A/MDS (Going very bad)
30 " " " Staging post (Going almost impossible)
50 " " " MDS (Going almost impossible)
60 " " " Mersa Matruh (per MAC)
50 " " " CCS (per hospital train)
150 " " " General Hospital (per hospital train)'[22]

Air evacuation offered one solution in the desert campaigns that had not been available in 1914-18. It enabled thousands of wounded men to be transferred to the base in a matter of hours, sparing them a long and uncomfortable journey. However, the arrangements for air evacuation in Libya were rather ad hoc and were constrained by the conditions pertaining in that theatre. There were few designated ambulance planes, which meant that there was no reliable service and that military rather than medical concerns were uppermost in considering the use of available freight planes: 'The benefits acquired by isolated air evacuations were very doubtful. It is a debatable point as to whether one badly wounded man is as valuable as 100% airplane with its 100% crew.'[23] Problems also arose because of a lack of suitable landing sites next to CCSs. The risks to the wounded, following emergency surgery, of undergoing a road journey along poor highways outweighed any benefits to be gained from rapid transportation to the comfort of a base hospital: 'The saying that no one is fit for the air who is not fit for the road became more than a saying, it became a rule.'[24] Air transport was, however, a positive boon for men with injuries such as a fractured femur who, although fit for travel, were vulnerable to disruption of their injury on a long road journey. By 1944, in Western Europe, a more systematic air evacuation service existed. Based on close co-operation between the RAMC and the RAF, this air evacuation service became 'a vital necessity':

'...air evacuation really came into its own, and without it evacuation of casualties back over war-scarred roads to Normandy would have been virtually impossible. As it was, the RAF, with the able guidance of Air Commodore Murphy and Group Capt Bruce Harvey, appeared with a Dakota and almost magical regularity on what seemed quite impossible fields almost alongside CCSs and surgical centres.'[25]

The principal medical problem encountered in Libya was the inability of the CCSs to provide surgery in the forward area. As in France, this gap was plugged by the

FAs undertaking greater responsibility for early surgery. Surgical teams were dispatched from the base hospitals to the MDSs and, reinforced by mobile transfusion units and bacteriological laboratories, they operated as 'improvised' CCSs. However, this was never a satisfactory solution, and 'no attempt was made to hide the fact that the whole standard of comfort was necessarily far below that achieved during the static war in France between 1914 and 1918'.[26] Indeed, early in the First World War the RAMC had recognised that FAs did not provide the stable conditions required for successful surgery. These limitations were apparent again in 1940:

> '...to give the seriously wounded man a chance of recovery it is essential that he receive full surgical treatment at the earliest opportunity and that he be held up to 10 days after operation before he is evacuated any further. So that under the present conditions one of two things happens:
> 1 The HQ of a FA becomes immobilised and cannot follow the Bde. forward.
> 2 To permit the FA to carry out its function and follow up its Bde., it is necessary to evacuate seriously wounded cases within a short time of operation. This results in the loss of a number of lives and limbs that otherwise could be saved.'[27]

The lesson of 1940-41 was that the RAMC could not persist with the evacuation model of the previous war. Medical Officers complained bitterly, throughout the campaigns in Norway, France and the Middle East, about the complete immobility of the CCSs.[28] The failure of these units to perform their intended function had serious implications for the wounded:

> 'It was observed that seriously wounded men had little if any hope of being saved if the RAMC relied wholly upon transporting them from the forward battle areas back to stationary casualty clearing stations where emergency operations are performed. Communication lines in this Libyan theatre are too long, and the prospects of infection setting in between the administration of first aid in the field and the arrival of the patient in the operating room is too great.'[29]

Some relief from the problem was achieved when the British were able to take over Field Hospitals abandoned by the retreating Italian forces. These hospitals themselves were victims of deficient transport, and consequently it had not been possible for the Italians to evacuate their patients: '...in most cases [they] were full of enemy sick and wounded. The Italian staffs of these hospitals worked willingly and well under British direction.'[30] The hospitals were of a standard design, consisting of a series of ward and operating tents, the number of which could be increased as demand required. Some of the tents had floors constructed from tiles or beaten stone. The hospitals were well-equipped with portable electric sets and X-ray installations. Altogether, these Italian hospitals provided comfortable conditions for the wounded, although the British were shocked to discover that there existed no organised latrines. One group of patients less favourably dealt with were the Libyans who were treated 'to a lower scale of hospital comfort', having to sleep on straw, and towards whom the Italian medical staff were 'openly contemptuous'.[31]

The utilisation of enemy hospitals provided a breathing space for the British, but the clear need in 1941 was for the organisation of effective mobile surgery in the forward areas. Surgery was brought nearer to the wounded by making the CCSs more mobile. They were divided into 'heavy' and 'light' sections, with the latter possessing their own transport. Greater mobility meant that, by the time of El Alamein, the CCSs were able to keep close to the advancing troops by leap-frogging over one another, thus creating a chain of staging posts between the forward areas and the base. Steps were also taken to formalise the provision of surgical treatment ahead of the CCSs by establishing mobile field surgical teams, which comprised a surgeon, an assistant surgeon and an anaesthetist, with a number of trained orderlies. These teams had their own staff car and a lorry. Lieutenant-Colonel Peter B. Ascroft regarded these mobile units as a significant departure because 'for the first time a real attempt was made to put the doctors on wheels, to take the surgeon to the patient rather than the patient to the surgeon.'[32]

The CCS light sections and the field surgical teams performed a similar role, but the former were more independent whereas the latter were reliant on support from a host unit, such as an MDS or a CCS in need of surgical reinforcements. By the time of the Italian campaign the surgical teams had become well-established mobile field surgical units. Together with the CCS light sections they successfully provided surgical treatment in close proximity to the fighting. During the rapid advance through Italy the CCSs were able to stay in touch by leap-frogging, as in the desert, with the result that a chain of medical units was established that stretched over 300 miles.[33]

The greater flexibility meant that the CCS was once again able to act 'as the key unit of field surgery', sited as near to the front as was compatible with providing the stable conditions necessary for the treatment and recovery of the wounded. In this respect the position was not dissimilar from 1914-18. But, in contrast, because of the innovations in forward surgical provision, the system was now much more capable of responding to the needs of those seriously wounded men in need of resuscitation and urgent surgery, who were unlikely to survive the journey to the CCSs. The bulk of this work fell to the field surgical units, whose facilities had been improved to provide beds and tents for the wounded. It also became the practice for advanced operating centres to be formed by an MDS with two surgical units and a transfusion unit attached to it. In Italy, a pool of medical orderlies, all with a minimum of one year's service with a CCS, was established at the Corps FA to provide the experienced nursing staff for the advanced surgical centres.[34] This was essentially the scheme of organisation employed in Western Europe in 1944. Here the contrast with the static medical units in 1914-18 was perhaps most marked, with two CCSs actually forming part of the attacking column in the 'Nijmegen corridor'.[35]

The emphasis on surgery in the forward areas reflected the importance of the wounded receiving surgical treatment as soon as possible after injury. There had been some resistance to the principle of forward surgery in the First World War.

Not until 1916, following pressure from Sir Anthony Bowlby, and thanks to the results achieved by surgeons such as Lockwood and Gask, was the case for forward surgery firmly established in the RAMC.[36] Surgeons in the Second World War, on the other hand, were armed from the outset with knowledge gained in 1914-18, and more recently in the Spanish Civil War, concerning the benefits of early surgery. During the operations in Western Europe, in 1944, surgeons noted that the vital time lapse between wounding and treatment was consistently under 12 hours.[37] Similarly, the organisation of the Soviet Medical Corps reflected awareness that 'the best results are obtained when wounds are treated within a few hours of their infliction'.[38]

In both wars, the standard of care given to the wounded in front-line medical units was recognised as having critical implications for their subsequent surgical progress. Peter Ascroft expressed a widely accepted opinion that it was in the forward areas 'rather than at the Base where the fate of the wounded man is so often decided'.[39] Particular attention was given by Medical Officers at RAPs and FAs to ensuring that measures were taken to prevent the onset of shock, including arresting haemorrhage, keeping the patients warm and giving them plenty of fluids. Peter Ascroft noted that, 'Every patient wants tea, the sweeter the better, and it should be available [wherever] they may be detained… A long drink of sweet tea does the average patient far more good than a pint of saline intravenously.'[40]

The forward medical units also undertook to ensure that the wounded were prepared for further evacuation by immobilising fractured limbs. During the First World War the principal means of immobilising fractures was the Thomas splint, which was in regular use from the Somme campaigns of 1916. In the view of Ambrose Lockwood it 'rapidly established itself as probably the most important agent of all war measures in combating shock and in saving life and limbs'.[41] In the Second World War the Thomas splint remained in use, but the principal means of immobilising limbs was plaster of Paris. Plaster provided greater comfort for the patient, and allowed a wide variety of splints to be constructed. One such was the Tobruk splint, first employed by Number 62 General Hospital, Tobruk. This proved particularly valuable for the immobilisation of fractured femurs and knee injuries. It involved traction of the wound with a Thomas splint encased in a plaster box. There was seldom need for redressing of the wound in transit, thus reducing the risk of infection.

The emergence of blood transfusion had been one of the most important medical developments during the First World War. Its use became regular from 1916, and by 1917 it was the practice in the CCSs to delay operation until a patient's blood pressure had been restored, following transfusion to replace blood lost from serious wounds. Specially trained Medical Officers were placed in charge of resuscitation teams, which dealt with severe cases of wound shock in the resuscitation wards. The result was a significant reduction in cases of operative shock. Sir Geoffrey Keynes, a leading figure in the popularisation of blood transfusion in Britain, noted that in the early years of the technique donors had been regarded as heroes. During the war, however, attitudes changed: 'A voluntary blood donor was given 14 days extra leave at home and volunteers were to be found by the hundred. The successful candidates were not regarded as heroes by their friends.'[42] Transfusion nevertheless remained a noteworthy event in 1917-18, and difficulties arose from incompatibility of blood type between donor and recipient. Also, the blood had to be taken from donors on the spot, which meant that 2 pints was the most that could be given at any one time. Knowledge of the technique remained limited and there was little provision for transfusion in advance of the CCSs.

Surgery in the Second World War benefited from significant advances in blood transfusion. Refrigeration enabled stored blood to become a standard resource, fluid and dried plasma was widely in use, and there was greater familiarity with the techniques of intravenous transfusion. In 1939 there was immediate recognition of the necessity to provide stored blood for military needs. An Army Blood Centre was established at Bristol, under Brigadier Lionel Whitby, where blood and plasma were collected and prepared for transport overseas. By 1943 the Army Blood Transfusion Service operated in 850 centres throughout the UK and had taken blood from over a quarter of a million donors. It trained Medical Officers who were then dispatched to oversee arrangements at base transfusion units in the theatres overseas. This organisation enabled Britain to supply whole blood to any theatre of war within reasonable distance. In 1941, for example, a Dakota regularly transported up to 300 bottles of blood to the British Eighth Army.[43] Medical units overseas also collected blood. On 9 November 1942 the commander of 19 General Hospital, at Fayid, noted that 5,000 pints of blood were collected in collaboration with the blood transfusion unit at Cairo.[44] The donors were all volunteers who were rewarded with a pint of beer. Compatibility between donors and recipients was ensured, as every serviceman had his blood group marked in his pay book. Transfusion was made mobile by the establishment of the Field Transfusion Unit, which was the smallest self-contained unit in the British Army. It consisted of one officer, four other ranks and a refrigeration vehicle. Its mobility meant that it was able to operate alongside FSUs, FAs, CCSs or General Hospitals, depending upon circumstances.[45] W. H. Ogilvie commended the achievements of the Army Transfusion Service as 'the greatest surgical advance' of the Second World War.[46]

During the course of 1914-18 developments in anaesthesia ensured that it became much more reliable, with the adoption of gas and oxygen by 1918. Throughout the war, however, there was little recognition of anaesthetists as skilled specialists.[47] The Second World War saw this situation transformed, as anaesthetists were given equal rank with surgeons. Developments in technique, with anaesthesia given intravenously, also enabled surgeons to save cases that would have proved fatal in 1914-18. This was particularly true of abdominal wounds, in which locally administered anaesthesia, supplementary to a general anaesthetic, radically improved the prospects for successful surgical intervention.[48]

In 1914 the British approach to war surgery was heavily influenced by the evidence from the Boer War, where wounds had healed rapidly and conservative surgery had produced good results. This approach proved disastrous on the Western Front, where the wounds quickly became infected due to the rich agricultural land over which the battles were fought. By 1915 more radical surgical intervention became the norm, with complete excision of infected wounds at the earliest opportunity. The latter involved the extraction of all foreign bodies from the wound, and the removal of all dead muscle, which by 1916 had been recognised as the breeding ground for gas gangrene. Once excised the wounds appeared free from infection and the temptation was to close them. This often led to amputations or death, as wounds were not sterile and bacteria became trapped inside. The practice therefore developed of excision followed by delayed primary suture. This approach produced excellent surgical results, but it worked less efficiently in the mobile warfare of 1918, as it took longer for the wounded to reach the surgeon.

Time was also a factor in the failure of delayed primary suture to be adopted in France during 1940, or in the Western Desert campaigns. Rarely were hospitals sited sufficiently close to the line to make delayed primary suture a viable option in the desert, 'and for the majority of young surgeons it was a forgotten if not unknown art'. In any case, the environment in the desert differed so markedly from that in France and Flanders that surgeons realised that a different surgical approach was more appropriate. The wounds were far less prone to be contaminated, and with reduced risk of sepsis surgeons were able to undertake more conservative surgical intervention – the practice of 'trimming' replaced the wound excision, which was now viewed as mutilation.[49]

Surgeons in the desert adopted the closed plaster method, following the practice developed by Trueta during the Spanish Civil War, in which wounds treated within 6 hours of receipt were immobilised in plaster casts applied directly to the skin.[50] However, as the lines of evacuation in the desert became extended, it was found that greater comfort and protection had to be provided for fractures. It was in these circumstances that padded plaster box splints, like the Tobruk splint, were adopted. The closed plaster approach was appropriate to conditions in which there was likely to be some delay before the wounded reached the stable environment required for further surgical treatment. Closing the wounds in plaster, though, had the disadvantage that it restricted access to the wound:

> 'Nearly all battle casualties are compound fractures; this inevitably involves an additional hazard, the inclusion within the wound of foreign bodies, bullets, pieces of shrapnel and the ubiquitous germs. Ideally these should be removed as quickly as possible… The surgeon is then faced with a dilemma especially as Plaster of Paris usually limits his further access to the wound. Experience has shown that it is often better to ignore the potential danger of the foreign body and germs for the greater benefits that Plaster of Paris bestows.'[51]

George Feggetter, however, believed that in the early part of the Second World War surgeons had been too heavily influenced by misguided assumptions about the surgical successes of the Spanish Civil War, and that most had been ignorant of the dangers of infection in war wounds. He found that when open wounds encased in plaster of Paris were revealed in the theatre:

> '…it was not uncommon to find numerous living maggots infesting wounds covered with healthy looking granulation tissue, other wounds were covered

with greenish sloughs and slimy, sticky discharge. (Indeed it appeared that those wounds harbouring maggots were sometimes healthier than those without them.) But when cleaned up long broad wound surfaces had a fibrous base adherent to underlying muscle and this accounted for the very slow healing process.'[52]

In fact, during the course of the campaigns in North Africa, surgeons were increasingly confronting infected wounds, and began to modify surgical practice accordingly. The climate and cultivated soil over which these battles were fought resembled more closely the conditions on the Western Front in 1914-18. Excision was increasingly favoured over 'trimming', and improvements in evacuation meant that delayed primary suture once again became an option. In Italy, those with experience of the First World War noticed that wounds were identical in character to those encountered 25 years earlier. All surgeons now had to adopt a radical approach. For the first time since 1939 the conditions in place prior to the Cassino assault, on 11 May 1943, enabled excision and delayed primary suture to be adopted as standard practice. The results were impressive according to Brigadier F. A. R. Stammers: '...it is no exaggeration to say that several thousands of men have been returned to duty much earlier than they would have without delayed suture and large numbers who otherwise would have been placed in Category "D" have been retained in the higher categories.' The surgical statistics from Cassino revealed that 90 per cent of the wounded were treated by delayed primary suture, and that these cases healed completely. In the advance on the Gothic Line, however, the lines of evacuation became extended and the consequent delay in treatment produced less favourable results: only 78 per cent of wounds showed perfect healing. The introduction of Delayed Primary Suture Centres in the forward areas saw a return to the success rate recorded at Cassino.[53] Thus, by the time of D-Day, surgeons were following the surgical practice that had operated in France during the First World War.

The fight against wound infection exercised medicine throughout 1914-18. Surgeons were completely unprepared for the treatment of battle casualties in 1914, expecting that the aseptic approach of civilian practice would be equally applicable to war surgery. The aseptic technique, however, simply avoided the further contamination of already infected wounds. The heavily infected wounds forced a return to Listerian principles. They were drained and initially treated with the older antiseptics, including carbolic and hydrogen peroxide. These antiseptics failed to combat the gas infection and many limbs were lost as a consequence. Almroth Wright criticised the use of antiseptics and developed a system of wound irrigation, using an hypertonic salt solution, that had good results, becoming the standard practice from 1915. The salt solution did not sterilise the wounds and research continued into the use of antiseptics. Alexis Carrel and Henry Dakin developed the most widely adopted method for treating wounds with antiseptics. Their approach used a system of tubes to allow the cleansing of wounds with a sodium hypochlorite solution. Other treatments used included BIPP (iodoform), developed by Rutherford Morrison, permanganate of potash and salicylic acid. The antiseptics did not sterilise the wounds but in a time before antibiotics they were the best that medicine could call on, and they did contribute to a decrease in the number of amputations.[54]

In 1939 surgeons had the benefit of newer antiseptics – the sulphonamide group, which included sulphanilamide, sulphapyridine and sulphathiazole. Alexander Fleming's research revealed that although these antiseptics did not kill bacteria, they did prevent the growth of infection, allowing the body's natural defences to get to work.[55] Their failure to kill bacteria meant that these drugs had to be used in conjunction with specific sera, such as those used against tetanus and gas gangrene. By stopping the spread of infection the sulphonamides did ensure that, even when prevailing circumstances militated against immediate surgery, there was no repetition of the severely septic wounds encountered in the Great War.[56]

The biggest advance in chemotherapy during the Second World War was undoubtedly the use of penicillin in the treatment of war wounds. Its employment contributed to vastly improved prospects for cases that were likely to have proved unsaveable in 1914-18, such as serious brain injuries. It enabled gunshot injuries to be closed by delayed primary suture and allowed surgeons to conduct reamputations of infected stumps.[57] It proved effective as a prophylactic against gas gangrene, and equally so as a complement to anti-gas gangrene serum in established cases. As in the First World War, however, there was a need to recognise the limitations of drugs. Stammers found that in the desert campaigns inexperienced surgeons had been too apt to attribute the successful performance of wounds to the impact of sulphanilamides. The drugs were not miracle workers; the decrease in infection as compared to 1914-18 was simply a reflection of the different climate and terrain. This became apparent when the desert environment was left behind. In fact it was clear that in the fight against wound infection 'even penicillin [is] no substitute for surgery. Surgery is the first line of defence: the drugs are adjuncts'.[58]

The increased surgical work of the CCSs during the Great War was facilitated by the formation of surgical teams. These consisted of a surgeon, an anaesthetist, a sister and two theatre orderlies. In 1917 it was also increasingly the practice for teams at particular CCSs to be responsible for certain types of wounds. However, throughout the war there were complaints that insufficient attention was paid to medical specialisms. The principle of teamwork was extended in 1939-45 and accompanied greater recognition of surgical specialisms, alongside a greater emphasis on mobility and treatment in the forward areas. Specialist mobile teams were organised, including ophthalmic, chest, neurosurgical, maxillo-facial and orthopaedic units.

The treatment of skull and brain injuries is indicative of the advance of specialisation in war surgery. Head injuries had never been systematically segregated during the First World War, although some individuals, such as Harvey Cushing, had begun to establish specialist centres. By 1939, however, the British Army had recognised neurosurgery as a specialism, and it entered the Second World War with clear plans for the employment of neurosurgeons and the segregation of head injuries. The newly created Army Head Injuries Service established the Mobile Neurosurgical Units, which were deployed in all the theatres of operations. The first such unit saw service in the Western Desert and consisted of 'two large trucks, two drivers, four army surgeons and four assistants from other ranks, in addition to all necessary equipment'.[59] Between 18 November 1940 and 6 February 1941, this unit dealt with over 350 cases and undertook 239 major operations. The unit recorded a mortality of just six patients, under treatment in the desert, and a further four following their transfer to the base.[60] This successful record pointed the way forward. Altogether, during 1939-45, the work of mobile neurosurgical units ensured that over 90 per cent of head wounds received immediate expert treatment; the death rate for penetrating head wounds was reduced to 5 per cent, and to less than 1 per cent for non-penetrating injuries.[61]

The work of field surgical teams was greatly assisted by the mobile specialist units. George Feggetter recalled the benefits of having a mobile orthopaedic team attached: '...[it] proved of great value in the treatment of simple and compound fractures caused by gunshot and mortar wounds thus allowing the surgeon to deal more speedily with serious abdominal and thoracic wounds.'[62] Whereas advanced sections of neurosurgical and maxillo-facial units would operate in the forward areas, it was, however, generally accepted that the orthopaedic teams were best employed at the base – here the patients could be held in the stable conditions required for prolonged skeletal traction.[63] The segregation of fracture cases into specialist centres reflected the growth in the status of orthopaedics, building on the work of Robert Jones in the First World War. The consequent improvement in the surgical care of fractures was a significant factor in the greatly reduced incidence of amputations in 1939-45 as compared to 1914-18.[64]

Burns were far more common in the Second War than they were in the First, reflecting the consequences of the greater use of petrol due to the increased mechanisation of warfare. Burns were particularly prevalent amongst aircrews, tank crews and seamen escaping sinking ships into seas covered in burning oil. As Andrew Bamji points out, however, the greater incidence of burns in 1939-45, and the work of plastic surgeons at specialist centres, such as the Queen Victoria Hospital, East Grinstead, has tended to obscure the achievements of Harold Gillies and his team at the Queen's Hospital, Sidcup, where modern plastic surgery and burns treatment really began. It was here that the team approach to facial surgery was born, with close co-operation between plastic surgeons, dentists, anaesthetists and specialist support staff producing excellent results in terms of facial reconstruction, and setting the pattern for the future development of plastic surgery.[65] In the Second World War burns patients benefited from advances in surgical understanding, which led to a recognition of their particular needs. The Medical Research Council appointed a sub-committee in 1942 to co-ordinate research on burns, and the war highlighted the need for specially trained teams to deal with these cases.[66]

Also, building on the undisputed achievements of plastic surgery in the First War, preparations had been made, prior to the outbreak of war in 1939, for specialist plastic surgery teams to be assembled under the guidance of Gillies. During the Second World War designated centres for plastic surgery were established across the UK. Plastic surgery in 1939-45 underwent significant improvements, reflecting advances in techniques of skin-grafting and the use of penicillin. The recovery rate of patients was also greatly improved by the provision of expert plastic surgery with the Army in the field. From the Italian campaigns of 1943, it became the practice for maxillo-facial units to operate in the forward area, in close co-operation with ophthalmic and neurosurgical units. The primary treatment of bone fragments, and the undertaking of primary bone-grafts and skin-grafts, contributed to reduced hospital stays for the patients, and a more rapid return to active duty.[67]

In both World Wars the calibre of the surgeons' work was of the highest. However, advances in surgical specialisms and the greater opportunities that they were afforded by the military medical organisation of 1939-45 ensured that the wounded of the Second World War had better prospects for survival and recovery.

In the First World War medicine was increasingly recognised as a vital factor in victory. Early in 1918, when asked if he could foresee an end to the war, Sir Douglas Haig replied, 'Yes, take the medical services away from both armies, and the war will cease in a few days because the combatants would refuse to fight.'[68] In the 1939-45 conflict, the importance of medicine became even more apparent. In the USSR Stalin compared the achievements of the medical profession to those of airmen and tank crews.[69] The medical services had a duty to prevent sickness and to ensure that those who became sick were rapidly returned to duty. This required Medical Officers to be vigilant of the emotional and physical impact on servicemen, and planning for the medical war needed to take account of the climate, environment and nature of the fighting in any particular theatre. In this regard the work of Battalion Medical Officers was particularly important. Captain H. M. Jones's summation of his duties is equally applicable to both wars: 'To maintain the health of the Battalion by preventable measures and amidst a great deal of minor ailments to distinguish the early signs of serious diseases should they arise.'[70]

The First War was a war of the divisions fought mainly in the small area of Northern France and Flanders. Although actually shorter in years than the Second, for survivors dreading yet another winter it seemed to bring a mixture of monotony and fear. The Second World War was a war of the crews fought in a series of rapid engagements across the globe, in the sky and on the seas. The crews fought in cramped conditions, with sudden movement, drastic changes in temperatures and an instant requirement for vigilance. It was reported of the Royal Navy:

'…during the war one ship … went from Algiers to Murmansk in three weeks in January, from a mean temperature of 70°F to one varying between 18°F and minus 30. Habitability problems, always severe in ships of war … were greatly increased by war-time conditions, including voyages of great length, long periods closed up at Action and Cruising Stations, black-out and a vast increase in "wild heat" generated by constant running of main engines and the maintenance of the reserve of energy needed to allow the availability of full power at short notice.'[71]

For the Army in the First War, sickness was a serious potential threat of losses, which would add further gaps in the line to those caused by battle casualties. There were 3.5 million admissions in France and Flanders from the sick or injured, and of these 1.03 million had to be evacuated overseas. In the Passchendaele offensive the ration strength of the Fifth Army fell from 537,035 on 4 August to 171,041 on 10 November. To the attrition of battle could have been added yet more attrition through sickness and lowering morale from the long, bloody inconclusive fighting. In practice, loyalty kept down the sickness rate. Dr Charles Moran, Medical Officer of the Royal Fusiliers, recorded that, 'During the battle of the Somme there were no sick. It was the creed of the Regiment. Part of their being.'[72] The survivors fought on in the 'many varieties of mud'. They even had their record in a poem reported by the battalion medical officer of the Black Watch:

> "Tis easy to smile when the skies are blue
> And everything goes well with you,
> But the man who could grin
> With his boots letting in,
> With a boil on his neck
> And its mate on his chin,
> With I.C.T at the back of each knee
> and P.U.O of 103,
> Was the fellow who won the war!'[73]

Moran recorded during the battle of the Somme, '…this morning a man came to see me with an abscess in his hand and some fever. Last night there were ten degrees of frost and his hand must have given him hell, throbbing throughout his cold watch but he would not hear of hospital, he would not even hear of rest. He meant to go back and when I had cut it, back he went.'[74] For others it could be different. Moran reported how he had seen the Colonel who was now spending most of his time sheltering in a deep dug-out:

> '"My dysentery is damn bad, Doc," the Colonel said, as he passed his hand through his thin hair as if brushing it back. And when I did not speak he went on: "I'm afraid I'll have to go sick. It's a nuisance isn't it?" His long back leant forward, his head drooped. His eyes kept blinking. He looked old and troubled. For a quarter of a century he had been a soldier preparing no doubt for the real thing. It had come and this was the end.'[75]

The sickness rate rose with fatigues and inactivity, particularly in wet weather. At the battle of the Ancre in 1916 conditions were so bad that for the only time in the war one senior officer had direct evidence that British troops deserted in considerable numbers to the enemy. This was due to the 'low nervous condition produced by the appalling surroundings to the battle'.[76]

Even before the numbers of sick began to swell with growing stress and war weariness in the last years of the war, men had unavoidably been taken ill. For some this may have been the chance of getting back to Blighty, and in the first two years most who were sick for longer than seven days were in fact evacuated. Others wanted to get back in the line as soon as possible. One senior doctor reported how in 1916 he had seen the Corps Commander, Lord Cavan, 'very sick with dysentery'. He soon discovered that he was 'fretting lest his illness should lose him the command of the XIV Corps'. The doctor went 'straight to Sir Douglas Haig and on his next visit was able to tell his patient that he would return to his Corps. Cavan later reported that from that moment on he began to pick up and by the end of six weeks he was back in the field.'[77]

Another Medical Officer reported of an officer with chilblains who was very keen to get back, so as not to lose his temporary rank. A senior officer 'with arteries made of red tape' was insisting that after seven days a man could no longer stay at the Divisional Rest Station for slightly sick and wounded. Instead he had to go back to the CCS and ipso facto was struck off the strength of the division. Extra days were, however, wangled for this fortunate officer.[78]

Sickness affected young and older men alike. A VAD recorded in 1915 on their 'newest arrival', a 'young boy with bad trench feet, purple, red, swollen and with big black blisters from which later we get a great amount of fluid.'[79] In the harsh winter of 1916 older men, even working out of the front line in transport, were prone to get pneumonia. Driver Thomas Arthur Wood, aged 35, reported sick, and on 15 December he was taken to a field hospital. Two days later he was at No 10 CCS. On 22 December a chaplain wrote to his wife:

'I am sorry to inform you that your dear husband is seriously ill with pneumonia at No 10 C.C.S.

Remember he has a good chance, but it is best for you to know that his condition is still serious. He is very comfortable and receiving the very best of care. Everything that medical skill can do is being done for him; of that you need have no fear.

When I last saw him he was, if anything, somewhat improved.

I will keep you informed as to his condition: or, if he is able he will write you himself.

I am not his Chaplain, but was sent for, to see him.

Now you must not worry: just try and be brave. I know you will be anxious, but he has a good chance and the doctor is very hopeful.

Should you write him address his letters to: No 10 C.C.S., B.E.7, France.

May God sustain you in this your time of anxiety and give you back your dear husband.

Believe me, your very sincere friend…'

On 3 January Driver Wood was sent to Boulogne, and on 11 January he left France for a hospital in England. By 1 April he was at a convalescent centre in Eastbourne. He was discharged at Woolwich, in medical category B1, in March 1919, and survived to work as a docker at the Colonial Wharf after the war.

For the first two years of the war the patient experience would have been of treatment in a tented hospital, followed, if he was sick for longer than a few weeks, by evacuation to England. The end of 1916 saw a change of policy towards treating as many people as possible in France, partly so as to expedite their return to the front line and partly to reduce targets for submarines in the Channel. Against French protests the British authorities began to establish hospital cities in

Boulogne, Etaples and Rouen. By late 1917 there were above 20,000 beds in each of these three centres, using prefabricated buildings rather than tents. Hospital trains ran there from all points at the front. The experience of the patient was more impersonal and more standardised with increased use of protocols. The services for the sick and the convalescent patients was concentrated in these back areas, while, as outlined above, the Casualty Clearing Stations developed much greater capability for surgery and the immediate treatment of battle casualties.

For many it was the first experience of being treated in hospital by nursing staff. It was an experience characterised by exceptional care and humanity, with communication across the classes. 'Most nervous patients are reassured by "chipping", for "chipping" is the language they best understand.' The dreaded moment was when a patient labelled 'sev' was admitted from the hospital train. 'All you can do, sister, is to make him comfortable.' The VAD recorded that there 'follow some of the bitterest moments one is called upon to endure... One welcomes any little need of the patients.' One poor boy one night whispered, 'I don't know what I want. I seem to be slipping away.' In response to his requests 'there were changed and changed again the pillows, the cushions, the position of the limb, the cradle, the bedclothes, his lips were moistened, his face wiped.' His response was to say, 'I know now why you nurses are called "sisters". You are sisters to us boys.'[79] Following the expansion in 1916 the quality of the service declined. The crisis expansion was partly brought about by increasing the numbers of beds in wards and placing trestle cots and mattresses instead of hospital beds in huts for personnel, dining rooms or other accessory buildings. At first there was no increase in medical and nursing staff and many of the locations were 'altogether unsuitable for the permanent treatment of patients'.[80]

By 1918 there was more of a settled system of treatment, with large numbers of beds and a network of convalescent depots where men were brought back to full fitness through good food and physical exercise. Many more of the patients were suffering from the diseases of stress such as soldiers' heart, effort syndrome, or trench nephritis. The predisposing causes of trench nephritis were said to be 'cold and humidity, hard work and overloading the soldier with heavy equipment'.[81] The incidence was greatest in the winter months. In the Second World War machines came to do some of the lifting, but in the First every shell and every sandbag had to be lifted by hand. The numbers invalided because of heart disease rose from 2,500 in the first phase of the war, until 31 May 1916, to 36,569 by May 1918.[82]

In addition, the invisible enemy sprang some surprises, including the louse-borne disease of trench fever, where recovery might take many months. 'The extent to which our own troops were lousy had to be seen to be believed, and the kilts of the Scottish soldiers might have been specially designed for the benefit of the louse, their pleats forming ideal shelters and breeding places for it.'[83] Trench fever was possibly increased by exposure to cold and wet, which 'act indirectly by inducing men to share blankets and sleep closer together, so that infected lice pass from one to another with greater ease.'[84] Out of the line the soldier 'naturally seeks gaiety, brightness and laughter'. For an increasing number this could lead to a stay in one of the specialised VD units where there were 60,099 admissions in 1918, or over 3 in 100 of ration strength. The use of protocols was developed and stigma reduced in the interests of encouraging early treatment.

The last year of the war also saw an increase in shell shock, hysteria and neurasthenia. In the 1939-45 war part of the condition was decriminalised by accepting the reality of fatigue for those who had been in service for a length of time, and even in the Great War there was a recognition that, 'The stress and strain of active service not infrequently result in a condition of mild confusion, which may merge into deep stupor'.[85] Lord Dawson found the war confirming his view that the diseases of stress were advancing as the diseases of invasion receded, and commented on 'that curious blend of the physical and the psychical which seems more and more to characterise the ailments of present day humanity'.[86] The 'common' problems of hysteria often meant months or even years in hospital. Paralyses and contractures, staring eyes, hysterical muteness and blindness all became much more common and more difficult to treat. It was only towards the end of the war that short-cycle psychotherapy began to be used successfully.

By 1918 there were many thousands of people in hospital in the UK with longer-term conditions and disabilities. The slow-stream hospital patient could be in an ex-asylum or a country house. The environment was relatively pleasant with many entertainments and gifts from the local population. 'Asylums and poor law infirmaries ... proved ideal buildings for war hospital purposes, as not only had they ample and attractive pleasure grounds and gardens, recreation fields, recreation halls and well-equipped stages for concerts and theatricals, but they were also going concerns with ample stores and kitchens.'[87] The history of war hospitals in Shropshire recorded how in one county alone there could be more than ten hospitals in country houses. Some patients could be discharged after 40 or 50 days. Others might have to stay for months or years undergoing repeated operations, such as the early guinea pigs for facial surgery at Sidcup.[88] The First World War left a legacy of long-term disability and hospital treatment. 'A soldier, walking slowly and painfully with the aid of two sticks, bending far forward, his arms and legs often shaking with the effort was a common sight in the latter part of the last War.'[89] By 1930 1,664,000 people had been awarded war pensions, 27.7 per cent of those who had served.[90] For many veterans the legacy of the war was disability, continuing pain, nightmares and reduced life expectancy. The experience of patients went on for many years after the war, with those with mental or psychotic illness rated as most likely to be permanently in hospital. They must have been some of the patients in the asylums reconverted in the post-war world.

The tropical and Mediterranean fronts in the First World War created a considerable number of non-battle casualties, especially in view of the limited fighting done in most of them, with the exception of Gallipoli. Salonika was not only the central powers' largest internment camp but also an unusual centre of disease. In Salonika, Palestine, East Africa and Mesopotamia the main threat was from malaria, and even in the First World War, of all the diseases responsible for casualties, 'malaria easily took first place' with almost half a million admissions.[91] Such diseases were to be an even more significant part of the total burden in the Second War. For the British Army in the first five years of the Second World War almost all fighting was in Mediterranean or tropical areas. Army patients were most likely to be those with heatstroke in the desert or in Southern Italy, dysentery in India or malaria in Burma. The Army put great effort into prevention and for all diseases stressed treatment close to the battle area so as to accelerate return and to minimise the problems of air evacuation. The experience of the patient was to be cared for in a small hutted or tented hospital on a temporary site with the dedication and cheerfulness of the nursing staff supplying the main element of continuity with the First World War.

Such patients were more likely to have had long service in the theatre. Army doctors noted a sharp rise in diseases affected by carelessness after 18 months away from home.[92] The Army waiting in Britain was in good health. In the First World War there was comment on 'the large number of men rendered ineffective by the simple ailments of everyday life, such as diseases of the respiratory and digestive systems, rheumatic fever and its allied conditions, local and general injuries, minor septic infections and influenza.'[93] The Army of the Second War was drawn from a population with far better health and the process of recruitment was more prolonged and carefully organised. The new problem was that of gastric illness and especially of ulcers. These patients in the UK were treated in separate wings taken over from ordinary hospitals. The vast construction and requisitioning programme was not repeated and again for most of the war the patients were in a few wards on their own rather than in large treatment areas.

The new 'patients' of the Second World War were members of crews in bombers, ships or tanks who had to undergo extreme stress. 'In good weather crews of heavy bombers and their fighter escorts may go out on daily missions lasting nine to twelve hours. The constant emotional stress which interferes with adequate relaxation is then superimposed on the physical fatigue so that the effect is increasingly cumulative.'[94] Immobility in long flights resulting in muscular tension, and low temperatures at high altitudes added more stress. 'Flak is impersonal, inexorable and as used by the Germans deadly accurate.'[95] The loss of friends in combat was another source of stress. Some crews developed somatic illness, which ultimately removed them from the war. Like Moran's colonel, this 25-year-old dive-bomber pilot developed severe diarrhoea, for treatment of which he was sent to a station hospital. He was treated several times but the problem kept recurring. He then 'developed malaria owing to his own carelessness', as he had not bothered to sleep under a mosquito net at the height of the rainy season.[96]

Some of the same stress factors were at work at sea, as in Arctic convoys. There could be sudden changes in temperature as a result of alterations in wind intensity and direction, leading to thawing or freezing. 'In bad convoys, fighting their way mile by mile, large numbers of the crew were at action stations, out in the open, for days on end.'[97] The noise was 'dementing' and 'behind it all was the awe-inspiring beauty of the Arctic with its cruel cold, its dreadful loneliness and what seemed to be the utter hopelessness of survival should the worst happen.'[98] As on the Somme, the pride in the service was the main motivating force. 'The object of training was to create in him [the sailor] such a personal pride that failure to do his duty would be unthinkable.'[99] For those who were badly injured, shore treatment was in the inadequate facilities in Kola and Archangel.

The military importance of medicine raised some awkward ethical issues concerning attitudes to the enemy. In June 1942 Sir Edward Mellanby, at the Medical Research Council, wrote to Sir Alfred Webb-Johnson, President of the Royal College of Surgeons, seeking advice on whether information pertaining to research on penicillin should be made public, as it was likely to prove valuable to the enemy. Already information had been withheld concerning the use of compounds for the prevention of lice because, at the time, there had been expectations that German troops, in Russia and the Balkans, were likely to succumb to typhus. Webb-Johnson replied that the view of the Royal College was strongly inclined to publication, believing that suppression of information on penicillin was 'not consistent with the glorious history of British medicine'. In any case, it was deemed that Germany was unlikely to benefit from the information until after the war. Generally, the Government view appeared to be that medical knowledge should be published in the wider interests of science and out of respect for 'the ordinary humanitarian view'. In the case of penicillin, the pages of the medical press provide evidence of this readiness to propagate information.[100]

The 'humanitarian view' appears to have been the one that generally informed attitudes towards the treatment of enemy wounded. A. A. Martin's conviction that 'there is no nationality amongst the men in a hospital' is a fair summary of attitudes on all sides during the First World War.[101] In the later conflict this attitude appears to have prevailed between the Western Allies and the German and Italian armies, and there is much evidence of co-operation between the medical services of opposing forces. One doctor recalled the treatment of German wounded following the Battle of El Alamein:

'Eventually over 40 German wounded overflowed into the British hospital… Most of the British staff were engaged in one way or another in tending to the German wounded. It was essentially an exercise in team work and I know that the German medical staff is deeply appreciative of the help we gave them.'[102]

Bald statistical evidence suggests that there is no comparison in the casualty experience between the First and Second World Wars. In 1914-18 British figures record 1,837,613 wounded and a further 677,515 men who were either killed, missing in action or later died of wounds. In 1939-45 the equivalent figures were 239,575 and 126,734 respectively. However, as John Ellis points out, when the figures for the Second World War are represented as a percentage of the number of men exposed to battle the casualty rates for both wars prove remarkably similar. The more telling difference between the wounded in the two wars was that those in 1939-40 were probably much fitter, prior to wounding, than their earlier counterparts – a fact that greatly aided the medics in their work. The wounded from both wars are, however, united by the bravery they displayed in their suffering. One doctor, who commanded four field hospitals during the course of the Second War recalled, 'My most enduring memories are the courage and stoicism of the men who were admitted as patients.'[103] Luther Wolff, an American doctor, shared this admiration for the wounded. He found it 'remarkable' that even the 'worst banged up' GIs refused to give in to their wounds.[104] Equally remarkable, as Dr Aitken found while serving as an RMO in Normandy, was the fact that the most seriously wounded could be oblivious to their condition: 'Curious – the one with both legs off only wanted to evacuate his bowels – otherwise he felt nothing.'[105]

To conclude, it is evident that in both wars there was a growing recognition of the vital role to be played by medicine in securing victory; an understanding that the fate of the casualty had a key bearing on the fate of the whole Army. This represented a triumph for medicine in the British Army and it compared well with the medical shortcomings that had been the focus of public criticism in the Crimean and Boer Wars. The physicians and surgeons of 1939-45, however, had the benefits of learning the lessons taught by their counterparts in 1914-18. Casualties in the Second World War benefited from advances in technology and medical knowledge, which resulted in more comfortable and faster evacuation; greater provision of specialist treatment and after care; the improvement of techniques, such as blood transfusion; and the adoption of drug treatments, including the application of penicillin in war medicine. On the other hand, the experience of the casualties and medical personnel could show as much diversity between theatres in the same war as they could between the two wars – contrast for example the experience of the Dardanelles with that of the Western Front in 1914-18, or the differing circumstances of the Western Desert and Italy in the Second War. The one constant in both wars was the devotion of the medical personnel and the bravery of the casualties in their care.

Notes on contributors

Professor Nick Bosanquet, Imperial College, University of London, UK
Nick Bosanquet is Professor of Health Policy at Imperial College. He is a health economist and formerly worked at the Centre for Health Economics at the University of York. He is a special advisor to the House of Commons Select Committee on Health Services. He contributed to Facing Armageddon (1996) and lists among his leisure pursuits visiting battlefields and brainstorming with Americans and others about military history.

Dr Ian R. Whitehead, The University of Derby, UK
Ian Whitehead is Lecturer in Modern British History at the University of Derby. He has recently completed a book, Doctors in the Great War (Leo Cooper, 1999), and has also contributed chapters to Facing Armageddon, Passchendaele in Perspective and Medicine and Modern Warfare.

Recommended reading

Cooter, R., Harrison, M. and Sturdy, S., *Medicine and Modern Warfare* (Amsterdam: Rodopi, 1999)
   War, Medicine and Modernity (London: Sutton, 1998)
Whitehead, I. R., *Doctors in the Great War* (London: Leo Cooper, 1999)

Notes

1   See Mark Harrison, 'Medicine and the Management of Modern Warfare: An Introduction' in Roger Cooter, Mark Harrison and Steve Sturdy, *Medicine and Modern Warfare* (Amsterdam: Rodopi, 1999) pp1-27

2   J. C. Watts, *Surgeon at War* (London: Allen & Unwin) p27

3   Colonel J. R. Mac, 'A Doctor Goes to War', Wellcome Institute for the History of Medicine (WIHM), Contemporary Medical Archives Centre (CMAC), RAMC 944, 16 April 1940, p55

4   W. H. Ogilvie, *Forward Surgery in Modern War* (London: Butterworth, 1944) pp1-2

5   W. H. Ogilvie, 'General Introduction' in Sir Zachary Cope (ed), *Surgery* (London: HMSO, 1953) p4

6   I. R. Whitehead, 'Third Ypres – Casualties and British Medical Services: An Evaluation' in Liddle, P. H. (ed), *Passchendaele in Perspective* (London: Leo Cooper, 1997) p190

7   I. R. Whitehead, *Doctors in the Great War* (London: Leo Cooper, 1999) pp198-9; 202

8   'Experiences of an RMO in a Retreat – France and Belgium, 1940', WIHM, CMAC, RAMC 761/3/2, p1-2

9   Ibid, p3

10 Ibid, p4

11 I. R. Whitehead, *Doctors in the Great War*, op cit, pp190-5

12, 13 'War Diary of 10 Field Ambulance', WIHM, CMAC, RAMC 801/13/3, p4
     Ibid, p7

14 Ian Samuel, *Doctor at Dunkirk* (London, Autolycus, 1985) pp22-4

15 Ibid, p40

16 Colonel J. R. Mac, 'A Doctor Goes to War', WIHM, CMAC, RAMC 944, 7 February 1940, p11

17 Major T. R. Maurice, 'My First Three Decades', extract from letter, 5 June 1944, p54, Imperial War Museum (IWM)

18 Ibid, 27 May 1940, pp76-7

19 Major General P. S. Tomlinson, 'Operations in the Western Desert – Medical Aspect', WIHM, CMAC, RAMC 761/3/6, 28 February 1941, p3

20 'Notes on Re-organisation of AMS', WIHM, CMAC, RAMC 761/3/7, 15 May 1941, p2

21 P. T. S. Morrison, 'Jottings of the Medical Administration of an Armoured Division during Active Service', p12, in papers of Lt-Col Peter B. Ascroft, WIHM, CMAC, RAMC 1154/2/9

22 Ibid. In other theatres of the Second World War the journey of the wounded could be even more arduous, with the wounded in Burma, for example, being in transit sometimes up to six weeks; see John Ellis, *The Sharp End: The Fighting Man in World War II* (London: Pimlico, 1990) p173

23 Ibid

24 Brigadier Charles Donald, 'With the Eighth Army in the Field', *British Medical Journal* (BMJ), 1944 (I), p743

25 Brigadier A. E. Porritt, Brigadier R. K. Debenham and Colonel C. C. Ross, 'B.L.A. Surgery', BMJ, 1945 (II), pp377-8

26 'Report on the Medical Aspect of the Cyrenaica Campaign', WIHM, CMAC, RAMC 761/3/5, p14

27 'Notes on Re-organisation of AMS', WIHM, CMAC, RAMC 761/3/7, 15 May 1941, p2

28 'Reasons for Rendering Mobile Certain CCSs for Work in the Western Desert', WIHM, CMAC, RAMC 761/3/9, p1

29 'The Mobile Medical Units', extract from a broadcast by Leslie Nichols, in papers of Lt-Col Peter B. Ascroft, WIHM, CMAC, RAMC 1154/2/12

30 Major General P. S. Tomlinson, 'Operations in the Western Desert – Medical Aspect', WIHM, CMAC, RAMC 761/3/6, 28 February 1941, p. 3.

31 'Report on the Medical Aspect of the Cyrenaica Campaign', op cit, p16

32 P. B. Ascroft, 'Experiences of a Mobile Surgical Unit in the Western Desert', WIHM, CMAC, RAMC 1154/2/27, p1

33 Brigadier Charles Donald, op cit, pp709-11

34 Ibid, p713

35 Porritt, Debenham and Ross, op cit, pp377-8

36 Ambrose Lockwood, 'Some Experiences in the Last War', BMJ, 1940 (I), p358
37 Porritt, Debenham and Ross, op cit, p379
38 Yefim Smirnov, 'The Medical Corps in Red Army Operations', BMJ, 1945 (I), p175
39 P. B. Ascroft, 'Experiences of a Mobile Surgical Unit in the Western Desert', op cit, p13
40 Ibid, p11
41 Ambrose Lockwood, op cit, p356
42 Sir Geoffrey Keynes, Royal College of Surgeons (RCS), MS Add 514, *MTE Journal*, October 1941, Vol 1, No 5, p10
43 'The Army Blood Transfusion Service', BMJ, 1943 (I), pp610-1; Harold C. Edwards, 'The Contribution of War to the Advancement of Surgery', *Journal of the Royal Institute of Public Health & Hygiene*, January 1956, pp17-8
44 Colonel J. R. Mac, op cit, 9 November 1942, p220
45 Brigadier Sir John Knox Smith Boyd, 'Blood Transfusion', WIHM, CMAC, RAMC 1816/6/1/1, pp1-3
46 W. H. Ogilvie, 'Some Applications of the Surgical Lessons of War to Civil Practice', BMJ, 1945 (I), p620
47 I. R. Whitehead, *Doctors in the Great War*, op cit, pp190-5
48 George Feggetter, 'Diary of an RAMC Surgeon at War, 1942-1946', WIHM, CMAC, RAMC 1776, p72; J. C. Watts, op cit, p90
49 Brigadier F. A. R. Stammers, 'Reports of the Consultant Surgeon to Allied Armies in Italy, 1 October 1944 to 28 February 1945: Appendix 2: The Role of the Forward Surgeon in the Policy of Delayed Suture: The Genesis of technique in Italy', WIHM, CMAC, RAMC 779, pp1-2
50 Douglas W. Jolly, *Field Surgery in Total War* (London: Hamish Hamilton, 1940) pp107-10
51 Colonel J. R. Mac, op cit, 10 August 1942, p210
52 George Feggetter, op cit, pp126-7, 161
53 Brigadier F. A. R. Stammers, op cit, p3 and pp1-2 in Appendix
54 I. R. Whitehead, *Doctors in the Great War*, op cit, pp153-4, 206-7
55 'Antiseptics in Wartime Surgery', BMJ, 1940 (II), p715
56 W. H. Ogilvie, *Forward Surgery in Modern War*, op cit, pp11-2
57 W. H. Ogilvie, 'Some Applications of the Surgical Lessons of War to Civil Practice', op cit, p621
58 Brigadier F. A. R. Stammers, 'Report of the Consultant Surgeon to Allied Armies in Italy, for quarter ending 30 June 1944', WIHM, CMAC, RAMC 779, p14
59 'The Mobile Medical Units', extract from a broadcast by Leslie Nichols, in papers of Lt-Col Peter B. Ascroft, WIHM, CMAC, RAMC 1154/2/12, p1
60 Ibid, p2
61 Sir Zachary Cope, 'Neurosurgery' in *Surgery*, op cit, pp377-87
62 George Feggetter, op cit, p43
63 Brigadier Charles Donald, op cit, p713
64 H. Osmond-Clarke and J. Crawford Adams, 'Orthopaedic Surgery' in Sir Zachary Cope, *Surgery*, op cit, pp234-70
65 Andrew Bamji, 'Facial Surgery: The Patient's Experience' in Hugh Cecil and Peter Liddle, *Facing Armageddon* (London: Leo Cooper, 1996) pp490-501
66 Sir Zachary Cope, 'Burns' in *Surgery*, op cit, pp288-90
67 Sir Harold Gillies, et al, 'Plastic Surgery' in *Surgery*, op cit, pp321-59
68 Ambrose Lockwood, 'Surgical Problems of War', BMJ, 1940 (I), p495
69 Anonymous Soviet doctor, 'Work of the Medical Corps in the USSR', BMJ, 1942 (II), p734
70 Captain H. M. Jones, 'The Work of a Battalion Medical Officer', IWM, p1
71 C. H. Joynt, 'The Royal Naval Medical Services' in A. S. Macnalty and W. F. Mellor, *Medical Services in War: The principal medical lessons of the Second World War* (London: HMSO, 1968) p21
72 Lord Moran, *The Anatomy of Courage* (London: Constable, 1945) p174
73 D. Rorie, *A Medico's Luck in the War* (London: Milne & Hutchison, 1929) p3. ICT is inflammation of connective tissues, PUO pyrexia of unknown origin
74 Lord Moran, op cit, p173
75 Ibid, p122
76 J. F. C. Fuller, evidence in *Report of the War Office Committee of Enquiry into 'Shell Shock'* (London:

HMSO, 1922)

77 F. Watson, *Dawson of Penn* (London: Chatto & Windus, 1950) p122

78 D. Rorie, op cit, pp14-5

79 O. Dent, *A V.A.D. in France* (London: Grant Richards, 1917) p47

79 Ibid, pp54-5

80 T. J. Mitchell and G. M. Smith, *Medical Services Casualties and Medical Statistics of the Great War* (London: HMSO, 1931)

81 Ibid, p90

82 A. Hurst, *Medical Diseases of War* (London: Edward Arnold, 3rd Edition, 1943) p193

83 Ibid, p448

84 Ibid, p205

85 Ibid, p107

86 F. Watson, op cit

87 W. G. Macpherson, *Official History of the War, Medical Services, General History*, Vol 1 (London: HMSO, 1921) p79

88 Andrew Bamji, 'Facial Surgery: The Patient's Experience', op cit, pp490-501

89 A. Hurst, op cit, p47

90 Mitchell and Smith, op cit, p315

91 A. Hurst, op cit, p333

92 F. Crew, 'The Army Medical Services', in Macnalty and Mellor, op cit, pp166-7

93 Mitchell and Smith, op cit, p59

94 R. Grinker and J. Spiegel, *Men under Stress* (London: Blakiston, 1945) p30

95 Ibid, p34

96 Ibid, pp109-10

97 C. H. Joynt, 'The Royal Naval Medical Services', in Macnalty and Mellor, op cit, p22

98 Ibid, p43

99 Ibid, p37

100 Sir Edward Mellanby to Sir Alfred Webb-Johnson, 19 June 1942; Sir Alfred Webb-Johnson to Mellanby, 2 July 1942, RCS, MS Add 507

101 I. R. Whitehead, *Doctors in the Great War*, op cit, p157

102 John Ellis, op cit, pp156-9

103 Colonel J. R. Mac, op cit, pi

104 Luther H. Wolff, *Forward Surgeon* (New York: Vantage Press, 1985) pp202-3

106 Dr Aitken, transcript diary, WIHM, CMAC, RAMC 1668, p20

Chapter 19

Spies, codebreakers and secret agents

M. R. D. Foot

C landestine action is always presented, especially by thriller-writers, as something original and new. In fact it has a long history. Feinting, for instance, on which strategic deception is based, is pretty well as old as hand-to-hand combat, far older than warfare; while Homer's *Odyssey* describes some classic escapes. Hardly anything clandestine was done in the war against Hitler that had not been done, in some comparable way, during the Great War that preceded it.

Just as war is one, like the sea, so is the world of secret action. For ease of working, separate secret services often handle the collection and analysis of news, propaganda, security, subversion and sabotage, help to escapers, or deception. Most of these services must depend heavily on each other, and need to learn not to waste their energies on inter-secret-service squabbles. This elementary lesson in service politics has been taken in slowly, or not at all, by too large a number of the secret services in many countries, thus providing a point of entry for sensationalists, who keep trying to wrest the whole subject away from serious historians. The former sell more, many more, books; the latter try to tell the truth.

No decent strategy can be founded except on a sound appreciation of the enemy's strength and intentions; intelligence services exist to provide data on just this point. A vast deal was already public knowledge in August 1914 about how large the armies and fleets on each side were; tactical doctrines, and mobilisation arrangements, were also well known. There should therefore have been no scope for strategic surprise. The Germans managed all the same to bring off a major surprise both on the Eastern and on the Western Front.

In the East, they secured their almost annihilating victory at Tannenberg through an intelligence accident. The Russian high command, rejoicing in the use of the latest technology, issued its operation orders by wireless telegraphy, but omitted to put them into any kind of cipher; this made life easy for Hoffman and Ludendorff, who had adequate listening staffs (just as the British had adequate listening staffs on the South Downs in the summer of 1940 to get a few minutes' advance warning of every large Luftwaffe raid on England, from pilots taxying out for take-off who chatted to each other in clear). Their triumph can be compared with the prodigies of Polish and British decipher technique, which by the summer of 1944 had laid the German Enigma cipher machine's secrets so wide open to

Germany's enemies that a great many operation orders were read by both sides, while the Germans supposed that they remained entirely private to themselves.[1]

English interest in decipher goes back at least to the 1580s, when it was used to unravel Mary, Queen of Scots. Churchill's account of how the High Seas Fleet's codebook was secured after the Russian Navy sank the *Magdeburg* is now well known. For most of the rest of the war, the Admiralty had access to the main tactical orders being given to the High Seas Fleet; though a faulty connection, inside the Admiralty itself, between the intelligence and the operational branches prevented Jellicoe from securing another Glorious First of June in 1916, the morning after the fight off Jutland. Care was taken, next time round, to make sure that there was a close link (by teleprinter and, at moments of crisis, by scrambler telephone) between the decipher staff at Bletchley Park and the operational intelligence centre off Whitehall, and that centre in turn worked closely with the First Sea Lord and the rest of the operational naval staff.[2]

The British success in breaking the German diplomatic cipher, which led to the crisis admirably surveyed in Barbara Tuchman's *The Zimmermann Telegram*[3], is well known; so is the success that Bletchley Park had in reading both Enigma and Geheimschreiber machine ciphers in the later war. It is less often remembered that the Germans too were capable of decipher; the Admiralty maintained for years that merchant ship captains could not manage complex codes, so up to 1943 the Germans read easily the Royal Navy's instructions to merchant ships forming up into convoys, a great help to U-boats' depredations. This crux was resolved when someone realised that it would save a great many lives if each merchant ship carried a handful of RN sailors and a Typex cipher machine, which the Germans never broke.

The Germans' second surprise in 1914, on the Western Front, lay in manpower deployment. Everyone who mattered knew, to within a thousand or two, how many men were serving in the German Regular Army when the war broke out; that the Germans were able to mobilise, and bring forward into battle, a substantial further army of students and others from what were later called 'reserved occupations', sprang a disagreeable surprise on the British Expeditionary Force under Sir John French at First Ypres. The riflemen of the BEF rose to the challenge – hence it became what the Germans remember as the Kindermord, the massacre of the innocents.

Potential or actual enemies' resources in manpower and womanpower ought to be a permanent preoccupation of intelligence services, not all of which rise to this challenge. The British secret (or special) intelligence service (SIS), put on a formal footing by a Cabinet decision in 1909, grew from its original staff of a single elderly naval officer to a staff of over a thousand (agents included) by the end of 1917, and produced a most valuable volume of data in the course of the Great War, remaining directly under that same officer's hand. He was (Sir) Mansfield Smith-Cumming, the original 'C', knighted after the end of the war in recognition of his services. He held, with Benjamin Franklin, that three can keep a secret if two of them are dead; and he liked to do everything of real importance himself, which of course limited his field of action. According to his biographer, he did not confine his work to the securing of that most precious of intelligence officers' finds, an accurate order of battle of the opposing forces; he diversified into supplying escape aids for prisoners of war, providing explosive devices for saboteurs, and engaging in propaganda.[4] During the next World War, the British escape service, MI9, the Special Operations Executive (SOE), and the Political Warfare Executive (PWE) that grew out of it, were formed to handle these extra tasks.

Cumming was hampered during the war (as well as before and after it) by constant attempts by other officers to overrule him or to take control of his service's work. This, again, was still Whitehall's behaviour towards various secret services through the Second World War; SOE in particular was several times the object of efforts to close it down altogether, or bring it strictly under the wing of SIS or of the Foreign Office.

Cumming managed all the same to secure intelligence of infinite value, which saved thousands of lives, from agents behind the German lines on the Western Front, most of them in a Belgian group (itself over a thousand strong, not counted in his estimate of strength above) called La Dame Blanche. After the war, the chief of police at Cologne confessed that it had been a 'fatal mistake' by the Germans to underrate the British secret service: 'We now know that they knew 100 times more about us than we knew about them and 1,000 times more than we gave them credit for knowing.'[5]

One of the pillars of La Dame Blanche, Walthere Dewé, went on to become chief executive of the Belgian telephone service, and came out of retirement in 1940 to set up a parallel, and equally efficient, successor to La Dame Blanche called Clarence, which provided masses of priceless intelligence to the British throughout the German occupation of Belgium in 1940-44. Early in 1944, Dewé himself was shot down in the street by Gestapo agents who would not let a priest near him, to administer the last rites, until he was quite dead; Clarence's efforts went on almost untroubled.[6]

They provide a good example of the similarities between last century's two World Wars; strict enemy police control, counter-balanced by widespread support from the general populace, usually made routine work feasible. Yet in both cases, if one developed any standing routine, it was liable to be noticed by the wrong people, thus increasing the chances of arrest; and once arrested, one was liable to get short shrift. Nazi Germany exercised still more widespread control over Europe than Imperial Germany had done, and in its policemen had a uniquely awful body of repressors; yet thousands of men and women were still ready to undertake the risks of spying against it, and a few of them secured the magical 'contact with London' that enabled the data they collected to be of some actual use to the prosecution of the war.

The existence of several governments in exile in London – and of the Free French headquarters, there and later in Algiers, unrecognised as a government (except by the USSR) until late in 1944 – did provide a perceptible difference between the two great wars; for it was often through these exiled regimes that patriots on the continent sought to establish their channels of passing out news.

Priceless as the data from spies often was, they did not of course provide the only sources of intelligence for Army or Navy staffs. Air reconnaissance (on which the future chief of the air staff, Portal, got much of his operational experience), equally priceless to gunners on both sides on the Western Front in 1914-18, was almost forgotten by the Royal Air Force between the wars, and had to be re-invented by Sidney Cotton, the industrialist, in 1939. It provided one of the soundest of immediate sources of what the enemy was doing and could often be co-ordinated with spies' efforts – in both wars – but this always called for extra-careful co-ordination, lest it imperil the spies.

The American share in the clandestine effort has often been misunderstood. Too many scholars (the present writer included) have maintained that they really had no foreign intelligence capacity at all until Colonel Dansey of MI5 (later vice-chief of MI6) went over to Washington in May 1917 to give them some starting hints. James Srodes in his *Allen Dulles*[7] exposes this as a mistake; the State Department as well as the Departments of the Army and Navy were already quite hard at work. Moreover, on the defensive side, the Federal Bureau of Investigation – still flourishing today – had been set up as long ago as 1908, by a great-nephew of the great Napoleon, who understood the need for the sort of police system of which a Fouché or a Metternich would have approved (ill though such a body fits in with the political correctness of today). Pershing's army in France, when it got there, was of course involved in all the front-line intelligence activities of the telephone-tapping type that were common form on the Western Front, but for which there was less room next time round, as on the whole land campaigns moved faster.

In the Second World War the Americans created Donovan's Office of War Information in 1941 and his Office of Strategic Services in 1942. The latter tried to combine the tasks of SIS and SOE under a single head, and backed them with a large research department as well; debate continues about how far he succeeded.

Escaping, as the reference to the *Odyssey* at the start of this chapter reminds us, has long been a well-known adventure, and there were plenty of escapers, British in particular, during both World Wars. Several memorable books arose from escapes in 1914-18, such as A. J. Evans's *The Escaping Club* (1921), or M. C. C. Harrison and E. A. Cartwright, *Within Four Walls* (1930); these were eagerly read from the libraries of preparatory schools attended by children of the officer class, who went into the next war as junior officers ready to repeat – if they had to – the exploits of their elders. H. G. Durnford's The *Tunnellers of Holzminden* (1926), later republished as an early Penguin, provided masses of technical details on how to tunnel; this was paralleled by an article in the *Journal of the Institution of Civil Engineers*, xx, 108-12 (April 1943) by Squadron Leader R. G. Brickell, RAFVR, who had been in charge of tunnelling in a camp set up by Vichy French forces in southern Tunisia in 1941.

There were three major differences, on the escape front, between the two World Wars. One was that in the Great War prisoners from the French Army took a frequent and leading part in attempting escapes, and made considerable nuisances of themselves while on the run in German territory – nuisances against which a senior German general was still inveighing when lecturing to troops in 1937.[8] In the following World War, the French Army had been even more thoroughly demoralised by propaganda by May 1940 than the German Army had been in the autumn of 1918, and most of the nearly two million Frenchmen who were shortly captured were content to remain incarcerated in Germany, waiting for the war to end. On the other hand, in the later war there were efficient services both in London and in Washington devoted solely to the fostering of escapes and what Crockatt, the head of the British one, called 'escape-mindedness'. Thirdly, there were many more airmen among the prisoners of war in German hands, both British Commonwealth and American. The British escape service has been written up by two former escapers, one unsuccessful – Foot – the other – J. M. Langley – so successful that he became the link man between the service and SIS in MI9. One aspect of the American escape service, MIS-X, the secret provision of tools for escape sent into camps, has been written up by a former participant, Lloyd R. Shoemaker.[9] In each war, escapers could look to international conventions that were supposed to govern how prisoners of war were to be treated; but in each war, captors did not go out of their way to stick to the rules laid down. In both wars, in the heat of combat, some surrendering troops were killed rather than being taken into captivity and, in the Second War, a few units were notorious for not taking any prisoners.

One reason why the French, on the whole, took a less arduous share in the escape effort in 1940-45 was the existence in France of what turned out to be a satellite regime of Nazism, under Marshal Petain at Vichy, which was trying to reverse the course of French politics for many decades past, and posed all sorts of difficult questions of allegiance for conscientious Frenchmen, any of whom could be forgiven for hesitating. Within France a few people threw themselves into resistance at once, and nine-tenths of the population had come to agree with them by midsummer 1944; within Germany, choices were still more tricky.

On the fronts of subversion and sabotage, in the First War the Germans did much better than their opponents; in the Second War, the reverse was the case. The Germans had a small but efficient team of saboteurs in the ports of north-eastern USA, supervised at a distance by the German military attaché in Washington until he was declared persona non grata. This man became notorious in world history in 1933, when he helped to engineer Hitler's arrival to power in Germany: his name was von Papen. He went on to be German ambassador to Turkey, where he played a part in the 'Cicero' mystery. Another early Penguin book, F. von Rintelen's *The Dark Invader* (1933), lays out in considerable detail how these saboteurs worked, and how von Rintelen controlled them. One of their devices, invented in 1917, helped the British to devise in 1940 the pencil time fuses of which over 12 million were manufactured for saboteurs' use against Germany in the following war.[10]

Still more important than sabotage was the German general staff's successful injection of Lenin, in April 1917, into newly liberal Russia, a blow that drove Russia out of the Great War within the year, and all but enabled Germany to win it. Just before he left Switzerland, Lenin made a last-minute appeal to the Americans – by telephone. No notice was taken of it, because he rang after the office had closed on a Friday afternoon. The young diplomat who took the call was already late for a tennis appointment with a girl he was hoping to seduce, and said it could wait till Monday; by which time Lenin was already sealed into his train. The diplomat, later a leading figure in the Cold War, was fond of telling this anecdote against himself – he was Allen Dulles.[11]

Dulles had a subversive role to play himself in 1942-5, as Roosevelt's representative in Switzerland, and provided another illustration of how the intelligence world is one. Cartwright, escaper from the previous war, had by now advanced to be a brigadier, and was the British military attaché at Berne. He showed the door to a man who said he was a German diplomat who wanted to spy for the Allies. Dulles took him up instead, and secured from him telegrams dispatched by the German Foreign Office, which were invaluable to codebreakers working on a new German diplomatic code.[12]

During the Great War, the Germans also attempted major subversion in France, spending for instance £300,000 on efforts in the United States by Bolo Pasha to incite peace propaganda that would rot the French will to resist.[13] These attempts, which reached as high as Joseph Caillaux, a former prime minister, failed – quite how narrowly has never been worked out.

Their achievement in Ireland was notable. With their backing, the IRA made a doomed attempt to seize political power in Dublin at Easter 1916, which was easily put down by a brigade of young British soldiers (who were cheered by the public as they marched from Kingstown, now Dun Laoghaire, into Dublin[14]); but the politicians in London made such a hash of reprisal that most of Ireland voted solidly for Sinn Fein, the political wing of the IRA, at the next General Election, and after two civil wars (one Anglo-Irish, the second Irish-Irish) an independent Eire has resulted. As Lenin remarked, the collapse of a part of the British Empire so close to its capital presaged the collapse of the whole.[15] In the longer run, unlike many prophecies by Lenin, this has turned out true.

On the other hand, there was one substantial British subversive effort in the Great War. It turned out, eventually, not to have much effect, but remains in the forefront of public belief about how subversion can work: it was the Arab revolt against Turkish control of South West Asia. The exploits of T. E. Lawrence, Lawrence of Arabia, have already passed from history into legend, and the legend remains powerful. Lawrence, the illegitimate son of an Irish baronet's son who had run away from his wife with one of the servants, had a powerful intellect and considerable courage; he also knew something of the Near East, where he had worked as an archaeologist (and, possibly, as a junior spy) before the war. What he managed to do, operating against the Hejaz railway behind the left flank of the Turks defending Palestine against Allenby's advance from Egypt, was comparatively puny in military terms, but provided a marvellous contrast to the dreary waste of mud and muddle that came to form the popular conception of the war on the Western Front. Militarily, it tied down a lot of Turkish troops and provided a significant distraction to the Turkish command. Politically, it turned out after the war was over not to have achieved the liberation of the Arabs from foreign control that Lawrence had sought; the dynasty he had supported, fobbed off with the throne of mandated Iraq instead of that of mandated Syria, was elbowed off the centre Arab stage by Ibn Saud of Arabia and eventually deposed by revolution in Iraq, though it still rules (Trans)Jordan.

Lawrence wrote a big book, *Seven Pillars of Wisdom*, that circulated among his friends in the 1920s, and was published in 1935, shortly after his accidental death. It contains a great deal of interest about the nature and conduct of irregular warfare, elaborating from his article in the first volume of the *Army Quarterly* on 'The evolution of a revolt' (October 1920). Unhappily it also contains some exaggerations of his personal sufferings, which have led sceptics to classify it as a historical novel rather than a history book. An abbreviated version of it, entitled *Revolt in the Desert*, did appear in his lifetime, in 1927, and helped to enhance his legend. Many of the agents of the SOE thought of themselves as his imitators, though none quite matched his strength of personality, depth of learning, or range of achievement. Other SOE agents took as their model Robert Jordan, the fictional hero of Hemingway's *For Whom the Bell Tolls* (1940).

SOE was formed, in a tearing hurry, in the summer of 1940 to play back against Nazi Germany the sort of devious tricks that the Germans were (it now turns out, quite wrongly) supposed to have played against their victims during the Blitzkriege of 1939-40. It was never a popular service in Whitehall, but it did make its mark on the history of Europe and of the Far East, mainly by supplying arms and advice to a dozen indigenous resistance movements, which were thus able to take an active part in the re-conquest of their countries from Nazi domination and to regain some of the national self-respect that they had lost at the earlier moment of military catastrophe. Foremost among its achievements can certainly be placed a small raid by nine Norwegians on a heavy water plant at Rjukan, west of Oslo, which deprived Heisenberg of the raw material he said he needed to make an atomic bomb. It also played quite as large a part as the Allied air forces in disrupting the railway networks of North West Europe during 'Operation Overlord', a critical task against an enemy that depended heavily on rail as well as horses to transport food, ammunition and reinforcements.

SOE's mainspring, after he joined it in November 1940, and its eventual Chief Executive, was (Sir) Colin Gubbins, a regular gunner brigadier, promoted to Major General during the war and knighted after it. He had learned the use of the urban guerrilla when on the losing side in Dublin during the Troubles of 1919-21. It seemed to him, and to a fellow student at Woolwich before 1914, the engineer J. C. F. Holland, that the methods of the IRA were far more economical in men than the methods of bombardment and massacre that had killed so many of their friends in France, and they both resolved to try one day to persuade the Army to take them up.[16] Holland had an appointment to the War Office in 1938 that enabled him to research on any subject he chose; he chose irregular warfare, and got Gubbins to join him. From their partnership SOE, among several other interesting enterprises (including MI9), arose. All staff colleges preach the importance of economy of force; only SOE and MI9 seem to have practised it (Crockatt ran MI9 on a slogan later famous, 'Small is beautiful').

Gubbins remained a soldier in his outlook, intensely political though all SOE's work had to be; he inclined, like so many British senior officers, to think that a sharp line can be drawn between strategy and politics (though we have Churchill's word for it that at the summit they are one). He was glad when eventually almost all his forces came under the strategic direction of the local Allied Commanders in Chief. They played a large part in securing de Gaulle's achievement of power in France, and Tito's in Yugoslavia, as well as sustaining morale and arming resistance in a great many other places. He was received with standing ovations by parliament both in Copenhagen and in Oslo shortly after the war.

He exercised SOE's substantial impact with a total force of some 13,000, of whom some 3,000 were women. Most of its women were on the staff or engaged in the conventional tasks of clerking and housekeeping, but SOE did send 50 women agents into occupied France, and a small number elsewhere. A few of these have been blown up by the news media into heroines of almost Lawrentian proportions, not always with due account of the amount of damage they actually caused the enemy.

Much more significant than any of the newspaper heroines were the myriad of ordinary women, most of them wives with children, who imperilled themselves and their families by acting as safe-house-keepers and couriers for the men who cared to engage in active resistance of any sort, or who worked to conceal from the occupier those who were on the run from them – either service escapers, in both wars, or Jews in the second struggle. To them the free world continues to owe an enormous debt, though history can identify and name hardly any of them.

There were two famous precedents for the clandestine use of women. One was the case of Mata Hari (who in private life was a Mrs Macleod), a leading courtesan in Western Europe in the years before 1914, now synonymous in the tabloid press with any woman spy. She seems to have had a little professional training from the Germans as a secret agent, but, in accordance with her life before the war, seems to have been ready to help anybody who asked her, to do anything. She fell into the hands of the French counter-espionage authorities late in 1917, when Bolo Pasha had just been arrested and Clemenceau's Government was anxious to make an example of somebody, to show how firmly it meant to go on resisting the Germans: Mata Hari was duly sacrificed, and Bolo Pasha soon followed. (Even Caillaux, too prominent to shoot, was kept in jail; compare Sir Oswald Mosley 20-odd years later.) The other, earlier, case was that of Edith Cavell, a British nurse – daughter of a Norfolk clergyman – who stayed behind in Brussels when the Germans occupied it, and continued to look after the sick, including many wounded soldiers, of both sides. Some British Tommies asked her to help them get away to Holland; she complied, and before the Germans caught her had moved well over a hundred down an improvised escape line. She was tried in secret, like Mata Hari; and, like Mata Hari, was shot dead. Worse fates awaited several of SOE's captured women agents in the later war, who were massacred (always without trial) in concentration camps.

Counter-espionage services flourish in wartime. One of Cumming's lasting difficulties was with Vernon Kell, who was appointed with him to the secret service bureau in 1909, and took charge of the part of it that turned into the security service, conveniently called MI5 (just as SIS is sometimes called MI6). Kell established a system of port controls that kept a reasonable check on German attempts to send spies into the United Kingdom, and was able at the very start of the war to capture most of the spies the Germans thought they had already safely established in it. Though the highest strategic quarters were dreadfully gossipy[17], none of the gossip seems to have got through to where it would do damage, and none of the leading personalities was assassinated. Fortunately, we now have a discreet in-house history of MI5[18], as well as a detailed official history for the war against Hitler, the fourth volume in Hinsley's magisterial series.[19]

Next time round, Kell was still in charge of MI5 in 1939. He was dismissed in the summer of 1940 by Churchill, who had been his term-mate at Sandhurst and reckoned Kell was worn out. Without him, the service brought off a substantial clandestine coup, which surpassed even his achievements in 1914-18. First, nobody who mattered was assassinated except for Lord Moyne, killed in Egypt by a gang of Jewish extremists that included a future prime minister of Israel; and second, MI5 managed to bring off a major feat of deception, baffling the German high command entirely. This was done in co-operation with several other bodies – the civil police, the deception service, the radio security service, and above all the decipher service – through the medium of the agents the Abwehr, the German armed forces' clandestine branch, believed it had working for it in the UK. Every one of these was either turned round by MI5, and worked for the British instead of the Germans, or tried in secret and executed – with a single exception, and he was found dead by his own hand with an unopened wireless telegraphy set beside him.[20]

It turned out to be possible, through these controlled agents, to deceive the Germans thoroughly about where the Allied invasion of North West Europe, which everybody knew was going to take place in 1944, was going to land.[21] Similar results were secured in the Mediterranean by A Force, a branch of GHQ Middle East set up by Wavell in 1940, which seems to have originated the idea of feeding one's enemy with an inflated idea of one's own order of battle.[22] This was all a good deal more sophisticated than the attempts that were occasionally made during the Great War at intercommunication between the then numerous Royal Houses of Europe, most of whose members were interrelated. Notoriously, at the very outbreak of that war the Kaiser and the Tsar – who were close cousins – had failed to prevent their general staffs from carrying them over the edge; and the Kaiser's brother brought away to Berlin a misleading account of a talk he had just had with another close cousin, King George V, from which the Kaiser wrongly concluded that the British would not intervene. (His general staff took for granted that they would.[23]) When the next World War broke out, the exiled Kaiser said to some friends, 'I see the machine is running away with him as it ran away with me.'[24]

Hitler did not run Germany on the same lines as the Kaiser. He had a fixed, unwritten rule that he would never allow any of his subordinates an entirely free hand. This led to a great deal of overlapping of authorities, which spread into the clandestine world. Goering had his private decipher service; Ribbentrop had another; both the Nazi Party and the armed forces had separate intelligence and security services, each with decipher (among many other) components. The judiciary was infected with party doctrines, to the detriment of due legal process; and the lines of demarcation between the police, the party and the armed forces remained obscure, being obscured further by the existence of Himmler's private army, the Waffen-SS, part at once of the police and of the fighting forces in the field. This helped to make life still more difficult for inhabitants of occupied countries who wanted to resist German occupation. An arrested resister's fate might easily depend on which service held him. Indeed, the satellite state of Vichy France ran to as many as 15 different police forces, of varying ferocity.

Police savagery against the opponents of Nazism was a tremendous boon to the Allied propaganda services, which exploited it whenever they could; the less directly controlled Allied press of the Great War had been similarly vociferous in its protests against particular atrocities, such as the execution of Nurse Cavell or of Captain Fryatt, a merchant sailor arrested and shot in 1916 after having tried (so it was alleged at his secret trial) to ram a U-boat with his steamer as it plied between Harwich and Rotterdam.

Exactly what degree of control the British, or indeed most other, governments exercised over the newspaper press during the Great War remains obscure. The British had a Department of Propaganda, based at Wellington House, in charge of Mr Gladstone's great-nephew-in-law C. F. G. Masterman; the shadowy figure of John Buchan the novelist, later Lord Tweedsmuir (Governor General of Canada when it declared war, in its own time, in September 1939), can be discerned in the background. Into the foreground stepped Alfred Harmsworth, Lord Northcliffe, a leading London press baron of strong temper and erratic disposition, who at that time owned both *The Times* and the *Daily Mail*. In February 1918 he took over the department from Masterman, and settled it at Crewe House, whence it supervised leaflet propaganda delivered by artillery into the German trenches in France, as well as more usual forms of spreading news and views. These leaflets exasperated the German high command, and may have helped to weaken German Army morale.

A work devoted to military history may be allowed an excursus into diplomatic history, which ends with a puzzle for history writers.

R. W. Seton-Watson, historian, impresario for Thomas Masaryk, and editor of *The New Europe*, a new journal devoted to the demolition of the Habsburg Empire, spotted rather early that the Great War was going to end; guessed, correctly, that the peace congress would be in Paris; and secured in September 1918 a year's lease on a flat in the Avenue Marceau there, with an option to renew for another year. As the rent was rather steep, he arranged to share it with his friend Wickham Steed, then editor of *The Times*, who had been directed by Northcliffe to attend the congress.

They discovered that they were near neighbours to President Wilson, cultivated Wilson's butler, and found that Wilson, who liked to read a newspaper over breakfast, was making do with six- or seven-day-old copies of the *New York Times*. The utmost efforts could not get the London *Times* to central Paris before 11am; meetings began at 10.30. They arranged with Northcliffe that one or other of them was to write each day's leading article in the Paris *Daily Mail*, which was part of Northcliffe's empire, and got Wilson's butler to serve that up to the President instead.

Working on the Paris peace negotiations, many decades ago, I needed to see these articles. No library in England seemed to hold the Paris *Daily Mail*, not even that of its London namesake; the Bibliotheque Nationale held no English newspapers except Galignani's *Messenger* (1814-1904). The Paris *Daily Mail*'s own file copy had been ceremonially burnt, in the street in front of the office, by German troops on arriving in Paris in June 1940, as an act of execration of Northcliffe's memory. However, both Seton-Watson and Steed had kept a private guard-book of his own articles. However, again – Seton-Watson's sons had mislaid their father's copy, and Steed's widow did not answer letters. This puzzle I leave to more dogged researchers...

The run-up to the war of 1939 was dominated by propaganda, much of it poured out by that exceptional master of the art, Dr Goebbels. The Chamberlain Government's ripostes seemed exceptionally inept. When Churchill succeeded Chamberlain, and founded SOE, Hugh Dalton, the first minister in charge of it, took propaganda under his own wing. SOE absorbed into itself, inter alia, section EH (or CS) of the Foreign Office, so named after Electra House, where it had worked, or Sir Campbell Stuart, author of *The Secrets of Crewe House* (1927), who was its head. Unluckily for SOE and for Dalton, 13 months of bitter infighting followed in London, between SOE, the Foreign Office, the new Ministry of Information, the Home Office, the BBC, the Post Office, and the chiefs of staff, not to speak of SIS. The end result was a treaty between SOE and the Foreign Office, under which the propaganda branch of SOE (called SO 1) was taken away from it and turned into a new secret service, called the Political Warfare Executive (PWE).

PWE then settled down to its job, and by the end of the war had exercised a perceptible, if not a quantifiable, impact on morale and on resistance throughout occupied Europe. When its in-house history joins MI5's (released in 1999) and SOE's (due for release in 2001), those interested will have a fascinating read – but (I understand) it has not yet been cleared.

Wherever there was a tyrannous occupier to fight, there was a clandestine press, just as there had been in Belgium in 1914-18. PWE did all it could to support these dangerous enterprises, SOE acting (jointly with the RAF) as travel agent and taxi-driver. Several books testify to the results – but one word of warning needs to be dropped in here. Newspapers or leaflets produced in such circumstances are inherently fascinating, and appear to be first-class primary historical sources; but their readers must recall the perilous circumstances in which they were composed and distributed, and remember to lay off, sometimes quite extensively, from what they appear to be presenting as the historical truth before being satisfied about what the historical facts really were. All sorts of awkwardnesses, personal and political, might prevent a clandestine newspaper editor from saying exactly what he meant; and he probably entertained political aims himself so strong that they were bound to colour his opinions.

The revolutionary regime that Lenin and Trotsky had set up in Russia was deep in propaganda and deception from its earliest stages; indeed, the 'Lockhart Plot' on which every Soviet child was brought up now turns out to have been Lenin's last throw, an entirely bogus deception plan to save himself from having to flee the country.[25] Lockhart, by the bye, went on to head PWE. Strict party control was, from the first, an essential in Bolshevik Russia, and remained the doctrine by which Stalin and Beria controlled their partisans who were operating behind the German lines in 1941-4. Propaganda too continued to play a vital part in Stalin's defence of the Soviet Union against German attack in the latter two-thirds of the war against Hitler; and he also, it is now clear from the Venona revelations and other sources, had an extensive and efficient espionage net in Great Britain and the USA, which countries believed themselves to be fighting on the same side.[26] This provides a suitably confused note on which to end a discussion of subjects that used to be wrapped in total secrecy.

Notes on contributors

Professor M.R.D. Foot, Formerly Professor of History, University of
Manchester, UK
M.R.D. Foot, an army officer all through the war against Hitler, sometime
Professor of Modern History at Manchester University, has written on
Gladstone, resistance, escape, and SOE. He helped Ian Dear with the Oxford
Companion to the Second World War (Oxford: Oxford University Press, 1995)

Recommended reading

Judd, Alan, *The Quest for C* (London: HarperCollins, 1999)

Evans, A. J., *The Escaping Club* (London: The Bodley Head, 1921; Panther, 1957)

Rintelen, F. von, *The Dark Invader* (first published 1933; London: Penguin, 1936)

Lawrence, T. E., *Seven Pillars of Wisdom* (London: Cape, 1935; Penguin, 1996)

Andrew, Christopher, *Secret Service* (London: Heinemann, 1985)

Masterman, J. C., *The Double-Cross System In the War of 1939-1945* (London: Yale University Press, 1972)

[J. C. Curry], *The Security Service 1908-1945* (London: Public Record Office, 1999)

W. J. M. Mackenzie, *History of the Special Operations Executive* (London: St Ermin's Press, 2000)

Notes

[1] See F. H. Hinsley and others, *British Intelligence in the Second World War*, 3 Vols in 4 (London, 1979-88) passim

[2] See Patrick Beesly, *Very Special Intelligence* (London: 1977)

[3] New York, 1958

[4] Alan Judd, *The Quest for C* (London: HarperCollins, 1999) pp394-8, 417-20

[5] Ibid, pp451-2

[6] See Henri Bernard, *Un Géant de la Resistance* (Brussels: 1971)

[7] Washington, DC, 1999

[8] See M. R. D. Foot and J. M. Langley, *MI9* (Boston: 1980), pp21-2

[9] In his *The Escape Factory* (New York: 1990)

[10] M. R. D. Foot, *SOE in France* (London: 1968) p3

[11] See James Srodes, *Allen Dulles* (Washington, DC: 1999) pp80-1

[12] Ibid, pp277-97

[13] *Encyclopaedia Britannica* (12th ed, 1922) xxx, p469a

[14] Private information from a diary kept on the spot at the time

[15] *Collected Works* (Moscow: 1964) xxii, p357

[16] See Peter Wilkinson and Joan Bright Astley, *Gubbins and SOE* (London: 1993) passim; and M. R. D. Foot, *War and Society* (London: 1973) pp57-69

[17] See Michael and Eleanor Brock (eds), *H. H. Asquith Letters to Venetia Stanley* (London: 1982) passim

[18] [J. C. Curry], *The Security Service 1908-1945* (London: Public Record Office, 1999)

[19] F. H. Hinsley and C. A. G. Simkins, *Security and Counter-Intelligence* (London: 1990)

[20] See J. C. Masterman, *The Double-Cross System In the War of 1939-1945* (London: Yale University Press, 1972)

[21] See R. F. Hesketh, *Fortitude* (written in 1945 but not published until 1999)

[22] See Michael Howard, *Strategic Deception*, the fifth and most important volume in Hinsley's series

[23] See R. C. K. Ensor, *England 1870-1914* (Oxford: 1936) p483n

[24] John W. Wheeler-Bennett, *A Wreath to Clio* (London: 1967) p181

[25] Gordon Brook-Shepherd, *Iron Mask* (London: 1998) pp81-118

[26] See Christopher Andrew in K. G. Robertson (ed), *War, Resistance and Intelligence* (London: 1999) pp203-25s

PART II
THE EXPERIENCE OF
LEADERSHIP

Chapter 20

Monarchy in wartime:
King George V and
King George VI

Hugo Vickers

There is no call for a modern monarch to be a Henry V in wartime. The days are long past when a King led his troops into battle; striking public oratory is not in his remit. He does not control the waging of war. But he is the nation's leader in a more representative sense. The King's first role in the 20th century was as a symbol of national unity. His duty was to inspire confidence in his people, to remain steadfast, despite knowing what the average citizen did not: the progress of the war, the perils to the country, and the doubts and dissension in government and high command.

Fighting for King and Country is a concept that over-rides party politics and local dissension, and it is the person of the King to whom all turn. The King represents the average Englishman, and while he is still going about his business, with quiet confidence, visiting his troops, the wounded in the hospitals, and decorating the heroes, his country thrives. For 300 years every constitutional monarch has required the gifts of ceremonial presence and a command of political manoeuvre, tempered by restraint. Never is this more needed than in wartime, but in the two World Wars of the 20th century the sovereign was eclipsed by a Prime Minister with almost dictatorial tendencies.

King George V had reigned for four years before war was declared in August 1914. These had been testing years, during which the King had to grapple with numerous constitutional crises, problems such as Home Rule in Ireland, the Parliament Bill (complicated by contrary advice given to him by his principal advisors, Lord Stamfordham and Lord Knollys), and the worsening European situation that led to war.

George V was a dutiful sovereign. At his birth in 1865 he was not expected to succeed to the throne, but the death of his inadequate elder brother, the Duke of Clarence, in 1892, made him the eventual heir, and after a suitable lapse of time he married his late brother's fiancée, Princess Mary of Teck. For 18 years he served as grandson, then son of the sovereign. In May 1910 the sudden death of King Edward VII at the age of 68 placed him on the throne.

Trained in the Royal Navy, George V had risen to the rank of Captain by the time of his marriage, and had commanded the cruiser HMS *Melampus*. He had travelled the world. He was a wholly dedicated man, who loved England and mistrusted 'abroad'. His prime recreations were the shooting of game-birds, great numbers of which he dispatched in his lifetime, combined with a sincere love of stamps, of which he made a fine collection. His tastes were simple, and he was almost certainly at his happiest in the cramped conditions of York Cottage on the Sandringham estate.

George V was not an intellectual, but he learned by absorbing wisdom from the experienced men around him. As such he was an exemplary constitutional monarch. When war came he was a selfless symbol of unity. As Kenneth Rose has written:

'He asked nothing for himself; popular acclaim he left to his ministers, glory to the fighting men. His own role was unobtrusive: to carry on the business of a constitutional monarch. He must know all yet relinquish ultimate responsibility, ease the path of his Government while safeguarding those prerogatives which in the stress of war could so easily be lost forever.'[1]

George V brought to the role of king his experience as a naval officer, his personal knowledge of many European countries, combined with his uncomfortably close blood relationship to the Kaiser in Germany, the Tsar in Russia, and most of the kings and princes of Europe. His sense of duty drove him to remain optimistic and resilient during however many years of war there would be. To each changing circumstance of war, the King adapted. He remained as a steadfast figure, supportive in the background, encouraging where possible, speaking his mind when he felt the need to do so.

The King held strong private views on many aspects of the war. By and large, the politicians did not want to hear them. Sometimes these views disturbed the politicians. George V did not at once fall prey to the hysterical loathing of all things German that suddenly engulfed the British nation. He soon realised that one of his problems was to overcome the public suspicion that he had German sympathies, because of his close family links with Germany. He had to be quietly influenced to sever these old loyalties. But most difficult of all was his wish to make an effective contribution. There were numerous occasions, on which he had to exercise restraint. This was how King George V approached the First World War.

His second son, King George VI, who ascended the throne after the brief, unfortunate reign of Edward VIII, was burdened by other handicaps. He was politically inexperienced; he was hampered by a stammer not wholly eradicated by the treatment of Lionel Logue, which dogged his public appearances; and his finely tuned temperament was subject to occasional outbursts of temper.

George VI is remembered as a fine constitutional monarch, who won the respect of his people by his example in wartime. Of the varying approaches to kingship, his was a shy one. Propelled to the throne with scant warning and no training, his aim was to be a good king and much of what he did he approached from the position of fearing that he was unequal and inadequate to the task. In this respect he differed from his father, who had a more robust and confident view of his role.

But George VI had more advantages than he realised. Robert Rhodes James wrote of him: 'Honest modesty is not a disability; nor is straightforward common sense. He made up for what deficiencies he had by sheer hard work, moral strength, and application.'[2]

Born in 1895, George VI had served in the Royal Navy at the Battle of Jutland in the First World War. Indeed, of all George V's sons, he was the one who experienced the greatest personal danger, the one for whom his father prayed hardest, and the one for whose safe emergence from battle George V was the most grateful at the end of the war.

As Duke of York, he had spent most of his early working life in England. His private life was impeccable. He had made an exceptionally popular marriage, in 1923, to Lady Elizabeth Bowes-Lyon, which was followed by the birth of Princess Elizabeth in 1926 and Princess Margaret in 1930. The King epitomised the virtues of the good Englishman, with an ideal family life. Although his brother, Edward VIII, had cast a shadow over the throne, George VI came to his heritage with the sympathy and understanding of the nation. In the background too was the rock-like support of his mother, Queen Mary.

The first years of George VI's reign were made testing by political problems and the imminent threat of war. In September 1939 all the King's best qualities were shown to advantage: his fierce patriotism, his concern for the fighting forces, his support of his ministers and his determination to display confidence when others might have despaired.

George VI emulated his father in his stamina in times of adversity. Both kings accepted that their role was to set an example, and both succeeded in this. They differed in approach, George V often wary for slights from his prime minister, or occasions when he was not given the courtesy of being properly informed. More than once, particularly during the premiership of Lloyd George, the first intimation the King had of an important piece of news was when he read it in the newspaper.

George VI was more modest in what he expected from his ministers, and he was more fortunate. He came to enjoy a particularly harmonious relationship with Winston Churchill, whose readiness to take him into his confidence proved one of the most enduring elements in Churchill's conduct of the war. There were times when George VI's calm presence tempered the ebullient and sometimes irresponsible bravado of his second wartime Prime Minister.

The image of war that has passed into history finds the King in his Palace, a symbolic figure, and the Prime Minister at 10 Downing Street, controlling the business of waging war. It was the duty of both kings to support the prime minister of the day, to work with whomsoever that may be while he retained a parliamentary majority. Both wars began with a prime minister who lost the nation's confidence; Asquith in the First World War, and Chamberlain in the Second, were variously succeeded by Lloyd George and Churchill.

The relationship between George V and Asquith was satisfactory without being rewarding to either party. Asquith was no great admirer of the King's conversation, which he found superficial and discursive. Nevertheless, he respected the King's views as reflecting those of the average Englishman. In September 1914, following the Home Rule issue, Asquith complimented the King on 'the patience and strict observance of constitutional practice, together with the tact and judgement, which in a time of exceptional difficulty and anxiety, Your Majesty has never failed to exercise.'[3] George V put several ideas of merit to him, notably his suggestion that more women be employed in munitions factories (possibly with Mrs Pankhurst as recruiting agent), to release extra men for military service.

Like his grandmother and father, George V believed that he had an important constitutional role to play in connection with the armed forces. He insisted on being consulted about important naval and military appointments, taking his supposed role as head of the armed services as more than ceremonial. In 1914 the King tried to resist the enforced resignation of his cousin and friend, Prince Louis of Battenberg, as First Sea Lord. It was judged inappropriate to have a German leading the Royal Navy, although Prince Louis had served in the Royal Navy with unflinching loyalty since the age of 14. But Prince Louis resigned, his German blood having played against him. The King shrewdly urged the Prime Minister not to appoint the volatile Lord Fisher as his successor, but was ignored. The King also extended his influence to ensure the formation of a Coalition Government in 1915, with Asquith still as Prime Minister.

The King was not directly involved in the issue of Asquith's resignation. Indeed, in December 1916 he recorded that he still had 'the fullest confidence'[4] in his Prime Minister. He was, however, the arbiter in the complicated matter of his successor. After Asquith resigned, the King followed constitutional convention and summoned Bonar Law, who was the leader of the party with the next largest majority in the Commons. Theirs was a difficult encounter, in which the King and Bonar Law disagreed on virtually every point. Bonar Law criticised Asquith for his mismanagement of the war. The King defended him. The King differed with him on the respective roles of ministers and the military, saying that the generals were the experts and should be allowed to conduct the war as they saw fit. He refused Bonar Law's request for a General Election, believing this to be inappropriate in wartime, and adhering to the constitutional practice that he would not give pledges to a man not yet prime minister.

Despite all this, Bonar Law tried to form an administration. His success depended on persuading Asquith to serve in it in a subordinate capacity. This Asquith refused to do, and the following day the King summoned a conference at the Palace. Asquith attended, as did Lloyd George, Bonar Law and others. After much discussion leading nowhere, the King was forced to remind the politicians that no decision had been reached. The result was that Lloyd George emerged as the only man with a chance of forming a working ministry.

Though the King did not welcome the rise to power of Lloyd George, he had performed his stabilising role as a constitutional monarch, acting as a mediator, while the politicians resolved their differences. He therefore saved Britain from entering a period of national disunity, ensured the safe transfer of ministerial power from one prime minister to another, and though not personally happy with the result, deserves credit for avoiding a dangerous crisis.

At the beginning of the new ministry in December 1916, George V was pleased that Lloyd George deferred to him over some of the new Government appointments. But George V soon felt excluded. Lloyd George tended to despise military men, in which category he placed the King. He thought the King's opinions both politically and strategically irrelevant.

Lloyd George was determined to be his own strategist and to wage war on his own terms. Since the final outcome of the war was victory, much can be forgiven Lloyd George. He nevertheless defied the King whenever it suited him, withheld decisions until it was too late for the King's views to be taken into account, and presented him with many a fait accompli. Not unnaturally, the King resented this lack of trust.

While Asquith had followed the example of his predecessors in sending the sovereign long hand-written accounts of cabinet meetings, Lloyd George deemed this a waste of time, as indeed it was. Lloyd George appointed the first Cabinet Secretary to record what was said. Printed minutes were then circulated, one set reaching the King; but frequently these arrived late or not at all. Not unreasonably, the King complained that his very existence was being ignored.

Yet in his memoirs, Lloyd George gave the King considerable credit for his visits to the munitions workers, where an encouraging word direct from him to the workers did wonders in boosting morale. Lloyd George wrote: 'It was this directness of personal contact, free from pomp or any trace of arrogance and aloofness, which made the King's visits to the munition areas such a valuable aid in the task of raising the workers' enthusiasm and breaking through the reluctance to accept new methods and regulations.'[5]

The King was a staunch supporter of Lord Kitchener, the Secretary of State for War, who spoke frequently of the 'unstinted and unswerving support'[6] of the King in the great military task assigned to him. The King was a close friend of General Sir Douglas Haig, a court favourite. He was not impressed by Field Marshal Sir John French, Commander-in-Chief of the British Forces in France since 1914. As his confidence in French weakened, the King asked Haig his opinion of French. Presently, the two men were conspiring quietly together. In 1915 the King took soundings from other generals and became convinced that French must go. The King pressed Asquith to remove French. Offers of a peerage, the promise of a monetary grant at the end of the war, and of immediate command of the Home Forces failed to achieve French's resignation. The King then pressed Asquith to act without delay, and French finally resigned. Kenneth Rose cited this as 'a notable victory for the King'.[7] The King asked Haig to report to him from time to time about the progress of the war, promised to keep such discussions as they had completely confidential, and kept his promise scrupulously. However, his constitutional limitations were exposed when he tried to protect General Robertson, who Lloyd George was determined to remove from the post of Chief of the Imperial General Staff. Lloyd George told the King that unless he gave way, he would have to find another prime minister. A frustrated monarch had no option but to submit.

George VI enjoyed an easier relationship with his two wartime prime ministers. He had more respect for Neville Chamberlain than was reciprocated, Chamberlain having little regard for the King's counsel. In the last years of peace, the King suggested that he might write to Hitler 'as one ex-serviceman to another', but was dissuaded by the Prime Minister. He wanted to meet Chamberlain at Heston Airport on his return from Munich, with the 'Peace for our Time' document, which at least gave Britain more time to re-arm. But he did invite Chamberlain to Buckingham Palace to congratulate him and to appear with him and the Queen on the balcony, responding to the cheers of a self-deceiving but relieved crowd. This largely forgotten image of history (wholly superseded by the 1945 photograph of Churchill with the Royal Family at the moment of genuine victory) was controversial, identifying the King too closely with the party politics of his Government. This evoked criticism of the King's role.

By March 1939 the King, if not Chamberlain, was convinced that war would come. In this he was influenced by his closest political friend, Lord Halifax. Even when convinced of this, and when he had in consequence lost faith with Chamberlain, the King saw it as his first duty to support his Prime Minister.

Towards the end of Chamberlain's premiership, there were times when the Prime Minister ignored agreements made in Cabinet and appeared to be acting entirely independently. He became lax in keeping the King informed about important developments in the war.

Like his father in the previous war, the King wanted a Coalition Government. This was only achieved after Chamberlain's resignation on 10 May 1940. George VI would initially have preferred Halifax as Prime Minister, but in due course he accepted that Churchill was the man of the hour. In the meantime Halifax had made it clear that he would withdraw from the contest. So Churchill was called to the Palace, and a Coalition Government was formed. The King's private secretary, Sir Alec Hardinge, recalled that Halifax was 'always the court favourite', and added: 'It took me a long time to get the King and Queen to look on the new Prime Minister with favour, but in the end the King at any rate made great friends with him.'[8]

It is generally assumed that because the King and Queen liked Chamberlain and had supported him over Munich, they were mistrustful of Churchill. Others have stated that the King may have held resentment over Churchill's support of his brother during the 1936 Abdication crisis. As with many solid relationships, that between the King and Churchill developed gradually and was accordingly stronger and more durable.

A shared interest in the welfare of the Royal Navy first drew the two men together. During the Battle of Britain the King suggested that the Tuesday audience should become a regular and more spacious lunch. The relationship improved. Servants were dispensed with and they helped themselves from the sideboard in order that they could talk more freely. Occasionally the Queen joined them. Churchill wrote that this was 'a very agreeable method of transacting business'.[9] They lasted for four and a half years, and were a regular feature when both men were in London.

At last the King felt that he was of genuine use. After he and the Queen had returned from innumerable visits throughout Britain, he was able to give Churchill first-hand reports of the public mood in the country. Buckingham Palace was bombed twice within three days in September 1940 – the Palace was hit nine times in all – identifying the King closely with his people. In 1941

Churchill wrote to the King: 'I have been greatly cheered by our weekly luncheons in poor old bomb-battered Buckingham Palace, & to feel that in Yr. Majesty and the Queen there flames the spirit that will never be daunted by peril, nor wearied by unrelenting toil.'[10]

In May 1944 there was an extraordinary clash of wills. Both the King and Churchill contemplated sailing in one of the bombarding warships on D-Day. Sir Alan Lascelles, the King's private secretary, dissuaded the King by asking him to brief Princess Elizabeth (then just 18) as to whom she should appoint as prime minister, in the event of the King and Churchill being killed. The King then saw the danger of such an escapade, in which the captain of the warship in which they sailed would feel inhibited from taking a robust part in the action.

Churchill proved harder to dissuade, and there began a period of bad-tempered negotiation. Determined to sail, he brushed aside fears of his being killed, and the need to find a new prime minister in the middle of the war. He bridled at the King's description of the trip as a joy ride. As the situation worsened, Churchill acted in open defiance of the King's advice. There came a point when the King even contemplated himself descending on Portsmouth to command his first minister not to embark. Churchill headed to Portsmouth by train, but finally succumbed to a telephone call from Lascelles. Even then, he wrote to the King, complaining about unnecessary curbs on what he called 'my freedom of movement when I judge it necessary to acquaint myself with conditions in the various theatres of war'.[11]

Churchill got his revenge by preventing the King from visiting his troops in India. George VI mooted the idea in November 1944 and hoped to travel there in February 1945, but Churchill was unwilling to face the political implications of such a visit. This the King resented.

Both kings recognised their wartime role of seeing and being seen by their people. Harold Nicolson produced the remarkable statistics that in four years of war, George V 'held 450 inspections, visited 300 hospitals, and personally conferred some 50,000 decorations'.[12] He paid five visits to the Grand Fleet, and seven visits to his armies in France and Belgium. He inspected 300 naval and military formations, toured industrial areas, visiting several hundred munitions factories and toured areas damaged by war.

On a visit to the Western Front, George V suffered a serious accident. It occurred at Hesdigneul in France on 28 October 1915, where he was inspecting the 1st Wing, Royal Flying Corps. The mare lent to him by General Haig was frightened by the cheers of the men, reared up, threw the King and fell on top of him. The Prince of Wales, who was present, wrote: 'I shall never forget the sight of the horse getting up, leaving my father still on the ground. For a few terrifying seconds I thought he was dead.'[13]

During the train journey home to England, George V remembered that he had been due to award the Victoria Cross to Sergeant Oliver Brooks, of the 3rd Battalion, Coldstream Guards. Such was his devotion to duty that, although in intense pain and suffering shock, he summoned the Sergeant to the train, had the citation read by his equerry and pinned the VC to the Sergeant's tunic as he knelt beside the King's impromptu hospital bed.

The extent of the King's injuries was underplayed at the time. He had suffered a fractured pelvis, which caused him intermittent pain and stiffness for the rest of his life. Harold Nicolson wrote that 'he was never quite the same man again'.[14]

Broadcasting was not a feature of the First World War, so George V was not able to use this medium to communicate with his people. Only towards the end of his reign in the 1930s did he become a brilliant and popular broadcaster. But by the Second World War, George VI was able to make full use of the reassuring role of broadcasting to his people in the nature of a fireside chat. He used this medium often, especially at Christmas. He was listened to both with admiration and a certain sympathetic anxiety, because of the impediment of speech that he never fully overcame. He hated broadcasting, but succeeded in hitting absolutely the right note. His people waited to hear him and, more than at any other time, looked to him as a father figure to the nation.

George VI also made overseas visits to his troops. The most famous was to Malta, to award the island the George Cross, the first time that it was given to a collective group (until Queen Elizabeth II bestowed it on the Royal Ulster Constabulary in April 2000). He also visited North Africa in 1943 and Italy, and, like his father, made it his business to decorate many servicemen personally.

During the First World War, in March 1915, prompted by Lloyd George, Buckingham Palace set an example to the nation by going 'on the water-cart', as it was called. No alcohol was served at the Palace for the duration of the war. George V hated giving up, but genuinely hoped that he was setting a good example. The 'King's Pledge' was not the popular success that Lloyd George hoped, few of the people following the King's example. Nor was it long-lasting as far as the King was concerned, since, following his bad accident in October that year, the doctors advised a little daily stimulant during his convalescence.

King George VI also set a fine example to the nation, best remembered by his many tours at home and overseas, but also evident in pictures of the King entertaining Mrs Roosevelt in a deserted and seemingly empty Palace.

Mrs Roosevelt's visit in October 1942 was of significant importance. The British war effort was given considerable help in both wars by the United States, without whose intervention the outcomes would have been different. Good personal relations with President Roosevelt were of particular importance in the Second World War. These originated with a personal invitation from Roosevelt to the King to visit him at Hyde Park, his home on the Hudson, before the war, in 1939. This was accepted, and, after a triumphant visit to Washington, the King spent some days with the President in his own home. George VI made copious notes following the visit, assessing Roosevelt as 'Charming personality. Very frank person. Easy to get to know & never makes one feel shy. As good a listener as a talker'.[15] The visit strengthened both their friendship, the personal confidence of the King, and Anglo-American relations.

Mrs Roosevelt had the chance to see what the British were enduring. Returning to the United States with a bad cold, the President's wife was able to give a personal account of the plight of the British at a time when news reports and photographic images still took some time to make their way across the Atlantic.

The problem for any King of the United Kingdom was his close relationship to most European monarchs, many of whom were Britain's enemies. It cannot have been entirely easy for George V to wage war on his first cousin, the Kaiser, a grandson of Queen Victoria. Unlike Edward VII, George V had maintained amiable terms with the German Emperor.

Even in peacetime, George V was not an international monarchist. He resented the expense of state visits to Britain and the dislocation of reciprocating them. During the First World War there were various exchanges between George V and other European sovereigns, but his replies were monitored and drafted for him by the Foreign Office. He was approached by envoys of foreign monarchs, notably from King Constantine of Greece, who thought it was in the best interest of his country to remain neutral and who did not, therefore, join the Allied cause. These visits prompted aggressive headlines in certain newspapers.

Perhaps the most significant personal meetings with George V occurred just before the war, when on two occasions, in December 1912 and again in July 1914, Prince Henry of Prussia, the Kaiser's brother, called on him, asking for an indication of what Britain would do in the event of Germany and Austria going to war with Russia. On both occasions, due to the inability of Prince Henry to report the views of his cousin, George V, correctly, and the Kaiser's wish to read only that which suited him, the wholly false impression was given that Britain had given an assurance of neutrality. (In the immediate aftermath of the war, Prince Henry exaggerated his role as peace-maker, declaring that these meetings indicated that the Kaiser had done everything possible to avoid a war.)

An issue of lesser importance, which nevertheless preoccupied the King, was the removal of foreign kings from the British orders of chivalry and from honorary positions in the British armed forces. In May 1915, pressed by his mother, Queen Alexandra, George V sanctioned the removal of the Garter banners of eight Extra Knights from St George's Chapel: Emperor Franz Josef of Austria, Kaiser Wilhelm II (the German Emperor), Ernst August, Duke of Cumberland, Prince Henry of Prussia, Ernst Ludwig, Grand Duke of Hesse, Crown Prince Wilhelm of Prussia, Charles Edward, Duke of Saxe-Coburg and Gotha, and King Wilhelm II of Württemberg.

The question of whether or not to give asylum to the Tsar of Russia haunted George V. The King almost certainly went to his grave believing that he had done his best by his cousin, whereas the opposite was unquestionably the case. It was one of the few occasions during the war when the King rejected Lloyd George's advice and succeeded in changing his mind. George V could probably have saved the Tsar soon after the 1917 Revolution in Russia, at a time when the new Russian Government might have preferred to let him go. He had some sympathy for him as a cousin and an ally, but objected to the idea of a fallen tyrant enflaming endemic republicanism in Britain. Predominant in the King's concern was the thought of having to welcome in England the Tsarina, a German, with whom even her closest family had lost sympathy. The King's fears grew as March 1917 turned to April, and he expressed concern as to the merits of inviting the Tsar to Britain, 'on general grounds of expediency'.[16] It was soon too late.

The King hoped that the Tsar could take sanctuary in a country like Switzerland, rather than Britain. He was not to know that the moderate Russian Government, which overthrew the Tsar, would be replaced within months by the ruthless

Bolsheviks. On 16 July 1918 the Tsar, the Tsarina and their young family were murdered. King George V mourned them publicly, but never reproached himself for their fate.

As the First World War drew to its close, George V became worried about the names and titles used by some of his German relations in Britain, some of whom were serving in the British armed forces. The King had in mind Queen Mary's two surviving brothers, the Duke of Teck and Prince Alexander of Teck, and his cousins, Prince Louis of Battenberg, Prince Alexander of Battenberg, and Princesses (Helena) Victoria and (Marie) Louise of Schleswig-Holstein. Certainly, the last-mentioned princesses had been insulted in public, while serving the English war effort, being unfairly treated as alien Germans domiciled in Britain. In May 1917 the King set in motion the business of eliminating the German titles, and in July 1917 these members of the Royal Family were converted into English aristocrats with peerages: Tecks became Cambridges (Marquess of Cambridge and Earl of Athlone); Battenbergs became Mountbattens (Marquesses of Milford Haven and Carisbrooke); and the name Schleswig-Holstein was quietly dropped.

From this concern about 'visible' German titles the larger question arose as to the name of the dynasty itself. Throughout the war the King had been haunted by accusations that he was German or pro-German; there had been snide comments in a variety of satirical publications and the lower echelons of the popular press. The King had to be reminded that the Royal House bore a German name, and that he and many of his family still bore Saxe-Coburg and Gotha titles; the Prince of Wales, for example, was still Duke of Saxony. Whether the Royal House was the House of Hanover, Saxe-Coburg and Gotha, or even (more correctly, though never used) the House of Wettin, Lord Stamfordham was adamant that the issue should be resolved.

After some discussion with ministers, the King declared that his family should be called the House of Windsor. To Stamfordham goes the credit for this new name, which recalled Windsor Castle, 'the best known and most beautiful of English silhouettes outside the capital: ancient, sturdy, benevolent'[17], as Kenneth Rose put it. Thus did King George V succeed in the important matter of re-branding the Royal House, which emerged from the war with a fine English name that has been borne by the British Royal Family ever since. Rose concluded: '[The King] deplored having had to sweep away so much of the past, yet was not ashamed of his handiwork. Carisbrooke and Cambridge, Milford Haven and Athlone: Shakespeare himself could not have composed a more resonant or patriotic call to arms.'[18]

A generation later, there was not a hint that George VI suffered the danger of being identified with German relations. As British sovereign, relatively secure in Britain, he sought to act as 'shop steward' for his fellow monarchs. He was willing to give them sanctuary, and he was energetic in keeping in touch with those kings who were more directly threatened by the Germans than he was. Indeed, he resented the Government's reluctance in allowing him to appeal to fellow heads of state, not only the notable case of Hitler, but his wish to communicate with Emperor Hirohito of Japan.

In 1940 there was a serious danger that both Queen Wilhelmina of the Netherlands and King Haakon of Norway might be taken hostage by the Germans. Queen Wilhelmina's flight was dramatic. She withdrew from Holland in May 1940, aiming to return, but soon realised that this was impossible. She telephoned George VI from the Hague at 5.00am on 13 May, begging to be rescued. A British destroyer was put at her disposal, she arrived at Harwich, and took a train to London. George VI, who had never met her before, came to the station to greet her, and she was his guest at Buckingham Palace.

Three weeks later King Haakon of Norway arrived. He was George VI's uncle (by his marriage to Princess Maud, who had died in London in 1938). Driven from Norway, he too was welcomed as a guest at Buckingham Palace, and lived there for several months.

George VI hoped that King Leopold III of the Belgians would set up a government in exile in Britain; instead he surrendered to the Germans. Churchill, looking for a scapegoat in order to save French pride, publicly blamed him for this exposing 'our whole flank and means of retreat'.[19] George VI took a more charitable view and had some sympathy for the King, insisting, when the question arose, that King Leopold remain as a Knight of the Garter.

The King was also supportive of King Boris of the Bulgarians, hoping that he would hold fast against Hitler. He was annoyed when old King Gustaf V of Sweden behaved badly in an attempt to have King Haakon replaced by his very young grandson, Harald, the present King of Norway. When King George II left Greece for Crete and then Egypt in April 1941, George VI let it be known that he would permit the King of Greece to come to Britain, but he would not have any young princes or princesses in line to the throne.

George VI sanctioned the removal of King Victor Emmanuel II of Italy from the Garter in 1940, having initially made friendly approaches to him by letter, and that of Emperor Hirohito of Japan in 1941, though the Emperor was almost certainly not aware of this until 1952. Prince Paul of Yugoslavia, Regent of his country, was also allowed to retain his Garter, and was the recipient of several stirring letters of support from George VI, a long-time personal friend. Churchill, on the other hand, took an alternative view of the Regent, calling him 'Prince Palsy'.

After Prince Paul's flight from Yugoslavia, George VI went to some trouble over the new King Peter, who was his godson. When the young King came to London, George VI took care of him, assisted him in his wish to marry Princess Alexandra of Greece, and gave support to the family, including housing the King's mother, Queen Marie.

Queen Mary supported King George V throughout his reign, subjugating her considerable personality to his. She was more of a background figure than Queen Elizabeth. But she was a born organiser, and hardly had war been declared than she set to work offering clothes and money to various relief schemes. An early application of her energy was the creation of The Queen's Work for Women Fund, to help those women who had been put out of work by the war to find useful employment in the war effort. She gave her patronage to the Central Committee for Women's Training and Employment, an all-party organisation to extend the work of the earlier fund.

She also accompanied the King on his many visits to the troops in Britain, and then again to hospitals, comforting the maimed and blinded after their return from war. This they both found a strain, though they never flinched. She wished that she could accompany him on troop visits to Europe, and on one occasion she succeeded. Her attitude is well caught in a letter to the King, written in 1915: 'I flatter myself that in these anxious times I am of some help to you & that you like having me near you, for tho' there is not much one can say or do, the mere fact of having sympathy near one is surely a help.'[20]

George VI was triumphantly supported throughout his reign by his wife, Queen Elizabeth. All credit for his growing self-confidence must be given to her. The King depended on his Queen for both private and public decisions. They were a magnificent team, with the quiet confidence that gave heart to a nation at war. The lasting popularity enjoyed by Queen Elizabeth in her 100th year in 2000 stemmed more from her heroic role as a heroine of the Second World War than from the later cliché image of 'Queen Mum', Britain's favourite 'granny', or 'great-granny', of which much play was made in the newspapers during her later years.

One of the subtle and effective ways in which Queen Elizabeth stood for Britain was by maintaining her image as a civilian. Throughout the war the Queen never wore uniform. It is indeed rare to see a picture of her in any uniform at any time of her life, although as Duchess of York she had occasionally worn that of the Red Cross. Shortly before the outbreak of war she had been photographed by Cecil Beaton in a number of extravagant costumes designed in white by Norman Hartnell, for the 1938 State Visit to Paris. The portfolio showed the Queen in the garden in a white lace dress, wide-brimmed hat and parasol, and in the state rooms of Buckingham Palace in a white Winterhalter evening dress and tiara. Hardly had these pictures been developed and printed than war broke out. There were anxious discussions as to whether they should be published in wartime, when the nation was geared for military action. But, wisely, it was agreed that they should be released, some at the end of 1939, and some more in March 1940, serving as one symbol of the pre-war peace for which the Britons were fighting.

Similarly, throughout the war pictures were released of the Queen and her daughters together at Windsor Castle, in the family circle, the two daughters cycling behind the Queen in her pony-cart. Such images stood in stark contrast to Nazis goose-stepping in sinister black uniforms.

The Queen's role went further than a display of imagery. Her determination to stay with the King in London and to keep her children with her evoked admiration. Not for her an easy refuge in Canada or the United States. The general public certainly believed that the King and Queen were permanently at Buckingham Palace, and the Royal Standard flew from the Palace flagpole even at times when they had retreated to the comparative safety of Windsor Castle.

Independently, the Queen started a knitting group at the Palace, and was photographed at work with her ladies. She made a broadcast to the women of Britain, she spoke in French to the women of France. She wrote President Roosevelt a 13-page letter in her own hand in 1940, and in October 1942 she was directly responsible for the invitation to Mrs Roosevelt to visit Britain, as her guest at Buckingham Palace.

In November 1939 the Queen gave her name to *The Queen's Book of the Red Cross*, which had contributions from 50 distinguished British authors and artists, including Hugh Walpole and Daphne du Maurier, Edmund Dulac and Rex Whistler. Queen Elizabeth commended it as a way of 'helping forward the great work of mercy on the battlefield'.[21]

Although neither the King nor Queen was initially favourably inclined to Churchill as Prime Minister, Queen Elizabeth and Churchill gradually came to terms of strong mutual respect. In his case, he admired the Queen's courage and her unremitting cheerfulness under stress. She once wrote out a poem from Napoleonic times in her own hand – '...the bad have finally earned a victory o'er the weak, the vacillating, inconsistent good' – to boost his morale for the fight ahead, something that appealed to the romantic side of Churchill's nature.

Above all she sustained the King, giving him support to set a good example in wartime, so that his quiet nature shone and the people of Britain looked up to him with renewed respect.

At the hour of victory, at the end of both the First and Second World Wars, it was the King who became the focal point for widespread demonstrations of affection and loyalty. Both Kings were summoned to the balcony of Buckingham Palace to receive the cheers of a war-weary but grateful crowd. Neither George V nor George VI claimed credit for the cessation of hostilities. Neither of them had been the power-force for victory. Credit for that must go to their Prime Ministers and their generals. Credit must also be given to the United States of America, significantly a powerful republic.

There is no doubt that the role of the constitutional monarch in Britain was weakened by the First World War. Lloyd George wrote of George V: 'His was the only throne in all the combatant countries which did not rock throughout all those critical years.'[22] Yet there was much work for George V in the remaining years of his reign to present the monarchy as a peaceful arbiter, working within a strictly constitutional framework. The King made a point of attending rugby matches and the like, sharing the simple pleasures of his people. When he celebrated his Silver Jubilee in 1935, within a year of his death, his position was strong.

George VI's approach had always been different from that of his father. He believed himself ill-prepared to serve as king, and his prime wish was to be a good king and of genuine use to his prime minister and to his people. This modesty served him well in the different times in which he faced a World War. He emerged strengthened by the war effort, the monarchy at a high point in its popularity. When he died in February 1952, worn down by the heavy burden placed upon him, and wasted by lung cancer, his wartime prime minister paid him this tribute:

'No British monarch in living memory has had a harder time. War came and never in our long history were we exposed to greater perils of invasion and destruction ... the late King lived through every minute of this struggle with a heart that never quavered and with a spirit undaunted.'[23]

The wreath that Churchill sent his sovereign bore the simple words: 'For Valour'. As for the leadership qualities of both kings, they succeeded in full measure to serve as figureheads. They represented the common goal of all British people to unite to win the war. Those wars were waged in the King's name, and the King's example inspired and reassured the people during those dark hours. Both kings employed diplomatic skills when dealing with their often difficult prime ministers. Both sought in different ways to protect the prerogative of the sovereign. Both operated restraint.

It would be wrong to under-estimate the role that both kings played in the war effort. Symbolism is important. By proving themselves steadfast in wartime, quiet but consistent representatives of the world of peace, they reassured, consoled and inspired their people.

Notes on contributors

Hugo Vickers, Independent writer, Ramsdell, Hampshire, UK.
Hugo Vickers is a biographer and writer, who has specialised in the Twentieth Century and is an acknowledged expert on the British Royal Family. He was born in 1951 and educated at Eton, and Strasbourg University. His works include: Gladys, Duchess of Marlborough, Cecil Beaton, and The Kiss (winner of the Stern Silver Pen for Non-Fiction, 1996). His authorised biography of The Duke of Edinburgh's mother, Alice, Princess Andrew of Greece will be published in November 2000.

Recommended reading

Bradford, Sarah, George VI (London: Weidenfeld & Nicolson, 1989)
Nicolson, Harold, King George V: His Life and Reign (London: Constable, 1952)
Pope-Hennessy, James, Queen Mary (London: Allen & Unwin, 1959)
Rhodes James, Robert, A Spirit Undaunted (London: Little, Brown & Co, 1998)
Rose, Kenneth, King George V (London: Weidenfeld & Nicolson, 1983)
Wheeler-Bennett, John W., King George VI: His Life and Reign (London: Macmillan, 1958)

Notes

[1] Kenneth Rose, King George V (London: Weidenfeld & Nicolson, 1983) p169
[2] Robert Rhodes James, A Spirit Undaunted (London: Little, Brown & Co, 1998) p344
[3] H. H. Asquith to King George V, 17 September 1914, quoted in The Dictionary of National Biography, 1931-1940 (Oxford: Oxford University Press, 1949) p324; George V by Sir Owen Morshead
[4] King George V's Diary, 4 December 1916, quoted in Kenneth Rose, op cit, p196
[5] David Lloyd George, War Memoirs, Vol 1 (London: Ivor Nicholson & Watson, 1933) pp321-2
[6] Harold Nicolson, King George V: His Life and Reign (London: Constable, 1952) p261
[7] Kenneth Rose, op cit, p193
[8] Sir Alexander Hardinge, Notes on his service as Private Secretary (Private papers)
[9] Robert Rhodes James, op cit, p206
[10] Winston Churchill to King George VI, 5 January 1941 (Robert Rhodes James, op cit, p210)
[11] King George VI's Diary, 2 June 1944, quoted in Robert Rhodes James, op cit, p259
[12] Harold Nicolson, op cit, p252
[13] HRH The Duke of Windsor, A King's Story (London: Cassell, 1951) p119
[14] Harold Nicolson, op cit, p268
[15] Robert Rhodes James, op cit, p165
[16] Kenneth Rose, op cit, p211
[17] Ibid, p174
[18] Ibid, p175
[19] Robert Rhodes James, op cit, p198
[20] James Pope-Hennessy, Queen Mary (London: Allen & Unwin, 1959) p500
[21] The Queen's Book of the Red Cross (London: Hodder & Stoughton, 1939) p5
[22] David Lloyd George, op cit, Vol 1, p322
[23] Report of Parliament, 11 February 1952

Chapter 21

Political leaders in wartime: Lloyd George and Churchill

George H. Cassar

In 1961 on the campus of the University of New Brunswick, renowned and controversial historian A. J. P. Taylor gave an engaging lecture on the rise and fall of Lloyd George.[1] At the very end, almost as a matter of course and without explaining why, Taylor observed that of Britain's two greatest wartime leaders in the first half of the 20th century, Lloyd George and Churchill, he considered the former to have been superior.[2] As a young student sitting in the audience, I overheard a professor whisper to a colleague and question whether it was fair to make a comparative judgement about two British prime ministers whose tenures were separated by a quarter of a century. Did he have a point? For unless the two men operated within the context of comparable situations, such an exercise would certainly be futile.

Although the Second World War differed from the First in many respects, it is important to note that Lloyd George and Churchill faced a stream of problems and challenges that were much the same. Hence an appraisal of their relative merits is a legitimate subject and one that I undertake with great pleasure. Before moving ahead, it would be useful to define what their work necessarily entailed. As John Ehrman has noted, there are three vital and overlapping functions that a prime minister engaged in a total war must perform: manage the war, mobilise the home front, and sustain the spirit and confidence of the nation.[3]

The two outstanding politicians whose careers overlapped and interacted had much in common. Each combined fluency in argument with restless energy, dogged determination, a fertile imagination and an extraordinarily agile mind. Both were egocentric, had a flair for self-advertisement and possessed unlimited ambition to dominate. They entered politics at an early age – Lloyd George was 27 and Churchill 25 – they had a passion for politics, they were unconventional and impatient of party discipline, they served together in various administrations, they never shrank from hard work or heavy responsibilities, and they were at their best in crises.

In contrasting the two men it seems natural to begin by discussing their backgrounds, which could hardly have been more dissimilar. Lloyd George's father was a headmaster who died of pneumonia 17 months after he was born. Together with his mother and sister, he went to live with his maternal uncle, Richard Lloyd, who managed the family shoe business. Lloyd George grew up in a stable and loving home and his education at the village school (Llanystumdwy in Wales) was followed by his training as a lawyer.[4]

Churchill sprang from the ruling class, the son of Lord Randolph, a descendant of the Duke of Marlborough.[5] He grew up a lonely and neglected child: his remote and unsympathetic father was swallowed up in politics and his vacuous mother centred her life around social activities. He was an indifferent student, notwithstanding his privileged education – which included a preparatory school, Harrow and Sandhurst – and, as he entered manhood, was no better trained intellectually than Lloyd George.

The differences in their upbringing do not explain their contrasting personal conduct. The one thing constant throughout Lloyd George's political career was the bankruptcy of his moral character. How this could occur to someone brought up on the Bible by his uncle, who was an unpaid Nonconformist minister, is anybody's guess. What is undeniable was his cynical disregard of commonly held values and principles – he was duplicitous, an inveterate liar, a serial philanderer, a practitioner of gutter tactics, an assassin of other people's reputations, a man who repaid loyalty with disloyalty and, in all likelihood, an embezzler of a war charity fund.[6] Few who knew him had anything kind to say about him as a person. John Maynard Keynes's chilling verdict was that he was 'rooted in nothing', that he was 'void and without content'.[7] Clementine Churchill once described him as a 'direct descendant of Judas Iscariot'.[8] Commenting on Lloyd George's absence of loyalty, Lord Selborne wrote: 'I would never wish to go out tiger hunting with him, not because I doubt his courage but because I know that he would leave anyone in the lurch anywhere if he thought it would serve his purpose.'[9] Well might even Taylor, an admirer of Lloyd George's political skills, concede that he had 'no friends and did not deserve any'.[10]

Churchill was a far bigger man than Lloyd George. Whether in public or in private, his behaviour was the same. 'There were no two faces, no mask that would drop when the audience would retire,' wrote his private secretary, John Colville.[11] Churchill had his faults, like everyone else, but he was a sensitive and warm individual with a host of friends, above board, loyal to associates and, as far as is known, faithful to his wife.

Both men gained power under similar circumstances. Lloyd George became prime minister in a restructured coalition on 6 December 1916, after the public and press repudiated his predecessor, H. H. Asquith, and demanded a better-directed and more determined war effort.[12] Churchill's hour came in May 1940 when a substantial segment of Conservative backbenchers, angry with Chamberlain's ineffectiveness, revolted in the wake of a badly bungled operation in Norway.[13]

At first glance neither Lloyd George nor Churchill appeared to have the authority of a normal British prime minister. Lloyd George came to power, not as the leader of a great party, but as an individual, and his survival rested on the support of the Unionists. In reality his position was quite secure, not so much because his allies possessed great faith in his leadership gifts as because they perceived that the alternative, the return of Asquith, might mean an ignominious peace or even defeat.

Churchill succeeded Chamberlain only because the favourite, Lord Halifax, correctly sensed that he was unsuited to the task of leading the nation in war. Churchill was the symbol of anti-appeasement and his energy and brilliance were recognised, but he was unpopular with the hierarchy of his own party, which perceived him as something approaching a rogue elephant. Consequently there were constraints on his freedom, even though his party held a comfortable majority in Parliament. Indeed many, including loyalists, expected his tenure to be brief.[14] They were wrong. What they could not foresee was the development in his character and judgement in the months that followed. Then, too, by establishing a true national Government, he avoided Labour and Conservative broadsides, thus boosting his own delicate position.

While Lloyd George exaggerated the extent of his innovations, Churchill tended to minimise them. Lloyd George gave the impression that his move to 10 Downing Street represented not merely a change of prime ministers, but a clear break with the past administration. On the surface he appeared justified. He introduced new methods, a new form of Cabinet Government, and additional controls and regulation. He created half a dozen new ministries to meet special problems caused by the war and staffed them with new men, mostly captains of industry with little or no political background. Recent studies have shown that no sharp break occurred at the end of 1916 and that, in fact, there was much administrative continuity between the regimes of Lloyd George and Asquith. If Lloyd George's Government took a more active hand in organising the economy, it was not because of an inherent commitment to state intervention, but rather as a pragmatic response to the changing nature of the conflict.[15] The difference between Asquith and Lloyd George appears to have been more style and tempo than substance.[16]

Churchill liked to emphasise that his Coalition Government represented a sign of unity rather than a repudiation of the past. There was no influx of new faces in his administration and he established only one new ministry.[17] Churchill divested himself almost entirely of domestic affairs so that he could concentrate on managing the war. As a witness in the earlier conflict, he did not have to be reminded of Lloyd George's failure to impose his will on the British High Command. Without any fanfare, he adopted a variety of measures to ensure civilian control over the military. No British prime minister in this century, if ever, wielded the degree of power that Churchill possessed during the Second World War.

The two prime ministers ran their wars differently. In place of the War Committee and historic Cabinet, Lloyd George set up a small War Cabinet, which exercised supreme authority under his direction. Of the five members only one – Bonar Law as Leader of the House of Commons and Chancellor of the Exchequer – had administrative and parliamentary duties and was not expected to attend regularly. The rest were free to concentrate all their energies on the war.[18]

In addition to the premiership, Churchill took charge of the Ministry of Defence, a new office designed to co-ordinate the work of the service departments. He was briefed on the activities of the Chief of Staff Committee (formed in 1924) by his representative General Hastings Ismay, although he often attended in person. The War Cabinet never possessed the authority that its counterpart had in the earlier war.[19] Unlike Lloyd George, Churchill saddled the other members of his War Cabinet with heavy departmental responsibilities. He did so deliberately, realising that they would be too busy to deal with complex military matters.[20] Thus after a few months, strategic policy was determined by Churchill and the Chiefs of Staff, then brought before the War Cabinet for formal approval.

As sombre as the military picture was in 1916, it was far darker in 1940. When Lloyd George assumed the reins of government the grisly four-month Battle at the Somme had just ended with only slight gain of ground. The Central Powers had overrun most of Romania (which had joined the Entente in August 1916) and captured its capital, Bucharest. After nearly two years of repeated attacks along a very narrow front on the Austrian frontier north-east of Venice, the Italian Army had advanced less than 10 miles. In June a great Russian offensive, begun too soon and without adequate preparations, had been halted and thrown back with horrendous losses.

Churchill entered upon his assigned role in the worst of circumstances. On the very day that the change of government occurred, 10 May 1940, the German armies struck without warning in the west. Invading the Low Countries, they bypassed the Maginot line and drove British and French forces back to a beachhead around Dunkirk on the English Channel. Through a miracle of improvisation, nearly the entire British Expeditionary Force, plus a considerable part of the French contingent, more than 338,000 men in all, were evacuated to Britain. On 13/14 June the Germans entered Paris and shortly after France signed an armistice. Britain was left alone to face the Axis powers. Its prospects seemed hopeless.

During both World Wars, the administrations of Lloyd George and Churchill discussed the possibility of a negotiated settlement with Berlin. Whether Lloyd George was as single-mindedly committed to a military victory as Churchill is a matter of dispute.[21] What is known for sure is that in the summer of 1917 Lloyd George and some of his colleagues were prepared to consider a compromise settlement in which British aims in the west would be achieved by concessions to Germany in Russia. At any rate the peace talks broke down because both sides refused to abandon objectives they considered too important.

Shortly before the fall of France, the Churchill War Cabinet debated whether there were grounds to initiate peace talks. Halifax was in the forefront of those who wanted to use the good offices of Mussolini to explore if Hitler would be amenable to terms that would guarantee Britain's integrity and independence, even at the cost of parts of the Empire. Churchill knew that Hitler was not a man to be trusted and that in any case he would not be content with anything less than the relegation of Britain to the status of a satellite or, at best, a second-rate power.[22] As he saw it, there was no alternative but to fight on. Churchill made his position clear in an emotionally charged speech at a meeting with his Cabinet Ministers. 'If this long island story of ours is to end at last,' he concluded, 'let it end only when each one of us lies choking in his own blood upon the ground.'[23] His defiant words were greeted by his colleagues with loud cries of approval and a number of them went up to him when he rose from the table and patted him on the back. Hugh Dalton,

Minister of Economic Warfare, described Churchill as 'quite magnificent' and the 'man and the only man we have, for this hour'.[24] The Cabinet's spontaneous and whole-hearted support for the continuation of the war deeply moved Churchill and fortified his resolve for the next and perhaps greatest challenge, the Battle of Britain.

As war-weariness spread in Britain during the latter half of the Great War, Lloyd George used his rhetorical skills to rally his countrymen, as Churchill would do, with even greater effect, in the early 1940s. There was an almost hypnotic quality about Lloyd George's voice, described by a historian as resembling that of 'a light tenor'. Seldom shouting, for he had no need to, he had mastered projecting his voice into densely packed halls.[25] He did not always write his speeches but he delivered them effortlessly, as though he was speaking off the cuff. By combining power and passion, occasionally in short rhythmic sentences in the style of a lay preacher, he could move an audience to tears.

Lloyd George appreciated, to a much greater degree than Asquith, Bonar Law's dictum that in 'war it is necessary not only to be active but to seem active'.[26] He was indefatigable in trying to project an image of a dynamic man of action, single-mindedly committed to winning the war. While there were occasions in the darkest of all days when he spoke confidentially as if he thought the war was unwinnable, he never gave the least hint of discouragement in public. As in the past, he cultivated and fed the press in return for editorial support and a conduit to mould public opinion. He was constantly on the move, addressing crowds, visiting the front, or attending inter-Allied conferences. Wherever he went, he made sure he was accompanied by a bevy of reporters and photographers to record and tout his activities. His vitality and buoyancy was contagious, imbuing the public with confidence, determination, and belief in ultimate victory.

Churchill's greatest single contribution to winning the war was his oratory or, to be more precise, his speeches.[27] He was not a great impromptu speaker and did not express himself on the platform with the same facility as Lloyd George. He spent hours composing his speeches, committing them to memory and rehearsing the manner of their delivery.[28] He had a slight stammer, a noticeable lisp and his voice was neither clear nor strong. Yet his gruff manner, measured cadences, exquisite sense of timing, and verbal artistry lightened by ironic humour, all combined to give his speeches a stirring quality. Churchill's best remembered speeches dramatised the events of 1940 and 1941 when Britain had no hope of winning the war alone and only a slender chance of survival unless help arrived from outside. Even today, more than half a century removed, it is difficult to listen to his words without experiencing a moving echo of the emotions they aroused at the time.

The radio – not readily available to the public during the Lloyd George era – meant that Churchill's voice could reach practically every household.[29] His broadcasts, following the 9 o'clock news on BBC, struck a responsive chord in the hearts of his countrymen, providing 'the fire and stimulus which were so badly needed'.[30] Later in the war Churchill appeared on film and his broadcasts to the nation were less frequent. The public saw him at work, surveying bombing damage and talking to survivors, meeting Allied leaders, touring munitions plants and aeroplane factories. Although Churchill had never rubbed shoulders with the masses, or knew much about them, newsreel and documentary footage enabled him to develop an intimacy with them in a way that Lloyd George was never been able to do in 1917 and 1918.

For Britain, a nation facing a total war both in 1914-18 and 1939-45, the home front was no less important than the battle front. By the time Lloyd George became prime minister the most difficult issues of the war, such as munitions and conscription, had already been resolved, and the state exerted controls over much of the economy. Nevertheless Lloyd George was confronted by new problems and it was left to him to bring the practice of war socialism to completion. Churchill profited from work done by others or by learning from their mistakes. He inherited from the previous administration a blueprint for control of key sectors and for the allocation of important resources. When Churchill took the reins of government, rationing and compulsory military service were already in operation, but other plans, notably the direction of labour, had not been applied.

Lloyd George's rise to power coincided with the growing unrest of labour, the co-operation of which was essential to winning the war. Responsible labour leaders had declared a truce at the outset and vowed not to resort to strikes to resolve differences with management. The instances of industrial action until well into 1916 were comparatively few, but friction developed from the demands of the war economy, and by the spring of 1917 stoppages and strikes had become serious. While workers understood that national sacrifice was a prerequisite to winning the war, most thought that their own interests were exempt.[31]

The turmoil was inspired, not by union officials, but by the shop stewards and by the workers themselves.[32] Grievances naturally varied from place to place but standard ones included wages in relation to rising prices, conditions of work, pressures of overtime and impediments to labour mobility. Although Lloyd George proclaimed the need for industrial discipline, he hesitated to use the Government's extensive legal powers too freely, preferring conciliation to coercion and co-operation to conflict. There were occasions when strike leaders were arrested and imprisoned for impeding war production, but Lloyd George understood that no lasting settlement was possible unless the workers' grievances were addressed.[33] Such a policy put a strain on the nation's economy, but at least it kept labour disturbances to tolerable levels.

Churchill was anxious not to alienate the labour movement and repeat the costly strikes that had marred the conflict of a generation before. His selection of Ernest Bevin, the leading union boss, to serve as Minister of Labour and National Service was a masterstroke. The acquiescence of organised labour to state regulations was essential if output was to be maximised and the war economy developed smoothly.[34]

Invoking the Government's vast legal powers as sparingly as possible, Bevin preferred to rely on the willing co-operation of the unions and on voluntary use of peacetime machinery for dealing with disputes over wages and conditions of employment. He set up a tribunal whose ruling was binding on both sides in cases where agreement could not be reached or where there was no arrangement to reach an agreement. The Government endeared itself to the workers by enlarging social welfare schemes as well as by stabilising living conditions through price controls and the fair distribution of food and other necessities. Unions were represented on regional war production committees and, at the factory level, management worked hand-in-hand with shop stewards to find ways to speed up output. A new spirit of co-operation between management and labour emerged. Not that strikes – in theory illegal – were altogether avoided, but, with few exceptions, notably in the coal industry, they were small and settled quickly. In all, the loss of working days due to strikes was only half that experienced in the First World War.

In 1917-18 and again in the early 1940s the Royal Navy fought off German U-boats to keep the Atlantic shipping lanes open. The resumption of Germany's unrestricted submarine campaign in February 1917 had resulted in a dramatic increase of Allied shipping losses. By April a quarter of British merchantmen had been sunk and the prospect of starvation became a genuine one. The Admiralty could offer no antidote beyond the early countermeasures of laying minefields, arming merchantmen and hunting down submarines – which were sinking U-boats at the rate of only one or two a month. Clearly, an alternative approach was required.[35]

When Maurice Hankey first suggested the adoption of a convoy system in February 1917[36], the Admiralty considered such a move impracticable. It contended that the convoys would be especially vulnerable to attacks and that it lacked the escorts to protect them. Lloyd George in his memoirs accused the Admiralty of being hidebound, obstinate and unimaginative.[37] His charges may have been correct, but it was his own attitude that allowed matters to drift. As late as the third week in April he was on record as saying that he did not consider the shipping crisis as seriously as Hankey had perceived it[38], a statement that defies comprehension in view of staggering British losses, which that month alone totalled 545,282 tons. It was not until Lloyd George read Hankey's latest carefully reasoned paper on the subject on 21 or 22 April that he changed his views.[39] The adoption of the convoy system, which solved the submarine crisis, ranks high among the decisive events in the war.

The latest scholarship has dispelled the myth that it was Lloyd George who forced senior Admiralty officials, in a face-to-face encounter on 30 April, to institute the convoy system. His action that day was really anticlimactic. By then the Admiralty, impressed by the recent successful Channel crossing of convoyed ships carrying coal, had already agreed to extend the experiment to other routes.[40] It is perhaps safe to say that Lloyd George's active intervention hastened the application of the principle, but the claim made by admirers that he saved the day is a gross exaggeration.

In the early 1940s the Germans resorted to the submarine once more in a bid to reduce the flow of food and vital war material to a level critical enough to force Britain's surrender. This time the Admiralty's convoy system proved ineffective, partly because of insufficient escort ships, and partly because German U-boats, their range, speed and destructive power far greater than in 1917, operated not singly, but in large groups, or 'wolfpacks'. British merchantmen were being lost faster than they could be replaced. From July 1940 to March 1941 Britain lost 2 million tons of merchant shipping, not to mention an additional 130,000 tons to

Italian submarines operating in the Atlantic for the same period. There was no let-up in the following months. Between April and December 1941 Axis submarines sank 1.5 million tons of shipping.

Churchill established and directed a committee of high officials to devise new tactics to surmount this mortal threat. In particular he was insistent that ways be developed to take the offensive against U-boats at sea or in port, before they could approach a convoy; and to fit merchant ships with fighters that could attack German bombers that were destroying British shipping from the air. More importantly he placed a greater premium on the construction of escort vessels than on capital ships; he negotiated with President Roosevelt a deal involving destroyers for bases; and he persuaded the United States to take an active part in defending shipping lanes in the western Atlantic, reducing the area that Britain had to patrol.

Naval critics like Stephen Roskill have reproached Churchill for committing long-range aircraft to strategic bombing offensives against Germany, instead of closing the Greenland Gap, a 300-mile swath running down the middle of the Atlantic where German submarines were immune to air attacks. Whether he was right or wrong, as John Keegan points out, is really academic.[41] There were too few long-range aircraft available to do the job, and by the time more had been produced the tide in the Atlantic had turned. Instrumental in winning the battle were the resources from the United States in the form of aircraft carriers and long-range bombers that eliminated the Greenland Gap; the acquisition of a German code scrambler, which enabled British cryptanalysts to intercept enemy messages to their forces in the field; radar, which helped locate surfaced German U-boats at night or in the fog; and sonar, a radar variant that detected submerged submarines. After March 1943 the number of Allied ships sunk declined steadily, while German submarine losses rose enormously. During the middle of 1943 the Germans were compelled to call off their U-boat campaign. The Allies had found, and again in the nick of time, the right antidote to the submarine menace.

Food and the disposal of scarce manpower resources were central dilemmas as much in the First World War as in the Second. Before Lloyd George assumed control of the Government, no real effort had been made to increase the production of food or to ensure economy in consumption. Civil authorities were confident of the Royal Navy's ability to keep the sea lanes open, not to mention that they were loath to disturb private trading and the normal process of production.

However, mounting shipping losses and the nation's poor harvest in 1916 induced Lloyd George to take drastic action. He put R. E. Prothero and Lord Devonport in charge of the production, supply and distribution of food. As President of the Board of Agriculture, Prothero, with a mandate to increase the production of food, faced a daunting task. There were severe shortages of essential material: agricultural workers, farm machinery and implements, and fertilisers. Prothero's programme included reducing by 50 per cent the area devoted to hops, encouraging farmers to plough more arable land by a five-year guarantee of prices, and using women and prisoners of war to lessen the difficulty of finding labour. Although it took time for Prothero's measures to take effect, the production of the potato and cereal crops rose by more than 3 million tons in 1917.[42]

On the other hand, Lloyd George's appointee as food controller, Lord Devonport, fell far short of expectations. Devonport had no precedents to guide him and his work was made more difficult by his colleagues' reluctance to consent to greater state intervention. His experiment with one meatless day per week for hotels and restaurants and voluntary rationing proved unsatisfactory and in May he resigned and was replaced by Lord Rhondda. Lengthening queues and rising public indignation drove the ministry towards price controls and a gradual introduction of a general rationing system during the early months of 1918. The regime's tardiness in implementing a full-blown rationing scheme was reminiscent of the previous government's handling of controversial issues.[43]

The experience in the First World War made it easier and less disconcerting in the Second to adopt state controls to harness the nation's resources.[44] In the opening days of the war, the Chamberlain Government pushed through Parliament all the requisite legislation to take quick control of the economy. But controls were imposed at an unhurried pace in order to avoid disrupting the economy. Chamberlain and his advisers initially sought to limit the nation's military commitment, placing their faith instead on the naval blockade and on holding the Germans at bay in northern France. British leaders were jolted out of their complacency when the 'Phoney War' ended early in the summer of 1940. The British Army's forced evacuation from Dunkirk and subsequent fight for control of the Channel airspace, enemy bombardment of cities and the threat of invasion, all served to convince the new Government that survival depended on the rapid adaptation to a full war economy. With the help of such experts as internationally renowned economist John Maynard Keynes, the Government set up a mechanism designed to control inflation, finance the war (which proved inadequate), allocate material resources where they were most needed, control prices and ration goods and services. There was much improvisation during the chaotic critical months, but, once the immediate danger from invasion and defeat receded, a coherent war economy began to take shape.

Rationing of clothing and basic necessities, begun on a limited basis in January 1940, became more thorough after heavy shipping losses and the switch from consumer to war goods. To help ease the food shortage, the Government mounted a drive to raise agricultural production at home. Farmers were given subsidies to reduce pasturelands, improve drainage and plough every inch of arable land. The space devoted to growing potatoes and grain increased from 12 to 18 million acres. City folks spent their spare time spading and weeding their gardens, and even the moat around the Tower of London became a vegetable patch.

The huge manpower losses incurred during the offensives in 1916 placed Lloyd George in the inescapable predicament of having to arbitrate between the competing needs of the Army and sectors of the economy vital to war production. That problem would not have risen if industrial conscription had been implemented at the same time as military conscription in 1916, but the Asquith Government, like its successor, feared the resistance of labour. It was left to Neville Chamberlain, the Director-General of National Service, to achieve results on strict voluntary lines. His authority did not extend beyond matters of civilian manpower, and even here he found himself in competition with established

Ministries, such as Munitions and Labour. His plan was a complete failure and in August 1917 a bewildered Chamberlain resigned.[45]

The Department of National Service was reconstituted under Auckland Geddes, former Director of Recruiting. As a consequence, Geddes was given authority over the whole field of manpower, military as well as civilian, with the power to close down non-essential industries. In April 1918 the National Service Act raised the age for conscripts from 41 to 51 and gave Geddes the right to review all exemptions from service. These expedients enabled Geddes to divert 70,000 men from industry to the Army without affecting the production of food or munitions. Had the war lasted longer it might have led to a reduction of industrial output. Even so, the arrival of large-scale American reinforcements would have lessened the strain. But in the short term, when the nation was about to face a military crisis in the spring of 1918, it was in a position to throw into the fray thousands of young men of the highest level of fitness.[46]

Since the Churchill Government's long-range objective was to build a massive army, there were limits on the extent to which the civilian economy could be drained of labour. Under Bevin's auspices a system was put into effect that directed and allocated labour. A series of National Service Acts empowered the Government to conscript all men between the ages of 18 and 50, either for the armed forces or for work in vital war industries. Before the end of 1941 women, aged 20 to 50, were subject to this provision and eventually over 2 million were employed in war-related work. War output rose dramatically, particularly in the aircraft industry, which produced 20,000 planes in 1941 as compared to 2,800 in 1938.

The ultimate purpose of a wartime government is, of course, to win. Much as they wanted to, neither Lloyd George nor Churchill really controlled the supreme direction of the war. They were unable to do so because they could not dominate their professional advisers. Lloyd George rarely got his way with Sir William Robertson (CIGS), and did not fare much better with his successor, Sir Henry Wilson. Representing only himself, Churchill was at a disadvantage when he went up against the Chiefs of Staff who possessed more technical military knowledge than he did and who could count on the backing of their service departments. With endless patience and at the cost of debilitating loss of sleep, they usually prevailed over Churchill, although there were occasions when he was able to coerce them into going along against their better judgement. While Churchill was sometimes reluctant to abandon schemes that were more romantic than realistic, he never overrode the judgement of his professional advisers and chiefs of staff. There was no rift between the 'brass hats' and the 'frocks', such as had occurred during the First World War.[47]

The eminence of both Lloyd George and Churchill as war leaders does not rest on their grasp of military strategy, which is open to question. Lloyd George had not taken an interest in military science before the outbreak of the war. He did not realise, as Balfour would correctly surmise, 'the depths of his own ignorance'[48], and approached strategy 'as an essentially simple subject which had been unnecessarily complicated by the professionals'.[49] As a military novice, he failed to comprehend that the course of war does not follow any scenario, however well reasoned, that it is unpredictable and that the first requirement in planning strategy is attention to detail and provision for all conceivable contingencies.

Churchill's weakness was that, while enjoying unprecedented authority for a chief executive in a democratic system of government, he was incapable of framing an overarching concept that would harmonise and balance future political considerations and military strategy. At times he clung too rigidly to preconceived plans despite changing circumstances; while waiting to exploit developments that never arose, he missed those that did. Furthermore, at the tactical-operational level, his knowledge was rather outdated. He did not fully grasp the extent to which mechanisation had revolutionised wartime operations.[50]

Convinced that decisive results were unattainable on the Western Front, Lloyd George favoured an attack through Italy, the Balkans or the Middle East, where progress was expected to be easier and the cost substantially less. His reference to Turkey and Austria-Hungry as props whose elimination would have the effect of bringing down Germany was not related to reality. It was Germany that propped up its allies, not the other way around. He flitted from scheme to scheme without fully taking into consideration logistics, interior versus exterior lines, topography of the land, and probable German response. Even if successfully carried out, Lloyd George's indirect strategy was not worth the investment. While it would bring some benefits, it would not by itself lead to the destruction of the German Army. There was no quick and cheap way to defeat the enemy. The war could only be decided on the Western Front, and even if the British Army had employed more imaginative tactics early on, the price of victory would have been tragically high.

The main British objective in the Second World War, as in the First, was to find a way to defeat the Germans. In the early years of the war Churchill and his generals adopted a peripheral strategy, designed to wear down the enemy. They had been struck by the British Army's lack of success against German forces in 1941-42, particularly in North Africa where it had enjoyed a numerical superiority and better intelligence. They had no desire to fight the German Army on the continent, unless it was on the verge of collapse. Otherwise, they assumed, a land campaign in western Europe, following an invasion, would end either in defeat or in a stalemate. That view has been challenged by John Grigg who argued in his book *1943: the Victory that Never Was* that a cross-Channel invasion in 1943 would have been successful and shortened the war. He points out that defences along the beaches of Normandy were non-existent and that, with most of the German forces on the Russian front, reinforcements were too far away to be of immediate help in France.[51] There are historians, myself included, that find it difficult to refute Grigg's thesis. Nevertheless, Churchill has his defenders, so the question of whether a Mediterranean strategy after 1942 was correct will never be resolved.

Churchill's peripheral strategy of attrition was interrupted by the Americans who favoured striking directly at the German Army as the only way to end the war quickly. Although Churchill was coerced into accepting the American approach, he resorted to various expedients to delay the planned invasion of Europe as long as possible. In 1942 he pressed the Americans to attack in French North Africa and they agreed. The following year he convinced President Roosevelt that a campaign in Italy was a preparatory move vital to the success of the invasion of western Europe. This too was meant to be another step in Churchill's attritional policy, but as it turned out the Anglo-American armies suffered far more casualties than the Germans. Churchill's expectations that Italy could be taken easily were unfulfilled when Hitler decided to fight every inch of the way. Churchill's loss of credit with the Americans left him with no choice but to live up to his commitment to invade Europe, even though Germany showed no signs of imminent collapse.

Churchill's preoccupation with Europe and the Mediterranean led him to neglect the British position in the Far East. When the Japanese attacked in December 1941, the British lacked the tanks and aircraft to resist effectively. Hong Kong and British Borneo fell almost immediately. Under the blows of Japanese bombs and torpedoes, two British warships, the *Prince of Wales* and the *Repulse*, helpless without air support, were both sent to the bottom off the Malayan coast. In Malaya the Japanese outwitted and outmanoeuvred the British, completing their sweep of the peninsula by the end of January 1942. On 15 February the 130,000-man garrison of Singapore yielded to a Japanese force half it size in what was the greatest single defeat in British military history. While this was going on, Japanese forces invaded Burma and captured Rangoon on 6 March.

The two prime ministers differed in their dealings with their commanders. Lloyd George's temperament and unconventional approach to war brought him into conflict with Field Marshal Sir Douglas Haig, C-in-C on the Western Front. Haig was undoubtedly right in insisting that the war could only be won in the west, but he was slow to learn the lessons of trench warfare. The Prime Minister was certainly within his rights to dismiss a commander with whom he disagreed sharply. Why he chose to retain Haig is a puzzle. Lloyd George's own explanation was that he would have been hurled from office if he had sacked Haig. Besides, he went on to say, he knew of no credible officer with the qualifications to replace Haig.[52] Lloyd George's reasons, to put it bluntly, are not credible.

Haig had important allies, particularly in political circles, but he was not invulnerable. Few in Britain had been spared the loss of a family member or close relative on account of his operations. On the other hand, Lloyd George's position was secure because there was no other potential war leader of his stature in the country. The Tories had reservations about Lloyd George's methods and resented his lack of moral character, but they preferred him to his immediate predecessor.[53] If Lloyd George had chosen to make it a issue that either he or Haig must go, there is no doubt that he would have won the test of strength. The other point made by Lloyd George, namely that he could not find a suitable replacement for a man he held in such disdain, is an insult to the reader's intelligence. General Herbert Plumer, for one, was a first-rate commander. His accomplishments at Messines and during the opening phase of the ill-fated Third Battle of Ypres had been brought to the attention of the War Cabinet. Lloyd George believed him competent enough to appoint him in command of an important expedition sent to shore up the Italian Army after its crushing defeat at Caporetto in the autumn of 1917.[54]

The question of why Haig was allowed to stay at his post must remain a matter of conjecture. My own view is that Lloyd George lacked the will to face the political fallout the removal of Haig would have caused.[55]

Thus the Prime Minister's underhanded manoeuvres against Haig continued. In the spring of 1917 Lloyd George subordinated Haig to the French C-in-C, General Robert Nivelle, and agreed to support just the sort of operation on the Western Front that he had wanted to avoid.[56] Mounted in April, Nivelle's offensive, like all previous ones, made minimal gains at great sacrifice in lives. Lloyd George's reckless gamble had backfired. Having staked a good deal on Nivelle's success, his credibility as a judge on military matters suffered and he lost ground in trying to control Haig. The upshot was that he was forced to preside over Haig's two bloody debacles during the last half of 1917, one at Passchendaele and the other at Cambrai.

Churchill's relations with his military commanders were conditioned by personal as well as professional considerations. Churchill required a personal rapport with his senior military officers before he could establish a professional one. He looked for field commanders who possessed vigour, creativity and the resolve to overcome obstacles, no matter how difficult. He bombarded them with memos, advising them on what tactics to adopt and urging them to show flair and take risks. British commanders would have preferred to be left alone and make their own assessments without having to defend them to an amateur strategist thousands of miles away. Churchill was loyal to his commanders, but those that displeased him, fairly or unfairly, were replaced. Lloyd George could not make the same claims.

With British fortunes at a low ebb, both Lloyd George and Churchill faced political challenges. Preferring to concentrate manpower on the economy for a war that he expected would last perhaps into 1920, the Welshman sent 174,000 men to the Western Front when Army leaders had requested 334,000. The question of whether Lloyd George deliberately held back reserves to prevent Haig from frittering them away in costly offensives is an extremely complex subject, which continues to exercise historians.[57] It is apparent that he underestimated the danger in 1918 and that his decision to give priority to the home front, rather than the Army, was a dreadful mistake that came perilously close to costing Britain the war.

The matter was aired publicly. In a letter to the press on 7 May 1918, Major-General F. B. Maurice, the former Director of Military Operations, accused Lloyd George of deliberately misleading the House of Commons about the strength of Haig's army prior to Ludendorff's massive assault of 21 March. There is no doubt that Maurice's charges were soundly based, but they were brushed aside. Lloyd George displayed his dazzling oratorical skill and, as the issue at hand was so technical and confusing, the motion of censure was defeated by a vote of 293 to 106. Many Conservatives voted against the motion, not because they believed Lloyd George, but because they recognised that if it was carried, it would return a discredited war leader to power.[58] The Maurice debate marked Lloyd George's first occasion since becoming prime minister to assess his support in Parliament and left him in a position of supreme authority for the remainder of the war.[59]

For Churchill the defeats in South East Asia were followed by more bad news. In North Africa, where the fortunes of war had shifted back and forth, Rommel started a major drive late in May 1942, and, with the capture of Tobruk, was in a position to menace the Suez Canal and British possessions in the Middle East. The mounting criticism over the way Churchill was conducting the war led to a challenge to his leadership. A motion of censure in the House on 29 June was defeated by a vote of 475 to 25, with 40 or so MPs abstaining.[60] This was perhaps less than the resounding triumph claimed by the Government. Since there was no official opposition, both Labour and Conservative leaders were able to pressure most of their MPs to fall into line. The general consensus was that whatever Churchill's mistakes, there was no one better to put in his place. Later in the year the turning tide of war stopped the slide in his political standing.

Britain's relations with its allies were less difficult and complicated in the First World War than in the Second. Throughout most of the war of 1914-18 British leaders had only to co-ordinate their activities in the west with the French.[61] As the two nations shared commitment to the defeat of the Germans and to the liberation of French and Belgian territory, their quarrels never threatened the stability of the alliance. Moreover, with the British Army shouldering the greater part of the fighting after the Nivelle offensive, Lloyd George was a dominant player at the inter-Allied conferences.

Britain's aims in the Second World War differed from those of the Soviet Union and the United States. Frequent meetings and conferences with Roosevelt and Stalin kept Churchill busy travelling around the world at an exhaustive pace and severely taxed his physical strength. His relations with Stalin were never cordial, marked as they were by mutual suspicion and mistrust. Nevertheless Churchill valued the Soviet Union as an ally and he sent 3,276 tanks and 2,665 aircraft to northern Russian ports in 1941 and 1942[62] – generous material support given at a frightful cost to the nation and which probably would not have made any difference in the outcome of the fighting on the Russian front. Britain's help was usually greeted by curt demands for more, and Churchill could not have found it easy to put up with the ingratitude of the Soviets and their constant nagging on the delay in opening a second front.

By contrast Churchill forged a special and intimate friendship with Roosevelt. Nevertheless Churchill disagreed with his American counterpart over such key issues as where the war effort should be concentrated and how vital supplies should be apportioned among the various fronts. Because the Americans could bring to bear massive resources, decisions for joint planning slipped increasingly into their hands, with Britain forced to accept the role of a junior partner.[63] From 1944 onward Washington called the shots. Churchill never felt comfortable playing second fiddle, but he accepted the realities of power when he agreed to the appointment of an American general as Supreme Allied Commander in the Normandy landings.

After all that has been said, what ought we make of Britain's two wartime prime ministers? When the fighting ended suddenly and unexpectedly in 1918, Lloyd George was proclaimed as the 'man who won the war'. That characterisation, which continues to find favour with some historians[64], is absurd. For one thing the war was not won by Britain alone but by a coalition of powers. For another there were many elements besides Lloyd George's leadership that were responsible for victory – the naval blockade, American help and Haig's new tactics, which abandoned the concept of a breakthrough in favour of a more effective strategy of limited objectives.

In assessing Lloyd George's role as war leader one thing is certain. His legacy does not rest on his management of the war. Here he did more harm than good. His strategy was faulty, his feud with Haig had a debilitating effect on the war, and his decision to withhold men from the British Army at a crucial moment led to a defeat that almost spelled ruin for the Allies. It was on the home front that Lloyd George left his mark: safeguarding shipping and maintaining food supply; increasing production; mobilising manpower; and providing an unflagging display of optimism and resolve when things looked bleak, giving the nation grounds for hope and persistence.

Churchill did not have to learn by experience in making the transition to a centrally managed economy. Having served in various posts between 1914 and 1918, he was able to avoid mistakes and to establish at once the full control that had come only in the latter stages of the First World War. He governed the country with admirable firmness and judgement, but his record in directing the war itself was far from spotless. He erred often on particular matters, but none, it must be added, came close to causing total defeat. Set against his strategic misjudgements was the unrivalled power of his words and personality. His inspirational leadership of the nation in its darkest moments ranks among the greatest feats of will and courage in the annals of British history. It is safe to say that without him Britain would have succumbed in 1940.

There have been, to the best of my knowledge, four previous essays analysing the careers of Lloyd George and Churchill.[65] All the authors involved have refrained from ranking one against the other. I confess that I am unable to exercise such restraint. In choosing Churchill over Lloyd George I have been guided by two considerations: first, which of the two faced the greater obstacles; and second, whether the achievements of either man could have been duplicated by someone else. On the first point there is little doubt that Churchill's military predicament was far more dangerous and immediate. Lloyd George inherited a fairly solid alliance system in 1916 and Britain was never in danger of defeat, except momentarily in the spring of 1918, owing, as has already been noted, to his own misguided action. On the other hand Britain fought alone from May 1940 until June 1941 (that is between the fall of France and the Soviet Union's entry into the conflict) against the most formidable military machine in the world with little or no hope of averting defeat. As for the second point, Lloyd George was not confronted with the nightmare of having to rescue his country from almost certain defeat. His work at home was significant but not decisive. Even if we concede that no rival could have handled matters as effectively as he did, the margin of difference would not have had a significant impact on the final outcome. By contrast it is virtually unanimous that no British politician other than Churchill could have galvanised the nation in an all out-effort when everything seemed lost. Single-handedly he saved Britain and Western civilisation from the horrors of Nazi tyranny. With all due respect to the late A. J. P. Taylor, it was not Lloyd George but Churchill who was the greatest British war leader of the 20th century.

Notes on contributors

Professor George H. Cassar, Eastern Michigan University, Ypsilanti, Michigan, USA.

Professor Cassar's extensive publications on various aspects of the First World War include Asquith as War Leader (1994) and the Forgotten Front. The British Campaign in Italy 1917-18 (1998). He is currently completing a study on Kitchener and British Strategy, 1914-1916

Recommended reading

Ben-Moshe, Tuvia, *Churchill: Strategy and History* (Boulder, CO: Lynne Rienner, 1992)

Charmley, John, *Churchill: The End of Glory* (London: Hodder & Stoughton, 1993)

Colville, John, 'Churchill as Prime Minister', in Peter Stansky, ed, *Churchill: A Profile* (New York: 1973)

Ehrman, John, 'Lloyd George and Churchill as War Ministers', in *Transactions of the Royal Historical Society*, 2 (1961)

Gilbert, Martin, *Winston S. Churchill* (London: Heinemann, Vols, 3, 6 and 7, 1971, 1983 and 1986)

Keegan, John, 'Churchill's Strategy', in Robert Blake and Wm Roger Louis, eds, *Churchill* (Oxford: Oxford University Press, 1993)

Jablonsky, David, *Churchill: The Great Game and Total War* (London: 1991)

Rintala, Marvin, *Lloyd George and Churchill* (Lanham, MD: 1995)

Taylor, A. J. P., *Lloyd George: Rise and Fall* (Cambridge: Cambridge University Press, 1961)

Woodward, David R., *Lloyd George and the Generals* (London and Toronto: Associated University Presses, 1983)

Notes

[1] The paper was published, with slight modification, as *Lloyd George: Rise and Fall* (Cambridge: Cambridge University Press, 1961)

[2] Taylor made similar remarks in his writings and lectures. See, eg, *English History, 1914-1945* (Oxford: Oxford University Press, 1965) in which he rates Lloyd George on one occasion as 'the greatest prime minister of the century' (p87n) and on another as 'the most inspired and creative statesman of the twentieth century' (p192)

[3] John Ehrman, 'Lloyd George and Churchill as War Ministers', Transactions of the Royal Historical Society, II (1961), pp105-6

[4] In Lloyd George's pre-political career, see John Grigg, *The Young Lloyd George* (London: HarperCollins, 1973); and Bentley B. Gilbert, *David Lloyd George* (London: Batsford, 1987) Vol 1, Chap 1

[5] Biographies of Churchill are published almost annually and would easily fill a volume. The official and most detailed life of Churchill was begun by his son Randolph and, after his death, carried on to completion with extraordinary thoroughness by Martin Gilbert.

[6] In 1917 S. R. Guggenheim gave Lloyd George £20,000 to distribute to war charities of his choice. The records show that, despite Guggenheim's repeated requests, Lloyd George never gave a satisfactory accounting of what happened to the money. This episode was unknown until brought to light by John Grigg in a paper delivered at a conference of British historians in Santa Barbara in 1980. I am grateful to John Grigg for correcting some of my earlier misimpressions of the affair.

[7] John Maynard Keynes, *Essays in Biography* (London: 1933) p36

[8] Cited in Martin Gilbert, *Winston S. Churchill: The Challenge of War* (London: Heinemann, 1971) iii, p623

[9] D. G. Boyce, ed, *The Crisis of British Unionism: The Domestic and Political Papers of the 2nd Earl of Selborne, 1885-1922* (London: 1987) p188

10 A. J. P. Taylor, *English History, 1914-1945*, op cit, p74

11 John Colville, 'Churchill as Prime Minister', in Peter Stansky, ed, *Churchill: A Profile* (New York: 1973) p114

12 The events that brought Lloyd George to power can be followed in Robert Blake, *The Unknown Prime Minister* (London: Eyre & Spottiswoode, 1955) Chaps 19-21; George H. Cassar, *Asquith as War Leader* (London: Hambledon Press, 1994) Chap 12; Lord Beaverbrook, *Politicians and the War, 1914-1916* (London: Oldbourne, 1960) Chaps 26-41; Roy Jenkins, *Asquith* (London: Collins, 1978) Chaps 26-7; John Grigg, *Lloyd George: From Peace to War, 1912-1916* (London: Methuen, 1985) Chap 17

13 Martin Gilbert, *Winston S. Churchill* (London, Heinemann, 1983) vi, Chap 15; Kevin Jeffreys, *The Churchill Coalition and Wartime Politics* (Manchester: Manchester University Press, 1991) Chap 1; John Charmley, *Churchill: The End of Glory* (London: Hodder & Stoughton, 1993) Chap 34: Robert Blake, 'How Churchill Became Prime Minister', in Robert Blake and Wm Roger Louis, *Churchill* (New York: Oxford University Press, 1993)

14 John Charmley, op cit, p396

15 Trevor Wilson, *The Myriad Faces of War* (Cambridge: Polity Press, 1986) p533

16 J. M. Bourne, *Britain and the Great War, 1914-1918* (London: Edward Arnold, 1989) p130

17 He kept about two-thirds of Chamberlain's Government and gave only 12 ministerial posts to newcomers

18 Lord Hankey, *The Supreme Command, 1914-1918* (London: Allen & Unwin, 1961) i, pp577-81; John Turner, 'Cabinets, Committees and Secretariat: the Higher Direction of the War', in Kathleen Burk, ed, *War and State, The Transformation of British Government, 1914-19* (London: Allen & Unwin, 1982) pp63-4

19 Kevin Jeffreys, op cit, pp36-7; Tuvia Ben-Moshe, *Churchill: Strategy and History* (Boulder, CO: Lynne Rienner, 1992) pp124-5; Martin Gilbert, op cit, vi, pp322-6

20 Grigg, 'Churchill and Lloyd George', in Blake and Louis, op cit, p110

21 For differing viewpoints see David French, *The Strategy of the Lloyd George Coalition* (Oxford: Oxford University Press, 1995) pp144-7; and David R. Woodward, 'David Lloyd George, A Negotiated Peace with Germany and the Kühlmann Peace Kite of September 1917', *Canadian Journal of History*, 6 (1971), pp75-92

22 The most recent study on the subject is John Lukacs, *Five Days in London: May 1940* (New Haven, CT: Yale University Press, 1999). For a summary of the talks see Martin Gilbert, op cit, vi, pp411-8; John Charmley, op cit, pp403-4

23 Hugh Dalton, *The Fateful Years: Memoirs 1939-1945* (London: Muller, 1957) p336

24 Ibid, p335

25 Marvin Rintala, *Lloyd George and Churchill* (Lanham, MD: 1995) p60; Bentley B. Gilbert, op cit, i, pp82-4

26 Blake, *The Unknown Prime Minister*, op cit, p290

27 Much of the material in the text on this subject was based on Robert Rhodes James, 'Churchill, the Parliamentarian, Orator and Statesman', in Blake and Louis, op cit. Churchill's wartime speeches can be found in Robert Rhodes James, ed, *Winston S. Churchill: His Complete Speeches* (New York: 1974; London: Chelsea House Publishers, 1974) vi and vii

28 Elizabeth Nel, *Mr Churchill's Secretary* (London: 1958). The author gives a vivid picture of Churchill composing his speeches.

29 D. J. Wenden, 'Churchill, Radio, and Cinema', in Blake and Louis, op cit

30 Norman Rose, *Churchill: The Unruly Giant* (New York: 1994) p330

31 Trevor Wilson, op cit, Chap 47; Bernard Waites, *A Class Society at War: England 1914-1918* (New York: Berg, 1987) Chap 6

32 James Hinton, *The First Shop Steward's Movement* (London: Allen & Unwin, 1973) – Part II deals with the war; Branco Pribicevic, *The Shop Stewards' Movement and Workers' Control, 1910-1922* (Oxford: 1959) Chap 5

33 David Lloyd George, *War Memoirs* (London: Odhams, 1938) ii, Chap 59

34 On Bevin's wartime activities, see Alan Bullock, *The Life and Times of Ernest Bevin* (London: Heinemann, 1967) ii

35 A. J. Marder, *From the Dreadnought to Scapa Flow* (Oxford: Oxford University Press, 1969) iv, Chaps 4-5; David Lloyd George, op cit, i, pp667-73; Richard Hough, *The Great War at Sea, 1914-1918* (Oxford: Oxford University Press, 1988) pp300-6

36 Secretary of the War Cabinet and unofficial adviser to both Asquith and Lloyd George, Hankey may have picked up the idea from junior officers. Stephen Roskill, *Hankey: Man of Secrets* (London: Collins, 1970) i, p356

37 David Lloyd George, op cit, i, p677

38 Hankey Diary, 22 April 1915, Hankey papers. Lloyd George's exact words to Hankey were, 'Oh well, I have never regarded that matter as seriously as you have.'

[39] Stephen Roskill, op cit, p382, 379
[40] A. J. Marder, op cit, iv, Chap 6; Richard Hough, op cit, pp308-9
[41] John Keegan, 'Churchill's Strategy', in Blake and Louis, op cit, p341
[42] David Lloyd George, op cit, i, pp758ff
[43] Trevor Wilson, op cit, pp534-5; José Harris, 'Bureaucrats and Businessmen in British Food Control, 1916-1919', in Kathleen Burk, ed, op cit, pp139-46
[44] The most detailed work on the subject of economic controls is the official history, W. K. Hancock and M. M. Growing, *British War Economy* (London: HMSO, 1949). A good summary of this study can be found in A. J. Youngson, *The British Economy* (London: Allen & Unwin, 1960) Chap 5
[45] Keith Grieves, *The Politics of Manpower, 1914-1918* (Manchester: Manchester University Press, 1988) Chaps 4-6; R. J. Q. Adams and Philip P. Poirier, *The Conscription Controversy in Great Britain, 1900-1918* (London: Macmillan, 1987) pp190-212
[46] Keith Grieves, op cit, Chaps 7-8; Trevor Wilson, op cit, pp535-36; Adams and Poirier, op cit, pp213-8
[47] David Jablonsky, *Churchill: The Great Game and Total War* (London: 1991) pp124-5
[48] Balfour to Cecil, 12 September 1917, Cecil papers, ADD 51071 (British Museum)
[49] John Ehrman, op cit, pp102-3
[50] For a detailed study of Churchill's strategy see Richard Lamb, *Churchill as War Leader – Right or Wrong?* (London, 1991); R. W. Thompson, *Generalissimo Churchill* (London: 1973); Tuvia Ben-Moshe, op cit; and David Jablonsky, op cit
[51] John Grigg, *1943: The Victory that Never Was* (London: Eyre Methuen, 1980)
[52] David Lloyd George, op cit, ii, pp1366-7
[53] That view was best expressed by Arthur Balfour, who had no illusions about Lloyd George's strategic intuition, in a letter to his cousin, Lord Robert Cecil, 12 September 1917, Cecil Papers, ADD 51071
[54] On Plumer see Geoffrey Powell, *Plumer: The Soldier's General* (London: Leo Cooper, 1990)
[55] Trevor Wilson, on the other hand, offers several other plausible explanations. He speculates that Lloyd George needed Haig as a whipping boy, for he anticipated further setbacks ahead. Another possibility he suggests is that Lloyd George recognised that the experience Haig had gained during his command on the Western Front would stand him in good stead when the opportunity to win the war presented itself. Trevor Wilson, op cit, p549
[56] David R. Woodward, *Lloyd George and the Generals* (London and Toronto: Associated University Presses, 1983) pp142ff
[57] The reader who wishes to probe deeper into this issue may be referred to John Gooch, 'The Maurice Debate, 1918', *Journal of Contemporary History*, 3 (1968), pp211-28; Nancy Maurice, ed, *The Maurice Case: From the Papers of Major-General Sir Frederick Maurice* (London: 1972); John Turner, *British Politics and the Great War* (London: Yale University Press, 1992) pp297-302; David R. Woodward, 'Did Lloyd George Starve the British Army of Men Prior to the German Offensive of 21 March 1918?', *Historical Journal*, 27 (1984), pp241-52
[58] Trevor Wilson, op cit, pp574-5
[59] Lord Beaverbrook, *Men and Power, 1917-1918* (London: Hutchinson, 1956) p260
[60] Kevin Jeffreys, op cit, pp99-100
[61] The only study on Anglo-French relations is William J. Philpott, *Anglo-French Relations and the Strategy on the Western Front, 1914-1918* (Basingstoke: Macmillan, 1996)
[62] Robin Edmonds, 'Churchill and Stalin', and Warren F. Kimball, 'Wheel Within a Wheel: Churchill, Roosevelt, and the Special Relationship', in Blake and Louis, op cit, are good brief examinations of Churchill's relations with the Allied leaders.
[63] John Ehrman, op cit, p112
[64] See, eg, Peter Rowland, *Lloyd George* (London: Barrie & Jenkins, 1975) and A. J. P. Taylor, *Lloyd George: Rise and Fall*, op cit
[65] In addition to the three mentioned in the above notes, there is Leopold Amery, 'Churchill and Lloyd George', in Martin Gilbert, ed, *Winston Churchill* (Englewood Cliffs, NJ: 1967)

Chapter 22

Erich Ludendorff and Tôjô Hideki: some comparisons

Peter Wetzler

General Erich Ludendorff (1865-1937) was, at the height of his power and influence between August 1916 and October 1918, first Quartermaster General of the German High Command (Oberste Heeresleitung, OHL). This meant that he was second in command to the Supreme Commander, Field-Marshal Paul von Hindenburg (1847-1934). He is treated here and not Hindenburg because, though superior in rank, '...Hindenburg was merely a symbol behind which stood the reality of Ludendorff'.[1] After the war a former member of the OHL, Colonel Bauer, told the historian Hans Delbrück that, 'In the end we did not even tell him [Hindenburg] where the army corps were.'[2] Ludendorff was the strategist who planned and executed the operations carried out under their command. He was also the source of the energy, vanity and pride that characterised their so-called military dictatorship during this period.

General Tôjô Hideki (1884-1948), Prime Minister of Japan from October 1941 to July 1944, was for the Allies 'the war premier'.[3] In Japan he is known for his uncompromising dictatorial policies, and he was often able to prevail over others nominally superior to him. Because of his narrow unbending interpretation and execution of military and political decisions he was called by many 'the razor' (kamisori).[4] Toward the end of his tenure in office Tôjô was so unpopular that there was apparently a plan to assassinate him.[5]

Ludendorff and Tôjô were both professional soldiers who never doubted the significance and honour of their calling, and who never doubted the just nature of the wars their respective countries prosecuted. Neither inspire(d) affection or widespread admiration. Both were extremely efficient staff officers known for their stern discipline, who demanded and received the loyalty of their subordinates. Yet each was affected personally by his wartime experiences in quite different ways. In turn, their respective reactions had very different implications for future events in their countries. This may be attributed in part to differences in these experiences. Ludendorff was actively involved in planning and carrying out military operations for most of the First World War. Tôjô once planned and led as a field-grade officer a very successful operation in northern China and Mongolia, but with this exception was not responsible for individual military operations.[6] As prime minister, he was more concerned with national policy in China and the Pacific during the Second World War.

Both men, as is well known, fought on the losing side. And it is in defeat that one sees most clearly the ways in which war weighed upon them personally. Ludendorff appears to have suffered a nervous breakdown in 1918 when things went badly for the German Army.[7] He never could admit his role in this defeat and spent many years after the war defending the military and himself. His extensive writings are in part factual and of interest to historians, but they also contain fantasies, self-laudatory accounts and racist diatribes that indicate emotional imbalance and possibly early senility.[8] He died an honoured if somewhat self-tarnished man. Tôjô was obliged to resign from office one year before final defeat. After Japan's surrender in 1945 he attempted to commit suicide immediately before his arrest by Allied authorities, but not in order to avoid responsibility for the war. He was perfectly willing to defend himself and the correctness of Japan's war efforts in court, but not as a war criminal. Arrest he regarded as an affront to his honour.[9] Later Tôjô accepted responsibility for beginning the war in the Pacific at the Tokyo War Crimes Trials, and for the defeat.[10] He never blamed others for his fate and never recanted his convictions about the justness of Japan's war aims. Tôjô was hanged as a war criminal, and most people in Japan preferred to forget he ever existed. In fact, he is still regarded as an embarrassment by many. For example, his family came from the city of Morioka, about 500 kilometres north of Tokyo, and in recent brochures published by the city and prefecture governments he is not included among the prominent historical figures from the area listed in them.

The training and education these men received no doubt conditioned their reactions to their wartime experiences. Ludendorff and Tôjô attended military academies in Prussia and Japan, and rose in the officer corps based on their abilities as staff officers. Their training and education was somewhat similar, because the Japanese adopted (and adapted) German education and military systems after they began to modernise and industrialise their society in the latter half of the 19th century.[11] Both were 'high achievers', but the military was not just a career, it was life itself. With respect to the effects of war on them personally, their feelings about religion, race and a nation's ability to conduct war were more important than their formal education in the strategy and technology of war. These spiritual factors were also similar in some ways due to earlier Japanese borrowings from Germany.

Itô Hirobumi (1841-1909), framer of the first Japanese constitution, commented in 1888 after several visits to Europe, especially Germany and Austria:

'In Europe, not only have the people become proficient in constitutional government since it first took seed, there was also religion, and this constituted the axis, deeply infusing the popular mind. In this the people's hearts found unity… In our country there is only the Imperial House that can become such an axis.'[12]

The goal was national unity and this was to be achieved through promotion of a religion-like cult centred on the emperor. The model for creating this unity Itô saw in the relation between Christianity and the modern state in Europe; unassailable state authority was based on universally accepted religious beliefs, and this was to be adapted to the Japanese milieu. Japanese were called upon to subordinate themselves to state policies, which were legitimised by a state religion based on native beliefs connected with the imperial house – State Shintô. This appeal was apparently quite successful as the people came to follow unquestioningly the mandates of their leaders. Tôjô, though a leader, was equally swayed by this propaganda. While prime minister he told his secretary in private:

> 'The emperor is a holy being [shinkaku]. We subjects, regardless of how important we become, cannot overcome our existence as human beings [jinkaku]. [Compared with the emperor] even the prime minister is unimportant. I have heard that previously in conducting politics it was important for a statesman to apprehend the will of the people, to formulate this will, and to move in the direction indicated. But this is not sufficient in Japanese politics. Which means, since our people are like the children of the emperor it is important to disseminate the imperial will to all corners [of the land]. At the same time the feelings [kokoro] of the people, who are children, must be bound together and united with the emperor. This is certainly an important duty of the prime minister and the other ministers.'[13]

Since this was a private conversation, published more than 40 years later, one may assume that it reflects Tôjô's personal beliefs. In the name of the emperor it was the duty of government leaders to unite the people in support of national policy, not because it was the policy decided upon by elected representatives of the people but because it was the policy of a 'holy being' – the emperor. In practice, Tôjô implicitly accepted popular religious beliefs propagated about the emperor as integral to uniting disparate people behind the policies of the imperial government. (Contrary to the assumptions of many persons outside Japan, regional, linguistic and political differences, combined with the social stress concomitant with industrialising a nation, precipitated serious divisive problems there for many years.)

In Germany Ludendorff felt similarly about national policy and national destiny. The OHL was supposed to be the instrument of this destiny, but without specific reference to the reigning German emperor. In the First Quartermaster General's words:

> 'The spiritual [seelische] unity of a folk, this is and certainly will remain the basis for prosecuting a total war; it is only to be achieved through the unity of racial inheritance and belief, and careful observance of the biological and spiritual laws and the characteristics of one's racial inheritance.'[14]

Interesting enough, he cited, in 1935, the Japanese as a splendid example of this sort of unity. The unity of the Japanese folk:

> '…is spiritual and is based principally on Shintô belief, which puts the Japanese necessarily in the service of the emperor, in order to preserve the way to an [after-]life with their ancestors. Living in accord with the gods means to

the Japanese service to the emperor, and thereby to the state. This is in conformity with Shintô belief which comes from the racial inheritance of the Japanese, and with the needs of the people and the state. We see today the manner in which the Japanese acknowledge this, how the Shintô religion is emphasised in Japan, and the holy nature of the emperor may not be questioned. The strength of the Japanese folk lies in the unity of her racial inheritance, belief, and in the way of life constructed thereupon.'[15]

The theoretical underpinnings of late-19th-century nationalism and imperialism were adopted, adapted and preserved so successfully by the Japanese that one of the foremost nationalists and imperialists of his day, Ludendorff, saw in them a noteworthy example of this mentality. References in Germany at that time to Japanese patriotism were not unusual. Ludendorff probably was as well sensitised to developments in the Far East as most, having studied at the War Academy under a former military advisor to the Japanese – Jacob Meckel (1842-1906), who was in Japan from 1885 to 1888.[16] He even predicted, in a report written shortly after graduation, against the prevailing climate of opinion, that in the event of a war between China and Japan, Japan would win.[17] And indeed, the Japanese won handily the Sino-Japanese War, 1894-95. There is no indication in his writings, however, that Ludendorff's knowledge transcended military matters, and that he was aware that the presumed Japanese spiritual unity was a result of the adaptation of Shintô to Chinese Confucianism, and to modern European nationalism – as perceived in large part in the German model. Quite the contrary – he believed that it derived from the Japanese 'racial inheritance'.

Finally, however, Ludendorff and Tôjô, reflecting differences in their respective assessments of their personal roles vis-à-vis god, Kaiser and country, came to their positions of power in rather different ways.

Ludendorff was described by Theobald von Bethmann Hollweg (1856-1921), Prime Minister 1909-17, as someone whose '…pan-German extravagance and self over-estimation knew no bounds with respect to his view of what militarily and politically was attainable'.[18] This conceit was based on Ludendorff's vision of Germany's heritage. He expressed more than once his convictions about the unique destiny of the German 'Volk'. For example, in 1922 in *Kriegführung und Politik*:

'Out of an object of history they [the Hohenzollern] made the German folk into a subject of history. The great achievement of this noble house is displayed in the fact that at the same time, in accord with our German origins, they gave us a special view of life which may be summarised in the word 'Prussian' [Preußentum].'[19]

He identified this destiny with his own such that he brooked no opposition to his policies. Even the emperor was subordinated to Ludendorff's self-centred, Prussian, megalomania. A later historian summarised that he was '…obsessed with power to the point of insubordination…'[20] Early on, for example, despite the Kaiser's support of Hindenburg's predecessor, their commanding officer, General

Erich von Falkenhayn (1861-1922, Chief of the General Staff 1914-1916), Ludendorff criticised him persistently and this criticism was an important factor in the latter's downfall. At a critical juncture when the Prime Minister and Falkenhayn had fallen out and the emperor's support was on the wane, Ludendorff attacked him again viciously in a lengthy note to the Under Secretary of State. Citing examples of well-known failures, such as Verdun, he accused Falkenhayn of incompetence. Wilhelm II himself, adverse to public pressure, distrusted Hindenburg's popularity and was none too anxious to appoint Hindenburg and Ludendorff to head the OHL. But in the end, faced with these and other attacks after the Wehrmacht's defeats, he had no alternative.[21]

Ludendorff was intent upon attaining power for himself through his patron Hindenburg, and he worked untiringly for the latter's appointment as Chief of the High Command General Staff. After Hindenburg attained the post, with Ludendorff as his deputy, the latter quickly began to assert his authority in political as well as military matters. According to Prime Minister Bethmann Hollweg, up to that time the High Command had tried to co-operate with political leaders while maintaining wherever possible the division between political and military functions:

> 'Very soon however [after Hindenburg's appointment with Ludendorff as his second in command] General Ludendorff changed the relationship. There were almost no political issues in which he not only demanded that the views of the High Command be taken into consideration but that the High Command was to make the decisions. This military interference was justified nearly always with the explanation that otherwise the war would be lost and Field-Marshal von Hindenburg could no longer carry the responsibility.'[22]

Using Hindenburg's popularity, Ludendorff blackmailed the Government into accepting his dictates. Obviously one important effect of the war on Ludendorff was that it whetted his appetite for power.

In Japan, military leaders also sought to dictate political policy similarly – by threatening to recall one or both of their ministers and to refuse to appoint a new one; this meant the fall of a cabinet. Tôjô personally, however, prior to his appointment as Army Minister, was not engaged politically outside normal activities within the Army itself. It is unlikely that he fomented or was involved in intrigues that led to his appointment. Post-war testimony indicates that he was chosen for purely administrative reasons; other officers superior to him could not be easily transferred, and previously as Chief of Staff of the Kwantung Army, Vice-Minister of War and in his post at that time, Inspector-General for Air, he had demonstrated outstanding executive ability. When the decision was made, he was travelling in Manchuria on an inspection tour. Only after his appointment, on 18 July 1940, was he ordered to return to the capital by plane, and was told of the appointment following his arrival.[23] During the time immediately after his appointment notes from conferences reveal differences between Tôjô, 'a child of the army ministry', and others who were mainly concerned with military operations as members of the general staff. These same notes do not show him treating others in an autocratic manner, but as alternatives were discussed from different points of view, Tôjô emphasised political as well as military considerations and did not shy away from confrontations with his peers, regardless of age and rank.[24]

Tôjô was a 'hard-liner' when it came to following rules and abiding by decisions made. Later, similar to Ludendorff, he assumed uncritically that only his policies would benefit the destiny of the empire. Unlike Ludendorff, he honoured the emperor as a 'god manifest' (*arahitogami*) and he does not appear to have been obsessed with power. Which is to say, war opens the avenue to power for some well-placed ambitious military officers, and Ludendorff readily, even greedily, grasped at this opportunity. Tôjô did not. The manner in which he came to be appointed prime minister, and his reaction to the appointment, demonstrate this clearly.

Tôjô's selection as prime minister was a surprise to everyone. His opposition to the previous premier, Konoe Fumimaro[25], caused the fall of that Cabinet, and under the circumstances it was considered poor etiquette, a very important consideration in Japan, for him to succeed his predecessor. When he received an order to report to the emperor, he was at the official residence of the Army Minister packing his bags. He assumed that he had been summoned to explain his reasons for opposing Konoe's policies. But Tôjô was told to form a new government, a mandate that was totally unexpected and about which he had serious misgivings.[26] Had he been intent upon retaining or increasing his power for power's sake, then he would have assumed a totally different posture. He fully expected that as a consequence of his bitter opposition to the prime minister – head of the foremost noble family in Japan, whose leaders were for centuries advisors to the throne – that he would be assigned to another post that had little to do with politics.

Tôjô opposed Konoe's policies for reasons of both form and content. Previously a decision had been made in an imperial conference that war should be decided upon by 10 October 1941. Nevertheless, Konoe was against war; the Navy was also against war but did not wish to openly express this policy, and Konoe did not want to make a decision under the circumstances. Tôjô believed that the decision, because of the emperor's presence at the earlier conference, and for military reasons, was unavoidable and that it should be in favour of war. He was selected to be the next prime minister due to the former stance and in spite of the latter: he was well-known for his unswerving loyalty to the throne. Decisions sanctioned in the presence of the emperor were unalterable, because a change would have amounted to lèse-majesté. At the same time it was assumed that if the emperor ordered him to ignore the former decision and conduct an impartial review of the situation, he would do this despite his personal convictions about the advisability of war. And equally important, he was the only person who could control the Army and unite the Army and Navy, whose long-standing disputes over military priorities made a coherent national policy impossible.[27] Tôjô himself worked for the appointment of someone else, Imperial Prince Higashikuni (1887-1990), who in his opinion was the only person who could accomplish the desired unity. But an imperial prince was not supposed to be put in a precarious situation – deciding for or against war – that might later endanger the existence of the imperial house. (It was thought, as affirmed by future events, that if war was decided upon and lost, the deciding authority would be held responsible by the victors and treated poorly.) Finally, the Navy also declined to have one of its officers assume this responsibility, and Tôjô was nominated to become the next prime minister because there was no one else available, and expendable, who might fill the bill.[28]

Officially, the Army Ministry and the general staff had little to do with the selection process. Behind the scenes, the emperor discussed it with his political advisor, Lord Keeper of the Privy Seal Kido Kôichi (1889-1977) and the departing prime minister; military leaders were consulted similarly, because if they refused to appoint Army or Navy Ministers a Cabinet could not be formed; finally the elder statesmen, former prime ministers, were informed of the trend of these consultations, and they made a formal recommendation to the emperor. Various contemporary sources – notes made by the general staff, Konoe, Kido, and others – show that Tôjô did not seek the office himself.[29] Once in office, however, he was not reticent about using his power.

Prime Minister Tôjô Hideki soon came to be known for the brutal use of his new authority. In particular he employed the military police (*kempeitai*) to enforce his will on political opponents.[30] As noted above, Ludendorff also sought to influence political policy from his position in the OHL. Nevertheless, their respective attitudes toward power, reflected in the way each came to a position of power, is a key to understanding their different personal reactions when things went badly.

At the end of their respective wars, Ludendorff and Tôjô reacted very differently to the defeat of their nations, their personal loss of power, prestige and honour. Both men had families that were also affected by the war. Ludendorff had two stepsons, and the loss of one in battle caused him considerable grief. Tôjô had seven children; none were lost in the war, and Tôjô was not known as a devoted family man. More important for both men personally was the fate of the nation, the Army, each's honour and memory in history. In particular their attitude toward the loss of power – the ability to cause others to do one's bidding – reveals poignantly their reactions to war. For this reason the way in which each came to power was treated above. Now their reactions to lost battles, power and eventually honour in war will be addressed.

Ludendorff never tired of blaming others for Germany's defeat. Germany's deteriorating military situation near the end of the war had a severe impact on him, and it appears to be no coincidence that the famous 'stab in the back' (*Dolchstoß*) legend and his nervous breakdown came at about the same time. This legend – that weak-kneed civilian leaders behind the lines and not the Army on the front lost the war – became the underlying theme of his many writings. It is, for example, implied at the beginning of his war memoirs written in exile (1919) in Sweden:

> 'The government went her own way, and with regard to the wishes of the High Command, did not fail to do anything which they deemed appropriate. But many things were left undone which in the interests of prosecuting the war were designated as urgently necessary.'[31]

At the end of the same account his choice of words was much stronger:

'That was the gratitude of the newly formed nation to German soldiers… The destruction of the German army, brought about by Germans, was a crime and a tragedy never yet seen in the world. A flood-tide has broken over Germany, and it is not a result of the elementary forces of nature, but proceeds from the weakness of the government represented by the chancellor and also from the paralysis of the leaderless folk.'[32]

This stab-in-the-back legend originated not in these writings, but before the end of the war when Ludendorff was grappling with defeat, personal loss of power and influence.

The last serious German offensives of the war came in the spring and summer of 1918: 21 March, 27 May and 15 July. The preparations for these offensives, according to Ludendorff, were very similar.[33] According to one later expert, the planning for these battles, especially the first, was 'brilliant', but the outcomes were unfavourable, in no small part because Ludendorff lost his nerve, intervened continually and ordering changes in tactics that in the end undermined the strategic concepts behind the offensives.[34] Then, with the French counter-attack on 18 July, the German position on the Marne was seriously threatened. Ludendorff broke under the stress and fell into a severe psychological depression. Many officers at the OHL thought he could no longer perform his duties satisfactorily. For example, Graf Schulenburg, General and Chief of Staff of the Crown Prince's army group, wrote:

'In my opinion Ludendorff's judgements of the situation are not correct objectively and much too optimistic. Since the middle of July a great deal of nervousness has become apparent in him personally. This was expressed especially in persistent, excited telephone conversations which have upset the entire front. Other persons appear to have urged that he be released from the High Command.'[35]

One of the other persons was the above-mentioned Colonel Bauer, a department head at the end of the war, who spoke to Schulenburg personally. Not everyone shared this opinion, but Ludendorff's ability to cause others to do his bidding was beginning to crumble. It was the beginning of the end.

Ludendorff was a soldier. He had built up not only his career but also his life as such, based on his prowess as a military planner. He became an important man because of this hard-won ability, and readily identified with his role as a 'power behind the throne' – the Kaiser's and also Hindenburg's command. When it became clear that he would no longer be able to fill this role, that power was slipping from his grasp and with it the respect and fear of others, his own self-esteem faded rapidly and he was unable to deal with this total loss of personal identity.

According to Ludendorff, 8 August 1918 was '…the black day of the German army…'. The spirit of the German Army wavered and in places broke.[36] In fact, the Allies achieved a major breakthrough on the Somme where well-trained, elite German troops broke and ran away in panic. Previously it had became obvious to many in the OHL that the German Army should only think about defensive operations, contrary to Ludendorff's basic policy up to that time. With support in his own staff failing and another large setback, Ludendorff's nerves collapsed completely. He was no longer able to assess professionally the war situation. Shortly thereafter he, too, proposed a war of attrition (*Ermattungsstrategie*) so that at least Germany would not lose the war.[37] By this time that was also an illusion. The men and material available simply were insufficient to the task.

Ludendorff's nerves and his ability to control and guide the OHL did not improve, and he was persuaded to seek the help of a doctor. He agreed to treatment for his 'over-work', the consequences of which he was aware. The treatment lasted from 6 September to 5 October 1918. He was advised to take a rest – sleep regularly, sing German folk songs, and enjoy the roses in the garden. Whether or not he followed all of this advice is unclear, but he did work far less than accustomed for some time.[38]

Nevertheless, he remained well-informed. On 28 September, as his period of recuperation came to an end, Ludendorff went to Hindenburg and told him that an armistice was necessary. Both still entertained the illusory notion that this would be a pause, not the end of the war. Somehow the danger of Bolshevism to the Allies as well as Germany would bring them to agree with this proposal.[39] Shortly thereafter, at the beginning of October, both Ludendorff and Hindenburg feared the collapse of the Western Front in the event of a new enemy offensive. Prince Max of Baden, who had been selected to form a new government, was told this in the early hours of the morning in Berlin on 1 October by a representative of the OHL. On the same day at the OHL, the 'stab-in-the-back' legend was born. Ludendorff told the section chiefs that an armistice must be signed as soon as possible, but he did not say the military situation demanded this. Instead the socialists had 'undermined morale and sabotaged industrial production'. They should be part of the new government and take responsibility for the conditions imposed during peace negotiations.[40] Ludendorff expressed this conviction clearly in a work published several years after the end of the war:

> 'The government and parliament abandoned the army, [national] policy, military leaders…
>
> The courageous army, which denies this charge, did not lay its weapons down. Rather, political policy forced it to do so…
>
> Finally the politicians disarmed … the army – undefeated by the enemy – and delivered Germany into the hands of an enemy intent on her destruction… That was the high point of the betrayal of war leaders and the people committed by the politicians, represented by the social-democratic delegates of the people.'[41]

Defeat, loss of power and respect, and a nervous breakdown, preceded the stab-in-the-back theory. One man's reaction to losing honour, prestige, power and a war appears to have had serious consequences for him personally, for his country, and for many more in the war to come.

Tôjô did not blame anyone for Japan's defeat in the next war. His feelings about his responsibility for the Pacific Theatre of the Second World War are reflected in the following statement to his wartime cabinet secretary, Hoshino Naoki (1892-1987), made while awaiting the Tokyo War Crimes Trial in prison:

'...Japan's going to war was unavoidable. It was never something we wanted. Therefore, prosecuting the war should not be treated as a crime.

...However if the victorious powers want to treat this as a crime, all responsibility lies with me only and no one else.

...The emperor did everything possible to avoid the war. That it finally came to war and war was unavoidable was due to my recommendations. That responsibility, formal as well as practical, lies with me alone.

...Other persons also voiced various opinions up until the final decision was made. But the person who finally made the decision and advised the emperor accordingly was none other than I myself.

...The result was a war, a war which ended with Japan's total defeat. If one believes that the fatherland has suffered damage and shame, and somehow someone must be called to account, naturally I must submit myself [for judgement].'[42]

Tôjô had little time for reflection. As noted above, immediately after the war he was tried as a war criminal and executed. Writings about and by him therefore have a different character from the thick volumes of prose left by Ludendorff. They consist mainly of notes made by subordinates during the war and reflections on loose-leaf paper from prison. During the war crimes trials Tôjô made virtually no effort to defend himself personally. Instead, he defended the correctness of the war effort, and assumed responsibility for the decision for war in order to ensure that the emperor was not saddled with this responsibility.

Previously, near the end of Tôjô's period of rule, as the Japanese military situation began to deteriorate rapidly, he demonstrated his resolve and emotional strength of character and conviction. In mid-February 1944 the Imperial Navy suffered a devastating defeat in the Caroline Islands, which left her with no combat aircraft in the area.[43] Tôjô and other leaders in Tokyo were shocked, well aware of the significance of this defeat, and the Prime Minister acted immediately. He had himself appointed Chief of Staff. The reasons behind this move have to do with Tôjô's penchant for direct action and the structure of the Government, little known or understood outside Japan then (and now). Practically speaking, the Imperial Army and Imperial Navy were independent resorts beyond the influence of the Cabinet or the Army and Navy Ministers in the Cabinet. The general staffs of each service were charged with planning and executing the operations of their respective services, responsible only to the emperor personally. As a result, aligning political and military policy was often impossible. Moreover, co-ordinating Army and Navy operations was equally problematic – usually limited to empty proclamations with no operative consequences.[44] Tôjô had himself appointed Chief of Staff (he was already Army Minister) and a trusted colleague, Navy Minister Shimada Shigetarô (1883-1976), was simultaneously appointed Chief of the Navy General Staff in order to overcome these difficulties.

The need to improve the co-ordination of military activities was apparent to all, but not everyone was happy to see Tôjô increase his power and authority. Among his critics were members of his own ministry and one of the emperor's younger brothers, Imperial Prince Chichibu.[45] In any case it was a last-ditch manoeuvre, the success of which was predicated on victories by Japanese military units overseas, which were not forthcoming. It was the beginning of the end of Tôjô's political and military career.

Until his resignation on 18 July 1944, Tôjô continued to try to improve the co-ordination of military operations. Notes in the *Tôjô Naikaku Sôridaijin Kimitsu Kiroku* (*Prime Minister's Secret Agenda During the Tôjô Cabinet*) show that as late as 14-15 July he proposed a unified command by establishing an Imperial Headquarters Chief of Staff (*Daihon'ei Bakuryôchô*), over the two Army and Navy Chiefs of Staff, who should be an imperial prince. The proposal was rejected by the Navy after considerable discussion.[46] These and other attempts to improve the command structure can and were interpreted as simple efforts to retain power. Nevertheless, after leaving office and after the war, Tôjô continued to maintain that this division of authority – Army, Navy, civil government – was a principal reason for Japan's defeat, an observation confirmed in post-war commentaries by Japanese contemporaries and former adversaries alike.[47]

By the early summer of 1944 another disaster loomed on the horizon: the Allied advance on Saipan. On 19 June, with the defeat of Japanese forces in the Marianas Islands, the importance and difficulty of defending Saipan became clear. From Saipan, US long-range bombers would be able to reach the home islands in six hours (Japanese calculation). Previously Tôjô had warned other members of the Government and military leaders that they must reckon with this eventuality. But as speculation turned to a concrete possibility the stress mounted on Tôjô and he, like Ludendorff many years before, appears to have engaged in unrealistic speculation about how Japan could still win the war, despite diminishing war potential and failing production capacity. On 20 June Tôjô told his secretaries enthusiastically:

'The strong point of the Japanese is that everyone risks all; we are daring, not afraid of death. Against one enemy aircraft carrier we send in one plane [ikki] and with it can defeat the carrier. This is the strength of Japan. Therefore if one thinks that when the enemy builds an aircraft carrier we also [must] build a carrier, if one simply resists using raw materials only, this probably would mean the defeat of our country which is lacking in productive power. In the end we make use of our strong point – with one plane we defeat one of the enemy's carriers. Using special boats, through suicide units [kesshitai] which defeat one enemy ship the enemy can be beaten. If the time comes when I too must embrace a bomb and jump into the fray, of course I will do it. Making use of this Japanese strength, we must somehow win out. Our young people offer up their lives for the nation. Through sacrifice one gladly lays the foundation for successfully completing the East Asia War. It is really great!'[48]

Tôjô was not a member of the Imperial Way Faction (*kôdôha*), and was not one of those who advocated fighting with 'human bullets' (*nikudan*).[49] However, as the war approached a conclusion he knew would be unsuccessful, he too grasped at spiritual straws hoping to achieve what was by all rational accounts impossible –

victory over an enemy obviously superior in material and manpower. This might be attributed to his desire to retain power, but, unlike Ludendorff, it did not reflect a loss of nerve or indicate a nervous breakdown. Fighting to the death has long been a respected part of Japanese tradition, as is idolising persons who fought and died for what was generally acknowledged as a lost cause. Tôjô was well aware of this tradition and identified with it. He readily used the power he acquired as prime minister, sometimes brutally. But as he did this, he saw himself as a military man in service of the emperor, come what may.[50]

On 7 July 1944 word reached Japan that the garrison on Saipan had met with an 'honourable death' (*gyokusai*). It had been wiped out. Intrigues against Tôjô now included members of the elder statesmen and the imperial court. Tôjô and his assistants knew this.[51] As noted above, he attempted to reform the command structure, and retain power. But when it became clear that the persons who had recommended him to the emperor, the elder statesmen, were solidly against him, he resigned. Not only did he resign as Prime Minister and Army Minister; he was also removed from active duty and little was heard from him until the war crimes trials after the end of the war.

In the Tokyo War Crimes Trials Tôjô was convicted and condemned to death along with six other defendants. (There were 28 persons on trial.[52]) One of the last things he told his family was that '...there should be absolutely no apologies'.[53] The word translated as 'apologies' (*iiwake*) can mean explanations, excuses, etc, whereby in Japan, as elsewhere, an explanation can be construed as an apology or excuse. Therefore Tôjô's exact meaning is unclear. To be sure, Tôjô had no intention to bow before the enemy, and admit to conducting an 'unjust' war as asserted by the Allies. At the same time he was deeply affected by the enmity of his own people, many of whom held him responsible for defeat, for the deaths of family members and relatives.[54] In this sense he was similar to Ludendorff, and then again not. Ludendorff's writings were in defence of the Army and himself; Tôjô felt misunderstood, asserted the righteousness of Japan's cause, and nevertheless forbade his family to engage in explaining or defending him. Tôjô maintained, 'One must await the critic (*hihan*) of history.'[55]

What then are we looking for when considering the reactions of (important) individuals to war? Personal suffering? Professional consequences? Here I have concentrated on how personal character and reactions to wartime stress influenced professional activities. The acquisition and loss of power were focused upon because this is something that is readily comparable in two very different men from different times and cultures. Moreover, their reactions had historical consequences. Their different attitudes – different reactions to war – were important. Ludendorff in crisis suffered a nervous breakdown, and during this time the 'stab-in-the-back' theory of Germany's defeat in the First World War emerged. Whether or not one precipitated the other cannot be ascertained definitively, but it is at least a tantalising coincidence. Later, this assertion helped a former soldier in Ludendorff's army, Adolf Hitler, to justify another war – the Second World War – and it helped to convince many Germans of the correctness of his claims – Germany had never really been defeated. It also led the Allies to demand from Germany and Japan unconditional surrender at the end of that war. It helped to justify the carpet-bombing of German cities, and the dropping of atom bombs on Hiroshima and Nagasaki.

The legacy of Tôjô's reaction to war is as yet not so clear. Obviously he was instrumental in deflecting war crimes charges against Emperor Hirohito (1901-1989), and in preserving the imperial institution in Japan. The continued existence of Emperor Hirohito personally and the imperial institution generally have been, up until now, beneficial or at worst of no consequence for the Japanese populace and the world. But since Tôjô and the military were held responsible for starting and losing the war, a serious side-effect has emerged: not only the late emperor but also most Japanese have been able to avoid confronting their personal and collective responsibility for the War in the Pacific. This continues to have negative repercussions on social and political relations in East Asia.

Erich Ludendorff and Tôjô Hideki both influenced the wars of their times, and events that came thereafter. This influence resulted not only from conscious planning, but also from their reactions to individual opportunities – among others attaining power – and to the stress ensuing from these wars – the loss of power. Ludendorff came to power through design and wilfulness, Tôjô through no fault of his own – almost by accident. The reasons for the loss of their respective wars and power are manifold. As for the critic of history awaited by Tôjô, synonymous with the 'judgement of history' expected by Ludendorff and many others, this appears to have been a significant factor with respect to their reactions to war: hoping to be remembered favourably by his future countrymen, Tôjô assumed responsibility for the war, shielding emperor and nation; Ludendorff engaged in self-serving assaults on home-grown enemies, which were detrimental to himself and his own people. Each in very different ways attempted to assure his personal place in history, during and after war. These attempts, like their flirtations with power and the wars they prosecuted, ended in failure.

Notes to contributors

Professor Peter Wetzler, East Asia Institute, Ludwigshafen Business School, Germany
Professor Wetzler received his doctorate from the University of California, Berkeley in 1977. He is currently Professor of Japanese Business, Politics and Language at the East Asia Institute, Ludwigshafen Business School, Germany. His writings include: Hirohito and War. Imperial Tradition and Military Decision Making in Prewar Japan (Honolulu: University of Hawai'i Press, 1998).

Recommended reading

Asprey, Robert B., *The German High Command at War: Hindenburg and Ludendorff Conduct World War I* (New York: William Morrow, 1993)

Browne, Courtney, *Tojo: The Last Banzai* (New York: Holt, Rinehart & Winston, 1967)

Butow, Robert J. C., *Tojo and the Coming of War* (Stanford: Stanford University Press, 1961)

Crozier, Andrew J., *The Causes of the Second World War* (Oxford: Blackwell, 1997)

Kitchen, Martin, *The Silent Dictatorship* (New York: Holmes & Meier, 1976)

Notes

1   Gordon A. Craig, *Germany 1866-1945* (Oxford: Oxford University Press, 1981) pp373-5 for this and the evaluation concluding this paragraph. See also Michael Geyer, 'German Strategy in the Age of Machine Warfare, 1914-1945' in Peter Paret, ed, *Makers of Modern Strategy, from Machiavelli to the Nuclear Age* (Princeton: Princeton University Press, 1986) pp527-97, 538-9.

2   Hans Delbrück, *Ludendorffs Selbstporträt* (Berlin: Verlag für Politik und Wirtschaft, 1922) p9

3   Tôjô was also Army Minister during this time. While prime minister he held a number of ministerial portfolios. See Miwa Kai and Philip B. Yampolsky, *Political Chronology of Japan 1885-1957* (New York: East Asian Institute of Columbia University, 1957) pp22-4. All Japanese names are in their normal Japanese order, family name before given name.

4   Robert J. C. Butow, *Tojo and the Coming of the War* (Stanford: Stanford University Press, 1961) pp42 and 307. This is the only reliable biography of Tôjô in a Western language. For Tôjô's uncompromising nature see, Hara Shirô, *Taisenryaku naki Kaisen* (*Beginning a War with no Great Strategy*) (Tokyo: Hara Shobô, 1987) p253

5   Tsunoda Tadashige, *Waga Tôjô Hideki Ansatsu Keikaku* (*Our Plan to Assassinate Tôjô Hideki*) (Tokyo: Tokuma Shoten, 1985)

6   Hosaka Masayasu, *Tôjô Hideki to Tennô no Jidai* (*Tôjô Hideki and the Era of the Emperor*) 2 Vols (Tokyo: Gendai Jânarisumu, 1979) Vol 1, pp109-11; Robert J. C. Butow, op cit, pp103-4

7   Martin Kitchen, 'Ludendorff and Germany's Defeat', in Hugh Cecil and Peter Liddle, eds, *Facing Armageddon: The First World War Experienced* (London: Leo Cooper, 1996) pp51-66, 56-58; Gunther Mai, *Das Ende des Kaiserreichs: Politik und Kriegführung im Ersten Weltkrieg* (Munich: Deutsche Taschenbuch Verlag, 1997, rev ed) pp150-1

8   See, eg, Erich Ludendorff, *Kriegführung und Politik* (Berlin: Verlag von E. S. Mittler & Sohn, 1922) 'Vorwort' and pp81, 110, 316-9; General Ludendorff, *Der totale Krieg* (Munich: Ludendorffs Verlag, 1935) pp11-28

9   Tsunoda Tadashige, op cit, pp16-9. Tsunoda cites notes made by Tôjô later in prison.

10 John R. Pritchard and Sonia Magbanna Zaide, eds, *The Tokyo War Crimes Trial (The Complete Transcripts of the Proceedings of the International Military Tribunal for the Far East)* 22 Vols plus Vols 26 and 27 (New York: Garland, 1981) Vol 15, pp36779-81

11 Carol Gluck, *Japan's Modern Myths: Ideology in the Late Meiji Period* (Princeton: Princeton University Press, 1985) pp19-20; Hosaka Masayasu, op cit, Vol 1, pp18-21. For the development of modern military units in Japan, see Ernst L. Presseisen, 'Before Aggression: Europeans Prepare the Japanese Army' (Association of Asian Studies Monographs & Papers, No XXI) (Tucson: University of Arizona Press, 1965). Also Georg Kerst, *Jacob Meckel, sein Leben, und sein Wirken in Deutschland und Japan* (Göttingen: Musterschmidt, 1970)

12 David A. Titus, *Palace & Politics in Pre-war Japan* (New York: Columbia University Press, 1974) p36

13 Akamatsu Sadao, *Tôjô Hishokan Kimitsu Nisshi* (*Secret Diary of Tôjô's Secretary*) (Tokyo: Bungei Shunjûsha, 1985) p33

14 General Ludendorff, *Der totale Krieg*, op cit, pp20-1

15 Ibid, p17

16 See note 11

17 Erich Ludendorff, *Mein militärischer Werdegang* (Munich: Ludendorffs Verlag GmbH, 1933) p33. See also Ernst L. Presseisen, op cit, pp140-1. An interesting 'footnote to history': Tôjô Hideki's father, Hidenori, was an instructor at the Japanese War Academy during Meckel's stay there (Hosaka Masayasu, op cit, Vol 1, p18)

18 Theobald von Bethmann Hollweg, *Betrachtungen zum Weltkriege* 2 Vols (Berlin: Verlag zum Reimer Hobbing, 1919/1921) Vol 1, p51; cited in Gunther Mai, op cit, p121

19 Erich Ludendorff, *Kriegführung und Politik*, op cit, 'Vorwort'

20 Gunther Mai, op cit, p87

21 Martin Kitchen, *The Silent Dictatorship* (New York: Holmes & Meier Publischers, 1976) pp30-1; Gunther Mai, op cit, pp84-7

22 Theobald von Bethmann Hollweg, op cit, Vol 2, p47

23 Robert J. C. Butow, op cit, pp143-4. Butow cites testimony from the Tokyo War Crimes Trials. Gunjishi Gakkai (Military History Association), eds, *Daihon'ei Rikugunbu Sensô Shidôhan, Kimitsu Sensô Nisshi* (*Secret War Diary of the Army Dept. Directorate, Imperial Headquarters*) 2 Vols (Tokyo: Kinseisha, 1998) Vol 1, p15

24 Ibid, Vol 1, pp68, 133-5

25 Konoe Fumimaro (1891-1945) was head of an elite extended family – the Fujiwara – the oldest noble family in Japan. He was Prime Minister three times during the pre-war years: June 1937-January 1939, July 1940-July 1941, July-October 1941. Tôjô served as Army Minister in the last two Cabinets.

26 Akamatsu Sadao, op cit, pp24-7

27 Ibid, pp22-3

28 See, for an authoritative narrative in English, Robert J. C. Butow, op cit, pp293-307

29 Higashikuni Naruhiko, *Higashikuni Nikki* (*The Higashikuni Diary*) (Tokyo: Tokuma Shoten, 1968) pp91-2. Konoe Fumimaro, *Heiwa e no Doryoku* (*Efforts for Peace*) (Tokyo: Nihon Denshin Tsûshinsha, 1946) pp97-8. Kido Kôichi, *Kido Kôichi Nikki* (*Kido Kôichi Diary*) 2 Vols (Tokyo: Tokyo Daigaku Shuppankai, 1966) Vol 1, pp234, 470; Vol 2, pp915-6. Gunjishi Gakkai, op cit, Vol 1, pp163-72

30 Ôtani Keijirô, *Shôwa Kempeishi* (*History of the Shôwa Military Police*) (Tokyo: Misuzu Shobô, 1987) pp442-57

31 Erich Ludendorff, *Meine Kriegserinnerung* (Berlin: Ernst Siegfried Mittler und Sohn, 1919) p6

32 Ibid, pp619-20

33 Ibid, p533

34 Martin Kitchen, op cit, pp52-5

35 Wolfgang Foerster, *Der Feldherr Ludendorff im Unglück* (Wiesbaden: Limes Verlag, 1952) pp71-2. Foerster quotes private papers. See for a discussion of the situation in the OHL and Ludendorff's psychological crisis, see pp71-81. Here the treatment by Dr Hochheimer, in Hochheimer's words, is reproduced. See also Fritz von Lossberg, *Meine Tätigkeit im Weltkrieg 1914-1918* (Berlin, 1939). Martin Kitchen, a historian who has written extensively about Ludendorff, shares the opinion that Ludendorff indeed was unable to perform his duties due to this depression. See, Martin Kitchen, op cit, pp55-6

36 Erich Ludendorff, *Meine Kriegserinnerung*, op cit, pp547, 550-1

37 Gunther Mai, op cit, pp148-9

38 Wolfgang Foerster, op cit, pp76-9, 138 note 40; Erich Ludendorff, op cit, p570; Martin Kitchen, op cit, p57

39 Erich Ludendorff, op cit, pp582-3

40 Martin Kitchen, op cit, cites secret documents from that time, pp60-1

41 Erich Ludendorff, *Kriegführung und Politik*, op cit, pp316-7, 319

42 'Hoshino Naoki Shuki' ('Hoshino Naoki Notes') in Jôhô Yoshio, *Tôjô Hideki* (Tokyo: Fuyô Shobô, 1974) p670

43 Robert J. C. Butow, op cit, p427

44 Ibid, pp420-2

45 Ibid, p428

46 Itô Takashi and Hirohashi Tadamitsu, Katashima Norio, eds, *Tôjô Naikaku Sôridaijin Kimitsu Kiroku* (*Prime Minister's Secret Agenda During the Tôjô Cabinet*) (Tokyo: Tokyo Daigaku Shuppankai, 1990) pp462-5

47 Satô Sanae, *Tôjô Hideki Fûin Sareta Shinjitsu* (*Tôjô Hideki, Sealed Reality*) (Tokyo: Kôdansha, 1995) pp127-8; Robert J. C. Butow, op cit, pp421-2, 426-7

48 Akamatsu Sadao, op cit, pp150-1. 'Ikki' normally refers to a fighter plane, but later in the text 'special boats' are also specifically mentioned.

49 Leonard A. Humphreys, *The Way of the Heavenly Sword: The Japanese Army in the 1920s* (Stanford: Stanford University Press, 1995) p106. This military 'thought' came from General Araki Sadao. See his *Kôgun no Hongi* (*Basic Principles of the Imperial Army*) issued in 1928.

50 See Peter Wetzler, *Hirohito and War: Imperial Tradition and Military Decision Making in Pre-war Japan* (Honolulu: University of Hawaii Press, 1998) pp70-4. On fighting to the death for lost causes see, Ivan Morris, *The Nobility of Failure: Tragic Heroes in the History of Japan* (New York: New American Library, 1975)

51 Akamatsu Sadao, op cit, p153

52 See Richard H. Minear, *Victors' Justice: The Tokyo War Crimes Trials* (Tokyo: Charles E. Tuttle, Co, 1971)

53 Satô Sanae, op cit, p254

54 Ibid, p256

55 Ibid, p255

Chapter 23

Foch and Eisenhower: Supreme Commanders

Frank E. Vandiver

Unity of command problems have plagued the long history of confusion, wrangling, posturing and wasted opportunities among allies. Some students argue that Napoleon's successes stemmed largely from the fact that he continually fought coalitions.[1] Command controversies still haunt 'interoperability' – witness recent experiences with NATO operations and UN commitments around the globe.

Complex allied problems during the First World War were confounded and multiplied by command conundrums. While a kind of entente cordiale smoothed relations between British and French combat leaders, the arrangements were personal, impromptu and uncertain. Field Marshal Sir Douglas Haig's relations with General Henri Pétain were good; the British commander frequently confirmed his strategic subordination to France's General-in-Chief. Still, full co-ordination eluded the Allies until 1918 and came then only in the backwash of crisis.

Not that unified command lacked supporters. Various Allied leaders had talked about it as far back as 1915. Always, though, nationalism delayed action. Not until France's General Robert Georges Nivelle – famed for his 'creeping barrage' technique – persuaded the French and British Governments to approve his plan for a decisive breakthrough along the Chemin-des-Dames in 1917 did an overall commander direct Allied operations. Prime Minister Lloyd George's haste to subordinate Haig to Nivelle shattered the British High Command's faith in the Government, but Haig loyally sustained his new superior. The flamboyant French general promised a great victory within 48 hours. Nivelle's persuasive powers were greater than his military prowess, and his April offensive drowned in a welter of blood. Failure at a cost of more than 100,000 casualties broke the French Army's morale. Widespread mutinies stalked French units, a fact desperately concealed by General Pétain, who succeeded Nivelle in late April 1917. The new French commander nourished a kind of pessimistic realism while he tried to rebuild morale. He clung to the defensive and waited for more Americans.

Now that Haig's doubts about Nivelle's attack were confirmed, he returned his attention to the Ypres salient.[2] In July 1917 he launched a major offensive against the Channel ports and Roulers. He pushed the battle against natural and enemy odds until his battered divisions took the ruins of Passchendaele in November – by then all the Flanders soldiers, British and German, were in mud and a stultifying fatalism.[3]

Haig and others recognised, as the battles ended, the brutal vulnerability of the hard-won Ypres position. No really strong barriers lay between the enemy and the Channel – a determined German drive might break through, recapture all the ground taken in the Third Ypres campaign, and divide the British and French armies in the exposed area around Amiens.

During the winter things worsened for the Allies. Russia collapsed in November, and its new Government accepted the draconian treaty of Brest-Litovsk in March; Romania, too, surrendered and almost 80 German divisions were freed for the Western Front.[4] As the balance of numbers shifted, Field Marshal Paul von Hindenburg and General Erich Ludendorff planned an offensive for March 1918 to do exactly what Haig feared: hit the juncture of the British and French near Amiens, divide them, push on to the Channel and end the war.

In the meantime, a massive Austro-German attack against the Italians in the Friuli area broke through at Caporetto in late October 1917, netted 300,000 prisoners, and was at last stopped on the Piave. One positive Allied result came from this disaster. Clearly, Allied efforts demanded co-ordination. Frightened military and political leaders created the Supreme Allied War Council, designed to bring some co-operation to the front from the Channel to the Adriatic. No council can act swiftly enough to manage armies in action; most Allied leaders knew that and accepted the Supreme Allied War Council as a stopgap, a first try at unified efforts. No one grasped the need for truly unified command more clearly than France's General Ferdinand Foch, and he pressed his view with the receptive new French Prime Minister, Georges Clemenceau.[5]

As the long-awaited German main drive, code named 'Michael', began on 21 March, Allied command arrangements shifted. The British Fifth Army under General Sir Hubert Gough took the hardest hit, bent, broke and opened a gap in the British line. Haig strove to hold on to Amiens and the French left. A hasty Allied conference convened at Doullens on 26 March, while German advances continued and it seemed likely that French troops would huddle southward to save Paris while Haig's men clustered on the Channel to get home.

A raging traffic jam around Doullens showed starkly the chaos engulfing the Allies. Against the persistent sound of German guns, lorries carrying reserves forward mixed with retreating guns, horses, ambulances, wagons, worn troops in a horrid montage of modern war.[6] That scene gave impetus to the meeting in the Hotel de Ville. The theme was unified command, but a good deal of uncertainty clouded proceedings. Clemenceau, optimistic in public, nursed doubts about Haig accepting subordination again to any French general – a worry quickly banished. Anxiety shaded the conference room as the meeting began at 12.20. Foch, head of the French general staff, exuded a lonesome confidence that captivated Clemenceau. 'I would fight without a break,' the rotund general said in his hard, cutting voice. 'I would fight in front of Amiens. I would fight in Amiens. I would fight behind Amiens. I would fight all the time.'[7]

Haig confessed that the British were hard pressed in front of Amiens, and said he could spare no more troops anywhere, but hoped to hold. Pétain thought he could send a few more divisions toward the British but guaranteed nothing. While this sort of general pessimism wafted across the table, the British War Cabinet Minister, Lord Milner, had a private talk with Clemenceau – he agreed, he said, with Haig that Foch be put in charge of Allied operations. The Tiger quickly agreed. By 2.30 a consensus was reached and was put into a minute: 'General Foch is charged by the British and French governments with co-ordinating the action of the Allied armies on the western front…'[8] American approval came quickly.

During a late lunch in Doullens, Clemenceau quipped to Foch, 'Well, you've got the place you so much wanted.'

'You should not say that,' answered the French Minister of Munitions. 'General Foch is accepting the command because he loves his country, certainly not for his own pleasure.'[9] Foch simply glowed in response.

Fortunately for Foch and his cause, the German drive slowed, and eventually came to a halt. Despite all efforts to sustain supplies over muddied, bloodied ground, a kind of dying rhythm stopped most Western Front offensives. Soldiers outran their food, ammunition, medicine, and even their morale as the dismal realities of war ground them down. When Foch took command, he guessed that Ludendorff would press on elsewhere, and the Allied leader ordered no more retreats. 'Instead of a British battle to cover the Channel ports and a French battle to cover Paris, we would fight an Anglo-French battle to cover Amiens, the connecting link between the two armies.'[10]

Foch's devotion to holding everything while building for attack inspired many but irked some. His swift visit to Gough's battered command produced more anger than inspiration. 'Why are you at your headquarters and not with your troops in the fighting line?' – more an accusation than a question. Gough said he was waiting for orders from the new commander. 'You should not wait for me in that way without ordering anything… Go forward; the whole line will stand fast, and so will your own men.' More accusations: 'Why did your army retire? What were your orders to your army?' Gough, keeping his temper, explained that he was following orders to fight a rearguard action until Allied reserves arrived. 'There must be no more retreat,' Foch shouted. 'The line must be held at all costs!' With that, Foch stormed out. Haig relieved the distracted Gough and gave his rallying remnants to General Henry Rawlinson – it was a political decision, a sop to British anguish.[11]

Victory everywhere greeted Kaiser Wilhelm II's visits to the front. Convinced of a war well won, the German Emperor basked in champagne-bathed glory behind Ludendorff's lines. But Ludendorff's problems escalated. Aware that 'Michael' had outworn itself, the German High Command shifted its aim toward richer ground. On 9 April Ludendorff launched the 'George I' offensive towards the River Lys.

By then, Foch realised that he lacked authority truly to direct Allied operations – he could only request action. If future enemy attacks were to be blunted by co-ordinated Allied efforts, he, or someone else, would have to have a Supreme Commander's powers. He got a good bit of what he needed at a conference in Beauvais on 3 April 1918 – he would co-ordinate all Allied operations on the Western Front. Italy and Belgium came under his control when he received the rank of Commander in Chief of the Allied Armies in France on 14 May 1918.[12]

Why Foch? He boasted some successes early in the war, but his reputation somehow grew as the war continued until almost all Allied leaders could accept him in command.

Born beneath the Pyrenees at Tarbes, on 2 October 1851, Foch early sought a military career, served briefly without combat in the Franco-Prussian War, and attended the fiercely selective École Polytechnique; his high success at the War College (1885-87) marked him for promotion. As a teacher of military history, strategy and applied tactics there from 1895 to 1900, Foch stressed the offensive, the power of the will, the certainty that battles are won by conviction of victory. He stressed, too, the need for information. Constantly he asked, 'De quoi s'agit-il?' because problems had to be understood to be solved.[13] Hampered by his Catholicism in the anti-Catholic French Army, Foch progressed slowly in peacetime, but in 1908 Premier Georges Clemenceau picked the new brigadier to lead the War College; in 1911 Major General Foch commanded a division, and in 1913 the elite XX Corps.

Foch's corps played an important part in France's vaunted Plan XVII at the start of the Great War. His men shared the Second Army's advance on Morhange and retreated stubbornly as Germany's initial drives sliced into France. As the Ninth Army commander, Foch fought hard and well against crucial German attacks in early September 1914 and took charge of France's Northern Army Group in January 1915. Foch learned a good deal in field command – mindless devotion to the offensive cost too many men, and he urged his mentor, Joffre, to recognise that trench warfare dimmed possibilities of a grand breakthrough. Instead of *attaque à l'outrance*, Foch urged a series of attacks on different sectors to wear down enemy strength.

All ideas withered in the wake of the German onslaught against Verdun in February 1916. Foch and his men fought devotedly, but with Joffre's removal from command in December 1916, new faces were the order of France's day. With General Robert Georges Nivelle's rise, Foch's star sank and for a time he was marginalised but without condemnation. He and his increasingly able assistant, General Maxime Weygand, worked on plans to thwart an improbable Central Powers attack against the Allied right flank through Switzerland. Weygand became an alter ego. Foch often spoke in parables supplemented by baffling gestures, a personal language Weygand understood and translated into usable orders and communications. Foch seemed a master of disorganisation who shirked details; Weygand tidied up for him. Foch's appreciation came in his oft-quoted comment that 'Weygand c'est moi'.

Foch won reprieve from his peripheral tasks when Pétain replaced Nivelle as commander in chief. The new French leader called Foch to be Chief of the French General Staff. From that position, he rose to Supreme Command.[14]

Foch surely had the experience for high responsibility. But had he forgotten enough to lead the Allied armies in 1918? B. H. Liddell Hart, in his perceptive biography *Foch: The Man of Orleans*, puts the issue this way: 'Foch's handicap was that he had to forget so much before he could learn… He had come to perceive that the single stroke must be replaced by the serial, that concentration must be endowed with variety, that compromise was as inevitable in strategy as in policy…

It is necessary, when one has been repulsed for from four to five days, not to change one's objectives, but to give them a new form in the guise of a new operation. Only at this price will you get obedience from men.'[15]

Foch's natural optimism sustained his credibility. He could, nonetheless, be a man of moods. An American officer who knew him well noted that Foch signalled his feelings by his walk and his cap. A measured gait, cap straight, showed him in sober concern; stick over shoulder, cap tilted toward his right ear, showed the battle going well. One morning, late in the war, the American saluted Foch on the street and the Marshal stopped to chat. The American observed that the Germans seemed to be getting more than they could handle. Foch 'came up close to me, took a firm hold on my belt with his left hand, and with his right fist delivered a punch at my chin, a hook under my ribs, and another drive at my ear; he then shouldered his stick and without a single word marched on…'[16]

Foch was lucky – an attribute much cherished by Napoleon. He took command at a crucial time, but at a time when his foremost enemy really lost control, not only of the war but also of himself. After 'Michael' and 'George I' failed, Ludendorff succumbed to the worst of military blunders – he shifted his Western Front attacks as he saw opportunities. Instead of sticking to Flanders as his objective, he shifted men and materiel from point to point and hence yielded the initiative to the Allies, even though German troops reached the Marne and were some 40 miles from Paris. Foch seized the moment, pirated reserves as he could and, in a daring gamble, hit the flank of the great German salient bulging between Reims and Soissons in a massive counter-attack in July 1918, which broke the back of the German Army. And opened the way to victory.

Then, in late 1918, Foch, acting as orchestrator of victory with the motto 'tout le monde à la Bataille', guided all the Allied armies in a series of attacks in 1918 against different objectives, kept the Germans off balance, never gave them respite, and finally forced them to ask for an armistice. At the end he urged strong armistice terms designed to prevent a resumption of the war.

His ultimate success suppressed criticisms that could have dimmed his reputation. In his role of orchestral leader he sometimes ran roughshod over subordinates. Haig, who respected Foch, had varied disagreements with him and cherished suspicions of sincere French help until the end of the war. General John J. Pershing, commander of the American Expeditionary Force, argued almost daily with Foch about objectives, support, even about American dedication to the war. Pétain's natural pessimism clashed with Foch's inveterate optimism and they argued through the summer of 1918 until Pétain's old élan returned and he drove fiercely at the end. These different personalities dictated Foch's leadership. He never really commanded the Allies, he co-ordinated their actions. He described his role accurately: 'I was no more than conductor of an orchestra… A vast orchestra, of course… Say, if you like, that I beat time well!… The true meaning of the unified command is not to give orders, but to make suggestions… One talks, one discusses, one persuades…'[17]

Foch's reputation faded as the First World War sank from popular concern. As time restores the war to memory so it restores Foch and his contemporaries. As the only truly Allied Supreme Commander in the First World War, Foch holds a special place in history, a place he filled with dash, verve, relentless courage and a flair essential to the moment.

Foch's role set a pattern for another, even harder, war.

On Monday 8 June 1942, Major General Dwight D. Eisenhower – 'Ike' to almost everyone – presented to General George C. Marshall, Chief of Staff of the US Army, a 30-page plan for unified command of all American forces going to Europe. Just back from an inspection trip to England and fully aware of the need for unity in a coalition effort, Eisenhower suggested that Marshall read carefully the proposed directive for a US commanding general in the European theatre – it was likely to be an important document. Marshall's reply surprised Eisenhower. 'I certainly do want to read it. You may be the man who executes it. If that's the case, when can you leave?' Three days later Marshall appointed the tall Midwesterner to a job whose limits Eisenhower would define.[18]

Foch's experience shaped much of the new American commander's thinking on unified command. General Fox Conner, a First World War veteran and an Eisenhower mentor, reminded his young protégé that in the next war, 'We must insist on individual and single responsibility – leaders will have to learn how to overcome nationalistic considerations in the conduct of campaigns…' Foch never had enough power.[19]

Lessons about nationalism Eisenhower grasped completely. As he prepared to take his new command, he became, first and last, a coalition man and insisted on the same devotion among his generals and staff – indeed, a story ran through Allied halls about his comment that he had no objection to an American officer calling a British officer a bastard, but if he said 'a British bastard' he would return swiftly to the States![20] He did, though, display some nationalism of his own by insisting that American troops remain American.[21]

London fog permeated everywhere in Allied relations. Eisenhower found plans conflicting and stretching fault lines in the coalition. Russia, sorely pressed by Hitler's armies, demanded a 'second front', and hoped for an early Allied attack across the English Channel. The new American commander favoured a nearly sacrificial feint into northern France to relieve Russia, but British leaders were opposed. Eisenhower realised the dangers – he thought the landing stood about a 20 per cent chance of success – but, typically, weighed possible losses against gains and argued that 'we should not forget that the prize we seek is to keep 8,000,000 Russians in the war'.[22] Besides, even a small lodgement on the continent would be aimed at the heart of Germany and might be expanded in the great cross-Channel effort Eisenhower and most Americans favoured.

This kind of aggressive optimism irked many British officers, who thought most Americans bumptious in their inexperience and dangerous in their naiveté. Other plans intervened. Since some Allied offensive had to be tried in 1942 – President Roosevelt ordered it – the British urged an invasion of French North Africa. If all went well, Field Marshal Erwin Rommel's army might be caught in a pincer between the British and the Americans and trapped in Tunisia. Code-named 'Torch', the North African invasion took shape midst many misgivings.

Eisenhower, convinced that a cross-Channel invasion of France was the best way to break into Hitler's *Festung Europa*, and of helping Russia, feared 'Torch' might preclude an effort toward France. There were disagreements, too, about where the North African landing or landings should occur. A surprised but pleased Eisenhower found himself named Supreme Commander of 'Torch', and thought a landing well inside the Mediterranean, as close to Tunis as possible, gave the best chance for trapping Rommel and his growing force. Higher-ups, especially Marshall, considered it too risky and dictated landings at Algiers, Oran and Casablanca, despite the distance from Tunisia and Bizerte. The decision stemmed largely from concern about the French garrisons in those major ports. If they stayed loyal to Vichy's Marshal Henri Pétain, they could threaten the whole Allied rear situation. Better to face them and subdue them if necessary. Dealing with competing French generals – Giraud, De Gaulle and Darlan – baffled Marshall, President Roosevelt, and even Britain's veteran negotiator, Winston Churchill. Eisenhower, who faced them at first with his usual candour, soon found them 'little, selfish, conceited worms that call themselves men'.[23]

All kinds of problems plagued the campaign. There were too few naval vessels, too few men, supply lines were uncertain, and when Allied Force Headquarters moved to Gibraltar on 4 November, Eisenhower – who relished being in command of Britain's symbol of power[24] – worried about the task force taking his men to battle. Inactive for a few days, he reflected and, on the eve of the landings, revealed some insecurity to Marshall: 'We are standing ... on the brink and must take the jump – whether the bottom contains a nice feather bed or a pile of brickbats!' Still, he felt confident that everything had been done for success.[25]

As the invasion forces landed on 7 November 1942, several Vichy French garrisons did resist and Eisenhower fumed that 'every bullet we have to expend against the French is that much less in the pot with which to operate against the Axis... I am so impatient to get eastward and seize the ground in the Tunisian area that I find myself getting absolutely furious with these stupid Frogs.'[26]

Eisenhower suffered from varied trepidations in his first Allied war command. Planning for 'Torch' occupied months, involved the usual staff studies familiar to him, but as jump-off time approached he sank into a quagmire of politics and jealousies that rankled his blunt military honesty. Like Foch an apostle of optimism in commanders, Eisenhower wallowed in uncertainties as he negotiated with Free French, Vichy French and African French officers and politicians for help with the landings, with supplies, port facilities and troops. In the first weeks of November Eisenhower stuck a deal with Vichyite French Admiral Jean Darlan to win a cease-fire among French troops in North Africa. Necessary as the deal seemed to Eisenhower, it nearly cost him his job. Many politicos in England and the United States – many military men as well – regarded Darlan as a hard-nosed Fascist, a man who represented all the things the Allies were resisting.

Stunned by the outcry against Darlan, Eisenhower realised that his diplomatic sense needed work and that his advisors had not served him well. Diplomacy made him uncomfortable and Marshall finally told him to leave it to others and get on with the war. He sometimes suffered from self-pity, depression, and irritation with subordinates and politicians, and had to blow off steam to somebody; he vented it in his open correspondence with Marshall, who understood his man growing into whole new capacities and supported him always.[27]

North African combat realities reshaped the general's ideas a good deal and he criticised himself. He had been slow getting his units in place, had allowed incompetence in his intelligence section, had not pushed hard enough to ensure the highest standards of security and action from some subordinates, interfered with field commanders, and he had lost the race to Tunis. Rommel, with Field Marshal Bernard Montgomery's Eighth British Army following all the way from El Alamein, stabilised the Mareth Line west of Tripoli and focused on protecting his rear by attacking American positions at Kasserine Pass. He broke through, chewed up several small units along with the US II Corps, inflicted heavy casualties – and escaped. When he saw that General Sir Kenneth Anderson (Allied ground commander) and Montgomery were, in fact, running the North African show and ignoring the Americans, the Supreme Commander took charge. He ordered a reluctant Anderson to give the US II Corps an important piece of the main Tunis attack – the Corps, now under General Omar Bradley, amply justified the order – and he relieved his British intelligence chief and finally relieved II Corps commander, General Lloyd Fredendall. Marshall approved; he had worried that Eisenhower was being too nice for his job and was glad to see steel behind the winning grin and easy manners.[28]

Marshall strongly supported Eisenhower at the Allied Casablanca Conference in January 1943, despite criticism of his management of some battles in North Africa and the resulting 70,000 casualties. The conferees decided that Eisenhower would retain his command, even receive the British Eighth Army as part of it, and would be in charge of Operation 'Husky', the invasion of Sicily, probably followed by an invasion of the Italian mainland. Aware of the complicated British attitude toward Eisenhower as a field commander, and aware, too, that several of his British staff outranked him, Marshall had him promoted to full General in February. The promotion signalled nearly the ultimate approval – Marshall and MacArthur were the only full Generals on the US rolls – and it brought with it increased self-confidence.

Allied strategic plans for the Mediterranean were no surprise to Eisenhower; he had been planning ahead for Sicily. Attacking Italy's mainland after that made good sense and would certainly tie up Axis forces. With increased confidence came increased luck for the Supreme Commander. He picked off the island of Pantelleria in June at the cost of one casualty – a British soldier bitten by a mule!

Sicily posed different problems. Eisenhower would deluge the island with almost half a million men. Italians constituted the bulk of defensive forces and were not expected to fight hard. The Germans there, totalling some 60,000 men, would surely show their usual veteran stubbornness. The battle went about as expected, except that Field Marshal Albert Kesselring's men exacted a higher price than expected for Allied victory in August – 20,000 casualties against 12,000. Kesselring's remaining troops escaped.

Now fairly confident in amphibious operations, Eisenhower turned to Italy, but here, again, he was tempted by political possibilities. Everyone at AFHQ knew of Italy's war-weariness, and when news came of a successful coup against Mussolini on 19 July, and the resurgence of King Victor Emmanuel III, hopes soared for a bloodless Allied march into Rome. Various secret negotiations, appallingly like those with the French before 'Torch', almost succeeded, but Hitler's quick insertion of large occupying forces scuttled the possibilities and a long, hard Italian campaign up Italy's boot consumed men and materiel beyond Eisenhower's expectations.

By the time German forces were driven back and Italy joined the Allies, Eisenhower knew he would have the greatest command ever given anyone in history – he would lead 'Overlord', the new code-name for the cross-Channel invasion now scheduled for 1944.

Imagination defied the scope of Ike's new assignment – not only Allied, but also service co-ordination of personnel, materiel, logistics, tactics and strategy after successful lodgement on the continent of Europe were his concerns. From the huge Allied base in England, he would direct a massive invasion effort involving thousands of men, thousands of ships, landing craft, boats, vehicles and immense stores of food, ammunition and miscellaneous supplies. Planning such an effort posed awesome problems in itself.

Why Eisenhower? Experience, not only Ike's but also of the Allies, tipped the scales. Ike expected Marshall to command the big invasion, had planned all along to hand over a carefully orchestrated effort to his cherished superior. Many others thought Marshall would get the job; Roosevelt himself wanted Marshall to have a chance for lasting fame.[29] With the chips down, though, Roosevelt knew he could not spare Marshall – as Pershing had said, no one else could manage a two-front war.[30] More than that, Ike's wondrous ability to win friends even among enemies, his obvious magic in forging teams from disparates, his steady growth from challenge to challenge, and his determined devotion to coalition warfare made him the only choice, even including Marshall.

History validated the selection. D-Day, 6 June 1944, capped months of planning, training, deception, uncertainties, worry, despair, and succeeded despite poor weather (Ike's most crucial decision was to made the attack in face of an uncertain barometer) and thin reserves. Even Stalin stood in awe of the complexities of Ike's achievement. 'The history of warfare,' he said, 'knows no other like undertaking from the point of view of its scale, its vast conception, and its masterly execution.'[31] Stalin was right. Nothing compares to D-Day. In the last lashings of rain and wind more than 5,000 ships sailed into the English Channel, an armada dwarfing Spain's, a vast, sprawling, iron-sided energy of men and machines, guns, landing craft, all covered by a canopy of planes, headed for the Normandy beaches. Some on the ships thought of Shakespeare's words:

'He that outlives this day and comes safe home,
Will stand a tip-toe when this day is named...
And gentlemen in England, now a-bed
Shall think themselves accursed they were not here'[32]

At day's end the Allies had won an astounding victory. More than 150,000 Allied soldiers were firmly ashore on several beaches – Hitler's Atlantic Wall was broken.[33]

With a firm foothold in Europe, Ike directed a careful build-up, supervised a breakout, designed a splendid double envelopment of German troops in the Ruhr area that netted 317,000 prisoners, and held to his strategy of a broad front attack against Germany – this despite Montgomery's urging of a pencil-like attack of his Army group straight for Berlin. Ike was probably right, though arguments about the two ideas continue.[34]

The Supreme Commander knew that invasion only began his problems. Orchestrating the Allied campaign in France and the Low Countries and Germany occupied him now and, with strategy approved from on high, he focused on tactical combinations, urging initiative on his ground and air commanders, pushing them hard to press the enemy, to give the Germans no respite. He made some mistakes – he still had trouble disciplining generals like Montgomery and Patton and let them almost run wars of their own, and he missed a chance to get Berlin when Churchill and others thought he should have tried[35] – but as Allied armies drew up along the Rhine and pierced across to bag prisoners galore, errors could be forgiven a man who did so much for victory.

Hitler's Thousand Year Reich crumbled as the Allies – Russians from the east, Americans, British, French and others from the west – squeezed German armies inexorably into central Germany. With resistance fading, Ike's hatred for the Germans abated not a bit; after their unconditional surrender, he sent a grimly laconic cable to the combined chiefs of staff: 'The mission of this Allied force was fulfilled at 0241 local time, May 7, 1945.'[36]

It is tempting to conclude by saying that Foch and Eisenhower are incomparable, each faced vastly different problems in vastly different wars. But is that true? Not entirely. There are similarities and comparisons worth noting.

First, the men themselves. Their different careers have tangents. Both were frustrated by being in a war early but denied combat – Foch in the Franco-Prussian War, Ike in the First World War. Both did well in their service schools and became instructors. Both finally had combat experience, Foch before he became Supreme Commander, Ike during his North African stint in that role. Both understood the problems of coalition warfare and both emphasised Allied co-operation. Both had the flexibility to rise above themselves, conceive strategic plans and let others carry them out. Both had thorny subordinates to work with – Foch with Haig, Pétain, and Pershing; Ike with Montgomery, Alan Brooke, Patton, De Gaulle.[37]

Second are the challenges faced by the Supreme Commanders. Both arrived at their high command at difficult times – Foch when the Allied cause in France teetered toward defeat, Eisenhower when America first entered the war and at a time of near British exhaustion from two years of fighting the Nazis. Both struggled to gain enough power to do their jobs – Foch by almost dragooning authority from political superiors who clung to personal nationalism, Eisenhower by making himself the foremost symbol of Allied efforts. Both shared a similar vision of strategy – Foch determined to press an Allied attack across his whole front, shoving the Germans constantly; Ike, with like determination, pressed his broad front offensive, again to permit no respite to a beleaguered foe. Both made epochal decisions – Foch to attack the Marne salient in 1918, Ike to cross the Channel.

Both were tough soldiers but diverged in the way they worked with people. Foch tended toward arrogance, was often truculent in giving orders and frequently raged at subordinates. Ike's temper became legendary, but he could, when the alliance needed it, charm the paper off the wall and his persuasiveness ranked a high cause of victory. Allied leaders came to have a deep regard for Foch's energy, his unflagging optimism, his sense of opportunities; the same for Ike, whose personality outshone Foch's and whose smile, one British general said, was 'worth an army corps in any campaign'.[38]

General De Gaulle thought the Allies lucky to have Eisenhower in Supreme Command[39] and a good many others agreed. Many thought, too, that the Allies were lucky to find, finally, Marshal Foch. In fact, both alliances were lucky that two men of good fortune rose to seize their challenges and forge them into victory.

Notes on contributors

Professor Frank E. Vandiver, Texas A&M University, College Station, USA
Frank Vandiver is Emeritus Professor at Texas A&M University. He is the author of numerous books on the American Civil War. He is the biographer of General John J. Pershing and is currently writing a biography of Field-Marshal the Earl Haig

Recommended reading

Ambrose, Stephen E., *Eisenhower* 2 Vols (New York: Simon & Shuster, 1983; London: Allen & Unwin, 1984)

Eisenhower, Dwight D., *Crusade in Europe* (New York: Doubleday, 1948; Baltimore and London: Johns Hopkins University Press, 1997)

Gunther, John, *Eisenhower: The Man and the Symbol* (New York: Harper & Brothers; London: Hamish Hamilton, 1952)

Liddell Hart, B. H., *Foch: The Man of Orleans* (Westport, CT: Greenwood Press, 1980; reprint of 1931 ed)

Marshall-Cornwall, James, *Foch as Military Commander* (New York: Crane, Russak, 1972)

Mott, T. Bentley, trans, *The Memoirs of Marshal Foch* (New York: Doubleday, Doran; London: William Heinemann, 1931)

Notes

[1] G. E. Patrick Murray, *Eisenhower versus Montgomery: The Continuing Debate* (Westport, CT: Praeger) pp54-5

[2] John Terraine, *Douglas Haig: The Educated Soldier* (London: Leo Cooper, 1990) pp282-306; Alistair Horne, *The Price of Glory: Verdun, 1916* (New York: Macfadden Books, 1964) pp314-7; A. J. P. Taylor, *The First World War: An Illustrated History* (Harmondsworth, UK: Penguin Books, reprint ed, 1987) pp175-7; James L. Stokesbury, *A Short History of World War I* (New York: William Morrow & Co, 1981) pp233-5; Richard M. Watt, *Dare Call It Treason* (New York: Simon & Shuster, 1963) pp169-74; John Williams, *Mutiny 1917* (London: Heinemann, 1962) pp31-42

[3] Frank E. Vandiver, 'Field Marshal Sir Douglas Haig and Passchendaele' in Peter Liddle, ed, *Passchendaele in Perspective: The Third Battle of Ypres* (London: Leo Cooper, 1997) pp35-40

[4] John Toland, *No Man's Land: 1918: The Last Year of the Great War* (Garden City, NY: Doubleday, 1980) pxix

5 See T. Bentley Mott, trans, *The Memoirs of Marshal Foch* (New York: Doubleday, Doran, 1931) pp225-30; Georges Clemenceau, *Grandeur and Misery of Victory* (New York: Harcourt, Brace, 1930) pp35-7; Gen Sir James Marshall-Cornwall, *Foch as Military Commander* (New York: Crane, Russak, 1972) pp206-13; Major General Sir George Aston, *The Biography of the Late Marshal Foch* (New York: Macmillan, 1929) pp249-63

6 John Toland, op cit, p88

7 Georges Clemenceau, op cit, p39

8 T. Bentley Mott, trans, op cit, pp261-4. The Doullens meeting is covered graphically in John Toland, op cit, pp88-94

9 T. Bentley Mott, op cit, p264; John Toland, op cit, p94

10 T. Bentley Mott, op cit, p265

11 John Toland, op cit, pp94-101

12 T. Bentley Mott, op cit, pp277-8

13 B. H. Liddell Hart, *Reputations Ten Years After* (Boston: Little, Brown, 1928) p155

14 For a succinct summary of Foch's career, see Holger H. Herwig and Neil M. Heyman, *Biographical Dictionary of World War I* (Westport, CT: Greenwood Press, 1982) pp151-4

15 B. H. Liddell Hart, *Foch: The Man of Orleans* (Westport, CT: Greenwood Press, 1980; reprint of 1931 ed) p451

16 T. Bentley Mott, op cit, pxxv

17 B. H. Liddell Hart, op cit, p454

18 This story is told in various sources. For Eisenhower's version, see his *Crusade in Europe* (New York: Doubleday, 1948) pp50-1

19 Conner is quoted in Stephen E. Ambrose, *Eisenhower* 2 Vols (New York: Simon & Shuster, 1983) Vol 1, p77

20 See John Gunther, *Eisenhower: The Man and the Symbol* (New York: Harper & Brothers, 1952) p74

21 Ibid

22 Stephen E. Ambrose, op cit, p180 (italics in the original)

23 Ibid, p204

24 Harry C. Butcher, *My Three Years with Eisenhower: The Personal Diary of Captain Harry C. Butcher, USNR, Naval Aide to General Eisenhower, 1942 to 1945* (New York: Simon & Shuster, 1946) p178b

25 John P. Hobbs, *Dear General: Eisenhower's Wartime Letters to Marshall* (Baltimore and London: The John Hopkins Press, 1971) p59

26 Harry C. Butcher, op cit, p204; John P. Hobbs, op cit, p14

27 For the problems bothering Eisenhower in this period, see John P. Hobbs, op cit, pp183-214; Harry C. Butcher, op cit, pp165-78b; Eisenhower, *Crusade in Europe*, op cit, Chap 6, pp95-114; John Gunther, op cit, pp75-6; John P. Hobbs, op cit, pp47-60; Don Cook, 'General of the Army Dwight D. Eisenhower' in Field Marshal Sir Michael Carver, *The War Lords: Military Commanders of the Twentieth Century* (Boston: Little Brown, 1976) pp509-37

28 For a concise survey of Eisenhower's battle lessons in the Tunisian campaign, see Stephen E. Ambrose, ibid, pp225-37

29 Ibid, p269

30 Ibid, pp270-1; Eric Larabee, *Commander in Chief: Franklin Delano Roosevelt, His Lieutenants, and Their War* (New York: Harper & Row, 1987) pp437-8

31 Quoted in Eric Larabee, op cit, p438

32 Ibid, p440

33 Stephen E. Ambrose, op cit, pp308-10

34 John Gunther, op cit, pp80-1

35 Eric Larabee speculates that Allied forces could not have beaten the Russians to Berlin. See op cit, p506

36 Harry C. Butcher, op cit, p824

37 De Gaulle and Ike achieved something close to friendship and respected each other. See Stephen E. Ambrose, op cit, p240; Charles de Gaulle, *The Complete Memoirs of Charles deGaulle* (New York: Simon & Shuster, reprint ed, 1972) pp435-7

38 Lt Gen Sir Frederick Morgan, quoted in Eric Larabee, op cit, p412

39 Charles DeGaulle, op cit, pp435-6

Chapter 24

General Brusilov and Marshal Zhukov, June 1916 and June 1944

John Erickson

In June 1916 the inconceivable, the impossible occurred on the Eastern Front. Russian troops under the command of General Aleksei Alekseevich Brusilov launched an offensive across a front stretching for more than 120 miles between the Pripet marshes and the Dniester, a massive breakthrough operation that overwhelmed Austrian defences, brought Russian troops into the Bukovina, into Galicia, and advanced them to within striking distance of the Carpathian mountain passes.[1] What came to be known as the 'Brusilov offensive' defied prevailing military logic and contradicted what passed for current military wisdom.[2]

The accepted prerequisites for successful offensive operations involved a huge assembly of men and a great weight of shell, a cumbersome and protracted process that by its very nature made a mockery of secrecy and ruled out surprise. A tactical breakthrough might be achieved by sheer weight of metal, shredding barbed wire, demolishing defensive positions, killing defenders. But what ensued too often turned into a chaotic nightmare. Crossing unfamiliar ground ploughed up by its own artillery, the attacking force struggling in this morass encountered fresh defensive lines and strong points. Supporting artillery could not move up fast enough. Enemy resistance stiffened, fresh enemy reserves moved up to counter-attack, their guns now decimating the attackers. Initial tactical gains could never be exploited to the full and transformed into success at the operational level.

Shortly after 7.00am on 21 February 1916 massed German guns opened fire on the French defences at Verdun, in the course of the next few days sweeping away barbed wire, collapsing trenches. Convinced that France had almost reached breaking point and Russia was increasingly enfeebled by internal problems, General Erich von Falkenhayn launched his fire-based offensive at Verdun, deliberate, brutal attrition designed to bleed the French Army white. German seizure of the initiative did not come as a complete surprise to General M. V. Alekseev, Chief of Staff since 1915 at the Russian Stavka (General Headquarters) and the real military personality behind a weak and wavering throne. Together with War Minister Polivanov, Alekseev had engineered an undeniable recovery from the disasters of 1915 and the tragedy of the 'Great Retreat'. General Brusilov was quick to notice the sea-change once weapons were finally available to Russian soldiers: rifles, cartridges, reserves of 400 rounds per rifle, field guns, shells, aircraft, gas-masks, wireless sets. Though not wholly convinced that the Russian Army was ready for offensive action, Alekseev now found himself committed to exactly that course of action, the result of an insurance policy that misfired. Intent on preventing a recurrence of the Allied 'abandonment' of Russia in 1915, Alekseev's representative at the Inter-Allied Conference at Chantilly proposed an agreement whereby a German attack on one ally would be met by the others launching immediate offensives to save it. In a matter of days the French, hard pressed at Verdun, seized on 'the resolutions' of the Chantilly conference, formally requesting that 'the Russian army begin urgent preparations for an offensive'.

The Stavka conference on 24 February recognised the inevitability of offensive action. On the Northern and Western Fronts Russian superiority in numbers was considerable, while on the South-Western Front rough parity prevailed. The shell reserve piled up. But the portents were not promising. The earlier Russian winter offensive directed against the Austro-Hungarian forces had failed, abundance of guns, largesse of shells, numerical superiority notwithstanding. So often in the past the shell-shortage had been blamed for Russian failures. Now adequacy of shell reserves and superior numbers worked a peculiarly insidious effect, persuading Russian generals that sheer weight of metal would neutralise enemy defences, opening the way for the infantry. If in doubt, pile up more shell. None, with a single brilliant exception, grasped the essentials of a breakthrough operation or how to go about planning one.

The Russian offensive launched on 18 March in the area of Lake Narotch, east of Vilna and south of Dvinsk, furnished horrifying proof of this lamentable state of affairs. Two army groups commanded by the generals Evert and Kuropatkin were to co-operate in attacking to the south-west and west. Russian superiority in men and guns at Lake Narotch was staggering – 350,000 men and 1,000 guns facing 75,000 Germans and 440 guns – yet the final outcome was little short of catastrophic. Mismanagement combined with criminal incompetence, plus appalling weather conditions, sealed the fate of more than 100,000 Russian soldiers. Not a single German division moved from the west. Russian generals lost what little will to win they had ever possessed, cowering behind mountains of shell never enough to overcome their fright. 'Shell-shortage' became the mantra of sclerotic Russian generals, mesmerised by the vast stocks building up on the Western Front, further belittling the Russian Army's prospects.

Not all, however, fell victim to this debilitating military virus. General Brusilov, commander of the 8th Army South-Western Front, was not persuaded of the validity of the 'shell-shortage' alibi. Officers on this front increasingly pointed to the importance of thorough preparation of the attack as opposed to simply drenching the ground with high-explosive. A surprising but momentous change came in March 1916 when General Brusilov replaced General Nikolai Ivanov as commander of the South-Western Front. It was left to Ivanov to sulk in his tent while the wind of change swept through Front HQ at Berdichev.

Born in 1853 in Tbilisi, Brusilov came of a distinguished military family and a cavalry background, seeing action in the Russo-Turkish war of 1877-78, where he was duly noted for his tactical skills. His career took something of a meandering course: confined to the cavalry, he was never accepted either within the privileged circle of the Genshtabisty (General Staff officers) or that of the War Ministry, yet apparently without serious detriment to his prospects. Between 1902 and 1906 he acted as Commandant of the Cavalry School, followed by divisional command (2nd Guards Cavalry) and corps command (14 Corps) in 1909. Promoted General of Cavalry in 1912, this stately but unspectacular progress advanced him to Assistant to the commander of the key Warsaw Military District and command of 12 Army Corps. Holidaying in Germany in July 1914, he hurried back to Warsaw in the nick of time, taking over command of the 8th Army deployed on the borders of Galicia.

Brusilov exhibited none of the narrow bigotry of the cavalry officer. He quickly grasped that what counted most on the modern battlefield was artillery and machine-guns. He was a conscious practitioner of 'combined arms', stressing the co-ordination of infantry and artillery. Under his command the 8th Army enjoyed early success, penetrating deep into the Carpathians and seizing the Dukla Pass. The enforced retreat of June 1915 virtually demoralised Ivanov, but amidst the chaos Brusilov's 8th Army fell back in good order, sufficient in itself to single him out. He assembled a proficient, technically competent staff, which undertook a serious examination of the failures in December 1915 and March 1916.

While many commanders singled out particular tactical shortcomings or pleaded 'shell shortage', Brusilov turned to the operational milieu, examining the importance of deception, surprise, momentum. Disruption of enemy reserves had highest priority. Deception would mask offensive preparations; surprise would ensure an enemy thrown off balance; simultaneous multiple attacks across the entire frontage would disguise the location of the main blow. Momentum would be maintained by holding reserves close to the front line in concealed positions, sustained by artillery providing close support to the infantry. Inevitably such a radical approach left Brusilov's superiors and subordinates alike appalled at the foolhardiness, or the impracticality of a scheme where superiority was only marginal and heavy artillery deficient. If one powerful attack across a narrow frontage deploying superior strength could not achieve success, what chance would four weaker attacks across extended frontages have?

On 15 April 1916, in the presence of the Tsar and on the orders of Alekseev, the Stavka assembled at Moghilev at 10 o'clock to debate what assistance Russia might lend to the forthcoming Allied summer offensive. Alekseev asserted that offensive operations were possible on one front only, to the north, involving a two-pronged attack on Vilna. Front commanders Evert and Kuropatkin held their heads in their hands, bemoaning the lack of heavy artillery, prophesying inevitable failure. A timorous Evert, huddled behind heavy guns, reluctantly agreed to a limited attack on a narrow frontage. Brusilov struck an entirely different note, declaring his readiness to attack in the summer without seeking major reinforcement in men and guns. The chances of success were not negligible. Even if the attack fizzled out, it might at least assist the Northern Fronts by pinning down enemy forces. More as an afterthought, Alekseev authorised Brusilov to proceed with his preparations. Yet this represented triumph of a kind for Brusilov, undermined and criticised by his own subordinates and fellow generals. Once Brusilov departed for his own HQ, General Ivanov sought out the Tsar, who had uttered not a word during the Stavka deliberations, to warn him that Brusilov's ill-conceived venture could not succeed and risked the loss of Kiev.

The successful Austrian offensive against the Italians in mid-May brought not only a dramatic alteration in the situation but also an enforced change in Alekseev's attitude towards the 'Brusilov offensive'. Increasingly desperate appeals from the Italians for a Russian offensive, including a personal approach to the Tsar from the King of Italy playing the 'dynastic card', ended Alekseev's vacillation. Attacking in the north was ruled out because of 'weakness in heavy artillery' – an unprepared attack spelled disaster. Above all, Evert was virtually immovable. There remained only Brusilov, who agreed to attack without delay, asking only for an extra corps once his offensive was launched but resisting Alekseev's pleas to reducing his frontages. Alekseev saved face on 31 May by authorising 'a powerful auxiliary attack on the Austrians', reserving the main attack to the Western Front.

Brusilov deployed four armies across the length of his front, Kaledin's 8th Army in Volhynia, Sakharov's 11th Army to the south, Shcherbachev's 7th Army in eastern Galicia, Lechitskii's 9th Army at the southern extremity, each army launching a separate attack across a relatively broad front, a minimum of 30 kilometres as opposed to Alekseev's plea for a reduction to 20 and a single massed blow. Brusilov tried energetically to sustain the concept of operational co-ordination, insisting that Evert in the north should launch simultaneous offensive operations if only to prevent German reinforcement reaching the Austro-Hungarian armies. Not surprisingly Evert temporised, pleading unavoidable postponement, until 14 June. At this juncture Brusilov had to satisfy himself with an undertaking from Alekseev that there would be no further delay.

Alekseev's nervousness had its counterpart in the faint-heartedness and fainting fits of Brusilov's own commanders. By dint of personal example and encouragement, through frequent front-line inspections, Brusilov gradually imposed his methods – above all, intensive training and meticulous preparation, the like of which no Russian front had ever witnessed. Artillery cohabited with the infantry; the infantry rehearsed assaults on mock-ups of the Austrian trenches, reminiscent of Suvorov's practice assaults on models of Turkish fortifications in 1791. Brusilov's intelligence organisation combined agent reports with aerial photography, disclosing the location of Austrian artillery batteries. A highly complex offensive entrenchment system brought Russian troops close to Austrian lines. Huge, skilfully concealed staging areas near the front line hid reserves intended to emerge at the last minute to provide immediate support for local breakthroughs.

On 4 June Brusilov's guns opened fire along the length of his 350-kilometre front, the fiery prelude to stunning Russian victories. Tactical surprise was complete. Brusilov directed his main blow at Lutsk in the northern sector of his front, committing General Kaledin's 8th Army against the Austro-Hungarian Fourth Army under the nominal command of Archduke Joseph Ferdinand, presented that day with a terrifying and unexpected birthday present. The Russian margin of superiority was slight, negligible in manpower, 200,000 to 150,000, 704 to 600 guns, but the meticulous preparation paid off handsomely in the breakthrough operations. The Russian guns had already registered their targets, fire directed by radio-equipped aircraft, the artillery commander behaving in Brusilov's words like 'the conductor of an orchestra'. Austrian guns were knocked out, wire obstacles blasted away, forward trenches destroyed, machine-gun positions wiped out, heavy artillery directed against the better-fortified dug-outs. Russian artillery fire destroyed the Austrian trench system, day-long bombardment in some sectors completely smashing in the first line of trenches and obliterating the barbed wire. Russian soldiers advancing on the second and third line of trenches found only 'ruins and shattered corpses'. Clouds of smoke and dust raised by bursting shells shrouded the battlefield with a gloom, which reduced visibility and impeded observation. The spread of noxious fumes further incapacitated the defenders, compounding the growing chaos. Those who survived in the deeper dug-outs were urged to surrender, otherwise they were killed with grenades tossed into their midst. Immured in these death-traps Austrians in large numbers chose surrender. By the evening of 5 June all three Austrian defensive belts had collapsed. The general demoralisation spread like wildfire, the tally of prisoners mounted.

In three days the Archduke's Fourth Army had been shattered and Austro-Hungarian defences pierced across a 70-kilometre front. Russian troops had closed on Lutsk, heavily defended with wire obstacles and concrete reserve positions. The defensibility of Lutsk depended on ensuring that the heights at Krupy held by Hungarians to the south of the town would be denied to enemy artillery, the very condition that the Austrian command failed to prevent. Once in possession of the heights Russians guns could fire directly into Lutsk and its defences. Russian cavalry then took the town. The Fourth Army panicked and ran in headlong flight, only to be trapped in its own barbed wire or crammed on to the pontoon bridges over the River Styr. Panicky demolition of the bridges by Austrian engineers left thousands stranded on the banks. The defence literally melted away. The Russians made another huge haul of prisoners, weapons and stocks of ammunition.

Brusilov's rolling thunder spread across the entire length of the South-Western Front. Three Russian armies, the 11th, 7th and 9th, struck with a speed and measure of success that in places compared favourably with that of the 8th Army. The key to much of the Russian success lay in what Brusilov had deliberately intended with multiple attacks across a broad front: the disruption of reserves. German reserves were concentrated to the north, facing the Russian western and northern fronts. Austrian reserves had already been diminished by the dispatch of six divisions to the Italian front, less than a handful now finding themselves switched erratically and too often pointlessly into rear areas stretching from Volhynia in the north to the River Dniester.

To the south of the 8th Army Russian successes in the centre, with Sakharov's 11th Army and Shcherbachev's 7th Army, were limited. Facing General Bothmer's German-Austrian *Sudarmee*, Shcherbachev overplayed his artillery

Above 'EROS' at 'Piccadilly', made from 4-gallon non-returnable petrol tins. 'A most useful landmark in the trackless desert.' *G. Hayward, SWWEC, Leeds*

Below Western Desert sandstorm: American servicemen with a problem. *H. J. Cavigli, SWWEC, Leeds*

Above Troops of the US 82nd Division inspect captured German shells, Meuse-Argonne, October 1918. *US Army Military History Institute*

Left Football match, Christmas Day 1941: Officers (2) v Sergeants (5), Sidi Bu Amid [sic], Tobruk. Squadron Leader 'Pop' Ault is challenging Sergeant McAuley. *A. J. M. Smythe, SWWEC, Leeds*

Above Twelfth Night at Stalag VIII B: Denholm Elliott, later to become a celebrated actor, is far left. *P. M. Peel, SWWEC, Leeds*

Below An Anglo-American Greek resistance group: Christo Jecchinis is in the middle of the front row. *Christo Jecchinis, SWWEC, Leeds*

Above Relaxation after secret work: 'Bobby' Hope-Robertson, an ATS assistant who processed experimental runs of sound on film recorded on purpose-built equipment to eavesdrop on people who might be attempting to pick up military intelligence from service personnel. The equipment was not in fact put into operational use. The photograph was taken at the Mena House Hotel swimming pool, adjacent to the Pyramids, during an afternoon off work. Bobby 'later married our Camp Commandant, leaving many broken hearts amongst all ranks in our unit.' *G. O. Hayward, SWWEC, Leeds*

Above Merrill's Marauders, 2nd Battalion, crossing the Tanai River over a native bridge of bamboo in March 1944. *Courtesy of Merrill's Marauders Organisation*

Left Russian soldiers of the First World War: General Polovtsev, commander of the Petrograd military district, with his soldiers in July 1917. *Per Sergei Kudryashov*

Above A soldier having a wound dressed: 42nd Division, Bertricamp, France, 26 April 1918. *US Army Military History Institute*

Below Indian troops of the Eighth Army move across Aquino airfield, Italy, on 29 May 1944. *US official photograph, SWWEC, Leeds*

GIs of the 936th Field Artillery Battalion and a 'liberated' wine barrel, Italy, Christmas 1944. *James J. Cooke collection*

Above Soon after the Armistice at the end the First World War, British troops march through Cologne. One wrote in a letter home that the streets were 'full of boys who I suppose will grow up to try and conquer the world again'. *Photograph J. C. H. Willett, quotation E. P. Neville, Liddle Collection, University of Leeds*

Below Gallipoli: the headstone commemorating Lt A. V. Smith VC in Twelve Tree Copse Cemetery, Commonwealth War Graves Commission, bearing as the next-of-kin's inscription a quotation from Alfred Tennyson's *Crossing the Bar. Bob Bushaway*

hand, the lengthy bombardment alerting Bothmer to the impending assault. The main Russian attack failed; only a subsidiary attack southwards on the right flank succeeded. The Austrians were finally forced back across the River Strypa. If progress at the centre was slow, Lechitskii's 9th Army at the southern extremity of Brusilov's front broke into General Pflanzer-Baltin's Seventh Army, a force noted for its comparative cohesion and the loyalty of its Hungarian and Croat components. Russian superiority was marginal, a factor that weighed heavily with Lechitskii, particularly his weakness in heavy guns, old models lacking any great stock of shell, numerically inferior to the Austrians. By strange coincidence both generals, Lechitskii and Pflanzer-Baltin, were indisposed, Lechitskii confined to a sick-bed, Pflanzer-Baltin brought to hospital from which he directed the battle by telephone. The Russian attack was carefully prepared, opening with an artillery bombardment supplemented by a gas attack. The tactical situation did not favour Pflanzer-Baltin. Impressive though his defences were, the bulk of his reserves were deployed too close to the front line, while the River Dniester split the Seventh Army's front, separating one half from the other.

The Russians enjoyed their first tactical successes on 5 June near the village of Okna, but a quite spectacular breakthrough was in the making. Intent on containing further Russian attacks, Pflanzer-Baltin deployed his main force south of the Dniester. Inevitably this starved the Austrian front north of the river, precisely where the Russians chose to attack on 7 June, forcing a precipitate Austrian retreat across the river. What was a disaster now turned into calamity. On 9 June Pflanzer-Baltin ordered a full retreat to the south-west, into the Bukovina, only to have his orders countermanded on German insistence by his own High Command: the Seventh Army would fall back westwards in order to retain contact with the Sudarmee. The effect was to rip the Seventh Army to pieces, elements falling back on the River Prut to the south, remnants fleeing west. The Seventh Army for all practical purposes had ceased to exist, Pflanzer-Baltin himself mourning the loss of 100,000 men.

The calamity visited on the Seventh Army was but one reflection of what had befallen the entire Austro-Hungarian Army in the east, which had lost half of its manpower in little more than a week, one-third of it, almost 3,000 officers and 200,000 men, trudging into Russian prison camps. The results of Brusilov's offensive now persuaded the Austrian High Command that any hope of victory in Russia was an illusion, yet without a victorious peace the very survival of the Habsburg Empire was in doubt. There was no alternative but to chain Austria to the German chariot, to hand control of what remained of the Austro-Hungarian forces to the German High Command, to 'corset' Austrians with German troops down to the lowest tactical level, the precursor to full German command of the entire Eastern Front, including Austrian forces.

The attention of both Brusilov and the German High Command was now directed to the north, to the possibility of Russian offensive operations launched by Evert and Kuropatkin. Brusilov's problem was how to bring Evert's enormous superiority in men and guns into action. The problem for the Germans, facing costly French resistance at Verdun, the likelihood of a British offensive, a crisis with reserves, was the 'worst case scenario', where superior Russian forces finally attacked in the north aiming at Riga. To Brusilov's unrestrained fury and Germany's undisguised relief the great 'northern offensive' proved to be something of a chimera. Brusilov also found himself the victim of his own brilliant tactical successes. The very essence of Brusilov's 'method' ruled out a great, cumbersome concentration of reserves, yet an operational method designed to prevent the enemy making timely use of his reserves simultaneously denied Brusilov resources for an 'exploitation echelon'. Brusilov argued that the Russian Army had an excess of cavalry. On his front the bulk of the cavalry was dismounted, providing extra infantry, simplifying supply problems, leaving only one cavalry division in reserve, the 12th Cavalry, commanded by Baron Carl Gustav von Mannerheim, veteran of the Russo-Japanese war, and Guards Cavalry Brigade commander in 1914.

Supply problems dogged the 8th and 9th Armies at both extremities of the front, pursuing the defeated Austrians, whereupon Brusilov temporarily halted Lechitskii's advance in the south-west and turned his attention to the north. The lure was Evert's military hoard of a million men, huge stocks of guns and ammunition. The problem was Evert's endemic pusillanimity. One date after another slipped for Evert's promised offensive. If a date was fixed, then the location was changed. Kuropatkin in the north-west displayed similar ignominious passivity. Brusilov rounded on Alekseev, who was well aware of the 'criminality' (*prestupnost*) of this inactivity, conniving in it because of his previous subordination to Evert and Kuropatkin during the Russo-Japanese war. On 2 July Evert's phantom offensive finally materialised, aimed now at Baranovichi. Massing men and guns on a narrow 7-kilometre front, as if the 'Brusilov method' had never existed, barrage followed barrage. The main assault was driven back by German artillery counter-attack, and the predictably confused, wasteful nightmare followed, Russian losses reaching the horrendous figure of 80,000 within one week. This disaster ended any further attempt at a multi-front operation, even the Tsar recognising the advantage in shifting men and munitions to Brusilov.

In autumnal rain, mud and fog, the 'Brusilov offensive' slowed to a halt. Early gains had been spectacular, hideous losses inevitable. Enemy losses exceeded a million and half men, 400,000 of whom were prisoners, plus great quantities of weapons and equipment lost to the Russians. Brusilov's South-Western Front paid a comparable price, losses of 1,200,000 for which 25,000 square kilometres of territory had been recovered – Russian armies in the south had actually penetrated into Hungary. The Austrian offensive in northern Italy was suspended in order to send eight divisions back to defend Galicia. German divisions withdrawn from Verdun stiffened wavering allies in the east. Falkenhayn fell by the wayside, replaced by Hindenburg as chief of staff. Brusilov's late August victories in Galicia and the Bukovina had important political consequences. Finally persuaded of the arrival of the 'the moment to march', on 27 August 1916 the wavering, neutral Romania declared war on Austria-Hungary, promptly invading Transylvania. German and Austrian retribution was swift.

Sceptical of Romania's potential value as an ally, suspecting only additional liabilities, Alekseev was proved right. Brusilov's successes had encouraged Romania to go to war, but they could not of themselves guarantee Romanian security. Strategically vulnerable, virtually indefensible, its army primitive and largely untrained, Romania proved to be the debilitating drain on Russia's limited resources as Alekseev feared. Winston Churchill observed acidly that 'the golden opportunity' for which Romania had long watched 'had not only come: it had gone'.[3] The 'opportunity' presented by the ruination inflicted by Brusilov on the Austro-Hungarian armies was frittered away in hesitation, negotiation and bargaining.

The Romanian imbroglio effectively doomed 'the Brusilov offensive'. The South-Western Front now found itself responsible for preventing the total collapse of Romania. Such a task not only demanded major reorganisation but also forced the abandonment of Brusilov's offensive in Galicia. Earlier in the summer the Stavka had been too slow to recognise and reinforce success. Now the growing crisis in Romania faced it with no other option but to underwrite manifest failure.

Exactly 28 years after the 'Brusilov offensive' the Red Army, in which General Brusilov himself had served from 1920-26, launched Operation 'Bagration', a massive breakthrough operation designed to accomplish the final destruction of its inveterate foe: Army Group Centre.[4] It was Army Group Centre's Fourth Army, striking due east on 1 December 1941 along the Minsk-Moscow highway, that posed an immediate and direct threat to Moscow, penetrating Soviet perimeter defences and closing to within kilometres of the Soviet capital. North and south of Moscow dangerous German armoured thrusts aimed to bring about a deep envelopment of the city. Decimated German and Soviet units grappled with each other on the approaches and in the very suburbs of Moscow.

General Zhukov, Western Front commander, had already presented Stalin on 30 November with plans for a Soviet counter-stroke designed to eliminate the German armoured wedges jammed into Soviet positions to the north and south.[5] To clear his left and right flanks and to strike in the centre Zhukov planned to use those reserves, which the German High Command believed did not – indeed, could not – exist. Nevertheless, the margin of Soviet superiority was slight, the large tank formation needed for breakthrough operations conspicuously lacking, artillery in short supply, ammunition available only to assault formations.

Zhukov intended to strike swiftly and secretly. Finally authorised by Stalin, Zhukov's 'counter-stroke' was launched on the morning of 5 December 1941. The first phase of what subsequently developed into a major counter-offensive ended in mid-December with the German pincers to the north and south blunted and Army Group Centre's flanks under immense strain. These early spectacular successes now excited Stalin's ambitions, who immediately proposed offensive strategic operations spanning the entire Soviet-German front, from Leningrad to the Black Sea. On 5 January 1942 the Stavka reviewed plans for a transition to a general offensive, the object being the destruction of German forces near Leningrad, west of Moscow and in the south. The main blow would be directed against Army Group Centre, a multi-front operation designed to bring about the destruction of German forces in the Rzhev-Vyazma-Smolensk area. In vain Zhukov protested that Stalin's plans subverted strategic logic. Rather than concentrating on the destruction of Army Group Centre and exploiting Western Front successes inwardly, the Stavka was to expand outwardly to every Soviet

Front. Inevitably, predictably, this first attempt to destroy Army Group Centre failed. Zhukov's furious efforts to sustain momentum, remarkable as they were, deploying cavalry corps in the deep rear, an airborne corps and air-lifted rifle regiments to 'strike deep', could not of themselves compensate for the absence of that brute strength, mobility, fire support and logistical capability necessary to deliver the coup de grâce to Army Group Centre.

Slowly, painfully, at excessive cost, the Red Army improved its tactical skills and renovated its doctrine, but many months were to pass before that critical 'trilogy' – doctrine, technology (armaments level) and *upravlenie voiskami* (troop control) – was fully aligned. Whatever the failures and disasters of the early summer of 1942, including the Kharkov debacle, the Stavka never abandoned its intention to resume major offensive operations and destroy at least one German Army Group. In the south at Stalingrad, Stalin and the Stavka prepared a major counter-offensive, 'Operation Uranus', but in the north General Zhukov planned and directed 'Operation Mars', an even more massive assault aimed at Army Group Centre in the Rzhev salient, the residual threat to Moscow's defences.

Launched on 25 November 1942 against a background of initial success at Stalingrad, by mid-December 'Mars' had come to terrible grief. German reserves checked Red Army penetrations, Soviet losses in men and machines mounted catastrophically. Success at Stalingrad quickly persuaded Stalin that the entire German southern wing was collapsing, presenting an opportunity after February 1943 to launch a fresh assault on Army Group Centre. But serious Soviet reverses in the south finally doomed Rokossovskii's offensive at the centre. His attacks ebbed away, leaving a huge Soviet salient jutting westwards: the famous 'Kursk bulge'.

Victor in the giant battle of Kursk in July 1943, the Red Army moved swiftly on to the offensive, demonstrating new, sophisticated operational techniques. German Army Group South was pressed back. At the centre, Smolensk was recaptured on 7 September 1943 whereupon the Stavka planned the liberation of Belorussia, launching multi-front offensive operations in November to seize Minsk and eastern Belorussia. Gains were impressive but not decisive, Army Group Centre veterans fighting doggedly and skilfully to contain Soviet attacks. The situation in Belorussia was temporarily stabilised, though it would not remain so for long.

The Soviet design for the third winter offensive, December 1943-April 1944, was for operations to unroll 'without pause', the aim being the destruction of German forces in the Leningrad area, in Belorussia, the Crimea and the Western Ukraine. The main attack would nevertheless develop in the South-Western theatre. A great avalanche of men and tanks was poised to crash down on Army Group South. When it materialised, the damage inflicted on German forces in the 'southern theatre' proved to be as unexpected as it was immense; Soviet operations continued uninterruptedly even during the spring thaw, the *rasputitsa*, leaving the Germans no respite and draining reserves. Marshal Zhukov, in temporary command of the 1st Ukrainian Front, found himself on familiar ground, the theatre where he first saw action in September 1916 as an NCO with the 10th Cavalry Division dispatched to General Brusilov's embattled, over-extended South-Western Front.

Zhukov splintered Army Group South with a massive cleaving blow. In the spring of 1944 the attention of Hitler and his commanders was riveted on the southern theatre, a major thrust into Poland and the Balkans presenting the obvious focus of the coming Soviet summer offensive. If this was obvious to the German command, what Stalin and the Stavka found equally obvious was that marking Army Group Centre down for death meant destroying those few German armies still relatively unscathed, cutting off Army Group North's line of retreat, clearing Soviet territory of German troops and placing the Red Army on the shortest line of advance to Berlin. The Red Army would pull down the so-called 'Belorussian balcony', the huge German salient jutting eastwards, freeing considerable Soviet strength tied down by Army Group Centre and thus eliminating the threat to Moscow from German bombers flying out of Belorussian airfields.

In March 1944 the General Staff completed its exhaustive analysis of the entire Soviet-German front, inspecting each Soviet strategic entity in turn. The destruction of Army Group Centre seemed to be the logical and desirable strategic objective, but, given past experience, was it feasible? Soviet armies on the 'western axis' had tried and failed too often, incurring grim losses. The General Staff concluded that even now German strength ruled out success for a single Soviet attack. Soviet experience, bought at high price, finally demonstrated the soundness of what pre-war doctrine prescribed as 'sequential offensives'. At the same time, in examining the misfortunes of the Western Front, the General Staff submitted that not only German strength but also Soviet 'organisational failures' must be held accountable. Heads had to roll. In April Stalin's all-powerful State Defence Committee, the GKO, completed its punitive mission under the direction of G. Malenkov, filling out the tally of 'subjective' and 'objective' shortcomings. General Sokolovskii was removed as Western Front commander, Artillery Marshal Voronov criticised for failures in the organisation and performance of the artillery, 'political' generals Bulganin and Mekhlis severely reprimanded. In the view of both the GKO and the General Staff, the Western Front, deploying five field armies and one air army, had dissipated its striking power, attacking towards Vitebsk, Orsha and Moghilev. It should therefore be split into two entities to form two new Fronts, the 2nd and 3rd Belorussian.

By mid-April the General Staff had completed the outline plan for the 1944 summer offensive, involving five or six Soviet Fronts deployed from north to south. The offensive would be opened in June by the Leningrad Front, the objective Vyborg, the aim to drive Finland out of the war. This would be the prelude to the massive Belorussian attack, where there was a reasonable prospect of attaining surprise and bringing about the destruction of Army Group Centre. Surprise and secrecy went hand in hand. The full operational plan was kept hermetically sealed within a circle of five men only, including Stalin, Stalin's Deputy Marshal Zhukov, and the Chief of the General Staff Marshal Vasilevskii. All telephone and telegraph traffic was rigorously controlled. At Front Headquarters the smallest possible number of officers worked on plans – all draft plans were hand-written – otherwise 'defensive' plans were ostentatiously distributed and discussed. Signal centres closed down the big transmitters, and formations in the field used only low-power sets, none located in the vicinity of the front-line. The General Staff set out to convince the German command that the Soviet offensive would unroll in the south and in the area of the Baltic.

At the beginning of May the two fronts selected to implement 'operational camouflage', the 3rd Ukrainian in the south and the 3rd Baltic in the north, received special orders to 'concentrate' and ensure 'offensive readiness' between 5 and 15 June. To lend further credence to the idea of a southern attack, all six Soviet tanks armies remained visibly deployed and displayed in the south-west. None of the Belorussian Fronts as yet deployed a tank army, even though the General Staff plan called for a powerful 'tank first' to strike along the Bobruisk-Minsk axis, not least to inhibit the movement of German reserves.

By mid-May the General Staff had completed the first detailed plan for the Belorussian operation. General Antonov, Deputy Chief of the General Staff, signed the hand-written operational brief, a few sheets of paper with attached maps, and duly submitted it to Stalin. Stalin asked what code-name had been assigned to the Belorussian attack. On learning that so far none had been selected, Stalin at once suggested 'Bagration' in honour of the Russian general Prince Peter Ivanovich Bagration, mortally wounded at Borodino in the 1812 war with Napoleon. The Soviet plan envisaged the elimination of the German salient in the area of Vitebsk-Bobruisk-Minsk, crushing the German flanks and breaking through the German defensive front with concentric attacks aimed at Minsk.

The General Staff had yet to take account of reports indicating greater German strength than previously suspected, but the attention of both Zhukov and Vasilevskii was fixed on securing one principal objective: the destruction of a 'significant' element of German strength during the actual breakthrough operation in the heavily manned German forward defences. The solution involved concentrating artillery and aircraft at each Front level, in particular 'artillery breakthrough divisions' with heavy-calibre guns. For success, it was essential to pin down and destroy German troops in the tactical defensive zone, inflicting the greatest possible damage there. Encirclement operations posed special problems. What Stalingrad and other operations had demonstrated was the amount of time needed to implement the actual encirclement followed by the destruction of trapped enemy garrisons. In Belorussia the German command could use that time to organise reserves, as well as exploiting the marshy and wooded terrain to impede Soviet attempts to build an encirclement front. German divisions had to be smashed in their defensive positions, remnants prevented from fleeing to the protection of swamp and forest. What agitated Zhukov and Vasilevskii had also plagued Brusilov: how to move from tactical to operational success, how to prevent the reconstitution of the tactical defence, how to speed up the actual penetration and, crucially, how to sustain the offensive into full operational depth, simultaneously depriving enemy reserves of the relative invulnerability afforded by operational depth. Through the application of momentum, deception and surprise, the Soviet command aimed to 'slice up' the main German groupings, isolate them and destroy them piecemeal.

Stalin convened a special two-day command conference on 22-23 May 1944. The two Stavka 'co-ordinators', the marshals Zhukov and Vasilevskii, were joined by the several Belorussian Front commanders, air force, artillery and engineering commanders, chief of 'rear services' (logistics). 'Bagration' emerged in its final form, the destruction of Army Group Centre opening with simultaneous blows on the German flanks to flatten them in the area of Vitebsk and Bobruisk, as well as wiping out German garrisons at Moghilev. The road to Minsk would then be open, Soviet troops could sever the German escape route, entrap Army Group Centre and destroy it 'piecemeal' with air attack, ground offensives launched by three Fronts and partisan operations. The May conference set 15-20 June as the probable period for the opening of 'Operation Bagration'.

The General Staff had already begun to organise a massive regrouping operation, which pulled armour and infantry from the interior military districts as well as withdrawing armies from the flanks. The General Staff wanted Rotmistrov's 5th Tank Army moved fully manned in order not to weaken it. Tank reinforcements moved discreetly into the central area, first pulled back into reserve, then re-assigned to the central sector, though weeks were to elapse before they were finally deployed. The Soviet command system had by now become extremely elaborate, with the Stavka 'representative' Zhukov 'co-ordinating' the operations of the 1st and 2nd Belorussian Fronts and Vasilevskii those of the 1st Baltic and 3rd Belorussian Fronts. For the first time these Stavka 'representatives' would not only 'co-ordinate' but exercise operational control, one of many innovations in Soviet strategic planning.

On 30 May the General Staff map was finally marked up with all the operations that would form the full complex of the 1944 'summer offensive'. The following day the Stavka issued the basic directive for 'Bagration' 1944, for once limiting immediate Front assignments to realistic objectives in stark contrast to previous directives, which prescribed wildly ambitious and wholly unrealistic objectives. The other distinguishing feature of 'Bagration' was intense debate and furious controversy over operational assignments and their execution, the most spectacular, celebrated and virtually unprecedented occasion being the dispute that erupted between Stalin and Rokossovskii, the latter insisting on a tactical double envelopment of German forces at Bobruisk much to Stalin's violent disapproval. After three 'presentations' Rokossovskii won his point and won out against Stalin, who at this juncture deferred to 'a general who knew his job'.

After all the General Staff investigations of German and Soviet strengths, it was apparent that the Red Army had not as yet been able to establish overwhelming numerical superiority over Army Group Centre. The reinforcement and redeployment designed to remedy this situation placed a colossal strain on Soviet rail and road facilities, continuous pressure being exerted by Zhukov and Vasilevskii at the front and more ominously by Stalin himself, who demanded an investigation of rail movement. The result was that traffic did speed up, but the provisional 'Bagration' timetable was beginning to slip. Four Soviet Fronts, the 1st Baltic, 1st, 2nd and 3rd Belorussian, were assigned to 'Bagration', deploying 14 combined-arms armies, one tank army, four 'air armies', two cavalry corps, eight tank or mechanised corps, 118 rifle divisions, 1,254,300 men (plus 416,000 men attached to the left flank armies of the 1st Belorussian Front), 2,715 tanks and 1,355 self-propelled guns, 24,000 guns and mobile heavy mortars lined up hub to hub, plus 2,306 Katyusha multiple rocket launchers, all supported by 5,327 combat aircraft (not including the 700 bombers of Long-Range Bomber Aviation ADD).

Every day 90-100 trains shifted fuel and ammunition to the four Fronts, while 12,000 lorries working for Front supply hauled up to 25,000 tons in one run, a fifth of the ammunition and a quarter of the fuel supply specified for a 24-hour supply period. In addition to base hospitals, Red Army medical services set up 294,000 forward dressing stations. Atop this huge pyramid of men, guns and tanks sat Marshal Zhukov, impatient to launch Soviet armies in a relentless assault on the last remaining bastion of German strength on the Eastern Front.

On 6 June British Prime Minister Churchill signalled Stalin that 'Overlord', the cross-Channel attack, had 'started well'. Stalin's response was a model of the most extreme discretion. He informed Churchill that in conformity with the agreement reached at the Teheran conference in December 1943, Soviet offensive operations would open in mid-June 'in one of the vital sectors of the front'. Two days later, 9 June, Stalin lifted the secrecy screen fractionally to inform Churchill that 'the first round' would begin on the Leningrad Front. The same day heavy-calibre guns opened fire on Finnish defences on the Karelian isthmus, followed by a 21st Army offensive on the western side of the isthmus, a ferocious assault supported by massive air attacks and the major armament of Baltic Fleet warships. As the Soviet offensive unrolled against Finland, the German command still clung to the belief that the main Soviet offensive would unroll in Galicia against the German Army Group North Ukraine, to which German reserves were increasingly directed. Army Group Centre was considered to be the object of diversionary attacks only, leaving the German Fourth Army with only one division in reserve and only one with Third Panzer, risky enough to cope with a subsidiary attack. Hitler forbade Army Group Centre to pull back to defensible river lines. Worse, the German High Command withdrew an entire Panzer corps in the Kovel sector from Army Group Centre, subordinating it to Army Group North Ukraine and thereby gravely weakening the central sector, depriving Army Group Centre from using reserves to block or deflect Soviet thrusts.

The Soviet build-up had not gone unnoticed. German military intelligence was aware that divisions were moving up to the central front from the Crimea and that the 5th Guards Tank Army was also on the move to the centre. Soviet deployments suggested operations to smother the German Ninth Army at Bobruisk, concentrations aimed at the Fourth Army in the Moghilev-Orsha area and a threat to the Third Panzer Army at Vitebsk from crack Soviet divisions. Massive Soviet air presence could not be entirely concealed. At the 14 June conference of all German Army Group commanders, the evidence of massive Soviet reinforcement opposite Army Group Centre was admitted but not regarded as 'conclusive'. A rapid build-up against Army Group Centre was considered feasible, but a Soviet offensive in Galicia was held the likeliest contingency. As late as 20 June the German High Command stuck to the view that the main Soviet attack would unroll in the south and that it might be expected when the Anglo-American armies had driven deeper from their coastal bridgeheads.

Before any Red Army units had crossed their start line Soviet partisans opened the battle for Belorussia, laying and detonating charges in the 'relsovaya voina', the 'war of the railway tracks', following instructions radioed to all Belorussian partisan units on the night of 8 June. During the short summer night of 19 June more than 10,000 demolitions ripped up German rail links west of Minsk, and for the next three nights 40,000 charges spread more destruction, disabling tracks and knocking out rolling-stock, the attacks concentrating on the lines connecting Minsk with Brest and Pinsk, the route German reinforcements might be expected to take. German anti-partisan operations inflicted heavy casualties but failed to eradicate the partisans. At the front the question of the line of advance of the 5th Guards Tank Army was as yet unresolved, a decision left temporarily to the Stavka 'co-ordinators', but the final decision would be Stalin's. Zhukov and Vasilevskii reported nightly to Stalin on their efforts to heave the Soviet armies into their attack positions, but pointed to dangerous delays in rail movements. Stalin repeatedly demanded assurance that the original timetable, 15-20 June, would be adhered to. In the event it was not.

The Red Army offensive opened on 22 June 1944, three years to the day since Hitler first loosed his shattering surprise attack on the Soviet Union. The Soviet offensive was staggered, the 1st Baltic Front in the north leading on 22-23 June, followed by the 3rd Belorussian and sequentially the 1st and 2nd Belorussian Fronts. The Soviet technique of 'developing reconnaissance into battle' confused the German command, suspecting only 'holding attacks'. A mass of bombers smashed the German rear. At 0355 hours on 24 June Rokossovskii's guns opened fire, his tanks advancing on roadways of logs looming up from swamp and bog to overwhelm German defences. One week after the initial Soviet operations, the first phase of the battle for Belorussia ended with the fall of Vitebsk, Orsha, Moghilev and Bobruisk.

The German defensive system at the central sector of the Soviet-German front had cracked wide open. Three German armies had lost more than 130,000 men – 66,000 taken prisoner – 900 tanks and thousands of vehicles destroyed. The Third Panzer was left with only a weakened infantry corps, in the centre the Fourth Army was in grave danger of being cut off in its long retreat to Minsk, and in the south the Ninth Army had the wreckage of its corps. The cost to the Red Army in casualties was high. On 28 June Stavka directives set the stage for a two-pronged drive on Minsk. One by one German escape routes were severed, and Minsk itself was threatened by Soviet columns moving to the north and south. The capture of Minsk doomed the Fourth Army, the Soviet encirclement trapping 105,000 men. Almost on the site where in late June and early July 1941 the Wehrmacht had carried out a huge encirclement of Soviet armies, a mass of German soldiers waited now either annihilation or capture in the great forests east of Minsk. More than 40,000 German soldiers were trying to escape encirclement. The last attempt was made on 5 July 1944, and three days later the acting commander of German XII Corps ordered a general surrender, but the battle for Belorussia had already been decided on 4 July. The Red Army had torn a gigantic gap in the German front. Army Group Centre was left with eight scattered divisions. The way ahead for the Red Army lay through Poland and Lithuania. The Red Army had achieved its greatest single success on the Eastern Front. For the German Army this was a catastrophe greater than Stalingrad, with between 25-28 divisions obliterated and 350,000 men lost.

Writing in 1945, Major General N. Talenskii drew an immediate comparison between 'Brusilov's genius in 1916', developing the concept of operational manoeuvre, and the genius of the Red Army in whose hands 'it acquired the character of a fully completed, highly perfected operational form of struggle'. 'This was especially so in its most developed form, that is, the rout of German Central Army Group in Belorussia.'[6] The immediacy of this comparison, while acknowledging elements of continuity between 1916 and 1944, cannot pass without some elaboration.

The circumstances under which Brusilov and Zhukov planned their breakthrough operations could not have been more different. Brusilov suffered a drastic paucity of resources, Zhukov a virtual plenitude. The Red Army in this later stage of the Soviet-German war became used to the notion of 'where Zhukov, there success', in itself largely a reflection of Marshal Zhukov's authority to demand and obtain what he deemed necessary for the successful conduct of his offensive operations. The gross disparity in material circumstances notwithstanding, the similarity of reaction on the part of both commanders is striking. Both were intent on maximising tactical ingenuity and innovation, improving command and control – *upravlenie* – staff organisation, intensifying troop preparation and training, and exploiting deception and surprise. In the case of Brusilov in 1916 it meant making a virtue out of a necessity, severe material constraints demanding radical tactical solutions and unorthodox operational planning. The relative abundance of Marshal Zhukov's resources in 1944 did not blind him to the need to refine operational methods and enhance tactical effectiveness. On the contrary, that relative military wealth was the spur to improve performance. Like Brusilov before him, Zhukov had mock-ups of offensive sectors prepared, Zhukov himself participating in the pre-attack 'gaming' conducted by 'operational groups' at army level.

Like Brusilov, Zhukov violently opposed the undifferentiated 'frontal blow' as the main operational method. The 'mechanisation' of the Red Army was not designed simply to enable it to launch frontal attacks. In 1944 the Soviet offensive designed to pull down the 'Belorussian balcony' extended across a frontage of 1,200 kilometres, with active operations planned across 700 kilometres. No fewer than six 'breakthrough sectors' were designated, with an operational depth fixed at 600 kilometres. If Brusilov learned from the disaster at Lake Naroch, Zhukov seems to have gained important insights from the failure of 'Operation Mars'. His 'operational credo', though not directly derived from the 'Brusilov offensive', bears some uncommon similarities to it: the emphasis on thorough, continuous reconnaissance in depth, rigorous training for command and staff, operational and tactical surprise, realistic assessment of the resources available for given assignments, no 'over-tasking', and the availability of adequate resources (the latter for Brusilov an elusive will o' the wisp).

In 1944 as in 1916 the problem was to devise methods that would transform tactical into operational success (and potentially strategic success). What distinguished the 1944 breakthrough from that of 1916 was Zhukov's deployment of 'mobile groups', committed after the breach of the tactical defensive zone, promising speedier movement into depth and the fragmentation of the enemy operational front. The meagre cavalry resources, the dwindling reserves of infantry and cavalry available to Brusilov to exploit the breakthrough paled into insignificance compared with Zhukov's tank armies, employed in echelons to complete the tactical breakthrough, the lead brigades operating with the forward elements of the combined-arms armies, the main body of the tank armies breaking into the second defensive belt. Speeding up the penetration, rapid development of the thrust into depth, was accorded top priority, intended to deprive enemy reserves of the 'relative invulnerability of operational depth'. Brusilov would have understood this situation, one by no means unfamiliar to him, and would have readily endorsed Zhukov's approach.

In the immediate aftermath of the war, in 1946, Brusilov and Zhukov were conjoined bizarrely in very select company: those whom Stalin would strike down. In the case of Brusilov it was a posthumous blow, the cause being Stalin's suspicions of anti-Soviet attitudes in a second volume of memoirs mistakenly ascribed to Brusilov, the result being the proscription of the name Brusilov. It was Marshal Zhukov's wartime achievements and reputation that proved to be his immediate undoing, provoking Stalin's envy and resentment and precipitating Zhukov's seven-year military exile passed in provincial military commands, sharing with Brusilov the fate of an 'un-person'. For General Brusilov and Marshal Zhukov the lightning struck not twice but thrice.

Notes on contributors

Professor John Erickson, The University of Edinburgh, UK
John Erickson FBA FRSE FRSA is Emeritus Professor of Higher Defence Studies and Honorary Fellow in Defence Studies in the University of Edinburgh. He is the author of The Soviet High Command 1918-41 (1962; 1984); The Road to Stalingrad, The Road to Berlin (1975, 1998, 2000), The Soviet Armed Forces 1918-1992. A Research Guide to Soviet Sources (1996) (with L. Erickson) and editor of BARBAROSSA, The Axis and the Allies (1994) (with David Dilks)

Recommended reading

Gackenholz, Hermann, 'The Collapse of Army Group Centre in 1944' in H. A. Jacobsen and J. Rohwer (eds), *Decisive Battles of World War II: The German View* (London: Andre Deutsch, 1965) pp335-82

Glantz, David M. and House, Jonathan, *When Titans Clashed: How the Red Army Stopped Hitler* (Lawrence: University of Kansas Press, 1995)

Jukes, Geoffrey, *Carpathian Disaster: Death of An Army* (London: Pan Books, 1971)

Stone, Norman, *The Eastern Front 1914-1917* (London: Hodder & Stoughton, 1975)

Notes

[1] For Brusilov, see A. A. Brusilov, *Moi vospominaaniya* (Memoirs), published in Moscow in five editions, 1929-63, 1929, 1941, 1943, 1946, 1963. See also A. A. Brusilov, *A Soldier's Notebook* (London: Macmillan, 1930). Sergei Semanov, *General Brusilov* (Moscow: Voenizdat, 1986), with a

foreword by Marshal of the Soviet Union K. Moskalenko, is a sympathetic, even laudatory, biography, emphasising that the offensive operations of Brusilov's South-Western Front in 1916 continued to be studied intensively in the Red Army during the 1920s and 1930s: see 'Vo glave fronta' and 'Russkaya armiya nastupaet!', pp170-229

² For the 'Brusilov Offensive', see Geoffrey Jukes, *Carpathian Disaster: Death of an Army* (London: Pan Books, 1971), especially 'Russia in 1916', pp76-96, 'Preparations for the offensive', pp96-116, and 'Decline of the army', pp142-9; John Keegan, *The First World War* (London: Pimlico, 1999), especially 'The Wider World and the Brusilov Offensive', pp321-31; and Norman Stone, *The Eastern Front 1914-1917* (London: Hodder & Stoughton, 1975), an indispensable account drawing on Russian, German and Austrian sources. See especially Chaps 11 and 12, pp232-81. For Russian sources, see I. I. Rostunov, *Russkii front v pervoi mirovoi voiny* (Moscow: 'Nauka', 1976), especially Chap 5 'Brusilovskoe nastuplenie', pp275-327, for a detailed military-political analysis.

³ Winston S. Churchill, *The World Crisis 1911-1918* (abridged revised ed, 1931; London: Landsborough, 1960) p754

⁴ For 'Operation Bagration', see Hermann Gackenholz, 'The Collapse of Army Group Centre in 1944', in H. A. Jacobsen and J. Rohwer (eds), *Decisive Battles of World War II: The German View* (London: Andre Deutsch, 1965) pp355-82. Gackenholz was responsible for Army Group Centre War Diary, 1943-45. David M. Glantz and Jonathan House, *When Titans Clashed: How the Red Army Stopped Hitler* (Lawrence: University of Kansas Press, 1995) Chap 13 pp195-215 'Operation Bagration: The Death of Army Group Center', on German and Soviet losses, pp214-5, and the invaluable notes and references, pp357-66. Otto Heidkamper, *Witbesk. Kampf und Untergang de 3 Panzerarmee* (Heidelberg: Vowinckel, 1954) pp144-62, for the Soviet assault, German break-out, withdrawal. Gerd Niepold (12th Panzer Division), Richard Simpkin, trans, *Battle for White Russia: The Destruction of Army Group Centre, June 1944* (London: Brassey's, 1987). A. M. Samsonov (ed), *Osvobozhdenie Belorussii* (Moscow: 'Nauka', 1974) is a major collection of detailed first-hand accounts of the planning and execution of 'Bagration'. S. M. Shtemenko, *The Soviet General Staff at War 1941-1945* (Moscow: Progress Publishers, 1985-86), Books One and Two. See Book One, Chap 12, pp297-333, 'Bagration'; this is a translation of *Sovetskii General'nyi shtab v gody voiny* (Moscow: Voenizdat, Vols 1-2, 1973-81). Finally, A. M. Vasilevskii, *A Lifelong Cause* (Moscow: Progress Publishers, 1981), a translation of *Delo vsei zhizni* (1973); see 'Prior to the Belorussian Operation' and 'For Byelorussian Land', pp356-88.

⁵ For Zhukov, see G. K. Zhukov, *Vospominaniya I razmyshleniya*, 3 Vols (Moscow: APN, 1990), the 10th edition of Zhukov's 'Memoirs and Reflections'. This edition contains names and passages that had been previously excised by the censor, the text reconstituted from Zhukov's own manuscript. See Vol 3, Chap 19 'Osvobozhdenie Belorussi I Ukrainy', pp128-69. See also N. Yakolev, *Zhukov* (Moscow: 'Mol Gvard', 1992) for a popular but well-informed biography, especially pp310-46

⁶ Major General N. Talenskii, 'The Development of Operational Art According to the Experience of Recent Warfare' in *The Evolution of Soviet Operational Art 1927-1991*, translated from the original by Harold S. Orenstein with an Introduction by David M. Glantz (London: Frank Cass, 1995) p160. For the original, see 'Razvitie operativnogo iskusstva po opytu poslednikh voin', *Voennaya mysl* (Moscow, 1945) Nos 6-7, pp15-30 (microfiche)

Chapter 25

Reflections on the experience of British generalship[1]

G. D. Sheffield

Field Marshals Sir Douglas Haig and Sir Bernard Montgomery were the two most prominent British generals of their respective wars. Their periods of high command were separated by a mere 25 years, yet their styles of generalship belong to completely different ages. Haig appeared as a remote patrician, impeccably attired, willing to take considerable risks and run up huge 'butcher's bills' in the pursuit of victory. Montgomery projected the image of a brash populLarist, who wore bizarre headgear and was a cautious general concerned to save lives. But in truth, how different was the British experience of generalship in the years 1914 to 1945?[2]

British generalship of the First World War is widely seen as incompetent. Likewise, during the 1939-45 conflict, the figure of 'Colonel Blimp' haunted the Army. British generals of both wars were accused of amateurism, being too old and members of socially elite regiments, which were supposedly anti-modern and resistant to technology. Thanks to recent research by John Bourne and David French, we now know a good deal about the nature of the British general officer corps. There were 147 commanders of infantry divisions in the Great War, 160 commanders of 'field-force' divisions in the Second World War. The average age of divisional generals when first appointed in 1914-18 was 51.5 years, with the mean age tumbling from 55.2 to 45.9 years in 1914 and 1918 respectively. At the beginning of the Second World War, the figure was 53 years; by 1945 it was 47.[3]

In 1914-18 the two Commanders-in-Chief of the British Expeditionary Force (BEF) were both cavalrymen. Socially elite units such as Rifle regiments and the Guards, as well as the cavalry, dominated the highest echelons of the Army, although the picture at lower levels of command was somewhat more mixed. By contrast, 1939-45 witnessed, in Stephen Badsey's words, 'the triumph of the English County Regiments in high command'. At divisional level, 61.5 per cent of commanders were drawn from the line infantry; the cavalry contributed 9.6 per cent and Foot Guards 7.0. In both wars the Regular Army kept its grip on command appointments of one star and above. It was difficult, if not impossible, for Territorial or temporary officers to break into the charmed circle. Given the small size of the Regular officer corps, particularly those who had 'psc' (passed staff college) after their name, British generals were drawn from a very small pool of officers indeed.[4]

The incestuous nature of the tiny officer corps may have enhanced the formation of cliques. As Badsey has noted, while historians have investigated the politics of faction in the late Victorian Army, the impact of faction on the Army in the two World Wars has been little explored. One, dramatic, example must suffice: the events in South East Asia in 1945, when Montgomery's protégé Oliver Leese attempted to remove Bill Slim from command, but ended up by being sacked himself. This was a struggle between factions at many levels: Eighth Army and the Mediterranean against Fourteenth Army and Burma; 'British' versus 'Indian' armies; aristocratic Guardsman versus middle-class line infantryman turned Gurkha – and a foretaste of the struggle between Montgomery and Slim for the leadership of the post-war Army.[5] British generals and factionalism in the two World Wars remains a rich seam for historians to mine.

The formative experiences of generals in the two conflicts were somewhat different. The generation of 1914-18 was brought up on colonial small wars. Even the largest of them, the second Boer War (1899-1902), was small by the standards of European warfare. By contrast, their successors of 1939-45 were overwhelmingly mostly veterans of the First World War. However, a surprising number of prominent Second World War generals had little or no experience of the Western Front, Auchinleck, Ismay, Slim and Horrocks among them.

The experience of generalship in both World Wars was conditioned by a number of factors that have influenced what Brian Holden Reid has referred to as the 'British style of command'.[6] The first is a general unreadiness of the British state to engage in protracted warfare. An important consequence is that British generals have had to cope with a good deal of improvisation, making use of scant resources in whatever situation emerges. Allenby's campaigns in Palestine, and the campaigns directed by Wavell in the Middle East and East Africa in 1940-41, both fit this pattern. In both campaigns 'British' armies used large numbers of Indian and white Dominion troops. Wavell's campaigns, which involved an extremely acute balancing of resources and commitments (most famously, in withdrawing troops from a successful campaign in North Africa and sending them to Greece in 1941), have been described as 'a thing of shreds and patches'.[7] This tag could be applied to a number of campaigns at the beginning of both World Wars, Antwerp, Gallipoli and Norway among them. By contrast, as high commanders Haig and Montgomery did not have to contend with the generalship of famine.

For most of its history, the British Army has been a colonial gendarmerie, capable of improvising an expeditionary force in times of trouble; the forces scraped together for the Norwegian campaign in 1940 are all too typical of the British experience. The British Army's experience of modern large-scale industrialised warfare is almost entirely confined to 1915-18 and 1942-45. Within the World Wars campaigns such as Mesopotamia, Palestine and East Africa in the First World War and Abyssinia, Eritrea, Syria and Iraq in the Second World War had more in common with each other than the Western Front or Normandy. The former, with relatively small forces deployed in a large area, large numbers of non-British troops and rampant 'ad hocery', have the 'feel' of large-scale colonial wars. This small wars heritage was not always a good preparation for total war. A commander like Wavell 'was not instinctively at home in a world of lengthy set-piece battles and wars of attrition'.[8] Similarly, Allenby was a relative failure on the

Western Front, but he thrived in Palestine fighting a more mobile campaign in a big 'small war'.

A third major theme was coalition warfare, in which it is difficult to take decisions unilaterally. Inevitably, coalition wars are fought by committees, and skill at diplomacy and bureaucratic in-fighting are valuable assets to the high commander. One reason why neither Haig nor Montgomery can be considered truly great commanders is their deficiencies as coalition generals, although the former was rather more adept at handling the French than the latter was the Americans. In both wars Britain had one close coalition partner, France in 1914-18 and 1939-40, and the United States in 1941-45. There were also other allies, of which some provided troops to fight alongside the British or even under British command. Moreover, by 1918 Dominion troops had to be treated as de facto allies rather than simply overseas appendages of the British Army. In 1941 Auchinleck discovered that, when faced with disputes concerning the organisation and deployment of Dominion troops, 'in such matters Australian demands, in [Australian General] Blamey's phrase, had to be treated like those of any other sovereign state and ally'.[9]

Several other factors can be mentioned briefly. The regimental system embodied enviable strengths, but it was not suited to large-scale industrialised warfare. The Army lacked a body of formal, intellectually rigorous doctrine, and while the staff colleges at Camberley and Quetta had their virtues[10], most training that British generals received for high command was informal and as often as not 'on the job'.

Throughout the period under discussion British generals laboured under the handicap of a lack of joint (that is, tri-service) structures and thinking. It is remarkable, given Britain's historical reliance on expeditionary warfare, that no effective machinery or doctrine for joint operations was in place in either 1914 or in 1939. In many cases, as at Gallipoli in 1915, goodwill and good working relations between soldiers and sailors made poor command arrangements work far better than they deserved.[11] Initially, there was no overall joint force commander for the Narvik operation in 1940. Worse, in the words of the naval commander, his army counterpart, General Macksey 'and myself left the UK with diametrically opposite views as to what was required'.[12] In 1940-41 in the Middle East matters were somewhat healthier. Through a mixture of goodwill and pragmatism General Sir Archibald Wavell emerged as, if not primus inter pares, at least as 'spokesman' of his fellow Commanders-in-Chief, Admiral Sir Andrew Cunningham and Air Chief Marshal Sir William Mitchell.[13]

During the Second World War the hard-won experience of joint operations in the Mediterranean theatre from 1940 to 1943 was used to create a fairly effective, although by no means flawless, joint command structure for 'Operation Overlord' in 1944. In this respect the experience of British generals in both World Wars was depressingly similar. Lacking an effective joint doctrine and machinery for joint command, ad hoc arrangements were the order of the day, which led to an avoidably large amount of sand being thrown into the works.

One enduring legacy of the First World War, which affected British generals of the Second, was the belief that an unacceptably wide gap had opened between the experience of high command on the one hand and regimental officers and soldiers on the other. 'Chateau generalship', the location of high commanders well behind the lines in grand and safe houses while the PBI huddled in rat-infested trenches at the 'sharp end', seemed to sum up everything that was wrong with British Army High Command in the First World War. As Major-General J. F. C. Fuller argued in 1933, 'Generals-in-Chief, forgetting the virtue of courage, [have] hidden themselves away in back areas to plot and to plan.' By not placing themselves in harm's way, in Fuller's words, they had 'broken that magic link which connects the heart of the general to the heart of his men.'[14]

Commanders of the vast armies of the Great War were victims of circumstances and technology. The only sensible place for a senior commander to be was behind the lines, at the end of a telephone. At Cambrai, on 20 November 1917, Brigadier-General Elles personally led the Tank Corps into action; this may have boosted the morale of his men but it is unlikely that it improved the handling of the battle. Conversely, the presence of senior officers in positions of danger could make soldiers nervous. As a warrant officer of the 16th Durham Light Infantry put it when complaining about the presence of General McCreery, up at the front line in Italy in 1943, 'You can't have generals being taken prisoner or killed.'[15]

The oft-repeated stories of the extreme isolation of Great War generals and their ignorance of conditions at the front are for the most part exaggerations, if not outright fiction. The figure of 78 officers of general rank 'who were killed in action, died of wounds or died as the result of active service' tells a story rather different from the traditional one.[16] Nevertheless, many of the generals of 1939-45 were extremely sensitive to charges of 'chateau generalship': commanders must be sure 'never to let the staff get between him and his troops', warned Wavell in his 1939 lectures on generalship.[17] Harold Macmillan noted in 1944 that Oliver Leese behaved towards the Eighth Army like a politician conducting 'an election campaign'. Macmillan went on to compare 'the remote, Blimpish' general of the Great War, with his casually attired successor who drove his own jeep into areas of danger: it was 'a remarkable contrast with the last war'. Macmillan's portrait was a caricature – for one thing, 57 fewer brigadiers and generals paid the ultimate price in the Second World War than the First, and for another, improved communications made it possible for generals to command from nearer the front line.[18] Yet many Second War generals drew the lesson that they had to be more approachable to their troops and share their danger. Thomas Rennie, commander of the 51st Highland Division in 1944-45, was of this type. He rose from the position of a junior staff officer in 1939, was '[un]pretentious', 'unassuming' and 'approachable', and was killed when his jeep was hit by mortar-fire – an indication of his proximity to the front line.[19]

Such men seem to have read the mood of their troops correctly. In part as a reaction to the experiences of 1914-18, British soldiers of the Second World War were less immediately deferential and more inclined to question orders than their fathers and uncles had been.[20] It is far from certain that British soldiers of the Great War would have appreciated their senior commanders adopting a more 'democratic' leadership style. As products of a hierarchical society, they expected their officers to be gentlemanly and slightly aloof. The evidence suggests that the likes of Haig made little impression on the consciousness of the other ranks; they might even have had difficulty recognising their divisional commander.[21]

It was not only the leadership style of the Great War generals that was rejected by some of their successors. Then British generals had spent lives freely in their pursuit of battlefield success (although British manpower resources were not unlimited). In the Second World War the Army's slice of the manpower cake was proportionately smaller, and the public, politicians and, indeed, many soldiers were not prepared to countenance losses on the scale of the Western Front. This influenced British strategy – which, between Dunkirk and D-Day, was based on avoiding fighting the main body of the enemy – and also influenced operations and tactics.

But for a simple twist of fate – a fatal plane crash – Lieutenant General W. H. E. 'Strafer' Gott, and not Montgomery, would have commanded at the second battle of Alamein. A fellow soldier commented that he believed that the responsibility would have weighed heavily on Gott:

'...particularly as the only way to carry it out appeared to be a reversion to 1914-1918 warfare with its heavy casualties, which he detested. He hated to see men killed and was determined to avoid the vast casualties for minor tactical gains which that type of battle involved... He had not the ruthless determination, one might almost say the callousness, which enabled Monty to face the colossal casualties in the first week of Alamein with equanimity...'[22]

Gott was one of the officers who, so keen were they to avoid the artillery-dominated attritional battles of 1914-18, attempted to fight an immature and largely unsuccessful form of manoeuvre warfare in the desert in 1941-42. Based in part on the half- digested theories of radical thinkers such as Liddell Hart and Fuller, this led to neglect of basic matters such as co-ordination between armour, infantry and guns, and concentration of force, especially artillery.[23] The early desert campaigns indicate that the old saw that generals always fight the next war using the methods of the previous conflict was, in this case, incorrect. It might have been better if they had.[24]

Pace the popular notion that the British Army fought the First World War on the Western Front in a militarily incompetent fashion, by the end of the war the British Army demonstrated a high level of tactical and operational effectiveness. The idea that the leaders of the inter-war Army were Blimpish, hippophile reactionaries who ignored the new form of warfare, based around the tank, is also open to challenge. David French has argued that the four CIGSs between 1918 and 1937 helped to set the Army along a path of analysing the experience of 1914-18, and the impact of new technology.[25] Yet official analysis of the lessons of the Great War did not receive the priority it deserved in the 1920s.[26] Reasons are not hard to find. One was repugnance at the thought of another Western Front. Another was the lack of any obvious continental enemy, allied to a lack of political direction – it was not until February 1939 that the Government reluctantly accepted that the British Army might have to be deployed to the continent to fight alongside the French. Moreover, the Army's primary role was to police the recently enlarged Empire.

Yet there was some analysis. The closest that the British Army had to a doctrine was its Field Service Regulations (FSR). FSR II of 1929 was a moderately progressive document that reflected some of the lessons of the Great War, and downgraded the primary role of infantry and horsed cavalry in favour of an all-arms approach with emphasis on mass firepower.[27] Even so, the 1932 committee on the lessons of the Great War, chaired by Lieutenant General Sir Walter Kirke, identified a number of weaknesses in existing doctrine. The Kirke committee was able to use the British official history, but unfortunately the volumes on the successful campaigns of 1918 had yet to be written.

The Kirke report contained much valuable analysis. It laid stress on surprise, which was linked to artillery, especially mechanised artillery; guns rather than tanks had represented the most advanced technology at the end of the Great War. When the report reproved FSR II 1929 because 'it has not quite got away from the old adage that "the infantry is the arm that wins battles"', it was the neglect of artillery, not tanks, that was being criticised. Kirke argued that attacks could succeed only if surprise was achieved, or by the use of artillery fire 'powerful enough to produce the effect of surprise'. The report recognised that the unwieldy nature of the Western Front-style artillery fire-plan might not be best suited to the modern mobile battlefield. As one scholar has commented, this type of thinking led the British Army down the tactical blind alley of excessive decentralisation of artillery, which had dire consequences in the desert campaigns.[28]

Kirke did not neglect armour. The report recognised the slow and unwieldy nature of artillery used in mobile warfare. The tank, by contrast, could give 'covering fire ... without elaborate fire plans' and that it 'combines the power both to blind and penetrate the defence – the roles formerly allotted to artillery and to infantry and cavalry respectively...' Kirke, in recommending 'permanent affiliations' between infantry and armour, which should train together, was pointing the way towards the armoured division.[29]

Perhaps the greatest weakness of FSR II 1929 was that it did not pay enough attention to the problems of converting a 'break in' to an enemy position into a 'break through'. Kirke and his team correctly identified poor communications as a major factor in preventing 'break throughs' on the Western Front; it made the timely employment of reserves all but impossible. In the absence of a solution to the problems of battlefield communications, Kirke suggested two broad approaches. One was to use the highly stereotyped plans of the Western Front. The second and preferable option was for higher commanders to 'delegate authority completely to subordinate commanders, trusting to their initiative in conformity with general instructions'.[30]

If poor communications was the first problem facing the Western Front commander attempting to convert initial success in breaking in to an enemy position into a break through, the lack of a usable instrument of exploitation was another. By 1932, this problem was less acute than in 1918. Kirke recommended employing:

'...a highly mobile reserve containing a powerful punch supplied by armoured fighting vehicles and mechanised artillery, with a sufficiency of cavalry or lorry borne infantry and mechanised machine-guns to secure bases from which to secure successive bases from which tanks can make a fresh bound. The whole must be under a selected commander and with a proper staff, signals and probably aircraft. The addition of low-flying aircraft ... is worthy of consideration...'

While this passage contains echoes of his Soviet contemporary Tukhachevskii, it is important to note that Kirke had to operate within tight financial constraints. Despite an evident lack of enthusiasm for horsed cavalry, the report recognised that it might have to be used in place of or in combination with motorised infantry to 'occupy, mop-up and secure communications' for the very good reason that 'it is unlikely that cross-country lorries will be available in sufficient numbers'. Moreover, Kirke made clear the committee's view on equipment purchasing priorities: 'If this [proposal] is accepted the necessity for an increase in tanks is obvious, unless we are to forego their assistance in all the preliminary operations.'[31]

The Kirke report has a number of blind spots. One is the scant attention paid to airpower, a fault common to much of the thinking of the British Army in the inter-war period, in part the product of inter-service rivalries; the examination of the air element was excluded from Kirke's remit.[32] Second, little attention was paid to logistics. On the Western Front the BEF's logistics coped well with static warfare, and tolerably well with the slow but steady advance of the Hundred Days. In the Kirke report there is no suggestion of further motorising of logistic services and no indication that in a future campaign the RASC might have to convey supplies over hundreds of miles behind an advancing mobile enemy. This may have been taken as a 'given', since the RASC was in the process of replacing horses with lorries, and by 1934 all Motor Transport companies were equipped with 3-ton lorries capable of cross-country movement.[33]

The report's apparent neglect of logistics is related to a third criticism: that the committee was still thinking of 1918-scale advances, of perhaps 40 miles, rather than the several hundred that their Soviet contemporaries were contemplating. This may account for the lack of provision for exploitation echelons to follow the initial breakthrough. Alternatively, it may simply reflect the brutal reality that in a small army there was unlikely to be a second echelon available. Certainly the Kirke committee did not seem to be envisaging the decisive blow at the enemy 'brain' that Fuller was propounding, or that shattering of enemy cohesion that lay at the heart of Soviet Deep Battle. It seems that the Kirke committee had not yet grasped the improvements in technology that made it possible to move from the mobile warfare of 1918 to the manoeuvre warfare of 1939-45.

For all its faults, the Kirke report was a firm basis upon which to develop a modern doctrine for the 1930s. Its publication did not induce the Blimpish reaction among senior officers that some, especially Liddell Hart, have claimed.[34] In 1935, during Montgomery-Massingberd's term as CIGS, a new version of FSR appeared that incorporated many of Kirke's recommendations. This was the version with which the British Army entered the Second World War.

The draft of FSR II 1935 was written by Colonel A. P., later Field Marshal Lord, Wavell, late Black Watch. Wavell was far from a Blimp. He was a progressive on the subject of mechanisation[35] and was described by a contemporary as 'a very great man ... he was an original thinker in the sense that he thought everything out for himself in a mind "well-furnished", as Bacon said by reading, and [was] very logical...'[36]

Through his writings we can trace the evolution of the military thought of a junior officer of 1914-18 who was to exercise high command in the Second World War, but failed initially to appreciate some important lessons of the Western Front.

There were two major themes in Wavell's thinking: the role of infantry and his experience of mobile warfare in Palestine in 1917-18. In an unpublished short story written in 1932 Wavell made a character say:

> 'If we would only label all the experience of the Western Front "Siege – to be left in store till called for", and base our ideas of warfare in the open field on the fighting in Palestine and on lesser fronts, it might help us.'[37]

Similarly, in that year Wavell argued that infantry had suffered a crisis of confidence in the Great War. In 1914 'I' was '"the arm that wins battles"' but in 1918 'emerged shell-shocked and machine-gun ridden, as the PBI' [Poor Bloody Infantry]. As a result, Wavell claimed that now, in 1932, infantry was patronised by other parts of the Army – presumably he had the armour radicals in mind.[38]

Wavell claimed that the reason for 'the failure of infantry' on the Western Front was obvious from the British *Official History*, although few had commented on this obvious fact: that the fighting was '"siege warfare", pure and simple'. Throughout history the siege had been the province of the sapper and gunner, not the foot soldier:

> 'Look … how the wretched infantrymen in France, practically untrained, were thrown at "breaches" that the umpires of Marlborough's time would seldom have passed as practicable. And to make quite certain that the poor mutt had no chance, he was loaded up for the assault… And on the inevitable failure is based the evidence for the decline of infantry.
>
> Where the infantry had a fair chance … in Palestine, Iraq, etc – they showed what infantry could do even against machine-guns.'[39]

Here, Wavell was generalising about the whole war from his experience of 1914-16 – he left the Western Front in October 1916 – and from his reading of the *Official History*, of which only the volumes for 1914, 1915 and 1916 had been published by 1932. Like Liddell Hart, whose failure to experience the campaigns of 1918 warped his understanding and writings on the First World War, Wavell in 1932 apparently failed to understand the major changes in warfare that occurred after the Somme. If he had, he might have acknowledged that infantry had been highly effective when used as part of an all-arms team during the Hundred Days.[40]

Wavell's vision of modern war was akin to his version of the mobile campaigns in Palestine in 1918. Wavell was absolutely correct in believing that reports of the death of infantry had been greatly exaggerated, but he probably underplayed the extent to which Allenby had applied 'Western Front' methods.[41] In Palestine he believed that siege warfare had been consigned to history, and 'light infantry', which in his words had the attributes of the 'poacher, cat-burglar, and gunman', came into its own.[42] Wavell's was a vision of a large 'small war', in which the Western Front experience of 1917-18 was discounted, and it bore a resemblance to the type of campaign that was actually to be fought under Wavell's direction in 1940-41.

Wavell's revision of FSR II in 1935 is testimony to his breadth of vision, because this document did incorporate, via Kirke, many of the lessons of the Western Front.

On the eve of the Second World War British doctrine was thus fundamentally sound and up to date. Many of the problems experienced by British generals in the early years of the war, as in 1914-16, were rooted in the absence of formal doctrine, in the sense of a body of ideas held throughout the Army that governed its thinking, organisation, tactics and training. Not only the radical thinkers Liddell Hart and Fuller, but also official publications, advocated an all-arms approach to warfighting. 'Unfortunately,' as two leading historians have commented, 'there is little sign that the army exercised itself to achieve such a close integration of combat arms.' Thus for a number of factors discussed above, good ideas on paper failed to translate into sound practice on the ground.[43]

The differences and similarities between generalship in the two World Wars can be highlighted by reference to two of the principal British commanders of the conflicts: Haig and Montgomery. One obvious difference is that Haig's scale of operations, and responsibilities, were far greater than Montgomery's. Haig's experience of high command was shaped by the fact that he had to deal directly with the Government. The Prime Minister, Lloyd George, militarily ignorant and highly suspicious of British high command, intrigued against Haig. Robertson, the CIGS, was the junior partner in his relationship with Haig. This limited the degree of 'top cover' he could offer the Commander-in-Chief, as did Lloyd George's suspicions of 'Wully' himself. As Prime Minister, Winston Churchill presented his generals with another if no less taxing set of problems. Churchill regarded himself as an expert on warfare and subjected his commanders to a barrage of advice and even direct orders. Alan Brooke's relationship with Churchill was such that the CIGS afforded Montgomery a degree of protection from political pressure – far more than Brooke's predecessor, Dill, had been able to give Wavell.

Douglas Haig is popularly remembered as the ultimate 'chateau general', with all the emotional and historical baggage that that term has accumulated. His General Headquarters (GHQ) was located at the town of Montreuil, some way behind the lines, with Haig and his closest staff living in nearby Chateau Beaurepaire. As discussed above, the location of higher headquarters in the Great War was largely dictated by the shortcomings of the communications of the era. GHQ was a substantial and complex organisation of 300 staff officers (with another 240 located elsewhere). For his major battles Haig set up a much smaller Advanced Headquarters closer to his subordinate formations and the front line. For the mobile battles of autumn 1918 he used a specially adapted railway train.[44]

In the next war, Montgomery took Haig's approach a stage further. He divided his HQ into 'Rear', 'Main' and 'Tactical', or 'Tac'. The donkey work was done at 'Main', while Montgomery spent his time at 'Tac', a collection of caravans close to the front line, where he had the time and mental space to think. In Normandy Tac was situated about 3 miles from the front line, although ironically enough in the grounds of a chateau. In considering the command arrangements of Haig and Montgomery, the similarities are at least as strong as the differences. Neither man was a front-line general in the Rommel mould, and Haig created his Advanced HQ for much the same reasons as Montgomery used Tac. One major difference was that the communications at Montgomery's disposal, which made possible the three-tier headquarters, were vastly superior to those available to Haig.[45] Another was that Montgomery adopted an ascetic life style; he slept in his caravan, rather than in the chateau. This is entirely consistent with Montgomery's personality, but was also perhaps a reaction to perceptions of the experience of 1914-18.

Both Haig and Montgomery used a system of liaison officers, junior officers who would go out to formations to act as the C-in-C's eyes and ears – the so-called 'directed telescope' system. Montgomery developed the system considerably, and he also had the advantage of J and Phantom services, which listened in on radio traffic of formations under his command, thus allowing him to keep his finger on the pulse of the battle. This was an asset of which Haig could have only dreamed.

One major innovation of Montgomery's was the establishment of a Chief of Staff (COS) system. On taking over at Eighth Army, he instructed that 'every order issued by [his COS, Major-General 'Freddie'] de Guingand must be accepted as coming direct from the Army Commander and obeyed without demur'.[46] Montgomery's creation of a powerful COS, who ruled the roost at Main HQ while he was at Tac, relieved him of the necessity to worry about details and allowed him to focus on big issues. The COS system does not always work, nor is it always necessary for success. Slim, for instance, did not operate such a system in Burma.

On balance, the COS system worked well for Monty, who always remained the senior partner. It also had its drawbacks. For much of the Normandy campaign the English Channel separated de Guingand at Main HQ from Montgomery at Tac. Thus Montgomery, cocooned at Tac with his surrogate (and highly talented) family of junior officers, was deprived of his COS's political antennae. This undoubtedly contributed to his increasing estrangement from developments at SHAEF and the problems he experienced with his fellow senior commanders, particularly the Americans. If Haig was mentally too remote from the front line, Montgomery was probably too close.[47]

In matters of 'jointery', Haig's lot was somewhat easier than Montgomery's. Haig had relatively few dealings with the Royal Navy[48], and on the Western Front the RFC/RAF saw support of the Army as its primary role. A comparison of Haig's and Montgomery's views on the importance of air/ground operation reveals a great deal of common ground.[49] However, by 1939 the RAF, partly as a consequence of its fight to retain an independent existence in the inter-war period, had adopted strategic bombing as its core doctrine and raison d'être and consequently neglected the army co-operation role. This was particularly damaging to the operational performance of the British Army. It took several years of hard fighting before the Army and the RAF achieved the level of co-operation that had existed in 1918.

In the absence of permanent joint command structures and doctrine, personalities were as important as ever. Montgomery's relationship with Air Vice-Marshal Harry Broadhurst, AOC Desert Air Force in 1943, was good, but in Normandy his relationship with another desert airman, 'Mary' Coningham, was very poor. In general, neither Haig nor Montgomery were well served by their personalities. Haig suffered from a remote, taciturn manner, while Montgomery's personality was such that he offended people impartially across the services (and indeed, across national boundaries).

Douglas Haig, who had been a successful cavalryman in the Boer War, was by training and instinct what would today be called a manoeuvrist. This led him, in his planning for the Somme, to attempt to make the BEF run before it could walk. Instead of the battle he had anticipated beforehand, the BEF fought a linear, attritional battle with a modicum of success. In 1917 Plumer's Second Army was at the forefront of mastering the art of conducting 'bite and hold' battles, applying attrition in a focused fashion to achieve a limited, but tangible, outcome. By the autumn of 1918 the BEF was capable of conducting a very successful form of mobile warfare. Adopting a more limited attritional approach earlier may not have saved lives, but it might have ensured that lives were expended for more concrete results.

Montgomery's arrival in Egypt in August 1942 brought about a doctrinal return to 1917-18, codified and modified by Kirke and FSR II 1935, but in defiance of Kirke's recommendations there was a return to the 'highly stereotyped, bite and hold' approach. Montgomery had had few illusions about the nature of training and morale of his citizen army. Scorning the imaginative if ill-founded attempts to fight naval battles on land, Montgomery recognised that the Eighth Army would be best used in a centrally controlled, stage-managed, artillery-heavy battle. This was a style of battle of which Montgomery had gained first-hand experience as a junior staff officer of IX Corps serving under Plumer in 1917. The Second Alamein in 1942 was an updated version of a battle such as Menin Road Ridge in 1917. Several other factors influenced Montgomery in his style of battle. It suited his cautious, methodical approach. He was as influenced as any by the post-war revulsion against the Western Front and knew that it was impossible on a number of grounds to expend men as Haig had done a generation before. In speeches to his troops he told them that he was going to be economical with their lives. Moreover, Montgomery was well aware that Britain was suffering from a manpower shortage, that the British Army was a wasting asset. A recent study has convincingly argued that Montgomery's operational approach in the North West European campaign of 1944-45 was shaped by his desire to minimise casualties and sustain his troops' morale. [50]

Ironically, Montgomery's attritional approach was thus intended to husband lives. Manoeuvre warfare offers great rewards if things go right but heavy penalties if things go wrong. It is noticeable that on the one occasion that Montgomery threw caution to the winds – 'Operation Market Garden' in 1944 – one factor in his thinking was that he seems to have believed, wrongly, that the war was nearly over and that, on an analogy with September 1918, it was time to take risks. Things went horribly wrong and in subsequent operations (such as 'Operation Veritable' and the crossing of the Rhine) he returned to type, and to his winning ways.

The difference in instincts between Haig and Montgomery helps to explain the difference in their methods of command. Montgomery was an exponent of the 'tidy battlefield', of exercising 'grip' over his subordinate commanders. In Normandy, his grip over Dempsey, the commander of the Second Army, was perhaps excessive. [51] With Haig things were different. In common with other senior officers of his vintage, Haig believed in setting broad objectives, then letting his subordinates get on with their operations. In principle this was ideal, but there was no real culture of devolved command, and some subordinates were incapable of exercising it – and Haig was inclined to interfere. In practice, on the

Somme in 1916 Haig's handling of Rawlinson lacked consistency and rigour.[52] A year later, before the Third Battle of Ypres, Haig failed to give Gough clear instructions as to whether he was to attempt a breakthrough or something more limited.[53] In the open warfare of the Allied offensives of 1918, when his subordinate commanders were more experienced and competent, his hands-off approach worked reasonably well. Haig was by no means as isolated as he is sometimes portrayed; he frequently visited his Army and other commanders, and it is by no means clear that he was as terrifying and resistant to advice as tradition would have it. But in comparison with Montgomery, Haig lacked 'grip'. Montgomery's approach was perhaps a reaction to the methods of his predecessor and, given that the forces he commanded were on a much smaller scale than Haig's, he found it easier to exercise centralised control.

By far the most obvious difference between the method of generalship practised by Haig and Montgomery was their personal leadership styles. Haig was a Victorian, the product of a highly stratified society in which people 'knew their place', and his army's officer-man relationship, a reciprocal, cordial mixture of deference and paternalism, worked remarkably well. Haig was certainly well aware of the importance of his troops' morale – he stood at the head of a vast organisation dedicated to its maintenance – and he regarded it as important to be seen by his troops. His method was to carry out inspections of troops on parade, which in the social conditions of the time was a perfectly appropriate response.[54]

Arriving in Egypt in August 1942 to take over an army that, if not demoralised, was certainly depressed, Montgomery seems to have recognised that the needs of the soldier of the Second World War were rather different from those of the First. Although his personality was not dissimilar to Haig's, he invented 'Monty', a vulgar, popularist showman, whose trademarks were eye-catching hats (an Australian bush hat covered in badges, a black beret with two badges), informal pep talks, and the handing out of cigarettes. This was truly a general treating his troops as a politician would have behaved towards potential voters. Not the least of Montgomery's achievements was to turn the Eighth Army into a 'brand name' with which soldiers and civilians could identify and of which they could be proud.

Nothing better demonstrates the changing nature of the experience of generalship than Haig and Montgomery's respective response to the media. The press had been a factor with which generals had to contend as early as the Crimean War. During the First World War the press was a vital element in achieving and maintaining consensus in Britain for the waging of a total conflict. In 1915 two incidents were to demonstrate that, more than ever before, handling the press had become a facet of command that generals ignored at their peril. The first was the behaviour of Colonel Repington, the military correspondent of _The Times_, who, egged on by Sir John French, attacked Kitchener over the so-called 'Shells Scandal' and thus precipitated a political crisis.[55] The second was General Sir Ian Hamilton's unhappy relations with the war correspondent Ellis Ashmead-Bartlett, which eventually led to a letter denouncing the conduct of the Gallipoli campaign reaching Asquith, the Prime Minister.[56]

Haig never came fully to appreciate the importance of cultivating and using the press. His mishandling of an interview with a French newspaper in 1917 further poisoned his relations with Lloyd George. Stephen Badsey has recently suggested that one reason why the BEF's victories of autumn 1918 remain comparatively unknown sprang from Haig's neglect of, and fundamental lack of interest in, the press. In September 1918 Haig wrote, 'I am not nor am I likely to be a "famous general".' For that must he not have pandered to Repington and the 'gutter press'? Badsey aptly comments that this comment might stand as Haig's 'professional epitaph'.[57]

There were some British commanders of the Second World War who handled the media in a similarly inept fashion, Percival's press conference just before the fall of Singapore being a case in point.[58] Montgomery quickly learned the importance of the media as an aid to building the morale of the troops. *Eighth Army News* and the weekly *Crusader* became important tools in Montgomery's leadership style. More than this, Montgomery recognised the importance of reaching out, also as he put it, to the soldiers' families. Whereas Haig was inarticulate and taciturn, Montgomery was on occasion suicidally candid. On 7 January 1945 he held a press conference at which he made some monumentally tactless remarks about American handling of the German Ardennes offensive. This occurred only a week after Montgomery's persistent and unsubtle attempts to force Eisenhower to re-appoint him as land forces commander had brought him within a hair's breadth of dismissal. Montgomery was not the last soldier to discover that the media can be a dangerously two-edged weapon.[59]

In retrospect, the experience of British generals in both World Wars was shaped by common factors: the influence of colonial warfare, the cult of unreadiness and improvisation, and coalition warfare; shortage of resources at the beginning of the war and abundance (of materiel if not of men) at the end; and the lack of joint structures and thinking. But in one important way the experience of the Second World War was different from the First. Many of the commanders of 1939-45 reacted against the Western Front style of generalship, with profound consequences, both good and ill, for the British Army of the Second World War.

Notes on contributors

Dr G.D. Sheffield, Joint Services Command and Staff College, Shrivenham, UK
Gary Sheffield is Senior Lecturer at King's College London, based at the Joint Services Command and Staff College, where he is Land Warfare Historian on the Higher Command and Staff Course. He has written widely on the history of the two world wars. His most recent publication is Leadership in the Trenches: Officer-Man Relations, Morale and Discipline in the British Army in the era of the Great War (Basingstoke: Macmillan, 2000).

Recommended reading

Bond, Brian and Cave, Nigel, *Haig: A Reappraisal 70 Years On* (London: Leo Cooper, 1999)
Fraser, David, *And We Shall Shock Them: The British Army in the Second World War* (London: Sceptre, 1988)

Hamilton, Nigel, *Monty*, 3 Vols (London: Hamish Hamilton, 1981-6)

Notes

1   I would like to thank Dr Stephen Hart and Dr Stephen Badsey for their comments on earlier drafts
     of this chapter. Portions were given as lectures to the Society for Army Historical Research and the
     2000 Higher Command and Staff Course. I would like to thank these audiences for their
     constructive criticisms.
2   In 1914-18 'one star' commanders were brigadier-generals; by 1939 they were simply 'brigadiers'.
     The term 'general' also encompasses 'Whitehall Warriors' such as Robertson and Brooke, as well as
     operational commanders and, of course, field marshals.
3   David French, 'Colonel Blimp and the British Army: British Divisional Commanders in the War
     against Germany, 1939-45' in *English Historical Review*, CXI, No 444 (November 1996), pp1185-6
4   Stephen Badsey, 'Faction in the British Army: Its Impact on 21st Army Group Operations in
     Autumn 1944' in *War Studies Journal*, 1 (1) (Autumn 1995), p15; David French, op cit, p1186; J. M.
     Bourne, 'British Generals in the First World War' in G. D. Sheffield, *Leadership and Command: The
     Anglo-American Experience since 1861* (London: Brassey's, 1997) pp93-116
5   Stephen Badsey, op cit, is a pioneering study. I an grateful to Dr Duncan Anderson for sharing with
     me the fruits of his as yet unpublished work on Slim. See also Hew Strachan, *The Politics of the British
     Army* (Oxford: Clarendon Press, 1997) especially Chap 9
6   What follows has been greatly influenced by Professor Brian Holden Reid's article of this name in
     his Occasional Paper, 'A Doctrinal Perspective 1988-98' (Camberley: Strategic & Combat Studies
     Institute (SCSI), 1998) pp29-42
7   Ronald Lewin, *The Chief: Field Marshal Lord Wavell, Commander-in-Chief and Viceroy 1939-1947*
     (London: Hutchinson, 1980) Chap 2
8   Ibid, pp30-1
9   Jeffrey Grey, *A Military History of Australia* (Cambridge: Cambridge University Press, 1990) p159
10   David Fraser, *And We Shall Shock Them: The British Army in the Second World War* (London: Sceptre,
     1988) p103
11   I owe this point to Professor Geoffrey Till.
12   Francois Kersaudy, *Norway 1940* (London: Arrow, 1991) pp89, 123, 126-7
13   Harold E. Raugh, *Wavell in the Middle East, 1939-1941: A Study in Generalship* (London, Brassey's,
     1993) pp39-40, 44-5
14   J. F. C. Fuller, *Grant and Lee: A Study in Personality and Generalship* (Stevenage: Spa Books, 1992 ed)
     p282
15   Quoted in Peter Hart, *The Heat Of Battle: The 16th Battalion Durham Light Infantry: The Italian
     Campaign, 1943-1945* (Barnsley: Leo Cooper, p80)
16   Frank Davies and Graham Maddocks, *Bloody Red Tabs: General Officer Casualties of the Great War,
     1914-1918* (London, Leo Cooper, 1995) p22
17   Field Marshal Earl Wavell, *The Good Soldier* (London: Macmillan, 1948) p13
18   Harold Macmillan, *War Diaries* (London: Macmillan, 1984) p529; Davies and Maddocks, op cit,
     p22
19   J. B. Salmond, *The History of the 51st Highland Division* (Edinburgh: Pentland, new ed 1994) pp151,
     239
20   G. D. Sheffield, 'The Shadow of the Somme: the Influence of the First World War on British
     Soldiers' Perceptions and Behaviour in the Second World War' in Paul Addison and Angus Calder
     (eds), *Time to Kill: The Soldier's Experience of War in the West 1939-45* (London: Pimlico, 1997)
     pp29-39
21   Niall Barr and G. D. Sheffield, 'Douglas Haig, the Common Soldier, and the British Legion' in Brian
     Bond and Nigel Cave, *Haig: A Reappraisal 70 Years On* (London: Leo Cooper, 1999) pp223-39
22   R. M. P. [later Field Marshal Lord] Carver to J. A. J. Agar-Hamilton, 1950, quoted in H. R. W.
     Vernon (ed), *'Strafer' Gott 1897-1942* (privately published, c1983) pp18-9
23   J. A. J. Agar-Hamilton and L. C. F. Turner, *The Sidi Rezegh Battles* (Cape Town: Oxford University
     Press, 1955) pp38-58; P. G. Griffith, 'British Armoured Warfare in the Western Desert 1940-43' in
     J. P. Harris and F. H. Toase, *Armoured Warfare* (London: Batsford, 1990); Brian Holden Reid, 'War
     Fighting Doctrine and the British Army', op cit, pp22-4
24   Brian Bond and Williamson Murray, 'The British Armed Forces, 1918-39' in Alan R. Millet and
     Williamson Murray, *Military Effectiveness*, Vol II 'The Inter-war Period' (Boston: Allen & Unwin,
     1988) p116
25   David French, 'CIGS: Unsung Leadership 1918-1937', *Army Quarterly*, 126 (3) (July 1996), pp288,

296

26 See, however, the analytical articles written by individual soldiers in the *Army Quarterly* and the *Journal of the Royal United Services Institution* as well as the works of Fuller and Liddell Hart

27 Compare Field Service Regulations Vol 2 (Operations, 1920) with the 1929 edition; David French, op cit, pp289, 95. For a more sceptical view, see Brian Bond, *British Military Policy Between the Wars* (Oxford: Clarendon Press, 1980) p129

28 'Report of the Committee on the Lessons of the Great War' [Kirke Report] (London: War Office, 1932) pp10, 14; Brian Holden Reid, op cit, p22

29 Kirke Report, op cit, pp13, 15; Shelford Bidwell and Dominick Graham, *Fire-Power* (London: Allen & Unwin, 1982) p189

30 Kirke Report, op cit, p19

31 Ibid, p20

32 Bidwell and Graham, op cit, p189

33 Ian Malcolm Brown, *British Logistics on the Western Front 1914-1919* (Westport, CT: Praeger, 1998) passim; G. Crew, *The Royal Army Service Corps* (London: Leo Cooper, 1970) p167

34 David French, op cit, pp293, 295. For adverse views on the reaction of Milne and Montgomery-Massingberd respectively, see Bidwell and Graham, op cit, pp189-90, and Liddell Hart, *Memoirs*, Vol I (London: Cassell, 1965) pp213-13

35 Brian Bond, *British Military Policy* (Oxford: Clarendon Press, 1980) p130

36 Major-General G. P. Dawnay to A. Whitworth, nd, Dawnay Papers, 69/21/3, Imperial War Museum

37 Field Marshal Earl Wavell, *The Good Soldier*, op cit, p82

38 Ibid, pp73-5

39 Ibid, pp73-4

40 See also his disparaging comments about Western Front-influenced post-war notions of open warfare; ibid, p74

41 A. P. Wavell, *The Palestine Campaigns* (London: Constable, 1938 ed) esp pp234-42; Matthew Hughes, *Allenby and British Strategy in the Middle East, 1917-1919* (London: Cass, 1999) pp43-59

42 Wavell, *The Good Soldier*, op cit, p102

43 Bond and Murray, op cit, p122

44 John Terraine, *The Smoke and the Fire: Myths and Anti-Myths of War 1861-1945* (London: Sidgwick & Jackson, 1980) pp173-8

45 That is not ignore the fact that by 1918 technology had advanced sufficiently to allow the BEF to develop a signals service capable of coping with semi-mobile warfare. See R. E. Priestley, *The Signal Service in the European War* (Chatham: Mackay, 1921) pp304-33

46 Ronald Lewin, *Montgomery as Military Commander* (London: Batsford, 1971) p51. See also Stephen Hart, 'De Guingand' in David Zabecki (ed), *Chiefs of Staff* (Boulder, CO: Lynne Reiner, forthcoming)

47 Alistair Horne with David Montgomery, *The Lonely Leader: Monty 1944-45* (London: Pan, 1995) pp134-5; Brian Holden Reid, 'British Style', op cit, pp39-40

48 Haig's relations during the planning for the abortive amphibious operation in 1917 were generally constructive; see Andrew A. Wiest, 'The Planned Amphibious Attack' in Peter H. Liddle (ed), *Passchendaele in Perspective* (London: Leo Cooper, 1997) pp201-12

49 J. H. Boraston (ed), *Sir Douglas Haig's Dispatches* (London: Dent, new ed 1979) pp301, 330-1; B. L. Montgomery, 'High Command in War, 21st Army Group, Germany, June 1945', pp5-8

50 Stephen Hart, *Montgomery and 'Colossal Cracks': The 21st Army Group in Northwest Europe, 1944-1945* (Westport, CT: Praeger, 2000)

51 Carlo D'Este, *Decision in Normandy* (London: Pan, 1984) pp352-4

52 Robin Prior and Trevor Wilson, *Command on the Western Front* (Oxford: Blackwell, 1992) p223

53 See Andrew A. Wiest, 'Haig, Gough and Passchendaele' in Sheffield, *Leadership and Command*, op cit, pp77-92

54 G. D. Sheffield, *Leadership in the Trenches* (London: Macmillan, forthcoming); John Terraine, *Douglas Haig The Educated Soldier* (London: Leo Cooper, 1990) pp178-9

55 A. J. A. Morris, *The Letters of Lieutenant-Colonel Charles a Court Repington* (Stroud: Sutton for Army Records Society, 1999) pp32-4

56 Robert Rhodes James, *Gallipoli* (London: Papermac, 1989) pp313-5. See also C. E. W. Bean, ed Kevin Fewster *Frontline Gallipoli: C. E. W. Bean's Diary from the Trenches* (Sydney: Allen & Unwin, 1990) pp159-60

57 Stephen Badsey, 'Haig and the Press' in Bond and Cave, op cit, pp186-7, 190

58 Clifford Kinvig, *Scapegoat: General Percival of Singapore* (London: Brassey's, 1996) pp200-1

59 Nigel Hamilton, *Monty: Master of the Battlefield 1942-1944* (London, Hamish Hamilton, 1983) pp79-81, 263-4, 532-5; Ronald Lewin, *Montgomery as Military Commander*, op cit, pp243-6, 271

Chapter 26

Coalition war: the Anglo-American experience

Dennis E. Showalter

'Yanks are like any other native troops, old boy. They'll do well enough with white officers.' Forty years after its delivery, this one-line comment brought a flush of rage to the face of the dignified senior professor who had been its victim as a junior officer in the aftermath of the 1943 Battle of Kasserine Pass. On the other side of the world, in the same time-frame, an American general exploded to his diary – and to anyone in hearing range – about 'Limeys' who neither wanted to fight nor knew how to fight for their south Asian empire.[1]

In two World Wars, one 'police action', and half a dozen peacemaking and peacekeeping operations during this century, British and US forces have stood side by side in combat. The 'special relationship' so beloved of Winston Churchill has been challenged at times by both parties. The alliance between the world's principal English-speaking powers is nevertheless generally recognised as a model of its type, sustained by a mixture of interest and affinity that to date has defied all solvents.[2] Even in the years between the end of the First World War and the Washington Naval Conference of 1932, the respective navies were rivals rather than potential enemies. The US contingency plans for war with Britain were taken no more seriously than Canada's army took its projections of a strike into the United States.[3] Brian Holden Reid appropriately likens the Anglo-American relationship, at least in the Second World War, to a long-term marriage on the companionate model, with both partners recognising the importance of mutual harmony publicly expressed. Mutual incomprehension tempered by occasional fundamental disagreements did not exclude 'a measure of tolerance and fruitful union'.[4]

On levels of policy and strategy the word 'large' might well be added to that quotation. The Roosevelt-Churchill connection, the Combined Chiefs of Staff and the Combined Bomber Offensive, the sharing of the Ultra secret, for example, remain archetypes of institutional co-operation during wartime. In personal contexts the turbulent Eisenhower-Montgomery and Montgomery-Patton relationships continue to inspire both scholars and popular writers. General Joseph Stilwell's sulphurous evaluations of Field Marshal Wavell and his contemporaries are balanced by Field Marshal William Slim's more subtle filleting of his American ally.[5] Such rocks and shoals, however, are generally presented in terms of personalities. Neither Montgomery nor Patton was regarded as an easy man in his own military culture; that they raised each other's blood pressure is no particular surprise. It was not the British who gave Stilwell the nickname 'Vinegar Joe', while his comments on his Chinese counterparts, including Chiang Kai-chek, make his strictures on the British seem almost affectionate.[6]

More common were expressions of warm mutual regard, such as those between Dwight Eisenhower and Admiral Sir Andrew Browne Cunningham. One was an American Midwesterner who had never seen a large body of water before coming to West Point. The other was perhaps the quintessential sea dog of the Second World War, one of the last of his kind in the Royal Navy. Yet Eisenhower described Cunningham as 'one of the finest individuals that I ever met', while ABC called Eisenhower 'forceful, able, direct, and foreseeing… We soon became fast friends.'[7] And if Eisenhower was notoriously conciliatory, Cunningham did not bestow his friendship lightly even within his own service, and had no reason to sweeten his opinion of Eisenhower when he wrote those words.

Such politesse should not be stretched too far. To extend Holden Reid's marital metaphor, it is not unusual for a companionate relationship to develop a significant affective element as well. That is not to be confused with passion – or with intimacy. In neither World War, and on no other occasion offering an alternative, did the British and the Americans interface directly on operational and tactical levels to a significant degree and as a matter of course. Exceptions did exist. The American destroyers and battleships dispatched to Europe in 1917-18 operated under British command and were integrated into the British system. They were also drawn from a fleet whose senior officers were on the whole strongly anglophile. It was scarcely accidental that the commander of the US force assigned to the Grand Fleet as the 6th Battle Squadron was a southern gentleman. Rear Admiral Hugh Rodman was skilled in playing bridge and composing a mint julep – and entertained no exaggerated notions about US operational independence. Admiral Sir David Beatty, his staff officers and subordinates offered a corresponding minimum of critical asides about American competence and American folkways.[8]

In general, however, both allies have operated under the principle that good fences make good military neighbours. During the Second World War the US 8th Air Force handled daylight operations; RAF Bomber Command took over by night. The escort and hunter-killer groups of the Battle of the Atlantic were nationally homogeneous. The closest thing to a joint ground formation in the English-speaking armies was the American-Canadian 1st Special Service Force – less than 3,000 men strong, and firmly under US command during its short operational life. In Korea the initial British contribution of a brigade was increased to an independent division within a year – not least to get out from under the thumb of a US Army whose performance to date had inspired little confidence in its allies.[9] In the Persian Gulf a British brigade again became a division as soon as enough troops could be borrowed from everywhere else.

That behaviour was in part objectively determined. In the Second World War fundamental differences in ship design and operational concepts made comprehensive integration of RN and USN a matter of mixing apples and oranges – both unpeeled. In 1945 mutually welcome wardroom exchanges of ice-cream for liquor did not obscure the British Pacific Fleet's limited adaptability to the long-range power projection operations in which the US Navy specialised. Even the ability of armoured British flight decks to shrug off kamikaze strikes was recognised in both navies as being compensated by reduced aircraft capacity, which in turn limited their ability to mount sustained mass attacks.[10] In the air, no one seriously argued that the Lancaster and the B-17 could effectively exchange roles under normal conditions. Apocryphal, but no less illustrative, is the story of the two fighter pilots arguing the respective merits of the P-51D and the Spitfire XIV. The Brit suggested resolving the question by a gun-camera duel – but backed down when the American stipulated the encounter take place over Berlin.

Americans in the Second World War might welcome British 'compo' rations as an alternative to their own forms of dietary monotony. British troops in Korea sought US-issue winter gear at every opportunity. Nevertheless, everything from right-hand-drive versus left-hand-drive vehicles to a difference of .003 in the basic calibre of small arms ammunition spoke for keeping British and US ground forces in their own administrative 'chimneys'. Nor could section/squad tactics shift readily between norms established by the Bren light machine-gun and the bolt-action Lee-Enfield and the essentially different requirements imposed by the superficially similar US mixture of Garands and Browning Automatic Rifles.[11]

Command styles differed significantly as well. To American officers, functioning in a staff system borrowed from the French and based on the methods of the first Napoleon, British headquarters sometimes seemed informal to the point of confusion. The British for their part had little difficulty finding American staff approaches inflexible and hierarchical. British senior officers carried arms as an afterthought. Pistols, carbines and hand grenades festooned even – or especially – American general officers. Even the languages of discourse could cause confusion. A vintage joke has a British officer commenting to a group of Americans that 'the men seem to have their tails well up', only to be greeted by blank looks and the question, 'Up what, sir?' In a similar anecdote the British company commander who informed a supporting US artillery battery that things were 'a bit sticky' in his sector was less impressed when the transatlantic gunners interpreted his communication as 'all reasonably quiet on the front'.

Yet far more than sea or air, land war interaction invited competition and comparison. Land-war performance increasingly set the standard of military effectiveness for both allies in both World Wars. In sharp contrast to the prevailing circumstances on the sea and in the air, the tools, the techniques and, not least, the enemy were more similar than different. On a deeper level, British soldiers in both conflicts prided themselves on an 'acquired professionalism' – a mixture of technical competence and 'character', artisanal, pragmatic, and with a skill at arms in no way diminished by a surface casualness. The British Army had by 1918 developed a comprehensive skill in large-scale operations unmatched in the world. For all the inter-war discussion of indirect approaches, Britain after Dunkirk also viewed itself as a land power – if for no better reason than that somehow, at some time, the Army would have to return to the continent in something other than a mop-up role. By late 1942 it was clear that sea and air power were not in any combination going to cause the demise of Nazi Germany in anything like an acceptable time-frame. Nor were the alternatives of allowing the Red Army to march to the Rhine, or becoming an auxiliary to the Americans, particularly appealing.[12]

Across the Atlantic the US Army applied to both World Wars a full-scale industrial model of mobilisation and preparation. Men were drafted, equipment produced, officers trained, and formations organised on assembly lines. Doctrine and training were both implemented on a uniform basis. Command competence was geared to a 'high average' standard, with 'defective parts' ruthlessly discarded at all levels. That last was achieved as much by random purging of unit officer corps as by any systematic processes. The result was nevertheless an inner-directed, performance-driven mentality that was confident in its own capacities to adapt and adjust, prone to take neither advice nor criticism on fundamental levels from outsiders.[13]

With such matrices it is scarcely surprising that grass-roots gear-stripping characterised Anglo-American interaction in ground operations during both World Wars. At the same time, tactical-level friction – with or without the fog of battle – not only diminished with contact, but also dissipated with a speed and comprehensiveness unusual, when not unique, in alliance relationships. This essay illustrates these related points by three case studies. The first is the training and combat experience of US units, especially the II Corps, with the BEF during the First World War. The second presents the relationships of another II US Corps to the British First Army in the North African campaign of 1942-43. The third goes deep into the D-Day campaign, to the side-by-side engagement of the British 43rd and US 84th Divisions at Geilenkirchen in November 1944, under a British corps performing a mission for the US 9th Army.

Scholars of the Burma Campaign may wonder why the experience of the Chindits under Stilwell in 1944 has been omitted. While there can be no doubt that Stilwell's prejudice against his allies did nothing to avert the virtual annihilation of the long-range penetration brigades placed under his command, Stilwell also destroyed the American counterpart of the Chindits, 'Merrill's Marauders', in essentially the same way and essentially for the same reason. His insistence that these light infantry forces engage in sustained combat whatever the cost was, in short, independent of their national identity.[14]

The fledgling AEF was willing enough to take its cues from Brits. Neither General John J. Pershing's insistence on maintaining American operational independence, nor his well-founded suspicion that American troops were regarded as a source of direct replacements by his exhausted allies, nor his conviction, less well-founded, that the British and French armies had become excessively trench-bound, kept him from recognising that the AEF had much to learn and little time to waste in becoming operationally effective.

Original proposals called for six American divisions to be moved to France in British ships and trained by the British, with the personnel available for combat duties in an emergency. A month's preliminary instruction, three weeks or so attached to British units in the line, and a final three to four weeks rear-area training at regimental level, was considered enough to fit the Americans for service under their own higher commands.[15]

Eventually a dozen AEF divisions would pass through British hands that wrote reports consistently praising the quality of the men and their eagerness to learn. The regimental officers are just as consistently described as possessing more good will than experience. The sharpest criticisms reflect American staff work, repeatedly described as slipshod and worse.[16] At bottom, the Americans felt welcomed. Correspondence, internal or with AEF headquarters, regularly expressed the open British desire to keep the Americans on their front, to the point of letting them fight as divisions and corps. To the increasingly self-confident Americans such a wish was only logical. The pleasure of being wanted was, moreover, relatively untainted by concern over the possible fate of AEF divisions at the hands of 'British butchers and bunglers'. Instead the everyday administrative abilities of British staffs seem to have made a generally favourable impression – a far cry from the images projected by Sassoon, Graves and Wilfred Owen.[17]

What might be called social antagonisms remained undeveloped – arguably, in part, because the Americans regarded attacks on their staff work as proof that the AEF came to France to fight, not keep books. At this stage of the war, moreover, British regimental officers were arguably drawn from a broader spectrum of society than the middle-class businessmen and professional men who largely filled the commissioned ranks of the National Guard and National Army regiments assigned to the British for training. Stereotypes involving 'hairy heels' and 'chinless wonders' had correspondingly less opportunity to develop.[18]

Taken as a whole, US and British soldiers found few points of common reference. Canadians and Australians, however, took to the Yanks as drinking partners and allies in the endemic rear-area brawls with Tommies and redcaps. Americans priding themselves on their toughness came to stand in near awe of the Australians' capacity for liquor and their quick reactions to a fellow digger in trouble. 'Cooo–ee' became a rally cry for the AEF as well as the AIF in some towns – to the disconcertion of already overextended military police.

The BEF's behaviour at higher levels also left frequent good memories. Normal British Army ceremonial, such as the playing of units into and out of a posting by regimental bands, made a substantial impression on the AEF's uniformed civilians, especially when bagpipes were part of the event. Nor did senior officers inevitably live down to American stereotypes of stuffiness. One divisional commander took a turn at bat in a baseball game and – presumably with some connivance – hit a home run, a feat far less usual in 1918 than at the end of the 20th century.[19]

British and Imperial regimental customs ranged from the ceremonial eating of leeks to the ceremonial beheading of buffalo, and swinging at a soft toss that did not even bounce was a correspondingly minor challenge to an old cricketer. Of more importance was Pershing's concern that his men were acculturating to the BEF a bit too well for his liking. The issue came to a head in July 1918. For weeks previously Sir John Monash, commander of the Australian Corps, had been planning a limited set-piece attack on the fortified village of Hamel. Monash, a leading exponent of the managed, semi-mobile battle whose doctrines were being developed in the BEF, intended Hamel as a test-bed for tactics to be used later on a wider scale, to crack open the entire German front. He had integrated into his planning, as mop-up troops, several companies from the US division attached to his corps for training. Two days before the attack Pershing learned of it and demanded that the Americans be withdrawn. Monash, as much prima donna as tactical artist, refused to mount the operation without them. The BEF High Command acceded to the man on the spot – its collective tongue firmly in its cheek.[20]

Hamel was a complete success, with the Americans doing particularly well. Pershing responded by asking, with more vigour than courtesy, that they be returned to American command. Sir Douglas Haig, who saw the end of the war in sight, negotiated the issue with more finesse than is usually ascribed to that dour Scots Presbyterian. In the end he succeeded in retaining two divisions. As a compromise, he also accepted the II Corps headquarters, which Pershing insisted should exercise operational command of them.

The 27th and 30th Divisions were what Russell Weigley in a later context would describe as 'well brought up'. They had their origins in the National Guard, the 27th from New York, the 30th from Tennessee and the Carolinas. Like all AEF divisions, transfers and drafts of personnel had heavily altered their composition, but the regiments' identities had remained local, with all the positive and negative aspects that implied. Both divisions had been with the BEF since early June. Elements of both had seen front-line duty. Obvious incompetents had been weeded out of the command structures. At their full strengths of 28,000 each, they were welcome in a BEF whose replacement depots were feeling the strain of a continuous offensive – the Australian battalions, for example, averaged fewer than 400 men apiece, and the corps staff was already planning to break up the weakest for replacements.

The progress of that offensive offered an ideal sector for their use. By mid-September the British advance had reached the main German position, the Hindenburg Line. One of its key features was the St Quentin Canal, and the logical choice to supervise its capture was Monash. The Australian Corps, however, was worn thin, and Monash's superior, Fourth Army commander Sir Henry Rawlinson, offered the Americans as compensation. The Yanks were fresh, there were a lot of them, and Monash had enough confidence in his planning abilities to believe that he and his experienced staff could compensate for American deficiencies in that area. One problem remained: what to do with II Corps headquarters? Monash suggested 'co-locating' it with his own HQ, with American officers informally understudying their Australian counterparts during the preparatory stages and exercising command once the attack began. Monash, of course, would command the entire operation. That solution was acceptable and more to Major General George Read. Assigned to command II Corps because no one obviously more qualified was available, he was a cavalryman and had a good cavalryman's situational awareness. Monash and his people knew how to do these kinds of things. Read was willing to swallow his pride and, knowing Pershing, abandon all hope of favour and preferment, accepting 'makee-learn' status for the good of the service and the sake of the men he commanded. May all two-star generals in any army have the same strength of character!

Read's decision was facilitated by his ability to read intelligence reports. The St

Quentin Canal sector's defences, based on an underground canal over 5 miles long dug in the days of Napoleon, were among the most formidable on the entire Western Front. Faute de mieux, moreover, the 27th and 30th Divisions were handed the sharp and sticky end of the job. Monash proposed to send them forward on a narrow front, by 1918 standards, of 6,000 yards to storm the main German position, cross the tunnel mound, and reach the secondary defences in an advance totalling 4,400 yards. They would then be relieved by two Australian divisions who would carry the attack forward.

Critics tend to agree that this proposal was not Monash at his best. He was expecting a longer advance from the Americans than he had ever demanded of his Australians, and against fixed defences. He was relying correspondingly on tanks and artillery to bring the green North Americans on to their objectives – most of the Fourth Army's artillery, and no fewer than 70 tanks. Firepower, however, had not been enough to bring inexperienced British divisions forward in the war's earlier stages. Rawlinson was sufficiently concerned to modify the general plan by extending the attack's front and incorporating a surprise crossing of the Canal itself further south. He did not, however, address the details of Monash's intentions for the American divisions – not least because he had more immediate problems with some of his British formations and their commanders.[21]

The devil proved to be in the details. Things began going wrong when American units were constrained to expend strength securing their own start lines because of the failure of worn-out British troops to do so. The 27th Division's preliminary operations in particular failed almost entirely. And 'almost' was the operative word. The division's reports described parties of New Yorkers holding on in the front German positions, with large numbers of wounded also remaining in no-man's-land.[22] Such information was typical from inexperienced troops in their first big 'show', but the Americans were allies, not clients. Their officers could not be ignored when they protested that the original artillery fire plan for the main attack would destroy their own men. Then a second decision, taken months ago, bore its unexpected fruit. US divisions were to be equipped with French artillery pieces. In consequence the artillery brigades of the AEF divisions training with the British had been detached and sent to French schools. So the 27th and 30th Divisions had none of their own gunners to take the moral responsibility of firing on wounded or isolated Americans. As a consequence Rawlinson ordered the artillery to avoid shelling German positions, and authorised the barrage accompanying the attack to begin 1,000 yards ahead of the 27th's start lines.

He did his allies no favours. At this stage of the war any experienced formation recognised the value of amicide: better to take 5 or even 10 per cent casualties from 'friendly fire' than to bear the consequences of losing the barrage. The artillery preparation itself, influenced by bad weather, was sufficiently below BEF standards as to be described as 'desultory' by the Australian official historian[23] – who was in a good position to notice. When the 27th Division went forward on the foggy morning of 29 September, its advance elements faced heavy fire from machine-gun positions they could not see, immediately supplemented by artillery batteries that escaped the initial barrage. The 27th had a full battalion of tanks supporting it, and even their Australian advisors expected much from the armour. But the tankers were American, as green as their infantry. The AFVs that did not ditch were destroyed by German guns. Over half the battalion's tanks were out of action in the first few minutes; the rest were more concerned with survival than support.

When the 3rd Australian Division moved forward, it found the American infantry engaged in a rat-fight with Germans who had been overlooked as they were overrun, reinforced by others emerging from passages in the canal tunnel. Instead of pushing forward themselves, the Australians became drawn into sector clearing. At day's end the main Hindenburg position was essentially intact in the 27th Division's sector.

The 30th Division had a better day – at least by comparison. It had the benefit of the kind of barrage veterans called fine enough to light pipes at. Its sergeants and lieutenants kept the leading elements close to the shell bursts. And if the southern boys who were still the heart of most rifle companies were not au courant with the latest forms of combined arms tactics, they knew how to use rifles, bayonets and grenades well enough to overrun the tunnel and push toward their final objective. But, like their British predecessors at Loos and on the Somme, the Americans paid too little attention to securing their gains. The supporting lines pushed forward instead of clearing dugouts and shell holes. The 5th Australian Division, as it advanced behind the Americans, encountered in some sectors virtually complete German positions, with the Americans fighting an increasingly desperate all-directions battle. Ironically, the amalgamation of American and Allied troops so feared by Pershing became at least a tactical reality here, with Australian subalterns and enlisted men assuming de facto command of groups of Americans willing enough to fight once someone showed them not so much how to fight, but where to look for enemies. By the end of the day the 30th Division's sector was clear, but little progress had been made in widening the breach it had made in the Hindenburg line's defences.[24]

The American divisions, as planned, were taken off the line next day. Rawlinson, initially inclined to scapegoat the Americans for the initial failure to achieve more against the Hindenburg Line, confined his strictures to his diary – and to a phone call to BEF headquarters on 29 September, suggesting that it would be necessary to withdraw the Americans from the battle at an early date.[25] BEF manpower shortages made that impossible. Instead a week later the Americans relieved the Australians, this time under command of their own II Corps. With one division leapfrogging the other, they fought their way forward steadily and unspectacularly until 20 October, when Rawlinson again pulled the Americans out. The 27th and 30th had suffered over 13,000 casualties between them while receiving no replacements, and were still combat effective – a tribute to the staying power of the big AEF divisions. Their fighting power was indicated by the award to the 30th Division of 12 Congressional Medals of Honor, more than any other AEF division.

Read had fought his corps competently in the last stages; he and his staff seem to have profited correspondingly from the close association with Monash. Despite some post-war challenges to specific criticisms of, in particular, the 27th Division's initial performance, reports, histories and the reminiscences of their officers and men combine to indicate that both the 27th and the 30th Divisions considered

themselves well treated and well handled in the BEF matrix. In the words of
General Read's report of 18 December 1918, 'it appeared to be the established
policy of the [British] Fourth Army to supply the II Corps with every possible
assistance and to protect American lives every whit as carefully as the lives of
British troops.' Read went on to acknowledge tactical shortcomings, which he
ascribed in part to training in open warfare that emphasised headlong advances
but neglected such niceties as liaison and mopping-up operations.[26] From almost a
century's perspective, in short, the experience of the II Corps suggests the wisdom,
in a limited military sense, of closer co-operation with the British than Pershing
was willing to consider.

The circumstances of the next Anglo-American battlefield interface could
hardly have been more different. 'Operation Torch', the 1942 invasion of French
North Africa, was the wrong war, or at least the wrong theatre, for both armies – a
sideshow to their respective principal concerns. In contrast to 1918, the forces
involved were small – especially relative to the headquarters committed. The
mentalities of each army differed significantly from its predecessor. This time it was
the Americans who were confident – almost exuberantly so at operational and
tactical levels. Instead of the improvised formations of 1918, the US was sending
divisions that had existed in their current forms since 1940. Their draftees,
National Guardsmen and regulars, had gone through some of the most elaborate
large-scale peacetime training in any modern army's history. Under forced draft
the US Army had developed doctrines and weapons systems specifically to wage
modern mobile war. Relevant combat experience was literally non-existent. Field
forces in fact manifested only 'the semblance of preparedness'. The Army had
nevertheless come far enough that, at regimental and divisional levels, Americans
believed that they had little to learn from allies that had spent the previous two
years showing their backs to the Germans.[27]

The British ground forces committed to 'Operation Torch', by contrast, were at
best uncertain – both of their general operational effectiveness and their specific
readiness to fight the kind of war expected in Tunisia. The Second BEF, driven into
the sea at Dunkirk, had since rebuilt itself, but essentially as a home defence force
and on a small-unit level. The British Army of 1942 was still learning how to fight
on divisional scales, to say nothing of corps and army levels. The formations sent
to North Africa were a distinctly mixed bag, ranging from the regulars of the 4th
through the second-line Territorials of the 46th to a 78th assembled from three
previously independent brigades, with a predictably low level of cohesion. As late
as May 1943 Major General Sir Francis Tuker, commanding the Eighth Army's
elite 4th Indian Division, described the training of the formations out from home
as deficient even after six months in the field.[28]

It was not a promising matrix for mid-level co-operation. Matters were not
improved by a complex command structure that provided a Supreme
Headquarters (joint), a field army (British) and two corps, one British and one
American, for an initial commitment of half a dozen divisions. If some of US II
Corps's problems in 1918 had been exacerbated by a high command that was too
busy to notice them, in 1942 underemployed staff officers of both armies would
have much to answer for as relations grew strained. And there was much to strain

them. Eisenhower, still feeling his way in command, tended to micromanage. First Army commander Sir Kenneth Anderson, who cultivated the persona of a dour lowland Scot, had to be reminded to submit his daily situation reports directly to Eisenhower instead of forwarding them directly to London.[29] US II Corps chief Major General Lloyd Fredendall reciprocated heartily despite admonitions.[30]

Initially, Allied commander Dwight Eisenhower and his subordinates intended to minimise opportunities for friction by keeping British and US contingents under their own respective higher commands. But troop dispositions in 'Operation Torch' were shaped by the distance between the landing zones and the operationally relevant ground further east. That required the Allies to deploy forward as fast as possible – and encouraged the tendency, already strong in both armies, to fight by improvised task forces rather than by tables of organisation.

The reasons for this phenomenon included reflex emulation of perceived German models – the battle group – and a misunderstanding of the nature of flexibility. Its consequences put too many units under strange commanders and alongside strange counterparts. Hart Force and Blade Force were the consistently reshuffled Combat Commands of the US 1st Armored Division – all the various combat teams and task forces were sources of uncertainty and confusion to inexperienced field and general officers. Anderson's suggestion to redesignate the First British Army the First Allied Army 'for local morale purposes' was eclipsed as the Germans opened the North African branch of their school of tactical tuition.[31] Erwin Rommel, Hans-Juergen von Arnim and their subordinates drew no significant distinction between British and American fighting power. If the Americans suffered humiliation on the larger scale, at Sidi Bou Zid and Kasserine Pass in February 1943, their British counterparts did no better in similar circumstances.

While negative evidence is always dubious, regimental-level records from both armies contain few recriminations against each other's fighting spirit or fighting power. In the first drive on Tunis during December 1942, British Guardsmen and American infantry bled side by side in the futile attack on Longstop Hill. British and American gunners formed a single fire unit to support a hard-hammered British brigade in the last stages of the fighting for Kasserine Pass. General George Patton, hardly a noted anglophile, personally decorated the commander of the 1st Derbyshire Yeomanry, whose armoured cars for months scouted for and fought alongside the Americans of II Corps, with the Silver Star. That is an award for valour in combat, not presence near it.[32]

Most of the problems of Anglo-US interaction, in short, were at higher command levels. In the spring of 1943 both the British and the US contingents in Tunisia responded internally to defeat – overhauling doctrines, relieving officers, restructuring training, and replacing equipment. Matters grew more complicated in January 1943 when Sir Harold Alexander was appointed Ground Forces commander in North Africa. Alexander, a man most histories legitimately praise for his tact, found Anderson and the Americans both professionally wanting. Anderson was sackable, and in fact saw no further field service. But Alexander's negative assessment of US fighting power was in sharp contrast to the BEF orthodoxies of a quarter-century earlier. 'They are soft, green, and quite untrained ... they lack the will to fight,' he declared to Brooke.[33]

One of Alexander's immediate solutions was to establish a system of schools and programmes to improve general levels of training. Intended for both armies, these were run by British officers. Alexander also established a network of liaison officers to advise their American counterparts. These men were as a group both experienced and competent. Their presence, however, was salt in an open wound to many Americans, despite Eisenhower's repeated insistence that he supported the policy.[34] Major General Ernest Harmon, for example, deliberately disregarded the brigadier assigned as liaison to his 1st Armored Division, preferring to risk relief by fighting his own battle.[35]

Alexander was not insensitive to the sensibilities of his allies. His policies as Ground Commander in Tunisia were not developed in response to that particular situation. Instead they replicated those he had implemented in the Western Desert in collaboration with Montgomery. There, too, Alexander had emphasised restoring unit cohesion and unity of command, working to create an army from what had become a structure of military fiefdoms. At this point Eisenhower took his first real steps toward great captain status – not in the field, but by an increasingly ruthless suppression of national backbiting wherever he found it. He informed Fredendall that when placing American troops under British command he did so '…unreservedly and expect any officer receiving an order from his next battlefield superior to regard that order as emanating from me and on up the line from the President himself'. No less remarkable in contemporary contexts was Eisenhower's blistering of the war correspondents, warning them that anyone persisting in attempts to initiate British-American controversy would be removed from the theatre.[36]

That recognition came more slowly than Eisenhower might wish, but it came nevertheless. In early April British IX Corps commander Sir John Crocker criticised in the presence of reporters the performance of a US division under his command. Alexander described the same division as being 'no good' – to George S. Patton, who had replaced Fredendall in command of II US Corps. Patton reacted by demanding in his diary that, 'God damn all British… I will bet that Ike does nothing about it. I would rather be commanded by an Arab.' His official response, however, was to tell Alexander that the division in question was a National Guard formation from the Midwest, where isolationism was prevalent. Its removal in disgrace from the front on the authority of a British general would have corresponding political repercussions![37]

Apart from suggesting that Patton well understood the strategy of the indirect approach, his point was not lost among senior Allied officers who increasingly recognised that neither Britain nor the US had divisions to waste – and that displacing one's own command anxieties on to counterparts with different accents led nowhere. Ernie Harmon reacted to Anderson's criticism of his plan to capture Bizerte by describing the Scot as a 'son of a bitch', then felt 'a little foolish' when Anderson warmly congratulated him on his eventual success.[38]

Alliance rivalry was also partly resolved by a paradigm shift. The catalyst again was Patton. One of his first official acts in command of II Corps was to issue a report deploring a 'total lack of air cover' for his troops. The officer responsible for tactical air support in the theatre was New Zealand-born Air Marshal Sir Arthur

Coningham. He had spent years attempting to correct what he considered the dilution of air power by the demands of ground officers who essentially regarded planes as flying artillery. He resented the slur against his USAAF subordinates, who had been following his orders and policies. He responded by suggesting that II Corps was not battleworthy in its present condition.[39]

This was exactly the kind of high-level situation Eisenhower was in position to address. He ordered Coningham to apologise. After a bitter personal exchange Patton accepted, and was further mollified when the theatre's senior air officers, RAF Air Marshal Tedder and USAAF General Spaatz, also visited his headquarters to cement relations – but relations between air and ground, not British and Americans.[40]

Senior officers in any military system are alpha personalities who reach the top by force of will and character at least as much as by demonstrated skill in warmaking. This is particularly true in a conflict's first stages. At all times, however, it makes for levels of stress and antagonism that can shock the hardiest academic veteran of departmental and common-room feuds, but are normative in high military commands. The best palliatives – there is no real cure – are experience and victory. As the Mediterranean campaign developed, British and US senior officers might not like each other. They might, to refer only to Alexander's relationship with Mark Clark during the Italian campaign, not even respect each other. They did, however, developed a culture of co-operation that not only survived the tests of Salerno and Anzio, but also incorporated a positive dimension. By 1945 both the US 5th and the British Eighth Armies were legitimate international commands, transferring divisions between them as the operational situation indicated, and each glad to have the other's divisions under its command when the going got worse than usual.[41]

The third case study is less familiar and on a smaller scale. It took place as the war in western Europe was entering its final phase, with the Allies bumping up against the Siegfried Line. The Westwall was less formidable than Nazi propaganda pronounced; its tank traps and pill-boxes were nevertheless intimidating enough to the British and Americans facing them in November 1944. The German town of Geilenkirchen was one of the strong points of the line's northern sector, a threat to the left flank of the US 9th Army's projected advance into the Reich and too well defended to be 'bounced'. Army commander Lieutenant General William Simpson saw a possible solution. The British XXX Corps, of 21st Army Group, in the aftermath of Arnhem, had just moved into the line on the 9th Army's left. Simpson drove over to visit its commander, Lieutenant General Sir Brian Horrocks. Would Horrocks extend his sector a bit further south and assume responsibility for clearing Geilenkirchen and securing Simpson's route of advance? Horrocks declared that since he had only a single division available, he was unable to assist. Simpson then reciprocated by inviting Horrocks to dinner. There was a surprise guest: Supreme Allied Commander Dwight Eisenhower. When asked, with the full force of the now famous Eisenhower charm, if he was going to take Geilenkirchen, Horrocks responded that he could not do it with one division. Eisenhower turned to Simpson and said, 'Give him one of ours.' Simpson offered the 84th Infantry – green but fresh and well trained. Horrocks demurred.

Was it fair, he asked, to send these men into their first action under a foreigner? When Eisenhower and Simpson brushed the issue aside, Horrocks found himself stuck with the bill for dinner: one strong point, to be delivered by the end of November.[42]

This incident indicated just how far Anglo-American co-operation had evolved in a quarter-century – or indeed in two years. Where Pershing grudged Americans in skirmishes under British command, Eisenhower was willing to commit a full division of them – and he had none to spare – to a frontal attack on fixed defences planned and executed by a British higher headquarters. Certain sub-texts of course existed. Geilenkirchen's capture was important to the 9th Army's general plans for attacking into Germany, but instead of having to allot two US divisions to the operation, the Americans were getting a fight at half price. Sir Brian Horrocks, moreover, was rightly regarded as one of the three or four best corps commanders in the Allied armies – the kind of general one wanted in command of a tough job with a short time limit.

Even when full allowances are made for these and similar factors, however, it is clear that Eisenhower was departing essentially from the Pershing matrix. And there is another kind of irony in a British general being seduced, sweet-talked, or conned – depending on one's perspective – by Americans into doing something against his better judgement. That shoe is stereotypically presented as being on the other national foot, whether Brits see themselves as playing the role Greece played to an unsophisticated Rome, or Americans grumble about allies far too clever for anyone else's good.

The two divisions committed to the Geilenkirchen operation similarly reflected and challenged national stereotypes. The British 43rd Infantry Division was as close to an archetype as anything the British Liberation Army could show. It was a pre-war territorial formation whose battalions were drawn from the West Country of England. Its Wessex character had been diluted by a steady influx of replacements drawn from almost every regiment in the British Army, plus a few Canadian officers 'loaned' to the British to make up for their heavy losses in subalterns. Most of the rifle companies had turned over their strength two or three times since the division first landed in France. The 43rd nevertheless stressed regimental identity and regimental pride as a central element of its fighting morale – even if a Bren gunner of the Dorsetshire Regiment spoke in broad Lancashire to his Number 2 from Nottingham in the Midlands.

The US 84th was a 'cookie-cutter' division. Created from a paper existence in the reserves in 1942, it drew its men from every state in the American Union, and for practical purposes created its own traditions. Where the 43rd had taken combat losses, the 84th, like most American divisions sent to Europe in late 1944, had been milked for cadres and replacements. Its ranks had been refilled with a mixture of men from the Air Force, the Army Service Forces, and a special programme for sending high-IQ draftees to college that was closed down when riflemen seemed more important than specialists. The division, however, had taken pains to assimilate its new faces and, despite the transfers, many of its men had been with their regiments and companies longer than their counterparts of the 43rd, and took corresponding pride in their outfits.

That pride showed in an initial emphasis on 'spit and polish' of a kind usually associated with the British. In contrast, the 43rd's casual attitude to uniform regulations might have almost been American. The respective commanding generals also challenged stereotypes. The 84th's Brigadier General Alexander Bolling was a West Point graduate whose appearance and demeanour would not have been out of place in the common room of a minor English public school, while the 43rd's Ivor Thomas looked and acted the archetype of a 'warrior stud' as described by David Hackworth – a hard man brooking no nonsense.[43]

Congruence and transgression increased with the final preparations for the attack. Briefings and orders groups included officers from both divisions – again providing opportunities to compare methods and mores. The British seemed informal to the point of carelessness. The Americans appeared to waste time on procedures. As was usual at this stage of the war, the artillerymen faced the least trouble developing common fire plans for both expected and emergency situations. During the next week British 25-pounders and American 105 and 155 howitzers would provide near seamless support throughout the corps sector.

That, however, was only a beginning of Allied tactical co-operation. When the Americans jumped off at 7.00am on 18 November, some of them at least were fortified by the pre-battle tot of rum to which they were entitled by virtue of being under British command.[44] They advanced behind British-manned flail tanks, specialised assault vehicles that beat paths through the German minefields with heavy chains, while American engineers on foot marked the safe routes. The flails were American: converted US Shermans. They were not the only armoured anomalies. One of the less familiar ironies of the D-Day campaign was that a US Army priding itself on its mechanised character was not always able to provide armoured support, even a single battalion, to its infantry divisions. British divisions by contrast seldom went into a major attack without having a full tank brigade, three regiments (equivalent to US battalions) under command.

The 84th was armourless, so Horrocks detached the Sherwood Rangers from the 43rd's supporting 8th Armoured Brigade and placed it under Bolling's command. The Rangers were mighty men of war, veterans of the Western Desert who adapted better than most of the old Eighth Army hands to the demands of war in Europe.[45] And in the words of one private of the 84th, 'their very name ... seemed to give then a dash of bravado which couldn't but help our morale.'[46]

The Rangers were equipped not with British tanks, but Shermans, exponentially superior to any British medium tank at this stage of the war. They now played a key role in a US division's attack in a form of reverse lend-lease never intended by Churchill or Roosevelt. The Rangers' leading tanks bogged to their bellies in liquid mud, but by 9.00am a few reached open country and caught up with the American infantry. They blasted pill-boxes with high explosives and machine-gun fire. They challenged minefields, with one officer blown out of three tanks in succession, then reading poetry to settle his nerves. When an American company was caught in the open, four Shermans of the Rangers charged to its rescue, silencing the pill-boxes while ignoring the anti-tank guns that knocked out all four in quick succession. Once in Geilenkirchen, British tanks blew up strong points while GIs kept away German bazooka men.

It was the same for the next five days. The 84th and the Rangers had never trained together, and would never fight together again. The division and the regiment were 'warriors for the working day', existing now only in records and memories. But over half a century the words of an American lieutenant resonate: 'I was sold on the British. Those boys were good. There's not a man in my company who will say there's anything wrong with a British soldier because of the support we got from those tankers.'[47]

British voices are less forthcoming. A soldier of the Somerset Light Infantry, on relieving an American regiment, described the Yanks as 'a very green lot ... always walking around in the open in broad daylight', and too ready to substitute flares and tripwires for aggressive patrolling. A British battalion commander gave an American counterpart a seminar on the advantages of depth in the attack when the latter officer failed to understand the throwaway warning, 'Don't put all your goods in the shop window'. Since British and American doctrines on that subject at battalion level were essentially the same, US Lieutenant Colonel Lloyd Gomes merits full marks for tact and flexibility under stress – the same stress that influenced his British counterpart's behaviour.[48]

The 43rd had no direct US equivalent of the Sherwood Rangers to change its collective mind in the next week. But at the same time the division showed no significant concern for its right flank. If anything, the British may have concentrated a bit too narrowly on the enemy to their front; patrols from the 84th reported frequent difficulty making contact with their British counterparts. And when a British battalion took one chance too many and was cut off behind German lines, it was the Americans that Horrocks contacted, asking them to push their advance in order to relieve pressure on the British.[49]

For two days Bolling's forward elements floundered forward in waist-deep water, across terrain where even the Rangers could not bring tanks, against artillery that had every yard of ground registered and pill-boxes with unchecked fields of fire. In the end fewer than a dozen of the trapped British made it back to their own lines. But no doubt was ever raised that the men of the 84th had done what they could, and more.

By nightfall on 23 November the battle for Geilenkirchen was over. Both divisions had been stopped by the same combination of mud, rain and Germans that had stabilised the entire front. The 84th reverted to US command. Its subsequent history suggests that it used Geilenkirchen as a springboard; that of the 43rd indicates that the division continued to be a hard fighting body of good plain cooks. Each remembered the other with appropriate and legitimate respect. In fighting power and fighting spirit there had been little to choose between them in front of Geilenkirchen.

In terms of fighting methods, two points characteristic of the campaign in general manifested themselves in this small-scale action. Independently of weather conditions, US units in Europe had consistent difficulty keeping combat power, as opposed to fire support, forward. Too often GIs found themselves tackling strong points and facing counter-attacks with what they could carry on their backs. For their part, British infantry were frequent victims of an organisation that kept rifle companies at a strength so low (usually under 100 in the line) that relatively few casualties reduced their fighting power to an unacceptable minimum.

The American problem was an indirect consequence of pooling. Giving each unit no more organic or attached resources than deemed absolutely necessary fostered a rearward control of support. The British seem to have been mesmerised by Sir Archibald Wavell's pre-war aphorism that the modern infantryman should be a combination of poacher, stalker, and cat-burglar; and kept their primary tactical unit, the rifle company, at a strength more appropriate for infiltration than breakthrough. In each case the consequence was the same.

In wider terms, Horrocks's sharp criticism of the 84th's failure to ensure that its forward elements had hot food and dry socks is an interesting reprise of 1918. He was answered to a degree by an American enlisted man, veteran of North Africa, Sicily and North West Europe, who responded, '...coming from America, the enlisted men were more self-reliant... From a British point of view our officers didn't take care of the men properly. From our own point of view, we didn't ask anybody to take care of us.'[50]

Boast or myth, it is a distinctively American statement – one, moreover, calculated to raise British hackles. Nevertheless, on those few occasions when the two armies have fought not merely side by side but arm in arm, the results in the trenches and the foxholes have replicated those at the levels of strategy and policy to a degree both soldiers and scholars might find unexpected.

Notes on contributors

Professor Dennis E. Showalter, Colorado College, Colorado Springs, USA
Dennis Showalter is Professor of History at Colorado College. He is President of the American Society for Military History, joint editor of War in History, and a Patron of the Second World War Experience Centre. His relevant publications include History in Dispute: World War II (2 vols. Detroit: St James, 2000) and Tannenberg: Clash of Empires (Hamden, CT: Archon, 1991).

Recommended reading

Hathaway, Robert M., *Ambiguous Partnership: Britain and America, 1944-47* (New York and Guildford: Columbia University Press, 1981)

Kimball, F. Warren (ed), *Churchill and Roosevelt: The Complete Correspondence* (Princeton: Princeton University Press, 1984)

Reynolds, David, *The Creation of the Anglo-American Alliance* (London: Europa, 1981)

Trask, David F., *The AEF and Coalition Warmaking* (Lawrence: Kansas University Press, 1993)

Woodward, David R., *Trial by Friendship: Anglo-American Relations, 1917-18* (Lexington: Kentucky University Press, 1993)

Notes

1   Joseph Stilwell, ed T. White *The Stilwell Papers* (New York: Sloan, 1948) pp163ff (and virtually passim)

2   On the wartime relationship see most recently F. Warren Kimball, *Forged in War: Roosevelt, Churchill, and the Second World War* (New York: HarperCollins, 1997); and Keith Sainsbury, *Churchill and Roosevelt at War: The War They Fought and the Peace They Hoped to Make* (New York: Macmillan, 1994)

3   Cf William R. Braisted, 'On the American Red and Red-Orange Plans, 1919-1939' in G. Jordan (ed), *Naval Warfare in the Twentieth Century, 1900-1945* (London: Croom Helm, 1977) pp167-85; and John Ferris, '"It Is Our Business to Command the Sea": the Last Decade of British Maritime Superiority , 1919-1929' in K. Nielsen and G. Kennedy (eds), *Far-Flung Lines: Studies in Imperial Defence in Honour of Donald Mackenzie Schurman* (London: Cass, 1996) pp124-70

4   Brian Holden Reid, 'Tensions in the Supreme Command: Anti-Americanism in the British Army, 1939-45' in J. White and B. Holden Reid (eds), *Americana: Essays in Memory of Marcus Cunliffe* (Hull: University of Hull, 1998) p336

5   Field Marshal Sir William Slim, *Defeat Into Victory* (London: Cassell, 1956) pp35-6, 220-2, 235-7

6   Stilwell, for example, regularly referred to Chiang as 'Peanut'.

7   This particular exchange is recorded in John Winton, *Cunningham* (London: John Murray, 1998) p278

8   Jerry W. Jones, *US Battleship Operations in World War I* (Annapolis, MD: Naval Institute, 1998) is the best overview. Rodman's *Yarns of a Kentucky Admiral* (Indianapolis: Bobbs-Merrill, 1928) show a solid 'good old boy' shrewdness and a retrospective amusement at the success with which he played his expected role.

9   This issue is a sub-text even in Jeffrey Grey's *The Commonwealth Armies and the Korean War* (Manchester: Manchester University, 1988) with its strong administrative/diplomatic focus. It is main text in almost every other British history of the war; see most recently Michael Hickey, *The Korean War: The West Confronts Communism* (London: John Murray, 1999)

10 Cf Correlli Barnett, *Engage the Enemy More Closely: The Royal Navy in the Second World War* (New York: Norton, 1991) pp877 passim; and Thomas Hone, Norman Friedman and Mark D. Mandeles, *American and British Aircraft Carrier Development, 1919-1941* (Annapolis, MD: Naval Institute, 1999) pp198-9

11 For some insight into the relatively uninvestigated issue of tactical differences at squad levels, see John A. English and Bruce I. Gudmundsson, *On Infantry* (New York: Praeger, rev ed 1994) pp108ff

12 Jonathan Bailey, 'The First World War and the Birth of the Modern Style of Warfare', Strategic and Combat Studies Institute Occasional Paper 22 (Camberley: SCSI, 1996) and David Fraser, *And We Shall Shock Them: The British Army in the Second World War* (London: Cassell, 1988) combine for a good overview of the Army's self-perception – which did not always dovetail with the evaluations of its numerous critics. Russell A. Hart, 'Learning Lessons: Military Adaptation and Innovation in the American, British, Canadian, and German Armies during the 1944 Normandy Campaign', Vol I (Dissertation, Ohio State University, 1997) offers a solid comparative analysis of the respective patterns of training and doctrine.

13 I am grateful to my former colleague at the US Military Academy, Captain Wade Markel, for sharing his preliminary research on the US Army officer corps of the Second World War. Peter Mansoor, *The GI Offensive in Europe: The Triumph of American Infantry Divisions, 1941-1945* (Lawrence: University of Kansas Press, 1999) pp16ff, is a good overview of US approaches to creating combat-effective divisions.

14 The most extreme denunciation of Stilwell's generally acknowledged mishandling of long-range penetration forces is David Rooney, *Wingate and the Chindits: Redressing the Balance* (London: Cassell, 1994). Cf the little-known but comprehensive work by Luigi Rossetto, *Major-General Orde Charles Wingate and the Development of Long-Range Penetration* (Manhattan, KS: AH/MH, 1982)

15 'Notes of a Conference with Representatives of the American Headquarters on the Subject of the Attachment of American Divisions to the British Armies in France, Feb 9, 1918' in *United States Army in the World War, 1917-1918*, Vol III 'Training and Use of American Units with the British and French' (Washington, DC: GPO, 1948) pp42-3

16 See, eg, 'Resume of Points Brought to Notice During Attachment of American 27th Division,

forwarded by XIX Corps BEF, Aug 13, 1918' in ibid, Vol III, pp213-5

17 As in Captain Henry Maslin, ed R. S. Sutliffe, 'To the Hindenburg Line and Through the Hospitals' in *Seventy-First New York in the World War* (New York: privately published, 1922) pp66ff

18 Tyrus Seidule, 'Morale in the American Expeditionary Forces during World War I' (PhD dissertation, Ohio State University, 1997) pp86ff, shows that almost three-quarters of the AEF officer corps included in one substantial survey had worked in business or the professions before commissioning; another 16 per cent were university students. In contrast, between February 1916 and the end of the war the majority of the more than 100,000 BEF officers who received temporary commissions had served in the ranks. See Keith Simpson, 'The Officers' in I. F. W. Beckett and K. Simpson (eds), *A Nation at Arms: A Social Study of the British Army in the First World War* (Manchester: Manchester University, 1985) pp79-83; and more generally, G. D. Sheffield, *Leadership in the Trenches: Officer-Man Relations, Morale, and Discipline in the British Army in the Era of the First World War* (Basingstoke: Macmillan, 2000)

19 For the AEF's acculturation see Edward M. Coffman, *The War to End All Wars: The American Military Experience in World War I* (Madison, Wis: Wisconsin University, 1986) pp286-7

20 On Hamel, see Robin Prior and Trevor Wilson, *Command on the Western Front: The Military Career of Sir Henry Rawlinson, 1914-1918* (Oxford: Blackwell, 1992) pp295-300; P. A. Pedersen, *Monash as Military Commander* (Melbourne: Melbourne University, 1985) pp227 and passim. John Laffin, *The Battle of Hamel: The Australians' Finest Victory* (East Roseville, NSW: Kangaroo, 1999) is a detailed popular narrative characterised by the author's familiar Brit-bashing.

21 On the run-up to the attack see most recently J. P. Harris and Niall Barr, *Amiens to the Armistice: The BEF in the Hundred Days' Campaign* (London: Brassey's, 1998) pp204-16; and Prior and Wilson, op cit, pp358-66

22 See the Australian Corps report in *United States Army in the World War*, Vol VII 'Military Operations of the American Expeditionary Force' (Washington, DC: GPO, 1948) p272

23 C. E. W. Bean, *The AIF in France May 1918 – The Armistice* (Sydney: Angus & Robertson, 1942) p958

24 Edward M. Coffman, op cit, pp293-7, is a narrative summary. Cf the reports of II Corps and 2nd Tank Brigade, AEF, in *United States Army in the World War*, Vol VII, pp276-82, 286-94

25 See Harris and Barr, op cit, p225; and Prior and Wilson, op cit, pp374-5

26 'Operations II Corps', 18 December 1918, *United States Army in the World War*, Vol VII, pp792, 793-94

27 Christopher Gabel, *The US Army GHQ Maneuvers of 1941* (Washington, DC: GPO, 1991) is a good introduction to the mind-set. The quotation is from Martin Blumenson, 'Kasserine Pass, 30 January-22 February, 1943' in C. E. Heller and W. A. Stofft (eds), *America's First Battles* (Lawrence: University of Kansas Press, 1986) p240

28 Sir Francis Tuker, *Approach to Battle* (London: Cassell, 1963) p354

29 Eisenhower to Brooke, 26 November 1942, in Alfred D. Chandler (ed), *The Papers of Dwight David Eisenhower: The War Years*, Vol II (Baltimore and London: Johns Hopkins, 1970) pp770-1

30 Eisenhower to Fredendall, 4 February 1943, ibid, p940

31 Eisenhower to Brooke, 30 January 1943, ibid, p933

32 Cf the respective official histories: George F. Howe, *Northwest Africa: Seizing the Initiative in the West* (Washington, DC: GPO, 1957) p277 passim; and I. S. O. Playfair and C. J. C. Molony, *The Mediterranean and Middle East*, Vol IV 'The Destruction of the Axis Forces in Africa' (London: HMSO, 1966) pp165-90, 287ff. Useful secondary accounts also include Martin Blumenson, *Kasserine Pass* (Boston: Houghton Mifflin, 1967) and Kenneth Macksey, *Crucible of Power: The Fight for Tunisia, 1942-1943* (London: Hutchinson, 1969). Paul M. Robinett, *Armor Command: The Personal Story of a Commander of the 13th Armored Regiment, of the CCB, 1st Armored Division, and of the Armored School during World War II* (Washington, DC: np, 1958) incorporates a telling narrative of the order-counterorder-disorder accompanying the early operations.

33 Quoted in Brian Holden Reid, 'Alexander', in J Keegan (ed), *Churchill's Generals* (London: Weidenfeld & Nicolson, 1991) p114

34 As in Eisenhower to Fredendall, 23 February 1943, *Eisenhower Papers*, op cit, Vol II, p981

35 E. N. Harmon, *Combat Commander* (Englewood Cliffs, NJ: Prentice Hall, 1970) pp132-3

36 Eisenhower to Fredendall, 22 February 1943, and Eisenhower to Alexander, 9 March 1943, *Eisenhower Papers*, op cit, Vol II, pp982, 1019

[37] Martin Blumenson (ed), *The Patton Papers*, Vol II 1940-1945 (Boston: Houghton Mifflin, 1974) pp217-8; Omar Bradley, *A Soldier's Story* (New York: Holt, 1951) pp67-8; Carlo d'Este, *Patton: A Genius for War* (New York: HarperCollins, 1995) pp483-5. The resolution of the question was also facilitated by increasing mutual recognition that the reasons for the American division's lack of success were by no means obvious, and included some dubious orders by the corps commander. The British *Official History*'s reference to 'injudicious comment' on the US performance (p384) makes the point by understatement.

[38] E. N. Harmon, op cit, pp130, 141

[39] For the background of Coningham's reaction see Vincent Orange, *Coningham* (London: Methuen, 1990) pp78-149. Coningham had had a similar earth-shaking row with Montgomery after El Alamein, for a similar reason.

[40] Cf Eisenhower to Marshall, 5 April 1943, and Eisenhower to Patton, 5 April 1943, in *Eisenhower Papers*, op cit, pp1071-2, 1073-4; and Omar Bradley, op cit, pp62-4

[41] Antagonism at intermediate levels was also checked by career considerations. Coningham, for example, mended his quarrel with Patton in part because of his hopes to command the British Tactical Air Forces in the invasion of Europe. Vincent Orange, op cit, p147

[42] For the matrix of the Geilenkirchen operation see Sir Brian Horrocks, *Corps Commander* (London: Magnum, 1977) pp152-3. Ken Ford, *Assault on Germany: The Battle for Geilenkirchen* (New York: Charles, 1989) is a detailed narrative.

[43] In addition to a plethora of regimental histories, Major General Hubert Essame, *The 43rd Wessex Division at War, 1944-1945* (London: Clowes, 1952), written by one of its brigadiers, ranks among the best Second World War British divisional histories. Patrick Delaforce, *The Fighting Wessex Wyverns* (London: Strodd, 1994) is one of a series for general readers. The 84th Division's history is also among the best of its kind – no accident, since the author of *The 84th Division in the Battle of Germany* (New York: Viking, 1946) was a young lieutenant named Theodore Draper, who went on to a distinguished career as an academician and public intellectual.

[44] H. P. Leinbaugh and John D. Campbell, *The Men of Company K: The Autobiography of a World War II Rifle Company* (New York: Morrow, 1985) p28

[45] T. M. Lindsay, *Sherwood Rangers* (London: Burrup, Mathieson, 1952)

[46] Ken Ford, op cit, p97

[47] Quoted in Theodore Draper, op cit, p43

[48] Quoted in Ken Ford, op cit, pp35, 44

[49] Sir Brian Horrocks, op cit, p155

[50] Ibid, p156; quotation in Ken Ford, op cit, p181

Chapter 27

Coalition war: Britain and France

William Philpott

I t is rare for two armies to find themselves fighting a coalition war against the same enemy on the same battlefields. Perhaps unique in 1939-40 was the fact that little more than 20 years earlier, in the ill-denominated 'war to end all wars', as junior officers on the Western Front the leaders of 1939 had learned their profession, and formed fixed opinions of their allies. Consequently, when in 1939 the French and British renewed their uneasy but ultimately victorious alliance of 1914-18, it was with a sense of déjà vu, and a certain foreboding. At heart there was an obvious disappointment that the efforts of 1914-18 had been in vain, and a perception that the Allied armies faced a harder task in defeating a resurgent Nazi Germany than they had in checking the earlier ambitions of the Kaiser's Empire. The shared experience of 1914-18 had not been a comfortable one, despite the mollification of ultimate victory and the sensitivities of inter-war Anglo-French relations leading to a certain playing down of Allied differences. Latent mistrust and dislike, firmly grounded in centuries of animosity and military conflict, were not easily put aside in the interests of the common anti-German cause.[1]

With their earlier experience not forgotten – indeed, ingrained over the intervening years of peace – both nations faced the prospect of a future coalition war with a certain degree of apprehension.

The British had put their faith in the French Army and the impregnable barrier of the Maginot Line[2], and the British Expeditionary Force (BEF) that was sent to France in September 1939 was a shadow of the force sent in 1914. As the senior commanders of the BEF settled into their headquarters near Arras, memories of their earlier stay in the region resonated in their thoughts. The possibilities of modern mobile warfare were not uppermost in their minds; rather dismay at the prospect of a repetition of that costly and ultimately indecisive struggle in the fields and villages of Flanders and northern France was deeply felt. As Major-General Sir Henry Pownall, the BEF's Chief of Staff, opined as plans for the coming campaign were deliberated with the French, 'We had a pretty full bellyful last time of fighting in the Flanders plain with all its mud and slime, not to mention the memories.'[3] The French had their own anxieties and prejudices. General Maurice Gamelin, French Commander-in-Chief in 1939, and formerly aide-de-camp to the French C-in-C of 1914, General Joffre, endured those anxious days of waiting for the British to arrive on the French left for a second time. Too little and too slow had been the judgement of France on British military effort at the start of the First World War, and nothing in British preparations for the Second had suggested any significant change to the French leadership.[4]

On a military level, long-standing differences about the strategic conduct of the war had proved impossible to resolve in peacetime. The maritime outlook of the British Empire – 'the British way in warfare' as inter-war British military theory had come to characterise it – caused anxiety in France, where German military superiority was a constant preoccupation.[5] While in the Great War the British had ultimately demonstrated that they were not there to fight to the last Frenchman, that conflict had seen two years of French blood sacrifice before the British Army had really made its presence felt in the main theatre. To the French, such an attitude was tantamount to abandonment, and pressure for the introduction of peacetime conscription and the creation of an adequate British Field Force equipped with the means for modern mobile warfare was a constant refrain of French political and military leaders in the lead-up to war. For the British the mantra of 'no more Sommes', at least among the appeasing element of the political establishment if not the military leadership, had to be balanced against the recognition that, without a clear demonstration of effective British military support, as France's military position worsened the prospect of a French deal with Hitler and the abandonment of the Anglo-French alliance increased.[6] Belatedly, peacetime conscription was introduced when Hitler demonstrated even to Chamberlain that he was not to be appeased, but by then the Allies had a lot of catching up to do in their military preparations.

Managerially, the coalition was better arranged than in 1914-18, although detailed analysis reveals that 1939 arrangements were in substance no more than those that had been arrived at with difficulty by 1918. When these arrangements for static attritional warfare were put to the test of modern mobile battle in May 1940 their deficiencies became clear. Before 1914 Anglo-French preparatory arrangements had been limited to joint staff talks to ensure effective naval and military deployment should war break out. Political considerations – divisions within the governing Liberal Party and the traditional British aversion to continental alliances – prevented any formal commitment to sending a military force to France, although materially and logistically the small BEF was ready to go at a moment's notice. Nevertheless, the political decision to support France could not be taken until war had actually broken out, and even then the elaborate logistical preparations were questioned as Britain's military and political leaders paused to review Britain's strategic options and obligations.[7] One thing that had never been considered before the war was the role of British forces once they arrived in France. The unquestioned assumption of the military planners was that the early battles would be decisive, British participation might tip the military balance in the Allies' favour, and that therefore there was no need to do more than to fall in with the French offensive plan. The other omission, which was to prove a perpetual source of weakness in the lengthy coalition war, was the failure to determine formally the relations between the British and French field commanders. Sir John French went to France with vague and contradictory instructions, a consequence of the British reluctance to accept French authority.[8] The consequences of this omission were to undermine military co-operation in the field until 1918, when in the face of imminent defeat the then British Commander-in-Chief, Sir Douglas Haig, overcame his personal reservations and accepted the authority of a French Generalissimo, General Foch.[9]

One lesson had been learned by 1939. The independence of action vouchsafed to Sir John French, which had so badly hampered Joffre's attempts to co-ordinate Allied operations in the early months of 1914, was denied to General Lord Gort, Commander-in-Chief in 1939. In the staff talks that preceded the outbreak of hostilities, it was agreed that the BEF would be formally incorporated into the French chain of command in a situation analogous to that which had developed by 1918. Gort found himself an army commander in the French First Army Group commanded by General Billotte, but responsible to General Georges, commander of the French armies on the North-Eastern Front, himself responsible to Gamelin, in charge of the strategy of the coalition as a whole.[10] Theoretically, orders for the BEF would come down the French chain of command, although the unique circumstance of having an allied army as part of a national force rendered this arrangement fragile. Like his First World War counterparts, Gort retained the right of appeal to his Government in the event of orders being issued that imperilled his command, so the formal authority of the French High Command was never complete. Yet Pownall commented favourably on the arrangement:

> 'We shall get unity of command in the field from the outset, instead of wasting three and a half years trying to get there. It may be a bold step but I'm sure it's right. Independent commands like that of French are all very well when times are good, fair or indifferent. But when times are bad they are most dangerous.
>
> We have learned a lot from the last war in these matters... I'm sure the French for their part have learnt their lesson too.'[11]

But once again in May 1940 the deficiencies of peacetime arrangements were exposed when times became bad.[12]

In other respects British military preparations for continental war in 1939 did not match up to those of 1914. In Britain's defence preparations the Army had come a poor third behind the other services, and political commitment to 'limited liability' on the continent had starved the Army of resources, until the realisation that war was imminent forced Chamberlain out of his appeaser's complacency. Six months was too short a time to make up for years of neglect, so the BEF of 1939 was both significantly smaller than that of 1914 (initially four infantry divisions in 1939, as opposed to six on paper in 1914) and poorly equipped for modern mobile warfare. Paradoxically, while the British military effort in 1939 was weaker, the French expected, indeed demanded, more than they had in 1914. Then a confident French High Command had put its faith in the élan of the French Army and the moral value of the offensive to check superior German numbers. In 1939 there was no such confidence. Demography and the defensive 'Maginot mentality' had fostered a resigned sense of military inferiority amongst France's political and military leaders. Any expectation that 'blue water' Britain would make up the manpower gap between France and Germany with a mass-conscript army ready for continental war was hopelessly naïve. Nevertheless, the issue of British military support, paralleled by British anxieties over French air weakness, was a major cause of friction between the Allies in their preparations for coalition war.

It was Britain's slow and limited contribution to the Allied cause in August 1914, rather than the commitment of ever-increasing resources to the Allied war effort, that was enshrined in the collective French memory between the wars.[13] Echoes of this earlier experience were soon apparent in the preparations for a second war. From the start Britain's leaders limited the military staff talks with France to purely technical questions to avoid any such moral obligation to France as had existed before 1914. Britain's strategic planners were playing the long game, preparing for a lengthy war of economic blockade in the mistaken belief that it had been the slow and steady pressure of maritime power, rather than the attrition and eventual defeat of the enemy army on the main fighting front, that had decided the earlier conflict. For France, however, it was axiomatic that the Allies could never win a long war if they had already lost a short war on the battlefield.[14]

As the French Army would have to meet the first German offensive, there was a desire to maximise the potential assistance that the British would provide in the early military engagements. The more realistic French leaders accepted that Britain's military contribution would initially be small, although they comforted themselves with the thought that an early token of British military support would, as in 1914, portend the full mobilisation of Britain's Imperial strength for the Allied cause. In the late 1930s the French therefore pressed the British for a small mobile expeditionary force equipped for continental warfare, especially with armoured formations, to make up for a perceived deficiency in the French Army's order of battle.[15] The BEF would be assigned a key role in the counter-attack to be delivered against the first German offensive against France. Thus British support would help to prevent an early Allied military defeat, and in time the military potential of the British Empire would be employed in a successful offensive against Germany after economic blockade had weakened the adversary.

Even this clear and limited military role was too much for Britain's political leaders, who feared a repetition of the costly stalemate of 1915-17.[16] Nothing that emerged from the early rounds of the pre-war military staff talks altered the initial French conclusion that any British military support on the outbreak of war would be 'limitée et tardive'.[17] The British themselves maintained for too long too rosy a picture of the French Army and French military capabilities.[18] Inspections of the Maginot fortifications, which greatly impressed British visitors, and an over-reliance on 'bean counting' rather than qualitative assessments of French strength and doctrine, led British leaders to conclude that French pleas for substantial British military support were paranoid – an underhand Gallic trick with echoes of the nagging demands of the last war. In these circumstances French demands for more formal military staff talks were refused at the highest inter-governmental level, placing an increasing strain on the fragile alliance.[19]

Pragmatic British self-interest eventually forced Chamberlain out of his rigid opposition to a military commitment in the spring of 1939. Without firm military support it was feared that defeatists would gain the upper hand in France and come to a separate accommodation with Hitler, depriving Britain of the French defensive shield on which she relied and leaving Britain to face the dictators alone.[20] Authorisation of high-level staff talks, the introduction of peacetime conscription to back a hasty and impractical commitment to double the Territorial Army and equip an expeditionary force of 19 divisions for overseas service, and the diversion of resources to re-equip the first echelon of the Field Force, came too late to improve significantly the military assistance Britain could send to France in the short term. But as an earnest of Britain's military commitment it was welcomed in France.[21]

The British contingent that arrived in France in the early weeks of the war was more than the French could have anticipated a year earlier. Anxiety in France persisted, however. The initial British contingent of four infantry divisions was adjudged to be inadequately trained and of questionable value[22], and there was a real fear that having done more than they promised at the start, the British would now rest on their laurels. As the French Army waited over the winter and spring of 1939-40 for the first German blow to fall, complaints about Britain's small, poorly equipped and tardy military contribution continued to cast a shadow over Anglo-French relations, just as they had done in the first year of the previous war.[23] German propaganda dwelled on the British fighting to the last Frenchman, and it was that which the French did their best to guard against. There was, the French ambassador commented perceptively, no Kitchener to improvise a continental-scale army in 1939.[24] Instead, there was the evasive and irresolute Chamberlain – who according to Harold Nicholson 'did not want this war, and is continually thinking of getting out of it'[25] – and the bumbling Secretary of State for War, Leslie Hore Belisha.[26]

In 1939 the Kitchener role of developing the British Empire's latent military strength fell to General Ironside, the Chief of the Imperial General Staff. He faced the same dilemma as his predecessor, balancing Britain's need to offer adequate support to the French Army on the Western Front with the defensive needs of the British Empire outside Europe. Kitchener had fought for the best part of a year to keep some strategic independence for the British Empire, before surrendering the bulk of his New Armies for the French front. Kitchener had been playing the long game of husbanding British resources for the final decisive phase of the war, but had eventually been forced to recognise that Britain could not afford for France to be overwhelmed in the short term.[27]

In 1939 Ironside, too, had a long-term perspective – there was little alternative given Britain's military unpreparedness. Ironside's contemplated 55-division Imperial Army fell far short of the 96 divisions that Britain had put in the field in the First War, and political and industrial constraints meant that it would take much longer to prepare. After Imperial defence needs were met only 20 of these divisions were earmarked for France. Whether the precise details of Britain's military effort were confided to the French is unclear; Ironside himself felt that having done as much and more than pre-war arrangements required, French political pressure should be resisted. Ironside, for his part, recognised the deficiencies in Britain's military preparations, but felt obliged to put his faith in the French Army in the short term. Nevertheless, he felt uneasy with Gamelin's strategic preparations to meet the anticipated German attack.[28] Leisurely British preparations offered little comfort to the French who feared an immediate German onslaught once Poland had been overcome. Although this did not materialise, French anxieties over British commitment to the Western Front, and British uncertainty over French strategic planning, continued to undermine the solidarity of the alliance during the 'Phoney War' period. It was not a matter that could be left to the generals, so these disagreements were played out at the highest political level.

In the area of political co-ordination similar late and slow preparation was apparent. While Lord Chatfield, the British Minister for Co-ordination of Defence, could honestly tell his audience at the end of 1939 that, 'we have the closest co-operation with *our great Ally*. Here again in the months before the war was organised the closest and most complete understanding. Not only had we at the outbreak of war a Supreme War Council, but Anglo-French staffs in all sections are completely organised and sit together daily to study the problems of war. It is true to say that never have allies started fighting with such a complete mechanism, such complete plans and such identity of spirit,'[29] it was a close-run thing. Political co-ordination ranked alongside military preparation as a sign of British commitment, so before 1939 French requests for some form of high-level political forum for co-ordinating policy and strategy were as unwelcome as their calls for military preparation. Belatedly, high-level political exchanges about the machinery for co-ordinating the alliance evolved out of the formal staff talks. By the time war broke out in September 1939 an elaborate Allied co-ordination machinery existed on paper, although the intention of ironing out its teething troubles in peacetime could not be realised.

This machinery took up where the last war left off – indeed, it even bore the same name, the Supreme War Council – and it demonstrated the same deficiencies of the earlier organisation in practice. Gamelin, who was to direct the coalition's military effort, had pressed strongly for military representation on the Supreme War Council and a clear definition of the respective responsibilities of soldiers and politicians.[30] This was not forthcoming, so after war broke out the same civil-military tensions that had compromised the efficiency of the alliance in 1914-18 re-emerged. While military representatives were called to the Supreme War Council when strategic matters were under discussion, they had little real input. Ironside, for example, reportedly never said a word at the Supreme War Council meetings he attended.[31] But he observed carefully. The proceedings were dominated by the politicians, particularly the respective Allied Prime Ministers, and long-winded; so much so that at the meeting on 28 March 1940 both the French Air Minister and Chief of Air Staff fell asleep, while the bored Chief of the French Naval Staff, Admiral Darlan, 'smoked his pipe all the time and drew pictures on his bit of paper'.[32]

Real decision-making took place outside the Supreme War Council, through unilateral exchanges between Ministers and Governments. The Supreme War Council would rubber-stamp these earlier agreements, and if matters came before the Council that had not already been agreed they would be talked out.[33] Moreover, it was a slow, bureaucratic and unfocused machine, a 'café de commerce' as Gamelin reportedly called it[34], the product of the long war of attrition that had originally spawned it, and dedicated to fighting a similar war by indirect means. Just as in 1918 the Supreme War Council had directed economic warfare and peripheral campaigns while the Allied armies had been winning the war on the principal front, so in 1940 Scandinavia and the Balkans preoccupied the Allies' political leaders while the enemy prepared its devastating blow on the main front. The Supreme War Council's press communiqués suggest its true purpose: 'Complete agreement was reached on the best method of combined employment of French and British forces for the most effective conduct of operations' was announced after the 17 November 1939 meeting.[35] It was a means of demonstrating Allied solidarity to the outside world, but not an instrument for the effective direction of modern war. Too much attention was devoted to the organisation of Anglo-French relations once peace had returned.[36] Little preparation was made for the war that would have to be fought first.

The foregoing analysis indicates that in 1940 the Allies were expecting events to develop much the same as in the last war, and their preparations had not looked beyond their previous experience. But for all their backward glances, the one thing that they did not prepare for was a repeat of the events of August 1914. Gamelin, as Joffre's aide-de-camp in 1914, had been a first-hand witness of the failure of the French Army's forward manoeuvre, and instrumental in planning the 'miracle of the Marne' that had saved the Allied cause. Yet, in 1940, Gamelin showed the same complacency that had upset Joffre's pre-war planning and early operations.[37] The Maginot Line now existed to protect France's eastern départements from invasion, and, as far as strict Belgian neutrality would allow, a plan had been developed to enable the Allied armies to meet a German invasion of the Low Countries by advancing to a strong defensive line in eastern Belgium. It took an Englishman, Ironside, to spot the weakness in this plan[38], although the British had such an unequal military voice that influencing the generalissimo's plans proved impossible.[39]

The French Army was the military mainstay of the coalition and, as in 1914, it proved easier to place faith in its fortitude than to contemplate the possibility of its failure. The British leaders in 1939 inevitably made comparisons with the French Army alongside which they had fought in 1914, some more favourable than others. Ironside wrote positively of his inspections of French troops and fortifications, but it would seem to be an impression born out of suspicion, uncertainty and resignation:

'I tried in my mind to sum up the state of the French Army and its fighting value. I must say I saw nothing amiss with it on the surface. The Generals are all tried men, if a bit old from our view point. None of them showed any lack of confidence. None of the liaison officers say they have seen any lack of morale after the long wait they have had, after the excitement of mobilisation. I say to myself that we shall not know until the first clash comes. In 1914 there were many officers who failed, but old Joffre handled the situation with great firmness. Will the Blitzkrieg, when it comes, allow us to rectify things if they are the same? I must say I don't know. But I say to myself that we must have confidence in the French Army. It is the only thing in which we can have confidence. Our own army is just a little one, and we are dependent on the French. We have not even the same fine army we had in 1914. All depends on the French Army and we can do nothing about it, but it is up to us to back it up and not deny it...

Gort has given me no inkling that he finds anything serious amiss in the French Army. None of his staff have even whispered doubts.'[40]

Some of the BEF's field commanders, however, had their doubts, from working closely with the French Army, which they communicated to Gort.[41] This opinion apparently went no further.

When the first clash came the French Army's deficiencies became glaringly apparent.[42] The events of May 1940 are well known. German armoured and mechanised forces penetrated the weak infantry screen opposite Sedan and split the advancing Allied armies in Belgium from their defensive mass in eastern France. The Allies found themselves facing a similar military reverse to that of August 1914; and just as in 1914 there was no contingency plan on which to fall back should the initial Allied advance fail. In 1914 the early teething troubles, if not resolved, were at least surmounted, and the German offensive into France that threatened to defeat the Allied armies in detail was checked and reversed on the Marne in early September. In 1940, despite the clearer chain of command, this proved impossible. While the defeat of 1940 cannot be attributed entirely to the weaknesses of Allied co-operation, this was a factor that contributed to the Allies' failure to mount an effective counter-stroke against Germany's armoured thrust across northern France.

It is undoubtedly a truism that alliances work better in times of triumph than adversity, and very quickly in May 1940 strains began to show. After a particularly exasperating round of co-ordination conferences Pownall confided privately to his diary; 'And my god how awful to be allied to so temperamental a race!'[43] Pownall's vilification was directed specifically at Billotte, appointed to co-ordinate the Allied armies in Belgium but unable to make up his mind and impose his authority on Allied commanders.[44] General Blanchard, who belatedly replaced Billotte after the latter's fatal injury in a car accident, proved no more effective.

The similarities with August 1914 are striking. Then the commanders of the BEF took their assigned place on the left of the Allied line at Mons with a certain confidence in the French Army, if not in its leadership, who had demonstrated their worst side in the anxious days of mobilisation and deployment. The initial defeat of the French Army, the purge of its High Command, and its precipitate retreat, apparently leaving the small British Army to fend for itself on the exposed flank of the Allied line, fatally undermined this confidence. Like Pownall, the BEF's Chief of Staff, General Sir Archibald Murray, took against the French, exercising a pernicious influence on his chief who himself felt the disappointment most bitterly, partly as a consequence of wounded amour-propre after Joffre took on himself the role of generalissimo of the Allied coalition.[45] Haig, too, at the time commanding the British I Army Corps, felt badly let down by supporting French troops; this initial disappointment was to overshadow his dealings with his Allies for the rest of the war.[46]

The natural reaction of a British commander staring defeat in the face is to look to his ports. French's intention in late August 1914, to abandon contact with the French Army, retreat on Amiens and if necessary 'go to Havre and home'[47], was a strange premonition of 1940. In May 1940 Gort demonstrated the same sprit of independence when the French strategic plan had failed. As early as 19 May GHQ staff were weighing up the options for retreat to the coast and evacuation through the French and Belgian Channel ports.[48] In 1914 a political solution to the crisis in the alliance was found – Lord Kitchener, Secretary of State for War, hurried to Paris to insist that French participate in Joffre's planned counter-attack. While this intervention was not immediately effective, Sir John French reconsidered the position, halted the BEF's retreat and within a week joined the successful counter-offensive on the River Marne.[49]

In 1940 the principle that there would not be political interference in the conduct of field operations was more clearly established. Since the BEF was integrated into the French chain of command, Gort was expected to fall in with General Weygand's plan for a counter-attack, approved by the Prime Minster, Winston Churchill, and the Supreme War Council. It was only too clear to the soldiers in the field that there was a large discrepancy between the schemes of the new Allied generalissimo and the forces available. Gort had already concluded that the battle in Flanders was lost, that his divisions were exhausted and overextended, that his allies were on the verge of collapse, and that the only course left for the BEF was a fighting retreat to the coast and evacuation. Gort could find no British forces for Weygand's counter-attack.[50] If a political intervention might have saved the situation, it was not forthcoming. Following the failure of Weygand's counter-attack, complete discretion was left to Gort over whether to retire the BEF to the coast and embark for home.[51] Repeated French entreaties made no impression on Gort, who had his eyes set on Dunkirk. A final disagreement, over the proportion of British and French troops to be evacuated through Dunkirk, set the seal on a humiliating series of events.[52]

Whether Weygand could with willing British support have achieved a 'miracle of the Somme' is questionable. What is clear is that the Allies had learned little from their experience of 1914 when it came to military co-operation. Although the alliance was not at an end, it was never to recover. The British 'miracle of Dunkirk' was to the French a clear demonstration of the British perfidy that they had long expected. In the south the French Army fought on, but British support, on the ground or in the air, was by now token. The Supreme War Council had not stood the test of real war, and was increasingly circumvented by personal diplomacy as the British strove to keep the French in the war. On the other hand, duplicitous British policy became increasingly geared to preparations to fight on alone. Churchill's meetings with the French premier, Paul Reynaud, were dignified with the title of Supreme War Council, but much of the business of these days was conducted in back rooms between liaison officers and in hastily arranged ministerial meetings. As a final gesture, borne more out of desperation than sincerity perhaps, Churchill proposed his famous scheme for 'Franco-British Union'. It was swept aside by the French Cabinet, a final gesture of contempt for their Allies before the armistice with Germany.[53] Britain's response, the destruction of the French fleet at Mers-el-Kébir, was to be a fitting epitaph to an alliance that had always been tense, and where differences – essentially the product of irreconcilable maritime and continental perspectives – were barely contained.

On the eve of war, Sir Edward Spears, a military liaison officer in the first conflict who became Churchill's political liaison in Paris in the second, offered a salutary reminder to those who were to mange the Anglo-French alliance:

'It is all too evident that centuries of peaceful intercourse will be needed to achieve what even the common suffering of the war failed to accomplish, a capacity to view a given situation from the point of view of the man of another nationality. To do so calls for a degree of education, knowledge and imagination that the men of the war generation did not possess.'[54]

It was a fair verdict on the problems of the first coalition, and a percipient premonition of the second. Although in 1939 the institutional framework of the coalition had been strengthened, with a belated acknowledgement of the weaknesses that had undermined the alliance in 1914-18, personalities still counted for much in the day-to-day management of alliance relations. The 'men of the war generation', with their lack of knowledge and imagination, were still in charge in 1940. If anything, the knowledge that they had was of the last war, and their imaginations were dominated by its costly and tragic trench stalemate. Hence, their preparations were based on false premises and unrealistic expectations, and the cast of their minds was fundamentally pessimistic. When battle was joined in earnest it became clear that war had changed, and that the Allies could not mount an effective response with the institutions and mind-set of an earlier generation. Perhaps uniquely among the senior statesmen and soldiers of 1940, Churchill, who had written the foreword to Spears's book, and who would appear to have taken his warning to heart, demonstrated the imagination and force of character to hold the alliance together in the difficult days of June 1940. Others from the earlier generation, old men by 1940, Marshal Pétain and Weygand, were most deeply scarred by their memories. Two venerated veterans of the First War and key architects of victory in 1918, they had ordered many young Frenchmen to their deaths to achieve that triumph, only to witness the steady erosion of French grandeur, the resurgence of Germany, and British bad faith. Well aware of the consequences of a second long struggle on French soil – years of blood sacrifice and devastation of the metropole – these Frenchmen of 1940, still at heart the men of 1918, proved unwilling to contemplate that alternative and pushed the French political leadership towards an armistice with Germany. It was time to save and renew France, rather than fight on for a Britain that had always qualified its commitment to the French cause.[55] It was a strange reversal of fortune. In 1914 British recalcitrance had threatened to break up the alliance; in 1940 French defeatism was to succeed.

Animosity between neighbouring nations is always more natural than cordiality. The British and French, with incompatible maritime and continental perspectives, and traditions of rivalry and war going back centuries, proved reluctant and quarrelsome partners when forced together by a bigger bullying neighbour. Their earlier experience of coalition war, while ultimately successful, had not been comfortable, and cast a long shadow over the events of 1939-40. Between 1914 and 1918 the legacy of early misunderstandings and poor co-ordination had bedevilled the coalition war effort. As late as 1917 Haig was railing against the unreliability of the French Army that he had experienced in 1914, and in private expressed the view that 'all would be so easy if I only had to deal with the Germans!'[56] With recollections of the Great War recently reanimated, for the British, France's capitulation in 1940, while a disappointment, was not a disaster. Most famously, King George VI expressed a sentiment that must have been warmly received in the corridors of power: 'Personally, I feel happier that we have no allies to be polite to and to pamper.'[57] Although Churchill described the decision to sink the French fleet at Mers-el-Kébir as the most difficult that he ever had to take, there were probably those who felt more comfortable that Britain was now standing alone, free of the encumbrance of a difficult and temperamental ally and spared a second costly attritional land campaign in northern France; and once again engaged in hostilities with the traditional maritime enemy.

Notes on contributors

Dr William J. Philpott, London Guildhall University, UK
William Philpott is Principal Lecturer in International History at London Guildhall University. He has published Anglo-French Relations and Strategy on the Western Front, 1914-1918 (Macmillan, 1996), and many articles on Anglo-French relations in the era of the two world wars. He is currently co-editing a volume on Anglo-French Defence Relations Between the Wars with Professor Martin Alexander. He is a Fellow of the Royal Historical Society and a Member of the Council of the Army Records Society

Recommended reading

Bedarida, F., *La Stratégie Secrète de la Drôle de Guerre: La Conseil Suprême Interallié, Septembre 1939-Avril 1940* (Paris: Presses de la Fondation Nationale des Sciences Politiques, 1979)

Bell, P. M. H., *France and Britain, 1900-1940: Entente and Estrangement* (London: Longman, 1996)

Bond, B. J., *Britain, France and Belgium, 1939-1940* (London: Brassey's, 2nd ed 1990)

Dockrill, M. L., *British Establishment Perspectives on France, 1936-40* (Basingstoke and London: Macmillan, 1999)

Philpott, W. J., *Anglo-French Relations and Strategy on the Western Front, 1914-1918* (Basingstoke and London: Macmillan, 1996)

Notes

1 See, eg, J. Keiger, '"Perfidious Albion?": French Perceptions of Britain as an Ally after the First World War' in M. S. Alexander (ed), *Knowing Your Friends: Intelligence Inside Alliances and Coalitions*

from 1914 to the Cold War (London: Frank Cass, 1998) pp37-52

2   This author has argued elsewhere that that faith was over-optimistic and misplaced. See M. S. Alexander and W. J. Philpott, 'The Entente Cordiale and the Next War: Anglo-French Views on Future Military Co-operation' in M. S. Alexander (ed), op cit, pp53-85

3   Pownall Diary, 18 September 1939, in B. J. Bond (ed), *Chief of Staff: The Diaries of Lieutenant General Sir Henry Pownall*, Vol I 1933-1940 (London: Leo Cooper, 1972) p235

4   The infamous outburst of General Lanrezac's Chief of Staff, Hély d'Oissel, when a delegation from British headquarters finally appeared in August 1914 – 'At last you are here, it's not a moment too soon. If we are beaten we will owe it all to you' – became a metaphor for British military policy in general thanks to the success of the post-war memoirs of General Huguet, principal French liaison officer at British Headquarters in 1914 and 1915. See Gen V. Huguet, *Britain and the War: A French Indictment* (London: Cassell & Co Ltd, 1928). The influence of this book is discussed in P. M. H. Bell, *France and Britain, 1900-1940: Entente and Estrangement* (London: Longman, 1996) pp101-6

5   There was a considerable degree of satisfaction in French military circles when, after Munich, Basil Liddell Hart, the prophet of 'limited liability', was forced to admit the need to strengthen the force the British contemplated sending to support the French Army. 'Compte-rendu, 10 February 1939' by Lelong (Service Historique de l'Armée de Terre (SHAT), Vincennes, 2N228/1)

6   M. L. Dockrill, *British Establishment Perspectives on France, 1936-40* (Basingstoke and London: Macmillan, 1999) pp132-3

7   'Secretary's Notes of a War Council held at 10 Downing Street, 5 August 1914', Cabinet Office: Cabinet Papers, 1915-16, Public Record Office, Kew (PRO) (CAB 42): CAB 42/1/2; W. J. Philpott, *Anglo-French Relations and Strategy on the Western Front, 1914-1918* (Basingstoke and London: Macmillan, 1996) pp8-10

8   Kitchener's instructions to French read: 'The special motive of the force under your command is to support and co-operate with the French Army... I wish you to understand that your command is a fully independent one and that you will in no case come under the orders of any Allied General.' Quoted in W. J. Philpott, op cit, pp15-6

9   Ibid, pp154-6

10 At the time that Gort, the then CIGS, made these arrangements with the French he did not expect to be in command of the BEF himself.

11 Pownall Diary, 3 July 1939, B. J. Bond, op cit, p211

12 For the comments of one who saw the deficiencies of these arrangements in operation, see Field-Marshal Montgomery, *The Memoirs of Field-Marshal the Viscount Montgomery of Alamein* (London: Collins, 1958) pp51-6

13 Largely as a consequence of Huguet's book. See note 4.

14 An assumption that ultimately proved incorrect, but was nevertheless valid in the political and strategic climate of the late 1930s

15 'Etude sur la collaboration des forces terrestres franco-britanniques en cas de conflit', 24 April 1938, SHAT, 2N227/3. The French had always taken a close interest in British mechanised warfare developments. They themselves had neglected this aspect of the military arts until the late 1930s. However, it soon became apparent that the early British promise had not been sustained and that the hoped-for mechanised Field Force was not going to materialise for some years. For details, see M. S. Alexander, *The Republic in Danger: General Maurice Gamelin and the Politics of French Defence, 1933-40* (Cambridge: Cambridge University Press, 1992) pp236-78 passim

16 Ironically, the mobile warfare of 1914 and 1918 had been far more costly in terms of casualties.

17 'Note sur l'appui militaire éventuel de la Grande Bretagne', 2 May 1935, SHAT, 7N2840/1

18 The product in part of inadequate intelligence assessment of their allies, and preoccupation with French weakness in the air. See Alexander and Philpott, op cit, pp73-5

19 'Conversations franco-britanniques des 28 et 29 Avril 1938: questions militaires. Conversations d'Etat-Major', SHAT, 2N227/3

20 M. L. Dockrill, op cit, pp113-31 passim

21 'Le situation internationale et l'opinion britannique' by Lelong, 9 February 1939; 'Synthèse, 30 March 1939 and 31 March to 6 April 1939', SHAT, 7N2816

22 'Information du Général: remarques relatives aux conclusions du Conseil Suprême Interallié du 12 Septembre 1939', 13 September 1939, Edouard Daladier papers, Archives Nationales, Paris, 3DA2/2b

23 For details see W. J. Philpott, 'Kitchener and the 29th Division: A Study in Anglo-French Strategic Relations, 1914-1195' in *The Journal of Strategic Studies*, XVI (1993), pp375-407

24 Corbin to Daladier, 18 October 1939, Daladier papers, 3DA2/3c

25 Nicholson Diary, 6 September 1939, quoted in E. M. Gates, *End of the Affair: The Collapse of the Anglo-French Alliance, 1939-40* (Berkeley, Los Angeles: University of California Press, 1981) p23

26 Hore Belisha's sacking in January 1940 caused mixed feelings among the French. While he was judged to be a friend to France and an admirer of the French Army, his over-zealous championing of their cause, and the tactless comparisons that he drew with the unprepared British Army, had not served French interests. It was felt that his replacement, Oliver Stanley, would put the French case more tactfully in London, although it was regretted that a more dynamic individual who would accelerate the pace of British military armaments had not been appointed. Note by Corbin, 9 January 1940, Daladier papers, 3DA5/2a

27 W. J. Philpott, 'Kitchener and the 29th Division', op cit, passim

28 Col R. Macleod and D. Kelly (eds), *The Ironside Diaries, 1937-40* (London: Constable, 1962) 6 September to 23 December 1939 passim, pp103-68

29 'Speech to National Defence Public Interest Committee Lunch', 13 December 1939 (Chatfield's emphasis), Admiral of the Fleet Lord Chatfield papers, National Maritime Museum, Greenwich, CHT/6/4

30 'Note sur la Collaboration militaire franco-britannique' by Gamelin, 23 November 1938, and 'Note sur la direction d'une guerre de coalition' by Gamelin, 10 June 1939, SHAT, 2N227/3 and 2N229/1

31 F. Bedarida, *La Stratégie Secrète de la Drôle de Guerre: La Conseil Suprême Interallié, Septembre 1939-Avril 1940* (Paris: Presses de la Fondation Nationale des Sciences Politiques, 1979) p32

32 *Ironside Diaries*, op cit, 28 March 1940, pp237-8

33 Ibid, p237

34 Ibid, 22 April 1940, p278

35 Press communiqué, 17 November 1939, Cabinet Papers: Registered Files, PRO (CAB 21): CAB 21/1337

36 F. Bedarida, op cit, pp43-7

37 For Joffre's mistakes, see W. J. Philpott, *Anglo-French Relations and Strategy on the Western Front, 1914-1918*, op cit, pp11-2 and 18-22

38 *Ironside Diaries*, op cit, pp116-20

39 For a detailed analysis of Allied planning during the 'Phoney War', see B. J. Bond, *Britain, France and Belgium, 1939-1940* (London: Brassey's, 2nd ed 1990) pp21-54

40 *Ironside Diaries*, op cit, 10 January 1940, pp203-4

41 Field-Marshal Montgomery, op cit, p59. Interestingly, Montgomery's impression was formed while visiting the Maginot Line in the same month as Ironside.

42 Pownall's conclusion, having observed the French Army in action, was that 'in the early stages of the campaign ... the French soldier did not fight as he should ... and the French high command [was] quite equal to the emergency'. 'Retrospect', June 1940, B. J. Bond, *Chief of Staff*, op cit, p366

43 Pownall Diary, 19 May 1940, ibid, p323

44 Pownall Diary, 17 May 1940, ibid, pp318-9

45 W. J. Philpott, *Anglo-French Relations and Strategy on the Western Front, 1914-1918*, op cit, pp21-4

46 W. J. Philpott, 'Haig and Britain's European Allies' in B. J. Bond and N. Cave (eds), *Haig: A Reappraisal 70 Years On* (London: Leo Cooper, 1999) pp130, 140

47 Clive Diary, 29 August 1914, Major-General Sir G. S. Clive papers, Liddell Hart Centre for Military Archives, King's College, London

48 Pownall Diary, 17 and 19 May 1940, B. J. Bond, *Chief of Staff*, op cit, pp319-23

49 W. J. Philpott, *Anglo-French Relations and Strategy on the Western Front, 1914-1918*, op cit, pp26-9

50 B. J. Bond, *Britain, France and Belgium, 1939-1940*, op cit, pp75-85

51 Pownall Diary, 26 May 1940, B. J. Bond, *Chief of Staff*, op cit, p343

52 P. M. H. Bell, *France and Britain, 1900-1940*, op cit, pp238-9

53 Ibid, pp240-8

54 E. L. Spears, *Prelude to Victory* (London: Jonathan Cape, 1939) p81

55 E. M. Gates, op cit, pp139-40; P. M. H. Bell, op cit, pp242-4

56 Haig Diary, 8 March 1917, Field Marshal Earl Haig of Bemersyde Papers, National Library of Scotland, Edinburgh

57 Quoted in B. J. Bond, 'The British Field Force in France and Belgium', in P. Addison and A. Calder (eds), *Time to Kill: The Soldier's Experience of War in the West, 1939-45* (London: Pimlico, 1997) p49

Chapter 28

Coalition war:
Germany and her allies,
Austria-Hungary and Italy

Gary W. Shanafelt and G. T. Waddington

When Josef Stürgkh, the Austro-Hungarian liaison officer with the German High Command, returned to Austrian headquarters early in 1915, he was taken aback at the sentiments he encountered there. 'Well, then, what are our secret enemies, the Germans, doing, and the German Kaiser, the play-actor?' demanded Franz Conrad von Hötzendorf, the Austrian Chief of Staff – not exactly words one might expect from an Austrian leader about his chief ally in the war.[1] By 1917, the last Austrian emperor could even declare flatly, 'A smashing German victory would be our ruin.'[2] Many Germans reciprocated such feelings. Max Hoffmann, the brilliant but acerbic German staff officer of Hindenburg and Ludendorff on the Eastern Front, had little good to say in his private diaries about his Austrian counterparts: 'I should like to go to war with them.'[3] The German ambassador in Vienna, Heinrich von Tschirschky, was equally blunt: 'God preserve my poor fatherland from ever again making war with Austria as an ally.'[4]

Coalition wars usually involve friction between the various states fighting together, as they strive to subordinate their individual differences to the larger goal of defeating a more dangerous common enemy. But few coalitions seem to have suffered from the level of friction that characterised the Austro-German war effort during the First World War, even though it was the culmination of an alliance going back to 1879. At the most basic level, the coalition never really found a single, unifying enemy at all. Both Germany and Austria-Hungary felt threatened by Russia before the war; but Germany had little interest in Austrian feuding with Italy, and Austria-Hungary was certainly not concerned about Alsace-Lorraine or battleship construction in the North Sea. Basic disagreements about war aims were aggravated by the disparity in power between the two states. By the 20th century the Dual Monarchy was clearly not in the same league as Imperial Germany. In 1914 an Austro-Hungarian infantry division was equipped with 42 light field guns and no heavy ones; the respective German numbers were 72 and 80.[5] Yet the Dual Monarchy's leaders still thought of themselves as rulers of one of the European Great Powers. They both admired and feared their more powerful, upstart neighbours, needing their strength but resenting their dependency on it.

German leaders acting even in the best of faith would have had difficulty dealing with such Austrian sensitivities. Often, however, they simply assumed that what was good for Germany was good for the alliance as a whole. Erich Ludendorff, in his post-war memoirs, contrasted Austrian jealousy and concerns over questions of 'so-called prestige' in military decision-making with Germany's lofty objectivity; for Germany 'considered military necessities and nothing else'.[6] These fundamental problems created tensions within the alliance even before 1914, but under the conditions of the war they assumed major proportions and seriously hindered effective conduct of a common war effort by the two powers.

The initial Austro-German campaigns of 1914 set the pattern for much of the subsequent wartime relations of the two allied states. Before the war, contact between their respective general staffs had been minimal, confined almost wholly to personal correspondence and occasional meetings between German Chief of Staff Helmut von Moltke the younger, and Conrad. In case of war, Moltke thought that the Austrians would engage the Russians while the bulk of the German Army carried out the Schlieffen Plan against France; while Conrad expected the German offensive in France, he nevertheless thought major German forces would be available to support the Austrians on the Eastern Front. There was no common plan of operations. To make matters worse, at the outset of hostilities Conrad botched the initial Austrian mobilisation and then, even without significant German assistance, attempted to take the offensive against the numerically superior Russian forces. The result was a disaster. By the autumn, the Russians had reached the Carpathians and seemed about to invade Hungary. The Austrians were bitter, but not just against the Russians. Austria-Hungary, Conrad asserted, had been left in the lurch by its ally.[7] The diplomats in Vienna agreed with him. 'The collapse of our Polish campaign is the fault of the Germans, whose agreed co-operation on the left wing failed to appear,' János Forgách wrote from the Austrian Foreign Ministry.[8] Leopold Berchtold, the Austrian Foreign Minister, even hinted to Berlin that the Monarchy might conclude a separate peace if more German assistance was not forthcoming.

In the meantime, the Germans won brilliantly at Tannenberg in East Prussia, making it easy for them to overlook their own defeat on the Marne. What they thought of their ally's initial performance is graphically apparent from Hoffmann's diary entries in the autumn of 1914. 4 October: 'Here everything is in excellent order, except for the Austrians! If only the brutes would move!' 18 October: 'We cannot place the smallest reliance on the Austrians, otherwise everything would be so simple.' 1 November: 'If only the Austrians had done what we told them!'[9] Ludendorff was no less blunt in his memoirs after the war. 'I got to know the condition of affairs in Austria-Hungary only in the course of the war. I had never had any opportunity previously. I was utterly amazed.' A Jew he encountered while campaigning in Russian Poland commented to him that Germany was allied to a corpse: 'He was right.'[10]

Paul von Hindenburg wrote after the war that anyone who thought Germany's allies 'merely a lot of cripples' betrayed 'a stupid ignorance of the truth' because they in fact tied down 'very superior enemy forces'.[11] Nevertheless, there is no question that Austro-Hungarian performance during the course of the First World

War left much to be desired. A major factor in its military shortcomings was its character as a multinational state, with no ethnic group constituting a majority of the population. While some German leaders recognised the language difficulties this created in the Habsburg Army, and even the need for its political system to take into some account the desires of the various national groups, most of them had little idea how the tie with Germany impacted the integrity of the Habsburg political system. Numerous Germans, including Kaiser Wilhelm, spoke in Darwinian terms about the First World War being a racial struggle between Teutons and Slavs. If this were true, then half of the Monarchy's population, which was Slavic, was fighting after 1914 on the wrong side. German and Magyar groups in the Monarchy saw victory in the war as an opportunity to buttress their own power in the Habsburg political system; as a result, it is unsurprising that non-German and non-Magyar groups were less than enthusiastic about the war effort. Not inappropriately, the most famous book about the Austrian Slavic population's participation (or non-participation) in the First World War is Jaroslav Hasek's novel *The Good Soldier Svejk*. The problem of how to motivate the Slavic nationalities of the Monarchy to fight wholeheartedly in alliance with Germany was never solved by the Austro-Hungarian leadership. Given the dynamics of the alliance, it was probably unsolvable. But with it in abeyance, the Habsburg war effort was inevitably less effective than it could have been.

As the Germans realised, Slavic disaffection was not the only problem hindering their ally's performance in the war. Austria-Hungary's seeming inability to utilise even its limited resources with reasonable efficiency became a chronic source of concern. There was no wonder in German eyes why German military units were better equipped than their Austro-Hungarian counterparts; for example, the Monarchy may have counted itself one of the Great Powers before 1914, but its military spending had ranked with that of Italy. When news began arriving of the first Austrian defeats, Hoffmann noted in his diary that for 20 years the Austrians had saved money on their army 'and now they are paying for it'.[12] The convoluted political structure of the Dual Monarchy made increases in spending on almost any common institution next to impossible. During the war, the situation got worse; production bottlenecks abounded, and by 1917 the Habsburg authorities were begging Germany for food supplies as well as military assistance, even though grain remained relatively plentiful in Hungary; what was available was often squandered. Conrad fantasised great battles of encirclement, but as Ludendorff later remarked in a moment of pointed understatement, 'Unfortunately, the Austrian Army was not always strong enough to carry out his bold plans.'[13]

If Habsburg generals failed to realise that frontal assaults without adequate artillery support were suicidal, the soldiers did, which probably contributed as much to their growing unreliability as did the Monarchy's nationality conflicts.[14] After the war the Austrian staff officer Theodor von Zeynek summarised the difference between German and Austro-Hungarian military operations: 'We unfortunately lived by improvisations, while on the German side the most solid organisation was the basis for every undertaking.' Hoffmann, as usual, was more blunt; the Austrians, he noted in 1916, 'can't seem to take the war seriously'.[15]

That lack of seriousness had fatal consequences. Austria-Hungary suffered more total casualties than any other power in the war, including Russia. Of that amount, however, around 32 per cent came from prisoners. By contrast, only 9 per cent of German casualties were prisoners, which speaks for itself about the combat effectiveness of the two military establishments.[16]

Habsburg weakness – if not outright incompetence – was something the German leadership could ill afford to ignore, for it threatened Germany's own prospects in the war. It practically invited extension of more and more German control over the overall war effort, as well as over the Dual Monarchy's own internal affairs, not always to good advantage for either. The German leadership generally thought the Monarchy's nationality conflicts could best be solved by supporting the Austrian Germans and Magyars against the 'slack' or treasonous Habsburg Slavs, particularly the Czechs, which merely risked alienating the Slavs further. There was, in any case, only a narrow line between seeing Austria-Hungary as a weaker ally needing help in the common cause, and, as German commitments to it deepened, seeing it as little more than war booty like Belgium or Poland.

A major German goal in the war was achievement of a single Austro-German *Mitteleuropa* with close economic and political ties. Falkenhayn wrote in the autumn of 1915 that the Monarchy should be forced to 'give up as much of its sovereignty as this requires'; and Gottlieb von Jagow, the German State Secretary for Foreign Affairs, bluntly informed his Austro-Hungarian counterparts that Austria's role in the new construction would be little more than that of the 'Germanic Eastern March' keeping the local Slavs under control.[17] Austro-Hungarian leaders understandably worried that German assistance came at a higher price than they could afford to pay. 'No one values our ally more than I, but they have the cute habit of grabbing at your entire hand as soon as you extend your little finger to them,' István Tisza, the Hungarian Minister-President, once declared.[18]

The following two years intensified the friction already apparent in the 1914 campaigns. With the failure of the Schlieffen Plan, Erich von Falkenhayn replaced Moltke as German Chief of Staff. Falkenhayn believed that the war – if it could be won at all – would be won on the Western Front. This made conflict with the Austrians inevitable, for the latter for obvious reasons wanted the emphasis placed on beating the Russians. To disagreements over military priorities was added the threatened intervention of neutral Italy and Romania. To keep them from the Entente camp, Germany advocated giving in to their demands for Habsburg territory, much to the outrage of the Austro-Hungarian leadership. German Chancellor Theobald von Bethmann Hollweg made clear his priorities to Ambassador Tschirschky: 'All considerations for our ally ... have to take second place to our concern for Germany's existence.' By March 1915 Austria-Hungary had agreed in principle to a cession of the Trentino to Italy, but only with very bad grace. Conrad fumed: 'If Italy could not be satisfied with this heavy sacrifice and made new demands, in his opinion it would be better to go to ruin and drag Germany along with them, than to give in to more of such blackmail.'[19] The protracted exchanges, which did not prevent Italy from entering the war in May, served little purpose except to further exasperate feelings in both Vienna and Berlin.

Militarily, 1915 was a year of success for the Central Powers. Even Falkenhayn realised that enough German troops had to be transferred east to stabilise the front, though he sent them there 'with a heavy heart' and only because he feared the alternative would be a complete collapse of the Dual Monarchy.[20] The resulting Austro-German offensive, spearheaded by a German breakthrough at Gorlice-Tarnów, rolled the Russians away from Hungary and, in fact, out of most of Russian Poland. In the autumn a joint German-Austrian-Bulgarian invasion overran Serbia. The Dual Monarchy contained Italy on the Isonzo while Romania remained neutral. Success, however, simply papered over the discord in the alliance rather than addressing it. Falkenhayn hoped that the loss of Poland would induce the chastened Russians to conclude a separate peace, something many Austrians dreaded as likely to come at their expense. In any case, he expected the Eastern Front to be quiet for a while, enabling a renewed concentration of German forces in the west. Knowing that his allies would not be happy about this, he simply hid from them his preparations for the Verdun offensive until mid-April of 1916.

The Austrians certainly were not happy, for they wanted German forces to be concentrated in the east until Russia was knocked out of the war entirely. More dangerously, the Austrian leadership tended to overlook the obvious unreliability of growing numbers of Austrian units even during the moments of success. And they forgot that both Poland and Serbia were bought with German troops. When Conrad attempted an independent campaign of his own in late August against the Russians, it was a miserable failure. 'With our troops, one can't plan any operations,' he moaned. 'In the whole war there was never anything as simple, as certain, as this operation, but it was still botched up.'[21] That realisation did not keep him after the fall of Serbia from ordering an independent Habsburg campaign in Montenegro and northern Albania without informing Falkenhayn, who was so incensed that the two ceased to be on speaking terms for a month. He also began preparations for an offensive out of the Tyrol against Italy. A campaign against the Monarchy's 'own private enemy', as Falkenhayn put it, would in his view simply be a dangerous diversion of resources; his admonitions were ignored by the Austrian High Command. The Germans were not even officially told of the upcoming attack until 9 May 1916. There were endless disputes between the diplomats about *Mitteleuropa* and the future of Poland. Unable to achieve their goals together, each side went its own way and did its best to keep the other in the dark about its plans, a disastrous lack of co-ordination considering the odds arrayed against both of them.

The dénouement came in 1916. Conrad's Tyrol offensive captured a few mountain villages, then fizzled out. Verdun became a bloody stalemate. Meanwhile, on the Eastern Front, which had been denuded of both Austrian and German units for these separate theatres, Russian General Brusilov launched his famous attack against the Austrian lines at Lutsk. In the three days following 4 June, 20 miles of Austrian lines ceased to exist. As Conrad begged assistance from Falkenhayn, his staff officer Karl Schneller drew the obvious conclusion: 'We are now totally and completely under the thumb of the Germans.'[22] The Germans were not long in pressing their advantage. 'It has to become clear to our allies that it will not do to go to the strong brother to get help in time of need, and then to empty his pockets after the danger is over,' Jagow wrote to Tschirschky in Vienna.[23]

It was massive German reinforcements, despite commitments at Verdun and the Somme, that finally stopped the Russians and threw back the Romanians when they entered the war in August. A unified command structure, blocked by Conrad in 1914, was imposed on the Eastern Front at last, with Austrian commanders under German leadership and usually paired with German chiefs of staff. German units were placed among Austrian ones along the line to 'stiffen' it. Germans undertook to retrain Austrian units, redo their trenches, and even build new Austrian railway lines. Despite all these efforts, it still required German forces to stop the 1917 Kerensky offensive after more Austrian retreats. And the famous Habsburg victory over the 'private enemy' at Caporetto in the autumn was likewise possible only with German troops and overall German command, provided only because the Germans once again feared an Austrian collapse, this time against even the Italians.

The debacle at Lutsk left Austria-Hungary few options for the rest of the war. Alone among the major powers, its leaders by the end of 1916 began seriously attempting to get out of the conflict rather than pushing themselves further into it. It took the Germans two additional years to realise that the war was lost, and by then any favourable bargaining position with the enemy coalition was gone. Emperor Karl ascended the Austro-Hungarian throne hoping to conclude peace as quickly as possible and to lessen his dependence on Germany. His new Foreign Minister, Ottokar Czernin, believed that a moderate Austro-German war aims programme – at least in the west – might open the door to a negotiated end to the war. The year 1917 saw a spate of secret Austrian peace feelers with various western contacts.

In Germany, however, the team of Hindenburg and Ludendorff, having replaced Falkenhayn in command of the Army, pushed a rigid annexationist agenda that could be achieved only through total victory. Berlin soon disclosed that it was much more willing to give up the Trentino than Belgium. Austrian opposition to unrestricted submarine warfare was simply brushed aside; and when Russia collapsed, the Germans set the pace of the negotiations at Brest-Litovsk. The Monarchy's only remaining leverage was the threat of its own impending collapse, which Vienna proclaimed repeatedly to Berlin – to no avail. To Czernin's pleas for moderation, Ludendorff replied bluntly: 'If Germany makes peace without profit, then Germany has lost the war.'[23] While Karl may have been tempted by the possibility of an Austro-Hungarian separate peace, most of the Habsburg leadership believed that the Monarchy's military and economic dependence on Germany made such an option impossible. By 1918 Czernin was describing himself – and Austria-Hungary – as being 'in the position of a man who finds himself on the fourth floor of a burning building and who jumps out the window as the only possibility of rescue.' Nikolaus Revertera, one of the contacts in the abortive peace feelers of the time, wrote in terms of similar desperation: 'We are bleeding ourselves white for grotesque ideas and nevertheless cannot separate ourselves from Germany without approaching a catastrophe.'[24]

To the extent that the war ended with the defeat of Germany and the total dissolution of the Habsburg Monarchy, the wartime alliance between the two powers can hardly be said to have been a success. German strength easily led to domination; Austro-Hungarian weakness, to Austrian over-extension of limited resources, which invited German control to rectify the situation. Much the same happened between Germany and Italy in the Second World War, though without the added complication of the Monarchy's nationality problems. Nevertheless, it is hard to see any better alliance combinations for either power. Austria-Hungary, eyed hungrily by Russia, Italy, Serbia and Romania, could hardly dispense with its ties to Germany. And Germany, encircled by the Entente, could certainly not afford to abandon its last halfway reliable ally in Europe. Ultimately, each was the lesser of the various evils available to the other.

Few individuals were more outspoken in their criticism of Austria-Hungary's performance during the First World War than the future German chancellor, Adolf Hitler, who in September 1939 plunged the peoples of Europe and ultimately the world into a further and yet more devastating conflict. An Austrian by birth, and a strident nationalist by persuasion, Hitler was particularly scathing about the failure of the Austro-German partnership, which had been so calamitous in its consequences for the Germanic mission. 'The fantastic conception of the Nibelungen alliance with the Habsburg state cadaver,' he wrote bitterly in *Mein Kampf*, 'has been the ruin of Germany.'[25] It was the planning of Germany's resurgence rather than the causes of its ruin that interested Hitler, however, and as early as 1920, two years before Mussolini and Fascism came to prominence, he was already preaching the necessity of an alliance with Italy, whose own grievances against the post-war settlement, coupled with her numerous intractable disputes with France, made her an obvious choice for the coming leader of the embryonic National Socialist Party.

Twenty years later the Greater German Reich and the Italian Empire, united by the Anti-Comintern Pact of November 1937 and the Pact of Steel of May 1939, presented to the world a daunting image of political solidarity and military prowess as their respective leaders converged on Munich in order to decide the fate of a defeated France and an enfeebled, isolated Britain. Beneath the surface, however, even at the apparent zenith of its power, the Axis alliance was plagued by as many if not more crises, problems and contradictions as its German/Austro-Hungarian predecessor. Such was Hitler's exasperation after almost five years of war in partnership with Mussolini that as his own hour of defeat approached he exclaimed to the inner circle: 'Ah! If only the Italians had remained aloof from this war! If only they had continued in their state of non-belligerence! In view of the friendship and the common interests that bind us, of what inestimable value to us such an attitude would have been!'[26]

The wartime failure of the German-Italian alliance cannot fully be understood without some preliminary consideration of the nature of the Rome-Berlin Axis and the circumstances in which it was forged during the mid-1930s. Contrary to the claims of Nazi and Fascist propaganda, which sought to stress the ideological and political affinity of the two regimes, in reality the Axis never amounted to much more than an awkward and unequal association to which competition rather than co-operation provided the dominant impulse. While there may have been certain superficial similarities between Fascism and National Socialism, though here too there were significant differences, nothing could disguise the fact that during the 1930s Germany and Italy were not only engaged in a fierce struggle for political and economic influence in South Eastern Europe, of which their quarrel over Austria was only the most obvious manifestation, but also intensely suspicious of each other's relations with the Western democracies, particularly Britain, with whom Hitler had more than once intimated his desire for a close understanding. Brought together partly in consequence of the failure of their respective policies towards Britain, and, in Italy's case, due to fears of isolation following the Abyssinian crisis, the Axis powers found much to dislike in the international order of the 1930s, yet spectacularly failed to devise between them a common strategy designed to adjust conditions to their mutual satisfaction. This failure in peacetime to co-ordinate policy and objectives, even at the most basic level, meant that during the war Germany and Italy inevitably pursued different agendas and fought separate wars for different ends.

The problem was compounded by the fact that whereas Hitler's foreign policy 'programme' had a discernible ideological dimension and was largely focused on Germany's position vis-à-vis Great Britain and the USSR, Mussolini, lacking any clear-cut objectives, tended to stumble from one imperialistic adventure to the next in an attempt, in his own ill-chosen words, to make Italy 'great, respected and feared'.[27] One consequence of this important difference between the two dictators was clearly demonstrated during the summer of 1940 when the impending collapse of France once more conjured up in Hitler's mind the alluring prospect of a settlement with Britain. From that point onwards the Italians suddenly became something of a nuisance in view of their designs on the British Empire. 'In the overall picture, some minor differences begin to stand out between Italy and ourselves,' noted Franz Halder with supreme understatement on 21 May. 'Italy's chief enemy now is Britain, whereas Enemy No 1 for us is France. We are seeking to arrive at an understanding with Britain on the basis of a division of the world.'[28] In the circumstances a more revealing admission of German priorities is difficult to imagine.

The lack of a common political strategy inevitably impacted on military relations. Conversations between the general staffs were not inaugurated until April 1939, and even then one of their chief purposes was to enable each side to keep an eye on the intentions of the other.[29] Between 1940 and 1943 the failure to establish anything resembling a joint command structure meant that senior Italian and German officers conferred so infrequently, and then only in the shadow of their respective political leaders, that any ties of friendship and mutual confidence, let alone any joint initiatives, were stifled from the outset. The failure of the Axis powers to co-ordinate their political and military plans before the outbreak of war is not the only parallel that may be drawn between their association and the Austro-German alliance of the First World War. Italy, like Austria-Hungary, was inherently much weaker than Germany in both economic and military terms. As a result, the more the war dragged on, the more she was forced to depend on the resources of her ally, and, inevitably, the more she came to resent that dependence. In German eyes, Italy's weakness, coupled with the palpable incompetence of her military establishment, of which there was abundant evidence from the outset, went from being the butt of *Schadenfreude* and cynical jibes in 1940 to an object of outrage and scorn by 1943, when her manifold deficiencies were predictably held responsible for Germany's own reversals.

Considerations of high politics and military strategy aside, the omens for a friendly relationship between the German and Italian people were in any case far from auspicious. The view of Italy entertained by the generation of Germans who had lived through the Great War was inevitably coloured by the perceived treachery of Italian policy in 1915 and the military disaster at Caporetto two years later. As a result of these and other factors, most notably Italy's opposition to an Austro-German Anschluss and her harsh treatment of the German population of the South Tyrol, there was no love lost for the Italians in post-war Germany, where they were roundly dismissed as a race of indolent and cowardly hedonists. For their part, the Italians similarly despised the Germans as a horde of godless and uncultured barbarians, whose unscrupulousness and savagery made them a constant menace to European peace. No alliance or pact, no state visit or propaganda campaign, could ever have reconciled these mutually antagonistic viewpoints, and to each population the national image of the other appeared to perform perfectly to type during the Second World War. Thus, just as it is unsurprising that German criticism of Italy's military achievements, or rather lack of them, was rife from the very day Italy entered the fray, so is it equally unremarkable that Italian civilian and military authorities refused on humanitarian grounds to co-operate with their German allies in the transportation of French and Greek Jews to the death camps.

Ironically one of the more unlikely tasks that Mussolini set himself was to imbue the Italians with some of the very characteristics that they themselves attributed to and so abhorred in the Germans. Aiming to 'prussianise' his people and make them less sympathetic to the plight of others, he hoped that they might one day become 'hard, relentless, and hateful – in fact, masters'.[30] When in March 1938 the Duce was informed of a British protest about recent bombing raids on Republican Spain, he expressed satisfaction that the Italians were at last horrifying the world instead of charming it with their virtuosity on the guitar.[31] It is no less ironic therefore that it was largely the musical and artistic talents of the Italians that so impressed and enchanted Hitler.[32] The prospect of fighting alongside them, however, particularly at a time and against enemies not of Germany's choosing, was quite another matter. The German leader was more than happy to avail himself of Italian diplomatic backing and its implied threat of military action in the crises of 1938-39 and during the Sitzkrieg, but from the summer of 1939 he was under no illusions about Italy's ability to sustain a major and protracted war effort. Indeed, how could he be when, barely one week after the Pact of Steel had been announced to the world with a fanfare of Axis propaganda, the Duce sent his Under Secretary of State for War to Berlin bearing a document in which were enunciated no fewer that eight concrete reasons why war with Great Britain and France should not break out until 1943?[33] Hitler may have admired the Italians, but as allies in wartime he wanted the modern-day equivalent of Caesar's legions, not the army that had taken eight months to subdue Ethiopia. In October 1936, shortly after Addis Ababa had finally fallen to the Fascists, Hitler was shown a photograph of Mussolini with the caption 'The greatest Roman of them all'. 'What a pity the rest are Italians!' was his laconic response.[34]

When war came in September 1939 the Axis was predictably plunged into a crisis of equal if not greater proportions to that which had shaken it at the time of the Anschluss in the spring of 1938. Having received repeated assurances from the Germans that there would be no war for several years, the Italian leaders were understandably horrified to learn in mid-August of the impending attack on Poland and the advanced state of the German negotiations with the Soviet Union. Frustrated at his inability to intervene either as warrior or peacemaker, and wary of a German backlash should he denounce the Pact of Steel, a course that he tellingly feared might even provoke a German attack on Italy[35], Mussolini finally and reluctantly opted for a policy of non-belligerence. Despite his anger at German duplicity, however, the Duce never seriously considered breaking fundamentally with Hitler, whose military triumphs were simultaneously an object of admiration and envy.

Nevertheless, by early 1940 he was sufficiently alarmed by the level of German-Soviet co-operation that he wrote personally to the Führer imploring him not to renounce his self-proclaimed mission to destroy Bolshevism.[36] When two months later Hitler deigned to respond, his main preoccupation was to assure himself of Mussolini's support in the forthcoming Western campaign. Accordingly, the arguments articulated in his reply, which were duly reinforced during a personal meeting at the Brenner on 18 March, were nicely calculated to produce the maximum psychological effect on Mussolini, whose itch for action was thereby undoubtedly stimulated.[37] The Western campaign, however, proved a massive disappointment to the Italians and brought Mussolini neither the military glory he craved nor the fruits of victory he coveted. In consequence he began to cast around for other theatres in which to conduct his 'parallel war', which, when it finally began in North Africa and on the Greek-Albanian frontier, so fatally compromised Italy's position within the Axis that it was never to recover. Although Hitler sought to spare Mussolini's feelings during their summit at Salzburg in January 1941, the recent Italian military reversals transformed the conference into what Denis Mack Smith has aptly termed 'a protracted torture of embarrassment' for the Duce, as it was now apparent to all that 'the parallel war was over and only the support of Germany kept the tragi-comedy of fascism in being.'[38]

Three weeks before this meeting took place Hitler had written warm words of encouragement to Mussolini in the spirit of 'the sincere comradeship of a man who feels that he has thrown in his lot with you for better or for worse'.[39] Irrespective of the circumstances then prevailing, there seems little reason to doubt that these words came from the heart. Having taken considerable inspiration in his early years from the example set by Mussolini, Hitler never entirely lost his affection and admiration for that 'extraordinary man' for whom he had feelings of 'deep friendship'.[40] Even in 1945, although long since disillusioned with Fascism, the Führer still admitted to considering the Duce his equal, perhaps in some respects his superior.[41]

Mussolini, however, was too saturated with arrogance ever to contemplate the possibility of an equal, and saw in Hitler at best an upstart, if a clever and gifted one, whose armed forces might one day secure for Italy that glorious future that alone she was singularly incapable of realising, and at worst a degenerate who had 'none of the decisive gestures or soldierlike demeanour that a dictator should possess'.[42] Ciano and Ribbentrop, the two Foreign Ministers, maintained a superficially civilised attitude towards one another in correspondence and during their personal meetings, but behind the diplomatic niceties their relationship bristled with contempt and suspicion. For Ciano Ribbentrop was a 'sinister being', a 'madman' who exercised a malevolent influence on events; in Ribbentrop's view his Italian opposite was a jealous, vain and deceitful rogue who was in 'permanent contact with the enemy'.[43]

Relations between the military personnel were similarly strained and grew progressively worse as the war continued. Italy's jackal-like intervention in the Western campaign created a baleful impression among the German military elite whose deep-seated suspicions of Italian incompetence were instantly and comprehensively confirmed. Years later this episode continued to provoke a lively reaction from the German leaders. Under interrogation in 1945, for example, Goering fulminated against Italy's 'treacherous' conduct in June 1940. 'The most ridiculous thing of all,' he complained, 'was Mussolini's speech at the conclusion of the French campaign, when he said that Italy's soldiers had accomplished the very difficult task of overcoming "tremendous fortified positions", and worst of all had triumphantly announced the capture of a certain mountain peak, which had always been Italian.'[44]

In late 1940, following a limited degree of collaboration in the Battle of Britain, one of the few things that united German and Italian airmen was a healthy respect for their RAF opponents; for each other, however, they felt only complete contempt.[45] Field Marshal Kesselring, the German commander best placed to provide a judgement on Italy's contribution to the war, later wrote that he had had no reason to doubt the 'goodwill' and 'enthusiasm' of the Italian armed forces, although this in itself might be considered sufficiently patronising and dismissive. Despite his admiration for the individual acts of heroism performed by Italian servicemen, Kesselring was appalled by the glaring deficiencies that existed in all three branches of the Italian forces.[46]

In the one area where Italy might have been able to render Germany valuable assistance, namely at sea, she again proved to be a colossal disappointment. Having already suffered a mauling at Taranto in November 1940, the Italian Navy sustained a further defeat off Cape Matapan in March 1941 when, at a cost to themselves of one aircraft and its crew, the British disposed of three Italian heavy cruisers and two destroyers. Following this engagement the *Supermarina* was instructed to keep its most powerful units within 100 miles of coastal air bases.[47] By mid-summer Italy's battleships had been immobilised by a shortage of oil, thus ending 'the small remaining chance of a temporary Mediterranean victory for the Axis'.[48] It was perhaps understandable therefore that Hitler should explain to the Japanese ambassador in March 1942 that it was a pity that the Mediterranean had not been patrolled by the 'excellent navy of Japan' instead of that of Italy. Had that been the case, 'he thought that the position there would long ago have been stabilised'.[49]

It would clearly be unwise to accept without question the criticism that is habitually meted out to the Italians in the memoir literature of former German military and political figures. Nevertheless, despite some recent attempts to reassess Italy's role in the Second World War, which have sought to focus attention on purported German shortcomings[50], it remains difficult to escape the conclusion that from start to finish Italy was poorly equipped and poorly led. It is certainly undeniable that the Italians were frequently disappointed in their requests for assistance from the Germans; it is equally incontestable that it was largely their own political and military blunders that made those requests such an urgent necessity in the first place. The ill-fated Italian operation against Greece in October 1940 is a case in point. Angered by the news of the dispatch of a German military mission to Romania, Mussolini exploded in a fit of pique: 'Hitler always faces me with a fait accompli. This time I am going to pay him back in his own coin. He will find out from the papers that I have occupied Greece. In this way the equilibrium will be re-established.'[51] Such were the immediate and hopelessly frivolous origins of an undertaking that was destined to result in abject humiliation for the Italians and, more importantly, to create for Germany a host of political and military problems in South East Europe at a time when she was most anxious to see order and stability maintained in that region. Further complications arose from Mussolini's extraordinary capacity for self-delusion and his stubborn refusal to heed expert advice. During the early stages of the Egyptian campaign, for example, considerations of prestige, coupled with serious misjudgements about the tenacity and quality of his own forces and those of his opponents, conspired to prevent him from accepting offers of German assistance until his own position had become virtually untenable.

The Italian failures in Greece and North Africa were made doubly deplorable in German eyes by the fact that Mussolini's leaping political aspirations bore no relation to his meagre achievements on the field of battle. On 21 April 1941, following an acrimonious round of negotiations concerning the new order in the Balkans, Ribbentrop remarked how fortunate it was that the Italians had scored no military victories, otherwise they would have been 'completely intolerable'. 'All that we need from them is to have their country at our disposal as a theatre of war, nothing more,' he announced to his astonished State Secretary.[52] Hitler, too, his eyes fixed on the forthcoming invasion of the USSR, had grown utterly weary of the Italians by mid-1941. On 29 May he told his advisors that one could not keep making concessions to somebody who was 'always running around with his backside beaten black and blue'. Once 'Barbarossa' was over, Hitler remarked revealingly, he would no longer need to show any consideration for the Italians.[53]

He showed precious little consideration for them in any case when three weeks later the Wehrmacht thundered across the German-Soviet border. Although the decision to attack Russia had been taken in principle in July 1940 and confirmed following the failure of the German-Soviet negotiations of the following November, it speaks volumes for the true nature of the Axis that Mussolini was only officially informed of this major and ultimately catastrophic extension of the

European war once the German invasion was under way. Mussolini's first thought upon receiving the news, which arrived in the form of a letter from Hitler, was to provide a contingent of Italian troops, although, as Ciano correctly divined, 'from what Hitler writes it is clear that he would gladly do without it'.[54] The German leader was indeed most reluctant to sanction anything more than a symbolic Italian participation in the Russian campaign. In Hitler's view the greatest contribution that Italy could make to the common cause would be to send reinforcements to North Africa and concentrate on air and naval warfare against the British in the Mediterranean.[55] To be sure, he would change his tune following the setbacks of the coming winter, but in the early months of 'Operation Barbarossa' Hitler was exhilarating in a personal crusade that marked the realisation of a long-standing ambition. As such he was by no means inclined to share the glory of the moment with others, particularly those who had failed him in the past. Moreover, the further his armies advanced, the more the old ideas returned to the fore, and within a month of the invasion the German leader was once more speaking of a 'durable friendship with England'.[56]

After June 1941 it became increasingly difficult to speak of the Axis as an alliance in any real sense of the term. Although the dictators continued to meet periodically in order to discuss the progress of military operations and matters of mutual political interest, a combination of ill-health, the weakening of his own position in Italy and a growing reliance on German support on all fronts made these conferences an increasingly frustrating and humiliating experience for the Duce. Moreover, they served chiefly to demonstrate that he and Hitler had altogether different priorities. For just as Mussolini was incapable of breaking Hitler's preoccupation with the conflict in the East, so too was the Führer completely unmoved by the Duce's tentative suggestions of a compromise with Stalin and the concentration of the entire Axis war effort on the Mediterranean. Following one such conference at Klessheim Castle in April 1943, during which he had listened in silence to a series of crushing monologues, Mussolini returned to Rome vowing never again to submit to the indignity of being lectured by that 'tragic clown'.[57] Two months later, when he was finally removed from office and taken into custody, what little remained of the Axis alliance, and indeed of Fascism, evaporated overnight.

Although the Germans subsequently liberated Mussolini and placed him at the head of the Republic of Salò, he spent the rest of the war as little more than a Nazi stooge with no real authority over the important areas of state business. Despite his pleas for increased executive powers, the Germans purposefully kept him on a tight rein, having no desire to risk any further setbacks or surprises. The plain fact was that, lacking an army to put into the field, and with his country partially overrun by the Allies in the south, and elsewhere collapsing into a state of civil war and open resistance to the German 'invaders', Mussolini was now of little practical value to Hitler. Moreover, the Duce was forced officially to admit that Germany should assume sole responsibility for the conduct of military operations, even those now being carried out on Italian territory. Convinced of Italy's unreliability, the Germans showed little enthusiasm for Mussolini's fantastic dreams of raising another army. They now had other uses for the Italians. As Ribbentrop explained to the Japanese ambassador shortly after the final meeting between Hitler and Mussolini at Rastenburg in July 1944:

'Italy wanted her troops better armed and their number increased. Although that was considered not unreasonable, the most pressing need was to win the war, and until that was done it would be best for Italy, taking an overall view of the situation, to send as many workers as possible to Germany and to help Germany in the industrial field. Germany too, of course, was deeply interested in promoting the formation of an Italian army, but with the Italian temperament to consider there was a limit at which they had to stop.'[58]

As the German and Italian dictators travelled their separate roads to defeat, each found time to reflect on the fundamental causes of his own downfall. In Mussolini's view the Italians themselves were naturally partly to blame, but a good measure of his wrath was reserved for the Germans, whose generals understood nothing of strategy and whose leaders knew little of politics. The Germans still had great potential as a nation, but they had deserved a better leader than Hitler who had failed to recognise the 'superior spiritual gifts' of the Duce.[59]   Hitler was rather more gracious in adversity and managed to refrain from any personal recriminations against Mussolini. Nevertheless, it had been a grave mistake to have entered the war with an Italian alliance that had been 'of more service to our enemies than to ourselves' and whose benefits had been 'modest in the extreme in comparison with the numerous difficulties to which it has given rise'. It would have been far better if Italy had remained neutral, for Germany would then have been spared a multitude of military and political complications that had fatally diverted her from her real aims. In the course of this monologue, recorded by the faithful Bormann on 17 February 1945, Hitler made a statement that might well be considered applicable to German alliance policy during both World Wars: 'We have everything to lose and nothing to gain,' he informed the assembled company, 'by binding ourselves closely with more feeble elements and by choosing into the bargain partners who have given all too frequent proof of their fickleness.' And although he claimed to have lost neither his personal affection for the Duce nor his 'instinctive' feelings of friendship for the Italian people, his own experience of the Italians as comrades-in-arms had effectively mirrored that of the leaders of the Central Powers during the First World War. 'I have often said that where you find Italy,' he concluded philosophically, 'there you will find victory. What I should have said is – wherever you find victory, there, you may be sure, you will find Italy!'[60]

Notes on contributors

Professor Gary W. Shanafelt, McMurry University, Abilene, Texas, USA. Professor Shanafelt received his doctorate from the University of California, Berkeley, in 1977. Since 1981 he has taught modern European history at McMurry University. His book, the Secret Enemy: Austria-Hungary and the

German Alliance, 1914-1918, deals with Austrian political relations with
Germany during the First World War. In addition to his interest in the Habsburg
Monarchy, he has also published work on Edith Durham and her life in the
Balkans before the war.

Dr G.T. Waddington, The University of Leeds, UK
G. T. Waddington took his B.A. and Ph.D. from the University of Leeds where
he is currently Lecturer in International History. He has published articles and
essays on Ribbentrop, Anglo-German and German-Soviet relations, and his
translation of the memoirs of Reinhard Spitzy appeared in 1997 as How We
Squandered the Reich (Norwich, Michael Russell). He is currently completing a
monograph on Ribbentrop and German foreign policy for Cambridge University
Press. He is also working on a book on Anglo-German relations between the
wars with Dr Frank Magee of Coventry University

Recommended reading

Ciano, Galeazzo, edited with an Introduction by Malcolm Muggeridge and a Foreword by Sumner
    Welles, *Ciano's Diary 1939-1943* (London: Heinemann, 1947)

Deakin, F. W., *The Brutal Friendship: Hitler, Mussolini and the Fall of Italian Fascism* (London: Weidenfeld
    & Nicolson, 1962)

Herwig, Holger H., *The First World War: Germany and Austria-Hungary, 1914-1918* (London: Arnold,
    1998)

Knox, MacGregor, *Mussolini Unleashed 1939-1941: Politics and Strategy in Fascist Italy's Last War*
    (Cambridge: Cambridge University Press, 1982)

Schreiber, Gerhard, Stegemann, Bernd and Vogel, Detlef, edited by the Militärgeschichtliches
    Forschungsamt, translated by Dean S. McMurry, Ewald Osers and Louise Willmot, *Germany and the
    Second World War*, Vol III 'The Mediterranean, South-east Europe and North Africa 1939-1941'
    (Oxford: Clarendon Press, 1995)

Schreiber, Gerhard, *Revisionismus und Weltmachtstreben: Marineführung und deutsch-italienische
    Beziehungen 1919 bis 1944* (Stuttgart: Deutsche Verlags-Anstalt, 1978)

Shanafelt, Gary W., *The Secret Enemy: Austria-Hungary and the German Alliance, 1914-1918* (Boulder:
    East European Monographs, 1985)

Silberstein, Gerard E., *The Troubled Alliance: German-Austrian Relations, 1914 to 1917* (Lexington:
    University of Kentucky Press, 1970)

Stone, Norman, *The Eastern Front, 1914-1917* (London: Hodder & Stoughton, 1975)

Wiskemann, Elizabeth, *The Rome-Berlin Axis: A History of the Relations Between Hitler and Mussolini*
    (London: Oxford University Press, 1949)

Notes

[1]   Josef Stürgkh, *Im Großen Deutschen Hauptquartier* (Leipzig: List, 1921) p116
[2]   Karl draft letter to Ottokar Czernin, 14 May 1917, quoted in Karl Freiherr von Werkmann,
    Deutschland als Verbündeter, Kaiser Karls Kampf um den Frieden (Berlin: Verlag für Kulturpolitik,

1931) pp170-2

3   Hoffmann Diary, 17 July 1917, Max Hoffmann, trans Eric Sutton, *War Diaries and Other Papers*, 2 Vols (London: Secker, 1929) Vol I, p188

4   Heinrich von Lützow, Peter Hohenbalken (ed), *Im Diplomatischen Dienst der k.u.k. Monarchie* (Vienna: Verlag für Geschichte und Politik, 1971) p220

5   István Deák, *Beyond Nationalism: A Social and Political History of the Habsburg Officer Corps, 1848-1918* (Oxford: Oxford University Press, 1990) p191

6   Erich Ludendorff, *Ludendorff's Own Story, August 1914-November 1918*, 2 Vols (New York: Harper, 1919) Vol I, pp259-60

7   Conrad to Bolfras, 27 August 1914 and 5 September, 1914; Franz Conrad von Hötzendorf, *Aus Meiner Dienstzeit, 1906-1918* 5 Vols (Vienna: Rikola Verlag, 1922-1925) Vol IV, pp551-2, 647

8   Forgách to Macchio, 30 September 1914, quoted in Gary W. Shanafelt, *The Secret Enemy: Austria-Hungary and the German Alliance, 1914-1918* (Boulder: East European Monographs, 1985) p45

9   Hoffmann Diary, op cit, Vol I, pp45-9

10 Erich Ludendorff, op cit, Vol I, pp138-9

11 Paul von Hindenburg, trans F. A. Holt, *Out of My Life*, 2 Vols (New York: Harper, 1921) Vol I, p210

12 Hoffmann Diary, 26 September 1914, op cit, Vol I, p43

13 Erich Ludendorff, op cit, Vol I, p89

14 A recent examination at the regimental level of the Habsburg Army's fighting efficiency finds ethnic disloyalty greatly exaggerated as a cause of its battlefield shortcomings; see John Schindler, 'A Hopeless Struggle: The Austro-Hungarian Army and Total War, 1914-1918' (unpublished doctoral dissertation, McMaster University, 1995)

15 Hoffmann Diary, 27 August 1916, op cit, Vol I, pp144-5; Zeynek memoirs, quoted in Gary W. Shanafelt, op cit, p44

16 Figures calculated from Niall Ferguson, *The Pity of War* (New York: Basic Books, 1999) p295, Table 32. The corresponding figures for the other Central Powers are 4 per cent for Bulgaria and 17 per cent for the Ottoman Empire.

17 Bethmann note on Falkenhayn's views, 15 October 1915, quoted in Gary W. Shanafelt, op cit, p77; Jagow memo, 13 November 1915, André Scherer and Jacques Grunewald (eds), *L'Allemagne et les Problèmes de la Paix Pendant la Première Guerre Mondiale*, 4 Vols (Paris: Presses Universaires de France, 1962-1978) Vol I, pp211-5

18 Tisza to József Vészi, 2 March 1915, István Tisza, Oskar von Wertheimer (ed), *Briefe (1914-1918)* (Berlin: Hobbing, 1928) p170

19 Bethmann to Tschirschky, 6 February 1915, quoted in Gary W. Shanafelt, op cit, p61; Common Ministers Council, 8 March 1915, Miklós Komjáthy (ed) *Protokolle des Gemeinsamen Ministerrates der Österreichisch-Ungarischen Monarchie, 1914-1918* (Budapest: Akadémiai Kiadó, 1966) p229

20 Erich von Falkenhayn, *The German General Staff and its Decisions, 1914-1916* (New York: Dodd, Mead, 1920) pp64-5

21 Kundmann Diary, 9 September 1915, quoted in Manfried Rauchensteiner, *Der Tod des Doppeladlers, Österreich-Ungarn und der Erste Weltkrieg* (Graz: Verlag Styria, 1993) p292

22 Holger H. Herwig, *The First World War: Germany and Austria-Hungary, 1914-1918* (London: Arnold, 1998) pp209-10

23 Ottokar Czernin, *In the World War* (New York: Harper, 1920) p275

24 Crown Council, 22 January 1918, Miklós Komjáthy, op cit, p631; Revertera to Berchtold, 17 October 1917, quoted in Gary W. Shanafelt, op cit, p156

25 Adolf Hitler, trans Ralph Manheimi with an Introduction by D. Cameron Watt, *Mein Kampf* (London: Pimlico, 1993) p575

26 François Genoud (ed), trans from the German by Colonel R. H. Stevens, with an Introduction by H. R. Trevor-Roper, *The Testament of Adolf Hitler: The Hitler-Bormann Documents, February-April 1945* (London: Cassell, 1961) p73

27 Christopher Hibbert, *Benito Mussolini: A Biography* (London: The Reprint Society, 1963) p94

28 Charles Burdick and Hans-Adolf Jacobsen (eds), *The Halder War Diary 1939-1942* (London: Greenhill, 1988) p156. See also MacGregor Knox, *Mussolini Unleashed 1939-1941: Politics and Strategy in Fascist Italy's Last War* (Cambridge, Cambridge University Press, 1982) pp113ff

29 Gerhard Schreiber, Bernd Stegemann and Detlef Vogel, edited by the Militärgeschichtliches

Forschungsamt, translated by Dean S. McMurry, Ewald Osers and Louise Willmot, *Germany and the Second World War*, Vol III 'The Mediterranean, South-east Europe and North Africa 1939-1941' (Oxford: Clarendon Press, 1995) p9

30 Galeazzo Ciano, translated and notes by Andreas Mayor, with an Introduction by Malcolm Muggeridge, *Ciano's Diary 1937-1938* (London: Methuen, 1952) pp128, 135

31 Ibid, p92

32 See, eg, Dr Henry Picker, *Hitlers Tischgespräche im Führerhauptquartier: Vollständig überarbeitete und erweiterte Neuausgabe mit bisher unbekannten Selbstzeugnissen Adolf Hitlers, Abbildungen, Augenzeugenberichten und Erläuterungen des Autors: Hitler, wie er wirklich war* (Stuttgart: Seewald, Jubiläumsausgabe, 1983) pp58-9

33 Raymond James Sontag, John W. Wheeler-Bennett, Maurice Baumont, et al, 'Documents on German Foreign Policy, Series D', 13 Vols (Washington, 1949-64) (hereafter DGFP, D) Vol VI, No 459

34 Hodsall to Norton, 24 October 1936, PRO, C7628/4/18, FO 371/19914. In April 1944 Hitler told Mussolini that he 'wished to provide the Duce with the nucleus of a reliable military force, but the soldiers must be determined to fight for the Duce like a Roman Legion; and he made it clear that he regarded this as an unlikely contingency.' Sir Ivone Kirkpatrick, *Mussolini: Study of a Demagogue* (London: Odhams, 1964) p595

35 Galeazzo Ciano, edited with an Introduction by Malcolm Muggeridge and a Foreword by Sumner Welles, *Ciano's Diary 1939-1943* (London, Heinemann, 1947) p128

36 DGFP, D, VIII, No 504

37 Ibid, No 663; IX, No 1

38 Denis Mack Smith, *Mussolini* (London: Weidenfeld, 1993) p264

39 DGFP, D, XI, No 586

40 *Hitler's Table Talk 1941-1944*, with an introductory essay on the Mind of Adolf Hitler by H. R. Trevor-Roper (Oxford: Oxford University Press, 1988) p267

41 *The Testament of Adolf Hitler*, op cit, p74

42 Denis Mack Smith, op cit, p261

43 *Ciano's Diary 1939-1943*, op cit, p160; *Ray Moseley, Mussolini's Shadow: The Double Life of Count Galeazzo Ciano* (New Haven: Yale University Press, 1999) p82; *The Ribbentrop Memoirs*, Introduction by Alan Bullock, translated by Oliver Watson (London: Weidenfeld & Nicolson, 1954) p189

44 Scavenger special report No 10, 1 June 1945, PRO, WO 208/4463

45 Kelly to the FO, 20 December 1940, PRO, C13593/5/18, FO 371/24385

46 *The Memoirs of Field Marshal Kesselring*, translated by Lynton Hudson (London: William Kimber, 1953) pp105ff, 174

47 Denis Mack Smith, op cit, p265; Gerhard L. Weinberg, *A World at Arms: A Global History of World War II* (Cambridge, Cambridge University Press, 1994) p218

48 MacGregor Knox, op cit, p283

49 Oshima to Tôgô, 29 March 1942, PRO, HW 1/482

50 See, eg, James J. Sadkovich, 'The Italo-Greek War in Context: Italian Priorities and Axis Diplomacy', *Journal of Contemporary History*, Vol 28 (1993), pp439-64

51 *Ciano's Diary 1939-1943*, op cit, p297

52 L. E. Hill (ed), *Die Weizsäcker Papiere, 1933-1950* (Frankfurt am Main: Propylaen, 1974) p248

53 Hewel Diary 1941, entry for 29 May, microfilm 2249, Brotherton Library, University of Leeds

54 *Ciano's Diary 1939-1943*, op cit, p360

55 Horst Boog, Jürgen Förster, Joachim Hoffmann, et al, edited by the Militärgeschichtliches Forschungsamt, translated by Dean S. McMurry, Ewald Osers and Louise Willmot, *Germany and the Second World War*, Vol IV 'The Attack on the Soviet Union' (Oxford: Clarendon Press, 1998) p1038

56 *Hitler's Table Talk*, op cit, p26

57 Denis Mack Smith, op cit, p290

58 Oshima to Shigemitsu, 25 July 1944, PRO, HW1/3136

59 Denis Mack Smith, op cit, p315

60 *The Testament of Adolf Hitler*, op cit, pp69ff

PART III
THE EXPERIENCE
OF OCCUPATION

Chapter 29

The experience of occupation: Belgium[1]

Mark Derez

At the outset of both World Wars Belgium hid behind its neutrality, which was imposed in 1914 and chosen in 1940.[2] There was no military tradition to fall back upon. A well-known anecdote recounts that Leopold II, when in Berlin visiting Kaiser Wilhelm II, actually put his spiked helmet on backwards.[3] Even more familiar is the school-book illustration of the monarch on his death-bed, signing with trembling hand the law introducing compulsory military service. That was in 1909. In that same year the leading Catholic politician, August Beernaert, an advocate of the King's colonial policy, but also of using arbitration to solve international conflicts, received the Nobel Prize for Peace. Both Catholics and socialists were adverse to the clatter of weapons. In 1940 the Army was in readiness for a repeat of 1914-18, but not for a Blitzkrieg with aeroplanes and parachutists. Every now and again sneaking doubts would present themselves. Was this really our war? Or was it yet another of the long series of wars being fought on our territory? Except for the collaborators whose motto was 'wartime is action time', and who saw this as a chance to get power, there was, by and large, little enthusiasm for any kind of military enterprise. Belgium expected that her safety would be guaranteed:

'We fully expected to be saved by the English, without asking ourselves for a moment whether, in defending their own interests, our prospective liberators would give any thought to our interests. Without thinking, my fellow-citizens placed themselves under the tutelage of a foreign power. Remark that this was the power – can it have been an accident? – which had stood at the cradle of the new Belgian state in 1830-31. Now Britannia was being asked for advice, sympathy and help. One is put in mind of certain African states who, after decolonisation, appeal unabashedly for help to their former overseers.'[4]

The general picture is thus one of passivity. The Belgians were overwhelmed by the war, and the country underwent an occupation not once, but twice. The people were hounded, the country beleaguered and demeaned. For those who stayed behind it was a matter of surviving in fear and trembling. Survival was often the task of the women, who relapsed into ancient daily duties. Here, then, are the themes of this tale of two wars: fleeing, plundering, bombings, women and survival, heroines and female traitors.

In the Flemish collective memory there is a very special niche for *de vlucht* (flight from the occupier), as though it were a separate stage of life. Indeed, a very large part of the population was affected, many more than the 350,000 Belgians in the trenches in 1914-18, and even more than the 600,000 Belgians who were mobilised in May 1940 for the Eighteen-Day Campaign (in actuality a retreat that lasted 18 days, from 10 to 27 May 1940). For many, this was not only the initial experience of the war, it was also an unexpected and an overwhelming experience.[5] In my grandparents' repertory of tales, for instance, the dominant motif was *de vlucht* and its many hardships. Indeed our family, not exactly reputed to be a tribe of heroes, still cherishes the cradle in which an uncle, then a new-born babe, was transported during our flight in the Great War, which was accompanied by his vociferous comments. In Flemish literature there is a persistent image of massive panic and collective madness, sustained not least by the popular author Stijn Streuvels, the baker-writer once considered a Nobel Prize candidate. 24 August 1914 is the day known as 'Flight Monday', when the rumour circulated that all the men would have to go fight along with the Germans. The stronger sex scattered and went into hiding in ditches and streams, in haystacks and cesspools, with the local luminaries and authorities leading the way. Some did not surface until days later, to the great amusement of the women who had stayed behind.[6]

Were they chicken-hearted, all those farmers, or was the land in the grip of some atavistic anxiety going back to the time of press gangs and marauding mercenaries, to Marlborough's campaigns and Napoleon's conscriptions? Survival instinct, it seemed, still continued to triumph over patriotism, which had never developed deep roots in the countryside. As the refrain had it, 'Fatherland, fatherland? My father has no fatherland. The only land he has is the ground in the flower-pot.' In France, the transformation of 'peasants into Frenchmen' was not effected until about 1914.[7] How, then, could the process of turning 'peasants into Belgians' be expected to go any faster? Despite military service, and notwithstanding the many lessons at school on the history of the 'fatherland', large segments of the population had little awareness of belonging to the new nation-state of Belgium; the nation's socialisation was far from complete. In the flat Flemish countryside the intellectual horizon often reached no higher than the spire of the parish church. In contrast to this *esprit de clocher*, the socialist workers had their *Organisationspatriottismus*. Following the example of their German comrades, they constructed their own small fatherland around the Maison du Peuple, or the Volkshuis, the House of the People. The fatherland that encircled the church tower or the Volkshuis was hardly the fatherland over which a war could be fought. A *schoolstrijd*, a battle between Catholics and free-thinkers 'for the beautiful soul of the child', in line with the German Kulturkampf, now that was something worth fighting over, yet that was only a home game, played for local supporters.[8] In the case of a real war it was best to take to one's heels.

In August 1914 20,000 volunteers joined the Belgian Army with a flower in their button-holes. With the exception of this initial spurt of patriotism, the

Belgians did not live in the high-tension sphere of heroism, unless it be the electric current in the barbed wire put up by the Germans in the spring of 1915 to prevent young Belgian volunteers from making their way through the Netherlands to enlist in the Belgian armed forces. Eventually, 32,000 volunteers would join up with the exhausted Belgian Army on the Yser Front. It is hard to say if this figure is a heroic one. There was also movement in the opposite direction – refugees in Great Britain and France whose sons turned 18 preferred to send them back to Belgium, rather than see them leave for the front. Both the British and the French police were authorised to turn draft-dodgers over to the Belgian military authorities. Well-known artists such as Rik Wouters in the Netherlands and Frans Masereel in Switzerland were not affected, for the Belgian statutes on military service could be ignored in neutral countries.[9]

In art it was the suffering of the individual refugee that was most often portrayed. Before the war Alfred Ost had worked in a rather stereotype idiom, depicting processions and peasant fairs. Now, using the same baroque style, he drew old people and displaced families, women with babes hanging on to their skirts. Though these skirts still lift and billow, the cause is not the tempo of the dance but the haste of the flight. The children are still as plump as those Hummel figurines that our occupying forces would later bring back with them from Germany, but their eyes are bulging with fear. Such images are rare in the art of the Second World War, although refugees were much more numerous then. It was the First World War that was the defining factor. It was the memory of the Great War that set half the country fleeing in May of 1940, contrary to Government orders. *Fama volat* – fame has wings. It was the Germans' fame, or rather their infamy, that preceded them. In August 1914 it was the rumours of German brutalities that caused people to run; in May 1940 the remembrance was still a haunting one. The Blitzkrieg burst upon Belgium, and the Belgians made a lightning exit. Bruges, which pre-war planning intended to be a point of passage and not a place of reception, had received some 420,000 refugees by the end of May, almost eight times the town's population. The annual May fair had to be shut down in all haste.[10]

Yet the refugee problems of the Second World War did not replicate those of the preceding war. Though both conflicts produced a gigantic movement of the population, the exodus of 1914 resulted in permanent exile for the duration of the war, whereas in 1940 repatriation was completed by the end of the summer. By that time some 1.5 to 2 million Belgians had returned from France, which had itself capitulated. In 1914 the fleeing Belgians totalled 1.5 million – about one-fifth of the population. A million went to the Netherlands, where the border villages north of Antwerp were inundated by a veritable sea of refugees two or three times outnumbering the local inhabitants. Here, when the winter had passed, there were still over 100,000 refugees remaining. The German occupiers encouraged the refugees to return, for they wanted to remain in good standing with the neutral powers, and most of all they did not want to provide the Allies with extra manpower or cannon-fodder. The Belgian authorities, for their part, feared that the emigration would become permanent, and took measures to prevent Belgians from sailing away on ships with transatlantic destinations. Canadian and American offers of this type were refused. Of the 200,000 refugees in England, over 170,000 were still there in

1917 and 125,000 had not yet left by November 1918. The number of refugees in France grew from 250,000 at the beginning of the war to 325,000 at its end. For all these displaced Belgians shelter and food needed to be found.

The problems were enormous. In the Netherlands chaos threatened, and the Army was brought in with tents, help centres and provisions. Following the emergency measures, the refugees were quartered with families or in camps that were generally self-sufficient with their own bakers, barbers and tailors, and with a school, a dispensary, a bath-house and a nursery. Living conditions varied from spartan to deplorable, as two British envoys reported in November 1914.[11] The British Government, which was greatly in need of skilled workers, and was thus not totally disinterested, decided to take in thousands of refugees. As for France, it made no distinction between its own refugees and those from Belgium, nor did it establish separate refugee units. In contrast to France and the Netherlands, where the authorities made subsidies available and where refugee accommodation was a combined effort, England candidly called upon civil society, whose contributions were generous.

Likewise, in the Second World War, the British Government was reluctant to spend one penny extra on refugee aid, for the war effort and the evacuation of the cities were consuming its resources. Again it was the civilians who responded to the need. In 1914 Belgian Refugees Committees sprouted like mushrooms in towns and villages. Not counting the cost, they passed out food, clothing, toys and layettes for newborns. At times they even extended their solidarity to the Belgian combatants, instituting *Le shilling pour la chaussette du soldat*. This all had its source in the traditional philanthropy of the notables, of wealthy women and clerics, and in the efforts of thousands of volunteers. In the Second World War it was the Women's Voluntary Services for Civil Defence that recognised the needs of the refugees and performed miracles with minimal means. There was even a professor of International Relations who pressed the 'Great Artveldt', alias Jacob van Artevelde, the Flemish William Tell, into service, together with the hundreds of weavers who had crossed the Channel with him in the 14th century.[12] Thus, in one professorial stroke the history of England was shown to be interwoven with that of the Belgian refugees.

J. B. Priestley intoned on the BBC in 1942: 'England is today the Ark of Liberty and Hope'. This message did not fall upon deaf ears, least of all among the clandestine listeners on the continent who, no longer able to escape, were now surmounting their original defeatism and were placing all their hope in London.[13] It is questionable, however, whether the message of a certain little Georgette reached its destination. Georgette had been separated from her family during an air attack on Charleroi, and eventually she was placed in a Red Cross Home in the English countryside. Via the BBC she sent this message to her parents:

'This is Georgette, your little girl speaking, to tell you that I hope you are all well, also Huguette, Roberte and Gaspard. I am living in a big house in the country, and am very well looked after. Everybody is very kind to me. I was given two dolls at Christmas, a boy and a girl. I am getting big, and hope to see you again soon. Lots of kisses to everybody…'[14]

For far-off Allies such as those in North America and Australia, financial aid to the Belgians was more a political act than a humanitarian gesture, as occasional curious reactions demonstrated. As soon as the Armistice was signed in 1918 a certain number of Japanese ladies abruptly stopped sending contributions for the support of their nine 'adopted' war orphans; after all, Belgium was now slated to receive reparation payments.[15] Not only far away but at home, too, solidarity tends to get eroded, especially in the wear-and-tear of war. In France and the Netherlands, where the authorities had strongly contributed to refugee support, civilian efforts continued. This was much less so in England, which had mainly called upon private initiative. One cannot go on extending charity for ever. When the whole humanitarian operation seemed due for repetition, patience ran out.

England in 1914 had not been prepared for an influx of refugees at all, except perhaps in South Wales and the South West, where refugees were expected from the civil war that threatened to break out in Ireland. After the start of the World War, Belgians were thus able to profit from preparations that had been made with others in mind. Irish or Flemish – it was all the same. In 1940 the British authorities were better prepared. They were certain of at least one invasion, expecting the arrival of an army of 200,000 needy persons, estimating that 40,000 would be from the Netherlands and the rest from Belgium. The actual number was far below the initial estimates. The Belgians were in fact the largest refugee group, but their number never went above 15,000. Many arrived more or less accidentally, their intended departure for France having been prevented by the swift advance of the Germans. At this juncture many families became separated. Madeleine van Eeteveld recounts:

'In May 1940 Mother, my sister and I went along with Father, who was a mobilised civilian. He worked for the Ministry of Public Works in the Albert Canal Division. Unfortunately, as we left Mechelen [Malines] we got separated. Father went ahead alone and we tried to follow him, but we got to England and he ended up in France.'[16]

There was no easy way for those who missed the boat to get to England. Escaping through France, Spain and Portugal was extremely risky, by no means a tourist trip. Further, the Germans did not permit even paddling along the Belgian coast – *Schwimmen verboten* – as though they feared bathers might take the opportunity to swim across to England. Those who arrived in England in 1940 did not come unannounced, yet this time their reception was cooler. The memory of the Belgians' previous stay was not a totally positive one. Further, the capitulation of the King of Belgium had produced sharp, even suspicious, reactions, as also in France. Then again, the British populace had the air raids to contend with.

In both wars the Belgian refugees constituted a heterogeneous group in which town-dwellers and Flemings predominated. As for the Walloon provinces, the rapid German advance had simply taken the people by surprise. In 1940 most of the refugees who washed up on the British coast had made their exit from Belgium's extreme west, the same area that had been called the Ypres Salient in the previous war. For the most part they were ordinary people who had no choice but to remain where they had landed. It was of course the wealthy burghers who had grabbed places on the last boats, or whose limousines, protected by a mattress on the roof, were in the vanguard of an endless procession of lorries, wheelbarrows, bicycles and pedestrians heading toward France in 1940. Ironically, in 1914 it was also the wealthy who were the most readily persuaded to return in order to protect their fortunes (and to avoid the taxes that the Germans threatened to impose on the émigrés). Peasants also returned, for they were at least certain of regaining their land.

For those refugees who remained abroad for the duration of the war, problems were myriad: difficulties in adapting, language problems, cultural differences, choosing between integration within the host country or solidarity and isolation. This matter of balancing disparate loyalties was one that no emigrant community could escape. Religious conflicts did not arise, even though most Belgians in this Protestant setting were Catholics. Yet it was as though a festive and guzzling race had suddenly found itself in a culture that prized total abstinence and Sabbath observance, and where sobriety and the seriousness of life were the norms. The Catholic Church in Belgium kept an eye on its scattered flock, however, and sent out some 200 spiritual shepherds in 1914 and about a score of them in 1940. Not all of these sheep were angels or saints, much less heroes, and this was viewed as regrettably inconsistent with their refugee status. Nor were all of the victims from 'poor little Belgium' worthy representatives of a higher moral order. It was especially among co-religionists that such irritation ran high. A Catholic priest in the Netherlands described the Belgians as frivolous, ignorant of the faith and thankless. The war with its hardships was by no means sufficient to bring them to repentance, and to this end they would need to undergo the plague, famine and other afflictions, and above all ten years of German control, or so he opined.[17] Though he was hardly a source of comfort, this irate pastor was right on one count: in 1918-19 Belgian Francophone nationalists would lay claim to strategic Dutch territory – so much for gratitude![18]

Many of the so-called religious or cultural differences were in fact differences of class. The Baroque intemperance of the Counter-Reformation was thoroughly imbibed by the common people, the partially de-Christianised proletariat. It was members of the well-to-do burgher class who were the first Belgian refugees to arrive in 1914. They were French-speakers, they were representatives of la Belle Epoque who had a good general education and a certain *savoir vivre*. In short, they were seen as worthy representatives of Western civilisation and Latin culture who had become caught up in unequal combat with the barbaric Hun. Even if they arrived penniless, they could expect solidarity from others of their class. Marguerite Mathy, proud of being a direct descendant of one of Emperor Charles V's better-known Flemish mistresses, had vivid memories of being given a princely reception in the home of the Cadburys, the Birmingham chocolate-makers. Indeed, upon arriving in London she had become separated from her sisters, who were immediately snatched up by other rich families.[19] There was a philanthropic race on – everyone wanted to have his or her own Belgian refugee.

However, when 'fortress Antwerp' fell, 500,000 common people in the areas surrounding the city were caught like rats in a trap, and by the time they had managed to swarm out, the willingness to receive them had markedly cooled. A London doctor let the remark slip that the Germans deserved to be defeated, if only for the reason that they had saddled England with the Belgians – a comment that was eagerly repeated by the German press.[20] The impression was that the scum of the nation had been washed up on Albion's coast. Yet all in all, it was not that bad. The number of undesirables, or those who were labelled so – the work-shy, the drunkards and the profligates – was estimated at no more than 2 or 3 per cent. In the other host countries the percentage was equally high, or low. In the tabloids, however, various *faits-divers* involving Belgians were worked for all they were worth. Paradoxically, it was the workers who eventually achieved integration and not the bourgeoisie, the white-collar workers or the intellectuals, who did not speak English well enough to be able to work at their previous levels. Workers, on the other hand, were swiftly absorbed into wartime production plants in both France and England. This met with initial opposition from the unions, especially in 1940 when Britain's 1 million unemployed had only recently found work in the arms industry.

The deployment of the refugee workforce was not always efficiently managed, as in the case of the aid organisation that in 1914 sent thousands of Belgian workers to Blackpool, a seaside resort where there was absolutely nothing for them to do. Belgian fishermen, however, found a welcoming haven in Brixham, Devon. There, with half the Belgian fishing fleet, they actively contributed to the British food supply.[21]

What appeared to be an army of have-nots in the summer of 1940 was found to be a substantial reinforcement of the British war economy the following summer. There was integration in the plants and factories, and in the schools, which accepted refugee children free of charge. Somewhat surprising was the severity of the measures that the Belgian authorities took in both wars against loiterers and layabouts, in sharp contrast to the far milder treatment of conscientious objectors and deserters. Again and again it could be observed, in this land of Bruegel, of carnivals and drinking parties, that even if the military was not highly valued, the work ethic certainly was. Still, the Belgians could not turn down the chance to wear the fool's cap. When the Duchess of Kent paid a visit, the children were decked out in the costumes of the Gilles carnival figures from the town of Binche, with headgear like 'a gigantic tarantula spider' – a sight that soon became part of the corporate image of Belgium.[22]

Yet it was still the refugees who got the short straw. Their situation remained precarious, and the ways in which they were viewed were both ambiguous and contradictory. The accumulating daily irritations and erroneous perceptions produced prejudices that were hard to refute; those who had work were ruining trade, and those who found none were exploiters who were living off society. It was to be expected that the propaganda machine would make use of the refugees. The Allies, of course, ascribed to Belgium the unenviable status of unfortunate victim, with her refugees as the perfect example. In German counter-propaganda there were two main images, that of the ragged proletariat, exploited by the Allies, and that of the cowardly, lazy ne'er-do-well, living a life of ease far from the front. The propaganda was not without effect, particularly in occupied Belgium. When the refugees returned they were often treated with contempt for having chosen to flee, that is for having taken the hare's path. During the First World War there were even sarcastic pamphlets produced, containing mock certificates of membership in the Order of the Hare (*l'ordre du lièvre*).[23] Though not actually presented, they did constitute attempts to influence opinion. There was a deep chasm between the diaspora and those who had kept watch at home during the occupation. Each group felt the other had had a much better time of it. Here the war erased yet another of society's lines of demarcation. In 1944 the returning refugees had to share in the incomprehension that was meted out to the Belgian Government in exile, 'the men of London', who were viewed by many in the same light as defectors.

War is always an extreme experience, but when it is characterised by flight, by uprooting and alienation, by isolation – in particular in the case of people as bound to their homes as were the peasants and villagers of Flanders – then that experience sticks in one's memory and the war becomes a singularly exceptional stage of one's life. And that stage is marked most of all by disorientation. Whoever flees becomes a wanderer. As Camille Boudry from Wulvergem near Ieper (Ypres), a woman of the people, said: 'Ah yes, fleeing. Fleeing is strange; you don't know where you are going and you don't know where it is that you must go.'[24] The refugee is in any case someone in need of help who is at the mercy of others. Even more than the person who stayed at home – no matter how unfavourable the conditions were there, during the occupation – those who spent the war in a foreign land have been marked by an existential experience; their fleeing has stigmatised them. Louise Parmentier, from Dranouter, who as a young woman had to flee from the Ypres Salient in 1914, is still perceptibly indignant at what she experienced as a refugee – disrespect, disparagement, exclusion. She does not even want to hear the word 'refugee'.

'Back then things were good for those who could stay at home. But the people who fled would always be refugees. You were always "the refugee". The name they gave you was "refugee". For the longest time, they would say, "She's a refugee." Sometimes I got angry when they said "refugee". It was a strange name to have. You couldn't help it; there you were, ruined, and to top it all off they called you a refugee. We just weren't anybody any more.'[25]

From a military point of view, Belgium was at most a bothersome obstacle on the way to the ports on the Channel coast, but for the German intendancy it was a source of economic profit to be brazenly plundered, not once, but twice. Apart from being a buffer state created in part by Britain and destined for a passive role in the diplomatic chess game, Belgium was primarily an economic project, the work of a bourgeoisie that had imported its parliamentary monarchy from Britain, after it had brought in the Industrial Revolution – using some industrial espionage as needed. Among the founders of the 'firm' of Belgium, there were Lieven Bauwens, who smuggled the 'spinning jenny' out of England and brought it to Ghent, the Cockerills, father and son, who developed the steel industry in Wallonia, and Stephenson, after whom the continent's first railway locomotive was named. Though somewhat of a parvenu among Europe's kingdoms, Belgium proudly proclaimed herself *la Belgique industrielle*. With Flemish textiles, Walloon steel and the densest rail system in Europe, the Belgium of the early 20th century was a highly developed industrial nation possessing raw materials (coal and iron ore), semi-finished products and a well-qualified labour force: in short, *gefundenes Fressen* for a rapacious neighbour.

It was only to be expected that the occupier would take over the conquered country's means of production to ensure the provisioning of the people, and to benefit its own troops. This did not even contravene the Hague Convention of 1907, which allowed for the costs of an occupation to be paid for out of the treasury of the occupied country, provided this was within that land's capabilities.[26] In both World Wars, however, what resulted was unabashed exploitation. On both occasions there was conflict on this subject between the local German military authorities, who wished to spare Belgian industry in the interest of the population and of keeping order, and the war lords in Berlin, who intended to take over Belgium's *industries rücksichtslos* on behalf of the German war effort. The outcomes differed. From 1917 Belgium's industry was systematically dismantled upon orders from Berlin, and its machines were melted down to make weapons. In the Second World War the means of production remained for the most part intact. This time the intention was to eliminate Belgian competition, for here was the opportunity that German industrialists had been waiting for since 1918; any competition was to be absorbed into a European market that Germany of course expected to dominate.[27]

The First World War lists of requisitioned goods are legendary. Every municipal archive in Belgium still has packs of posters from 1914-18 with items to be confiscated.[28] It began with telephones (3 November 1914), followed by automobiles and bicycles, fire extinguishers (except those in buildings occupied by the Germans!), brooms and brushes (how would the famously clean Belgian housewife now keep her front steps spotless?). The requisitioning of copper and wool, usually performed in conjunction with unlawful entry, was perceived as an assault on ancestral heirlooms, for Flemish households were still quite traditional, and such items were passed from generation to generation, in dowries and as wedding gifts.[29] The 'copper thieves' went so far that by the end of August 1918 they were even requisitioning doorknobs and window latches. The continuous confiscations and ransacking were no laughing matter, and the population was bent low under the recurring demands. It is no wonder that after the war, at the time of the reparation payments, there were those who were reluctant to allow the vanquished to retain even so much as a toothpick.

The Germans, too, learned something from the First World War. Their approach to plundering in 1940-45 was more subtle. This time they bought up the whole country, at the expense of the Belgian treasury, making it possible for economic collaborators to dip into the pot, too. Requisitioning now came from the central authorities, and the amount to be turned over was linked with income – a sort of hidden social approach. This did not prevent the Germans from pulling out of the streets the large copper nail heads that marked pedestrian crossings. Now even these ultimate symbols of Belgium's colonial wealth, which had abundantly adorned the surface of the mother-country's roads, were forced into submission.[30]

In both wars non-ferrous metals were the object of special German interest. Copper and tin household utensils went underground and disappeared into clandestinity, along with the brass instruments of the village band. Bells found it harder to go into hiding. One could hardly tell the Germans that they had gone to Rome – the neutral Rome of Pope Benedict XV, who was labelled *Deutschfreundlich* – though this is what Belgian children were told each Good Friday when the bells began their silent Easter vigil. In the first war, when the Belgians were thought of as a nation of bell-ringers, thanks to Sir Edward Elgar's 'Carillon' piece, the Germans left their bells relatively undisturbed.[31] In 1916 plans were made for a general bell census, but apart from the bells along the front, no other bells were carted away to Germany. There was, however, a general prohibition on bell-ringing for the duration. All those 'tongues of bronze' that were celebrated in the songs and occasional verse of both pro-Flemish and pro-Belgian enthusiasts, were now silenced. In 1941 the bells again became fair game. Once again the church towers would become mute. Protests from the episcopate and from the Vatican did at least postpone the confiscation until 1943. The stealing of the bells aroused much indignation. A slogan went from mouth to mouth, 'Die met klokken schiet, wint de oorlog niet' ('He who shoots with bells will not win the war'). The collaborators replied, 'Beter een kerk zonder klok dan een klok zonder kerk' ('It is better to have a church without a bell than a bell without a church').[32] During the Second World War in this 'land of chimes', as Thomas Hardy had dubbed Belgium in 1914 in his 'Sonnet on the Belgian Expatriation', the civil war between patriots (the whites) and collaborators (the blacks) was fought in part with bells.[33]

Though Belgium's industries were not dismantled in the Second War, the occupier did raid its art treasures – taking Van Eyck's 'Lamb of God' from the cathedral in Ghent, and Dirk Bouts's 'Last Supper' from Leuven (Louvain) – two icons of the country's artistic heritage. Such looting created an uproar. Yet this mercantile nation had not always shown such concern for its artistic patrimony. In the 19th century, when the church roof leaked, the impoverished parish council would sell off a panel by Van Eyck or Bouts to some German museum. This could later have political implications, for the Treaty of Versailles had stipulated that such missing panels would have to be restored so that polyptychs could be reconstituted in situ. This made the Germans look as though they had also stolen art works during the First World War. In the following war this was indeed the case.[34] The Bouts and Van Eyck polyptychs became spoils of war and disappeared into an Austrian salt-mine together with the 800kg Madonna by Michelangelo, which was taken from the Church of Our Lady in Bruges. Reichsmarschall Goering, who had the reputation of being a great art lover, did not restrict himself to filching works of art. He did not beat about the bush:

'It is my intention to plunder on an enormous scale, beginning with the Netherlands and Belgium, and I am going to send a great many purchasers with special powers to those countries. They will have until Christmas to buy up everything that is attractive in the shops and department stores. I will make it all available to the German people in the shops here.'[35]

That was the Christmas Action of 1942. On offer were cosmetics (the largest segment!), dolls' prams, umbrellas and crutches... True to form, Goering made it graphically clear that inflation was about to break loose, so that the Belgian franc would be 'worth less than a certain familiar piece of paper that was used for a certain familiar purpose'. This recalled another scrap of paper by means of which Chancellor von Bethmann-Hollweg had contemptuously demolished Belgian neutrality in 1914. Since 1914, however, language in Germany had become more *völkisch* and earthy.

As though the large-scale plundering in both wars was not enough, the occupier also laid hand on a nation's most precious possession, its workforce, its human resources.[36] Between October 1916 and June 1917, 170,000 Belgians were deported to Germany, where they were forced to work in war plants. Although officially there were categories to be excluded, there were 4,000 women and 3,000 children in this number.[37] These draconian measures coincided with the granting of certain Flemish requests, such as making Dutch (Flemish) the language of instruction at the University of Ghent, and this did nothing to increase support for the Flemish cause among the general population. In the Second World War the occupiers applied their measures less bluntly, but they continually tightened their control: to begin with, voluntary work in Germany; from March 1942 onward, compulsory work in Belgium, preferably in war-related industries; by October 1942, compulsory work in Germany. This affected almost 2 million men and 900,000 women.[38] In the summer of 1943 the university students were conscripted, and the Rector of the University of Leuven, who refused to turn over the list of his university's students, was arrested.[39] Belgians were definitely not eager to leave friends and family to go and work in the enemy's country in factories that were bombed by the Allies almost daily. Eventually there came to be a 'work objector' in every family, and he or she had no choice but to go under cover. They were continually hunted down, with the Belgian collaborators joining in the chase. When the search for individuals produced insufficient results, razzias were instituted, carried out on Sundays, preferably, in the cafés, at football matches and at funfairs.[40] The Belgians could not have detested their captors more.

Before and after their plunder frenzies, the Germans were at pains to introduce Belgium to their newest weapons. A Leuven professor, known as an anglophile, apparently viewed the war as a sporting competition between friends, and protested privately but furiously that it was unfair of the Germans to attack Belgium with unfamiliar weapons. Fighting with unequal arms could distort the final outcome. That is one way of looking at it. The Germans were not impressed. Belgium, which had been considered in many ways a *terre d'expériences* at the beginning of the century, would be a testing ground for the means of war for the rest of the ill-starred century.[41]

It was the Ieper (Ypres) region that had the deplorable privilege of receiving the first large-scale gas attack in history.[42] On 22 April 1915, French, Algerian and Canadian troops in proximity to the Belgian sector near Steenstraat were attacked with chlorine gas. It was a fine spring day with a gentle north-easterly breeze, and a yellow cloud drifted slowly toward the Allied lines, where it spread death and, above all, panic. This was the beginning of the Second Battle of Ypres (22 April to the end of May 1915). At the beginning the hapless soldiers had no other way of protecting their lungs than to urinate on their handkerchiefs and hold them to their noses. Soon each soldier was issued a primitive gas mask as standard equipment. Ypres had the dubious distinction of lending its name to an even viler type of gas, yperite or mustard gas, which causes blistering, affects the eyes and attacks the lungs. Its first use on 17 July 1917 at Passendale (Passchendaele) occasioned dramatic losses on the British side.

Chemical warfare may have seemed about to put its mark on the century, but it was in actuality not so *epochemachend*. Poison gas assumed, for the most part, the role of a spectre. So it was in the Second World War, when the various belligerent nations possessed enough such gas to obliterate whole populations. Gas masks were passed out to civilians en masse. Cradles and prams were fitted with gas filters. Soldiers of every nation, including Germans, dragged gas masks about with them for years. Special hoods with filters were produced for the horses that pulled wagons and cannons – the Second World War was far less motorised than many imagine. There was a mutual chemical deterrence, analogous to later nuclear fears, and the various sides had a stranglehold on each other in a sort of balance of terror. Above all, it was the uncontrollability of gas and the instinctive, almost archetypal fear of poison that averted more such horror. Moral abhorrence and deeply rooted fear need not cancel out one another. This may explain why in the First World War nearly all the German commanders protested against using poison gas, and why even Hitler feared to unleash gas on the battlefield.[43]

Hardly anyone knows that the first air raid in history took place in the Belgian city of Liège. This unenviable 'first' occurred on 9 August 1914 with the advent of the first Zeppelin, one of six employed in German service.[44] Not much later there was one hovering over Antwerp, as we know from Allied propaganda prints. Just as abruptly, Zeppelins made their appearance in the poetry of Antwerp's avant-garde poet, Paul van Ostaijen, whose collection, *Bezette Stad* (*Occupied City*), was strongly influenced by German expressionism. They are presented as pictorial poems that literally adopt the shape of a Zeppelin, and in the immortal couplet: 'Jef Jef Jef ne Zeppelin / Kruipt algauw de kelder in' (loosely 'Jef, Jef, Jef, a Zeppelin there! / Hurry, hide down under the stair').[45] Not until 1915 did the Zeppelin raids on London begin. Van Ostaijen must have learned this from the newspapers, for he honoured Britain – *beata insula* – with a another typographically conceived poem. This time it was 'Good-bye Piccadilly, farewell Leicester Square' written out in the form of a Zeppelin. It can be no accident that the fame of another Antwerp artist, Panamarenko, born in 1940, has reached even London, though the Zeppelins he exhibits are anything but 'airworthy'. They are the artisan-like output of a typical Belgian do-it-yourself handyman that make poetic reference to a time when technical progress was not yet perverted by the *Materialschlacht* of modern warfare. The true Zeppelins were indeed instruments of war. These aircraft, which were called almost fondly 'flying cigars', created massive panic whenever they appeared. They floated slowly and ominously through the sky, and one could never know where they would drop their deadly cargo. Their unpredictability, and their seemingly arbitrary choice of targets, intensified the totalitarian impression that this technological warfare produced.

To that extent they were similar to the flying bombs that came at the end of the Second World War. They too were targeted to hit Belgium first. These new weapons, the V1s and V2s, were again aimed first of all at Antwerp and Liège – a strategic port city and a hub of communications. The fact that they were not manned doubtless increased their sinister reputation. Now the war acquired a new aspect, that of a war of the robots, against which the civilian was even more powerless. The military-industrial complex had now permanently assumed hair-raising totalitarian characteristics. Antwerp was hit by 3,700 flying bombs, resulting in over 3,500 deaths and more than 5,800 severely wounded victims.[46] Taking into consideration the area covered, Antwerp's fate was worse than that of London. The story of the V1 direct hit on a cinema during the matinée performance on 16 December 1944, with all of its 1,200 seats occupied, mainly by children and servicemen, has now entered the domain of urban legend. It was nevertheless bitterly real – and life had to go on. Dockworkers received extra wages because of the danger, the famous *bibbergeld*, or 'trembling money'. The people of Antwerp, keeping in character with their nickname 'Sinjoors', remained in the city – except on Sunday, for then they made excursions to the surrounding fields and heathland to see the spectacle of the whistling V-bombs and the shots fired by the artillery. There they treated their protectors to beer. (In the spring of 1945 there were 23,000 of these gunners: Britons, Poles and a great many black Americans.) In the evening they would get back on their bikes and pedal homeward, exhausted, the only thing passing them on the way to the city being those bombs that had escaped the artillery's fire, passing over their heads humming like insects. Until, that is, their morale finally broke down. Fifty-eight months of occupation and war – that simply had to have an effect. Toward the end of the war a reporter from *Time* was struck by the deathly silence of the city. On 27 March 1945 the last flying bomb fell on Antwerp. As in London, the end of the ordeal was greeted with boundless relief.

In the period following the First World War there grew up a whole arsenal of wartime imagery depicting the active fighting man and the passive, suffering woman. The woman is seen as the soldier's spiritual and physical mainstay. Having a woman nearby raised the troops' morale. She gave the warrior pleasure and support. Her supporting role is demonstrated in war memorials where she holds a tired, wounded or dead soldier.[47] The pleasure part was not perpetuated in stone. The well-bred ladies of La Belle Epoque who took the unexpected step of entering the war cautiously confined themselves to nursing and charitable works. They had expertise in charity. Soon they were involved in the distribution of food. This was undertaken on so large a scale, under American supervision, that charity could no longer be compared to a drop falling into a sizzling pan, but became a structural response to an acute need.

As for nursing, that was not really their meat. In the Belgian Army's medical services there was not one single woman nurse. Nursing was exclusively placed in the hands of nuns. Since their modesty with regard to the male body prevailed over notions of hygiene, this was not always beneficial to the healing process. Nurses were viewed askance in the military – a bit like spies or harlots. An upstanding Belgian officer would rather see his sister in a shroud than wearing a nurse's uniform. Despite all this, a veritable army of volunteer nurses grew up in no time at all. The positive image they earned during the war attained post-war mythic proportions, partly owing to the symbolic presence at the front of the Queen-Nurse.[48] Whereas the top brass had once turned up its collective nose at nurses, suddenly an odour of sanctity was ascribed to the 'White Angels'. Yet the amateurism of Belgian nurses was in undoubted sharp contrast to the professionalism of their British counterparts, whose legendary reputation had grown steadily since the days of the Crimean War and Florence Nightingale.

The society ladies never got near any real military business on the field. As for those women of the people who had become refugees, they found work in the Allies' war industry. On the home front or in occupied territory, employment opportunities were often limited to the red light districts behind the Allied lines or the institutionalised German army brothels. There it was not exactly a matter of military activity as such, though women of ill repute attached to the armed forces were often dubbed the 'light cavalry'. The German military leadership was apprehensive that these might be patriotic Amazons ready to infect the occupying troops with syphilis for sheer love of country.[49]

Belgian women did not return to the clatter of weapons until a few of them joined the British Army's Women's Auxiliary Air Force (WAAF) in the Second World War. After a short period of training they were given tasks commensurate with their previous qualifications, such as typist or translator. In this way women were again incorporated into the military's logistical services. 'Allied women fight for freedom' announced an Allied poster that found its way to Belgium after the war. It shows not only the obligatory nurse and women air mechanics, but also a woman in fighting gear and martial stance. One might almost suppose that these posters were intended primarily for post-war archives, but the sphere of heroism and adventure, of comradeship and communality that they show, was authentic. The war, as it was experienced in Britain, could be compared to one long adrenaline kick. Being demobbed was hard, somewhat like 'cold turkey'. Hear Josette Bens:

> 'Being demobbed and coming back to civilian life was much harder for me than being in the service in England. I have had a lot of difficulty adjusting to life as a civilian in a country that used to be mine, but where I have not lived for six years … and I miss the contact with the others. We used to live as a community, and now we were alone again… I had the feeling that there was a broad gap between 1940 and 1946, a gap that would be difficult to bridge.'[50]

Then, too, there was the difference between the war as it was experienced on the other side of the fence and the depressing situation in occupied Belgium. In both wars women had their hands full simply trying to survive. Belgium, thickly populated and heavily industrialised, depended on imports to supply three-quarters of its food. During hostilities all those imports were menaced. To make matters worse, in 1914 the British proclaimed a continental blockade, which produced severe food shortages. Germany refused to feed this occupied population as long as Britain continued the blockade. Eventually the British opened a very small door, reaching an agreement with the Germans, mediated by the neutral United States, Netherlands and Spain, that allowed foreign products to be imported for the exclusive benefit of the Belgian civil population. With winter at hand, 7 million Belgians were in danger of starving.

It was Herbert Hoover, the future American President, who took the initiative in London in October 1914 to set up the Commission for Relief in Belgium.[51] Whatever the Commission was able to purchase (with money from the Belgian Government and private donations) was distributed in Belgium by the Comité National de Secours et d'Alimentation.[52] This committee had been started by a 'club' of notables who organised soup kitchens in the spirit of bourgeois paternalism. However, it gradually assumed the role of occupied Belgium's Government in exile, and constituted a sort of shadow cabinet. This was all the more remarkable since it was in the hands of the Brussels bourgeoisie, who were liberal and unchurched, whereas the Government was still in the strong grip of the Catholics. As for the Commission for Relief in Belgium, which had been started as a private organisation, it had its own flag, issued passports and entered into negotiations with sovereign states. As one British voice put it, the Commission conducted itself like a 'piratical state organised for benevolence'.[53] The Belgian people were immensely grateful. After it was forbidden to wear national emblems, people wrapped themselves in the Stars and Stripes. Each American holiday was enthusiastically celebrated, and even Valentine's Day took on the air of a national day.[54] Thanks to this combination of traditional philanthropy and American pragmatism, the CRB developed into an exemplary humanitarian aid organisation. The Commission had 50 observers who rattled round the country in a fleet of brand new automobiles. The Germans looked upon them as obnoxious busy-bodies. It is not surprising that in 1940 the German authorities decided to keep food distribution in their own hands.

In fact, fearing foreign meddling, the occupying Germans established the Winter Help organisation in October 1940 to provide support and aid. Winter Help ran on contributions and lotteries. Since it had been set up by the occupier, it was at first considered to be tainted with collaboration. Radio London and the clandestine press helped to tarnish its reputation, and Winter Help (Winterhulp/Secours d'Hiver) was soon called Hitler Help (Hitlerhulp/Secours d'Hitler).[55] At length, however, with the blessing of the Cardinal, adorned with the halo of the late and much loved Queen Astrid, and, most of all on the basis of its achievements, Winter Help earned the people's confidence. Nor would the Belgians be Belgians had they not managed to re-route Winter Help to help their Jewish fellow citizens and demobilised Belgian soldiers. Perhaps it was only in this undisciplined kingdom that the aid organised by the Nazis could be re-directed to give help to the occupying regime's victims and opponents.

Yet provisioning remained precarious in both wars. However much the Germans complained that thanks to the actions of the Commission for Relief in Belgium and American food aid, the Belgians were better fed than the Kaiser's own subjects, the fact was that food imports fell drastically. More food was imported in 1913 than in the four war years together. In the Second World War the huge distribution system fell apart almost immediately. The official ration of 1,300 calories instead of the normal 2,400 was already inadequate. Up to the harvest of 1942, food production could not meet more than 30 to 50 per cent of that figure. In such conditions, feeding the mouths in her care was the housewife's daily challenge. The frugality that domestic science schools had kept harping on about, and which was primarily a means of maintaining social discipline, now turned out to be amazingly useful. Pre-war feminists were now writing cookery books for wartime based on this-for-that substitutions, and these books sold like hot cakes. The clocks had been turned back half a century. In the First World War, Grandmother's spinning-wheel and flour-grinder were brought down from the attic. In the Second World War useful items re-emerged after having been tucked away since the previous war. Among them were the churns and coffee-roasters whose forgotten charms were now the stuff of advertisements. What we see here is not mere technological recycling; the actors and structures may seem to change from war to war, but it is the women who embody a general continuity.

Women reverted to their ancient roles of gathering food and protecting life. They hoarded victuals and haggled on the black market. This is a traditional role indeed, and old atavisms came to the fore. At heart, it is a basic concern for survival. And when life itself is threatened, then they copy the women of the Ancien Régime, who disturbed public order and took to the streets demanding bread. Such were the women who defied the occupier in 1941-42, chanting 'Bread! Potatoes!' These were the isolated actions of angry housewives, but sometimes the resistance was involved. De Roode Vaan (the Red Banner), the clandestine organ of the Flemish communists, stirred up its feminine readers: 'Imitate the women of Andenne and Rumbeke and Aalst, who sent delegations to the mayor and the provisioning service demanding coal and potatoes.'[56] A few months later they were given a new challenge: 'Women of Flanders, follow the example of your fellow-Walloons; demonstrate against the reduction of provisions.' No general hunger uprising took place. Still, certain women activists had already been captured by the occupation authorities. They can be included among the 20 per cent of resistance members who were women, who, unlike the silent majority, did not sit and wait for the final victory, but made an active choice for the Allies – at the risk of their lives. They were motivated by anti-Fascism, or patriotism, or by the need for bread, or a combination. True resistance work was of course more than be-ribboning oneself with the national tri-colour on the national day (11 November), which commemorated the last triumph over the present victor. Yet there were those who progressed, almost without realising it, from symbolic actions and passive help to full-blown-action.

Those who were motivated by pure love of country could look to the heroines of the First World War. The resistance was unarmed then, and this may have encouraged a larger number of women to participate. Most of them were involved in escape routes or in intelligence networks, just as in the Second World War. The largest intelligence service that worked for the British, the Dame Blanche, had a thousand agents, over 300 of which were women. On an average, 30 per cent of resistance members in the First World War were women. In contrast to the Second World War, being in the resistance was clearly the feminine alternative to military involvement. The risks were not negligible – 11 women were executed. One of them was Gabrielle Petit, a saleswoman, who was sentenced to death on account of tramway espionage for which she received payment from the British intelligence service. Her execution, during the war, went almost unnoticed, but afterwards she came close to canonisation as a 'national heroine'. In 1919 Mgr Keesen declaimed in the senate, 'France has Jeanne d'Arc. Belgium has Gabrielle Petit. The meaning is the same. Let us not be jealous of our neighbours.'[57] With the permission of the Minister of Justice, her cell in the Brussels prison of Sint-Gilles/Saint-Gilles was turned into a chapel to which people could come on pilgrimage.[58] The Germans, however, had learned their lesson, and they carefully avoided creating women martyrs in the Second World War. Not one execution was made public. Most of them disappeared into *Nacht und Nebel*. Of the 1,511 Belgian women sent to the Ravensbrück Frauenkonzentrationslager, 443 never returned.

The heroines of the First World War received recognition, but no recompense – certainly not politically. High expectations that the vote would be given to women were crushed. Universal suffrage for men was introduced after the First World War, but the only votes for women were those that went to war widows and war mothers, substitutes, as it were, for their dead husbands and sons. The process of emancipation skipped a generation – that of the war. Britain's example of giving women the right to vote in 1918 was not followed by Belgium until 30 years later, in 1948. Indeed, after the Second World War there was even a kind of backlash, for in the first post-war election even war widows were no longer permitted to vote. Ironically, it was the more Leftist parties, the Liberals and Socialists, who excluded women from the voting booth, out of fear that the *Kinder, Kirche, Küchen* syndrome would drive women into the arms of the Right.

Between the wars more and more women stayed home as 'mother by the hearth' (*moeder aan de haard*). Before the First World War there had been many more Belgian women who worked outside the home. Paid work for women hit an all-time low after the Second World War, and not until the early 1960s did the level return to what it had been in 1910. To think that one had to wait until the 'golden sixties' for women to reclaim their pre-war (1914, that is!) share of the labour market. The causal relationship between war and emancipation is thus somewhat problematic. With hindsight, one can say that both post-war periods were characterised by a return to 'normalcy', to familiar ways of life and traditional role models.

War offers opportunities not only for heroes, but also for traitors. When the water rises, the rats emerge. The lowest form of betrayal was to be an informer. In one sample selection it turned out that in the Second World War 60 per cent of the informers were women.[59] That agrees with the generalised preconception that was also present in the First World War, and that made life difficult for the women spies who worked for the Allies. Women in general were suspected of being a threat to the 'infrastructure of silence' so essential to the work of the resistance. The most banal, but also the most human, form of betrayal was the so-called horizontal collaboration of girls who were all too accommodating where the enemy was concerned. After the war, they were the first victims of street justice and public revenge, which provided an outlet for all the sexual frustrations of four years of austerity. The most conspicuous ritual that this entailed, after both wars, was the shaving of the girls' heads. Though never openly expressed, the sexual connotation was clear to see. There was also another dimension to this act. It generally took place outdoors, after which the scapegoat was chased through the village. As in the ancient Flemish *ommegang* procession, the good townsmen could once again take possession of their public space, which had been usurped by the occupiers for four years. This witch-hunt – yet another atavism brought back by the war – thus took on the characteristics of a collective purification.

The motivations underlying both collaboration and resistance could well be the same, oscillating between idealism and opportunism, ie social advancement, economic gain, patriotism (here there were two choices, Belgium or Flanders) and, in the Second World War, being for or against the New Order. One's perception of who is a traitor and who is a hero will depend on one's ideological stance. This is especially so in Belgium, where the First World War already carried within it the seeds of conflict of national loyalties. 'Language had been a problem in Belgium; now it was the problem of Belgium. In this sense, August 1914, the finest hour of the idea of Belgium, was also the beginning of its end.'[60] In the Second World War, this national question became intertwined with Left-Right hostilities, and the upshot was that the threat of civil war was not far off. After each war tension continued to increase. Even after the First World War there were many who believed that the wave of reprisals was the work of anti-Flemish instigators. Starting in 1929, those who had been declared traitors were allowed to return to Belgium, but no general amnesty was ever declared. It was against this background that Flemish nationalists even brought the 'Walloon heroine', Gabrielle Petit, forward in 1937 to ask for forgiveness for the 'pro-French and Walloon cowards who were refusing justice [ie amnesty] to the Flemish people'.[61]

After the First World War it was still possible for society to display some amount of tolerance, whereas after the next war society was more fractured and the breaches were deeper. Now traitors were also branded as being anti-democratic. The day of retribution turned into a festival of hate. Many so-called 'Blacks' or traitors ended up behind the bars of the Antwerp Zoo, where some time before the last rhinoceros had been slaughtered for food. Across the board, antipathy toward traitors was much more intense after the Second World War. Certain instances took on symbolic proportions. Such was the case of Irma Laplasse, condemned to death in 1944 as a traitor and informer. The Flemish Movement made use of her as an example of unjust repression. The case was re-opened 40 years later and there was a re-trial. In 1996 she was condemned, posthumously, to life imprisonment.[62]

Irma Laplasse was not only a mother, she was also a member of the Flemish Nationalist Party. Within this party, from the very beginning of the war, the last of the orthodox democrats had been held hostage by the pro-German die-hards of the New Order.[63] After the war the die-hards were expurgated, just as the Activists had been after the preceding war. It was especially the wives of these so-called victims of the repression who turned out to be the true die-hards. While their husbands were doing time in prison, they had to support their large families. Later, they had to endure the social degradation of their husbands; often these were intellectuals who could only find work as door-to-door vacuum cleaner salesmen.

These women became bitter.[64] Their husbands, on the other hand, had to accommodate themselves to normal social life somehow or other after their return. When necessary, they had to be opportunistic, though inwardly they never recanted, keeping their ideas to themselves and their own circles. The women by the hearth lived on in anger. In their isolation, they clung desperately to an ideology that was no longer acceptable to society. Like an adder at the breast, they cherished their bitterness, which sometimes got passed on to the next generation in their mother's milk, as it were. The resentful dregs left after repression and reprisal could only further poison the atmosphere. The amnesty question was never settled – not after the First World War, nor after the following war, when the Walloons refused to grant amnesty to those Flemings who had committed the same offence, sometimes twice over.[65] That would be a persistent, contributing factor to the growth and deepening of anti-Belgian feelings within the Flemish community.

After 1945 the discussions in Belgium on matters of national and group import were conducted for deaf ears. Those who wanted more Flemish autonomy gained no hearing from those who favoured a united Belgium, and vice versa. The same incomprehension reigned between Flanders and Wallonia, and between the Right and the Left. On the one side, there were those who underestimated the divisions in the country, the frustrations of the Flemish and the separatist aspirations of the Flemish Movement. On the other side, there were those who used their pro-Flemish frustrations as an excuse for having collaborated, yet who refused to recognise that in so doing they had embraced the Germans' New Order in its totality, with its implied dictatorship, and that they had made a devil's pact with a criminal regime and all its elements, anti-Semitism included.[66]

Unfortunately, the collaborators continued to play the role of victim; they used the word 'repression' in the exclusive sense to mean only the punishment that had been meted out to them after the war. When they spoke of terror, they meant the mob justice, or street terror, that they had experienced, whereas they themselves had worked for a repressive system based on organised state terror. Disturbing, too, is the way 'right-thinking' circles in Flanders ridiculed the resistance, lumping it together with the last-minute resistance joiners of 1944, the so-called September resistance men.[67] All this was compounded by the veterans, whose isolated stances bore no relationship to the line of demarcation that divided the two linguistic communities. The very fatherland of the veterans' pro-fatherland organisations was being torn apart by regionalistic and linguistic bickering.[68] The patriotic rhetoric of the veterans, which was still that of the war, was miles apart from the political pragmatism of the regionalisation process that had begun with the post-war generation. Now one could speak, albeit with a certain pathos, of 'the historical process of the disintegration of the unified state'. Identities were shifting.[69] This meant the demise of the outmoded *Belgique à papa*, where French-speakers set the tone, and where bilingual Flemish civil servants kept the system functioning. In the meantime, however, Flanders had brought forth an elite of its own. Then again, regional differences of economic and social development became so marked that at times their elites chose opposing strategies for survival or change. All of these confrontations were always heavily laden with historic ballast. In both wars a self-proclaimed vanguard of the Flemish nation had opted for *la fuite en avant*. Conservative French-speaking Belgians forgot their own collaboration with Degrelle and the Rex Movement. The past, and the war most of all, had a long-lasting polarising effect.[70] Time, however, heals all wounds. To the next generation, the two World Wars will seem as far in the past as the Thirty Years' War.

Notes on contributors

Mark Derez, The Catholic University of Leuven, Belgium
Mark Derez is an Archivist whose speciality is the history of the University. He contributed to Facing Armageddon (1996), Passchendaele in Perspective (1997) and At the Eleventh Hour (1998).

Recommended reading

Conway, Martin, *Collaboration in Belgium: Leon Degrelle and the Rexist Movement 1940-1944* (London: Yale University Press, 1993)

Deprez, Kas and Vos, Louis (eds), *Nationalism in Belgium: Shifting Identities, 1780-1995* (London: Macmillan, 1998)

Devolder, Kathleen, *La Belgique occupée 1914-1918: dessins, estampes et photos des archives de guerre conservés aux Archives Générales du Royaume* (Brussels: Archives Générales du Royaume, 1998)

Michman, Dan, *Belgium and the Holocaust: Jews-Belgians-Germans* (Jerusalem: Yad Vashem, 1998)

Schaepdrijver, Sophie de, 'Occupation, propaganda and the idea of Belgium' in Roshwald, Aviel and Stites, Richard, *European Culture in the Great War: The Arts Entertainment, and Propaganda, 1914-1918* (Cambridge: Cambridge University Press, 1999) pp267-94

Notes

[1] I wish to thank Mrs Ardis Dreisbach (Stockholm) for the excellent translation and Johna de Vis for material support.

[2] Daniel H. Thomas, *The Guarantee of Belgian Dependence and Neutrality in Belgian Diplomacy, 1830s-1930s* (Kingston, RI: 1983)

[3] Georges H. Dumont and Louis Haché, *België in beeld: Van prehistorie tot heden* (a history of Belgium in cartoons) (Deurne: Uitgeverij Baart, 1979) p53

[4] Pierre (d'Outryve) d'Ydewalle, *Mijn oorlogsjaren* (Tielt: Lannoo, 1997) pp28-9

[5] This part is mainly based on: Albert Chatelle, *L'effort belge en France pendant la guerre (1914-1918)* (Paris: 1934); Peter Cahalan, *Belgian Refugee Relief in England during the Great War* (New York: Garland, 1982); M. Bossenbroek et al, *Vluchten voor de Groote Oorlog: Belgen in Nederland 1914-1918* (Amsterdam: Bataafsche Leeuw, 1988); Karen Celis and Anne Godfroid, *Vrouwen en Oorlog 16e-20e E.* (Brussels: Algemeen Rijksarchief, 1997); Kathleen Devolder, *Bezet België 1914-1918: Tekeningen, prenten en foto's uit de oorlogsarchieven van het Algemeen Rijksarchief* (catalogue) (Brussels: Algemeen Rijksarchief, 1998); Pierre Alain Tallier, 'De Belgische vluchtelingen in het buitenland tijdens de Eerste Wereldoorlog' in Anne Morelli (ed), *Belgische migranten: Oorlogsvluchtelingen, economische emigranten en politieke vluchtelingen uit onze streken van de 16de eeuw tot vandaag* (Berchem: EPO, 1999) pp21-42; Luis Angel Bernardo y Garcia, 'De belgische vluchtelingen in Groot-Brittanië tijdens de Tweede Wereldoorlog' in Anne Morelli (ed), op cit, pp43-57; Evelyn de Roodt, *Oorlogsgasten: Vluchtelingen en krijgsgevangenen in Nederland tijdens de*

Eerste Wereldoorlog (Zaltbommel: Uitgeverij Europese Bibliotheek, 1999)

6 Stijn Streuvels, *In oorlogstijd: Het volledige dagboek van de Eerste Wereldoorlog* (Brugge: Uitgeverij Orion; Nijmegen: Uitgeverij B. Gottmer, 1979); Luc Schepens, *14/18 Een oorlog in Vlaanderen*, p56

7 Eugen Weber, *Peasants into Frenchmen: The Modernisation of Rural France 1870-1914* (London: Chatto & Windus, 1977); Antoine Prost (ed), *14-18: Mourir pour la patrie* (Paris: Edition du Seuil, 1992)

8 Carl Strickwerda, *A House Divided: Catholics, Socialists and Flemish Nationalists* (Lanham, MD: 1997)

9 Joris van Parijs, *Masereel: een biografie* (Antwerp: Houtekiet, 1995)

10 Luc Schepens, *Brugge bezet 1914-1918 1940-1944*, pp55-7

11 Pierre Alain Tallier, op cit, p24

12 Norman Bentwich, 'Belgian Refugees in Britain' in *Message: Belgian Review* (February 1942) pp46-50; Sophie Rottiers, 'Jacob van Artevelde, de Belgische Willem Tell?' in Anne Morelli, *De grote mythen*, pp77-95

13 Pierre d'Ydewalle, op cit, pp27-8

14 *Message: Belgian Review* (February 1942) p51

15 Pierre Alain Tallier, op cit, p39

16 F. Raes, 'Femmes belges réfugiées en Angleterre pendant la seconde guerre mondiale: Une histoire orale' (thesis, History Department, Université Liège, 1995) p22, quoted in Celis and Godfroid, op cit, p63

17 G. Jaspaers, *Les Belges en Hollande 1914-1917* (Amsterdam: 1917), cited by Pierre Alain Tallier, op cit, p30

18 Sally Marks, *Innocent Abroad: Belgium at the Paris Peace Conference of 1919* (Chapel Hill: 1981)

19 Interview with Mrs Marguerite Mathy, Brussels, September 1997. For the better-off refugees, see also the highly literary family chronicle by Eric de Kuyper, *Drie zusters in Londen: uit de familiekroniek 1914-1918* (Nijmegen: SUN, 1996)

20 Louis Piérard, *La Belgique sous les armes, sous la botte, en exil* (Paris, 1917) p254, cited by Pierre Alain Tallier, op cit, p21

21 Norman Bentwich, op cit, p48

22 Luis Angel Bernardo y Garcia, op cit, p48

23 Kathleen Devolder, op cit, p34

24 Elfnovembergroep (ed), *Van den grooten oorlog: Volksboek* (Kemmel: Malegijs) p42

25 Ibid, p47

26 Etienne Verhoeyen, *België bezet 1940-1944: Een synthese* (Brussels: BRTN, 1993) p162

27 Ibid, p9

28 Luc Schepens, *Brugge bezet*, op cit, pp74-5

29 René Vermandere, *De Duitsche Furie te Antwerpen*, cited by Weverbergh, Julien and Opbroecke, Roland van, *De bezetter bespied* (Antwerp/Amsterdam: Uitgeverij C. de Vries-Brouwers, 1980) p102

30 Charel de Schipper, *België 1940-1945: Oorlog en bezetting* (Paris: Jacques Granger, 1998) p75

31 Herbert Foss, 'Belgium and England in music' in *Message: Belgian Review* (July 1942) pp31-3; Hans Triebels, *Muziek en woord: in de ban van de Eerste Wereldoorlog* (Nijmegen: Openbare Bibliotheek, 1998)

32 Luc Schepens, *Brugge bezet*, op cit, p101

33 Thomas Hardy, 'Sonnet on the Belgian Expatriation', in *King Albert's Book: Een hulde aan den Koning der Belgen...* (Dutch version; London: *The Daily Telegraph*, 1914) p21

34 Jacques Lust, 'Beeldende kunst tijdens de tweede wereldoorlog in Vlaanderen' (thesis, History of Art Department, University of Ghent, 1985)

35 John Gillingham, *Belgian Business in the Nazi New Order* (Ghent: Jan Dhondt Foundation, 1977) p109, quoted by Etienne Verhoeyen, op cit, p165

36 Robert B. Armeson, *Total Warfare and Compulsory Labor: A Study of the Military-Industrial Complex in Germany during World War I* (The Hague: 1964)

37 Celis and Godfroid, op cit, pp44, 58

38 Frank Selleslagh, 'De tewerkstelling' in *1940-1945 Het dagelijks leven in België* (Brussels: ASLK, 1984) p32; Celis and Godfroid, op cit, pp72-3

39 Dirk Martin, 'Les universités belges pendant la deuxième guerre mondiale', *Revue du Nord* (1987) pp315-36

40 Etienne Verhoeyen, op cit, p209
41 Henri Charriaut, *La Belgique moderne: terre d' expériences* (Paris: 1910) cited by Sophie de Schaepdrijver, *De Groote Oorlog*, p40
42 Luc de Vos, *Van gifgas tot peniciline: vooruitgang door oorlog* (Leuven: Davidsfonds, 1995) p19
43 Charel de Schipper, op cit, p16
44 Luc Schepens, *14/18 Een oorlog in Vlaanderen*, op cit, p61
45 Paul van Ostaijen, *Bezette Stad (Verzameld Werk)* (Antwerp/Amsterdam: 1952) no pagination
46 Charel de Schipper, op cit, pp138-49
47 Mariëtte Jacobs, *Zij, die vielen als helden…: Inventaris van de oorlogsgedenktekens van de twee wereldoorlogen in West-Vlaanderen* (an inventory of war memorials) 2 Vols (Brugge: 1996) pp122-4
48 Willem Erauw, *Koningin Elisabeth: over pacifisme, pantheïsme en de passie voor muziek* (Ghent: Stichting Mens en Kultuur, 1995) pp82-6
49 Denise de Weerdt, *Vrouwen van de Eerste Wereldoorlog* (Ghent: Stichting Mens en Kultuur, 1993) p201
50 Celis and Godfroid, op cit, p66
51 George H. Nash, *The Life of Herbert Hoover: The Humanitarian 1914-1917* (New York and London: W. W. Norton & Co, 1988)
52 Liane Ranieri, *Emile Francqui ou l'intelligence créatrice (1863-1935)* (Paris and Gembloux: Duculot, 1985)
53 Jay Winter and Blaine Bagett, *The Great War and the Shaping of the Twentieth Century* (New York and London, 1996) p356; 'Commission for Relief in Belgium (1914-1930): A Register of its Records in the Hoover Institution Archives' (Stanford University: 1996), historical note
54 Sophie de Schaepdrijver, *De Groote Oorlog*, p115
55 A. Collignon, 'Secours d'Hiver, Secours d'Hitler', *Jours de Guerre* 6 (1992) pp65-88
56 Celis and Godfroid, op cit, p87
57 Cyrille van Overbergh, *Gabrielle Petit: De Nationale Heldin* (Brussels: Revue de la Presse et des Livres, 1919)
58 Denise de Weerdt, op cit, p199
59 Celis and Godfroid, op cit, p83
60 Sophie de Schaepdrijver, 'Occupation, propaganda and the idea of Belgium' in Aviel Roshwald and Richard Stites, *European Culture in the Great War: The Arts Entertainment, and Propaganda, 1914-1918* (Cambridge: University Press, 1999) p294
61 *Nieuwe Encyclopedie van de Vlaamse Beweging* (Tielt: Lannoo, 1998) Vol 1, p278
62 Willy Moons, *Het Proces Irma Laplasse* (Groot-Bijgaarden: Scoop, 1999)
63 Bruno de Wever, *Greep naar de Macht: Vlaams-nationalisme en Nieuwe Orde: Het VNV 1933-1945* (Tielt: Lannoo, 1994)
64 Huguette Bleecker-Ingelaere, *Vrouwen in de Repressie 1944-1945* (Ghent: Federatie Vlaamse Vrouwengroepen, 1985)
65 Luc Huyse and Steven Dhondt, *Onverwerkt Verleden: Collaboratie en repressie in België 1942-1952* (Leuven: Kritak, 1991)
66 Bruno de Wever, 'Van wierook tot gaslucht: De beeldvorming over de Vlaams-nationalistische collaboratie tijdens de Tweede Wereldoorlog in de Vlaamse historiografie' in *Docendo discimus: Liber americorum Romain van Eenoo* (Ghent: Academic Press, 1995) Vol I, pp607-14; Louis Vos, 'Nationalism, Democracy, and the Belgian State' in Richard Caplan and John Feffer, *Europe's New Nationalism: States and Minorities in Conflict* (New York and Oxford: Oxford University Press, 1996) pp85-100
67 Johan Anthierens, *Zonder vlagvertoon: Over de weerstand tegen het verzet* (Leuven: Uitgeverij Van Halewyck, 1995)
68 Alain Colignon, 'La Belgique, une patrie d'ancien combattants?', *Cahiers d'histoire du Temps Présent* 3 (Brussels, 1997) pp115-42
69 Kas Deprez and Louis Vos (eds), *Nationalism in Belgium: Shifting Identities, 1780-1995* (London: Macmillan, 1998)
70 Rudi van Doorselaer, 'Steeds wordt een andere oorlog beschreven: Recente tendensen in de oorlogshistoriografie in België', *Spiegel Historiael* (1994) pp144-50

Chapter 30

The experience of occupation: Northern France

Margaret Atack

'Ainsi donc, sur ce coin de terre française
Vous avez, mornes Allemands
Marqués de notre sang, couverts de notre glaise
Déversé vos lourds régiments.'[1]

To most people, the German Occupation of France means the four years of German rule that lasted from the defeat of the French Army and the evacuation of the British forces from Dunkirk in 1940 until the D-Day landings and the Liberation, encapsulated in de Gaulle's triumphant walk down the Champs Elysées in August 1944. For those living in the north of the country, however, this was an experience they had undergone before. Marc Blancpain is not the only Frenchman to be able to say, 'I have spent about 9 years of my life in German hands.'[2] Indeed, for anyone over 70 years of age, it would be their third experience of seeing German soldiers on the streets. The invasion of 1870-71 left a powerful mark on both the French and the Germans, playing a significant part in shaping the attitudes and experiences of both sides when the Germans occupied substantial parts of northern France from August 1914 to November 1918. The experience of this occupation had in its turn a most significant impact on the attitudes and actions of the French in the north when faced with another invasion, another occupation, 21 years later.

On 10 May 1940, after seven months of 'Phoney War', the German Army invaded France, passing to the north of the famous Maginot Line, which was to have served as France's safeguard against further invasion from the east, driving forward through Belgium and through the Ardennes, and routing the French Army (and the British Expeditionary Force). Their dramatic victory led to Marshal Pétain asking for an armistice on 17 June 1940; one of the most telling indications of the psychological, cultural and political importance of the memory of the First World War framing, at least initially, the experience of the Second, was the fact that on 22 June the armistice agreement was signed at Rethondes, in the same railway carriage in the forest where the Germans had signed their own capitulation in 1918. The fact that several million French people had taken to the roads as the German forces advanced, to a certain extent rendering the task of the

French Army even more difficult than it might have been, was also eloquent testimony to the strength of the memory of the First World War, and the severity of that occupation.

It is not surprising that one of the first reactions to the outbreak of hostilities in 1939 was a widespread feeling of dread that it should be happening again, so soon. In August 1914 there had been a general conviction that the war would be brief – the troops would be home for Christmas. Only gradually did it become grimly clear that there could be no rapid settlement of this conflict of entrenchment. While in September 1939 the months of inactivity that followed the declaration gave an eerie sense to the war, Pétain's request for an armistice after the total chaos of exodus and rout seems to have been greeted by many with a feeling of sombre relief. The historian Marc Bloch, who would be shot by firing squad for resistance in 1944, left behind his eye-witness account of his experiences as an officer in the French Army during the campaign in the north, chronicling the extraordinary chaos and bewilderment provoked by the inability of the French High Command to impose order and control, in part because their heads were still in another war: 'Our leaders, among many contradictions, have sought, above all, to recreate, in 1940, the 1915-1918 war. The Germans were waging the 1940 war.'[3]

It is important, therefore, to recognise that in both wars, French soldiers and French civilians were not entering the conflict or the subsequent occupation unprepared, with 'blank minds'. This is especially true of the north, which had been occupied during the 1870-71 conflict with Prussia; the German soldiers, too, had kept alive the memory of opposition from the civilian population. Civilian resistance on the part of the French, ascribed to *francs-tireurs* by the Germans, was judged by them to be contrary to military codes; reprisals were savage, and in proportion to the terror projected as well as inflicted.[4] 'Each nation came to believe that it alone was upholding civilisation against a race of barbarians which could only be bullied into submission by brute force. Forty-four years later that belief was to be even more disastrously revived.'[5] By universalising what was at stake, universalising the confrontation as being between good and evil, each side succeeded in 'diabolising the enemy'.[6] This fear of 'the other', fear of atrocities, fear of unprovoked, 'unlawful' attack, provoked angry and harsh reprisals, and the great exodus of refugees. That of 1940 remains in the collective memory, but in 1914, too, many thousands took to the roads. Georges Leroy described his experiences as he left his village and family, keeping away from the roads crowded with troops, including English troops moving towards the front, and walked across fields down to Saint Quentin. He recorded his continual surprise at the ever-increasing closeness of the sounds of the guns, his one reliable indication of the state of the military balance of power, and one that was quite at odds with the reassuring accounts of French successes in the press.[7]

For all the combatant nations, the soldier in the trenches is the symbol of the war, and France is no exception. As Becker points out, one must give the full force to the word 'sacré' in the patriotic and inspiring 'union sacrée' around which the French united with a religious fervour. The defence of the French land from the aggressor was a sacred duty that involved willing acceptance of the sacrifice of oneself. The *poilu* in the trenches was the supreme embodiment of this patriotic immolation for French soil.[8] The result of this is that the experiences of those in the occupied territories disappear from view. Already in 1925, Georges Gromaire was lamenting the fact that the civilians in the occupied part of France had been forgotten in the public commemorations:

'The public knows in vague terms that [the Germans] did not behave in an exemplary manner and all can recount stories of violence and abuse of power. People are aware that this occupation was not like those of enemy armies in the previous wars, but so far there has been no detailed explanation that this was the result of the application of systematic exploitation and total exhaustion of the region.'[9]

Efforts have recently been made to break this 'veil of forgetfulness'[10], which has prevented the memory of the 'liberated regions' being kept alive. Annette Becker points out that even in the occupied territories, the war memorials commemorate the heroes of the trenches, only occasionally drawing attention to the misery suffered by those living under German occupation:

'How does one commemorate the victims rather than the heroes? How does one commemorate that which defies commemoration, namely hunger, cold, forced labour, rape, hostages, deportations, forced evacuations, requisitions, fines, tuberculosis?'[11]

The area behind the front line and under German occupation in 1914-18 stretched from Alsace and Lorraine in the north-east, across Champagne, and up through the départements of Nord and Pas-de-Calais, along or near a line of towns – Saint Quentin, Arras and Lille – to the Belgian border. This physical demarcation underlines the extent to which France was fractured and fragmented; France's fate in both World Wars was to be broken into segments, with the very context of the experience changing from area to area. Those in the occupied zones in the First World War shared with their compatriots the anxieties about loved ones at the front of whom they had no news, but they also experienced very specific privations and hardships. They were also a frontier zone – Lille was a mere 15 kilometres from the front, and daily life was carried out to the continual background noise of the guns. Continual troop movements, and the presence of refugees from towns virtually on the front line such as Chauny, meant that the war itself was never forgotten. But while for the rest of France behind the front daily life went on, for those undergoing German occupation normal life came to a full stop.

In Lille, as elsewhere, the first days of the war were marked by great hopes of a rapid French victory, but these were quickly countered by reports of the rapid German advance through Belgium, provoking many to try and leave the town.[12] On 2 September the Prefect ordered all men liable to conscription to leave, and 28,000 did so. The first German soldiers were seen in Lille on 6 September, but quickly left. In October 1914, however, fierce fighting broke out; men caught trying to leave the town this time were rounded up and sent to camps in Germany. Lille was under siege from 10 to 12 October, and on 13 October the Germans entered a town seriously damaged by the 5,000 shells that had rained down on it. One townswoman commented: 'We heard a huge, wild sound, backed up by a noise like that of hundreds of castanets... It was the triumphant shouts of the soldiers at the sight of the town in flames, accompanying themselves by banging on all kinds of objects.'[13] At least 100 civilians died during the destructive taking of the town.

Other towns in the north that also appeared to be about to experience a military occupation in fact found themselves behind the lines on the French side as the armies dug in for the long years of trench warfare. Amiens[14] saw thousands of conscript troops pour into the centre of town in the first few days of August, arriving to join their dépôt; horses were requisitioned, and the crops stood in the fields with no one to bring in the harvest. The news in the local press of the excellent progress of the French troops was brutally interrupted by miserable reality. An official communiqué on 29 August announced: 'The enemy is in our département.' The large numbers of refugees from Belgium and from the French regions further to the north also told their own story. At the end of August, the town was officially abandoned, provoking once more the exodus in panic of those who could get away. The German troops arrived on 2 September.

In the event, the occupation was to last just 14 days, and for some of that time no German troops were visible, the people of Amiens wondering whether they were occupied or not. But during the brief days of the German presence, there was a clear foretaste of the experiences to come elsewhere: the requisitioning of various materials, particularly toilet paper, (much to the locals' later amusement), the taking of hostages to ensure that German demands were met, and the deportation of men to German camps. One person who had attempted to open fire on the invading troops at the end of August was rapidly overcome by the French; the mayor had already announced that any revolt against the situation could have dire consequences for the town and its families. The total destruction of the town of Orchies, situated to the south-west of Lille, was a brutal indication of the punishment that would follow when aggression against German soldiers was suspected. Major von Meyring's notice was a chilling warning to the civilian population, as well as further proof of the power invested in the notion of French atrocities within the German Army:

'Unfortunately I have been obliged to apply the most severe measures dictated by the laws of warfare against the town of Orchies. In this place, doctors and other members of the German medical staff were attacked and killed, and about twenty German soldiers murdered. The most dreadful atrocities were carried out in a manner which defies belief (ears cut off, eyes torn out, and other bestialities of this kind).

I have therefore had the town destroyed. Orchies, once a town of 5,000 inhabitants, no longer exists: houses, town hall, and church have disappeared, and there are no more inhabitants.

Valenciennes, 27 September 1914.'[15]

By contrast, in Amiens, those few days when Germans were in the shops and dealing with the local population seemed to belie the terrible stories of atrocities that had preceded them. They were behaving 'correctement'[16], an ironic anticipation of the famous phrase so widely used at the beginning of the 1940-44 occupation: 'Ils sont corrects.' Elsewhere, the Germans put up notices stressing their goodwill towards the civilian population who meant them no harm, as an early 'Proclamation to the Inhabitants of Lille' signed by Wanschaffe, Généralmajor, indicated:

> 'The German Army is waging war only on the French, English, and Belgian armies, not on the civilian population which is not taking part in the war. It guarantees all properties to the citizens of Lille, provided that no hostile acts are committed on the German troops.'

He concluded by hoping that good relations would be established between the Lillois and the German soldiers.[17] In the event, the scenes of devastation, deportation and requisitions were a much more accurate curtain-raiser to the years of occupation to come.

The fragmentation of experience, and the isolation of those in the north, was even more marked in the Second World War. After the defeat and Petain's request for an armistice, France became a land divided into various zones; a 'demarcation line' separated the north, under German rule, from the south, a veritable internal frontier, shown dramatically in the opening scenes of René Clément's famous film about the resistance of the railway workers, *La Bataille du rail* (1945), with nervous passengers being subjected to border controls and identity checks by German officers as the train stops at the 'line', on the other side of which lay the southern or unoccupied zone, the 'so-called free zone' as it was so often referred to, under the rule of the Vichy Government. In July 1940 the National Assembly had voted to transfer full powers to Maréchal Pétain, as head of the new Etat Français, and the new Government established itself in the spa town of Vichy.

But in addition to these two zones (whose separate relationship formally ended when the Germans invaded the southern zone in November 1942, in response to the Allied landings in North Africa), the regions of Alsace and Lorraine, lost in 1871 and returned to France in 1918, were annexed into German territory, and the inhabitants subjected to German law, including conscription into the German Army. Also, to the north of a line running from Amiens, passing between Laon and Reims and south down the Vallée de la Marne to join the demarcation line in the Jura, were the *zone interdite*, to which refugees were forbidden to return, the *zone réservée*, covering the industrial départements of the north-east, and the *zone rattachée*, governed directly from Brussels.[18] The 12 départements of the north, including some of the richest, most highly industrialised and most populous in France, were thus removed from French control – every effort made by the Vichy Government to exercise power or authority was systematically rebuffed – and indeed, as Henri Amouroux notes, from the French community.[19]

As the German Army swept through the Ardennes and Belgium, reaching Sedan on 13 May and the Channel on 28 May, hundreds of thousands, remembering the 'atrocities' of the First World War, left their homes in panic and terror. By 11 June, Evreux in Normandy had 172 inhabitants remaining out of a population of 20,000[20]; Tourcoing's population dropped to 700, while the small town of Beaune-la-Rolande, some 30 kilometres north of the Loire, went from 1,700 to 40,000.[21] In the chaos of this aptly named exodus (estimates vary between 6 and 10 million refugees), families were separated and individuals lost on the road, as the sad announcements and appeals in the newspapers testify: 'Madame Mary, who lived in the Ardennes, is seeking her husband, and also her three carts and her four horses.' 'Their mum has lost Marc, Luc, Jean, Marie-Françoise, and Michel, on 17 June. They stayed with the suitcases at Poitiers station. Write to her immediately at La Tremblade.'[22] The Red Cross would restore 92,000 lost children to their families by 1942.[23]

Returning home was complicated not only by the demarcation line put in place on 25 June, but also by the parlous state of the railways, with bridges, stations and sections of line destroyed. The trains started running again in August, slowly bringing people back to their deserted towns and cities. Only 700,000 Parisians had been there on 14 June to witness the arrival of the Germans, since 2 million had left between 19 May and 14 June (repeating the experience of 1914 when 1 million fled the capital in the first month of the war). Half a million had returned by the end of August, and overall the French authorities estimated that 3.5 million refugees were back in their own homes by the beginning of October.[24] This could not, however, be the experience of those who had left the northern départements that now formed the *zone interdite*.

Those living in the *zone interdite* were once more the forgotten ones of the war. Once more there was at best a vague awareness of hardship being worse in some areas:

> 'Few French people in 1940-1942 were aware of the drama being lived in the forbidden zone. With the vast number of communiques, the tide of events and so many personal anxieties, how many of those who did not live in the relevant areas, paid any attention to the announcement on 23 July of the creation of a zone to which it was impossible to return.'[25]

The River Somme became another demarcation line, a hermetically sealed 'iron frontier' with police and border controls that it was virtually impossible to cross[26], and behind which a whole region ruled from Brussels lived in isolation. The fear of annexation was a very real one, creating a very different attitude towards the Germans. The inhabitants of the zone were effectively hostages. Even the experience of the military invasion and defeat was much harsher here than elsewhere; the départements of Nord and Pas-de-Calais came first and fourth in the list rating the severity of destruction.[27] The obsession with the *francs-tireurs* was as strong as ever, leading to hostages being taken, and also to massacres. Twenty-one villagers of Etrun were herded into a farmyard and shot. A notice pinned up outside, in French and German, stated that 'the inhabitants have been shot for having finished off two injured Germans'. At Oignies, the Totenkopf Division reacted with severity to the German losses of the fighting in the British and French counter-attacks from 21 May onwards: 80 civilians were rounded up and shot in public. In what some considered the first war crime, 99 British soldiers who had been cornered and surrendered, were shot. The German officer in charge was reprimanded. All in all, 500 civilians and prisoners of war, British, French, and Moroccan, were murdered during the campaign, fulfilling all fears that this war represented a nightmarish return to the experiences of 1914-18.[28]

For all that, the one sentiment that typifies the contrast between the experience of occupation in France in the First and the Second World Wars, is that in harshness and brutality the Second bears no comparison with the First. In the published accounts of historians and survivors, and private conversations, this is the message conveyed by those who experienced both:

'Those who only experienced the second occupation after 1940, even those living in the zone interdite, cannot begin to imagine the extreme harshness, the sheer scale and the meticulous thoroughness of the pillaging, the requisitions and the dishonest financial manoeuvres which for more than four years were the daily lot of the territories and inhabitants "governed" by the imperial German army.'[29]

On 22 October 1918, a few days after the liberation of Lille, two Members of Parliament from the city spoke in the National Assembly about their experiences.[30] The members of the National Assembly were shocked to see how exhausted and drawn M Delory looked.[31] From November 1916 to April 1917 he had been one of a group of 200 hostages from the north deported to a camp in Germany as a reprisal against similar measures by the French against Germans in Alsace.[32] Delory spoke of the women and girls hauled out of bed in the middle of the night, of men – ie the very young and the very old – used for building shelters for the German soldiers, a few kilometres away from the front, 'which means that many were wounded by fire from our own lines'. He spoke of Lens, flattened, of Douai, where the buildings stood, but empty, no inhabitants, no furniture. Ragheboom's account carried the same message, of severe oppression and hardship:

'Yes, the Germans had, for example, forbidden people to pass from one commune to another. They would be fined if they did. For having spoken to one of her cousins, my wife saw a German raise a hand to her, and heard herself called "grande salope" [great bitch]. Fifteen-year-old children were hung by their wrists, then locked up for three days without food, for having refused to work for the enemy.'

He went on to describe men being rounded up and forced to march for three days and three nights, young girls sorting soot from mud to try and keep warm, surviving on a diet of 150 grams of sugar, half a pound of rancid bacon or salt beef a fortnight.[33] Both députés closed their speeches with rousing cries that the experience would not, could not be forgotten – peace must mean justice. Writing in 1925, Georges Gromaire voiced common sentiments in linking the hardship endured and reparations:

'The picture of the ravages inflicted by the Germans is the justification for the articles of the Versailles Treaty which demands reparations. The unprecedented point to which the exhaustion of all the resources of the area was taken will show the necessity for justice which demands compensation.'[34]

According to some, the invaded territories were treated more like colonies, subject to the invaders' needs in every aspect of life.[35] As Ragheboom noted, movements were strictly controlled, the inhabitants having to pay for an *ausweis* to go from one village to another. 'Everything remained frozen in the state in which the Germans found it in 1914. Nothing came in, nothing went out, and thus it was possible to draw up an inventory of the contents and use it all for the better interests of the invader. The Germans did not fail to do this.'[36] Houses were given numbers, streets were given names, German names, and the people were issued with identity cards, all being seen as parts of the total control of the territory.[37] Notices were posted listing the materials and objects being requisitioned. For example, Avesnes was told to provide four dressing gowns; five days later, it was a pair of boots, puttees, and 'elegant' gloves[38]; from Etrœungt, 100 bedsheets, 600 shirts, 600 leggings, and 600 pairs of socks were demanded.[39] In 1916, everyone had to provide inventories of their total house contents.[40] Notices even went up regulating the mode of collecting nettles for payment.[41]

Charles Delesalle was Mayor of Lille during the occupation, and one of those in the front line of negotiation with the German command. The letters written by Delesalle to Maître Louis Selosse and his colleague, M Jacquey, seeking their advice about the German demands and the national and international legal framework, reveal the pressures on those placed in the front line of dealings with the enemy during an occupation, and to the nature of daily life at this time.[42] The Prefect, M Trépont, was deported in 1915 for protesting against German demands.[43] From 2 November 1914 onwards, Delesalle consulted with these legal experts about civilians forced to work for the German soldiers, about the hostages, and about the financial demands being made. On 9 December 1914 he protested to von Heinrich about the demand for 800,000 francs for the costs of German troops, having already paid 7,420,000 francs as a 'contribution to the war', as well as money for feeding the troops, and a ransom of 320,000 francs.[44] By 1916 he judged the cost to Lille of the occupation as running at 1 million francs a month, and sought to oppose von Heinrich's new demands for 23 million francs, which would put the money extorted to 4 million francs a month.[45]

With prices going up, profiteering became an issue. Some were not above sweetening further with ground beans the unfortunately named German flour 'K.K.' (its homonym, 'caca', being the childish French word for excrement).[46] The mayor of Valenciennes posted a notice about chewing food properly to extract the maximum food value.[47] Famine became a real possibility until the American Commission for Relief in Belgium intervened with a supply of flour.[48] But the appalling diet took its toll. The Mayor of Lille appealed for help from Paris, explaining that the people of Lille were having to live for a fortnight on food that would normally be eaten in three or four meals.[49] Medical statistics showed the weakened state of the population, as revealed by Dr Albert Calmette, who had been appointed by Pasteur himself to the new Institut Pasteur in Lille at the beginning of the century[50], and who stayed in Lille throughout the occupation, being prevented by the war from taking up an appointment at the Institut Pasteur in Paris:

> 'Morbidity and mortality are at frightening levels. 15,000 young people are in need of special meals, for tuberculosis is fatal here in a few days. Cardiac disorders, kidney infections, and rickets in children are becoming widespread.'[51]

From January 1914 to December 1918, there were 8,534 births and 22,951 deaths; the mortality rate soared from 18.98 per 1,000 inhabitants in 1913, to 41.55 in 1918.[52]

Equally difficult was the whole question of obliging the people of Lille to work for the Germans, asking them to abandon 'the most sacred of all duties', the defence of 'la patrie'. Delesalle worried whether Germans were within their rights under international law or not; the Germans wished local people to make sandbags and planks for the trenches, they wished local businesses to move to production for them. The German response to workers' refusal to do this was to propose that, in order to protect the workers from any difficulties once peace had been concluded, they would give them a certificate testifying that they had done this work under coercion.[53] But they also insisted that the hostages should spend every night at the Citadelle until the question was resolved. In October 1914 it was announced that 17 named hostages, including Delesalle, Trépont and Monseigneur Charost, the Bishop of Lille, had to go to the Mairie every morning.[54] They would often be held in the Citadelle, especially in tense situations such as these. Maître Selosse had advised Delesalle on the legal distinction between active and passive help for the occupying army. Making sandbags for German trenches was an active contribution, and thus outlawed by the conventions; indeed, most businessmen refused to co-operate, and there was great indignation at the attempt to coerce women and children into such work.[55] The inhabitants could not, however, be held directly responsible for any passive contribution they may make. In *Invasion 14*, van der Meersch gives a dramatic reconstruction of the dilemmas being posed. A group of businessmen and industrialists wrestle with the situation, weighing the financial implications for their workers if the factories close on patriotic grounds, against the possible or even probable recriminations after the war if they do not.[56] On top of this, at Easter 1916, 25,000 inhabitants of Lille were rounded up and deported to the countryside to work the land.

The demands were backed up by severe punishment, from initial notices in October 1914 announcing the death penalty for anyone who helped enemy soldiers, or hindered the German troops[57], to the random brutality of requisitions, punishments for insults large and small, such as the four days' prison sentence meted out for insulting a German horse as reported in the German newsheet *Bulletin de Lille*[58], or the four days' prison sentence for being caught in possession of a watch or clock not on German time (one hour ahead of French time)[59]. A woman who denounced two policemen to the authorities for calling the German soldiers 'pigs', one of whom was punished with six months in prison, was sentenced in absentia, in the French courts after the war, to deportation to the îles du Salut, the islands off Guyana that included the Devil's Island to which Dreyfus had been sent, a sentence that was not only for life, but also involved confiscation of all the person's goods.[60]

As if in recognition that the experience of occupation set the French of the north apart from the rest of France, and did indeed cut them off from the community of the nation, they had to face a harsh lack of comprehension elsewhere in France. The Germans sent out of the region the 'bouches inutiles' ('useless mouths'), useless to their war effort and a burden on limited resources.[61] But they were met with hostility and suspicion in France, not sympathy, even being called 'les boches du nord'.[62] This was the experience of those who managed, through Belgium, to get themselves back into France after the town of Lens was forcibly evacuated in April 1917.[63] The same thing would be said in the second occupation of those from the zone interdite; a managing director allowed to visit Nantes for business reasons was told: 'The North? Oh it's no longer France up there.'[64] An envoy remarked in August 1941 on the gulf between the occupied zone and the zone interdite, the ignorance and indifference of the former only surpassed by the even greater insensitivity shown in the unoccupied zone: 'There are towns in the Midi where they are called the "Boches" of the North; there are schools in the Midi where they are bullied because the "Boches" of the North have a different accent from their schoolmates.'[65]

Even when the whole country was occupied, then the French of the north were again in special circumstances, both because of their intimate knowledge of being occupied and the formative role this played in their attitudes, and because of the different conditions. The military importance of the region in relation to the war with Britain, first offensively, then defensively, meant that the north saw large numbers of troops and troop movements compared to elsewhere in France. Once the bombing raids on Germany started, Allied airmen were baling out on their return flights over northern France, and smuggled back to Britain through well-established rescue networks. So the military situation, the fear of annexation, the experience of the earlier occupation, and strong pro-British sentiments, forged after their liberation by British troops in 1918, and reinforced by witnessing the fierce English resistance in 1940[66], combined to prevent those in the north from sharing the views of the rest of France on the armistice; in the north, the war went on.

The widespread pillaging during and after the military campaign meant that when the refugees were allowed back, they returned to devastated homes. Requisitioning was still a fact of life; the occupied lands were to serve the ever-increasing demands of the German war economy, in goods and in people. It is ironic to hear von Ebrennac, the German officer billetted in a French home in Vercors's famous clandestine story 'Le Silence de la mer', complaining, in the context of cultural relations between France and Germany, that 'one can take nothing from France', since the more usual sentiment from the French was 'they are taking everything from us'. 'Hitler's hoover empties the country in no time,' as Valmy, a resistance newspaper in the occupied zone, put it.[67]

People, too, were needed in Germany. After efforts on the part of Vichy to persuade the French to volunteer to work there by bringing in 'La Relève', a scheme whereby for every three skilled workers who left France, one prisoner of war was returned, a scheme that failed miserably to attract enough numbers to meet Germany's demands, the Service du Travail Obligatoire was imposed, effectively deporting young people in large numbers – about 650,000 in all.[68] This pattern of increasing repression, fuelling increasing resistance to the Occupation, is replicated in other domains. Vichy's anti-Semitism, which found early expression in the laws of October 1940 laying down the definition and status of Jews, intertwined with German measures against Jews in France. All Jews had to be registered, carry identification, and report regularly. The yellow star was introduced in the occupied zone in 1942, a development that was not well received among the population as a whole; expressions of sympathy and support were frequent and public. From summer 1942 began the mass arrests and deportations of Jews, both recent refugees from Germany and elsewhere, and naturalised Jews settled in France for generations. In all, 70,000 Jews were deported from France to the death camps; about 2,500 survived. In the north, all the Jews living in the coastal region of the *zone interdite* were rounded up and expelled in 1940. There had been many Jews in the exodus of May 1940; the Jewish community in Lille went from 4,000 to under 2,000. Jewish refugees were forbidden to return to their homes after the armistice; massive arrests and deportations swept Lille and other towns in September 1942. There were many refugees from Eastern Europe in this region, who not only found it virtually impossible to escape detection, because of obvious language and cultural differences, but who also met with some anti-Semitic reactions from local French people, in spite of the fact that well-attended meetings had been held in Lille in the wake of the Kristallnacht attacks to rally support against the German regime's anti-Semitic policies and actions. Some 1,647 Jews were deported to their deaths from the Pas-de-Calais.[69]

But the industrial strength of the north created a special situation. While some skilled workers and miners were sent to work in Germany right at the beginning of the occupation, it is also the case that the Germans were very concerned to get production going again, to exploit the industrial strength of the region. But the fact that this was a strongly industrialised area, with major strikes and much social conflict in the 1930s, had its effect. When escalating food prices and scarcity of goods meant that people were going hungry, with their poor diet having the predictable consequences in diseases such as tuberculosis and rickets, public protest began. There were food riots, demonstrations, work stoppages and strikes, though the latter were dealt with harshly.[70] The politicised workforce and history of conflict intersected with the situation in particular ways. The miners considered that the 'bosses' would collude with Vichy. While anti-German attitudes stretched across the classes, particularly given that some of the old industrial dynasties had not forgotten the harsh treatment in the First World War[71], the anti-communism of the industrialists, as well as the memory of the 1930s, tended to encourage support for Vichy. Social conflicts were exacerbated, not attenuated, in this occupation.[72] The north was Gaullist, communist, anti-German and anti-capitalist.

There was anger within the *zone interdite* at the abandonment by the French authorities. People looked to Pétain and the Vichy Government for some mention of their plight, some reassurance in public speeches, but none was forthcoming.[73] In December 1940 the Prefect, M Ingrand, reported back to Vichy on the hostility to the armistice (widely seen as being concluded in the interests of the southern half of the country), on anger at Pétain's meeting with Hitler at Montoire, and characterised the attitude of the population as anglophile and Gaullist, with a total rejection of any collaboration.[74] Vichy's envoys sent even firmer messages in May 1941: 'In Vichy, it's the armistice and, very soon, peace. In Paris, it's the occupation. In Lille, it's war.'[75] The Bishop of Arras, Monseigneur Dutoit, was strongly in favour of Vichy's National Revolution, and also preached obedience to the Service du Travail Obligatoire. Many of his priests had to censor parts of the letter, aware of the anger that would be aroused among their parishioners on hearing such views.[76] But as elsewhere in France, antagonism to Vichy and support for de Gaulle was often combined with support for Pétain, who retained an aura of trustworthiness. But here too, when disaffection did set in towards the end of war, it was much more pronounced in the *zone interdite* than elsewhere.[77]

It was a major cause of resentment in the First World War, too, that the French authorities in the 'pays libre' did not think to keep their fellow countrymen in the occupied territories informed of developments.[78] From 15 November 1914 appeared the *Bulletin de Lille*, a paper produced under German control, publishing decisions and notices of the German administration.[79] In contrast to the second occupation, clandestine production was limited. But Abbé Pinte managed to tune into the wireless from the Eiffel Tower and the English transmitter at Poldhu, and when the first issue of *La Patience* appeared, dated 23 February 1915[80], not surprisingly it devoted much space to war news, for example the declarations of the Russian Government. Each issue requested secrecy and prudence from its readers. After various changes of title, it disappeared when, together with his colleagues, MM Dubon and Willot, Pinte was arrested on 19 December 1916.[81] Escape and information networks were also set up. Louise de Bettignies was arrested with two other women resisters and sentenced to death – a sentence later changed to indefinite imprisonment; Léon Trulin was executed in La Citadelle for leading an information network for the Allies; and Eugène Jacquet and four others who became known as 'les fusillés de Lille' were executed on von Heinrich's orders for hiding French soldiers and helping an English pilot to escape.[82]

In 1940-44, resistance started much earlier in the occupied zone, including the *zone interdite*, than elsewhere in France. Escape networks for Allied airmen and others were established with the Special Operations Executive. They became famous for their exploits, and many of their prominent leaders were betrayed, arrested, and shot.[83] Acts of sabotage, at factories, on the railways, were a significant feature of Resistance work.[84] Many important Resistance newspapers, around which Resistance movements also grew, developed: *La Voix du nord*, *L'Homme libre*, *L'Enchaîné*. They provided information on the war, and countered German and Vichy propaganda. *La Voix du nord* kept memories of the first occupation alive on commemorative dates, such as an item on Armistice Day, 'Anniversary of Victory', which recalled 'the insolent arrogance of the German soldiers [suffered by] the inhabitants of the invaded territories'[85], as well as celebrating actions and protests of miners and other workers.[86] Resistance is always more than engaging in direct action. Morale, attitudes, knowledge and interpretation of the complexities of the situation are all essential components of behaviour. Tracts, literature, poetry, songs and poster art were all exploited as part of what in the Second World War would be called the intellectual resistance. Two poems were published in the sixth issue of *La Patience*, in March 1915. Both bear witness to the physical hardships of the German occupation, in matters of food, requisitions and submission expected from the civilian population, as can been seen in the shorter one, 'Von Heinrich's Ten Commandements':

Le pain KK tu mangeras
Et digéreras péniblement

Tout ton argent nous donneras
Sans protester, docilement

Nulle cocarde ne porteras
A ton corsage, crânement

Tous les Boches, considèreras
Toujours admirablement

Après 5 heures ne sortiras
Sous peine d'emprisonnement

Des affiches ne te ficheras
Du moins pas ostensiblement

A nul groupe ne te mêleras
Pour former des rassemblements

Les pires bourdes goberas
Sans réfléchir aucunement

Aux prisonniers rien ne diras
Quand nous les sortons gentiment

La situation tu comprendras
Ou sinon, gare au châtiment'[87]

In March 1941, *Valmy*, a newspaper produced in the occupied zone, carried a stylistically similar poem, but one that reveals also the prominence placed on the internal divisions between the French during the second occupation, alongside the purely national and patriotic confrontation between the French and the Germans:

'La BBC écouteras
Chaque jour avidemment.
Radio-Paris laisseras:
Car il est boche assurément.
Avec de Gaulle te battras,
Au grand jour du débarquement.
Ceux de Vichy mépriseras

Et leurs propos avilissants.
Laval, Déat, tu châtieras
Et leurs complices mêmement.
Et quand leur tête on coupera,
Tu danseras joyeusement.
La Carmagnole chanteras
Quand crèveront tous les tyrans.'[88]

Geographical divisions were not complicated by political divisions during the First World War in the way that they were in the Second. After the bitter arguments leading up to the outbreak of war between 'nationalists' and pacifists, the declaration of war itself was quickly followed by the establishment of the 'union sacrée'; collaboration motivated by a sense of cultural, social or ideological complicity, such as holding a reception for the Kronprinz, was much more rare in the First World War than the Second.[89] Collaboration was usually a case of profiteering and economic collusion. During the Second World War, the active complicity of promoting the Nazi vision, or promoting Franco-German collaboration as an ideological cause, greatly affected everyone's lives, although in the *zone interdite*, the experiences of the previous occupation hardly encouraged any spirit of collaboration. Some rallies were organised by extreme right and collaborationist movements, and there was encouragement from the authorities for the anti-French, separatist movements, but numbers were small.[90] Nonetheless, the sensitivity surrounding such issues explains the fact that Pierrard devotes pages of detailed analysis to the history of Lille during the First World War, yet covers Lille in the Second World War only briefly, on the grounds that it is too early to say anything about it; and this is in 1964.[91]

At the end of a discussion of a presentation of the public pronouncements of the prominent local figures Monseigneur Dutoit and Monseigneur Liénart, several listeners felt that Liénart's at times cautious statements should never be read as sympathy for Vichy or the Germans; he was well known to support the Allied cause, and the limitations on what he could or could not say clearly were also understood: 'There is a great gap between the bare coldness of the texts commented on and the atmosphere in which one was able to live at that time.'[92] The complexities of civilian life in situations of war and occupation, awkwardly defying the clarities of the interpretative grids by which we seek to make sense of them, can be traced in many aspects of the two occupations. The situation of women, particularly, refracts many of these issues – as non-combatants, they highlight the wide variety of situations such occupations entailed. In 1914-18, women and young girls were torn from their families and deported to work the land; but there were also women who are described in many a contemporary account as being of 'loose morals', having liaisons with German soldiers. There were women who reduced German soldiers to suicidal despair by the vehemence of their protests against the ferrying or deportations of prisoners.[93] And there were those who found that their only protector was a German soldier, bringing them food and the means to warm themselves when they had nothing:

'A soldier is staying with a woman, working class home. He sees her boots are torn, he asks her to lend them to him, he takes them to the barracks; and the next day he brings them back to her, mended. Resoling a pair of shoes costs between 12 and 15 francs. How could one ask that woman to be uncivilised towards that soldier?'[94]

Some were shot or deported for resistance. Louise Thuliez was arrested with Louise de Bettignies in 1916, and would also be a prominent resister in the second occupation.[95] The food rioters of 1941 onwards were mainly women, and yet at the end of that second occupation the spectacle of women having their heads shaved became an extraordinarily powerful icon of collaboration and its punishments.

The story of the two occupations is also a story of the changing nature of warfare. The confrontations between civilian authorities and occupying powers over the nature and extent of demands on the occupied lands and its people, the attempts to apply the international conventions governing military rights and obligations, are related to the traditions of military codes of warfare; civilian resistance as transgression of military codes, repression by the occupying forces as transgression of internationally agreed obligations, are both present in the long months of German presence on French territory. André Ducasse quotes a lengthy piece by Stephan Zweig, written in the 1930s, lamenting the passing of an honourable, military understanding of war in the name of total war[96]; in fact, this clash between the old world and the new is already present in the 19th century. It fuels German anger after 1870-71; it influences German actions and French anger in 1914-18. It can still be traced in 1940-44. In May 1940 the Germans recognised the French defenders of Lille by according them the honours of war; the defeated French soldiers paraded before the German Army in Lille's central square. This is the same army associated with Oignies and other shootings of civilians and prisoners of war. Moreover, honouring the French soldiers so infuriated the German High Command that they relieved the officer in charge of his command.

The two occupations of the northernmost areas of France have much to teach us about the complications of wartime experience, and about the extent to which the crucially important experiences of this area, in 1914-18 and in 1940-44, have been in danger of disappearing in the blind spots of conventional narratives of France's wars.

Notes on contributors

Professor Margaret Atack, The University of Leeds, UK
Margaret Atack is Professor of French at the University of Leeds. Her publications include Literature and the French Resistance: Cultural Politics and Narrative Forms 1940-1950 (1989), Contemporary French Fiction by Women: Feminist Perspectives (co-editor, 1991) and May 68 in French Fiction and Film: Rethinking Society, Rethinking Representation (1999).

Recommended reading

Becker, Annette, *Journaux de combattants et civils dans la France du Nord dans la Grande Guerre* (Villeneuve d'Ascq: Presses Universitaires du Septentrion, 1998)
　Oubliés de la Grande Guerre: Humanitaire et culture de guerre, populations occupées, déportés civils, prisonniers de guerre (Paris: Noêsis, 1998)
McPhail, Helen, *The Long Silence: Civilian Life Under the German Occupation of Northern France* (London: I. B. Tauris, 1999)
Ousby, Ian, *Occupation: The Ordeal of France 1940-1944* (London: Pimlico, 1999)
Revue du nord, special issue, *Guerre et occupation 1914-1918*, No 325, Vol 80, 1998
Taylor, Lynn, *Between Resistance and Collaboration: Popular Protest in Northern France 1940-1945* (Basingstoke: Macmillan, 1999)

Notes

1 First lines of the poem 'Occupation', published clandestinely in Lille in 1915. 'And so thus, on to this corner of French soil/Sinister Germans, you have/poured your heavy regiments/Bearing the marks of our blood, and covered with our clay.'

2 Marc Blancpain, *Quand Guillaume II gouvernait 'de la Somme aux Vosges'* (Paris: Fayard, 1980) p11

3 Marc Bloch, *L'Etrange défaite: témoignage écrit en 1940* (Paris: Gallimard, Folio, 1990) p84

4 Annette Becker, 'Mémoire et commémoration: les 'atrocités' allemandes de la Première Guerre mondiale dans le nord de la France', *La Revue du nord* 74 (295) (1992) pp339-54; Marc Derez, 'The Flames of Louvain: The War Experience of an Academic Community' in Hugh Cecil and Peter H. Liddle (eds), *Facing Armageddon: The First World War Experienced* (London: Leo Cooper, 1996) pp617-29; John Horne and Alan Kramer, 'German "Atrocities" and Franco-German Opinion 1914: The Evidence of German Soldiers' Diaries', *Journal of Modern History* 66 (March 1994) pp1-33; Michael Howard, *The Franco-Prussian War: The German Invasion of France, 1870-1871* (London: Rupert Hart-Davis, 1962)

5 Michael Howard, op cit, p381

6 Horne and Kramer, op cit, pp12-4

7 Annette Becker (ed), *Journaux de combattants et de civils: de la France du nord dans la Grande Guerre* (Villeneuve d'Ascq, Nord: Presses Universitaires du Septentrion, 1998) pp110-1

8 Ibid, p13

9 Georges Gromaire, *L'Occupation allemande en France (1914-1918)* (Paris: Payot, 1925) p7

10 Marc Blancpain, op cit, p291. See Annette Becker, *Oubliés de la Grande Guerre: Humanitaire et culture de guerre, populations occupées, déportés civils, prisonniers de guerre* (Paris: Noêsis, 1998)

11 Annette Becker, 'Introduction', *La Revue du nord* special issue: *1914-1918, guerre et occupation* 53 (325) (April/June 1998) p254

12 For this account of the invasion of Lille, see Pierre Pierrard, *Lille et les Lillois* (Paris: Blond & Gay, 1967) pp258-60; 'Lille, ville allemande' in *L'Histoire, Mourir pour la patrie: France 1914-1918* (Paris: Seuil, 1992) pp242-52

13 Pierre Pierrard, op cit, p260

14 This account is taken from Bruno Barbier, *La Grande Guerre à Amiens* (Amiens: Encrage Edition, 1992) pp41-52

15 Reproduced in André Ducasse, Jacques Meyer and Gabriel Perreux, *Vie et mort des Français 1914-1918* (Paris: Hachette, 1959) p32

16 Bruno Barbier, op cit, p49

17 Reproduced as an epigraph to Martin-Mamy, *Quatre Ans avec les barbares: Lille pendant l'occupation allemande* (Paris: La Renaissance du Livre, 1919)

18 See map in Ian Ousby, *Occupation: The Ordeal of France* (London: Pimlico, 1999) ppxvi-xvii

19 Henri Amouroux, *La Vie des Français sous l'occupation* (Paris: Fayard, livre de poche edition 1961) Vol 1, p97

20 Robert O. Paxton, *La France de Vichy* (Paris: Seuil, collection Points, 1973) p24

21 Ibid, p62

22 Quoted by Henri Amouroux, op cit, Vol 1, p83

23 Ibid, p96

24 Ibid

25 Ibid, p97

26 E. Dejonghe, 'Reprise économique dans le Nord et le Pas-de-Calais', *Revue d'Histoire de la deuxième guerre mondiale* 20 (79) p91

27 Ibid, p83

28 Hubert Claude, 'L'Evêque, le maréchal, la collaboration 1940-1945', *Revue d'histoire de la deuxième guerre mondiale* 34 (135) p54; Yves le Maner, 'L'Invasion de 1940 dans le Nord – Pas-de-Calais', *Revue du nord* 76 (306) pp478-9; in the same volume, Kléber Deberles, 'Les Atrocités commises par la Division S.S. Totenkopf', pp519-22

29 Marc Blancpain, op cit, p135

30 Maurice Thiéry, *1914-1918: Le Nord de la France sous le joug allemand, d'après des témoignages*

authentiques (Paris: E. de Boccard Editeur, 1919) pp11-5
31 Pierre Pierrard, op cit, p279, n10
32 Claudine Wallart, 'Déportations de prisonniers civils au "camp de concentration" d'Holzminden', *Revue du nord* 80 (325) (1998) p445
33 Maurice Thiéry, op cit, p15
34 Georges Gromaire, op cit, p7
35 Marc Blancpain, op cit, p88
36 George Gromaire, op cit, p85
37 Ibid, p77; André Ducasse et al, op cit, p243
38 Georges Gromaire, op cit, pp88-9
39 Ibid, p94
40 Ibid, p90
41 Reproduced in André Ducasse et al, op cit, p246
42 'Me Louis Selosse avec le concours de M Jacquey, Guerre de 1914-1918, Occupation de Lille par les Allemands: Consultations données à la mairie de Lille' (Paris: Société anonyme du Recueil Sirey, 1927) pp38-9
43 Pierre Pierrard, op cit, p265
44 'Me Louis Selosse', op cit, p7
45 Ibid, pp49-50
46 Maxence van der Meersch, *Invasion 14* (Monte-Carlo: Editions du livre, 1948) Vol 1, p150
47 Reproduced in André Ducasse et al, op cit, p244
48 Ibid, p243
49 Pierre Pierrard, op cit, p279
50 Nathalie Vidal, 'Physique ou tuberculeux? Le discours lillois sur la tuberculose à la Belle Epoque (1895-1914)', *Revue du nord* 76 (304) (1994) p91
51 Pierre Pierrard, op cit, pp279-80
52 Ibid
53 Letter from von Heinrich, reproduced in 'Me Louis Selosse', op cit, p15
54 Jean Lorédan, *Lille et l'invasion allemande 1914-1918: Abandon, martyre et délivrance de Lille* (Paris: Perrin) p163
55 Renée Martinage, 'Les Collaborateurs devant la cour d'assises du Nord après la très Grande Guerre', *Revue du nord* 77 (309) p103
56 Maxence van der Meersch, op cit, Vol 1, pp171-80
57 Georges Gromaire, op cit, p65
58 Quoted in ibid, p18
59 Maurice Thiéry, op cit, p23
60 Renée Martinage, op cit, p110
61 Georges Gromaire, op cit, p29
62 Marc Blancpain, op cit, p49
63 Dominique Gallez, 'Lens, cité-martyre 1914-1918', *Revue du nord* 65 (259) (1983) p695
64 Etienne Dejonghe, 'Le Nord – Pas-de-Calais pendant la première année d'occupation: un régime d'exception', *Revue du nord* 76 (306) (1994) p494
65 Ibid
66 Etienne Dejonghe, 'Le Nord – Pas-de-Calais', op cit, p496
67 Claude Bellanger, *La Presse clandestine 1940-1944* (Paris: Editions Kiosque, 1961) p59
68 Jean-Pierre Azéma, *De Munich à la Libération 1938-1944* (Paris: Seuil, 1979) p179
69 René Rémond, *Le Fichier juif* (Paris: Plon) pp98-102; André Kaspi, *Les Juifs en France pendant l'occupation* (Paris: Seuil, 1997); Danielle Delmaire and Yves-Marie Hilaire, 'Chrétiens et juifs dans le Nord – Pas-de-Calais pendant la seconde guerre mondiale', *Revue du nord* 60 (1978) pp451-6; Michael Marrus and Robert O. Paxton, *Vichy France and The Jews* (New York: Schocken Books, 1981); David Knout, *La Résistance juive en France 1940-1944* (Paris: Editions du Centre, 1947)
70 See Lynne Taylor, *Between Resistance and Collaboration* (Basingstoke: Macmillan, 1999) Chaps 5 and 6
71 Etienne Dejonghe, 'Le Nord – Pas-de-Calais', op cit, p495
72 See Didier Daeninckx, *La Mort n'oublie personne* (Paris: Gallimard, 1989) for a recent exploration

in fiction of class conflict and the occupation in the Pas-de-Calais

73 Etienne Dejonghe, 'Le Nord – Pas-de-Calais', op cit, pp494-5

74 Marc Sueur, 'La Collaboration politique dans le département du Nord (1940-1944)', *Revue d'histoire de la deuxième guerre mondiale* 34 (135) (1984) p4

75 Quoted in Etienne Dejonghe, 'Le Nord – Pas-de-Calais', op cit, p488

76 Hubert Claude, 'L'Evêque, le Maréchal, la collaboration', *Revue d'histoire de la deuxième guerre mondiale* 34 (135) pp64-5

77 Etienne Dejonghe, 'Le Nord – Pas-de-Calais', op cit, pp495-6

78 Marc Blancpain, op cit, p49

79 Jean Lorédan, op cit, p162

80 Bibliothèque d'information contemporaine, Université de Nanterre, 4° P 18 Rés

81 *Invasion 14* reconstructs the story of this paper in Vol 1, Chap IV

82 Pierre Pierrard, op cit, pp272-4, 262

83 M. R. D. Foot, *SOE in France* (London: HMSO, 1966); and Michel Rousseau, 'Deux réseaux britanniques dans la région du Nord: le réseau "Garrow-Pat O'Leary" et le réseau "Farmer"', *Revue d'histoire de la deuxième guerre mondiale* 34 (135) (1984) pp87-108

84 Lynne Taylor, op cit, Chap 4

85 No 18, 11 novembre 1941, p1. It is worth noting that it is also keeping alive the practice in the first occupation of referring to the area as 'invaded', not 'occupied', underlining the context of war.

86 Cf 'Honneur aux travailleurs de Fives-Lille', relating their hostile reception on the occasion of a visit by Vichy's Minister of Industrial Production, M Lehideux, 22 février 1942, No 25

87 'Thou shalt eat KK bread /And digest it with great difficulty/Thou shalt not wear a cockade/On your shirt front, boldly/Thou shalt not go out after 5 o'clock/Under pain of imprisonment/Thou shalt not join any group/In order to form a gathering/Thou shalt not say anything to the prisoners/When we kindly take them outside/Thou shalt give us all your money/Without protesting, meekly/Thou shalt consider all Boches/At all times admiringly/Thou shalt not mock written notices/At least not openly/Thou shalt swallow the worst lies/Without thinking about it at all/Thou shalt understand the situation/Or else, look out for punishment' *La Patience*, No 3, March 1915, pp24-5

88 'Thou shalt listen to the BBC/Eagerly every day./Thou shalt leave Radio-Paris alone,/Since it is certainly Jerry's./Thou shalt fight with de Gaulle/On the great day of the landings./Thou shalt have only contempt for the men of Vichy/And their degrading words./Thou shalt punish Laval and Déat/And their accomplices just the same./And when their heads are cut off,/Thou shalt dance for joy./Thou shalt sing the Carmagnole/When all the tyrants die.' Quoted in Claude Bellanger, op cit, pp61-2. Pierre Laval was Prime Minister under Pétain. He was tried and executed after the war. Marcel Déat, leader of the extreme right movement, was the author of the famous question in May 1939, whether it is worth dying for Dantzig.

89 Renée Martinage, op cit, p99

90 Claude Lévy, 'Sur le Nord et le Pas-de-Calais', review, *Revue d'histoire de la deuxième guerre mondiale* 20 (1970) pp125-6

91 Pierre Pierrard, op cit, p297

92 'Intervention of M Catrice, 1977 Conference on Churches and Christians in the Nord – Pas-de-Calais', *Revue du nord* 60 (1978), p291

93 Maurice Thiéry, op cit, pp20-1

94 'Journal de David Hirsch', Annette Becker, *Journaux de combattants et de civils*, op cit, p297

95 Pierre Pierrard, op cit, p272

96 André Ducasse et al, op cit, pp480-2

Chapter 31

The experience of occupation: Poland

Anita J. Prazmowska

During both the First and Second World Wars Polish territory was the battleground on which highly mobile military confrontations took place. The civilian population in both cases could not escape the consequences of fighting, and during both wars territories inhabited by Poles were occupied over a prolonged period of time. In the minds of the Poles both periods of occupation are associated with extreme hardship, economic devastation and genocide. In the case of the First World War, Russia, Germany and Austria all pursued policies that were haphazard and wasteful. Nevertheless, their approach to the Polish Question was always affected by long-term considerations. This led them to view Poland as a military zone in the present and any future wars. During the Second World War similar considerations dictated harshness and exploitation of the Polish areas by Nazi Germany and the Soviet Union. Ideology dominated the Nazi's occupation policies, adding to the already unbearable burden of hardship. Soviet occupation policies towards occupied Polish territories during the period September 1919-June 1941 were likewise affected by ideological considerations. Occupation policies were aimed at exploiting resources and consolidation of military advantages.

Nevertheless, the experiences of the First and the Second World Wars were distinct. The outbreak of the First World War marked the end of the consensus between the three powers that had, 100 years earlier, destroyed Polish independence and that had successfully prevented the re-emergence of a Polish state. In 1914 Austria-Hungary and Germany were pitched in a war against the Russian Empire. Not unreasonably, the Polish population in each of the three Empires presumed that whatever the outcome of the conflict, it would inevitably result in a reconstruction of Poland. Thus the First World War was, in spite of the hardship and destruction experienced by Poles, a time of hope and growing certainty that foreign oppression would be at best destroyed, at worst modified. The outbreak of the Second World War was a tragic time for Poland. The state, so recently rebuilt, was militarily defeated, diplomatically isolated and occupied. Soviet and German co-operation in September 1939 signalled the renewal of consensus on the subject of Poland. When Hitler attacked the Soviet Union in June 1941, Allied dependence on the Soviet war effort still raised doubts in the

Poles' minds about the Allies' ability and willingness to guarantee the restoration of an independent Poland after the war.

During the First World War national leaders in Poland, and those in exile, optimistically sought to prepare themselves and the nation for the moment when military defeat of either the Central or Allied powers would allow them to stake a claim to an independent Poland. Differences between various groups of self-appointed national leaders were inevitable, but the common aim was to prepare for the assumption of power. The Second World War was a time of deep conflicts between Poles in occupied territories and those in the West and the Soviet Union. Fratricidal conflicts in occupied Poland were mirrored by deep political divisions between, on the one hand, Poles who sought British and US support and, on the other, those who believed that the Soviet Union was the only guarantor of liberty and revolutionary change. The end of the war and the liberation of Polish territories by the Soviet Army meant that while German oppression was destroyed, a new, perhaps more complex chapter in Polish history was opened.

The responses of Polish nationals to the outbreak of war in August 1914 depended very much on where they lived and how the area was treated by the occupying power. In the first months of the conflict most politically active Poles hoped that autonomy within the existing Empires could be secured. As fighting continued inconclusively, the neutral states became focal points of diplomatic endeavours either to prevent them from joining the enemy side, or in order to secure their support. The Poles realised that in so confused a situation they might be able to demand independence in return for support for the war effort. In Paris, Washington and London, self-appointed Polish committees attempted to secure assurances that independence for Poland would become a war aim. At the same time, in Moscow and Vienna governments and military leaders were lobbied by the Poles to give assurances that Polish territories would be granted autonomy or at least special status within the Tsarist and/or Habsburg Empires. These negotiations were conducted by prominent community leaders, or simply famous Poles, as was the case of the pianist Ignacy Paderewski, who toured the US in an attempt to draw attention to the Polish issue. In the meantime developments in Polish-inhabited areas took their own course.

Before the outbreak of the war Austrian rule had been least oppressive. As a result, during the summer months of 1914 Poles in the Austro-Hungarian Empire still thought in terms of Polish autonomy within the Empire, rather than independence. While it was generally noted that the Polish peasant population of Galicia was unmoved by nationalist slogans, the intellectual and political elites took the initiative in negotiating with the authorities. Even as the war broke out there was caution in calling for outright independence.[1] The basis for co-operation between the Austrian authorities and the Polish community leaders was a shared desire to defeat the Russian Empire. Thus Poles willingly took arms and rarely avoided mobilisation. Polish nationalist movements, united in a Confederation, declared that Poles should be 'an active force' in the forthcoming war, thus indicating that military co-operation should be rewarded by the granting of increased rights within the Empire.[2] The Austrian authorities were not in a hurry to respond to these invitations, as clearly the pursuit of the war was a priority. Only when the military situation dictated the need to be conciliatory towards the national minorities was it possible for the Poles to extract vague promises that their demand for the same status as that enjoyed by the Hungarians would be considered favourably in the future.

The first attempt to spur on Poles in the Russian Empire to rise against the Tsarist authorities ended in a sad debacle, thus warning the Austrian authorities against making too hasty promises for changes in their hitherto carefully balanced minority policies with the Empire's nationalities. At the beginning of August, Józef Pilsudski, a self-appointed Commander-in-Chief in the still to be formed Polish national government, which he hoped would emerge in Warsaw, marched with a detachment of riflemen from Austrian Galicia into the Russian-held Dbrowa Basin. The anticipated mass uprising did not take place. The local peasants, wary of another military unit, which they expected to rob them of their meagre resources, showed no interest. When the enterprise was abandoned, Polish leaders in Austria henceforth concentrated their efforts on diplomatic negotiations in anticipation of either the Allies or the Central Powers winning and liberating Polish territories.[3]

In the spring of 1915 Austrian and German military action prevented the Russian Army from breaking through the Carpathian Mountains. By the summer of that year German and Austrian troops entered into the hitherto Russian-held Kingdom Poland. German troops occupied Warsaw on 2 August. Henceforth the Polish Question would depend on German and Austrian decisions, and the civilian population would be subject to their whims and changing military fortunes.

Russian policies towards Poles had been particularly harsh since the last great national uprising in 1863. Because of this, Polish community leaders in exile and in the so-called Kingdom Poland, maintained hopes for a nationalist rising. In fact by 1914 disappointment with previous uprisings and harsh repression, judiciously balanced by Russian investment in the Polish areas of the Empire, combined to destroy the insurrectionist spirit within the Polish communities. This was replaced with a pragmatic desire to gain for Poles a stable position with the Tsarist Empire. Thus in the summer of 1914 Poles, in common with most Russians in the Empire, wished to see Germany defeated. Only the revolutionary section of the Polish Socialist Party opposed the war and called for a revolution. Nevertheless, attempts to extract from the Tsarist administration concessions in return for loyal support for the war effort were only limited. While the Russians accepted the need for the establishment of town and local councils, they were unwilling to allow for the creation of a Polish central administrative authority.[4]

During the course of the war the Russian authorities tried to minimise the loss and destruction of industrial capacity by evacuating whole factories from areas close to the front into the Russian interior. Where enterprises were thus moved, workers and their families were expected to follow. Approximately 130 major enterprises were moved from Polish territories. In the wake of German and Austrian military successes in 1915 the evacuations were stepped up, but became more haphazard and thus caused more disruption and panic among the civilian population. In May 1915, facing the imminent loss of Polish territories, the

Russian High Command ordered the destruction of all property that could be of use to the enemy. Since the Polish community was also seen as an economic and military resource, the civilian population was uprooted and taken by train into the Russian interior.[5] While it has never been possible to calculate the exact numbers of those forcefully displaced, it has been accepted that the number was in the region of tens of thousands.

Once the German and Austrian authorities were in control of Polish territories, they could not escape addressing the Polish Question. The matter was bound to arise in all talks concerning war aims and as a potential source of disruption in the continuing war against the Tsarist Government. Nevertheless, they tried to postpone making plans for the end of the war as military issues remained in the forefront of all considerations. Germany did not want to allow its Austrian ally to assume control over the Polish Question, as any decisions made would have repercussions on any future negotiations with the Russians. Thus for administrative purposes the occupied Polish territories were divided into areas that came under the jurisdiction of the German or Austrian authorities; Germany retained control of Warsaw. The willingness of the German authorities to co-operate with citizens' councils, which had sprung up in all major cities, sent out a positive signal to the Poles. Reversing the policy of 'Russification', the use of the Polish language in schools and in public life was permitted. Additionally, a Polish university and scientific university were opened in Warsaw.[6] The Russian Government had abolished both after the last nationalist uprising in 1863.

Notwithstanding the generally good impression made by the first German and Austrian administrative decisions, Kingdom Poles continued to show indifference to the Central Powers' war effort. At the end of 1915 the military situation was still fluid. The economic policies of the Central Powers betrayed anxiety about their ability to hold on to areas captured during the summer campaign, and this anxiety rather than a long-term commitment to keep the Poles pacified dictated decisions in occupied areas. The German authorities proceeded to exploit Polish territories under their control, which in turn decreased the stock of goodwill towards them. German military victories had ended the evacuation and flight of population eastwards, but harsh economic exploitation of the occupied areas caused extreme hardship. By the autumn of 1915 most stocks of industrial raw materials and products were confiscated. This led to the reduction of local manufacture and as a result also to unemployment and shortages in the local economies.

German economic policies towards occupied Polish territories went beyond exploitation for military purposes. The German military administration authorised the selective destruction of certain branches of industry in the Kingdom Poland areas in order to undermine any competition with German industry that might arise after the war, as had been the case before the war. Textile and steel production was in particular identified as likely, in the long term, to compete with German industry. Coal mining and agriculture were fully exploited; forests and timber were in particular heavily affected, as ancient woodlands were destroyed and the ecological structure of whole regions undermined. German occupation was characterised by indifference to the economic difficulties that these policies caused to the local population.

As a result of German occupation policies, up to 70 per cent of those employed before the war in industry lost employment. Food rationing reduced the Polish community to starvation levels, and the policy of deliberate exploitation and destruction increased hostility towards Germany. The consequences of these policies were faced in the winter of 1915-16 when it was realised that Germany was short of manpower, and this in turn affected production levels. Since voluntary recruitment to work in Germany was not successful, in 1916 Poles were conscripted to work in German industry.

In the autumn of 1916 a number of German politicians put forward the idea that Germany should continue the war in the east under the guise of supporting the national aspirations of the local populations. General Erich Ludendorff, the German Commander-in-Chief, supported this idea, and as a result Germany made a commitment to the creation of an independent Polish state at the end of the war.[7] In November 1916 an interim Council of State was created in German-occupied Warsaw. In fact, the German military authorities had no genuine interest in the creation of an independent Polish state; the commitment was made merely to facilitate recruitment of Poles into the German Army. This duplicity was exploited by Pilsudski, who insisted on the creation of Polish units, thus preparing a nucleus of a Polish Army for action in the event of the collapse of the Central Powers.[8] In September 1917 the German authorities made a further attempt to control the growth of potentially disruptive Polish nationalist aspirations. From German and Austrian occupied territories a Polish Kingdom was created with a Regency Council assuming governmental powers. This move was only partially successful in defusing discontent in Poland, as the simultaneous imprisonment of Pilsudski, who had become a national hero, contradicted the earlier initiative. On 10 November 1918 Pilsudski was released from prison, and the political and intellectual elites in Poland accepted his authority. As the German war effort collapsed and troops were withdrawn from Poland, Pilsudski assumed the role of Provisional Head of State. During the next two months he initiated talks with other national leaders in Poland and in Paris, where in the meantime a National Polish Committee had secured the Allies' recognition. In January 1919 the first elections took placed in a free Poland.

During the whole of the course of the First World War the issue of direct Polish participation in the military conflict figured prominently in the minds of the community leaders. At the beginning of the war each of the partitioning powers conscripted Polish nationals into their armies, Tsarist, Austrian and German. But Polish community leaders had no means of extracting concessions in return for the use of Polish manpower. Thus in order to highlight the Polish cause they sought permission for the creation of distinctly Polish military units. On the whole all three governments tried to avoid making concession of this type, either because they feared that it would lead to other national groups demanding similar privileges, or because concessions would have highlighted the Polish war effort and this in turn would lead to demands for special treatment. As the war progressed the issue only increased in importance. In the course of the war manpower shortages experienced by both sides made it possible for the Poles to return to the issue of separate formations.[9]

The Tsarist Army was estimated to have conscripted several hundred thousand Poles. Even then there was no willingness to allow the Poles to have separate units. The idea had been put forward in August 1914, but that was as far as the matter had progressed. After the February Revolution, Minister of War Alexander Guchkov considered that it would be a good idea to encourage the creation of distinctly Polish units. He calculated that if on entry into Polish territories the Russian Army was accompanied by well-equipped Polish troops, this would build pro-Russian sentiments in Kingdom Poland.[10] A few months later the next Minister of War, Alexander Kerensky, opposed the idea of separate Polish units, so the matter was delayed until General Kornilov, the Commander-in-Chief, gave permission for the creation of a Polish corps in July 1917. By then fighting in the east had come to a halt, and though a Polish Legion was created, it made little impact on military and diplomatic developments.

In the west, the issue of raising Polish units was also closely connected with hopes that the Allied Powers would make a commitment to the re-creation of an independent Poland after the war. Poles in the US campaigned for the creation of the Kosciuszko Division, though the plan was defeated by the complexities of laws governing the rights of US citizens to volunteer to fight in foreign armies, so again the issue was postponed. However, large numbers of Polish migrant workers in France made it possible to plan for a Polish Army to fight in the west. This proposal seemed most likely to succeed because of France's interest in destabilising Germany, but the proposal was opposed by France's Russian allies, who did not want to make commitments to the creation of an independent Poland. In all cases the presence of Poles among the captured prisoners of war made it possible to put forward plans for the raising of units from the ranks of the POWs. But as in the Austrian and Russian case, the French and US Governments were willing to discuss the issue but not to commit themselves to Polish independence until this was militarily expedient. Towards the end of 1916 German initiatives added urgency to the need to address the Polish Question, thus making plans for the use of Polish manpower more realistic. To the Poles, on the whole it did not matter who they supported, as they were primarily concerned with the reconstruction of an independent Poland. When fighting ended with the signing of the armistice with Germany in November 1918, the Poles, who already had an embryo national army in the units that had been created within the German and Austrian armies, were in a strong position to settle border disputes by the use of force and to lay claim to contested areas.

Social stability was not established in Poland for some time. The outbreak of a revolution in Russia had affected Poles from the Kingdom Poland areas. Polish Socialism had developed organisationally and intellectually in the background of and in conjunction with developments in Russian lands. Polish and Russian revolutionaries frequently shared the same political experiences even if they differed on the subject of the Polish independence. Briefly, in November 1918 a Provisional Government of the Peoples' Republic was declared in the Polish town of Lublin. This was supported by the revolutionary sections of the Polish Socialist Party, the Jewish Socialist Party, the Bund and workers' councils. Workers council and Red Guard units had also sprung up in other major industrial towns of

Kingdom Poland. These ultimately either withered or were removed from power by the authority that had emerged in Warsaw.

In the years following the war successive Polish Governments would have to weld together areas that during the past hundred years had been administered by three different powers. In each, distinct political circumstances had led to the development of different political ideas. The economic policies of each of the occupying powers had created very different social structures. Nevertheless, the First World War and its outcome was seen as a victory for the Poles, enabling them to create their own national state.

Germany attacked Poland with the full force of her Army and Air Force on the morning of 1 September 1939. The Poles, notwithstanding their bravery, were badly prepared for the conflict. The military regime, which had ruled Poland since 1926, had laboured under a number of delusions – the military prowess of Polish soldiers had been overestimated and the development of military doctrines and study of modern warfare had been neglected. French and British support for Poland had been overrated. Most critically, the Polish Government ignored the possibility of Nazi Germany and the Soviet Union coming to an agreement.[11] By 17 September, Poland's defeat was a foregone conclusion. Germany's military success was overwhelming and the entry of Soviet troops into Eastern Poland, in accordance with the Ribbentrop-Molotov Pact, completed the disaster. Neither Britain nor France took direct or indirect military action to relieve the ferocity of Germany's attack on Poland.

During the course of the fighting the Polish Government and High Command were forced to evacuate Warsaw. In anticipation of the need to make a quick escape they moved in the direction of the south-western corner of Poland, which, once the news of the entry of the Red Army had been confirmed, enabled them to cross into Romanian territory. The Romanian Government interned the Poles and this in turn made it possible for the French Government to assist the francophile General Wladyslaw Sikorski to form a Polish Government in exile in Paris.

Poles in occupied territories were left to cope with the full implications of the military defeat and of the departure of the Government into exile. Most political leaders, prominent personalities of leading parties and the cultural elites left Poland. The Catholic Primate of All Poland and the Commander-in-Chief accompanied the Government in its flight to Romania.[12] German troops did not leave Poland until 1945, only to be replaced by the Soviet Army, which while defeating the Nazis assumed a direct interest in the area. The Government in exile was not to return to Poland after the war, while new political forces emerged to influence developments in the period immediately after the liberation. Unlike the First World War, the Second World War was a time of despair with only the vaguest hope for future independence.

The eastern part of Poland, which was occupied by the Red Amy in September 1939, contained an ethnically mixed population of Belorussians, Poles, Ukrainians and Jews. Heavy-handed and insensitive treatment of national minorities by the Polish Government during the inter-war period had led to the emergence of strong anti-Polish sentiments among the inhabitants or the region. The fact that the Soviet authorities did not seem to have a clear idea as to what policies they would pursue in relation to the occupied areas added to the already volatile situation.

During the second half of September 1939, as the Polish Government and High Command headed towards the Romanian border, infantry units seeking to regroup and continue fighting against Germany were confronted by bands of hostile Ukrainians and Belorussians. In some cases the Belorussian and Ukrainian communities delighted in seeing the hated Polish Army defeated. The Ukrainian population in particular had reasons for joy as the Army had in the 1930s been used to pacify the Ukrainian villages. Initially, the Red Army appeared to behave as if its main task was to impose order in the face of the flight of the Polish authorities. Polish soldiers were arrested and after a screening process, which was meant to separate the officers from the conscripts, the former were transported into the interior. In the first weeks after the end of military action the Soviet zone of occupation still contained refugees from Central Poland, including Jews who had fled the advance of the German Army. The Soviet administration pursued a haphazard policy of seeking out so-called 'class enemies' from among the Poles; prominent community leaders, Catholic priests, landlords and officers were arrested. Under Soviet supervision peasants were obliged to elect village councils and these proceeded to break up the great landed estates. Ex-Polish Communist Party members (the Polish Communist Party had been disbanded on the orders of the Communist International in 1938) do not appear to have been favoured, nor was the party reconstructed. Soviet occupation was haphazard in its consequences, apparently lacking purpose and frequently driven by the desire to make the most of a visible higher standard of living in the newly occupied regions.[13]

Bewilderingly, the Soviet authorities then attempted to legitimise their occupation of Eastern Poland by calling elections on 22 October. As a result of blatant vote-rigging, these resulted in the creation of national assemblies, which proceeded to Moscow, where they requested the incorporation of Western Ukraine and Western Belorussia into the Soviet Union.[14] The charade continued with the elections of delegates to the Soviet of the Union in March 1940.

In the meantime the legal status of the inhabitants of the occupied regions was defined. By a decree dated 29 November 1939 Soviet citizenship was bestowed on all inhabitants of areas incorporated into the Soviet Union. At the same time, as a result of agreements concluded by the German and Soviet Governments an exchange of populations was initiated. In February 1940 128,000 ethnic Germans who had in the past centuries settled in Russia lands and in the Baltic States were obliged to cross into German-controlled territories. The Soviet authorities also took the opportunity to rid themselves of Polish and German Jews who had earlier fled eastwards but had refused to take Soviet passports.[15]

In 1940 the Polish population was forcefully removed from areas incorporated into the Soviet Union. In February, without prior warning, approximately 220,000 people were put on trains and sent to Siberia and northern Russia. In April a further 320,000 Poles were thus removed from what increasingly was a security zone between the Soviet Union and Germany. In both cases Poles endured weeks of travel without having the right to decide where they were to go, being dispersed in camps and collective farms.[16] In some cases they waited for months at railway junctions. The plight of some of these deportees was dramatically changed with the signing of the Sikorski-Maisky agreement in London on 20 July 1941. As a result of the German attack on the Soviet Union and of the ensuing British decision to treat the Soviet Union as an ally, the Polish Government in exile was persuaded by Churchill to establish diplomatic relations with the Soviet Union. The military agreement, which was then signed by the Poles and the Soviet leadership, provided for the creation of Polish military units in the Soviet Union. The Soviet authorities released thousands of Poles from prisons, labour camps and compulsory places of settlement so that they could enrol with the Polish Army. However, the news caused a mass movement of Poles to the recruitment centres.

Within the next few months, in addition to building up Polish units, the Polish recruiting officers assumed responsibility for dependants of those recruited, for orphans and destitute Poles who flocked to them. In December 1941 the concentration points were moved south to Tashkent. Finally, because of the breakdown of relations between the Soviet authorities and General Anders, the Polish Commander-in-Chief of forces in the Soviet Union, some of the already formed units and all accompanying civilians were moved to Iran, where they became the responsibility of the British authorities.[17] By the summer of 1942 Stalin came to regret his earlier decision to allow the Poles to recruit and form military units in the Soviet Union. Remaining Polish units were made to leave and civilians also accompanied them. While a precise estimate is not possible, it is likely that approximately 50,000 non-combatants left the Soviet Union together with another 100,000 men fit for military service. The civilian population was temporarily housed in camps in British colonies and dependencies and after the war was allowed to settle in Britain. Few of those who had left the Soviet Union returned to Poland after the war.

The breach between the Polish Government in exile and the Soviet Government was completed with the German discovery of mass graves containing bodies of Polish officers in April 1943. In the meantime the Soviet authorities established a new organisation to represent the interest of the remaining Poles. The Union of Polish Patriots, while not ostensibly a Communist organisation, brought together pro-Soviet Poles as well as Communists who hoped for a revolution in the wake of the impending entry of the Red Army into Polish territories. In due course Polish military units were formed from Polish volunteers. These took part in fighting Germany in the east and entered Poland together with the Red Army. Notwithstanding these initiatives, the fate of Poles in the Soviet Union after 1942 continued to be tragic. In 1943 they were compulsorily awarded Soviet citizenship. To some joining the Kosciuszko Division, to fight with the Red Army was an escape from Soviet labour camps and represented the hope of returning to Poland. After the liberation of Poland only ethnic Poles who had lived in the areas occupied by the Soviet Union in September 1939 were in due course allowed to return to Poland.

German brutality in occupied territories manifested itself from the very moment the Wehrmacht entered Polish towns and villages. That this was not merely the by-product of military activities but had been part of an earlier prepared plan was confirmed by the fact that in areas where there had been a sizeable

German minority, Poles who had been associated with the nationalist movement or, as was the case in Silesia, where there had been a series of uprisings in support of the incorporation of the region into Poland, were immediately arrested. This suggested that lists of potentially dangerous Poles had been prepared in advance by the German community and handed over to the incoming troops. Public executions were a method of intimidating the local population even before any organised opposition manifested itself. A harrowing picture of such action is recounted in a recently published history of the Jewish community of the Polish town of Konin. The author had ascertained that on 21 September, having first taken an equal number of Polish and Jewish hostages, the German authorities decided to execute a Pole and a Jew.[18] These scenes were repeated all over occupied Poland.

In the long term the real issue was how the German authorities proposed to govern occupied areas. On 12 October 1939 Hitler issued an order designating Poland as occupied territory. Whereas Western Poland was incorporated into the Third Reich, the remaining central areas, approximately one-third of pre-war territory, including Warsaw, became the Generalgouvernment (GG), separated from the Third Reich. Hans Frank was nominated as the Governor General.[19] The economy of the GG was to cover the cost of occupation, and its residents were seen a slave labour. In addition this was an area where 'undesirable elements' from the Third Reich were to be dumped.

Initially, some attempts were made to identify potential collaborators. The leader of the peasant movement, Wincenty Witos, who had been imprisoned by the military regime of the inter-war period, was briefly considered. When he refused to play such a role, a number of prominent Polish personalities were unsuccessfully tried. Intriguingly, attempts made by the leader of the Polish fascist movement, Boleslaw Piasecki, to form a collaborationist administration were not successful. Though, initially, the Germans showed some interest in encouraging him, nothing was done actually to give the Poles any authority. In April 1940 Hitler forbade his military commanders from making further plans, and henceforth all talk on the subject of a Polish administration and a nominally independent state was finished. Thus, the reason why Poland never had a 'Quisling' was not because a sufficiently prominent person could not be persuaded to co-operate, but because the German authorities had no interest in granting the Poles authority.[20] In view of the impending attack on the Soviet Union, Poland remained a militarily sensitive area.

German occupation is associated with major resettlement programmes. Even before the war, Polish territory had been the object of extensive racially motivated studies to ascertain how the Germanic presence in Eastern Europe could be strengthened and expanded. By 1942 nearly half a million people had been removed from their homes and settled elsewhere. Poles and Jews were forced out of Western Poland, which was incorporated into the Third Reich. In their place ethnic Germans from the Baltic States, Romania, Czechoslovakia and other areas in Eastern Europe were transported and settled on farms vacated under duress, and their presence was to consolidate German control.[21] The whole process was economically wasteful and ultimately destroyed agricultural production for the duration of the war. To all involved, both those displaced and the Germans who were to take over their farmlands, the re-settlement was a tragic episode, resulting in numerous deaths. Poles removed from the Western areas were dumped in the GG, dying in great numbers. Additionally, approximately 40,000 Polish children, deemed to have Germanic racial characteristics, were forcefully parted from their families and were adopted by German families.

In areas incorporated into Germany Polish state property, factories and most industrial stockpiles were confiscated. In the GG area, industry, state property that belonged to charities, the property of political parties and trade unions and most Church property was taken over by the German administration. This meant that Poles lost employment, and co-operatives and charitable associations ceased to function.

Human resources of the occupied Polish State were once more used to maintain industrial production in Germany. Approximately 1.5 million Poles (though some estimates mention 3 million) were forced or induced to go to work in German industry and agriculture. Their treatment was brutal and arbitrary; in effect, they were slave labour with no right to leave their place of employment. In agriculture the situation was more complex, primarily because not until 1941 did the need for food cause the German occupiers to set strict quotas for agricultural deliveries. The issue of what food was necessary to guarantee a tolerable standard of living for Poles in the GG was not one that concerned the German administration. When the need arose, in particular after 1942, food delivery quotas were raised arbitrarily. The fact that the Poles were starving was not considered to be relevant, for the gradual extermination of the Polish race through hard work was considered to be the ultimate objective of the racially motivated economic polices.

All aspects of civilian life were affected by German occupation. All Poles aged 14 and upwards were obliged to work; thus all forms of higher education were destroyed. In these circumstances some secondary and higher teaching continued in conspiratorial groups, though this was always precarious and dangerous. The Germans had targeted the intellectual elites, and most university lecturers and professors had been arrested and incarcerated in concentration camps. Parish priests and the Catholic hierarchy were also arrested. Life in occupied Poland created preconditions for corruption, exploitation and fratricidal conflict. The fate of the Jews in particular provided innumerable opportunities for blackmail. Since sheltering of Jews was punishable by death, both Jews who tried to hide outside the boundaries of the ghettos and those aiding them were easy targets for blackmailers. While all but the extreme nationalist underground movements condemned those who exploited the fate of the Jews, little could be done to protect them. Some nationalist groups of Poles welcomed the German extermination policies. Anti-Semitism, encouraged by the nationalist policies of the pre-war Government and fanned by the fundamentalist Catholic ideas common in Poland, meant that within the Christian community there was little empathy with the fate of the Jews.

The extermination of the Jewish communities from all over Europe was almost entirely completed in sites in occupied Poland. Some camps, like Majdanek, Sobibór and Treblinka, were from their inception extermination camps. Others, notably Auschwitz-Birkenau, were labour camps, which were expanded to also become extermination camps. In addition to the extermination of Jews, these were camps in which other 'undesirable' national and social groups were sent. The Roma communities from occupied areas, political prisoners and religious dissidents died in the camps in Polish territories. Soviet prisoners of war and Polish prisoners were the two largest groups that were worked to death in camps in Poland and Germany.

Notwithstanding the degree of demoralisation in civilian life, Poles created one of the more successful underground movements in occupied Europe. The fact that the German authorities did not depend on a collaborationist Government, and that Poland was treated as occupied territory throughout the war, meant that a high degree of unity of purpose was possible. When the Government and High Command left Poland in September 1939, those officers who stayed in Poland undertook to organise the underground movement, the so-called Home Army. Impressively, the Home Army leadership reached agreements with most pre-war parties, uniting them behind a common programme of fighting for liberation. This required the postponement of potentially divisive plans for post-war reforms.[22] In addition to creating an underground army, a skeleton of the post-war Government was also prepared.

Nevertheless, the biggest problem was that of relations with the Government in exile. By the summer of 1940 agreements were reached whereby the underground movement accepted the authority of the London Government, but for operational purposes the Home Army had total freedom of action. The Home Army embarked only on a limited campaign against the occupiers, the severity of German retaliations discouraging all but the most vital act of terror. The Home Army instead concentrated on preparing plans for the capture of power when the German Army would be in retreat, which it was feared would be accompanied by a revolutionary upsurge. In August 1943, when it became apparent that the Red Army would be most likely to liberate Polish territory, the Home Army made the fateful decision to stage an uprising in Warsaw, which, it was hoped, would pre-empt the Soviet plan to create a puppet Communist Government in the capital. In July the Soviet Union had granted recognition to a Communist-dominated Committee established in the liberated town of Lublin.[23] The failure of the Warsaw uprising and the inability and unwillingness of the Western Allies to assume responsibility for liberating Poland, on which the Home Army had based all its military plans, destroyed the underground structure, so painfully built up during the course of the war.

Other forms of opposition, in particular based on revolutionary and progressive ideas, emerged at the same time in occupied Poland. These were connected with the pre-war left sections of the Socialist Party and with the trade unions. The village-based Peasant Battalions, though committed to the London Government in exile, wanted a commitment to land reform after the war. The Communist partisan movement, which emerged at the end of 1942, was most difficult to define. Though it was dissuaded by the Soviet authorities from putting forward a radical or revolutionary programme and ostensibly concentrated on unity with the purpose of fighting the occupiers, organisationally it was subordinated to the

Comintern and later to the Lublin administration. Although the Communist-led Armia Ludowa partisan units were active in attacking and sabotaging German communication lines during the crucial years of 1942 onwards, the Soviet Union never supplied them with enough arms to make them into a force of any consequence within occupied Poland. When Red Army units entered Poland these and other partisan units were disarmed.

The German policy of applying different laws to Jews and to non-Jewish Poles, combined with the creation of closed Jewish settlement areas, separated the two communities, assigning each to their distinct tragic fates. From the outset the German administration applied different laws to the Jewish communities. These appear not to have been entirely consistent until the German attack on the Soviet Union, when the 'Jewish Question' was tackled with a greater degree of clarity and determination than hitherto. In areas incorporated into the Third Reich, Jews were forbidden to move freely. They were forced to leave major towns and were then incarcerated in re-settlement camps, pending further decisions. Plans for the creation of separate areas into which all Jews would be ultimately moved went in parallel with local solutions. In occupied Poland the German administration had the freedom to follow its own policies unhindered by the need to seek agreements with the collaborationist administrations. Whereas the French Vichy Government successfully opposed the creation of closed Jewish areas in France, in Poland there were no such obstacles. In the GG local military administrators instigated laws restricting the Jews' right of movement, and Jewish people were forced to wear distinctive markings on their clothes, usually a star of David, and to observe very restrictive curfews. Those in state employment were summarily dismissed. Jewish property was confiscated and bank accounts blocked, and all Jewish religious and charitable organisations had their property confiscated. The policy of robbing and pillaging and lack of food led to mass starvation.[24]

The German administration used collective responsibility as a means of both controlling and exploiting the Jewish population in occupied Poland. The Judenrat councils, usually headed by community elders, became responsible for delivery of workers, distribution of food and, when the ghettos were established, for housing arrangements. Approximately 400 ghettos were created in Polish areas, with characters that varied enormously. The first was established in Piotrków Trybunalski in October 1939 and the Warsaw ghetto was consolidated in September 1940, while the Lódz ghetto, which was to become the largest in the Third Reich, was established in April 1940. Each was distinct depending on its location, on the German administrative and economic policies, and finally on the initiative of each Judenrat. The two ghettos that represented the opposite extremes were those in Warsaw and Lódz. In the former the ghetto was sited within the city and was never entirely separated from it; postal and telephone contact was maintained until the ghetto's destruction. In addition, Jewish workers were taken to the 'Arian' side for work, and Poles were able to enter the ghetto. In Lódz the ghetto was totally physically cut off from non-Jewish life. The Judenrat had contributed to this isolation by believing that by making the ghetto economically indispensable to the Germans, it would have a stronger negotiating role. This in turn reduced opportunities for escape and survival.[25] Into the big ghettos, primarily that in Warsaw, were dumped Jews from Germany and other Western European countries.

When Germany attacked the Soviet Union, the Werhmacht entered territories that had been occupied by the Russians in 1939. By then the Nazi policy on the 'Jewish Question' had undergone a change. Previous ideas for the removal of Jews from German-dominated Europe to Madagascar, or by means of emigration, were abandoned. As German troops entered new areas, extermination units moved in to murder the Jewish inhabitants immediately. At the same time preparations were made for the mass extermination of all remaining Jews in Poland and in occupied countries. At the beginning of 1942 Jews were increasingly concentrated in the larger ghettos, and leaders of the Judenrats in the main ghettos of the GG found out about the mass murders in the newly occupied areas. In March 1942 the first consignments of Jews were sent from the Chelmn to a purpose-built extermination camp in Belz. At the end of May inhabitants of the Kraków ghetto were deported to their deaths in Majdanek. In June the first stage of exterminating Jews in the Warsaw ghetto was under way, and by 21 September 1942 254,000 Warsaw Jews had been murdered in Treblinka.[26] In some ghettos, morally freed from the oppressive principle of collective responsibility, the young surviving Jews staged uprisings. On 19 April 1943 a planned military uprising took place in the Warsaw ghetto, and fighting continued until 16 May; a similar uprising took place in Bialystok and Bedzin. The last large ghetto to survive was in Lódz, where the head of the Judenrat, Mordehai Rumkowski, had succeeded in postponing its liquidation until June 1944, mainly because of the Germans' economic dependence on the work done within its boundaries.

At the end of the war it was impossible to estimate how many Polish Jews had survived the Shoa. It is estimated that within the Polish territories, thus excluding those who had fled east in advance of the entry of the German armies, approximately 30,000 to 150,000 Jews survived. These figures can never be accurate.

Notes on contributors

Dr Anita J. Prazmowska, London School of Economics, UK

Dr Prazmowska is Senior Lecturer in the Department of International History, London School of Economics. She is the author of Britain, Poland and the Eastern Front, 1939 (Cambridge: Cambridge University Press, 1986); Britain and Poland 1939-1943 (Cambridge: Cambridge University Press, 1995); and Eastern Europe and the Outbreak of the Second World War (Basingstoke: Macmillan, 2000). She is currently researching the establishment of Communism in Poland, 1943-48.

Recommended reading

Garlicki, Andrzej, *Józef Pilsudski, 1867-1935* (Aldershot: Scholar Press, 1995)

Garliñski, Józef, *Poland in the Second World War* (Basingstoke: Macmillan, 1985)

Jan T. Gross, *Revolution from Abroad: The Soviet Conquest of Poland's Western Ukraine and Western Belorussia* (Princeton: Princeton University Press, 1988)

Korbonski, Stefan, *The Polish Underground State: A Guide to the Underground, 1939-1945* (Boulder: Columbia University Press and East European Monographs, 1978)

Leslie, R. F., *A History of Poland since 1863* (Cambridge: Cambridge University Press, 1980)

Sukiennicki, Wiktor, *East Central Europe During World War I: From Foreign Domination to National Independence* (Boulder: East European Monographs, 1984)

Sword, Keith (ed), *The Soviet Takeover of the Polish Eastern Provinces, 1939-1941* (Basingstoke: Macmillan, 1991)

Notes

[1] Januz Pajewski, *Podbudowa Państwa Polskiego, 1914-1918* (Warszawa: Państwowe Wydawnictwo Naukowe, 1978) pp72-5

[2] Ibid, p75

[3] Andrzej Garlicki, *Józef Pilsudski, 1867-1935* (Aldershot: Scholar Press, 1995) pp70-1

[4] Janusz Pajewski, op cit, pp64-6

[5] Ibid, pp89-90

[6] Ibid, pp96-7

[7] Wiktor Sukiennicki, *East Central Europe During World War I: From Foreign Domination to National Independence* (Boulder: East European Monographs, 1984) Vol 1, pp242-6

[8] Andrzej Garlicki, op cit, pp83-4

[9] Ibid, pp96-7

[10] Wiktor Sukiennicki, op cit, pp328-9

[11] Anita J. Prazmowska, *Britain, Poland and the Eastern Front, 1939* (Cambridge: Cambridge University Press, 1986) pp174-9

[12] Anita J Prazmowska, *Britain and Poland, 1939-1943: The Betrayed Ally* (Cambridge: Cambridge University Press, 1995) pp1-8

[13] Jan T. Gross, *Revolution from Abroad: The Soviet Conquest of Poland's Western Ukraine and Western Belorussia* (Princeton: Princeton University Press, 1988) pp61-6

[14] Ibid, pp106-8

[15] Yosif Litvak, 'The Plight of Refugees from the German-Occupied Territories' in Keith Sword (ed), *The Soviet Takeover of the Polish Eastern Provinces, 1939-1941* (Basingstoke: Macmillan, 1991) pp64-9

[16] Z. S. Siemaszko, 'The Mass Deportations of the Polish Population to the USSR, 1940-1941' in Keith Sword (ed), op cit, pp219-24

[17] Anita J. Prazmowska, *Britain and Poland, 1939-1943*, op cit, pp126-38

[18] Theo Richmond, *Konin: A Quest* (London: Jonathan Cape, 1995) pp72-6

[19] Jan Tomasz Gross, *Polish Society under German Occupation: The Generalgouvernment, 1939-1944* (Princeton: Princeton University Press 1979) pp45-8

[20] Antoni Dudek i Grzegorz Pytel, *Boleslaw Piasecki: Próba biografii politycznej* (London: 'ANEKS', 1990) pp107-9

[21] Anna C. Bramwell, 'The re-settlement of ethnic Germans, 1939-41', in Anna C. Bramwell (ed), *Refugees in the Age of Total War* (London: Unwin Hyman, 1988) pp121-5

[22] Stefan Korboński, *The Polish Underground State: A Guide to the Underground, 1939-1945* (Boulder, Columbia University Press and East European Quarterly, 1978) pp15-9

[23] Ibid, pp168-9; Jan Ciechanowski, *The Warsaw Uprising of 1944* (Cambridge: Cambridge University Press, 1974)

[24] Jerzy Tomaszewski (ed), *Najnowsze Dzieje ydów w Polsce* (Warszawa: Wydawnictwo Naukowe PWN, 1993) pp278-82

[25] Ibid, pp291-3

[26] Ibid, pp318-23

Chapter 32

The experience of displacement: refugees and war

Guy S. Goodwin-Gill

If it is a truism that conflict produces flight, less well appreciated is the extent to which the nature of conflict changed during the 20th century, and with it the extent of displacement. The increasing vulnerability of civilians is illustrated by some crude statistics. Up until, and into, the First World War, civilian casualties in conflict numbered no more than 5 per cent of the whole; during the Second World War, they amounted to some 45-50 per cent; by the end of the century the original relationship of military to civilian casualties had been reversed, with civilians and non-combatants now making up 95 per cent of casualties. Indeed, in the last years of the century, wars were commonly waged against the civilian population and the civilian infrastructure.

Ironically, both this targeting of civilians and their generally heightened exposure to risk have paralleled the further elaboration of principles of international humanitarian law and human rights law, which might be thought to signal greater security. In fact, as a matter of law, civilians and civilian objects have long been recognised as deserving protection. King Richard II, for example, issued 'Ordinances of War' in 1385, which prohibited robbery and pillage, and the killing and capture of unarmed persons belonging to the Church; Henry V's 1419 Ordinances were even more protective of the population.[1] Closer to the present day, Francis Lieber drafted a Code in 1863 for the use of the Union Army during the American Civil War, Article 23 of which optimistically remarked that 'Private citizens are no longer murdered, enslaved or carried off to distant parts…'[2]

Following on the long-standing endorsement of such general principles, the laws of war today lay down a basic prohibition on the forcible displacement of civilian populations, which draws heavily on German practices during the Second World War in many of the occupied countries.[3] But some exceptions have always been recognised, and were taken into account even in the war crimes tribunals that followed the peace. For example, in the case of List et al, General Lothar Rendulic was accused of having breached the Hague Regulations by, among other things, having destroyed land, property and installations as he retreated, and for having ordered the involuntary evacuation of the indigenous people of Finnmark in northern Norway in October 1944. It was shown that no loss of life resulted directly from this order, however, and the court concluded that urgent military necessity could be held to have justified the action, even if the accused might have made an error of judgement.[4]

On the other hand, in the case of von Lewinski, aka von Manstein, Field Marshal Erich von Manstein was denied the defence of military necessity when he ordered the mass deportation and evacuation of civilians from the Ukraine in the summer of 1944.[5] It was argued that this was necessary 'for the security of the troops … [and] to deprive the enemy of labour potential'. However, the court ruled that the defence of military necessity was available only where military commanders considered that the safety of the civilian population required their removal from the theatre of operations.

Nevertheless, and in principle, civilians and non-combatants are 'protected persons'. This is illustrated by Article 48 of the 1977 Additional Protocol I to the 1949 Geneva Conventions[6], which provides that the parties to a conflict 'shall at all times distinguish between the civilian population and combatants and between civilian objects and military objectives and accordingly shall direct their operations only against military objectives'. Article 51 goes further, requiring that the civilian population and individual civilians shall not be the object of attack and prohibiting acts or threats of violence intended to spread terror among the civilian population, as well as indiscriminate attacks and reprisals. Similar provisions are made in Articles 13-18 of Additional Protocol II on non-international armed conflicts (civil wars). The displacement of the civilian population is also forbidden, 'unless the security of the civilians involved or imperative military reasons so demand', and even then, all possible measures are to be taken to ensure their reception under satisfactory conditions of shelter, hygiene, health, safety and nutrition. Moreover, 'civilians shall not be compelled to leave their own territory for reasons connected with the conflict'.

The 1949 Geneva Conventions were drafted in light of the bitter experience of the Second World War, where principles of general application were too often inadequate to their purpose. Even today, practice frequently departs from principle, to the point that the scale of actual or resulting displacement may be seen by the United Nations Security Council as a potential threat to international peace and security, and therefore as a reason for collective enforcement in one form or another. Whether this is always or necessarily to the advantage, benefit or satisfaction of the displaced is another matter, as events in Kosovo and Bosnia and Herzegovina have shown.

The history of displacement as a result of war is eternally the history of loss. The statistics in the following brief and necessarily selective review are staggering, but they are also numbing. The sense of individual tragedy should never be diminished by the numbers, and neither should one lose sight of the personal dimension so vividly captured by the German-Jewish philosopher Hannah Arendt, herself a refugee:

'We lost our occupation, which means the confidence that we are of some use in this world. We lost our language, which means the naturalness of reactions, the simplicity of gestures, the unaffected expression of feelings. We left our relatives in the Polish ghettos and our best friends have been killed in concentration camps, and that means the rupture of our private lives.'[7]

Though it may be odd to begin with an item of achievement in the way of international co-operation, the displacements of the First World War and the Russian Revolution led directly to the appointment of the first High Commissioner for Refugees and to the first international organisation to be charged with improving some at least of the formal and material disadvantages of the displaced. On the other hand, that its successor organisation, the Office of the United Nations High Commissioner for Refugees, remains active into the 21st century is perhaps the starkest reminder of the fact that conflict has an impact far exceeding any contact between armed forces.

In 1921 Gustave Ador, President of the International Committee of the Red Cross, addressed the Council of the League on behalf of nearly a million Russian refugees scattered throughout Europe, without protection or status.[8] They included some 50,000 former prisoners of war unwilling to return, civilians who had fled the Bolshevik revolution, and members of the various defeated armies that had opposed the revolutionaries during the first years. Russian agriculture had also collapsed as a result of forcible acquisitions, and the famine of 1921 is believed to have killed over 5 million people and to have forced as many to flee.

But the Russian displacement had already begun during the war, as the Russian Army began a massive retreat from German attack. Civilians fled the moving tide of conflict, as they had done earlier still in Poland and Galicia.[9] Military objectives – the denial of resources to the invading forces – played their role in the uprooting; the premises of Lieber's 1863 Code, that 'Private citizens are no longer murdered, enslaved or carried off to distant parts...'[10] carried no weight now, if ever they truly had. Over 2.7 million refugees were counted in Russia in December 1915, for whom practically nothing was done:

'Clashes broke out when desperate, exhausted fugitives from the war zone landed among settled populations in the interior. Anti-Semitic riots flared up often when Jews arrived in this way. By the beginning of winter the refugees began to jam major Russian cities. In Moscow crowds of starving fugitives gathered to be fed at the Alexandrovskii railway station in the bitter cold; in Kiev there was near panic...'[11]

Mobile patrols were organised to rescue babies abandoned by the roadside, and efforts made for lost children, many of whom knew not even their names or villages. All this chaos grew, of course, with the revolution of 1917 and later Bolshevik coup; enemies and opponents of the revolution added to the displaced, while intense conflicts between nationalist, revolutionary and counter-revolutionary forces only accentuated the horror of the 'terrible years of War Communism'.

Trainloads of refugees criss-crossed the vast spaces of Russia, carrying starving fugitives from town to town, spreading malaria, cholera and typhus from one end of the Soviet State to the other.[12]

As it became clear that the new Soviet Government was not going to collapse, the displaced moved westwards, even as increasing numbers of dissidents were sent into exile. Two decrees of October and December 1921 took away the Soviet citizenship of certain groups residing abroad, exacerbating their destitute and unprotected status.[13]

It was to meet the practical needs of the undocumented that the League of Nations turned its attention to Gustave Ador's appeal, with the first arrangement following in 1922 for the issue of identity certificates to 'any person of Russian origin who does not enjoy or no longer enjoys the protection of the Government of the Union of Soviet Socialist Republics and who has not acquired another nationality'.[14] That same year some 900,000 Russian refugees were estimated to have found their way to 'virtually every country bordering the former Russian Empire…'[15], with some 365,000 in Poland, 250,000 in Tunisia and Algeria, 95,000 in Romania, 50,000 in Bulgaria, 50,000 in Serbia, 50,000 in Greece, 20,000 in Finland, 10,000 in Lemnos, Cyprus and Egypt, and smaller numbers in other countries.

The effects of the First World War did not stop there, however. The European map was to be rewritten with the laudable aim, among others, of promoting self-determination and avoiding minority persecution. Germany would have to pay, however, and Alsace-Lorraine would be passed back to France, northern Schleswig would go to Denmark, and Eupen and Malmédy to Belgium. German refugees quit the Baltic States, Poland, Danzig and Upper Silesia. Hungarians moved into their 'new' but shrunken State from Romania, Czechoslovakia, and Yugoslavia.[16]

In the south, the attempt to impose the incorporation of Smyrna/Izmir into Greece on the Ottoman Empire led to further conflict, a huge exodus of Anatolian Greek and Armenian refugees, and the massive human tragedies of population exchange.[17] The Armenians fled a conflict with much earlier roots; massacres had already came to a head in 1915, when close to a million are estimated to have been killed, accused by the Turks of assisting the Russian invasion in the Caucasus. With the end of the war, an Armenian Republic seemed briefly to offer haven to the displaced[18], but international support was lacking. Famine and disease again struck the ranks of the refugees and the displaced; those who still could flee, and who avoided the massacres at Smyrna in 1922, found their way into Europe and into the now extended mandate of the League's High Commissioner; in 1924 their numbers were estimated to be not less than 321,000. As one contemporary commentator observed:

'These Russians and Armenians without support or protection, deprived of everything, lived in extremely miserable conditions, and had to count on charity if they were not to die of hunger. If it seemed natural to the conquerors to rid themselves of the conquered without pity, the entire world could not remain unmoved before these unfortunates, of whom some had believed it right to serve their cause, while others were merely innocent victims.'[19]

In succeeding years, the League was to act for many other groups, large and small, such as the Assyrians and Assyro-Chaldeans, Christians under the Ottoman

Empire who joined forces during the First World War with the Russians and later the British. The creation of the Kingdom of Iraq in 1925 effectively cut in two the lands they had previously inhabited, and those 'left behind' in Turkey were soon expelled. Assyrian aspirations for independence clashed with those of the new State of Iraq, and yet one more outward movement began, fuelled by massacre, violence and forcible conversion.

Beginning in the 1920s came the flight from fascism, augury of flights to come, first from Italy, then from Spain, and finally from Germany and its conquered or incorporated territories in the 1930s. Some 10,000 Italian anti-fascist exiles joined an already large expatriate community in France, where the economy was receptive; neither there nor elsewhere was international action required on their behalf. More than political difference was at the root of the exodus from the Third Reich, of course, founded on the ideology that none but 'the members of the nation may be citizens of the State. None but those of German blood … may be members of the nation'.[20] A first significant exodus was from the Saar, after a plebiscite held in January 1935 to decide the future of the territory on termination of the League of Nations administration. The majority voted for its return to Germany, and some 7,000 social democrats, communists and Jews left, mostly for France.[21]

As Nazism consolidated its hold, and as racial and political persecution and economic proscription became all-pervasive, the League of Nations took the first cautious, but ultimately inadequate, look at the plight of those who managed to leave. The exodus was seen as an economic, financial and social problem, but Germany's membership of the League initially compounded the contemporary reluctance of States to deal either with consequences or with causes.

In 1933 the Office of the High Commissioner for Refugees (Jewish and other) coming from Germany had been established, but outside the League of Nations; two years later, the High Commissioner, James G. McDonald, resigned in frustration. In a letter to the Secretary-General, dated 27 December 1935, he observed that private and international organisations could only mitigate an increasingly grave and complex situation. Given the condition of the world economy, resettlement opportunities were few and the problem had to be tackled at source. In an annex to his letter, McDonald focused on human rights in Germany, on that country's international obligations towards minorities, and the violation of the rights of other States, including their territorial sovereignty, that was involved by forced migration, denationalisation, and withdrawal of protection.[22]

No commitment to deal with root causes was forthcoming, although some agreement was reached during 1936 on the status of refugees coming from Germany[23], and was confirmed two years later.[24] This group was defined in such a way as to include nationals, former nationals and stateless persons who were proved not to enjoy, in law or fact, the protection of the German Government, but also to exclude those who had left Germany for reasons of 'purely personal convenience'.

Any impression that these limited arrangements might give of a prompt and adequate response to flight is belied by the history of the period, more renowned for its catastrophic failure to resolve refugee problems than for successes in regulating status or documentation.[25] It is true that with the collapse of republican Spain in 1939, more than 400,000 found immediate refuge in France, but no solutions were found for the German exodus, which an inter-governmental meeting at Evian in July 1938 described as 'the question of involuntary emigration'. In a resolution defining the functions of yet another international agency, the proposed Intergovernmental Committee on Refugees, participating States noted first that the movement was 'disturbing to the general economy', since those in flight were seeking refuge at a time of serious unemployment.

Thus, it was not humanitarian need that counted for States, but the economic, social and public order problems, and the 'severe strain on the administration facilities and absorptive capacities of the receiving nations'. Racial and religious problems were rendered more acute, it was said, international unrest increased, and 'the processes of appeasement in international relations' might be hindered.[26]

In what today seems folly or wilful naiveté, the answer was thought to lie in co-ordinating involuntary emigration from the Third Reich within existing immigration laws and practices; the country of origin, it was argued, should allow involuntary migrants to take property and possessions with them in an orderly manner.[27] Governments, meanwhile, carefully re-asserted their entitlement to take account of immigrants' economic and social adaptability, and to warn potential candidates that they could expect changed, ie lower, living conditions.[28]

Meanwhile, the exodus continued. On 1 October 1938 Germany occupied the Sudetenland, and several tens of thousands of anti-Nazi Germans, Czechs and Jews fled into what remained of Czechoslovakia, until that too was invaded in March 1939, spurring further onward movement. After Kristallnacht in November 1938 the flight of Jews from Germany spiralled again, up to the outbreak of war in September 1939, when it was estimated that some 400,000 refugees had fled since 1933.[29] Claudena Skran observes that:

'When the Second World War started, refugees from the Third Reich were scattered throughout the world. Palestine surpassed all European countries in its absorption of the products of this diaspora: about 90,000 Jewish refugees, or 25 per cent of the total, settled there. Britain accepted 56,000, and the United States about 100,000. Refugees ended up as far away as Shanghai, the only port in the world where passengers could disembark without a passport; it hosted 10,000 refugees by May 1949.'[30]

The multiple, often relatively small-scale, refugee problems of Europe in the 1930s were soon dramatically overtaken by those created by the war, by events elsewhere, and by the policies of the Third Reich. The joint German and Soviet invasion of Poland in 1939 spurred a variety of forced migrations, some from the re-drawing of national boundaries, others from the compulsory transfer of minorities. The German invasion of Western Europe drove an estimated 6 to 8 million Dutch, Belgian, Luxemburger and French civilians, together with some 140,000 refugees from central Europe, towards safety in the south.[31]

At the end of May 1940, the Red Cross reported that 2 million French, 2 million Belgians, 70,000 Luxemburgers, and 50,000 Dutch in northern France were seriously destitute. With the invasion of France, an estimated one-fifth of the French population fled as all roads to the south filled. Although many would return home, 1 million remained uprooted in southern France a year later.[32]

During the course of the next few years, an estimated 8.5 million foreign workers would be drafted into Germany, while ethnic German settlers were sent to colonise the various conquered territories. Among the major moves of ethnic Germans were those from the South Tyrol, further to agreements with Italy in 1939 and 1940; from Baltic countries, further to agreements with Estonia and Latvia in October 1939; from Bessarabia and northern Bukovina, further to a treaty with the USSR in 1940; from southern Bukovina and Dobruja, based on agreements with Rumania in 1940; and from Lithuania, further to agreement with the USSR in January 1941.[33]

The policy in the conquered territories was to eliminate native populations as a source of danger, by Germanising those considered racially valuable and politically susceptible to Nazi ideology, and by deporting and eliminating the undesirable. Poland and a number of other countries were targeted first, and the policy would in time have been extended throughout occupied Europe. Always described as voluntary, the programme's importance and the vigour of its implementation present a somewhat different picture.

It was estimated that some 12 million were displaced during the Second World War, otherwise than as a consequence of military operations, but as a result of campaigns of terror, population displacement, and deportation to forced labour.[34] By 1944 one worker in five in Germany was a foreign civilian or prisoner of war.[35]

Peter and Anna Naumoff left home precipitously in 1944 when German occupation forces rounded them up with other Ukrainian farmers. Their trip west was a brutal three-week journey in a cattle car. They were shipped, ahead of the Soviet Army, into Austria, where they were installed in a factory camp to work for the Third Reich. At the war's end they had nobody to go home to, so the couple, now with an infant son, were placed in a refugee camp to the west. By 1950 they were in a fourth camp with a fourth child. Because Peter Naumoff had contracted tuberculosis at the wartime factory, it would be 1960 before a country could be persuaded to accept them and they would begin civilian life again.[36]

At the war's end, some 30 million Europeans overall had been displaced by the conflict.

The United Nations Relief and Rehabilitation Agency (UNRRA) was established during the war and, despite its name, actually predated the UN Charter. In November 1943, 44 governments signed the constituent agreement and set out its responsibilities; as its name and time imply, UNRRA's role was to 'plan, co-ordinate, administer or arrange for the administration of measures for the relief of victims of war in any area under the control of the United Nations through the provision of food, fuel, clothing, shelter and other basic necessities, medical and other essential services.'[37] Even before the end of hostilities in Europe, UNRRA teams (of which there were more than 300 by mid-1945) were operating in the field, and by the end of its first full year of operation it had assisted the Allied military in repatriating over 6 million people.[38] UNRRA was intended principally to provide assistance to civilian nationals of the Allied nations and to displaced persons in liberated countries, with the expectation that it would assist in their repatriation and the return of prisoners of war. It was conceived as a temporary institution, and its only concern with refugees arose from its relief responsibilities. By the end of 1945, however, a further 1 million displaced remained, many of who simply did not want to go back.

Among the numbers of the unwilling to return were all the casualties of war and partition: Balts, for ever bounced between Russia and Germany and now faced with the transformation of their countries into Soviet Socialist Republics; Poles who remained loyal to the Government in exile in London, now replaced by a communist regime; other Poles who hailed from the east, now part of the Soviet Union; Jews from east and central Europe; Yugoslavs loyal to the King; a host of 'inter-war refugees', including White Russians, Armenians, Assyrians, even Spanish refugees from the civil war; and finally the German minorities expelled from east and central Europe.

Ironically, the end of the war brought not only a massive repatriation movement for those displaced by the conflict, but also another generation of involuntary migrations. The Yalta Agreement of February 1945 paved the way for large-scale forcible repatriations to the Soviet Union[39], and the Potsdam Agreement concluded in August 1945 provided for the expulsion to Germany of the German minorities in Poland, Czechoslovakia and Hungary.[40]

Between June and September 1945, several thousand British and American prisoners of war were moved westwards, and several million Soviet citizens were sent east, whether they liked it or not. The Allies slowly changed their position on repatriation. The US had never accepted that Balts should be returned, and inclined to see Yalta as requiring facilitation of return, rather than forcible repatriation. By the time the British reached the same position, most Soviet citizens had anyway been returned, although the French, who had their own agreement with the USSR, continued the forcible repatriation of very small numbers until July 1947. What exactly happened to those returned is still a matter of deep controversy.

With the Eastern European countries calling for the return of much-needed labour, UNRRA tried to encourage return. 'Operation Carrot', believe it or not, offered 60 days rations for those returning to Poland, and was preceded by a campaign of 'positive publicity', such as films, radio, encouraging letters from home, all downplaying the resettlement alternative. The British were sceptical, believing the reasons for non-return to be political, not economic. Salomon doubts that the carrot had any significant effect in the returns of October–December 1946, given the size of movements anyway, but thinks that it might have helped create an atmosphere that encouraged repatriation.[41]

When UNRRA tried to revive repatriation with carrots in the spring of 1947, the United Kingdom declined to participate, still doubting the efficacy of the scheme, but also concerned to promote its own labour recruitment scheme. By then, the high point for repatriation was over. Between the end of the Second World War and June 1947 some 6 million displaced persons were repatriated under UNRRA auspices, mainly from the western occupation zones in Germany.

The Cold War had also extended into the camps, where anti-repatriation groups were particularly active. The growing possibility of local settlement or settlement in a third country worked its magic, while the assumption and consolidation of power by the Communists undoubtedly increased apprehensions. An UNRRA poll revealed that the primary objection to return was political, with economic reasons running a close second and inextricably linked to the first.[42] Perhaps more interesting, however, are the differences between nationalities and, to some extent, classes. Baltic nationals, for example, many from the intellectual, white-collar and middle classes, saw their homelands as still under foreign occupation, which indeed was why many had fled. Poles, however, had been forcibly relocated and had not generally left for political reasons, even if they might have suspicions about the new government.

Fortuitously, labour shortages began to appear, spinning the wheels of resettlement in the late 1940s; miners were wanted in Belgium, France, the Netherlands and the United Kingdom; the United Kingdom also wanted hospital workers; and the United States, Australia, and Canada just wanted immigrants, as did Brazil and other Latin American countries.

UNRRA did not have the authority to find solutions for refugees considered as those who 'for any reason, definitely cannot return to their homes, or have no homes to return to, or no longer enjoy the protection of their Governments...'[43] Despite its remarkable success in overseeing the return movements of the displaced[44], by June 1947 nearly 650,000 still remained without solutions, most of them East Europeans and many of them refugees from the events of the post-war – among them, 380,700 Poles, 125,000 Yugoslavs and 186,500 Balts.

It was to aid in the completion of the remaining refugee tasks that members of the United Nations set up, first, the International Refugee Organisation (1947-1952), then the Office of the United Nations High Commissioner for Refugees (1951-). Under the IRO, repatriation played a lesser role, as most of those who wanted to go back had already returned.[45] For political reasons, the IRO's repatriation responsibilities appeared to be a priority, but in practice resettlement was the order of the day. During 4½ years of IRO operations, only about 5 per cent of displaced persons (numbering 73,000) and refugees under mandate returned home, whereas some 65 per cent (about 1 million) were resettled.

It would be 1960 before the last of the refugee camps in Europe would be cleared, and the remaining refugees of the war finally found a solution either in Europe or further field. An internal UNHCR document from the 1950s summed up the dispossession and the loss:

> '...families, wives who have lost their husbands and children who have lost their parents ... the old and the solitary, who have lost everything ... the physically sick, the one-third with TB ... the others, after years of destitution and misery in camps, mentally ill. The physician, not allowed to practice in her country of asylum; the craftsman, now an occasional labourer; emigration and integration governed by economics, not humanitarian need; the refugee family from the war, 14 years in the camp, their 12-year-old son knowing no other life; the sense of a waste...'

By the time the camps were cleared, of course, war and persecution had brought forth yet more of the displaced ... and so it is to this day.

It is often forgotten how many millions of Germans were uprooted after the Second World War, as a result both of the Potsdam Agreement of August 1945 and of unilateral actions by a number of States.[46] The Potsdam Conference supposedly paved the way for the 'orderly and humane' transfer of the German population of Poland, Czechoslovakia and Hungary to Germany, but in practice the operation was less than humane or orderly, and the overall numbers considerably exceeded those anticipated; for example, 5-6 million Germans were removed from Poland, where 3.5 million were expected, and 2.7 million from Czechoslovakia, against 2.5 million.[47] Other countries followed with their own expulsions, such as Romania, Bulgaria and Yugoslavia, even though they were not specifically mentioned in the Potsdam Agreement. By September 1950 it was estimated that some 12 million German refugees (*Vertriebene*) had been relocated to Germany, mostly in the west, but also in the east.[48]

As can be seen from the above, the end of war did not mean the end of displacement. In the period immediately following the end of hostilities in Europe, the impact of the refugee question continued to be felt, and occupied more time in the United Nations than any other topic after international security. The highly politicised, East-West debates[49] illustrate perceptions that continue to this day. In the United Nations Third Committee, for example, Yugoslavia emphasised that certain political aspects required attention. It would be unfortunate

'...if the United Nations become responsible, directly or indirectly, for perpetuating the presence outside their own countries of groups of persons who were either war criminals ... or at least hostile to democratic ideas, and therefore to the purposes of the United Nations.'[50]

The Yugoslav representative distinguished between Spanish republican refugees and German Jews, who deserved support, and other groups, such as the terrorist Ustachi, who did not. At the political level, also, the Egyptian, Iraqi and Lebanese representatives wanted a clear distinction to be made between 'the political and humanitarian aspects of the Jewish question'.[51]

The Netherlands favoured not returning refugees who might be repatriable technically, but who did not wish to go home; unless liable to extradition, their wishes should be respected. Denmark called attention to the dangers inherent in the large-scale migrations of German refugees, and also to its own problem of some 210,000 German civilians brought into the country by the Nazi authorities in early 1945. The Belgian delegate suggested that an international agency be entrusted with so-called political dissidents, those unwilling to return to their countries for reasons of political conscientious objection.

For the representative of the Ukrainian Soviet Socialist Republic, a major problem was the number of war criminals and traitors still at large. They should be extradited, the repatriation of soldiers and civilians uprooted by the war must be facilitated and encouraged, and elements hostile to the return of the displaced must be silenced. The Byelorussian representative in turn stressed the importance of appropriate arrangements between countries of origin and countries of refuge. For the USSR, repatriation was also 'the essential solution'; the League of Nations had perpetuated the refugee problem by assisting 'those who for political reasons stayed away from their homes and even pursued hostile policies against their country of origin'. The repatriation issue, particularly where it appeared to imply the return of refugees against their will, became the dividing factor between East and West.[52]

A foretaste of things to come is already apparent in the plenary session of that year. The Soviet delegate, Andrei Vyshinsky, claimed that fascist propaganda was spread in refugee camps, which were housing military adventurers; he challenged the 'thesis of unrestricted freedom' that seemed to license such activities. Yugoslavia declared that 'whole regiments of quislings' were now abroad, endangering good relations and understanding between States. Eleanor Roosevelt, the United States representative, countered with human rights arguments in support of free choice and freedom of speech.[53]

Nevertheless, the United Nations decided to act and the International Refugee Organization (IRO) was set up as a specialised agency in 1946, beginning and eventually ending its operations in a period of heightening East-West tension. It remained funded by only 18 of the 44 governments that were then members of the United Nations, and it is hardly surprising that its policies should be caught up in the politics of the day. Still, many tens of thousands of refugees and displaced persons were resettled under IRO auspices, through government selection schemes, individual migration, and employment placement, beginning new lives – 634,000 in the United States, Australia, Canada, and Israel alone, with others going to New Zealand, Latin America and South Africa.[54] Many States wanted more workers, to rebuild economies and to counter depopulation through natural decline and the wastage of war. Refugee resettlement policies also served broader political interests, however, allowing the West to make its points against the East[55], even as the humanitarian needs of individuals were often met.

In the aftermath of the Second World War, refugees had political significance, if classifiable as victims of persecution. There was no interest then in protecting those who had fled armed conflict or economic exploitation. The international refugee regime that emerged in the late 1940s and early 1950s sprang from an unholy alliance of competing interests. Created through confrontation, refugees were defined by the politics of denunciation in a persecution-oriented definition that continues to spawn a substantial edifice of gloss in today's national refugee determination systems.

At the beginning of the 21st century, refugees no longer have political significance. War still has its greatest impact on civilians, is still often directed against them; war still causes people to take flight, but little enough is done to prevent conflict, to mediate and bring it to a speedy end. Again, the primary costs, the human costs, are borne by those who are not involved – at serious risk if they remain, yet obstructed if they move. Whether they flee persecution or war, refugees today are seen mostly as a burden to be avoided, as an undifferentiated mass to be kept as far as possible from the national threshold. Their loss, captured in the stories of individual lives, is ever at risk of obliteration.

Notes on contributors

Professor Guy S. Goodwin-Gill, Wolfson College, Oxford University, UK
Guy Goodwin-Gill is an international lawyer and Director of the Centre for
Socio-Legal Studies, Oxford. He is the author of The Refugee in International
Law (Oxford: Clarendon Press, 1983, 1996) and The Role of the Child in Armed
Conflict (Oxford: Clarendon Press, 1994) (with Ilene Cohn).

Recommended reading

Bramwell, Anna C. (ed), *Refugees in the Age of Total War* (London, Unwin Hyman, 1988)

Marrus, Michael, *The Unwanted: European Refugees in the Twentieth Century* (New York: Oxford
University Press, 1985)

Skran, Claudena, *Refugees in Inter-War Europe* (Oxford: Clarendon Press, 1995)

Notes

1   T. Meron, *War Crimes Law Comes of Age* (Oxford: Clarendon Press, 1998) pp2-3
2   General Order No 100, Article 23, 1863, written for and issued to the Union Army during the Civil
   War; reprinted in D. Schindler and J. Toman (eds), *The Laws of Armed Conflicts* (Dordrecht: Nijhoff,
   3rd ed 1988) p3
3   These practices included not only the deportation of local populations, either generally or for the
   purposes of slave and forced labour, but also the transfer of German civilians into occupied
   territories. Such deportations were held by the International Military Tribunal to fall under the
   Nuremberg Charter, as being contrary to article 6(b) – war crimes – and article 6(c) – crimes against
   humanity. A. M. de Zayas, 'A Historical Survey of Twentieth Century Expulsions' in A. C. Bramwell
   (ed), *Refugees in the Age of Total War* (London: Unwin Hyman, 1988) p15. T. Meron, 'Deportation
   of Civilians as a War Crime under Customary Law' in T. Meron, *War Crimes Law Comes of Age*, op
   cit, p142. See now Article 49, Fourth Geneva Convention, 1949.
4   Ann Dig 16 (1948), p632
5   Ann Dig 16 (1949), p509
6   The texts of the four 1949 Geneva Conventions and the two 1977 Additional Protocols are
   reprinted in A. Roberts and R. Guelff, *Documents on the Laws of War* (Oxford: Oxford University
   Press, 3rd ed 2000)
7   Hannah Arendt (ed), *The Jew as Pariah: Jewish Identity and Politics in the Modern Age* (New York:
   Grove Press, 1978) p56
8   *League of Nations Official Journal* 2 (2) (1921) p227. Estimates of numbers vary; for different
   assessments, see Claudena Skran, *Refugees in Inter-War Europe* (Oxford: Clarendon Press, 1995)
   p33, n9; J. H. Simpson, *The Refugee Problem* (London: Royal Institute of International Affairs,
   1939) pp67-9
9   Michael Marrus, *The Unwanted: European Refugees in the Twentieth Century* (New York: Oxford
   University Press, 1985) pp53-4
10   See above, note 2
11   Michael Marrus, op cit, p54
12   Ibid, p58
13   See J. Fisher Williams, 'Denationalization', *British Yearbook of International Law* 8 (1927) p45
14   League of Nations Treaty Series, 13 (No 355) (Arrangement of 5 July 1922)
15   Claudena Skran, op cit, p35
16   Michael Marrus, op cit, p72
17   Claudena Skran, op cit, p43; Michael Marrus, op cit, pp74-81; C. Meindersma, 'Population

Exchanges: International Law and State Practice – Part 1', *International Journal of Refugee Law* 9 (1997) p335; 'Part 2', *International Journal of Refugee Law* 9 (1997) p613

18   The Treaty of Sèvres, 10 August 1920, recognised the independent State of Armenia, but less than a year later this was undone by the London Conference, at which the powers recognised no more than a 'national home' for Armenians on the western frontiers of Turkey. Even this was abandoned at the Lausanne Conference in 1923. J. H. Simpson, *Refugees: A Preliminary Report of a Survey* (London: Royal Institute of International Affairs, 1938) pp21-2; Michael Marrus, op cit, pp74-81, 119-21. 'Arrangement relating to the Issue of Identity Certificates to Russian and Armenian Refugees of 12 May 1926', League of Nations Treaty Series, 84 (No 2006); also 'Arrangement concerning the Extension to other Categories of Refugees of certain Measures taken in favour of Russian and Armenian Refugees of 30 June 1928', League of Nations Treaty Series, 89 (No 2006)

19   Hsu Fu-yung, *La Protection des réfugiés par la Société des Nations* (Lyon: Riou, 1935) p6 (translation by the author)

20   Cited in J. H. Simpson, *Survey*, op cit, p59

21   J. H. Simpson, *Survey*, op cit, p66; Michael Marrus, op cit, p133; *League of Nations Official Journal* 16 (6) (1935) p634; League of Nations Treaty Series, 16 (12) (1935), pp1681-2

22   See Michael Marrus, op cit, pp161-6; R. Y. Jennings, 'Some International Law Aspects of the Refugee Question', *British Yearbook of International Law* 20 (1939) p98

23   'Provisional Arrangement concerning the Status of Refugees coming from Germany of 4 July 1936', League of Nations Treaty Series, 171 (No 3952)

24   '1938 Convention concerning the Status of Refugees coming from Germany', League of Nations Treaty Series, 191 (No 4461). The scope of this convention was expanded the following year to include Austrian refugees; see '1939 Protocol', League of Nations Treaty Series, 198 (No 4634)

25   This is clearly described in Michael Marrus, op cit, pp166-207

26   *League of Nations Official Journal* 19 (8-9) (1938) pp676-7

27   The Committee's migration-oriented recommendations aimed to encompass 'persons who have not already left their country of origin (Germany, including Austria), but who must emigrate on account of their political opinions, religious beliefs or racial origin', and those who had left for such reasons but had not yet established themselves elsewhere.

28   Michael Marrus, op cit, pp170-7

29   Claudene Skran, op cit, pp48-54; Michael Marrus, op cit, pp122-207

30   Claudene Skran, op cit, p54

31   Michael Marrus, op cit, pp200-2

32   Leslie Page Moch, *Moving Europeans: Migration in Western Europe since 1650* (Bloomington: Indiana University Press, 1992) p167

33   International Refugee Organization, 'Manual for Eligibility Officers' (nd) pp44-50. In the course of debate in the UN Third Committee in 1949, the Chilean delegate expressly referred to the question of population transfers, the manner in which States had thus rid themselves of ethnic minorities, or sought to augment their labour resources. He cited the expulsion of Greeks from Asia Minor in 1923, and the removal of Germans from the Italian Tyrol in 1939. Provoked by USSR criticism of Latin American migration policies, however, he gave particularly detailed accounts of various agreements between the Nazi and Soviet authorities. He cited, for example, the Germany-USSR agreement of 16 November 1939 regarding the transfer of inhabitants of Volhynia, 15 (9 November 1949).

34   E. Kulisher, *The Displacement of Population in Europe* (ILO, Montréal: 1943)

35   Leslie Page Moch, op cit, p168

36   Ibid, p162

37   See, generally, George Woodbridge, *UNRRA: The History of the United Nations Relief and Rehabilitation Agency*, 3 Vols (New York: 1950)

38   Michael Marrus, op cit, pp317-24

39   See, generally, N. Tolstoy, *Victims of Yalta* (London: Hodder & Stoughton, 1977); N. Bethell, *The Last Secret* (London: Deutsch, 1974)

40   Eugene M. Kulisher, *Europe on the Move: War and Population Changes 1917-47* (New York: 1947) estimates at 4 million the number of ethnic Germans who, before the Potsdam expulsions, fled

former areas of the German Reich, that is what became Poland up to the Oder-Neisse line. The expulsions themselves added another 2 million in the period to 1 July 1947; in addition, some 300,000 Sudeten Germans fled to Austria and Germany during the war and in the months immediately following. See, generally, A. M. de Zayas, *Nemesis at Potsdam: The Anglo-Americans and the Expulsion of the Germans* (London: Routledge & Kegan Paul, rev 2nd ed 1979); Michael Marrus, op cit, pp326-31. Significant numbers of Germans were also expelled from or fled Bulgaria, Rumania and Yugoslavia.

[41] K. Salomon, *Refugees in the Cold War* (Lund: Lund University Press, 1991) pp92-164

[42] Ibid, pp145-6

[43] See para 22, proposal concerning refugees submitted by the United Kingdom: UN doc A/C.3/5, annexed to GAOR, Third Committee, 1st Sess, 1st Part, 1946, Summary Records: UN doc. A/C.3/SR.1-11

[44] It has been estimated that by the beginning of 1946, three-quarters of the displaced in Europe had been sent home; Michael Marrus, op cit, p320. By July 1947, when UNRRA ceased operations, some 7 million persons had been assisted and returned to their countries or places of origin.

[45] See further below. Generally, see Louise W. Holborn, *The International Refugee Organization: A Specialized Agency of the United Nations: Its History and Work* (London: 1956)

[46] de Zayas estimated that some 16 million were uprooted, and that some 2 million died in the process; A. M. de Zayas, 'International Law and Mass Population Transfers', *Human Rights Law Journal* 16 (1975) pp207, 228

[47] J. Vernant, *Les réfugiés dans l'après-guerre* (1953) p106; and, generally, A. M. de Zayas, *Nemesis at Potsdam*, op cit

[48] J. Vernant, op cit, pp107-8

[49] The period in question saw the inauguration of the Truman doctrine and the Marshall Plan in 1947; Communist Governments consolidated their hold in Eastern Europe with the takeover in Czechoslovakia in 1948; the Berlin blockade and airlift took place; the People's Republic of China and the conflict in Korea entered the scene in 1949; and that same year, NATO was set up, the German Federal Republic and the German Democratic Republic were established, and Yugoslavia and the USSR split.

[50] GAOR, Third Committee, 1st Sess, 1st Part, Summary Records, 4th Meeting: UN doc A/C.3/SR.4. Poland was also concerned by the political dimension; ibid, SR.5

[51] UN doc A/C.3/SR.7, pp18-20 (4 Feb 1946). Lebanon noted that 'the political aims of Zionism ... might well create another problem of displaced persons...'

[52] See the views of New Zealand and the United States: UN doc A/C.3/SR.8; see also, generally, UN docs A/C.3/SR.5, SR.6 and SR.7

[53] GAOR (I), 1st Sess, 1st Part (1946), Summary Records, pp412ff

[54] L. Holborn, *Refugees: A Problem of our Time: The Work of the United Nations High Commissioner for Refugees, 1951-72* (Metuchen, NJ: Scarecrow Press, 1975) p31

[55] See G. Loescher and J. Scanlan, *Calculated Kindness: Refugees and America's Half-Open Door, 1945 to the Present* (London: Collier Macmillan, 1986) pp15-24

Chapter 33

The experience of genocide: Armenia 1915-16 and Romania 1941-42[1]

Mark Levene

'Who, after all, speaks today of the annihilation of the Armenians,' Hitler is purported to have remarked.[2] The statement has often been taken as evidence of Hitler's intent to destroy the Jews, just as the Turkish Government of 1915, the Ittihad or Committee of Union and Progress (CUP), had set out to destroy its Ottoman Armenians. The idea of a causal link is a compelling one. A number of genocide scholars have pursued the similarities in the causes and contours of these two mass exterminations.[3] But, perhaps, we ought to be a little cautious, if only because Hitler in August 1939 was not talking about his intentions towards the Jews but towards the Poles. That may act as a reminder that Nazi medium-range goals for their racially organised New Order involved genocidal intentions against a whole range of peoples, particularly Slavs, over and above their most focused and immediate aim of making Europe *judenrein*.[4] Nor were genocidal policies confined to Nazi Germany.[5]

Though there were major atrocities committed by armies during the First World War, only the CUP-attempted extermination of Armenians is directly comparable as an example of genocide. Although there is no shortage of Second World War genocides with which the Armenian massacres could be compared, it is the Romanian genocide of Jews, specifically those from Bessarabia, Bukovina and the wartime region of 'Transnistria', in the years 1941-42, that will be considered here, for it is in this record that we will find the closest parallels with what happened to the Armenians in the First World War.

For this purpose, analysis of the historical causation of these two genocides, important as it is, will be subordinated to a consideration of the experience. That in itself raises not a few problems, not least because it somehow assumes that we can implicitly differentiate this experience from other experiences of war. What made the victims of genocide aware that what they were enduring was different from the privations, horrors, physical and emotional traumas, not to say mass violent death by bombing, bullet, siege, rape or other atrocities, that were visited on many millions of other combatants and, more particularly, non-combatants? Turkish and Romanian apologists, both at the time and later, would forcefully repudiate Armenian or Jewish suffering as quantitatively or qualitatively distinct from that endured by their populations as a whole, though with the frequent (and contradictory) caveat that they, the Armenians and Jews, were to blame for what had specifically happened to them by dint of actions or behaviour that, allegedly, had put the rest of the Turkish or Romanian people, their armies or states at risk. It is a noteworthy feature of the contemporary Romanian response to its Jewish genocide that it increasingly mirrors that of Turkish regimes, whether perpetrator or successors, in their consistent denial of the existence of, let alone acceptance of responsibility for, the fact.[6]

Raphael Lemkin, the Polish-Jewish international jurist who coined the term in 1944, characterised genocide as a co-ordinated plan aimed 'at the destruction of the essential foundations' of the life of a national, ethnic or social group 'with the aim of annihilating the group itself'.[7] Genocide, in other words, is not a military strategy in the way that the bombing of German or Japanese cities was argued to be a method to defeat armed and belligerent enemy states. Indeed, if genocide is a form of warfare, it is a very peculiar one, in that there are no regiments of soldiers or air defence systems to stand in the way of the perpetrator. If genocide is, nevertheless, pursued by military as well as other means, it is against a population where the men are not able to defend the women and children and where its successful conclusion involves the extermination both of men and women, children and babies. In this sense genocide is profoundly biological in its intent in a way that even the outrages of Dresden or Hiroshima could not be. Genocide thus often involves calculated and systematic efforts to deprive the victims of 'personal security, liberty, health, dignity, and even their lives'.[8] This, in turn, suggests both a long-term process of degradation and dehumanisation, which may not necessarily entail 'immediate destruction' but in which 'the disintegration of the political and social institutions of the group'[9] become evident, succeeded by a radical new phase, possibly even a definite rupture, often under the cover of more general war, in which the perpetrators' genocidal preparations are realised in a sustained killing process that may last for weeks, months, or even years.

So far, Lemkin's observations might be applicable to all genocides. The particularity and similitude of the Armenian and Romanian cases lie in a feature, which might be summarised in the term 'death march', that although common in other genocides, crystallised, developed and was completed in these two, in a pattern not obviously replicated elsewhere.[10] As a result, these Turkish and Romanian processes of deportation-cum-extermination often display an intimacy, messiness and gratuitous viciousness that not only defies notions of organised, routinised and systematised mass death, but also in both instances was remarked upon and, in some instances, protested against by individuals or official spokesmen among their German allies and notional masters.

This does not mean that ultimate responsibility and culpability for these genocides lies other than with the highest authorities of the Ottoman Turkish and Romanian states. Abundant Romanian official documents, used extensively in post-war trials by the successor Communist regime, confirm that deportation with the aim of liquidating Bessarabian and Bukovinan Jewry was not only an immediate Antonescu war aim but also a very minimum one insofar as Romanian

Jewry as a whole was concerned.[11] Enough has been pieced together from otherwise missing or destroyed Turkish official sources, particularly when aligned to relevant German and Austrian diplomatic material, to conclude that the extermination of the Armenians was a preconceived and planned CUP objective.[12] As early as November 1915 an official *British Blue Book*, compiled by the historian Arnold Toynbee, minutely detailed the scope, scale and nature of the deportations on the basis of a wide range of survivor and other eyewitness testimony.[13] This report, which was subsequently published by the British Government, has been repeatedly dismissed by Turkish or pro-Turkish analysts on the grounds that it is nothing more than black propaganda perpetrated by a wartime enemy. Yet Toynbee's information is not only corroborated by the many accounts of serving German officers as well as diplomats, professionals and missionaries, then in Turkey in various capacities, but also by a number of other largely disinterested sources.[14]

However, if we were to take the public claims of Turkish wartime policy towards its Armenians at face value, we would have to conclude that its purpose was not to harm them at all but on the contrary to protect them. Talat's public communiqué of 26 May 1915, entitled 'The Temporary Law of Deportation', advised that part of the Ottoman Armenian population living in three *vilayets* (provinces) affected by the fighting between Turkish and Russian armies on the eastern Anatolian front, as well as those living further to the south-west in Cilicia where there was a danger of Anglo-French landings, would be deported to a designated region south of the Baghdad railway, then still in the process of construction.[15] The argument that this was in their best interests, and with guarantees that their persons and properties would be protected by order of the Government itself, was emphasised in further communiqués over the following weeks. Among other things these promised that the deportees' abandoned properties and their contents would be registered by a specially created Commission; that these would be guarded in their absence; that if allocated to other migrants from the war zones that they would be responsible not only for their upkeep but for any damage incurred; and, if sold, the Kuvale Metruke, the Commission for Abandoned Properties, would send on the proceeds to the deportees in their new places of settlement.

What is so extraordinary about these communiqués is not just the travesty of the reality then in the making, but the almost surreal messages implicit in them. Even supposing all of its intentions were honest, and the CUP really had organised the safe and competent conveyance of its hundreds of thousands of Armenian charges to their designated destination in the *vilayet* of Deir Zor, what hope of mass settlement and colonisation could there have been in a desert region between Syria and Mesopotamia? But this is to miss the point. For many months prior to the communiqués, reports of major anti-Armenian massacres in the eastern war zone, particularly in the wake of the first great Turkish military disaster of the conflict, at Sarakamish, in the winter of 1914-15, had been filtering out of Constantinople and into the foreign press. It was in response to these stories that the Allied Governments, on 24 May, publicly declared that they would hold 'personally responsible … all members of the Ottoman government and those agents who are implicated in such massacres'.[16]

The Ottoman Armenian population was socially and occupationally multi-layered, not to say religiously diverse, given its Protestant and Catholic as well as traditional Christian Gregorian elements. This made it a rather typical component of an Ottoman society that was nothing if not multi-ethnic and multi-linguistic. But nowhere, even in the three most obviously Armenian *vilayets* of Bitilis, Van and Erzerum, were they anything close to a majority, while elsewhere in Anatolia and beyond they were widely dispersed both in the big cities like Constantinople and Smyrna and in smaller towns. This demographic vulnerability was exacerbated by other factors. As Christian *dhimmi* in a Moslem-dominated society, they were not entitled to carry arms. When Abdul Hamid had unleashed major massacres against them in the period 1894-96, the results had been horrific. Nor, unlike the indigenous Greeks, did they have a neighbouring state to which they might turn in times of danger. Though mostly peasants, the increasingly significant town-based element in Armenian society not only included a sizeable upwardly mobile and bourgeois core, but one that was also very Western-orientated. In the climate of constant crisis and military disaster at the hands of foreign powers that pervaded the period of CUP rule, this hardly endeared them to increasingly restive, xenophobic and fundamentalist elements of the dominant Turkish or other – notably Kurdish – populations.

In marked contrast, the CUP leadership saw the war not only as an opportunity to overturn long-term Ottoman decline but also to strike out on an entirely new course of overtly nationalist territorial aggrandisement in the east. The Armenian heartlands, both in Ottoman Anatolia as well as on the Russian side of the border, physically – if not psychologically – straddled this pan-Turanic route to salvation. Though the evidence still remains fragmentary, it is clear that at least some preparations for Armenian elimination were well in train before the spring 1915 crisis. The key players in these preparations were the Interior Minister, Talat, and the War Minister, Enver – in other words, two-thirds of the ruling CUP triumvirate – plus a number of leading figures from the now much radicalised Ittihad inner circle, most notably the medical doctors, Sakir and Nazim. The juxtaposition of the two key ministries here, as in the Romanian case, is of the utmost significance. Despite the known personal rivalry between Enver and Talat, it meant that there would be close co-operation between the Interior Ministry's National Security Office and Department II (Intelligence) of Ottoman Army Headquarters. A third arm was to be provided through Nazim and Sakir. The Teshkilat-i Makhsusiye, or Special Organisation, already had a shadowy existence under the aegis of the War Ministry with a remit to counter domestic subversion. In the immediate pre-war context this involved intercepting and destroying opposition groups, Armenian and otherwise, moving to and fro across the Caucasus into Russia. Though regular army officers were supposedly in charge, operations were mostly conducted by *cetes*, bands of often Kurdish or Circassian fighters, who were a law unto themselves. This type of 'dirty' war was utterly brutal and merciless even before the CUP ideologues had taken more direct control of it. What Nazim and Sakir did was to wield the organisation, with all the accoutrements that the War Ministry could provide, into a party-led instrument for the destruction of the Armenians. Vahakn Dadrian, the leading researcher and expert on the relevant Turkish records, notes that Sakir was already in Erzerum with Special Organisation operatives in August 1914, with the ink on the text of the secret Turko-German alliance hardly dry.[17]

If this suggests that the Turkish leadership had thought out its genocidal plans and had worked out its necessary staffing and logistics in advance, some documentary evidence from this early period suggests that there still may have been lingering doubts – at least by some participants – as to how far it was going to be taken.

For Armenians, however, the genocide is remembered as beginning on the night of 23-24 April 1915, when 235 of their leading figures in Constantinople, including politicians, intellectuals and other luminaries, were arrested. Less than a day later, the British made their landings, not far down the coast at Gallipoli. Further arrests both of communal leaders and thousands of other young Armenians, from all social classes, followed. Within days they were deported to the interior where the vast majority were slaughtered.[18]

In this way the Turkish state combined the logical, if unlovely, aim of beheading the Armenian community, so that devoid of its male leadership it could not effectively resist, with what appears to be a pathological need to torture and mutilate Armenians as much as possible before killing them. Nor was this procedure limited only to able-bodied men. In the three *vilayets*, from which according to Talat's 26 May communiqué the Armenian population was supposed to be deported, not only was massacre – not deportation – the norm, but also in the most horrific ways. In Bitilis it involved herding the remaining women, old people and children into haylofts and stables where they were burned alive. It is estimated that some 70,000-80,000 died thus. Soon after, in Mus, Djevded also adopted this killing method, utilising churches, schools and orphanages for the purpose, but not before, according to a German missionary, hundreds if not thousands of Armenian women had 'their eyebrows plucked out, their breasts cut off, their nails torn off'. The account continues, 'Their torturers hew off their feet or else hammer nails into them just as they do in shoeing horses'.[19]

Manpower requirements to undertake these tasks in Mus and many other towns in the area forced Djevded to employ units of the Third Army, at a time when its military position vis-à-vis the Russians was precarious. This did not, however, prevent him or his Third Army co-author, Khalil Bey, from enjoying their remit or, indeed, from exceeding it by killing all the other Christian Chaldeans, Syrio-Catholics, Nestorians and Jacobites they could lay their hands on.[20] Meanwhile, in the coastal *vilayet* of Trebizond, the CUP authorities, employing 15,000 troops for the purpose as well as police agents and volunteers, resolved to short-cut the sheer size of their Armenian problem by packing thousands of deportees on to caiques, which were towed on to the Black Sea or on to the fast-flowing Deyirmen Deré River and capsized in order to drown their incumbents.[21]

If military and para-military units or party members were the main instrument of the Trebizond killings, it did not, however, stop with them. Much further to the south, in Urfa, a last-ditch effort by its Armenians to resist the encroaching reign of terror was quashed in September with not only soldiers bayoneting or sabring to death their captives 'one by one' but also the population in general participating in these public executions of men and women. One eyewitness reports that a mullah took it into his head that among the Armenians still sheltering in the Apostolic church 100 male children under 1 year of age should be sacrificed by decapitation, a procedure he undertook himself.[22]

If immediate, in situ and general massacre proved the rule at the very epicentre of the Armenian genocide – as well as in many other places – the alternative experience of deportation proved no less horrific or ultimately final; it was simply more drawn-out. Modes of conveyance for the lucky few were quickly stolen or withdrawn, resulting in the march continuing entirely on foot. In the intense summer heat, the less strong became quickly dehydrated and exhausted. Soon they were being openly robbed not only by the gendarmes but also by villagers and brigands, who – in the account of a wealthy lady from Baibourt – appeared on the road in large numbers with rifles, guns and axes. Placing lira coins round her young daughter's neck or sewing them into her clothes proved no protection against them.[23] In another account, a robbery of a young woman's beautiful hand-made embroidery, a traditional element of Armenian dowries, had her sobbing uncontrollably until she was slapped back to her senses by an older woman.[24]

In comparison with what was to come, this incident may seem trivial, even petty. Yet the sense of personal violation involved is significant, not least because it provides a prelude to the much worse ordeals that increasingly characterise these death marches, as death marches of women. This was the case, not least because usually very early on in the process the men, priests included, were taken aside and slaughtered, either in full view of the convoy or out of view over a hillside. Not all killings, however, were gender or age conscious. For instance, the steep Kamakh gorge on the upper Euphrates was early identified in the Toynbee report as a site where convoys from Erzerum, Erzindjan and elsewhere were repeatedly ambushed by *cetes* or regular army units on a revolver-shot signal from the convoy guards. Here, according to one survivor, 'hundreds of children were bayoneted by the Turks and thrown into the Euphrates ... men and women were stripped naked, tied together in hundreds, shot and then hurled into the river'. The scale of the killing was so great here that the thousands of dead bodies created a barrage, forcing the river to change 'its course for about a hundred yards'.[25]

The finality of killing sites such as Kamakh Bogaz aside, the convoys that remained on the road after weeks if not months of suffering and depredation were very largely women and children. The result was that not only were they prey to constant hunger, thirst, extremes of heat and cold through constant exposure to the elements, lack of any facilities or night-time shelter whatsoever, pillage and, of course, murder, but also, and especially in the case of the younger women, the fear – or actuality of – sexual molestation and repeated rape. Without any notional protection from male family members, these most vulnerable women were thus thrown back on what emotional and physical support and sustenance they could offer each other or could be offered by equally exhausted but surviving older female relatives, whether mothers, mothers-in-law, aunts, sisters, grandmothers or, indeed, whoever was still clinging to life. Survivor testimony reminds us, too, that these many of the married women were close to their full term when they set out on these marches and gave birth literally on the road. These, alongside nursing mothers and others with little or older children in train, had to cope as best they could with all that this entailed.[26]

Eyewitnesses, mostly men, have tried to describe what they saw. The American Consul in Aleppo, Jackson, in a report on the fate of two convoys of women from Harput and Sivas, offered a description close to biblical catastrophe:

'On the 60th day when we reached Viran Shehir, only 300 had remained from 18,000 exiles. On the 64th day they gathered all the men and the sick women, and children, and burnt and killed them all. The remaining were ordered to continue on their way... On the 70th day, when they reached Haleb, 35 women and children were remaining from the 3,000 exiles from Harput, 150 women and children from the whole caravan of 18,000.'[27]

It is easy to assume from Jackson's description of the Sivas survivors he himself encountered in Aleppo, a major transit point en route to the desert, why so many had already died. Having had all their clothes torn off or stolen and having just completed a five-day forced march in their nakedness in temperatures of 105 to 115 degrees, these surviving women were burned through sun exposure, emaciated through starvation and dysentery to the point of skin and bones, and disgustingly filthy beyond description with their eyes, noses, mouths and hair covered in lice. If death came for many on the road because they were too sick, because they had seen and smelt too much, because they could not face the shame of violation, like the hundreds of young girls each day who, according to survivors, held hands and threw themselves in groups into the Euphrates[28], or because they had become too traumatised through the loss of relatives, especially of babies or children abandoned en route or sold for a few piastres to Turks, even this sort of attrition cannot account for the final death toll. Sivas, for example, had an estimated Armenian population of 300,000 before the deportations, of which Jackson could only account for some 5,000 survivors in August 1915.[29]

Of course, many thousands of young women, girls – and some boys – were 'saved' through being sold, or more simply abducted by the Kurdish, Turkish and sometimes Arab despoilers of the convoys.[30] But what actually happened to the vast majority is more obviously gleaned from the investigations conducted on horseback by Davis, the American Consul in Harput, accompanied on one occasion by an American missionary, Dr Atkinson, in the remote mountainous area some distance from Harput, around Lake Goeljuk (Hazar Golu), in the autumn of 1915. Atkinson seems to have been so upset by the experience that it may have caused his death two months later. Here is part of his report – as transcribed by his widow – on what he saw:

'Near the foot of the mountain were a great many bodies with their clothes on. But around the lake ... there were between five and ten thousand all entirely naked, nearly all women and children ... nearly all the women showed signs of mutilation, let us hope after death ... killed in various ways. Some were shot, some beheaded, many were hacked or cut with hatchets or knives. In one place ... a ravine ... the bodies lay four or five deep just as they had fallen.'[31]

Clearly Atkinson was trying to convey that vast numbers of these women had been killed in a sado-erotic fashion, though he was too coy or traumatised to spell out his own inference that they had had their genitalia and breasts hacked off while still alive. A somewhat more detached Consul Davis was able to add further details on how they met their deaths. The varying degrees of decomposition of the bodies around the lake suggested that the convoys had been taken to different valleys in order that they would avoid knowledge of what had happened to their predecessors. Ordered to rest in a designated valley by their gendarme guards, local Kurds would arrive on the scene a day or two later in order to do the actual killing. Davis was later able to confirm that what regularly transpired between the gendarmes and the Kurds was a financial transaction in which the latter, in return for payment of an agreed sum to the former, could then take whatever pickings they wished from those they had killed. This explains also why large number of bodies had been burned – not, it appears, for obvious sanitary reasons – but in order to locate gold coins, rings and so on that had been swallowed or hidden in orifices.[32]

Davis's information provides an important clue to how so many people not in uniform could be mobilised to participate in the killings. Opportunity for plunder was a primary goal. What he could not know was that his was not the only 'slaughterhouse *vilayet*', but that there were also mass killing sites all over Eastern Anatolia. There were indeed so many mutilated or bloated Armenian bodies strewn across its highways and byways, let alone its more obscure parts, and these were exciting so many complaints from German observers, that Talat sent an urgent coded message in mid-December 1915 to all *valis* ordering their local underlings, on threat of dismissal for non-compliance, to bury these corpses and accompanying debris forthwith.[33] One reason why there was now added urgency was the fear that dysentery, cholera and typhus epidemics – already running rampant among what was left of the convoys east of Aleppo – would spread to the rest of the population. In fact, it was already too late. De Nogales, a Venezuelan officer serving in the Ottoman Army, reports that in the year following August 1916, 50 per cent of villagers between Aleppo and Mosul in the main zone of Armenian 'resettlement' had died from typhus, rising to 88 per cent around Ras ul-Ain, a major deportee concentration point at the then terminus of the Baghdad railway.[34] Whether this 'hygiene' factor was at all responsible for renewed bouts of mass killing of the deportees in 1916 is difficult to discern.

By then, convoy survivors were spread along a broad swathe of the lower Euphrates River from Meskene to below Deir Zor, where they were confined to ramshackle, open-air concentration camps or allowed to fend for themselves. Here, also, were many additional thousands of Armenians who had been deported by railway truck from the Mediterranean coastline around Adana or from communities further west, such as Konya. A more fortunate few had also found their way further south to Lebanon and Palestine, where they were relatively safe from the threat of massacre and where charitable aid for them from the still neutral United States was beginning to filter through. In September 1916 Auguste Bernau, a German national working in Aleppo as a US oil company agent, was given diplomatic assistance by Consul Jackson to dispense aid to the Armenians in Deir Zor province. Travelling through Meskene he reported hundreds of mounds marking Armenian mass graves, saw slave labourers at work, and groups of dirty, verminous women and orphans desperately searching through horse dung for barley seeds to eat. Somehow 15,000 deportees in this area, he estimated, were still alive, though some 60,000 had succumbed, through hunger, typhus and intestinal disease. Further south, around Deir Zor itself, many more people had survived because the Mutessarif, Au Souad Bey, had gone against the CUP agenda, in attempting to provide the deportees with what nominal care and provision he had at his disposal.[35]

The regime of Ali Souad Bey, however, proved the exception to the rule. In early August he was replaced by a much more typical CUP nominee, Zeki Bey, who had already distinguished himself as a torturer-cum-killer in the Kayseri region. Under his aegis, the killings in Deir Zor resumed with a vengeance. In one single incident, on 9 October 1916, affirmed in a deposition by an Armenian lawyer, Mustafa Sidki, the police chief of Deir Zor 'ordered to pile great stacks of wood and spilt 200 cans of petroleum on the whole stack. He lighted it and then had 2,000 orphans, bound hand and feet, thrown into the pyre'.[36] This predilection for the literal idea of 'holocaust' spread back up the Euphrates to the camps at Meskene, Abu Hreera, Haman, Rakka, Zierrat and Sabka, and also along the adjoining River Khabour – where the deportees sheltering in Deir Zor had been driven – all the way to Ras ul-Ain. At Sabka it is reported that as many as 60,000 died in one week alone, through the generous use of kerosene. Herding thousands of people into caves, and starting a bonfire at its closed head, in order to asphyxiate them, was another common method of disposal, as occurred at Shedadi in the Syrian desert. Or simply tying them together on the edge of the river then shooting one so that the dead body would then carry the rest to their watery graves, as happened at Margada, another recently uncovered and remote killing site on the Khabour.[37] The hands-on role of Turkish, Circassian and Kurdish ex-convicts in the majority of these killings suggests once again the continuing guiding hand of the Special Organisation.[38]

If the CUP's passionate determination to exterminate Armenians was ostensibly finally spent in this ultimate wave of killings in late 1916, one could argue, contrarily, that it simply marked the first phase in a concerted Turkish national effort aimed at the 'the political and physical extermination of Armenia', this being CUP-successor Ataturk's top secret instruction to Karabekir, his commander operating in the east in November 1920.[39] Putting this issue to one side, it is likely that not less than 1 million Armenians died in the 1915-16 genocide, and this out of a total Ottoman Armenian population that could not have greatly exceeded the 2 million mark.[40]

Like the Turks in relation to the Armenians, the Romanian genocide was predicated on the assumption that its Jewry was not only a thorn in the side of Romanian society but that it also posed an imminent threat to the body politic. The sense that Jews were dangerous was, of course, rather deep-rooted in the European psyche. Nearly all the leading figures in inter-war Romanian political life were rabidly anti-Semitic. But the acute vulnerability of the Romanian Jewish minority only became fully apparent in the wake of the international crises that convulsed the country from 1938 onwards. Romanian territory had swelled dramatically, with Western Allied endorsement, at the end of the First World War, at the expense of neighbouring Russia, Austria-Hungary and Bulgaria. In the ebb of Munich, and under the guiding hand of the Germans, this now went into almost equally dramatic reverse. The Second Vienna award of the high summer of 1940 and the almost concurrent Treaty of Craiova, which returned land to Hungary and Bulgaria, were viewed as bad enough. But it was the secret clauses of the Nazi-Soviet non-aggression pact leading, in June 1940, to the absorption into Soviet Russia of the northern part of Bukovina and all of Bessarabia that really rocked the Romanian boat, with ultimately fatal consequences for their Jews.

From an outsider's perspective, the lather that Romanian nationalists worked up over the loss of these two provinces might seem excessive. Both remained on the social and economic periphery of the Regat heartlands, a profile underscored by the fact that though they contained sizeable Romanian-speaking populations, these were actually highly multicultural societies of long standing. Could it have been perhaps this very fact that so preoccupied the new Antonescu regime of self-styled 'national and social restoration' and that made it so determined to not only 'liberate' these territories but also in so doing absorb them for all time into Romania integrale?

For Antonescu and his supporters, the obstacle to this agenda was the provinces' supposedly pro-Bolshevik Jews. Again, as with the CUP and the Armenians, this tells us much more about the paranoid anxieties of the Romanian leadership than it does about its object. Though less than 11 per cent of the population in Bukovina and 7.2 per cent in Bessarabia[41], the Jewish presence in these provinces was significant. This was especially true in the towns where their demographic weight was not only much greater but where they also provided the core of the trading and professional classes. Nevertheless, the Jewish social and occupational profile was not of a piece any more than its political orientation. If there was a strong modernising, Westernising tendency accentuated by the extreme traditionalism and politically reactionary nature of surrounding society, there were also extremely traditional Jewish communities, especially in the more rural areas where Hasidic-style religiosity was often combined with acute poverty. Moreover, Bukovinan and Bessarabian Jewry were in critical respects unlike each other, as they were unlike their Moldavian, Wallachian or Transylvanian counterparts. Those of the Bukovinan capital, Czernowitz, for instance, tended to look back fondly to the Central European civic culture and security they had enjoyed under the Habsburgs. For Bessarabian Jewry, centred on Kishinev, the great moment of hope and liberation had been the first – non-Bolshevik – Russian revolution of 1917.[42]

It is hardly surprising that neither group could enthuse about incorporation into Romania. The kingdom's pre-1918 record on Jewish rights was the worst in Europe outside Russia. It had set its face against international demands for reform at the Treaty of Berlin in 1878, just as had the Porte vis-a-vis its Armenians, while the more recent attempts to guarantee Jewish citizenship at the Paris Peace Conference were viewed by Antonescu along with free elections, public opinion, humanism and the League of Nations as just so much 'Jewish morality' aimed at doing Romania down. Antonescu was not alone among Romanians in believing that there really was an international Jewish conspiracy and that salvation could only come through its destruction.[43] While successive Romanian Governments had blocked Jewish rights and were quick to introduce Nazi-style discrimination and expropriation, the self-styled legionary movement of the fascist Iron Guard openly attacked and butchered Jews, not least in September 1940, when they offered their support for Antonescu's military coup against the discredited King Carol by dragging scores of Bucharest Jews to a slaughterhouse to behead them with the mechanical instruments normally reserved for cattle.[44]

If one might propose that here might be grounds enough for Bukovinan and Bessarabian Jewry to back Bolshevism, and even welcome the Soviet invasion with open arms, a Romanian Secret Service Intelligence (SSI) report from July 1940 – claiming that the Jews there were indeed collaborating with the Red Army by committing acts of assassination, terrorism and vandalism against fleeing Romanians[45] – hardly tallies with the fact that thousands of them were at this very time being deported by the Soviets alongside other potential 'enemies' to the Gulag. Complex realities, however, tend not to impress those who have already made up their minds, especially, perhaps, when blame needs to be apportioned elsewhere to cover up one's own colossal failings. Nothing, for instance, could ever deflect Ion Antonescu from his deep conviction that Romania's impoverishment was the fault of millions (sic) of 'yids' taking over the country, just as later he would openly and publicly blame them for the thousands of Romanian soldiers killed on the Eastern Front. Now, in 1940, it was their collective treason that was responsible for the loss of the provinces, an accusation whose mendacity conveniently deflected attention away from his unilateral binding of Romania to the Nazi interest, delivering Romania's oil fields, steel plants and agricultural production completely to German military occupation and German-controlled corporations.[46]

That the Romanian Conducator enjoyed the unusual personal confidence of the Führer does have significant bearing, however, on Romania's autonomous Jewish genocide. For one thing, we know that Antonescu came away from his third meeting with Hitler, on 12 June 1941, not only knowing that 'Operation Barbarossa', in which the Romanian Army would be participants, was imminent – he already knew of its intention several months earlier – but also with knowledge of Hitler's initial guidelines for the treatment of Soviet Jewry. Judging from other remarks Antonescu later made about surviving Jews being deported across the Urals[47], one can assume that the flurry of 'Jewish' orders flowing from his Prime Minister's office over the next few preparatory weeks were not only geared towards bringing Romania's anti-Jewish operations into line with those of the Nazis on the wider Eastern Front, but also towards taking full advantage of the opportunity that they seemed to have provided. Antonescu spelled out what this would entail at a cabinet meeting on 8 July:

'There is no place here for saccharine and vaporous humanitarianism... I do not know when, after how many centuries, the Romanian nation will again enjoy this total freedom of action, with the possibility for ethnic purification and national revision. This is the hour when we are masters of our own territory. We must take advantage of it. I do not mind if history judges us barbarians. The Roman empire performed a series of barbarous acts against its contemporaries, and yet it was the greatest political establishment. History will not offer us other moments of grace. If need be – use machine-guns.'[48]

There would be no formalities or laws that would prevent this accomplishment, the Marshal assured his colleagues. They would have complete freedom. Of course, there was something extremely paradoxical in this statement. Only under German aegis was the anti-Jewish drive conceivable. Romania's independence of action on this score was bought at the expense of a much wider loss of independence. Nevertheless, for the Marshal's clique, the ability – and right – of the 'national totalitarian state' to destroy the Jews itself, and of its own volition, without the helping hand of the Germans, and, of course, without the censure of the League of Nations, or Western powers, became the chosen route by which Romania would reform and redeem itself. There would thus be no sub-contracting of this important 'Romanising' project to the zealots of the Iron Guard. Its legionaries, anyway, were no longer available for the task, having been bloodily crushed by the Romanian Army – with Hitler's acquiescence – in their abortive bid for sole power, in January 1941. This was the last time the fascist legionaries would provide an exemplary object-lesson on how to dispatch Jews.[49] Their efforts would be utterly dwarfed by what the official instruments of state could achieve.

Lined up on the Soviet border, as part of Axis Army Group South, the Romanian Third and Fourth Armies' advance across the River Prut into Bessarabia and Bukovina commenced on 3 July 1941, 11 days after the opening of 'Operation Barbarossa'. They did so with personal orders from the Marshal to Army HQ for the identification of 'all the Yids, communist agents or sympathisers' pending further action, and more specific ones directed only to the Pretoriat – the policing wing of the Army – for the removal of all communists across the Dneister, the first finishing-line in the projected advance – excepting Jewish communists, who were to be summarily exterminated.[50] If these secret directives, chilling as they were, were in line with Hitler's own notorious commissar orders, there was, however, a further directive that confirms that the Romanians were prepared to go much further than the Nazis, at this stage, in ridding themselves of Jews.

This directive emanated from the office of Antonescu's Prime Minister and deputy, also – confusingly – with the surname Antonescu, and was in the first instance only communicated verbally – prior to the start of 'Operation Barbarossa' – to the senior officers of the para-military Gendarmerie legions, which were then being formed to return 'the lost provinces' to civil rule subsequent to military liberation. However, there was nothing very civil about the three measures in the directive that they were required to perform. These were: 'on the spot extermination of all Jews found in rural areas'; incarceration of all urban Jews in ghettoes; and the arrest and dispatch of all those who had served the previous Soviet regime.[51]

As a consequence, many tens of thousands of north Bukovinan and Bessarabian Jews were massacred in this first great wave of the Romanian genocide in July and August 1941, possibly even exceeding the numbers killed by the Einsatzgruppen in this same period, and certainly more indiscriminately given that the Germans were – at this stage – mostly targeting only able-bodied Jewish men, while the Romanians were making no distinctions as to age or gender.[52] Yet, with an estimated 315,000 Jews[53] in the two provinces (though Antonescu thought the figure much higher) high-level planning was, paradoxically, predicated on the assumption that de-Jewing them could not be achieved – for the most part – by on-the-spot massacre but only by getting rid of them to somewhere else. In the circumstances of 1941 that could also only mean east and north-east across the Dneister, a forced migration to be accomplished by putting those who could be on trains in that direction or – for the vast majority – force-marching them there. But the assumption had one critical flaw. Whatever had been privately agreed between Antonescu and Hitler before 'Barbarossa', soon thereafter the Wehrmacht authorities, in control of the territory on the river's far side, were having none of it. This led to a perverse situation where deportees who had already crossed the river were being shot or drowned by the Germans as they were being forced back across, or shot or drowned by the Romanians trying to prevent it. However, the remaining deportees from this first wave – perhaps as many as 90,000 or 100,000 people – found themselves stranded in a huge log-jam, a situation for which Antonescu – with all his predilection for constant updates, graphs, tables and meetings to follow the progress of his directives[54] – had made no contingency planning whatsoever.

Forewarning of this breakdown had been coming in to Antonescu since mid-July. On 17 July General Topor had sent a terse wire on the surviving, rounded-up Jews from the Baltic district to GHQ: 'There is no one to guard them. There is no one to feed them. I request instructions on what we should do with them.'[55] He might well have asked. The Baltic Jews were just a fraction of those who were now strung out in vast, often open-air, lagers on the road between home and the main still extant river crossing at Atachi, or spread further still along the banks of the river from Hotin through to Secureni and down beyond Soroca. Antonescu's answer to Topor's plea – put them to work – proved no answer at all, as no work-scheme existed. At Vartujeni, south of Soroca, a new commandant – appointed in September – Colonel Agapie Vasile, attempted to improvise by putting all the 23,000-plus Jews there to hauling up stones from the bottom of the Dneister to pave the town's roads. These people were starving and largely naked, having been robbed of everything, yet Agapie's men still used rifle butts as a goad. The treatment only added to a soaring mortality rate of hundreds a day[56] in conditions in which the inmates were crammed into chicken pens, cellars, attics and quite literally gutters, and in which the only water supply was from a few wells at which they had to queue for hours. Gregore Nicolau, a magistrate, testifying at the post-war trials, confirms that none of this prevented Agapie amassing '12 gold watches, 30-40 gold chains, hundreds of gold coins with precious stones, 3 or 4 Persian rugs and so on' at the inmates' expense, or his subordinates, Captains Radelescu and Burdescu, from having all-night orgies with the camp's girls 'who screamed and wept all night'.[57]

If Vartujeni was bad enough, conditions at Marculesti, a clearing camp on the road between Balti and the river, were arguably worse. Another post-war testifier, a jeweller, St Dragomirescu, brought in to help value jewels and precious metals 'purchased' from the deportees on behalf of the Romanian National Bank (RNB), stated that there were corpses absolutely everywhere, in cellars, trenches and yards; those still alive were starving, unwashed and wallowing in their own filth, yet the situation was deteriorating as rain set in and the lager was beset by rats and mice that chewed everything, and 'vast number of flies [that] made sleep impossible'.[58]

Perhaps, in such circumstances, it is not surprising that Mihaescu, the senior RNB official there, decided to ignore the already ludicrously low purchasing prices for valuables in favour of direct confiscation while also robbing new arrivals of identity papers, bedding, soap, coffee and whatever else they had with them, primarily on his own behalf. He achieved all this by the simple expedient of making people undress, then beating them.[59] At Tataresti camp, the gendarmes found another expedient for dealing with the situation – they shot the inmates and dumped their bodies in the Dneister. This was in fact becoming common practice. A survivor from a convoy en route to Atachi stated in a post-war indictment that 861 Jews were killed one night by the roadside.[60] Another convoy, survivors from the massacre at Noua Sulita, reached the Dneister on 6 August to see it covered with the floating bodies of previous victims. No wonder by this time, Gendarmerie reports from the camps kept warning of the 'danger to public health'[61]; the human remains clogging up the rivers Prut, Raut and Dneister were testament enough to that.[62]

As the situation reached and passed breaking point, Antonescu, however, was let off the hook of his immediate problem. Part of the reason the Wehrmacht had previously denied the deportations across the Dneister was because they were still securing Soviet territory to the east. An agreement signed between them and the Romanians at Tighina, on 30 August, regularised a new situation. The Romanians were to have control of a southern Ukrainian sector between the Dneister and the Bug, the implication being that the Germans might later allow this to be added to the Romanian state as compensation for its territorial losses elsewhere, assuming that all went well, of course, in the continuing military struggle with Russia. Antonescu was now in a position to use the new territory, 'Transnistria', as at least a temporary dumping ground for the deportees.

Indeed, no sooner had the Tighina agreement been signed than Topor's 2nd Department – the unit that had made such a startling botch-up of overseeing the original deportation effort – got to work with a new set of instructions for the imminent Jewish exodus across the Dneister. On paper, these seemed to improve somewhat on the previous shambles. The Gendarmerie were required to draw up accurate reports on the number of Jews in the camps and elsewhere in Bessarabia and Bukovina; transport for their journey was to be provided by the provinces' governors, with 40 or 50 wagons for each convoy of 1,600 people; and the Romanian Federation of Jewish Communities (RFJC) in Bucharest was even notified to provide warm clothes for them.[63] Later, General Voiculescu, the Governor of Bessarabia, reported to the Marshal that the operation had been 'well organised and carried out in a civilised manner'.[64]

Yet, as with the Armenian deportations, the discrepancy between Germanic-style declarations of good order and murderous practice was gaping. From mid-

September, the Governors and Gendarmerie struggled to clear the estimated 54,000 Jewish backlog in the camps[65] so that a second wave of deportations from southern Bukovina and Dorotoi could commence early the following month. In the case of the Vartujeni exodus, for instance, the size of each convoy was arbitrarily doubled to 3,200, while at the same time more or less dispensing with the accompanying wagons; this, remember, for deportees who were already literally on their last legs, wracked by illness, and especially typhus. Even so, they were expected to cover 30 kilometres a day, now in conditions moving from blinding rain to the first onset of what would become, in this region, the most vicious winter in living memory. Family groups were split up, men often in one convoy – where they were not put into labour battalions – women and children in others. Worse, the log-jam at Atachi meant that the Vartujeni, and some other convoys, were now re-routed over increasingly muddy tracks down the river to the damaged bridges at Rezina and Cosauti, a further excuse for simply burning or drowning those who made it this far.[66]

What all this was like for the deportees can again be partially understood from post-war trial, eyewitness and survivor testimonies. One survivor from Hotin, deported in the last convoy from Secureni camp, relates how the gendarmes informed them that anybody too ill to leave would be shot. Not surprisingly, this led to people with typhus fever and nursing mothers dragging themselves along in agony in the mud. Knowledge that the previous convoy had been robbed and partially liquidated acted as a goad. People abandoned everything just to keep moving.[67] But for many convoys the danger was not just from the gendarmes – or not just the gendarmes alone. While in many places en route to Cosauti, according to a Lieutenant Popovici, the local peasants would hide close to the execution sites so that they could pilfer the corpses at the first opportunity, there is also evidence that on this same route gendarmes or accompanying paramilitary guards would 'sell' a Jew, or more specifically the clothes he or she was wearing to a peasant, in return for a fee of 1,000 or 1,500 lei for the necessary 'dispatch'.[68]

The mounting chaos and logistical breakdown at the Dneister River crossings, however, continued to be unrelieved not least because by mid-October the still departing camp deportees were being swamped by the new arrivals from southern Bukovina. These latter people were thrown into this maelstrom without any forewarning of what awaited them. Their complete evacuation was meant to take place in a period of ten days – this time primarily by train. The experience, as conveyed by Dr Meyer Teich, the president of the 3,500 strong Jewish community of Suceava, is remarkably reminiscent of the deportation of Armenian Harput a quarter of a century earlier. The unsigned 'evacuation' order was, in fact, presented to Teich in person at 5.30am on Thursday, 9 October, by a prefecture official. The deportation was to begin that same day but, owing to a lack of cattle trucks, would have to be completed the following one (in fact it was not concluded till the Saturday). The evacuees would be allowed to take with them eight days' food and small baggages only. Great insistence was made that all valuables, jewellery, foreign currency as well as keys to dwellings were to be handed over to the local officials of the recently created National Centre for Romanisation at the town hall prior to departure. No such items were to be deposited with Gentiles. Non-compliance was to be regarded as a capital offence. For the Jewish inhabitants at large these orders were announced by drum-roll.[69]

It was left to the German embassy in Bucharest to raise the question of whether getting rid of all the Jews so quickly – including those with specialist skills – might not undermine the smooth running of the Romanian economy (and of course German interests therein).[70] By contrast, Antonescu's economic rationale for these same actions seemed to be predicated on the idea that the state's rapid enrichment would follow, the National Centre for Romanisation serving this purpose as the vehicle for the return of what, according to his own perverted logic, rightfully belonged to it in the first place. Putting aside the obvious fact this was simply a very unsubtle cover for state expropriation, the other problem was that practically every official, military officer, gendarme and private citizen involved in the process seemed to assume that this was also occasion for his own self-enrichment too.

Thus, returning to Teich's testimony, we find the Mayor of Suceava, on the same day that the last Jews were departing, calling together the populace for a grand public celebration at the town hall, with all the 'abandoned' jewels, money and other valuables laid out for everybody, the BNR official included, to see, while providing a suitably flowery speech in which Antonescu, the Germans and God were thanked for having delivered the town from its Jewish yoke. Yet it later transpired that not only had large numbers of valuables ended up in the hands of the police chief and other officials – in direct defiance to the deportation order – but that the Prefect together with various municipal officials and their cronies had given away many of the best items to their friends while also organising a grand public sale of 'abandoned' furniture and goods, the proceeds of which they personally pocketed.[71]

Of course, one might argue that, from the experience of the victims, having one's best coat, wedding ring, child's toy or life savings filched was as nothing compared to having family members or friends tortured, raped or butchered in front of one, or indeed, losing one's own life. But this would be to miss the point. Expropriation and murder were intimately connected. Having survived the cattle truck journey, during which their wagons were fired into by Romanian soldiers, having arrived at Atachi in scenes of pandemonium, having seen bodies strewn all over the place, Teich nevertheless makes a point in his testimony of recalling his fellow Suceavans' shock at finding out that they were being required to exchange their Romanian money – and other valuables – for roubles, at one-fifth of the former's value.[72] For many others, this confiscation directive, plus the further one that the maximum sum they would be allowed to take with them – 2,000 lei – would not be enough to live on even for a short time, proved the last straw. While heads of communities wrote frantic pleas to Wilhelm Filderman, the head of the RFJC, asking him to intercede with Antonescu for an evacuation delay, Jacques Truelle, the Vichy ambassador in Bucharest, reported in November that many deportees were simply burning their money and committing suicide.[73] Those who hung on by attempting to conceal their valuables on their persons, still had to contend with the 'searches' conducted by Gendarmerie officers at the river crossings. The rivermen, too, made constant taunts about wanting to see the miracle of the Red Sea repeated before hurling men, women and children into the river after having stolen whatever baggages and clothes they could.[74]

Like Dante's Inferno, however, the experience of genocide can conceivably involve different regions of hell. What happened in Odessa on three days in late October 1941 – the very time when the second wave of deportations across the Dneister was in full swing – surely confirms the point.

The Army Group South's advance towards the Black Sea metropolis and – from the Romanian viewpoint – great prize in its Transnistrian aggrandisement was, by October, as elsewhere in 'Operation Barbarossa', increasingly slowing up in the face of hardening Red Army resistance. Romanian casualties were mounting and it was only after a two-month siege that Odessa was finally occupied by their Fourth Army on 16 October. Romanian frustration in the face of obstacles, especially suspected partisan action, had already been demonstrated in the early days of the campaign, as when, at Noua Sulita, 50 Jewish 'suspects' were summarily shot.[75] When in Odessa, in the late afternoon of 22 October, a delayed-action mine blew up their newly installed 10th Division HQ – in the recently evacuated NKVD command post – killing the commanding General and almost his entire staff, the most senior surviving officer, General Trestioreanu, took it upon himself to order the appropriate reprisals. By noon the following day, not only had hundreds of people been strung from the lampposts of Odessa squares, but up to 5,000 had been shot. Nearly all those killed were Jews.[76]

Worse was to follow. There were, it is estimated, at least 80,000 Jews who had been caught inside the besieged city. For Antonescu it was they who were to blame for the explosion, they who were the fifth column within, should the Red Army – as it was feared – attempt a seaborne landing to retake the city.[77] On the evening of 22 October the Conducator weighed in with his own reprisal orders – 200 communists to be executed for every officer killed in the explosion, 100 for every dead enlisted man. All communists were to be taken prisoner 'as well as one person from each Jewish family'.[78] Given that Jew equalled communist and vice versa, only one result could ensue. On 23 October, in addition to the 5,000 who had already died, another 19,000 Jews were squeezed into a square near the port. Some reports say that they were burned alive, having been sprayed with petrol.[79]

Even then the Romanian's need to kill Jews was not satiated. The next day, 24 October, a detachment of the 10th infantry regiment escorted anything up to 25,000 more of them towards Dalnik, a district on the outskirts of Odessa. This time the numbers included a much higher percentage of women and children. To begin with the victims were tied together in groups of 30 to 40 and shot in anti-tank ditches. But the officers in charge decided that this was too slow and wasteful of ammunition. So they continued the proceedings by cramming the remaining people into four large warehouses – some 2,000 women and children in each of three of them, the men in the fourth. Then, one by one, they machine-gunned the three 'female' warehouses through breaches in the walls. They also used hand grenades. However, not everybody was killed; the soldiers could hear the women still screaming and see their attempts to throw their children out of the windows and through holes in the roof. So, with night approaching, they flung straw into the entrances of the buildings and set them alight using petrol and kerosene. This time everybody died. On the next day, 25 October, it was the turn of the fourth and final warehouse filled with men. At 5.35pm, the time of the HQ explosion three days earlier, it was shelled to smithereens.[80]

The Romanians had exacted their revenge and in the process surpassed in numbers the single largest massacre to this point – that at Babi Yar – perpetrated by the Nazi killing machine. Yet, incredibly, it was not over. The Romanians were to surpass even themselves in one final sequence of mass murder, though this time the German factor was to be of crucial significance.

In spite of the Odessa massacre, there were still tens of thousands of surviving Jews in the city and the surrounding region. From the end of October onwards the Romanians seem to have been in a frantic hurry to remove the provincial ones to the furthest extremity of the area under their rule – the Golta prefecture on the banks of the Bug. Here they were assigned by Colonel Modest Isopescu to the warehouses, stables, pigpens and half-destroyed houses of three farms, Bogdonovca, Domanovca and Acmecetca. Though designated as camps, they were – like those that had formerly fouled the shores of the Dneister – nothing more than holding pens. Like them, too, the absence of water, food, or any other facility pointed not only to the usual Romanian incompetence but also, more tellingly, to Antonescu's refusal to be deflected from his Hitler-informed conviction that all the Jews in the Romanian sphere were soon going to be removed from such convenient transit sites to a final destination much further east. The only problem by late 1941 was that Hitler was no longer in any position to deliver; there was – thanks to the Soviet state's refusal to fall apart in the face of 'Barbarossa' – nowhere further east for the Jews to go.

The stage was thus set for a replay of that earlier stand-off between the Romanian and German military authorities over the spillage of Jews – this time across the frozen Bug – into the latter's territories, a situation that could only have been exacerbated in mid-December when a petulant Antonescu began the deportation of the remaining Odessa Jews to these same camps.[81] The German authorities, however, had their own trump card. They had learned that a major epidemic of typhus had broken out in the Golta camps' population, now numbering some 70,000, threatening not only neighbouring communities including – for them – significant Volksdeutsche ones but also their own armies. Public health thus became the authority upon which the nearest German Gebietskommissar demanded the removal of the Jews back deeper into Transnistria. The Romanians' response, however, was to undertake their own systematic – German-style – mass murder.

The orders for this operation, which began at Bogdanovca on the morning of 21 December – the last day of the Jewish holiday of Chanukah – clearly came from the highest level of the Romanian state, but were verbally entrusted to Prefect Isopescu, who in turn passed them on to his deputy, Aristide Padure, and so down to the mixed killing units of gendarmes, Ukrainian auxiliaries and local volunteers. The killing began with some 4,500-5,000 people too sick to go any further than the straw-covered stables into which, flooded with kerosene, they were burned alive. While this was in train, groups of 300 to 400 men, women and children at a time were marched through nearby woods to a killing site by a ravine.

It was reported that there were scenes of great lamentation from many of the women when they realised what was happening.[82]

They were ordered to undress – in temperatures dipping to minus 40 degrees – finally stripped of their last possessions and shot in the back of the neck. Grenades were again also used. There were between 40,000 and 50,000 Jews at Bogdanovca.[83] Too cold, exhausted or ill to do anything other than simply wait their turn to be killed, they sheltered as best as they could on banks or in pits close to the frozen river, often using corpses as wind breaks. The killing was halted for Christmas celebrations on 24 December – enabling Isopescu to organise a sleigh ride round the site for Bucharest friends and relatives he had specially invited – resuming again on 28 December and finally being completed, apparently at something of a stretch, just in time to welcome in the New Year. In spite of the effort, Isopescu seems to have enjoyed the proceedings, not only tormenting many of those about to be killed but also sending some of his own photographs of the results to Bucharest papers.[84] For the victims, one of just a handful of survivors, Chaim Kogan, later testified that he was put to work with 200 other 'hand-picked' men – most of whom were later shot – to clear the site.[85]

The 18,000 inmates at Domanovca were liquidated in a similar fashion, though over a longer period in January and February, while the 4,000 people in the camp at Acmecetca were simply cordoned off from the outside world and so 'exterminated by hunger'.[86] In this same period the last 20,000 Jews of Odessa were also sealed into German freight trains – which the Romanians delightedly called 'funeral trains' – and conveyed 60 kilometres north to a transit camp at Berezovka en route to those in the Golta district. So many of their 'cargo' were already close to death from typhus, starvation and the appalling conditions in the largely destroyed Slobodka area of the city where they had been ghettoised, that they quickly succumbed to the freezing weather on the journey. Vast bonfires were prepared to burn their bodies on arrival. The majority of the rest died soon after from the same causes, or at the hands of execution squads, largely composed of local Volksdeutsche units. Many of the Jews' Odessa homes were reportedly assigned to ethnic Germans.[87]

However, if the killings on the banks of the Bug mark the apotheosis of the Romanian genocide, it was not to be carried to its logical conclusion. True, Transnistrian Jewry – those at least who been unable to flee with the retreating Red Army – had been almost completely wiped out by the Romanians. Yet after mid-1942 there were no more major deportations across the Dneister, despite Transnistrian Governor Alexianu's sworn testimony at Antonescu's post-war trial that he had been led to expect further instructions regarding Regat Jewry, once the Bukovinan and Bessarabian operation was completed.[88] Instead, in the high summer of 1942, Antonescu, inveterate Jew-hater that he undoubtedly was, began to change his tune. German proposals for the implementation of 'the final solution' in Romania, to be enacted by wholesale Jewish deportation to the death camps in Poland, were stonewalled. Continuing pressure into 1943 from Eichmann's office, and from higher up the Nazi hierarchy, including Hitler himself, was similarly resisted. By November 1943, when news reached Antonescu of a major massacre perpetrated by Einsatzgruppen in the Golta district, he was blustering to his Ministers: 'I do not tolerate such killings.'[89] In fact, he was in no position to prevent repeated German incursions into the Romanian zone to take Jews for labour or to liquidate them.[90] But this emphasises the fact that by this time the greatest threat to those Bessarabian and Bukovinan Jews still alive in Transnistria was a German, not a Romanian one.

The reason, of course, was simple. Antonescu had sensed the way the war's wind was blowing and that this was no longer in the direction of a German victory. It was not that he had changed his mind about Jewish responsibility for the war, or his agenda for getting rid of them, simply that with increasing danger to the Romanian regime and state, a different tack was needed. Antonescu strove to re-open his lines to the Western Allies, not least by attempting to push his regime's crimes under the carpet. In March 1944 this led, by an extraordinarily circuitous route, to a decree ordering the repatriation of the deportees. One of the first tangible acts associated with this new agenda was the exit of a group of 300 camp orphans who were allowed to proceed to British Palestine. Antonescu's attempt to signal his new-found humanitarian credentials came too late to save him or his regime, which was overthrown that August as the Red Army entered Bucharest. One country that was able to flaunt its humanitarianism, however, was the one that had allowed the orphans free passage – Turkey.[91]

Jean Ancel estimates that the Antonescu regime was responsible for the deaths of 350,000 Jews, of whom 100,000 were 'Transnistrian'.[92] Armenian deaths exceeded these by threefold, if not more. But then again the Romanian genocide was only a small fraction of the European-wide Holocaust. Numbers of fatalities alone rarely provide grounds for direct similitude. But then, once we get into the numbers game, we start having to note so many other experiences of war where deaths ran into the millions. If many experiences can be genocidal without necessarily being genocide, they must also emphasise that there can be no single or uniform experience of that which is truly genocide. Nevertheless, if one takes the multitude and variety of the victims' experiences described in these two case-histories as a whole, they do have a quality that marks them out as distinct from other experiences of either the First or Second World Wars.

The Turkish Armenian and Romanian Jewish genocides were efforts to kill off whole peoples, for all time. The perpetrators wanted not only the people dead but also their cultures obliterated, so that there would be no future trace of them. They were prepared to pursue these agendas across internationally recognised borders, killing, in both instances, Russian subjects or citizens in the process, and also attempting to destroy other smaller groups who were similarly marked down as national 'enemies'.[93] Such flagrant violations of human rights flew in the face of what Antonescu sneeringly referred to as the 'demo-liberal world'.[94] As such, they could only be pursued under the most extraordinary wartime circumstances. It is significant that in both instances the attempt was made in the context of alignment with the one great power in both wars – Germany – that was prepared to challenge the values as well as the reality of the international system and in so doing, in the Second World War, attempt its own all-embracing, trans-continental genocide. The CUP and the Antonescu regimes were technically not comparable fascist regimes. But surely only ultra-nationalist, authoritarian and militaristic ones, which also exhibited the most extreme ideologically driven phobias about their victims, could even contemplate versions of which ultimately only the Nazis were complete masters.

Yet, if this is the case, what is surprising is how few people from the general population were prepared to stand in their way. The example of the Gentile Mayor of Czernowitz, Traian Popovici, who, in October 1941, stood up to the Jewish deportation order from his town and had it partially – though, as things turned out, ephemerally – rescinded, is all the more extraordinary because at this level of Romanian officialdom it is the only example of dissent of which we know.[95] Lower down the hierarchy there were certainly gendarmes on the marches who tried to protect their charges or refused to participate in the killings[96], just as in the Armenian genocide, there were similar stories. There were, too, friends and neighbours who went out of their way to save and protect the potential victims, Alevi Kurdish families coming notably to the Armenians' assistance, though with far fewer examples of good neighbourliness in the Romanian instance.[97]

The general picture, however, is much bleaker. It was not just those with particular sadistic and pyromaniacal tendencies – of whom we have come across a small sample in these pages – who were responsible for mass murder. Indeed, 'the need to find new ways of killing'[98] seems to have gripped thousands of ordinary participants both in uniform and out of it. Sheer hatred for the victims explains some of it. Misogyny, too, clearly played a major role in the specific degradation, violation and mutilation of women, though with the added bonus for the perpetrators that this also degraded and traumatised whole victim families and communities. But there was also something else – the enjoyment factor. With no Nazi-style race laws to warn of defilement or contamination, and no orders from on high demanding that mass murder be conducted in a purely mechanistic fashion without passion or feeling, the participants were free to dream up whatever form of pain, torture or humiliation as a vehicle to their victims' agonising deaths they could devise. The ravines of the Euphrates, the great sweep of the Dneister, were not incidental to these designs. They became part of the spectacle, a geography of death in which human ingenuity in killing was sanctioned by the state. It is a picture, alas, with which we have, in the final genocide-strewn decade of the last century of the second millennium, become all too familiar.

Notes on contributors

Dr Mark Levene, The University of Warwick, UK
Mark Levene is Senior Lecturer in History at the University of Warwick where he specialises in Jewish history and comparative genocide. His publications include War, Jews and the new Europe. The Diplomacy of Lucien Wolf, 1914-1919 (Oxford, 1992) and The Massacre in History (Oxford, 1999) co-edited with Penny Roberts.

Recommended reading

Butnaru, I. C., *The Silent Holocaust: Rumania and its Jews* (New York and London: Greenwood Press, 1992)

Hovannisian, Richard G. (ed.), *The Armenian Genocide in Perspective* (New Brunswick, NJ, and London: Transaction Books, 1986)

Ioanid, Radu, *The Holocaust in Romania: The Destruction of Jews and Gypsies under the Antonescu Regime, 1940-1944* (Chicago: Ivan R. Dee, 2000)

Melson, Robert F., *Revolution and Genocide: On the Origins of the Armenian Genocide and the Holocaust* (Chicago, University of Chicago Press, 1992)

Walker, Christopher J., *Armenia: The Survival of a Nation* (London: Croom Helm, 1980)

Notes

1   I would like to thank Dr Armen Sahakian of London, Dr Rouben Adalian of the Armenian National Institute (ANI) in Washington, Dr Jo Reilly of the Wiener Institute, London, and Dr Radu Ioanid of the United States Holocaust Memorial Museum for help and advice in the preparation of this contribution.

2   From the notes of Admiral Canaris, 22 August 1939, Quoted in L. P. Lorchner, *What about Germany?* (New York, 1942) p2

3   See, notably, Helen Fein, 'A Formula for Genocide: Comparisons of the Turkish Genocide (1915) and the German Holocaust (1939-1945)', Comparative Studies in Sociology 1 (1978) pp271-93; Vakahn N. Dadrian, 'Towards a Theory of Genocide incorporating the Instance of the Holocaust', Holocaust and Genocide Studies 5 (1990), pp129-243; Florence Mazian, *Why Genocide? The Armenian and Jewish Experiences in Perspective* (Ames: Iowa State University Press, 1990); Robert F. Melson, *Revolution and Genocide: On the Origins of the Armenian Genocide and the Holocaust* (Chicago: University of Chicago Press, 1992)

4   Michael Berenbaum (ed), *A Mosaic of Victims* (New York: New York University Press, 1990); Gerhard Hirschfeld (ed), *The Policies of Genocide, Jews and Soviet Prisoners of War in Nazi Germany* (London: Allen & Unwin, 1986); Gotz Aly and Susanne Helm, *Vordenker der Vernichtung: Auschwitz und der Plane fur em neue europaische Ordnung* Frankfurt am Main: Fischer Taschenbuch Verlag, 3rd ed 1994); Donald Kenrick and Grattan Puxon, *Gypsies under the Swastika* (Hatfield: University of Hertfordshire Press, 1995); Alan Fisher, *The Crimean Tatars* (Palo Alto, Cal: 1978)

5   See, eg, Robert Conquest, *The Nation Killers: The Soviet Deportation of Nationalities* (London: Macmillan, 1970); Aleksandr Nekrich, *The Punished Peoples: The Deportation and Tragic Fate of Soviet Minorities at the End of the Second World War* (New York: Norton, 1978); Nicolai Tolstoy, *Stalin's Secret War* (New York: Holt, Rinehart & Winston, 1981)

6   For analyses of Turkish and Romanian denial see Rouben Adalian, 'The Armenian Genocide: Revisionism and Denial' in Michael N. Dobkowski and Isidor Walliman, *Genocide In Our Time: An Annotated Bibliography with Analytical Introductions* (Ann Arbour, MI: Pierian Press, 1992) pp85-105; Roger W. Smith, 'Denial of the Armenian Genocide' in Israel W. Charny (ed), *Genocide: A Critical Bibliographic Review* (London: Mansell Publishing, 1991) Vol 2, pp63-85; Radu Ioanid, 'Romania' in David S. Wyman (ed), *The World Reacts to the Holocaust* (Baltimore and London: The John Hopkins University Press, 1996) pp225-55; and 'When Mass Murderers Become Good Men', *The Journal of Holocaust Education* 4 (1) (1995) pp92-104

7   Raphael Lemkin, *Axis Rule in Occupied Europe* (Washington DC: Carnegie Endowment for International Peace, 1944) p79

8   Ibid

9   Ibid

10 Interestingly, the nearest modern, but pre-1914, comparison is the US deportation of the remaining eastern seaboard tribes of native Americans, most infamously the Cherokee 'Trail of Tears' in the late 1830s. See Gloria Jahoda, *The Trail of Tears: The Story of the Indian Removals* (New York: Holt,

Rinehart & Winston, 1975)

11 See Jean Ancel (ed), _Documents Concerning the Fate of Romanian Jewry during the Holocaust_ (New York: Beate Klarsfeld Foundation, 1986) 12 Vols (hereafter Ancel, _Documents_)

12 The outstanding work in this field is that of Vakahn N. Dadrian. See his 'Documentation of the Armenian Genocide in Turkish Sources' in Israel W. Charny, op cit, Vol 2, pp86-138, and 'Documentation of the Armenian Genocide in German and Austrian Sources' in Israel W. Charny (ed), _The Widening Circle of Genocide: A Critical Bibliographic Review_ (New Brunswick and London: Transaction Publishers, 1994) Vol 3, pp77-126. Also Rouben Adalian, 'Source, Evidence and Authority: Documenting the Armenian Genocide against the Background of Denial' in Roger W. Smith (ed), _Genocide: Essays Towards Understanding, Early Warning and Prevention_ (Williamsburg, VA: Association of Genocide Scholars, 1999) pp67-77

13 (Arnold J. Toynbee, ed), 'The Treatment of Armenians in the Ottoman Empire: Documents Presented to Viscount Grey of Falloden', Misc No. 31, Command 8325 (London: HMSO, 1916) (hereafter Toynbee, 'Treatment')

14 See, notably, Johannes Lepsius, _Deutschland und Armenien 1914-1918: Sammlung diplomatischer Aktenstucke_ (Berlin-Potsdam: Tern pelverlag, 1919)

15 Ara Sarafian (ed), _United States Official Documents on the Armenian Genocide_, 3 Vols (Watertown, MA: Armenian Review Books, 1994, 1995) Vol 1, pp170-1

16 Quoted in Richard G. Hovannisian, 'Historical Dimensions of the Armenian Question, 1878-1923' in Richard G. Hovannisian (ed), _The Armenian Genocide in Perspective_ (New Brunswick, NJ, and London: Transaction Books, 1986) p31

17 Vahakn N. Dadrian, 'The Role of the Special Organisation in the Armenian Genocide during the First World War' in Panikos Panayi (ed), _Minorities in Wartime_ (Leamington Spa: Berg, 1993) pp50-82

18 Christopher J. Walker, _Armenia: The Survival of a Nation_ (London, Croom Helm, 1980) p209

19 Toynbee, 'Treatment', p90

20 Rafael de Nogales, _Four Years Beneath the Crescent_ (New York, Scribner's, 1925) pp134, 137, estimated that 200,000 non-Armenians were massacred in Siirt and district.

21 Toynbee, 'Treatment': testimony of Signor Gorrini, Italian consul, pp291-2

22 Ephraim. K. Jernazian, _Judgement under Truth: Witnessing Armenian Genocide_ (New Brunswick and London: Transaction Books, 1990) p88

23 Toynbee, 'Treatment', p240

24 Ephraim K. Jernazian, op cit, p102

25 Toynbee, 'Treatment', p239. See also the Safrastian account on p238

26 See Donald E. Miller and Lorna Touryan Miller, _Survivors: An Oral History of the Armenian Genocide_ (Berkeley and Los Angeles: University of California Press, 1993) Chap 5, 'The Experience of Women and Children'. On the broader implications of this line of enquiry, see Roger W. Smith, 'Women and Genocide: Notes on an Unwritten History', Holocaust and Genocide Studies 8 (3) (1994), pp315-34; Alexandra Stigimayer (ed), _Mass Rape: The War against Women in Bosnia-Herzegovina_ (Lincoln, Neb, and London: University of Nebraska Press, 1994; English ed)

27 Ara Sarafian, op cit, Vol 1, Jackson, 16 October 1915, p108. See also his longer report 'Armenian Atrocities', 4 March 1918, pp142-58

28 Miller and Miller, op cit, pp103-4

29 Ara Sarafian, op cit, Vol 1, re Jackson

30 Miller and Miller, op cit, Chap 5

31 Leslie A. Davis, _The Slaughterhouse Province: An American Diplomat's Report on the Armenian Genocide, 1915-1917_ (New Rochelle, NY: 1989) p31

32 Ibid, pp82-6

33 G. S. Graber, _Caravans to Oblivion: The Armenian Genocide, 1915_ (New York: John Wiley & Sons, 1996) p104

34 Rafael de Nogales, op cit, pp179-80

35 Ara Sarafian, op cit, Vol 1, Bernau to Jackson, 10 September 1916, pp129-35. See also 'Armenian Atrocities', note 27 above; Christopher J. Walker, op cit, pp227-9

36 Vakahn N. Dadrian, 'Naim-Andonian Documents', pp353-4, n96

37 See Aram Adonian, _The Memoirs of Naim Bey_ (Newtown Square, PA: American Historical Research Association, 1965 (1920)); Robert Fisk, 'Armenia's Holocaust', _The Independent Magazine_

4 April 1992, pp22-30, for Shedadi and Margada

38 Ara Sarafian, op cit, Vol 1 'Armenian Atrocities', pp148-9

39 Quoted in Vakahn N. Dadrian, 'The Role of the Turkish Military in the Destruction of Ottoman Armenians: A Study in Historical Continuities', *Journal of Political and Military Sociology* 20 (2) (1992) p282

40 The total casualty figure can be conservatively construed on the basis of Toynbee's carefully considered estimate of 600,000 deaths through to the end of 1915 and adding again the minimum figures derived from Adonian and others, with regard to the mass killing in or around Ras ul-Ain, Intilli and Deir Zor into late 1916. See Toynbee, 'Treatment', pp648-51; Robert F. Melson, op cit pp145-7 for a careful analysis of the figures. See also Vakahn N. Dadrian, 'Warrant for Genocide', Appendix, for the fierce and tortured demographic debate.

41 Radu Ioanid, 'La Destruction et La Survie des Juifs Roumains pendant La deuxième guerre mondiale: A La lumiere des documents des archives de Roumaine, Ukraine et Moldavie' (unpublished, 1993) p39

42 See Ezra Mendelsohn, *The Jews of Europe between Two World Wars* (Bloomington: Indiana University Press, 1987) Chap 'Romania'

43 Jean Ancel, 'Antonescu and the Jews' in Michael Berenbaum and Abraham J. Peck (eds), *The Holocaust and History, The Known, The Unknown, The Disputed and the Reexamined* (Bloomington and Indianapolis: Indiana University Press, 1998) pp465-8

44 Julius S. Fischer, *Transnistria: The Forgotten Cemetery* (New York and London: Thomas Yoseloff, 1969) p27

45 Ancel, *Documents*, Vol 10, SSI Report, 4 July 1940, pp29-34

46 See Jean Ancel, 'Antonescu', op cit, pp464-66; Julius S. Fischer, op cit, pp72-4, for Antonescu letter to Filderman, 19 October 1941, revealing mind-set on Jews. Also pp28-9

47 Jean Ancel, 'Antonescu', op cit, p469

48 See Jean Ancel, 'The Romanian Way of Solving the "Jewish Problem" in Bessarabia and Bukovina, June-July 1941', Yad Vashem Studies, 29 (1988) p190, for protocol of Government meeting, 8 July 1941

49 Martin Gilbert, *The Holocaust: The Jewish Tragedy* (London: Collins, 1986) p141

50 Ancel, *Documents*, Vol 5, p1; 'Romanian Way', op cit, p191

51 Ancel, 'Romanian Way', op cit, pp207-8

52 Ancel, 'Romanian Way', op cit, p231, argues that 150-160,000 died in July-August 1941. Radu Ioanid, op cit, p42, disputes this figure, arguing that it is based on a significant underestimate of those who were deported by, or fled with, or were mobilised by the Soviet Union. He proposes a figure of 65,000 dead for this period.

53 Radu Ioanid, op cit, p42, but with his caveat that as many as 124,000 Jews (compared with Ancel's figure of 30,000-40,000) may have exited the provinces eastwards before the Romanian 'liberation'.

54 Jean Ancel, 'Antonescu', op cit, p468

55 Julius S. Fischer, op cit, p42

56 Ancel, *Documents*, Vol 8, testimony of Israel Parkiman, pp575-81

57 Julius S. Fischer, op cit, pp51-2

58 Ibid, p53

59 Ibid

60 Ancel, *Documents*, Vol 5, Reifer testimony, 1945 trials, pp145-58

61 Ibid, Gendarmerie reports, 6-8 and 10-12 August 1941, pp41-2

62 Jean Ancel, 'Romanian Way', op cit, p226

63 Radu Ioanid, op cit, pp1-2

64 Jean Ancel 'Antonescu', op cit, p469

65 Julius S. Fischer, op cit, p55

66 Radu Ioanid, op cit, p10

67 Ibid

68 Ibid; Julius S. Fischer, op cit, p57

69 Radu Ioanid, op cit, pp24-30. For Harput comparisons, see Leslie A. Davis, *The Slaughterhouse Province*, op cit, pp54-5

70 Ancel, *Documents*, Vol 5, Bucharest embassy report, 12 August 1941, p53

71 Radu Ioanid, op cit, p26. See also Raphael Lemkin, op cit, pp237-8, for more on the National Centre for Romanisation

72 Radu Ioanid, op cit, pp28-9

73 Ibid, pp37-8; Ancel, *Documents*, Vol 5, President of Jewish community, Radauti, to Filderman, 22 October 1941, p88

74 Radu Ioanid, op cit, pp29-30; Julius S. Fischer, op cit, p100

75 Jean Ancel, 'Romanian Way', op cit, p302

76 Dora Litani, 'The Destruction of the Jews of Odessa in the Light of Rumanian Documents', Yad Vashem Studies, 6 (1967) pp135-54

77 Jean Ancel, 'Antonescu', op cit, p473

78 Ibid, p470; Radu Ioanid, 'When Mass Murderers', op cit, p101

79 Martin Gilbert, op cit, p218

80 Figures on the numbers who died at Dalnik differ. Jean Ancel in 'Antonescu', op cit, p470, opts for a figure of 20,500. Dora Litani, op cit, puts the figure higher at 25,000-30,000.

81 See Jean Ancel, 'Antonescu', op cit, p470, for an extract of Antonescu's 16 December 1941 speech to his Council of Ministers on this score

82 Ibid, pp472-3; Julius S. Fischer, op cit, pp122-3

83 Julius S. Fischer, op cit, p122

84 Ibid, p123; Hilberg, *Destruction*, p142

85 Quoted in Jean Ancel, 'Antonescu', op cit, p475

86 Julius S. Fischer, op cit, p123

87 Ancel, *Documents*, Vol 5, p204; Martin Gilbert, op cit, p289

88 Radu Ioanid, op cit, p1

89 Ancel, *Documents*, Vol 10, Antonescu statement, 17 November 1943, pp329-30. More generally, see Jean Ancel, 'Plans for Deportation of the Romanian Jews and Their Discontinuation in the Light of Documentary Evidence, July-October 1942', Yad Vashem Studies, 16 (1984) pp381-420

90 See Julius S. Fischer, op cit, pp107-13 for details

91 Martin Gilbert, op cit, p637

92 Jean Ancel, 'Antonescu', op cit, p476. This would closely tally with the 1943 estimates of Karl Koib, the IRB representative in Romania, for Bukovinan and Bessarabian Jewish dead at 241,057. See Ancel, *Documents*, Vol 5, pp536-8. Radu Ioanid, 'When Mass Murderers', op cit, p100, and Julius S. Fischer, op cit, p134, opt for lower figures of above 250,000 and 200,00 respectively.

93 John Joseph, *The Nestorians and their Muslim Neighbours: A Study of Western Influences on their Relations* (Princeton: Princeton University Press, 1961) p135, estimates that perhaps one-third of the Ottoman Hakkari population of Nestorians were killed or died during their flight or in subsequent wartime vicissitudes. Similarly, most sources seem to agree that of c30,000 Roma deported to Transnistria, some 24,000-25,000 perished. See Radu Ioanid, 'When Mass Murderers', op cit, p96

94 Jean Ancel, 'Antonescu', op cit, p467

95 Radu Ioanid, op cit, pp20-3; Julius S. Fischer, op cit, p128

96 Radu Ioanid, op cit, p13; Jean Ancel, 'Romanian Way', op cit, p203

97 On traditional Alevi and other sectarian group assistance to Armenians in times of persecution, see Tessa Hoffman and Gerayer Koutcharian, 'The History of Armenian-Kurdish Relations in the Ottoman Empire', *Armenian Review*, 39:4 (1986) pp6-7, 24-5. Also, more generally, Miller and Miller, op cit, pp182-6; see Jean Ancel 'Romanian Way', op cit, p198

98 Jean Ancel, 'Romanian Way', op cit, p226

Index